THE MUNICIPAL BUILDING, NEW YORK

THE AMERICAN VITRUVIUS:

AN ARCHITECTS' HANDBOOK OF

CIVIC ART

BY
WERNER HEGEMANN
AND
ELBERT PEETS

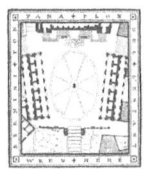

MCMXXII

NEW YORK:THE ARCHITECTURAL BOOK PUBLISHING CO:
PAUL WENZEL & MAURICE KRAKOW:31 EAST 12TH STREET

FOUNDATIONS IN URBAN PLANNING - HEGEMANN & PEETS
Edited by Thomas C. Myers, Jr.

De Facto Publishing • 2010

Published by De Facto Publishing
www.defactopublish.com

For information on volume purchases, licensing, or
educational adoption, please visit the publisher's web
site or email info@defactopublish.com.

Originally published in 1922 by
The Architectural Book Publishing
Company, New York.

ISBN: 1453762477
EAN-13: 9781453762479

THE
AMERICAN VITRUVIUS

AN ARCHITECTS' HANDBOOK OF

CIVIC ART

BY

WERNER HEGEMANN

AND

ELBERT PEETS

$40.00 net

EDITOR'S INTRODUCTION

The publication of Hegemann and Peets' *American Vitruvius* is an unlikely but important event in the history of American urban planning. Published in 1922, during the very infancy of this new form of planning, their *Civic Art* established a foundation for the subsequent nine decades of this discipline's rapid evolution. Today, their work enjoys newfound relevance to movements such as New Urbanism which seek to address postwar suburban sprawl with neighborhood centric design.

The *American Vitruvius*, which has been called a "landmark" and the beginning of a "new era," is the product of a restless German planner-architect and a young Midwestern landscape architect. The very fact that Werner Hegemann and Elbert Peets should produce this monumental work is unlikely. Their few years spent working together on planned communities like Wyomissing Park and Washington Highlands (see pages 280-283 of this volume) sparked an interest in the inherent challenges with planning in the Modern era; we are fortunate to have inherited the product of their thorough investigations and keen insights

from a pivotal point in the history of American city planning.

The volume's title itself warrants closer inspection since it effectively marks the challenges of early twentieth century city planning. By calling their work the "American Vitruvius" and further referring to it as "an architects' handbook," Hegemann and Peets clearly define their intended audience—not the professional planner but rather the practicing architect. The authors clearly viewed architects as necessary progenitors of quality city design and architecture's focus on the building in isolation from its surroundings as contributing to a decline of modern urban form. As they point out in the introduction, "The well designed individual building in order to be enjoyed fully must be part of an esthetically living city, not of a chaos."

The next important observation arises from the use of the phrase "civic art" to describe their work—one which is often used today as shorthand when referring to the volume. Hegemann and Peets clearly saw planning as an art form, and their reflections on classicism and its romantic ideals are prevalent throughout. Additional emphasis of Camillo Sitte's work, aptly titled *City Planning According to Artistic Principles*, and parallels with the Garden City and City Beautiful movements further this distinction.

In many ways, *Civic Art* can be viewed as a reaction to modernism's impending rise. The loss of human scale and the picturesque in favor of cold, calculated, almost scientific forms was unthinkable to Hegemann and Peets and further threatened the unity they believed necessary for good urban design.

It is interesting to note that following its publication, traditional urban design did succumb to modernism through most of the remainder of the century, the likes of Le Corbusier taking center stage with Contemporary City and Radiant City concepts. American cities experiencing explosive growth in the suburbs to the detriment of their cores. It was only later that Hegemann and Peets' work regained the attention it deserved, and its relevance to contemporary urban design was secured.

In terms of its format, *Civic Art*'s roughly twelve hundred illustrations and images effectively outline the key questions of modern planning— the relationship of buildings to one another, to public spaces such as plazas and streets, and the functioning of districts and cities from social, transportation, logistical, and aesthetic standpoints. Their scope is no less daunting, placing into perspective issues from their classic Greek and Roman origins through modern, turn of the twentieth century American design.

Hegemann and Peets' *American Vitruvius* could have been structured a number of different ways: temporally, functionally, geographically, or even from a design process orientation. However, the authors chose none of these, further reinforcing the book's objective—to serve as a guide for further investigation and reflection. Their work challenges the status quo from a historical and aesthetic basis; it does not provide definitive answers.

Civic Art draws heavily on the observations of Camillo Sitte in his *City Planning According to Artistic Principles*. The entire first chapter, "The Modern Revival of Civic Art," is devoted to a review of Sitte's principles of building placement and scale based on hundreds of examples throughout Medieval and Renaissance Europe. Interestingly, their overview provided the only English language access to Sitte's work for several decades after its publication—another important contribution of the *Civic Art*. For Hegemann and Peets, the artistic is the foundation upon which urban design should be based.

In subsequent chapters, the authors build upon Sitte's work and investigate progressive levels of scale in the built environment. From the individual building, Hegemann and Peets progress through adjacent public spaces such as streets and plazas. They then investigate groupings of buildings such as college campuses, civic centers, and hospitals, and after further consideration of street and garden design, review the full set of design elements as unified examples.

Throughout the volume, the authors rely on examples over written explanation. Captions to illustrations and images provide the majority of narrative, with direct explanation kept to a minimum. Readers are encouraged to think about the concepts being presented and form their own opinions. Such is the appeal and timelessness of its approach.

Contemporary relevance of Hegemann and Peets' work is undeniable, especially with the rise of New Urbanism and its associated approaches. Many are direct offshoots of *Civic Art*, and others are fully supported by its examples. As an acknowledgement of its importance, Duany, Plater-Zyberk, and Alminana modeled *The New Civic Art* on Hegemann and Peets' original, in both name and in structuring its content.

With a sporadic publication history, this edition aims to make Hegemann and Peets' original work accessible to a new generation of students and practicing planners and architects. It is reduced in size from the original volume's massive folio format, into a more portable and affordable size in the hope that it can better achieve this goal.

T.M. – August 2010

CONTENTS

FOREWORD

There are various more or less external circumstances, relating to the origin and purpose of a book of this sort, which ought to be made known to its readers as a preliminary, even, to asking them to accept an introduction to the book itself. One of these, and to the authors it is of first importance, is the acknowledgment of indebtednesses. Work on the book was begun in New York at the Avery Library of Columbia University, where every assistance was extended in the use of the Library's wonderful collections, and where permission was given to have photographs made of many old plans and engravings. At Milwaukee, where the work was continued, the staff of the Public Library has been extremely helpful in finding material and in permitting its use for the making of reproductions. Important help has also been received from the John Crerar Library in Chicago. And no book which is in any degree a record of the past can be written in the English language without direct or indirect indebtedness to the inexhaustibly rich and friendly Library of the British Museum.

To individuals, also, and of course especially to architects and city officials, the authors are indebted for many courteous favors, only a few of which have been specific-ally acknowledged in the captions. The greatest of these obligations is to Mr. Franz Herding of the architectural firm Herding and Boyd, of St. Louis, who has made for the book a series of pen drawings which constitutes one of its principal esthetic assets.

Yet, in spite of the help which they have asked and been so freely given, and in spite of the considerable number of the illustrations here presented, the authors are perfectly aware that they are offering only a gleaning from the broad field of civic art. The attitude of approach which was adopted neither permitted nor required completeness. The purpose was not to make a history of civic art, nor to formulate a well-rounded theory of its practice, nor to produce a full record of its present state. The objective has been the compilation of a thesaurus, a representative collection of creations in civic art, so grouped and so interpreted in text and captions as seemed best suited to bring out the special significance of each design. Sometimes the massing together of the work of a particular school or city has seemed the best way, by their cumulative effect, to force a recognition of the beauty of each example. In other cases the almost random selection of similar or contrasted designs from many different times and places has been employed to show the universality of the principles of art and to prove that one set of difficult conditions is as possible of artistic solution as another, if only the will be there.

It has been in the selection of modern American material that an interesting design has most often been omitted, reluctantly, and that it was often found impossible to secure satisfactory illustrations of work which the authors should have liked to have shown. In some cases a design which is very well known has been used in order to fill out a cycle or to drive home some point which could only be made by a close visual juxtaposition. In yet other cases it may seem that material has been selected for the very reason that it is little known; into such a classification would quite naturally fall these examples of their own work which the authors have ventured to include. Those who know how much labor has been expended upon these pages will not begrudge the authors the light tribute of attention which they thus levy upon their readers.

The size of the engravings is not always to be taken as an index of the authors' feeling as to the comparative importance of the designs. The size was often restricted by the suitability of the originals from which the reproductions were made. Some engravings were purchased or borrowed, and some had been prepared for previous publications by the authors or their friends. In many cases, too, as the making of the "dummy" progressed, reproductions had to be scaled down to fit the available space.

No attempt has been made, in text or captions, to attain scholarly fullness or exactness of historical or descriptive information. Only those facts have been stated which seemed essential to the interpretation of the design in question. Such phrases as "the Italian Renaissance" have been used with no illusion as to the impossibility of exactly defining them, and all American architecture preceding the Gothic revival has economically been classed as "Colonial". In making bibliographical

references, also, and in citing sources, the aim has been to record only a working minimum of information,— enough to make it possible, with the aid of more complete bibliographies and catalogues, to trace the illustration to its origin. The list of books which precedes the index contains only the names of works from which illustrative material has been used.

If this moment of confidences may be protracted yet a little, the authors wish to say another word about themselves. One of the advantages of collaboration is that the co-workers have different ideas as to what to say and how to say it, and the resulting work is usually better for that very reason. But if differences do persist, even after the milling and sifting which co-authorship involves, one or the other idea has to be chosen for incorporation in the book, with the result that one of the authors may in subsequent writings seem guilty of inconsistency. So it may be well to state that, with the exception of the last chapter, the text was drafted by the senior collaborator. Yet the authors have made every effort to make the text, both in form and in content, an expression of their common judgment, and it is only because complete coincidence of ideas is not to be expected in so large a field, that the junior author is not to be held accountable for every detail of the opinions expressed in the chapters indicated. It is to the first chapter that this disclaimer is especially relevant. For the captions responsibility is about equally divided. Many of the drawings and plans signed by but one of the authors were, in conception, the product of collaboration.

This "foreword" of explanation and acknowledgment would be incomplete without an expression of the authors' indebtedness to Mr. Wenzel and Mr. Krakow for their constant and valuable assistance and for the faith in the usefulness of the book which led them to support each extension of the original scheme. Their friendship is not the least of the authors' rewards for having undertaken this work.

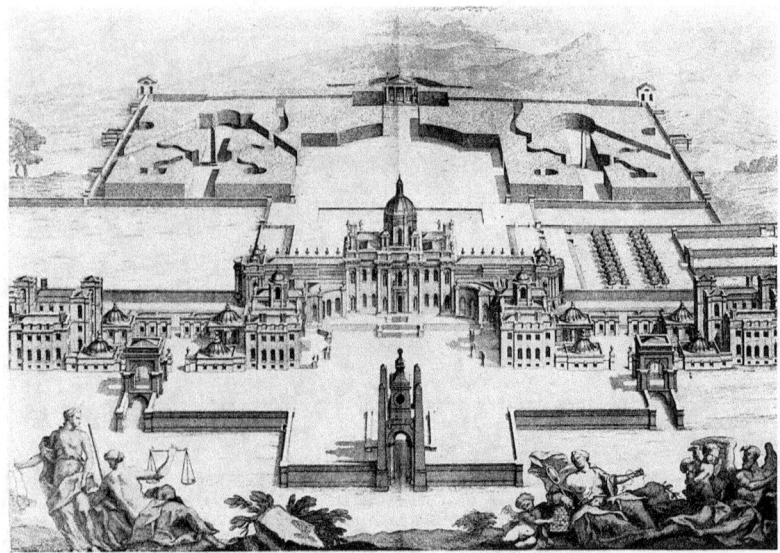

FIG. 1A—CASTLE HOWARD. A FEUDAL CIVIC CENTER

The symbolical figures in the foreground are to be found nowadays on the walls of court rooms and council chambers.
Designed by Sir John Vanbrugh, 1702. (From Campbell's "Vitruvius Britannicus.")

INTRODUCTION

"Vitruvius gives me much light, but not so much as would be sufficient."
Raphael (in a letter by his hand, written 1514).

Even architects — not to speak of their clients — are often unaware of the severe odds against which a good designer has to contend. They are apt to overlook the fact that for the enjoyment of a pleasingly designed individual structure there are essential conditions over which, thus far, they rarely have control. Still, without this control the spending of time and money for the design and the erection of a beautiful individual building is a hazardous enterprise. Only under rare circumstances will a fine piece of work be seen to advantage if thrown into a chaos, and dignity, charm and unassuming manner are preposterous when the neighbors are wantonly different or even obnoxious. The hope that good work will show off the better for being different from its surroundings, which are to act as a foil, is an illusion. The noise produced at county fairs by many orchestras simultaneously playing different tunes is a true symbol for the architectural appearance of the typical modern city street. The fact that one of the orchestras may play Beethoven will not resolve the chaos. "For chaos is the only word that can justly apply" says one of America's master designers in describing New York's Fifth Avenue, where much of the finest American work is exhibited. In the general riot harmony and even decency are being lost. Under such conditions sincere designers are not given a chance. It is painful to see them work hard trying to give their best; architects who unhesitatingly commercialize their output have something like an excuse to offer.

This condition is detrimental to the advancement of the arts and it must be changed. One of the foremost aims of this book on civic art is to bring out the necessity of extending the architect's sphere of influence, to emphasize the essential relation between a building and its setting, the necessity of protecting the aspect of the approaches, the desirability of grouping buildings into harmonious ensembles, of securing dominance of some buildings over others, so that by the willing submission of the less to the greater there may be created a larger, more monumental unity; a unity comprising at least a group of buildings with their surroundings, if possible entire districts and finally even, it may be hoped, entire cities.

Against chaos and anarchy in architecture, emphasis must be placed upon the ideal of civic art and the civilized

FIG. 2.—CHAOS.
Cartoon from the Architectural Review, 1904.

city. In the design of individual façades and of individual plans, American architects have created an extensive body of excellent work. What is now required is better correlation of the individual buildings. It is to facilitate work in this direction that there has been brought together in the following pages a large collection of compositions, with plans and material elucidating them, showing such examples and suggestions as will help to design and place individual constructions as harmonious parts of their surroundings, whether a group, an ensemble, a street, a plaza, a park or in short: a city or civic organism. The well

FIG. 1—ROMAN RUINS. (Piranesi)

designed individual building in order to be enjoyed fully must be part of an esthetically living city, not of a chaos.

This book may be useful as an atlas for imaginary travelling with the client when his insistence on casual short cuts (producing "informal" shapelessness) must be met with examples of orderly design. Unfortunately it is not the client alone whose morale needs strengthening. The artist himself, running continuously against the opposition of the so-called "practical" man with his "lack of funds" and his untrained imagination, gradually learns to make concessions and to be satisfied with compromise; whether these were finally executed or remained an artist's bold dream is not important. Be it remembered in this connection that the French Renaissance in important respects was deeply influenced by drawings and ideas many of which were suggested to Du Cerceau in Italy, not by work actually executed, but by bold projects which their creators never saw realized. Within the sketchiest suggestion, as de Geymuller points out, may lie the germ of great creations.

In writing at the top of the title page the name of Vitruvius, in what might be called an honorary title, the authors have meant to fly at their masthead a sign of their allegiance to the classical ideals associated with the Vitruvian tradition. And the greatest of those ideals,

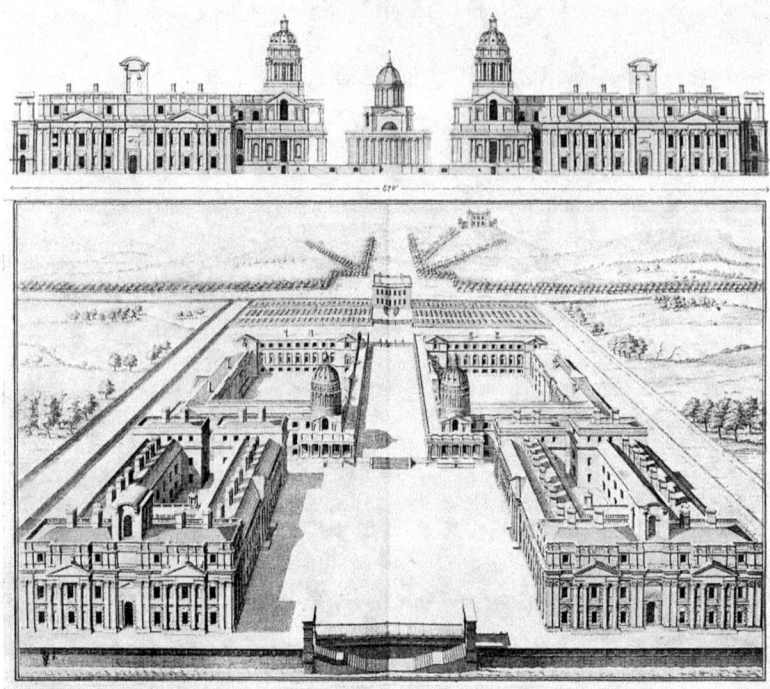

FIG. 3—GREENWICH. THE ROYAL HOSPITAL.

The elevation shows Sir Christopher Wren's proposal. The bird's-eye view shows the buildings as they existed at the time of the publication of Campbell's Vitruvius Britannicus, from which both engravings are taken. The block at the right, near the river and the Queen's House in the background were built by Inigo Jones. Wren's work began in 1699. According to the "Parentalia" Queen Mary's "absolute determination to preserve" them and of "keeping an approach from the Thames quite up to the Queen's House, of 115 feet broad" "naturally drew on the Disposition of the Buildings, as they are now placed and situated. The principal Front of this great Building lies open to the Thames; from whence we enter into the Middle of the royal court, near 300 foot square, lying open to the North, and cover'd on the West with the Court of King Charles II and on the East with that of Queen Anne, equal to it; and on the South, the great Hall and Chapel."

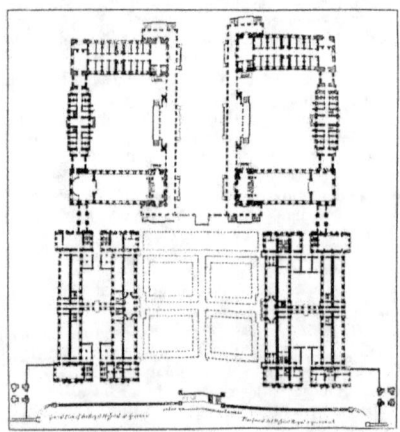

FIG. 4—GENERAL PLAN OF THE ROYAL HOSPITAL AT GREENWICH.

From "Vitruvius Britannicus." The group covers an area about seven hundred by eight hundred feet.

though in these days of superficial individualism it is often forgotten, is that the fundamental unit of design in architecture is not the separate building but the whole city. The authors have meant also to make a bow of respect and admiration to Colen Campbell and his classic "Vitruvius Britannicus," which was published early in the eighteenth century.

In the subtitle to his book, Campbell defines the meaning of his title: "Vitruvius Britannicus or the British Architect, containing the plans . . . of the Regular Buildings and the Geometrical Plans . . . of Gardens and Plantations." The definition of the term Vitruvius which this title and the book itself constitute has two important phases. In the first place the term did not imply a discussion of the "orders" and architectural details, and in the second place, it was definitely understood to apply only to "regular" buildings and "geometrical" plans.

Among the illustrious subscribers to the Vitruvius Britannicus we find "Sir Christopher Wren, Knt., Surveyor General of His Majesty's Works". The spirit that guided Colen Campbell and the century following Christopher Wren is responsible for all indigenous art in the United States. It is the spirit of this evolution which the present volume is intended to serve. To this evolution America with her Colonial art, her university groups,

FIG. 5—THE GREENWICH HOSPITAL SEEN FROM THE WATER
From a steel engraving of about 1840.

world's fairs, civic centers and garden cities, has made valuable contributions and is promising even greater ones through the development of the skyscraper, of the zoned city, and of the park system.

Of so-called "informal" plannings, therefore, only such examples will be included in this book as seem to illustrate a respectable endeavor to triumph over an inherent weakness (resulting from shapelessness of site or limitation of means or otherwise) as is the case with so many plans of the Gothic period. A seemingly shapeless plan can ingeniously be made to give in execution a realization of order and symmetry and many historic plans therefore have become of peculiar practical interest.

Colen Campbell's precedent of including in his Vitruvius Britannicus only English material did not induce the authors of this book to confine themselves to American work. The artistic ideal which inspired the Vitruvius Britannicus is peculiar neither to England nor to America. It is the same spirit that wrought architectural wonder all over Europe. Harmonious development of architecture requires equally both appreciation of tradition and bold development of inherent capabilities of such tradition into new precedent. While in the matters of detail of exterior form, it may be disputed whether it is wise to wantonly break away from the precedent created by the Georgian epoch or by that period of European (mainly Italian) art from which the Georgian is derived, it is certainly beyond question that in matters of plan and mass inspiration can be found wherever builders strove for order, symmetry, balance, and harmony, or whatever name one may give to that deep craving for rhythm structurally expressed.

In judging the public or private character of the creations illustrated in Colen Campbell's Vitruvius the casual American observer may doubt the "civic" character of many of them. The Vitruvius Britannicus illustrates Covent Garden, London—"this noble square, which for the Grandure of Design, is certainly the first in Europe" — which nobody would hesitate to call a creation of civic art. But Campbell's Vitruvius also shows many aristocrats' "magnificent places" and "noblest seats in the Kingdom". It must not be forgotten, however, that under the peculiar organization of Euro-

pean society before the revolution of 1789, the king's and noblemen's castles truly were civic centers. In Versailles or Carlsruhe all roads lead to the castle. The idea of separating White House and Capitol is of later date and the arrangement of axes in the plan of Washington is the first stately expression of this new idea.

When Colen Campbell praises a castle and says that the "noble Lord, from a place that could pretend to nothing but a Situation capable of improvement, with vast Labour and Expense, has now rendered it one of the

FIG. 6—THE GREENWICH HOSPITAL SEEN FROM THE HILLS
An engraving dating from about 1840. In the foreground Inigo Jones' Queen's House and the colonnades tying it to the rest of the composition.

noblest Seats in the Kingdom", he believes that a civic service has been performed. The terms in which he speaks of such achievements are not very different from the "boosting" customary in advertising the show points of American cities.

The public square of Covent Garden was built for the Earl of Bedford; Versailles, the creation of King Louis XIV has influenced the plan of Washington; the "Tuileries" and "Palais Royal" in Paris were always pleasure grounds of the people, and about "the stupendous Structure" of the Royal Hospital at Greenwich, Colen Campbell says in his Vitruvius: "This Royal Hospital was at first intended by King Charles II for a Royal Palace but was given by King William and Queen Mary for the Re-

FIG. 7—HOPETOUN HOUSE. Designed by Robert Adam. (From Swarbrick.)

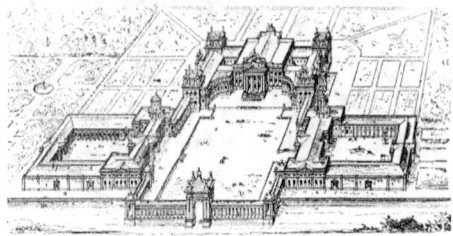

FIG. 8—BLENHEIM PALACE, BY VANBRUGH, 1705

(From Cornelius Gurlitt.)

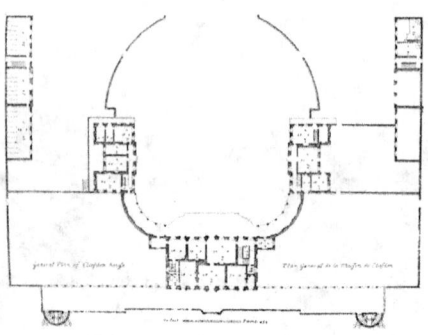

FIG. 9—GENERAL PLAN OF CLIEFDEN HOUSE

Overall width 435 feet. (From "Vitruvius Britannicus.")

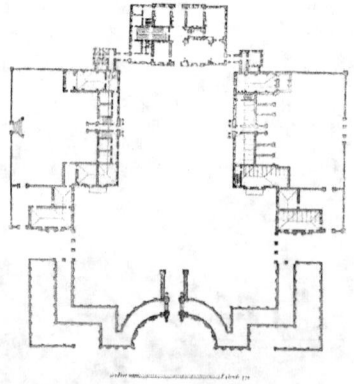

FIG. 10—PLAN OF LORD LEIMPSTER'S HOUSE

Finished 1713; designed by Hawksmore. Overall width 370 feet. (From "Vitruvius Britannicus.")

lief of decay'd and disabled Seamen" and he praises it: "for Magnificence, Extent and Conveniency the first Hospital in the World".

Like Colen Campbell, who was "architect to his Royal Highness the Prince of Wales", old Pollio Vitruvius, sixteen hundred years earlier architect to a Roman Emperor, was preeminently an apostle of civic art. Far from being an architect in the narrow sense often given to the term in decadent periods, as one who confines himself to the design of elevations and house plans, he had an equal interest in city and rural planning. Long chapters of Vitruvius's own book, as he wrote it originally for Emperor Augustus, dealt "of the design of plazas and streets within and of roads without" the cities. To Vitruvius the conception of architecture as being anything but civic art was impossible.

Therefore the architect who looks for inspiration as to grouping public buildings to best advantage into "civic centers" and laying out public parks and pleasure grounds, will study with advantage the achievements of the builders of former times; and will find that these compositions, whether called castles or otherwise, often were truly civic centers of great artistic quality, containing in actuality everything the modern civic reformer wants to bring together: council chamber, law court, chapel, library and picture gallery, dance hall and pleasure grounds, which under normal conditions were accessible indeed to all who made proper use of the facilities offered. And these centers in many cases were brought into thoroughly satisfactory esthetic relation to the town surrounding them.

Most American cities have fallen victims of a gridiron arrangement of streets along which buildings of different character are lined up indiscriminately. It is hard under such conditions to place buildings to advantage. The inconsiderate introduction of diagonal streets often made matters worse instead of improving them. How churches and other important buildings were placed and made prominent in former times and how their surroundings and approaches were treated and protected is a study well worth while to the American architect.

No part of this book will be found to treat of the engineering aspects of city planning. Indeed, the authors feel that the young profession of city planning is drifting too strongly in the directions of engineering and applied sociology. This is perhaps natural, for there are problems of such tremendous importance in these fields, problems of a practical importance which newspapers and public officials can appreciate and even property rights can be induced to recognize, that men in the profession are attracted in that direction. Besides, it is much easier and more respectable to be an engineer, an "uplifter", or a business man, than it is to be an artist. But, unless our efficient civilization is to produce nothing but its own efficiency, our cities must not be shaped solely by engineers. No city planning project should be undertaken nor report issued without the sanction of at least one trained man whose primary interest is in the dignity and beauty of form and color.

There need be no illusions as to the difficulty under modern conditions, of creating, on a large scale, uniform or even harmonious compositions of civic art. The individual architect may well feel that in spite of his knowledge and desires he can do nothing: the public does not know what a beautiful city is and would not get together to create one if it did. But, if the public inaction in the field of civic art is due to a lack of appreciation and the difficulty of cooperation, it is not easy for the architectural profession to allege the same reasons. Civic art is their peculiar field; the number of practitioners is small; their tastes and training are much more uniform

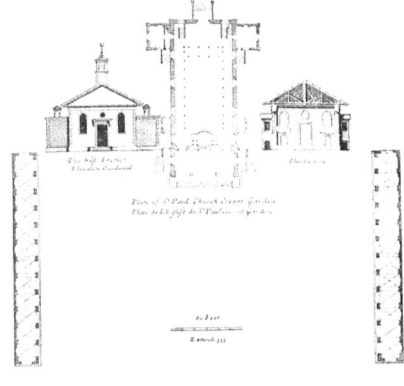

FIG. 11—PLAN OF THE GREAT PIAZZA COVENT GARDEN
Designed 1631 by Inigo Jones. (From "Vitruvius Britannicus.")

FIG. 13—PARIS. COURT OF THE PALAIS ROYAL, 1834

Looking south toward what originally was the Palais Richelieu; to the right and left the apartment houses built in 1829 upon the ground of the old palace garden. The theater of the Comédie Française appears above the roofs.

trained men without which an organization is worse than useless, the less hope one has of help from this direction.

Voluntary associations of the property owners in certain streets or sections constitute a more hopeful instrumentality, especially when a common material interest, such as the threat of reduced land values, forces them into common action. And it is between streets and districts of the same city, rather than between separate cities, that economic competition and local pride should be depended on to motivate work in behalf of civic art.

But architects who think of their profession as an art and not merely as a business can do a great deal for civic art even inside the ups and downs of the usual practice. If the house is to stand at the end of a street-vista it can be placed exactly on axis and can be designed symmetrically, so as to make it part of the street and

than among the general public; strong professional societies exist. Whatever may be the merits of the guild system it at least carries with it a feeling of corporate responsibility to the art and to the public. The public would concede that responsibility and follow the leadership of an architectural guild if the profession itself could attain some unity and positiveness of conviction. The medical profession can and does cooperate in the service of the public in every great emergency. It looks upon an uncontrolled epidemic as a stain upon the honor of the profession,—and was there ever a more deadly plague than the ugliness of a modern city? The best hope for mitigation lies in the strong unified action of the architectural profession.

It would be easy to draw up schemes for the organization of municipal civic art instrumentalities, bringing the architectural and commercial organizations into cooperation with city officials and employing the various leverages of regulation, persuasion, and education to weld the city gradually into some sort of harmony. But the more one knows of city governments and of the scarcity of the

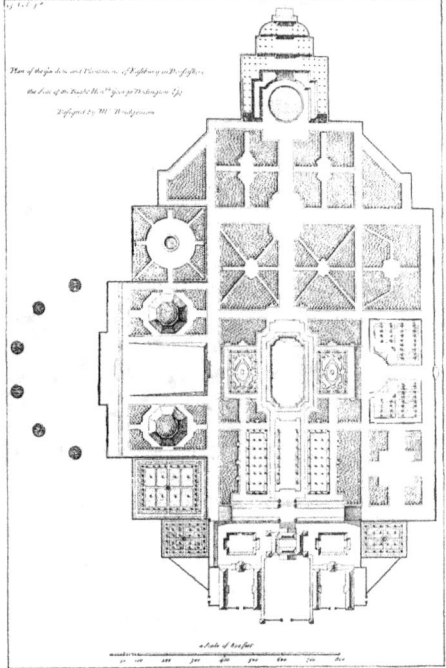

FIG. 14—PLAN OF THE GARDENS OF EASTBURY

Designed by Charles Bridgeman, 1718. Though a private estate, the plan is equally suited to the requirements of a public park. (From "Vitruvius Britannicus.")

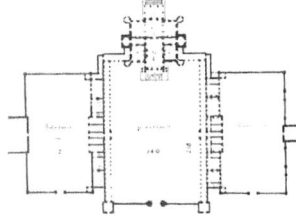

FIG. 12—PLAN OF SEATON DELAVAL
Designed by Vanbrugh, 1721.

the street part of it. If the office building is to stand on a corner there may happen to be a building of similar mass on the other corner to which, in color, scale, and dominant lines, the new building can be made to respond, thus creating a pair of entrance pylons for the street. Every new piece of street architecture should be designed as part of the block or street in which it stands, or if the existing buildings are hopeless, it can at least sound a note which is suited to serve as the keynote in the future rebuilding of the block. In these ways an architect can practice civic art without asking the cooperation of outsiders. Those cities which now hold competitions for the best-designed store-building, apartment house, and so on, of the year, ought to add a prize for the building which is best adapted to its place in the city plan or the city picture. Rome was not built in a day. Public opinion can gradually be induced to demand the right thing, even before it is sensitive enough to appreciate it. Propaganda can do other things besides win wars. Architects, in sketching in "entourages" and in preparing exhibition drawings must not be too sensitive about being called "idealistic". Good civic art can be made a current ideal long before it can be realized in steel and stone, but once it becomes a popular ideal opportunity will inevitably be found, here and there, to realize some well-designed project.

In architecture, as in every art, there are producers and consumers,—those who create and those who recognize and enjoy the creations. Always, too, the best consumers are the producers themselves. Members of the artistic professions make their skill and knowledge not merely their breadwinners but also the cultural inspiration and justification of their lives. And there is a mutual interplay, for the critical appreciation of the work of other men and other times must facilitate and enrich imaginative production. There are many pages in this book which will inevitably serve the cultural rather than the work-a-day lives of the readers. No architect will ever be employed to make such a plan as Piranesi's "reconstruction" of the Campus Martius, but to study that plan, to imagine it in three dimensions, to wander through its fantastic mazes, cannot but be, to the mind which is capable of it, a vivid and unusual pleasure.

To make the great classical works of civic art more familiar than they now are to the American architect, and a more ready and useful part of his daily thought, to show how much modern civic art has learned and has yet to learn from the old work, and to demonstrate to what great nobility and beauty the art of building cities can attain,—those are the dominant purposes of this book.

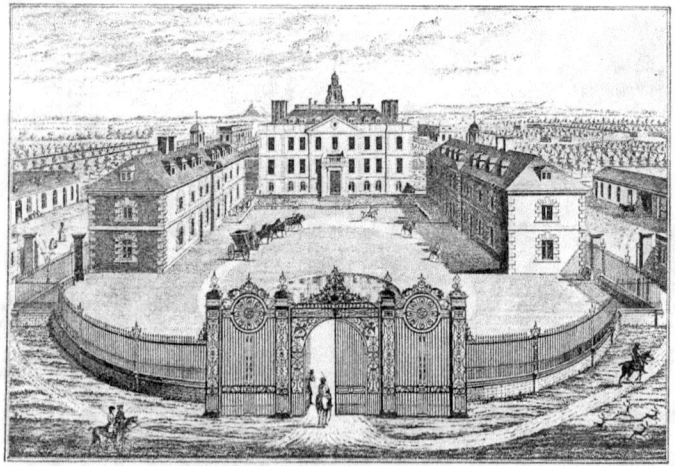

FIG. 15—EATON HALL.
Built about 1695; attributed to Vanbrugh. From an engraving by Badeslade and Thoms; 1740.

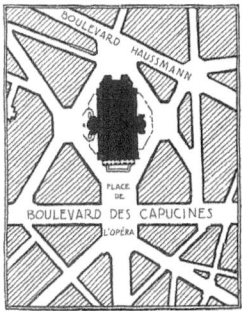

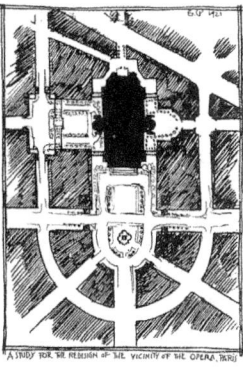

FIG. 16—VICINITY OF OPERA

A traffic center of the engineering
type. See Garnier's comment.

FIG. 17—AEROPLANE VIEW OF THE OPERA, PARIS

A STUDY FOR THE REDESIGN OF THE VICINITY OF THE OPERA, PARIS

FIG. 18

CHAPTER I

The Modern Revival of Civic Art

The engravings accompanying this chapter were mainly used by Camillo Sitte (of whose book the chapter is largely a synopsis) to illustrate his teachings and to serve as the basis upon which these teachings were built up. They are taken, for the most part, from the French edition of Sitte. Others, of which the sources are usually given, supplement Sitte's illustrations or represent designs which are known to have influenced him. Some of Sitte's own work is reproduced and one design by his followers. The small plaza plans are mostly at a scale of 330 feet to the inch.

Civic Art is a living heritage from classic, medieval and Renaissance times. Before starting, however, upon the road which seems destined to lead it to such high architectural achievements in twentieth century America, it went through a period of utter decline during the nineteenth century. The revival dates from the comparatively recent discovery that the customary gridiron street planning of most American cities, as well as the diagonal (or triangular) and radial street planning of Baron Haussmann's Paris or even of L'Enfant's Washington, to take two much praised examples, produce very unsatisfactory settings for monumental buildings. While many modern critics are unduly hard upon the gridiron system they frequently are still biased, especially in America, in favor of the diagonal or radial systems. But radial or triangular systems are like the gridiron system in having at the same time practical advantages and disadvantages and in producing esthetically satisfactory results only if handled with much discretion and taste. The wisely handled gridiron system as found in the original plans for Philadelphia, Reading, and Mannheim offers charming possibilities which should not be overlooked by critics to whom Baron Haussmann's work in Paris appears to be flawless. Indeed close students of Haussmann's engineering, which involved Paris in an expenditure of two billion francs, have frequently denounced it. One of the most interesting documents in this connection is the crushing criticism made in 1878 by Charles Garnier, the great designer of the Paris Opéra, of the failure of Baron Haussmann's methods to provide a satisfactory setting for the Opéra (Figs. 16 and 17; further illustrations in next chapter). Parts of Garnier's moving utterance deserve to be quoted, as it ought to have special weight with those American architects who are in sympathy with the traditions of the Ecole des Beaux-Arts of which Garnier was a star disciple. In order to appreciate how gigantic was the failure of Haussmann in connection with the Opéra site it is well to remember, before reading Garnier's criticism, that Thiers, shortly before his assuming office as the first president of the French republic, in a memorable address on city planning directed against Haussmann, especially dwelt on the latter having spent thirty millions

for the mere preparation of the Opéra site. If Haussmann's work, which aimed mainly at military, sanitary and engineering objects, should at all be judged from an esthetic point of view, the setting of Garnier's Academy of Music is the most ambitious piece of it.

This is what the architect whose building stands on the site prepared with such great effort, has to say about Haussmann's esthetic achievement:

"I know of no monument, ancient or modern, which was set amidst surroundings more deplorable than those of the new Opéra! Of some the view has been obstructed, others are almost hidden, still others stand on steep hills or in deep holes; yet all of them, be their setting what it may be, at least are spared from having to fight against surroundings which are regularly irregular, against houses larger than they are, against viewpoints whence foreground, sides, and background are banal buildings, ill-placed and symmetrically criss-crossed, and against open areas too small to set the monument free and too large to give it scale! The Opéra is, in a word, jammed into a hole, pushed back, and buried in a quarry! and, truly, if I had n't such a real admiration for the great things M. Haussmann has done, I should feel a furious rage against him! But, as I have had time to calm myself since he chopped the region of the Chaussée-d'Antin up into triangular fragments and put a hump in the roadway of the Boulevard des Capucines at the same time that he cut a notch out of the Boulevard Haussmann, when he ought to have done just the contrary, I console myself with the thought that in some hundreds of years there shall come to Paris a prefect who shall have (as ours have, nowadays) a desire to disengage the monuments of the Paris of those times, and that he will be inspired to disencumber the Opéra by razing the whole region! . . ."

"Whatever it may be in the Paris of the future, the Opéra of the present is surely ill placed; the site upon which it is built is narrow in front, narrow in back, and bellies out in the middle, in such a sort that the enclosure of the site, having to follow its outline, seems to hold its arms akimbo like a paver's ram; also, and still more terrible, the site has a side-slope and forcibly drags with it, in its descent, that same unhappy enclosure, which

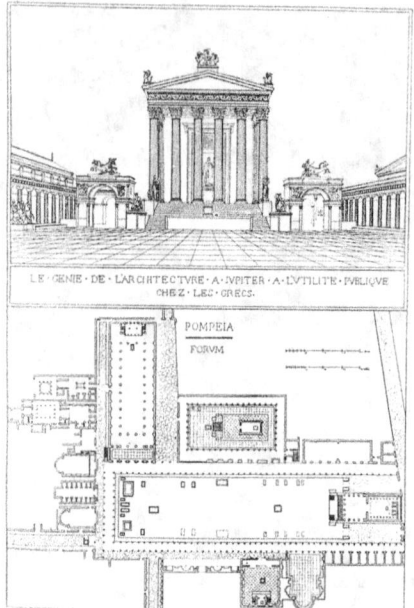

LE · GENIE · DE · L'ARCHITECTURE · A · IVPITER · A · L'VTILITE · PVELIQVE
CHEZ · LEC · GRECS.

POMPEIA
FORVM

FIG. 19—THE NEW FORUM IN POMPEII

Reconstructed view and plan (from J. A. Coussin, 1822). The less
attractive but probably more correct reconstruction published by Sitte
gives two stories to the colonnades surrounding the forum.

FIG. 21—PORTICO DEGLI UFFIZI, DESIGNED BY GIORGIO
VASARI, 1560.

This gate opens to the river; the other end of the colonnaded court
opens on the Piazza della Signoria as indicated in the plan, Fig. 20.

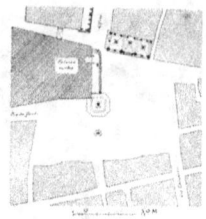

FIG. 20—PIAZZA DELLA
SIGNORIA, FLORENCE

This is the plaza around which
Michelangelo proposed a scheme of
arcades continuing the Loggia del
Lanzi (illustrated Fig. 798). (From
Brinckmann.)

clings to nothing at all and which, instead of serving as
frame to the monument, produces the effect of a picture
propped up at an angle in the very center of a salon!"

Garnier continues, incidentally giving some ideas on
city planning characteristic of his period, to which it will
be interesting to refer in a later part of this chapter, and
he concludes with the following sarcastic remarks about
the customary failure to grant the architect sufficient influence in the development of the site he has to build
upon:

"I was consulted, to be sure", says Garnier, "for at
least five minutes" — in 1861 when the plans were taken
to the Tuileries. The Emperor asked Garnier's opinion
of the site. Garnier regretted "the triangular form given
to all the blocks of houses." The Emperor agreed and
chided Haussmann with an overfondness for "fichus".
"His Majesty even made with his own hand a sort of
little sketch on the plan of the vicinity, eliminating the
bias streets and substituting rectangular plazas, and I
felt sure that with this imperial protection some change
in the project would be made." But the triangles were
built, just the same, and when Garnier remonstrated on
the occasion of the Emperor's only visit to the work, in
1862, "His Majesty Napoleon III answered me exactly
thus: 'In spite of what I said, in spite of what I did,
Haussmann has done as he pleased! !. . . .' And to think
that it is perhaps always thus that a sovereign's will is
done!"

The problem of the Paris Opéra site will be touched
upon again in the following chapter.

It happens that L'Enfant's plan for Washington —
it dates from the same period (1791) as the "plan of the
artists" (1793) which is responsible for the better ideas
to be found in Haussmann's plan — aside from the very
admirable sites for Capitol, Washington's Monument and
White House, contains specially reserved sites for fountains, monuments, or public buildings which have even
more impossible shapes than Haussmann's Opéra site.
Garnier's insight into the deficiencies of such sites has
not prevented modern city planners from following L'Enfant's and Haussmann's examples. There have been
made in America, even quite recently, numerous designs
for the civic centers of large cities where prominent
buildings are brought into equally bad situations and all
over Europe similarly poor work was turned out during
the nineteenth century.

Ineffectual as Garnier's and many contemporary
critics' casual outcries have been, they may be taken as
a prophecy of the comprehensive criticism of nineteenth
century city planning which appeared in 1889. In that

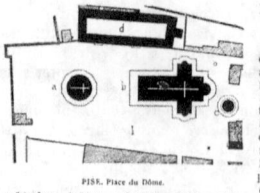

PISA. Place du Dôme.
a Saint-Jean   b Dôme.   c Campanile.   d. Campo santo.

FIG. 22—PISA. PIAZZA DEL
DUOMO

The finest group of the Tus-
can Romanesque period, built
about 1063-1280. The Baptistry (a) stands (like the one
in Florence) on axis of entrance to cathedral. The Baptistry is 200 feet from the
cathedral. No traffic is admitted to the plaza, which is
in grass. The frame consists
partly of a high wall. For view
of Campo Santo (d) see Fig.
959.

year was published "An architect's notes and reflexions upon artistic city planning" by Camillo Sitte which had deep and lasting influence upon all city planning thought and soon acquired the character of a classic. The book went through numerous editions, the latest of which appeared in Paris (second French edition) in 1918 (L'art de bâtir les villes; notes et reflexions d'un architect). The French translator, Camille Martin, points out in his introduction that Sitte's book for France, as for so many other countries, has become something like the point of departure for the new "urbanisme", urbanisme being the newly created French term for the art of building cities. If the French introduction also claims that Camillo Sitte's book even to-day preserves the value and timeliness it had when it first appeared over thirty years ago, this is true not only for France, where the discussion of city planning matters was almost lacking during the last generation, but even for America, where since about 1893 valuable contributions to civic art have been made.

As there does not yet exist an English translation of Sitte's book a synopsis will be attempted here, accompanied by the interesting plans and views as they appeared in the last French edition. From this synopsis the American architect can gather how much is still to be learned from Camillo Sitte and to what extent he must be judged as a son of his period.

The book investigates the causes that created the peculiar esthetic charm of the cities of former centuries and finds them in the old and unfortunately forgotten methods of setting buildings. This is demonstrated with "verve and enthusiasm" — to quote again the French translator's appreciation — by a large number of practical and theoretical examples.

The fora of the Romans, as at Pompeii (Fig. 19), like the plazas of Florence, Pisa, and Siena (Fig. 20 to 27) formed well designed forecourts for well placed buildings. Incidentally such plazas furnished fine locations for statuary. While modern routine is apt to place statues exclusively in the center where they often block valuable façades and main entrances, the civic designers of former periods placed their statuary either against the wall of their plazas where an effective background was secured, or in studied relation to well selected lines of

SIENNE
S. Pietro alle scale.

SIENNE
S. Vigilio.

SIENNE
V. di Abadia.

SIENNE
S. Maria di Provenzano.

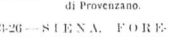

SIENNE
I. Piazza Vittorio Emanuele
II. Mercato Vecchio.

FIGS. 23-26—SIENA. FORE-COURTS OF FOUR CHURCHES

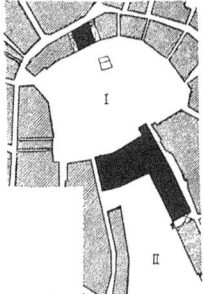

I

II

FIG. 27

FIGS. 27-27A—PLAN AND VIEW OF PIAZZA DEL CAMPO AND OLD MARKET. SIENA. The main plaza is located in a natural amphitheater between three hills. The streets following the ridges and valleys run radially into the plaza; some connect with the plaza by stairs; most street entrances are bridged over. The city hall dominates two closed plazas.

SIENA,
Mercato vecchio e
Piazza Vittorio Emanuele

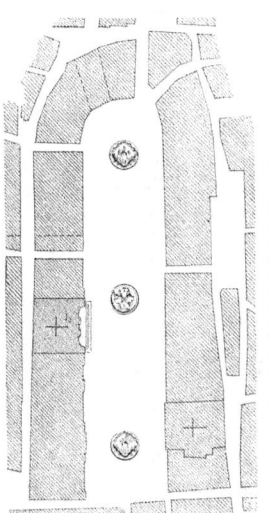

FIG. 28
PIAZZA NAVONA, ROME

The plaza goes back to Roman antiquity, when a circus occupied the site. A Renaissance proposal to surround the plaza with harmonious façades was not carried out. The long area is rhythmically subdivided by three fountains which have large and very low basins. In hot summers the area of the plaza is said to have been flooded and used for pleasure boating. (From Brinckmann.)

100 M.

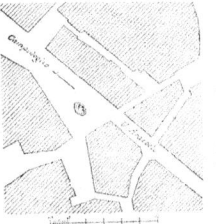

Fontana de' Moti

FIG. 29

Designed by della Porta. At the foot of the Roman Capitol; makes good use of a sharp street intersection.

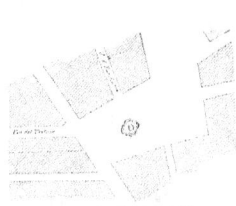

Fontana Barberini

FIG. 30

By Bernini, placed at the intersection of two street axes. (Figs. 29 and 30 from Brinckmann.)

FIG. 31

Donatello's bronze equestrian statue appears silhouetted against the sky if seen from the two most important entrances to the plaza. Dotted line shows old cemetery enclosure.

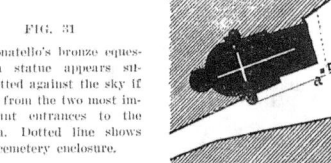

PADOUE. Piazza del Santo.
a Colonne.   b. Statue de Gattamelata.

vista and the esthetic centers of gravity of the plazas (see Fig. 20 and Figs. 28-31).

Public buildings were preceded by a plaza or surrounded by plazas, without which no important building can be well seen. As to the relation of the main building to the walls of the plaza Sitte finds that it is damaging to scale and effect of the main building to stand unrelated to neighboring buildings and that a physical or seemingly physical connection with such neighboring buildings is desirable. Out of 255 churches in Rome Sitte counted 249 thus connected with other buildings, and only six freestanding. Such physical connection with neighboring buildings incidentally permits concentration of the exterior decoration to one or two façades, instead of four, making greater splendor possible for the main building. For modern conditions, with plenty of land available, it might be added that a similar connection and support can be secured by dense tree plantings, preferably along formal lines, brought close to the buildings to which one wants to give a setting. (Figs. 32 and 33.)

In order to be effective the walls of the plaza laid in front of the building to be set must appear to be continuous, thus creating a seemingly enclosed area for the support of the main building. During the Middle Ages and the Renaissance architects found ways of producing such closed forecourt effects, even without using the colonnades customary in antiquity for the encircling of the forecourt areas. "The secret consisted in not permitting streets to debouch upon the plaza except in a direction perpendicular to the line of sight of the spectator" who stands on the plaza and looks at the prominent building of which the plaza is the forecourt.

The corners of the plaza are most in need of firmness. In most cases, therefore, not more than one street was permitted to come in at a corner of the plaza; other streets were intercepted before reaching the plaza or were made to come in at different angles instead of running parallel. Thus it was often managed that there was hardly a point within the plaza from which one could see more than one opening in the walls of the plaza (Figs. 34-40; 20; 48 D, J and T). If, against this rule, streets do come in, breaking the wall of the plaza, they are made to be so narrow that the break is insignificant.

Another method of closing a plaza was the simple covering of undesirable street openings with arches. These arches were often made to form a part of the design of the adjoining buildings. (Figs. 41-47.)

The desirability of giving a closed effect to parts at least of a plaza, has become even greater in modern times with the increase in the width of streets. What to-day is the width of a street, in former times would have been sufficient to form the width of a plaza to act as forecourt to a large public building. The enormous increase in the size of modern plazas that went parallel with the widening of the streets has made it more difficult to create a satisfactory relation between building and plaza and did not make it any easier to arch the disturbing gaps torn by street openings into the walls of the plazas.

Plazas to set off public buildings should be either long or deep. The same plaza can, at the same time, be called either long or deep according to its relation to the building in connection with which it is seen, i. e. whether this building is located on the narrow or on the long side of the plaza. In front of a building which is taller than wide, say a towered church façade, a deep plaza can suitably be used; for a building wider than tall, say the Basilica in Vicenza (Fig. 77 and 48 O), a long plaza is well suited. Too small a plaza instead of setting off a large building is apt to choke it. The enormous plazas which have been attempted in modern times often dwarf the surrounding buildings, making them appear like far-off villages utterly incapable of dominating

FIG. 32—TRIER. VILLA MONAISE

(See caption, Fig. 33.)

FIG. 33—TRIER. VILLA MONAISE

The little château was built in 1780. This is Osteudorf's study for the setting of the building which now stands unsupported as shown in the illustration above. The change in effect is similar to the change Sitte desired to secure in the setting of public buildings by avoiding unrelated freestanding sites.

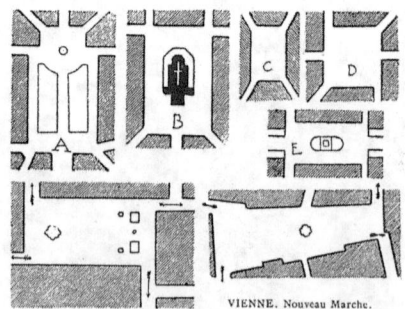

VIENNE. Nouveau Marche.

FIGS. 34-40—STEREOTYPED PLAZA DESIGNS CONTRASTED AGAINST SITTE'S RECOMMENDATIONS

Cuts A-E show plazas the walls of which are too much broken up. The plan of the New Market in Vienna and Sitte's proposal to the left of it contain suggestions for making the walls of a plaza appear closed. It might be said however that even in plazas of the type A to E satisfactory units could be created by a combination of uniform architecture with planting of dense tree rows and hedges.

FIG. 42

FIG. 43—PIAZZA DEI SIGNORI.

For plan see Fig. 41. This plaza furnishes one of the many Italian examples where an architectural motive from a prominent building framing the plaza is carried across the street openings at its sides.

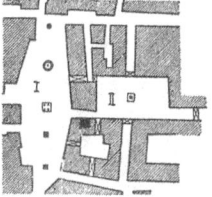

VERONE
I. Piazza Erbe.   II. Piazza Signoria.

FIG. 41

Plan and view of Piazza Erbe, Verona, quoted by Sitte as a typical example of an irregular plan made to look regular on the ground. Compare Fig. 106. Piazza Erbe and Piazza dei Signori (Fig. 43) form a civic center around which many historic buildings are located.

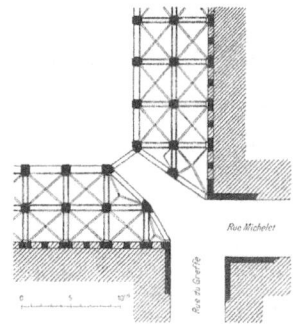

FIG. 45—MONTAUBAN; PLAN OF ARCH OVER ENTRANCE TO MARKET SQUARE

From Brinckmann, who describes Montauban, laid out 1144, as the first regular layout in Europe after the fall of the Roman Empire.

FIG. 44—VIEW OF CLOCK-TOWER, BERN

The tower, formerly the entrance gate to the city but now standing in its heart, closes the view down the main street (Kramgasse) so completely that the arcaded avenue gains the character of a well framed plaza.

FIG. 47—GRAND' PLACE, BRUSSELS

Immediately to the left of the City Hall appears a small building arching over part of Rue Charles Buls. It was reconstructed there to reduce the gap in the wall of the plaza after hasty street widening had deprived the City Hall of its esthetic support.

FIG. 46—MONTAUBAN.

Drawing by Franz Herding. For plan see Fig. 45.

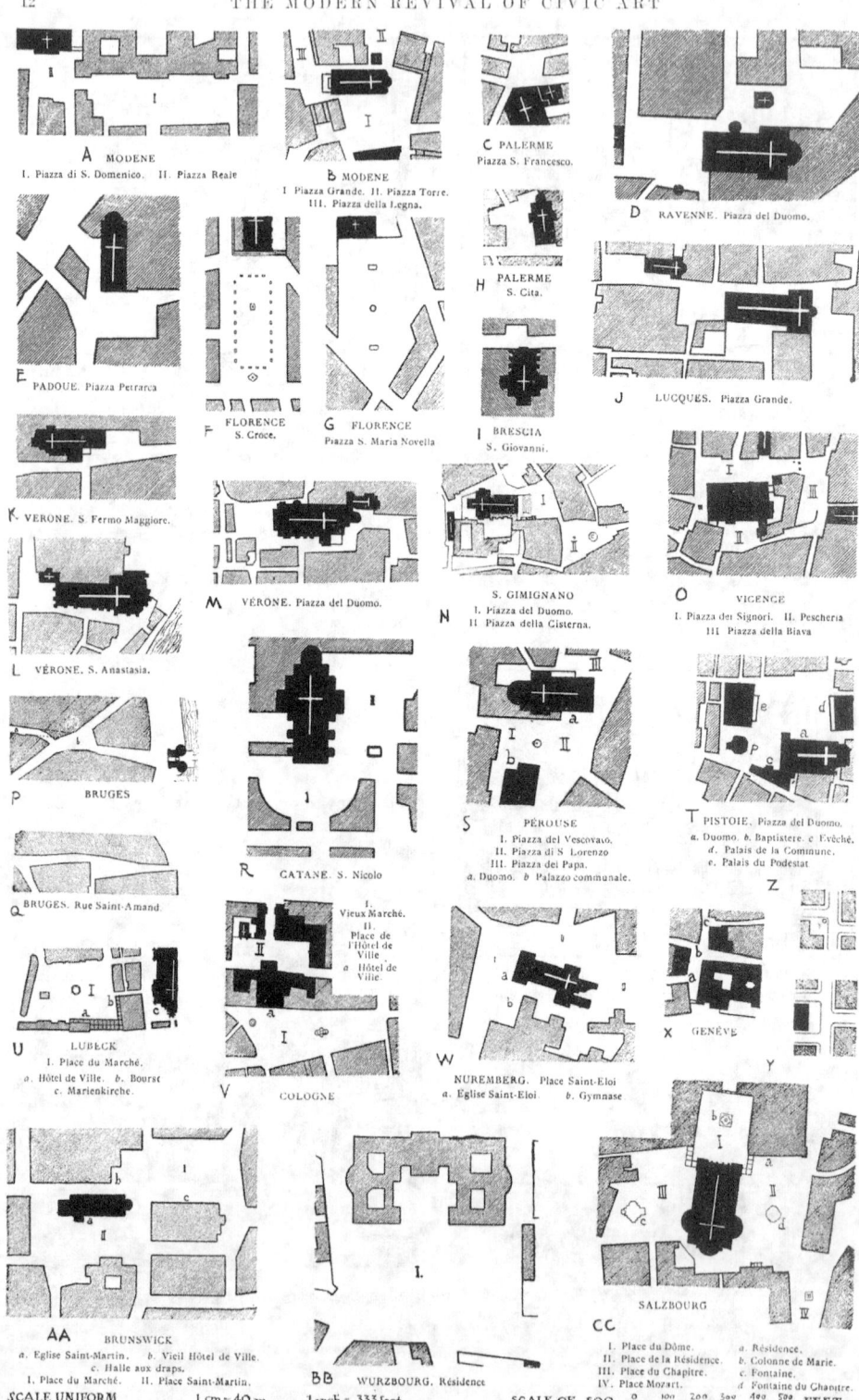

A MODENE
I. Piazza di S. Domenico. II. Piazza Reale

B MODENE
I. Piazza Grande. II. Piazza Torre.
III. Piazza della Legna.

C PALERME
Piazza S. Francesco.

D RAVENNE. Piazza del Duomo.

E PADOUE. Piazza Petrarca

F FLORENCE
S. Croce.

G FLORENCE
Piazza S. Maria Novella.

H PALERME
S. Cita.

I BRESCIA
S. Giovanni.

J LUCQUES. Piazza Grande.

K VERONE. S. Fermo Maggiore.

M VÉRONE. Piazza del Duomo.

N S. GIMIGNANO
I. Piazza del Duomo.
II Piazza della Cisterna.

O VICENCE
I. Piazza dei Signori. II. Pescheria
III Piazza della Biava

L VÉRONE. S. Anastasia.

P BRUGES

Q BRUGES. Rue Saint-Amand.

R CATANE. S. Nicolo

S PÉROUSE
I. Piazza del Vescovato.
II. Piazza di S. Lorenzo
III. Piazza dei Papa.
a. Duomo. b Palazzo communale.

T PISTOIE. Piazza del Duomo.
a. Duomo. b. Baptistere. c. Evêché.
d. Palais de la Commune.
e. Palais du Podestat

Z

U LUBECK
I. Place du Marché.
a. Hôtel de Ville. b. Bourse
c. Marienkirche.

V COLOGNE
I. Vieux Marché.
II. Place de l'Hôtel de Ville
a Hôtel de Ville.

W NUREMBERG. Place Saint-Eloi
a. Eglise Saint-Eloi b. Gymnase

X GENÈVE

Y

AA BRUNSWICK
a. Eglise Saint-Martin. b. Vieil Hôtel de Ville.
c. Halle aux draps.
I. Place du Marché. II. Place Saint-Martin.

BB WURZBOURG. Résidence

CC SALZBOURG
I. Place du Dôme.   a. Résidence.
II. Place de la Résidence. b. Colonne de Marie.
III. Place du Chapitre.   c. Fontaine.
IV. Place Mozart.   d Fontaine du Chapitre.

SCALE UNIFORM   1 cm = 40 m.   1 inch = 333 feet   SCALE OF 500   0 100 200 300 400 500 FEET

FIGS. 48-76 (A-CC)—TWENTY-NINE PLANS, AT UNIFORM SCALE, FROM CAMILLO SITTE

FIG. 77—VICENZA, PIAZZA DEI SIGNORI

For plan see cut "O" on preceding page. This is a "long" plaza in relation to Palladio's Basilica, and a "deep" plaza in relation to the campanile, which is set forward, thus creating, together with the two columns, a smaller transitional plaza connecting with the Piazza della Biava.

FIG. 78—STRASBOURG, CATHEDRAL.

The Rue Mercière leads right to the central entrance of the cathedral. The effect is good because the street is narrow and short (see plan Fig. 354) and the houses lining it are not too high. The appearance of the highly symmetrical central features of the western façade can thus dominate the view. If the street were longer and wider the unsymmetrical tower development and perspective diminution would become disturbing factors.

VICENZA, Piazza dei Signori   HH

STRASBOURG, Cathédrale   HB

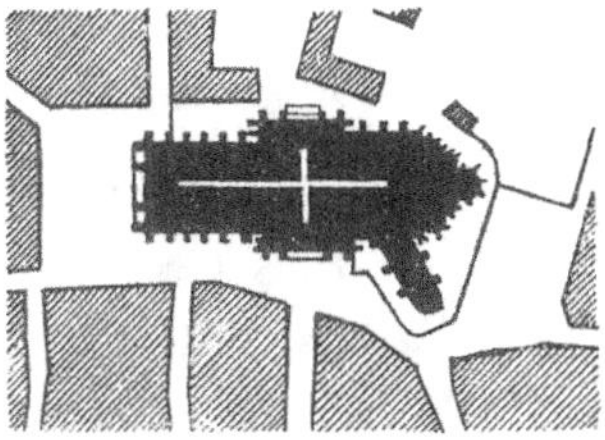

AMIENS Cathédrale.

A

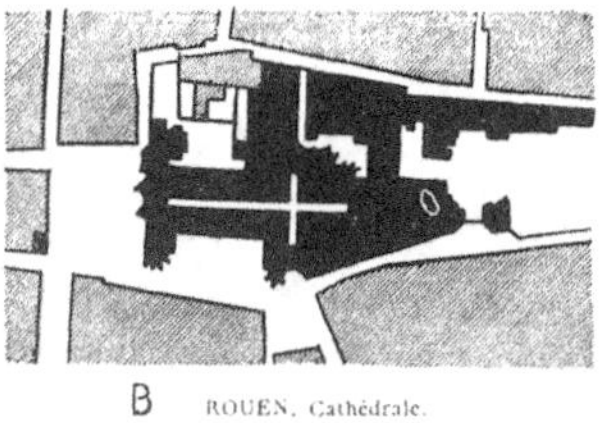

B   ROUEN, Cathédrale.

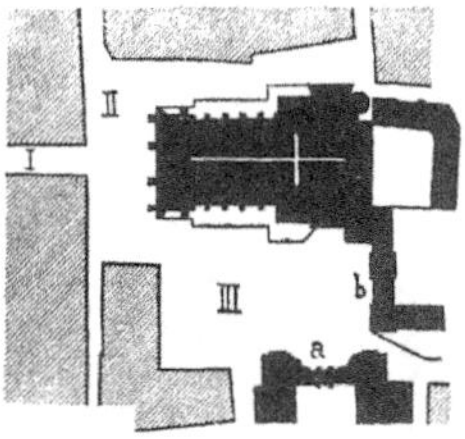

C   STRASBOURG
I. Rue Mercière   II. Place du Dôme
III. Place du Château.
a. Château de Rohan.   b. Lycée

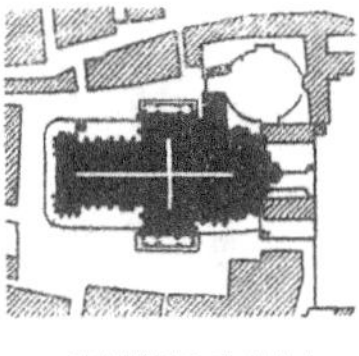

CHARTRES. Cathédrale.

D

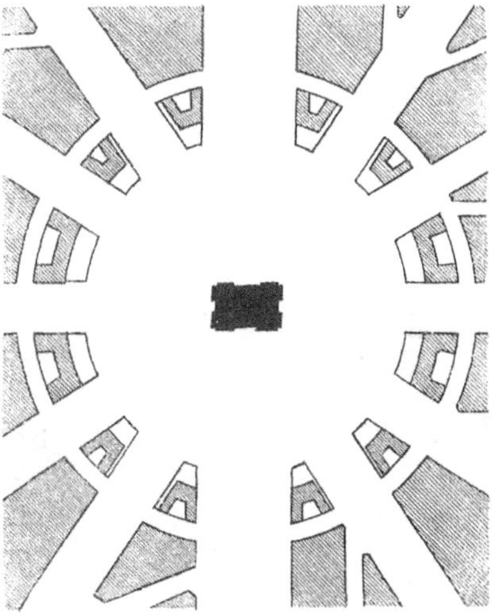

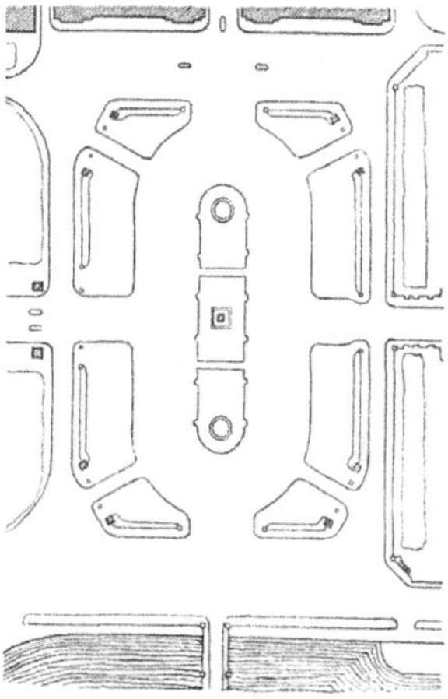

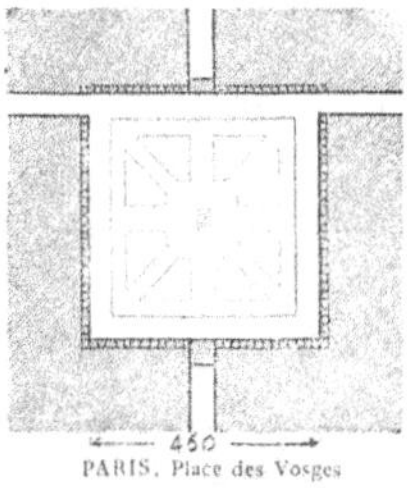

PARIS, Place des Vosges

E

PARIS, Place de l'Etoile

0   100' 200' 300' 400' 500'

1 IN.= 333 FT.

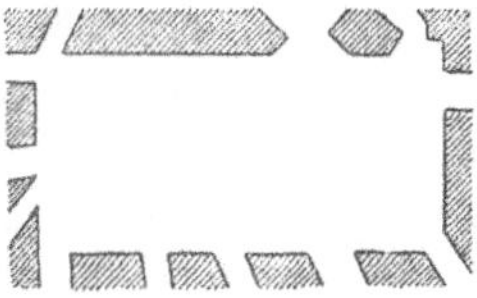

PARIS, Place de la Concorde.

G

H   MARSEILLE Place Saint-Michel

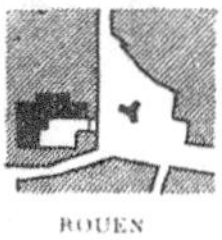

ROUEN
Place de la Pucelle

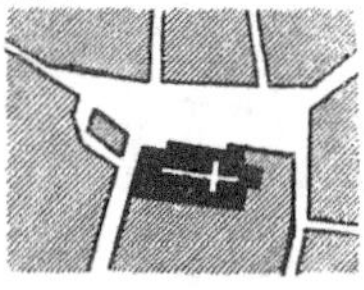

J   STRASBOURG, Saint-Thomas

K   STRASBOURG, Place Kleber.

FIGS. 79-89 (A-K)—ELEVEN PLANS FROM CAMILLO SITTE

At a uniform scale, except cut "E." The Place de l'Etoile in the center (for view see Fig. 254) and Place Saint-Michel, Marseilles, are shown as bad examples, the walls of these plazas being cut up too much. In the case of the Place Saint-Michel this defect of the architectural frame has been remedied by the planting of dense tree rows framing the inner area. The plan of the Place de l'Etoile is reversed.

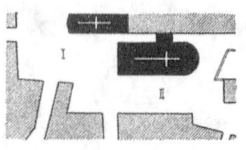

REGENSBURG

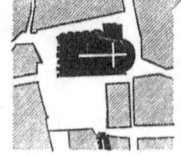

VICENCE. Piazza del Duomo

LUCQUES. S. Michel.

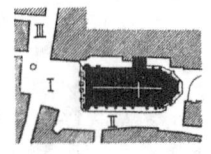

RATISBONNE

COLOGNE

I. Vieux Marché.
II. Place de
l'Hôtel de
Ville.
a, Hôtel de
Ville.

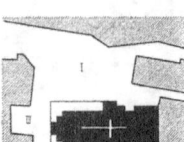

FIGS. 90-94—FIVE PLANS FROM
SITTE

Fig. 90—Regensburg
Fig. 91—Vicenza
Fig. 92—Lucca
Fig. 93—Ratisbon
Fig. 94—Cologne

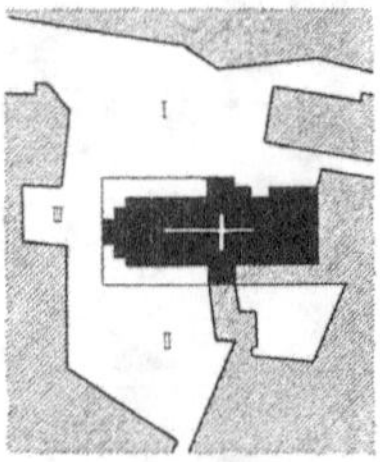

FIG. 95

Sitte describes the plazas grouped
around the cathedral of Hildesheim
as the naive effort of the highly cultivated Bishop Bernward to reconstruct the fora of Rome at a time
(1031 A. D.) when notions about
ancient Rome were very hazy.

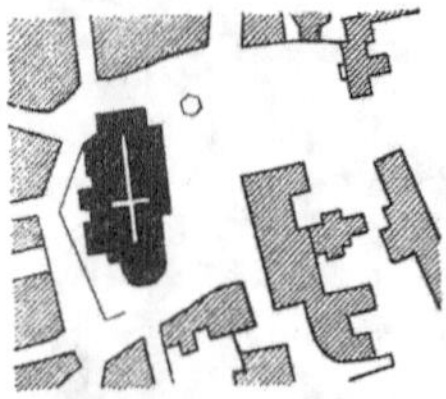

HILDESHEIM

AUTUN
Place Saint-Louis et fontaine Saint-Lazare

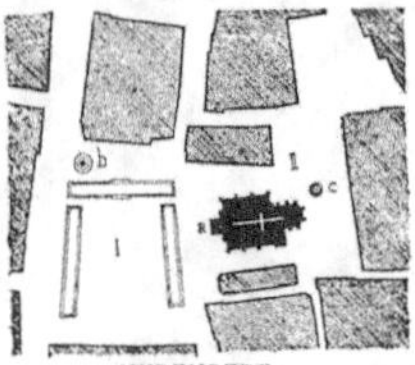

NUREMBERG

I. Place du Marché. Marché aux fruits.
a. Eglise Notre-Dame.
b. Belle Fontaine.
c. Fontaine du gardeur d'oies.

FRIBOURG-EN-BRISGAU. Cathédrale.

BRUGES
Cathédrale Saint-Sauveur.

FIGS. 96-99—FOUR PLANS FROM SITTE

Fig. 96—Autun; Fig. 97—Nuremberg; Fig. 98—Freiburg; Fig. 99—
Bruges.
    Scale about 330 feet to the inch except the Nuremberg plan which
is at a smaller scale. It shows the large market place cleared in the
fourteenth century in connection with an early reclamation scheme
razing the old ghetto. For view see Fig. 100.

the plaza. Few problems have set more architects busy
than has the question of how suitably to reduce the size
of the Koenigsplatz in Berlin (see Fig. 318), which much
to the detriment of the buildings adjoining it (especially
the large Parliament building) is ten times larger than
the Piazza San Marco in Venice. Similar problems were
created by the Champ de Mars in Paris, the City Hall
Square in Vienna, and others. The solution is often
sought in abandoning the idea of treating such oversized areas as architectural units and transforming them
into parks, filled with large trees and bordered by houses.

The question just what should be the proportion between the mass of the building and the plaza designed
to set it off, or vice versa, what mass should be given to
a building which is to face a given plaza, cannot be
answered by setting down a hard and fast rule. Experience shows that the dimensions of a plaza must be
at least equal to the height of the principal building
facing the plaza and that the maximum dimension depends upon "shape, purpose, and style of the building". Twice the height is often sufficient. (The question
of sizes of plazas will be discussed in the next chapter.)

The plazas must have, or appear to have, some symmetrical shape and axial relation to the important building facing them. Sitte emphasizes that the irregularity
of the Gothic plazas was neither wanted nor artificially
created by the Gothic designers, and that moreover it
was a thing they tried to hide as a "blemish" and often
did hide very successfully. "The irregularity so typical
of old plazas, results from a gradual historical development. One is seldom mistaken if one attributes this surprising tortuousness to practical causes". In developing
the façades of their plazas the Gothic designers relied
upon the fact that it is difficult for the eye to check up
even considerable "blemishes of symmetry" and that
things are apt to appear more regular on the ground
than in the plan. (Fig. 41, 42, 106 and 103-5.)

Amazing insight into the requirements of architectural
effect is shown by the grouping of old plazas around
prominent buildings. Often two or three elevations of a

FIG. 100—NUREMBERG MARKET PLACE AND "BELLE FONTAINE"
See plan, Fig. 97.

building are each made the object of a special setting by a special plaza most skillfully designed, as to size and height of walls, to meet the peculiar features of the elevation to be set off. The effect becomes supreme for the observer who moves from one plaza into an adjoining one and experiences the resulting changes of scale, light and shadow. Examples from Modena, Lucca, Vicenza, Perugia (Figs. 48, B, J, O, S) and other cities, are taken to prove that such plazas were designed as settings for the buildings after their construction and not vice versa, as it is unlikely that a set of plazas could have been designed previously, leaving it to a church to afterwards adapt its various façades to those differently shaped plazas.

Closing his remarks about connecting plazas with a study of the wonderful group dominated by San Marco in Venice (Fig. 107-110) — the main plaza being deep in relation to St. Mark's Cathedral, and long in relation to the two Procuratia palaces facing each other — Camillo Sitte makes this timely suggestion: "Let one try to imagine the Cathedral separated from its intimate connection with the walls of the piazza and put in the center

FIG. 106—PIAZZA SANTA MARIA NOVELLA, FLORENCE

For plan see "G" on p. 12 (Fig. 48-76). Sitte says regarding this plaza: "The difference that exists between the plan representation and the real aspect of Piazza Santa Maria Novella in Florence is surprising. In reality the plaza has five sides but in the memory of more than one traveller it has only four, because on the ground one can never see more than three sides of the plaza at once and the angle formed by the other two is always behind the observer. Furthermore it is easy to make a mistake in estimating the angle between these sides. The perspective effects make such an estimate difficult even for professional men when they make use of no other instrument than their eyes." The view is taken from an old guidebook.

of a huge modern plaza, and think of the palaces of the procurators, the library, and the campanile, now tied well together, as scattered over a wide area edging upon a boulevard 200 feet wide. What a nightmare!" One cannot but be struck with the resemblance this description bears to some of the recent projects for American Civic Centers.

However warm may be Camillo Sitte's appreciation of the civic designers of the Middle Ages who did such exceedingly fine work in the face of very adverse conditions, his fullest admiration belongs to the art of the Renaissance and especially to the seventeenth and eighteenth centuries, which had the opportunity of working out the great ideals of architecture much less hampered by practical necessities. Sitte also feels that the modern architect has to look for inspiration to the period of the Renaissance and the "Baroque" because these periods, like Hellenistic and Roman antiquity, and much more so

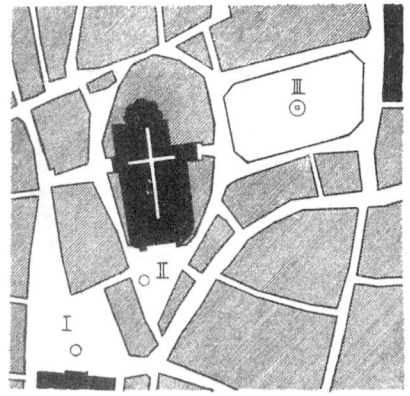

ANVERS
I. Grand Place.   II. Marché aux gants.   III. Place Verte.

FIG. 101—ANTWERP CATHEDRAL

A typical example of a medieval cathedral surrounded by plazas without giving a full view of its elevation except the façade. The irregular side elevations are screened, full views from the plazas being given only to the transepts.

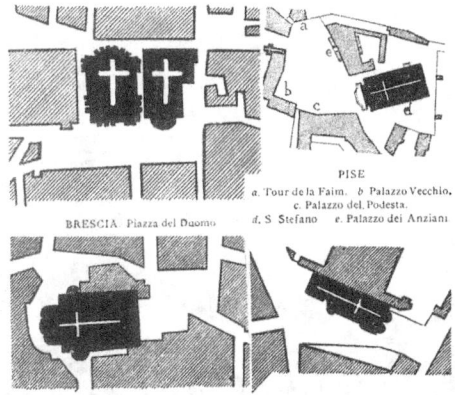

PISE
a. Tour de la Faim.   b Palazzo Vecchio, c. Palazzo del Podesta.
BRESCIA Piazza del Duomo   d. S Stefano   e. Palazzo dei Anziani

PADOUE. Piazza del Duomo   PADOUE. Piazza dei Eremitani.

FIGS. 102-105—FOUR PLANS FROM SITTE
Fig. 102—Brescia; Fig. 103—Pisa; Figs. 104, 105—Padua.

VENEZIA, la Piazzetta   HH

FIG. 107—PIAZZETTA, VENICE

FIG. 108—PIAZZA SAN MARCO, VENICE

View looking away from the Cathedral. (Photograph by courtesy of Edwin Cramer, architect, Milwaukee.)

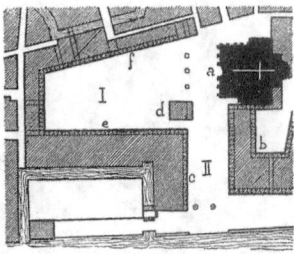

VENISE

I. Piazza di S. Marco.	c. Bibliothèque.
II. Piazzetta.	d. Campanile.
a. S. Marco.	e. Nouvelles Procuraties.
b. Palais des Doges.	f. Vieilles Procuraties.

FIGS. 109-10—AIR VIEW AND PLAN OF THE PIAZZA SAN MARCO

This group is the work of a thousand years. The campanile "d" was begun in the year 888, the cathedral "a" about 967; the two columns towards the water (Fig. 107) date from 1180, the Palace of the Doges "b" from 1423, the old Procuratia "f" by P. Lombardo, 1480, the Library "c" by Sansovino, 1536, the new Procuratia "e" by Scamozzi, 1584, and the building closing the plaza at the narrow end opposite St. Mark's (Fig. 108) was built as late as 1810. Nevertheless, the whole forms a harmonious ensemble.

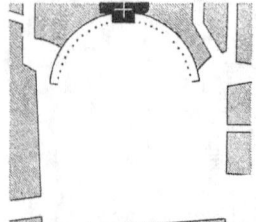

FIG. 112—PIAZZA DEL PLEBISCITO, NAPLES, PLAN

FIG. 111—PIAZZA DEL PLEBISCITO, NAPLES

This semicircle is designed as a setting for the church of San Francesco di Paola, a copy of the Pantheon built 1817-31, and forms the west wall of a plaza the other walls of which are formed by the Royal Palace and two other public buildings. In front of the church, framing—not blocking—the entrance, are two equestrian statues which remind one of the Piazza de' Cavalli in Piacenza (Fig. 159). The colonnades in front of the church are a good illustration of the extent to which a very inharmonious mass of high buildings can be screened by low colonnades and a comparatively orderly aspect secured under adverse conditions. (Photograph courtesy of Mr. Edwin Cramer).

FIG. 113—LE FAMEUX CAPITOLE
A ROME.

Old engraving by Rossi (from Mawson). Compare Fig. 162.

It is interesting to learn from
this engraving that in the old days
carriages discharged their passen-
gers at the foot of the ramped Cordonnata, instead of meandering up
a steep drive and entering the plaza
at one corner, as carriages do now.
The old stately approach on axis and
the banishment of carriages from
the floor of the plaza display much
the keener sense of the dignified
place of architecture in the drama
of civic life.

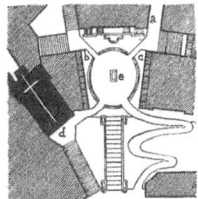

ROME. Place du Capitole.
a. Pal. del Senatore. b. Museo Capitolino.
c. Pal. del Conservatore.
d. S. Maria di Aracoeli.
e. Statue de Marc-Aurèle.

FIG. 114
PLAN OF THE CAMPIDOGLIO

For a larger and more detailed
plan of the Campidoglio see Fig. 163.

FIG. 115	FIG. 116	FIG. 117
SAN CARLO	PIARISTENPLATZ	HAYDN PLAZA
MILAN	VIENNA	VIENNA
125 feet wide	155 feet wide	135 feet wide

Three forecourts to churches created by simple indentation of
street. Sitte praises highly this type of plaza as giving on account
of its strong frame the effect of great spaciousness in spite of its
limited size. See Fig. 118-19. From Stuebben.

FIGS. 118-19—VIEW AND
PLAN OF JOSEPHS-
PLAZA, VIENNA

"The beauty of this plaza
which has hardly been surpassed anywhere is largely
due to the perfect closing
of three of the walls of the
plaza, which was made possible by using two arches,"
(Sitte). Designed by Fischer von Erlach, 1726. This
plaza and those shown in
Figs. 116-17 are interesting
also as the settings of
monuments with central
locations similar to those
illustrated in Figs. 368-72.

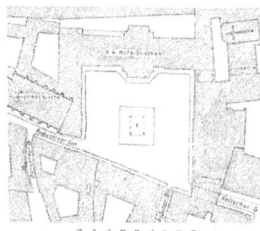

FIG. 121—ZWINGER, DRESDEN, CENTRAL COURT

This old view of the Zwinger produces much more the effect of a
public plaza than do recent views which show the clipped trees and
flower beds which now almost fill the area. The new gardening is well
done, but the old flatness and simplicity probably produced a better
total effect.

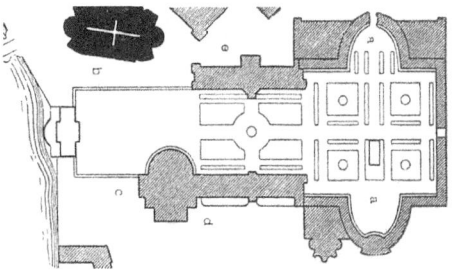

FIG. 120—ZWINGER, DRESDEN

Plan of Semper's project to connect the Zwinger-garden with the
river Elbe, "a" Zwinger, "b" Hofkirche, "c" Royal Theater, "d"
Orangerie, "e" Museum.

The Zwinger, one of the most brilliant achievements of Baroque
art, originally (1711-22) was built (by Poppelmann) as the outer forecourt of a castle planned to be erected on the river. As a plan feature
it therefore corresponded to the outer courts of similar plans as shown
in Figs. 392 and 469-12 (Madrid and Stuttgart). The side toward the
river remained open; but the castle was never built. When Semper
was called (about 1870) to build the new picture gallery he proposed
to follow the original idea transforming it as shown in Fig. 120, "e"
showing the location of the new gallery. His proposal was not appreciated and instead he had to close the open side of the Zwinger with
the new museum. The Zwinger, originally used for tournaments, is
to-day a charming garden area with a light elegant frame.

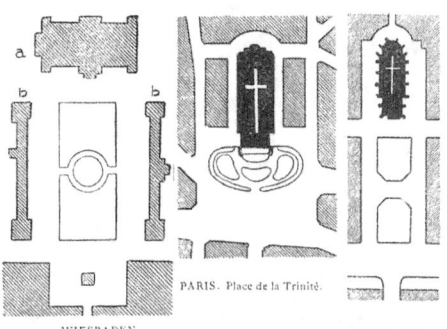

PARIS. Place de la Trinité.

WIESBADEN   WIESBADEN
a. Kursaal.   b. Colonnades.   Eglise catholique.

FIGS. 122-24—THREE PLANS FROM SITTE

Comparatively good modern plazas, the design of which however
could have been improved if the street entrances could have been partly
eliminated or closed by arches and colonnades.

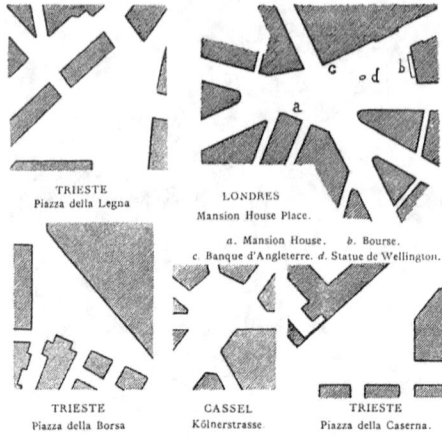

TRIESTE
Piazza della Legna

LONDRES
Mansion House Place.

a. Mansion House.   b. Bourse.
c. Banque d'Angleterre. d. Statue de Wellington.

TRIESTE
Piazza della Borsa

CASSEL
Kölnerstrasse

TRIESTE
Piazza della Caserna.

FIGS. 125-29—FIVE AWKWARD STREET INTERSECTIONS

Given by Sitte as examples of the thoughtless routine planning of
his time, producing situations hardly capable of artistic improvement.

than the Gothic age had to conceive large plans for immediate realization, very much in contrast to the slow, almost vegetable, growth of civic building during the Middle Ages. He points out how city planning art since the beginning of the Renaissance vied with painting and sculpture in the development of great perspective effects. The frontispiece of his book is an engraving of the Piazza of St. Peter in Rome. But the Piazza di S. Pietro still is influenced by the classic ideal of the closed forum as the ideal setting for a public building and with all its perspective effects is still conceived as a plaza enclosed on all sides — in the shape of a Roman circus — while the most important contribution of the Renaissance period, as Camillo Sitte recognizes, is the plaza closed on three sides only, the perfect prototype of which was achieved in the Piazza del Campidoglio in Rome (Figs. 162-63). It may be called the discovery of Michelangelo, heralding the greatest period of civic art, that the quality of support and esthetic security, which a closed plaza can give as a setting for a public building, may be gotten from a plaza which is closed on three sides only, leaving the fourth side open for the enjoyment of well framed vistas into far away perspectives. The visitor to the Piazza del Campidoglio climbing the stairs gets a view of the Capitol which is well framed by the palace of the Senate and the Museum; turning his back to the Capitol he enjoys an open view over the eternal city. The plaza framed on three sides, with the fourth one thrown open to the city, with well framed vistas towards interesting points nearby or far away becomes the type upon which the seventeenth and eighteenth centuries bestowed the most wonderful refinement. Sitte, who happened to have been educated in a school facing a fine specimen (Fig. 117) of this type of plaza so especially suited for modern conditions, and who had grown up in Vienna with its characteristic late Renaissance face, (Figs. 118-9 give a fair example), would never tire of calling attention to how much we can learn from seventeenth and eighteenth century art. He was right in foretelling that it would take many volumes even to inventory the wonderful achievements of civic art in the seventeenth and eighteenth centuries — these volumes have since been written by his followers — the traditions of which have unfortunately been lost to the men who in modern times are intrusted with the designs of city plans.

Sitte's remarks about the laying out of streets as made in the original edition have been amplified in the French edition in which the translator with the cooperation of Sitte's disciples added a special chapter on street design. Sitte has often been criticized for being responsible for the wantonly crooked streets the affectation of which disgraces many town plans made since the appearance of his book. This is unjust. Camillo Sitte had a sincere appreciation of the grandiose and monumental effect of the straight street especially if it has an interesting terminal feature. Where Haussmann's work in Paris, following eighteenth century precedent, provides for such streets Sitte specially commends them as the one redeeming feature of Haussmann's plan. But he did not want the straight street used continuously just as a matter of routine without regard to the configuration of the soil or esthetic requirements. He wanted every street to be an artistic unit, which is difficult to achieve with straight streets of interminable length without artistic interpunctuation. He is well justified in recommending deviation from the straight line at the junction of two streets to avoid a sharp angle (Fig. 48P). This gives him a welcome break in a monotonous length which he is satisfied to get by other means (Fig. 48Y and Z) when the streets intersect at right angles. He points out the esthetic necessity of giving architectural recognition to a high point in the street, a requirement which can and should be satisfied in the case of modern straight streets just as well (Fig. 693). If some of Camillo Sitte's remarks have been construed — some think unjustly — as recommendation of purposely designed sinuous streets, contrary to the spirit of Renaissance art, it will be interesting to remember that the great theoretician of the early Renaissance, Alberti, has recommended sinuous streets partly for esthetic reasons. This attitude was abandoned with the progress of the Renaissance movement and it is on the whole more the spirit of the seventeenth and eighteenth centuries than of Alberti's time that speaks from Camillo Sitte's writings.

Here should, however, be mentioned a delicate point which occasionally may bring about a difference of attitude between Sitte, and his modern followers. Sitte says: "Practically any system of street design can be brought to an artistic effect provided it is not carried out with that brutality which may s a t i s fy the local spirit of modern American cities and which, unfortunately, has lately acclimatized itself in Europe" (Fig. 125-129).

The request that the designer of the street system should make occasional concessions to the requirements of the monumental setting for individual public buildings certainly sounds moderate, but it is a delicate matter to determine how far these concessions should go. A practical illustration may be found in the plan for Carlsruhe which Sitte condemns and which the authors of this book must commend though without overlooking its one weakness, consisting of a number of rather undesirably shaped corners, a weakness it shares with similar regular plans like Christopher Wren's plans for London or the plan of the city of Versailles. While Sitte objects to regularity bought at so dear a price and calls it "playing with geometrical patterns", the modern followers of Sitte, while quite agreeing with him about the undesirability of certain awkward corners, would rather have them than sacrifice the big schemes, which occasionally produce them. Modern designers must hope to please even so sensitive a critic as Camillo Sitte by gradually working their way toward the conception of big schemes which avoid the awkward corners by ingenious location of streets or make them less objectionable by ingenious architectural treatment.

On every page Camillo Sitte's book is a spirited exposure of that inartistic fake symmetry and thoughtless formalism of the T-square, by which gridiron, diagonal, or radial street systems have been applied to our

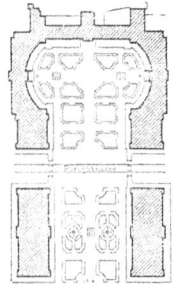

FIG. 130—PLAN OF SEMPER'S
HOFBURG PLAZA, VIENNA

The plaza is about 500 feet wide.

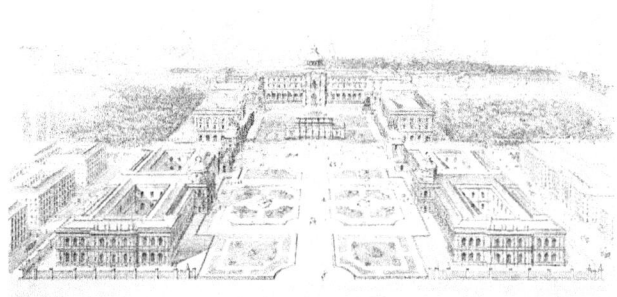

FIG. 131—IMPERIAL FORUM, VIENNA

This drawing by Semper and von Hasenauer shows Semper's original proposal (dating from about 1869) to throw a plaza from the imperial castle across the new Ringstrasse to the old imperial coachhouse. The street openings are shown bridged over by triumphal arches. The greater part of this project has been executed (see Fig. 138) but even so it is hard to judge the final appearance. In proportion to the very large size of the plaza the well placed monuments have to be enormous; the central statue of Empress Maria Theresa including the high pedestal measures 64 feet; the two equestrian monuments in the semicircles, 53 feet. (The original monument in the Place de la Concorde was 40 feet high.) The open area of the entire plaza is about 25 acres, while the Place de la Concorde in Paris measures only about 20 acres. While the latter however has an architectural frame (80 feet high) on one side only, the Imperial Forum in Vienna is to be framed on all sides, the buildings (105 feet high) being one third higher than Gabriel's colonnades. Furthermore the Vienna design is subdivided into two courts by the old gate which was left standing in the center.

modern cities, turning them into dreary places where it is hard or impossible to show fine buildings to advantage. Even the better productions of the system of T-square geometry which he was fighting appeared unsuitable to him for architectural development by an artist. (Fig. 34-40, 122-24. To this list the French translator adds the Place de l'Etoile in Paris, Fig. 79, which in its present shape is a creation of Haussmann who increased the number of converging streets and thereby reduced the walls framing the plaza. The repose of the plaza was destroyed and a restless street intersection remained).

Camillo Sitte has two bêtes noires, equally familiar to the American architect: the plaza which is not designed by an artist but is an ugly leftover which results from permitting many streets to intersect indiscriminately at one point, producing no effective building sites; and the casual way in which public buildings which are not adapted to stand free are so often dropped somewhere into plazas ill suited to set them off.

Camillo Sitte's thinking had been deeply influenced by the not always satisfactory experiences, gained from the first Viennese city planning competition called in 1858 and resulting in the plans for the Ringstrasse (Fig. 137-8) with the large groups of new public buildings constructed under Sitte's eyes. He warmly commends the forum designed by Semper for the Ringstrasse and other designs by the same architect (Fig. 130-1 and 120-1).

Camillo Sitte's book closes with a number of designs of his own by which he shows by theoretical examples and by practical solutions of outstanding problems of his time

FIG. 131A—THE HOFBURG, VIENNA

(See Figs. 130 and 131.)

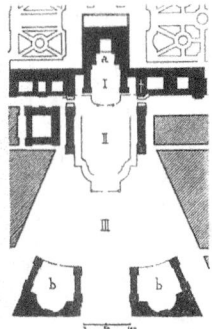

FIG. 132—VERSAILLES.

ENTRANCE COURTS

The area "II" is sometimes called the Court of the Ministers. "I" is not the Cour de Marbre but Cour Royale. The Cour de Marbre is the little area above the letter "a". Around it Lemercier built of brick and stone a hunting lodge for Louis XIII in 1624. Louis XIV preserved the charming façade and made it the heart of the spreading suite of courts produced by the constant extensions. Instead of the fence indicated between "I" and "II" there is an equestrian statue of Louis XIV, at the center of the three radiating avenues. These avenues, of course, were suggested by the Piazza del Popolo. In place of the two churches, the larger scale suggested two horseshoe shaped courts (the stables, "b") which are admirably suited to their places in the design.

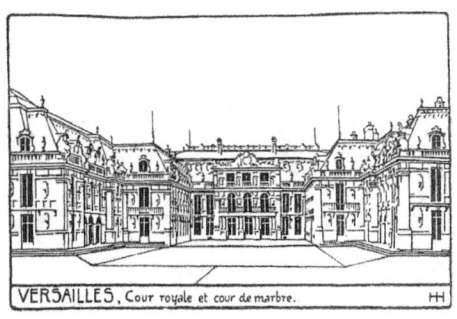

VERSAILLES, Cour royale et cour de marbre.   HH

FIG. 133

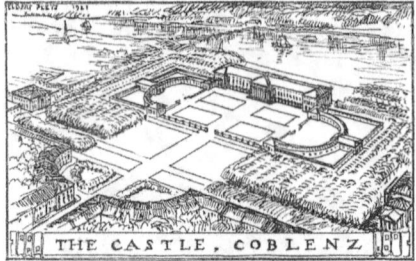

FIG. 134—COBLENZ

This sketch "visualizing" the setting of the royal palace at Coblenz
is partly based on an engraving of 1817. The castle was built 1778-'85
from plans by Dixnard, revised by A. F. Peyre.

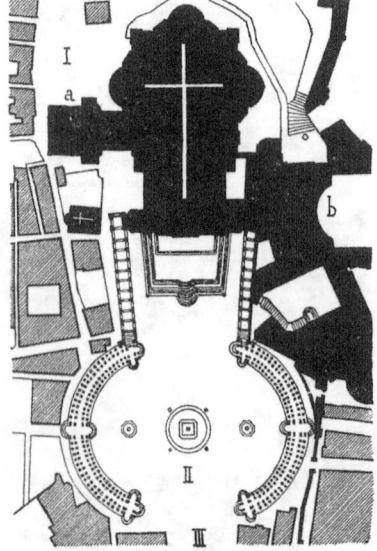

ROME

FIG. 136—ST. PETER'S, ROME

This plan is reproduced here to facilitate comparisons of size, it
being at the same scale as most other plans from Sitte. For other
material relating to St. Peter's see Figs. 243-50.

FIG. 137—THE RAMPARTS OF VIENNA BEFORE 1858 WITH ST.
CHARLES BORROMAEUS CHURCH IN THE DISTANCE

The charming rampart walks of old Vienna were destroyed to make
way for the Ringstrasse.

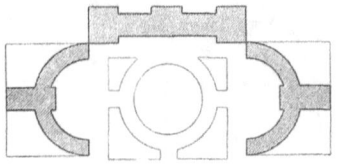

FIG. 135—COBLENZ
Plan of the "Schloss," from Sitte.

how modern public buildings ought in his opinion to be
set. (Fig. 139-42). These designs together with some of his
plans for the re-design of or addition to old cities (Fig.
150-51) show clearly how strongly his work tended in the
direction of formal design in the best sense of the word.

Camillo Sitte's followers are of two kinds. The
majority of them had the romantic inclinations of their
period—inclinations similar to those professed by Charles
Garnier (see p. 23). Thus they mistook Cammilo Sitte's
exposure of routine geometry as a defense of "informal",
picturesque, or "medieval" design, and did much very
poor work. The intelligent followers of Camillo Sitte
turned their attention mainly to the art of the Renaissance, Renaissance in this connection being understood,
in the broadest sense of the word, as comprising the
period 1400 to 1800, especially the seventeenth and eighteenth centuries. Among these are writers like Raymond Unwin, Patrick Abercrombie, A. E. Brinckmann,
Cornelius Gurlitt, and F. Ostendorf, whose publications
will frequently be made use of in the following pages.
Raymond Unwin in his town plans and writings stood up
for the town planning traditions of Christopher Wren and
Carlsruhe, which had not been understood during the romantic depression of the 19th century. A. E. Brinckmann, in his discerning books followed Camillo Sitte's
advice and has collected and analyzed the great work
achieved in civic art during the seventeenth and eighteenth centuries. Similar lines are now being followed
by the leading city planning periodicals, especially the
"Town Planning Review" of Liverpool, "Der Staedtebau", and, recently, "Stadtbaukunst".

"Informal" design, diametrically opposed to the spirit
of Classic and Renaissance art as it is, nevertheless deserves a paragraph in an American book on civic art,
because it had a great following not only in Europe but
even in America—although here it never had a traditional
basis or the practical cause of lack of space which often
had been its excuse in the old world. After the Renaissance had disposed of informality the tiring eighteenth
century and the disorganized post-revolutionary period
came back to it and imputed to it all kinds of new charms.

While the appearance of informality as a whole might
be thought of as the weakening of nerves preparatory and
parallel to the romantic demoralization of the arts which
generally is supposed to have reached its American climax in the Philadelphia exposition of 1876, it must not
be forgotten that there are several kinds of informality.
After the Renaissance had turned decidedly against the
informality of the Middle Ages, involuntary and dictated
by conditions as it often was, the designers of the Post-
Renaissance period made it a point to break the laws
which had been considered immutable during the Renaissance. Michelangelo meant to "burst the toils and
chains" of architectural rules, ancient and modern. That
does not mean, however, that he and his followers wanted
to be without rules; on the contrary in place of the old
simple rules that were broken, new and more complicated
ones were established and the new ones grew continuously more intricate, finally evolving the superrefinement of
Rococo.

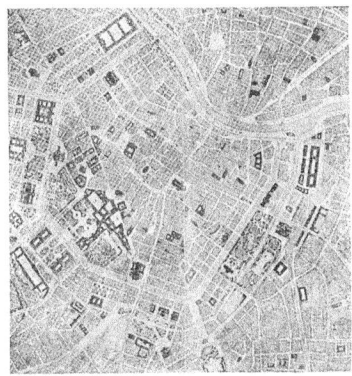

FIG. 138—THE RING OF VIENNA WITH THE PUBLIC BUILDINGS
BUILT SINCE 1858

The building of the Ring and transformation of Paris were probably the most important events in the city planning history of the nineteenth century. While Haussmann's work aimed mainly at military, sanitary, and other engineering objectives, in Vienna artistic purposes predominated. The "first city planning competition" of 1858 (called so to contrast it against the "second competition" of 1893) and its results raised the artistic aspiration of Vienna to the highest pitch and kept it there for decades. The work done represents much of the first groping for new standards in public building. While most of the work was good, some features have been justly condemned. One of the two big groups of new buildings, the Imperial Forum shown in the southwest corner of the plan, has been illustrated and commended in Figs. 130 to 131A. The group consisting of City Hall, Parliament, Theatre and University with the Votivkirche north of it (the group is shown in the middle of the left side of the plan Fig. 138) was made the object of special criticism by Camillo Sitte who proposed redesigning it as shown in Fig. 139.

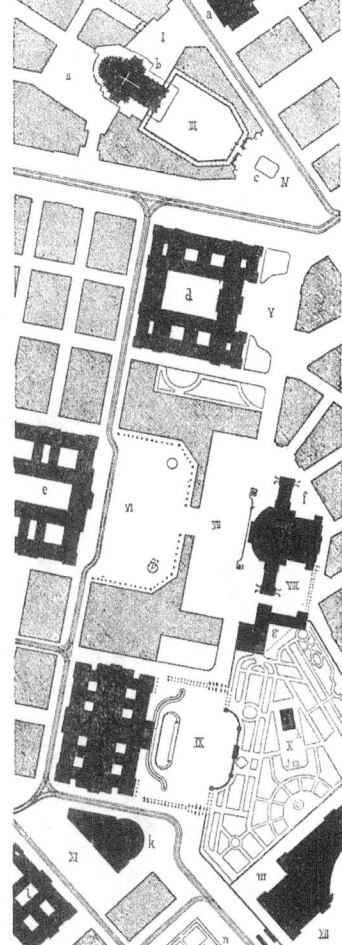

FIG. 140—VIENNA.

The large inarticulate triangle in front of the Votivkirche for which Sitte made a new design (Fig. 139) which was further developed by Ohmann (Fig. 141).

FIG. 141—VOTIVKIRCHE, VIENNA.

F. Ohmann's proposal for the development of the area of which the present condition is shown in Fig. 140. He suggests two large apartment houses one at each side, placed symmetrically to form a niche for the church. The lower stories of these apartment houses are pulled forward to frame the atrium in front of the church. The low buildings framing the atrium set a scale which accentuates the great height of the church. In front of the atrium is a monument, pulled far enough forward to be seen from the Ring.

FIG. 139—VIENNA, CIVIC CENTER AS REDESIGNED BY CAMILLO
SITTE

(a) Chemical laboratory, (b) Votivkirche, (c) Plaza for a large monument, (d) University, (e) City Hall, (f) Theatre, (g) Proposed annex to theatre, (h) Temple of Thesens, (j) Proposed location of Goethe Monument, (k) Proposed new building, (l) Palace of Justice, (m) Part of Imperial Forum, (see Fig. 130), (n) Triumphal Arch (part of the Imperial Forum).

The group consisting of the city hall, with the theatre facing it, and the adjacent university and parliament buildings (IX) leaves an area between the buildings which is too large for a monumental plaza. It is at present filled up with trees (see Fig. 138). Sitte proposed to partly cover it with buildings thereby producing a series of small plazas such as VI, a plaza in front of the city hall and communicating with VII, a plaza in front of the theatre. Between the theatre (f) and the proposed annex (g) another small plaza (VIII) becomes possible as on this side there is land available which is not the case on the north side of the theatre. In front of the parliament a plaza (IX) is partitioned off by a large scheme of colonnades and walls. In front of the Palace of Justice (l) an awkwardly shaped area is regularized by absorbing the awkwardness in a proposed new building (k) leaving a well shaped long plaza (XI). The Gothic church (b, Votivkirche) at present stands upon a large triangle as shown in Fig. 140. This triangle Sitte proposes to organize by framing off in front of the church a colonnaded parvis (III) as atrium to the church. In front of this atrium was to be a plaza (IV) for a large monument (c). The proposal for the area around the Votivkirche has been further developed in the project reproduced in Fig. 141.

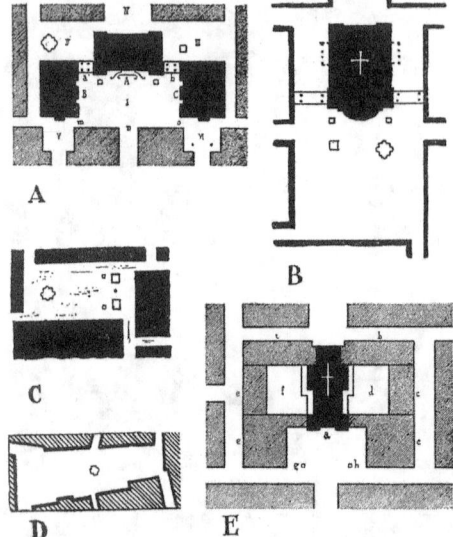

A

B

C

D

E

FIG. 142—FORMAL PLAZAS, PROPOSALS BY CAMILLO SITTE

A—Group of three large buildings connected by bridges over arcades and arranged together with the surrounding buildings, to form six plazas. B—Setting of a church; the façade supported by colonnades. C—Design of plaza formalizing suggestions given by the old Neuemarkt, Vienna, shown in D. E—Setting of a church in the center of educational buildings; design of the forecourt suggested by Pfarrplatz (see Fig. 116). It is characteristic of the misinterpretation of which Sitte's work has been a victim that a prominent city planning handbook in reproducing Sitte's plans A and E omits in three instances the formally located pairs of monuments by which Sitte proposes to flank three of his façades in the way of customary in the Renaissance (see Figs. 157-59 and 111) thus supporting instead of blocking the façades.

FIG. 143—PARIS. NOTRE-DAME BEFORE THE NINETEENTH CENTURY

From an engraving by Israel.

Situation primitive.

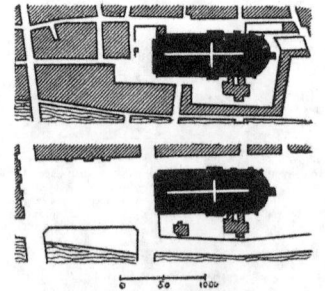

PARIS. Notre-Dame.

Situation actuelle.

FIGS. 144 AND 144A

The original setting of Nôtre-Dame de Paris was typical for medieval settings, low buildings in the immediate neighborhood of the church giving scale to the central monument. The clearing away of the low buildings and the erection of tall structures around the oversized area in front of the church does incalculable harm to the appearance of Nôtre-Dame as seen from many points of view.

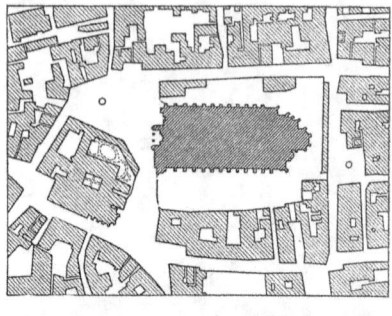

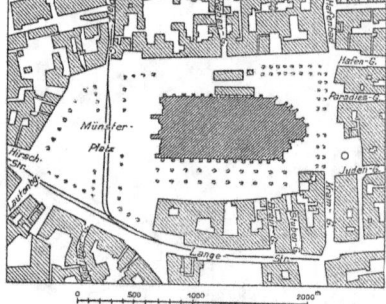

FIG. 146—ULM CATHEDRAL AFTER THE CLEARING OF THE NEIGHBORHOOD

This plan represents the conditions upon which the two proposals below seek to improve through the reduction of the size of the open area in front of the church.

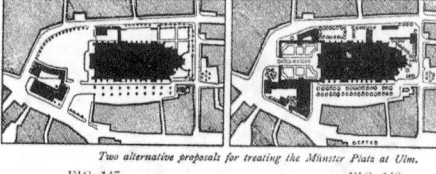

Two alternative proposals for treating the Münster Platz at Ulm.

FIG. 147　　　　　　　　　　FIG. 148

After the neighborhood of the cathedral had been cleared, for which money had been raised laboriously by popular subscription, the bleak appearance of the isolated building brought about a competition for the redesigning of its setting. Fig. 147 shows a proposal which aims at reconstructing very nearly the original condition. Fig. 148 follows Camillo Sitte's proposal for a formal atrium in front of Votivkirche (Figs. 139 and 141). The juxtaposition of the two plans (Figs. 147 and 148) illustrates well two schools of civic designers; the one trying to copy medieval informalities, the other, following Camillo Sitte, boldly casting them aside as most likely the old Gothic designers would have done if they had had a chance. (From Raymond Unwin).

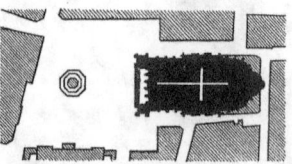

PARIS. Place Saint-Sulpice.

FIG. 149

The plaza in front of St. Sulpice was built by the first Napoleon as a setting for the Renaissance church. The design is interesting for the way in which the short lengths of wall at each side of the church are kept well back from the plane of the façade in order to give good views of the two towers.

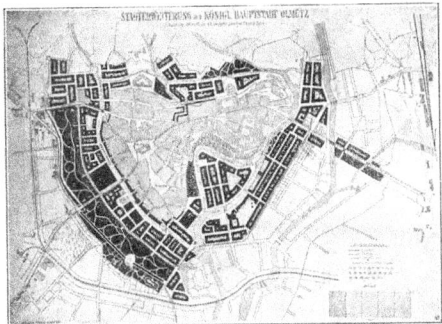

FIG. 150—OLMUETZ. PLAN FOR THE SUBDIVISION OF THE
LAND SURROUNDING THE OLD CITY. BY CAMILLO SITTE.

The old city lies on a plateau and the land surrounding it consists
largely of steep slopes. Sitte subdivided it into long narrow blocks
(from 125 to 140 feet wide) which have been built up connectedly
with continuous interior gardens.

This playing at the game of breaking old laws in order
to make more complicated new ones, which may be considered as one of the key notes of Baroque and Rococo
art, found its last perverse expression in the wilful desire to make believe that no laws had been considered at
all; Queen Marie Antoinette, the supreme arbiter of refinement, thus enjoyed dressing as a milkmaid and having
in her "Little Trianon" the fun of looking perfectly naive.
The informal gardens of Japan, following upon the stately majesty of the old temple settings, may perhaps find
a similar explanation as the informality of Little Trianon
in the immediate neighborhood of the "esprit classique"
of Versailles.

There is another kind of informality which is little
more than a misunderstanding. Well-meaning people
who grew up during the disorganized post-revolutionary
period or in pioneer countries without tradition or without a true sense of its value, imagined that by living in
the woods and by appreciating and imitating "nature"
the shortcomings of the old civilization could be avoided
and art would be regenerated. To them informality
seemed to possess all kinds of charms. Incidentally, informality was supposed to be democratic and expressive of
the fine taste of the Middle Ages. This supposed preference for irregularity, imputed to the designers of the
crystalline cathedral plans, appears just as fictitious as
the idea that the builders of the Propylea, the Erechtheion, or the Forum Romanum had a preference for irregular plans, when in reality their freedom of expression
had been interfered with by practical and economic necessities that made them deviate from symmetry. (See
below p. 29).

Since the death of traditional art had left the field
free for mechanical formalism of the worst kind even
such fine minds as Downing, Richardson and the elder
Olmsted found no other way of expressing their revolt
than to profess "informal" tendencies, traces of which
can still be found in present day architecture and in the
design of parks and land subdivisions.

Indeed "informalism" found support from the most
unexpected quarters. It is very surprising to hear for instance a man like Garnier — when, "after fifteen years
of worry about the bad location of his Opéra, he unbur-
dens his heavy heart" — advocating informal design.
From his utterances one gathers that he is well satisfied to have his Opéra surrounded by rectangular plazas
and porticos, but that outside of these plazas he wishes
for narrow streets, purposely designed to be tortuous,
with irregular façades. No street is to be straight; no
houses are to be of equal height. He seems to believe it

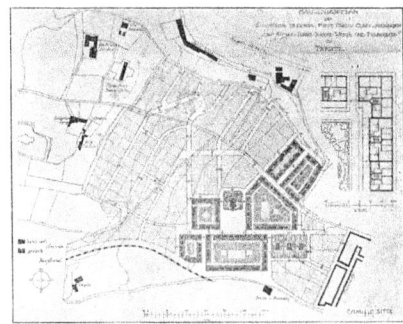

FIG. 151—TEPLITZ. SITTE'S PLAN FOR THE SUBDIVISION OF
A LARGE SLOPING AREA ADJOINING THE CITY

The emphasis is laid on obtaining straight streets and a formal
plaza in spite of the sloping territory. Large interior parks.

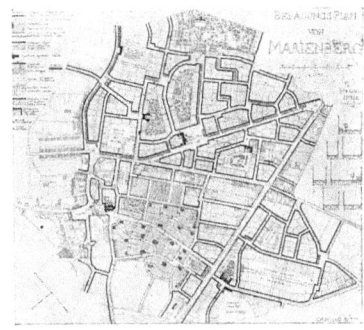

FIG. 152—MARIENBERG. CITY PLAN BY CAMILLO SITTE

The territory is so irregular, that the forecourt of the church had
to be terraced. The main avenue leading to the city hall plaza has
trees on the north side only. The market is laid in the interior of a
large block. The main avenues are straight; the minor streets avoid
sharp street intersections though keeping as close as possible to the
complicated property lines.

Figs. 150-52 were exhibited at the International city planning exhibition of 1910 by Sitte's son as a demonstration of his father's
preference for straight streets. He points out that in spite of irregular
topography and strict adherence to existing property lines Camillo
Sitte used curves, breaks, and changes of street axes only when there
were obvious practical reasons.

possible to purposely copy the contrasts that present themselves in old cities where spacious formal plazas without
much relation to the street system of the city have been
created by princely enterprise in the midst of congested
and inevitably very informal quarters. He may have had
in mind the startling impression that one gains, when,
after wandering through the labyrinth of the Borgi, one
comes upon the Piazza del Campidoglio or of S. Pietro in
Rome. As if he — the Beaux-Arts man — were a disciple

FIG. 153—EXAMPLE OF THE TYPE OF SINUOUS MEDIEVAL
STREETS ADVOCATED BY MANY SELF-STYLED FOLLOWERS OF
CAMILLO SITTE.

The picturesque effect of façades seen at an angle results without
having to be artificially produced, from the breaks in street direction
which frequently are enforced by topographical or other practical
reasons.

FIG. 154—PROPOSAL FOR ZURICH CITY HALL AND FORECOURT MADE BY SEMPER, 1858.
The city hall is tied into the plaza by two-storied arcades whose cornice lines are taken up by elements in the façades of the apartment houses at the sides of the plaza.

FIG. 155—CITY HALL, HERNE
The purpose of this view of the model is to show the method of "closing" the plaza visually even though it had to be opened for the convenience of traffic.

FIG. 156—CITY HALL PLAZA, HERNE

In a competition held in 1909 for the design of a civic center to comprise city hall, court house, postoffice, and office buildings and covering an area of twenty-two acres, this plan by Kurzreuter, Harro, and Moell was selected for execution. It entered the competition under the motto "Camillo Sitte" and is typical of the interpretation Sitte's writings were given at the time by many young architects. Note location of equestrian monument in one corner of the plaza. (From plan and model shown at the Berlin City Planning Exhibition).

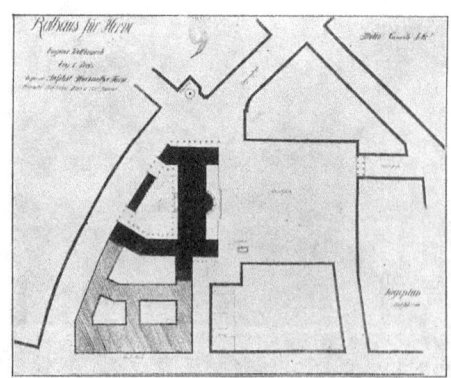

FIG. 156A—CITY HALL PLAZA, HERNE

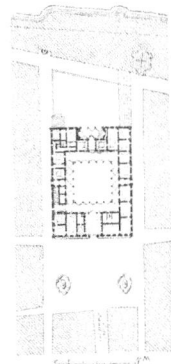

FIG. 157—ROME. PIAZZA FARNESE
(From Brinckmann.) See Fig. 158.

FIG. 158—ROME. PIAZZA AND PALAZZO FARNESE

This view of the Palazzo Farnese is not from an old engraving but was designed (by Ostendorf) with the vanishing point in the center following the method of old engravings. Except for the irregularity of the minor houses the setting is perfect. The narrow streets on both sides of the Palazzo close in the perspective without however touching the identity of the self-reliant cubical mass which is the representative type of the nobleman's residence of the period. A street enters the plaza on axis of the entrance to the palazzo; it was this axis which Michelangelo wanted to continue by a bridge across the Tiber into the gardens of the Villa Farnesina. In admiring the majestic balance of the façade it must be remembered that behind the even rows of windows are rooms of various sizes. In other words Sangallo and Michelangelo thought it more important to give the plaza a well balanced wall than to express the interior requirements.

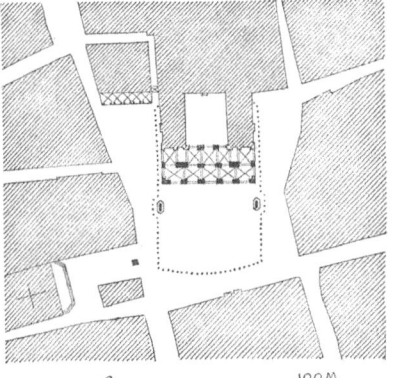

FIG. 159—PIACENZA. PIAZZA DE' CAVALLI

The forecourt to the Palazzo Comunale, built 1281, is the regular area flanked by two equestrian statues (1620-24) set off by posts about two feet high. The plaza is framed by fairly uniform houses four stories high. The Palazzo Comunale has only two stories but the lower story, an open arcade of light marble, is as high as the surrounding four story houses. The equally high second story, of red brick and terra cotta, resembles in color the surrounding houses over the roofs of which it is raised. (From Brinckmann.)

of Viollet-le-Duc, he expresses his hope for a "revival of the picturesque". This is the very picturesqueness in civic art which Camillo Sitte has so often and so unjustly been accused of propagating, which, no doubt, many of his followers have tried to attain, and which is so diametrically opposed to the spirit of traditional art in America, the spirit of Vitruvius, Palladio, Christopher Wren, the Adams, and Thomas Jefferson.

The emphasis Camillo Sitte lays on the closed-in effect of plazas is another point of his teaching which has often been criticized. The critics say: the effect of closed-in plazas may have been all right for the congested towns of former times, but the modern city with unlimited areas opened up by good transportation facilities does not want closing in but opening up; a much looser texture is desirable and perhaps more beautiful. The answer to this criticism is that the looseness of texture which may be brought about by reducing the number of houses per acre does really hardly affect esthetic requirements. The artist wants beautifully shaped spaces in our cities and

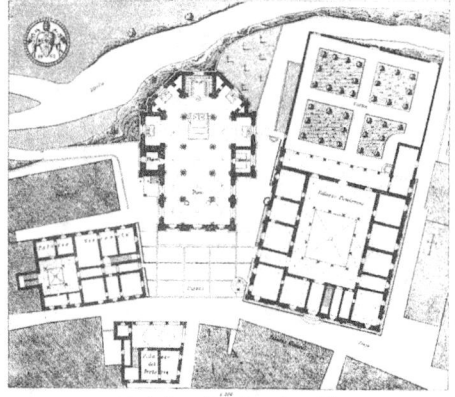

FIG. 160—PIENZA. CENTRAL PLAZA (From Mayreder.)

FIG. 161—PIENZA. CENTRAL PLAZA.
Built (1458-'62) by Bernardo Rossellino for Pope Pius II. For plan of Pienza see Fig. 979.

VUE GÉNÉRALE DE LA PLACE ET DES ÉDIFICES DU CAPITOLE au X.ᵉ

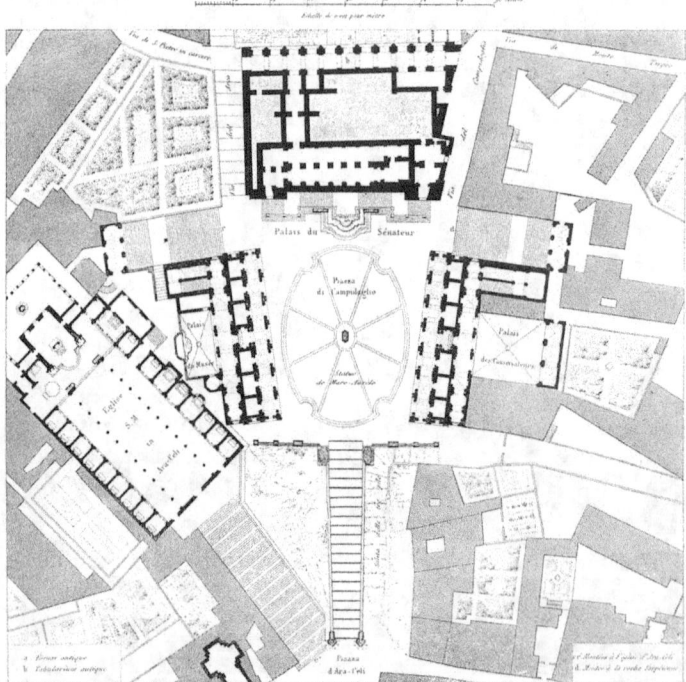

FIGS. 162-63—ROME, PIAZZA DEL CAMPIDOGLIO.   VIEW AND PLAN

The stairs to the left leading to Aracoeli date back to 1348. The monument was placed by Michel-angelo in 1538. The carrying out of his plans for the buildings took until 1598, thirty-four years after Michelangelo's death. (From Letarouilly.)

FIG. 164—ROME. PIAZZA DEL CAMPIDOGLIO
View looking away from the capitol over the city.   (Courtesy of
the Chicago Plan Commission).

suburbs independent of whether there are few or many
buildings to the acre. Plazas and even streets, like beautiful rooms, may have many windows with fine views but
they cannot do without strong frames and boundary lines.

In looking at a building one wants more than a feeling of distance; one wants to have the feeling of being
related to the building, which means that there must be
links and lines of connection, other than the floor, between
the building and oneself. These connections must be created by side walls. One practically wants to find oneself in
a beautiful room, one of whose walls is formed by the
principal building, while the other walls — they may be
buildings, colonnades, tree-rows or hedges — make the
connections with the monument. Without this intimate
connection the feeling of scale and proportion is interfered with. The intersection of the foreshortening horizontals at one's right and left with the horizontals of the
building one is facing is an essential part of the satisfactory effect in a plaza. In a circular and therefore cor-
nerless plaza the connection between the side wall and
the building one is facing is even more continuous and
strong. Civic art in the seventeenth and eighteenth centuries developed a great preference for inserting fine perspectives — like windows — into the walls of a plaza.
Instead of setting and framing a prominent building an
entire plaza can be designed to frame a fine perspective
across water (as in the Piazzetta of Venice) or a view of
high mountains (as one often finds in mountain towns, a
famous example being Innsbruck in Tyrol) or perspectives
into well terminated and not too long streets or into
connecting plazas giving the effect of a deep stage, or even
— perhaps most beautiful of all — a well framed, highly
concentrated perspective into infinite space, as in Versailles looking west.

When the early Renaissance in a gigantic effort shook
off the Gothic traditions of ornamental detail and covered the huge cubes of the Gothic palaces with the newly regained ornament in the classic style, one might think the
architects, for a little while, would have been inclined to
disregard the wisdom of the Gothic builders who knew
how to design plazas. But they took great pains to follow them in essential matters, doing freely and superbly
what the Gothic designers did under handicaps. Indeed
in plan the Palazzo Farnese (1520) seems to stand independent (Fig. 157-8); but this location practically only
repeats and improves on the setting of the great Palazzo
Communale (1281) in Piacenza (Fig. 159). The gaps on
its sides are narrow lanes less than 25 feet wide; they are
so narrow that they almost at once close perspectively;
looking down along the axis of these short lanes the eye
meets two well designed street endings, a church façade
and a fountain.

Rosselino's charming little piazza in Pienza (Fig. 160-
1) and its successor, Michelangelo's Piazza del Campidoglio (Figs. 162-4) are two other interesting examples of
plazas where corners on both sides of the main building
remained open. Both piazzas lie high above their surroundings and the special effort made by the designers
to open the corners by making the plazas broader in back
than in front is justified by the fascinating long distance
views thus secured. By no means are the corners casual
gaps. What here under peculiar circumstances and for
artists of the first rank was possible, cannot become a
thoughtlessly applied rule applicable to flat country. A-
gainst these two examples of plazas with open corners
there were built during the great period of the seventeenth and eighteenth centuries countless wonderful plazas with closed corners and it was left to the period of decline and of routine geometry in civic art to indulge in
plazas the corners of which stand open carelessly and
the sides of which are torn up by wide gaps between insufficient wall areas, but with none of the qualities of the
Piazza del Campidoglio.

There is one point in Camillo Sitte's teaching where
criticism might be justified. He was so thoroughly im-
bued with the spirit of the seventeenth and eighteenth
centuries that it looks as if he had lost the power of appreciation for the ideal of the sixteenth century architect, one of the finest ambitions conceivable in architecture, namely the placing of freestanding buildings, especially the placing of the perfectly symmetrical monument,
the "central building", in the center of a perfectly symmetrical plaza. (This matter will be dealt with a little
more fully later on. See p. 49.) Even in this respect it
must be recognized that Camillo Sitte has proposed surrounding a prominent columnar monument of Vienna with
a circular plaza of uniform architecture and has given
special praise to the beauty of central settings as, for instance, those shown in Figs. 113-19 and 130.

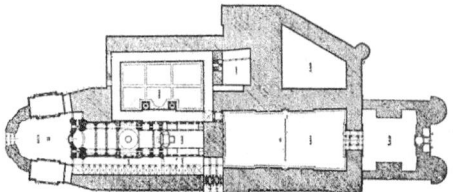

FIG. 165—MELK. MONASTERY IN AUSTRIA

FIG. 166—MELK. SEEN FROM THE DANUBE
The forecourt to the church (built 1702-26 by Prandauer) has a
plan somewhat similar to those of the Campidoglio and Pienza. The
view out from the main façade over the surrounding country is concentrated by a tall framing arch with a Palladian window effect.
(View from W. Pinder and plan from C. Gurlitt.)

FIG. 167—PERGAMON, ALTAR OF ZEUS.

Built about 180 B. C. The group setting the altar of Zeus with
its sculptured podium and a U-shaped Ionic colonnade surrounding
the platform of sacrifice was the fitting climax to the enormous scheme
of the new Acropolis. Reconstruction by R. Bohn.

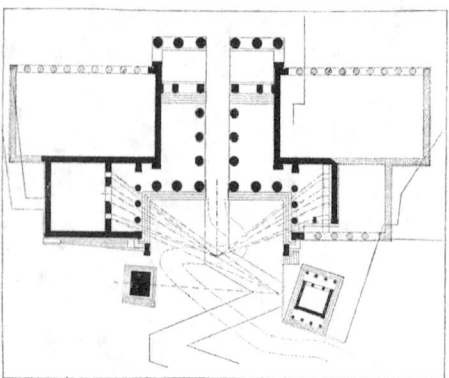

FIG. 168—ATHENS. PLAN OF THE PROPYLAEA

The original plan according to the researches of Doerpfeld, Elderkin and others. The plan also shows the zig-zag road (full line) con-
jectured by Elderkin, from the turning points of which well balanced
aspects of the buildings could be enjoyed. (From G. W. Elderkin.)

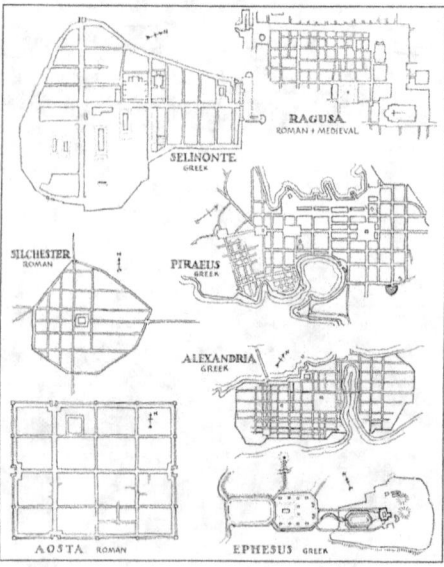

FIG. 168A—ANCIENT TOWN PLANS

These sketch plans are intended to show the generally regular
character of ancient planning and the close relation of the public open
spaces to the street plan.

FIG. 169—ATHENS. ORIGINAL PLAN OF THE ERECHTHEUM

"The Erechtheum as originally planned was an altogether symmetrical building . . . . With the Parthenon and the Propylaea it was
to form a group of symmetrical monuments to crown the Athenian
Acropolis in a manner worthy of the Periclean age." (From G. W.
Elderkin.)

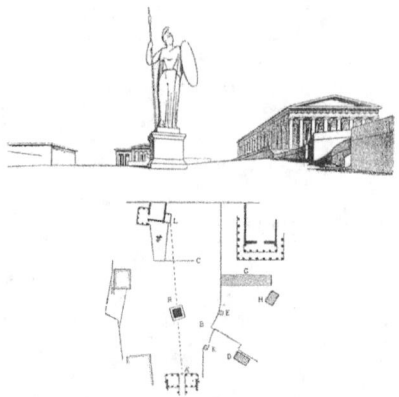

FIG. 170—ATHENS, ACROPOLIS

Plan and view from point A (Propylaea) towards the Erechtheum
(L) showing the giant statue of Athene (R) balancing against the
large mass of the Parthenon (G). "Le désorde des acropoles grecques."
(from Choisy.)

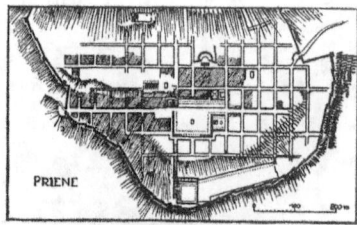

FIGS. 171 AND 171A—PRIENE

Plan and view showing corner of forum looking up hill. The
colonnade on the opposite side stands on higher ground. The city was
probably laid out for Alexander the Great, about 330 B. C. The whole
layout of the city on a gridiron plan (with exact north-south orientation
of streets) required cuts into the rock as much as 30 feet deep. (From
Theodore Fischer.)

Cospetto d'un regio Cortile nel cui mezzo vi stà una Loggia ove i cui intercolunny si vengono Fontane, Statue, ed altri ornamenti, si vengono pure in lontano luoghi rotondo con cristalli secondo il moderno costume.

FIG. 172—A ROYAL CORTILE. DESIGNED AND ENGRAVED BY PIRANESI.

CHAPTER II

Plaza and Court Design in Europe

The most important way of giving good settings to monumental buildings is to relate them to a plaza, which is another term for grouping them. Architectural grouping, as the previous chapter tried to show, is almost identical with plaza-design. A plaza is an area framed by buildings, this frame of buildings being an essential part of the plaza and the shape of the plaza being designed to show off the frame to best advantage. A plaza is not an area of land around which casual buildings may be dotted.

Modern civic art can learn most from a study of the achievements of the seventeenth and eighteenth centuries which in turn were deeply influenced by classic antiquity. But while the modern architect has learned long since to study most carefully even the smallest detail of the buildings of the classic and Renaissance periods, the far more important setting of the buildings from which he takes his details has interested him but little. Many Greek, Roman, and Renaissance buildings have been faithfully copied in America, but have been set into situations so entirely different from those for which the originals were designed that the effect is far less satisfactory. It is therefore well worth while to investigate the original setting of famous buildings.

Greek and Roman Precedents

The Acropolis in Athens and those in others of the oldest Greek cities, and the Forum in Rome, were not originally laid out according to orderly plans. The streets in Athens and Rome, like the streets in old sections of New York or Boston, were narrow and tortuous and the old Civic Centers had grown historically upon limited sites. Gradually old modest buildings had been replaced by wonderful reconstructions. In these new buildings the prevalent idea of symmetry could not always find full expression; sometimes space was so cramped that, even in

constructions of comparatively small size, orderly symmetry could not be achieved. It has been established that the Erechtheion and the Propylæa, as we know them, are not a realization of the original plan of their designers (Figs. 168-9). Considering the plans of ancient civic centers Choisy very properly speaks of the "désordre du Forum Romanum et des acropoles grecques", and shows the means by which the lack of symmetry in the plan was remedied to some extent by the use of what he calls an optical or picturesque symmetry. Thus, on the Acropolis, a picturesque symmetry was secured by balancing the colossal figure of Athena against the mass of the Parthenon (Fig. 170). The difficulty of the irregular rocky site in front of the Propylaea was economically overcome by placing a big statue to balance against the little Temple of the Wingless Victory (Fig. 168).

Vitruvius, living three hundred years later, belongs to a period in which limitations of site and means could more easily be disregarded. He and his Hellenistic teachers would not have sympathized with the "informal" city planners who during the last decade of the nineteenth century laid out civic centers purposely copying the quaint crookedness of medieval towns cramped into fortified sites. However highly the Hellenistic and Roman architects admired the work of their fathers, especially the wonderful detail of the Periclean period, so far as the plan of the ensemble was concerned the picturesque disorder of the Athenian Acropolis and the Roman Forum was by no means copied. The Hellenistic designers, under the guidance of Hippodamos of Miletus, laid out entire cities, as Piraeus, Rhodes, and Priene (Figs. 171, 171A), on straight lines. The civic centers of the Hellenistic colonies (the best preserved and probably one of the most beautiful was Pergamon, second century before Christ, Fig. 167), taught the Romans to admire perfectly balanced compositions which were quickly imitated by

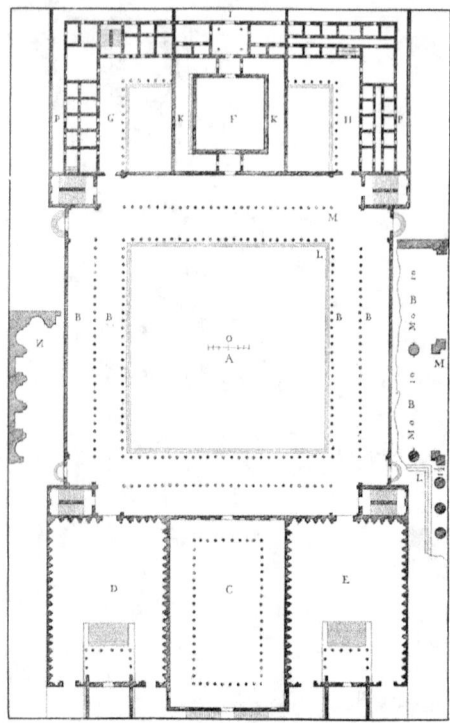

FIG. 173—PALLADIO'S IDEAL PLAN OF A "PIAZZA OF THE GREEKS"

Forum in the center; basilica and temples below; and curia, mint, and prisons above.

It is interesting that Palladio should use the word "piazza" in reference to the Roman forum and Greek agora. Such an identification has value as suggesting the fundamental similarity of public places, whether they be created within single buildings or by the enlargement of a street or the grouping of buildings. This identity, which has largely been lost (perhaps because of modern disparity between outdoor and indoor traffic), must be regained, as it was in the California fairs of 1915, if we are not to lose some of the most valuable effects of which architecture is capable.

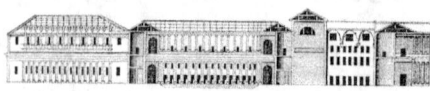

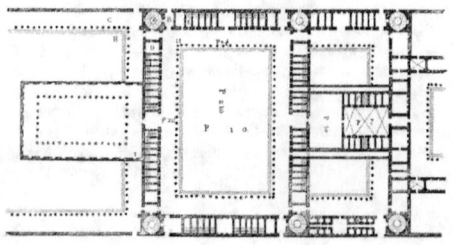

FIG. 174—PALLADIO'S IDEAL PLAN OF A "PIAZZA OF THE ROMANS"

The central forum is surrounded by porticos upon which open the shops of the bankers and artisans. Basilica at the left; prison and offices at the right.

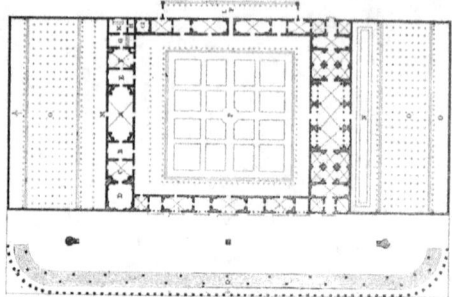

FIG. 175—PALLADIO'S IDEA OF A CLASSICAL XYSTUS.

A recreation center with running track, groves, and exercising areas. Figs. 173-75 represent interpretations of Vitruvian ideas.

the emperors, who in Rome and in numberless new cities of Italy and the colonies built civic centers of strictly formal plan. Almost unlimited wealth was at their disposal. Hilly or cramped sites were not permitted to interfere with the requirements of the design. Nero was not the only emperor who destroyed insalubrious quarters of Rome to create room for his new developments. Amazing grading projects were carried through. In the new colonies formal designs could be executed economically on virgin soil unhampered by the limitations of crowded sites. These new formal ideas, largely of Hellenistic origin, are those Vitruvius sets forth in his book, though it must be remembered that he lived at the very beginning of the period of great building that was dawning upon the Roman empire. He knew nothing of the great imperial fora in Rome or the astounding developments in Heliopolis, Palmyra, or Gerasa. Even of the splendor that had been achieved in the preceding Hellenistic period his book gives only a feeble picture. But he pointed in the direction of the great development to come.

"The Greeks made their fora square", Vitruvius asserts, "with a spacious double portico . . . . In the cities of Italy however . . . because the ancient custom prevails of exhibiting the shows of the gladiators . . . the width is obtained by assigning to the forum two-thirds of its length . . . which makes it convenient for the purpose of shows." (Fig. 173-5 Reconstruction by Palladio). Vitruvius speaks with satisfaction of his own cooperation in building the forum of the imperial colony of Fano (Fig. 176). He built the basilica in the center of one of the long sides of the forum on axis with the Temple of Jupiter which stood at the center of the opposite side. The Temple of Augustus, separated from the forum by the basilica, had also an axial relation to the basilica and to the Temple of Jupiter.

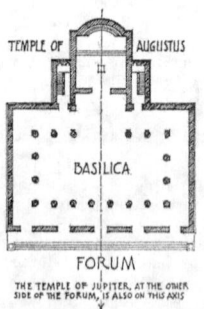

FIG. 176—PLAN OF BASILICA BUILT BY VITRUVIUS AT FANO

FIG. 177—SECTION THROUGH PORTICO
OF TEMPLE

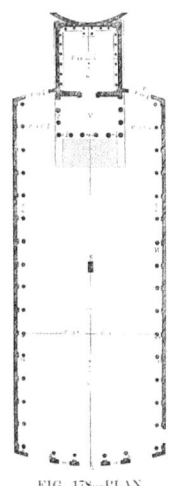

FIG. 178—PLAN

FIG. 179—TEMPLE AND FLANKING
ARCH

PALLADIO'S RECONSTRUCTION OF THE TEMPLE OF NERVA

In describing the above reconstruction, Palladio says that the columns buttressing the great wall of the plaza were set low that the temple might gain eminence. To confirm his admiration of this plaza as a setting for a monumental equestrian statue Palladio tells this story:

"Before this temple there was a piazza, in the middle of which the statue of the said emperor was placed: And writers say, that so many and so wonderful were its ornaments that they astonished those that beheld them, as not thinking them the work of men, but of giants.

"Hence the emperor Constantinus when he came first to Rome, was struck with the rare structure of this edifice; then turning to his architect, said, that he would in Constantinople make a horse like that of Nerva, to his own memory. To whom Ormisida answered (so was that architect's name) that it was first necessary to make him such another stable, showing him this piazza."

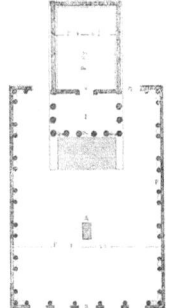

FIG. 180—PLAN

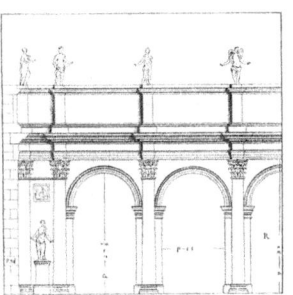

FIG. 181—ELEVATION OF WALL

PALLADIO'S RESTORATION OF THE TEMPLE OF ANTONINUS AND FAUSTINA

This reconstruction by Palladio is not archeologically correct but has value as his design of a forecourt plaza. "In the entrance opposite to the portico of the temple, there were very beautiful arches, and everywhere round it were columns, and a great many ornaments. On the sides of the temple there are two other open entrances, which were without arches. In the middle of this court there was the statue of Antoninus on horseback, of bronze, which is now in the piazza of Campidoglio."

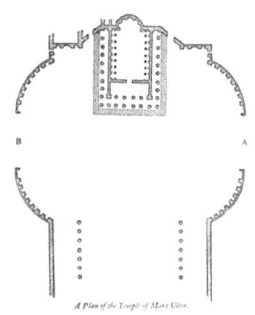

A Plan of the Temple of Mars Ultor.

FIG. 183—WREN'S RECONSTRUCTION OF THE TEMPLE OF MARS ULTOR

Wren's plan (from the "Parentalia") goes farther than Palladio's, forming a great plaza in front of the temple.

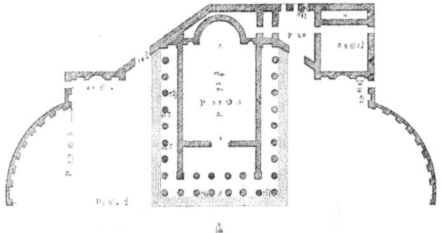

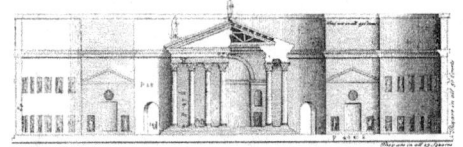

FIG. 182—PALLADIO'S RECONSTRUCTION OF THE TEMPLE OF MARS ULTOR

This reconstruction is a vivid demonstration of the classical and Renaissance conception of a public place as a great outdoor room. The lofty wing walls here are like the walls of a room or like a huge building turned inside out. In this way is created an impression of a space enclosed for its own sake, and not merely as the incidental result of the grouping of several buildings. In such a setting as this a classical temple would attain the complete dignity and mastery which were the consummation of classical design. The peculiar plan is very skilfully made to concentrate upon the temple and to tie it in place. The two straight pieces of wall (on which Palladio has indicated suppressed pediments) are essential elements in the composition. They quiet the movement of the curved and angular walls, give magnitude and firmness of position to the temple, and because they are parallel to the front of the temple the depression, in perspective, of their cornices (at the same height as the cornice of the temple) would express the depth of the plaza. Thus one would have a vivid perception, even when one could see only the façade, of the third dimension of the temple. Among the details which supplement this plastic expression are the equispaced niches. Even in the direct elevation they announce the concavity of the quadrant wing walls.

Palladio ascribes the unusual disposition of the wing walls to the willingness of Augustus to preserve the neighboring houses. The plan is reversed (see Fig. 189), and the elevation is somewhat confused by an error in the representation of the arched openings at each side of the temple.

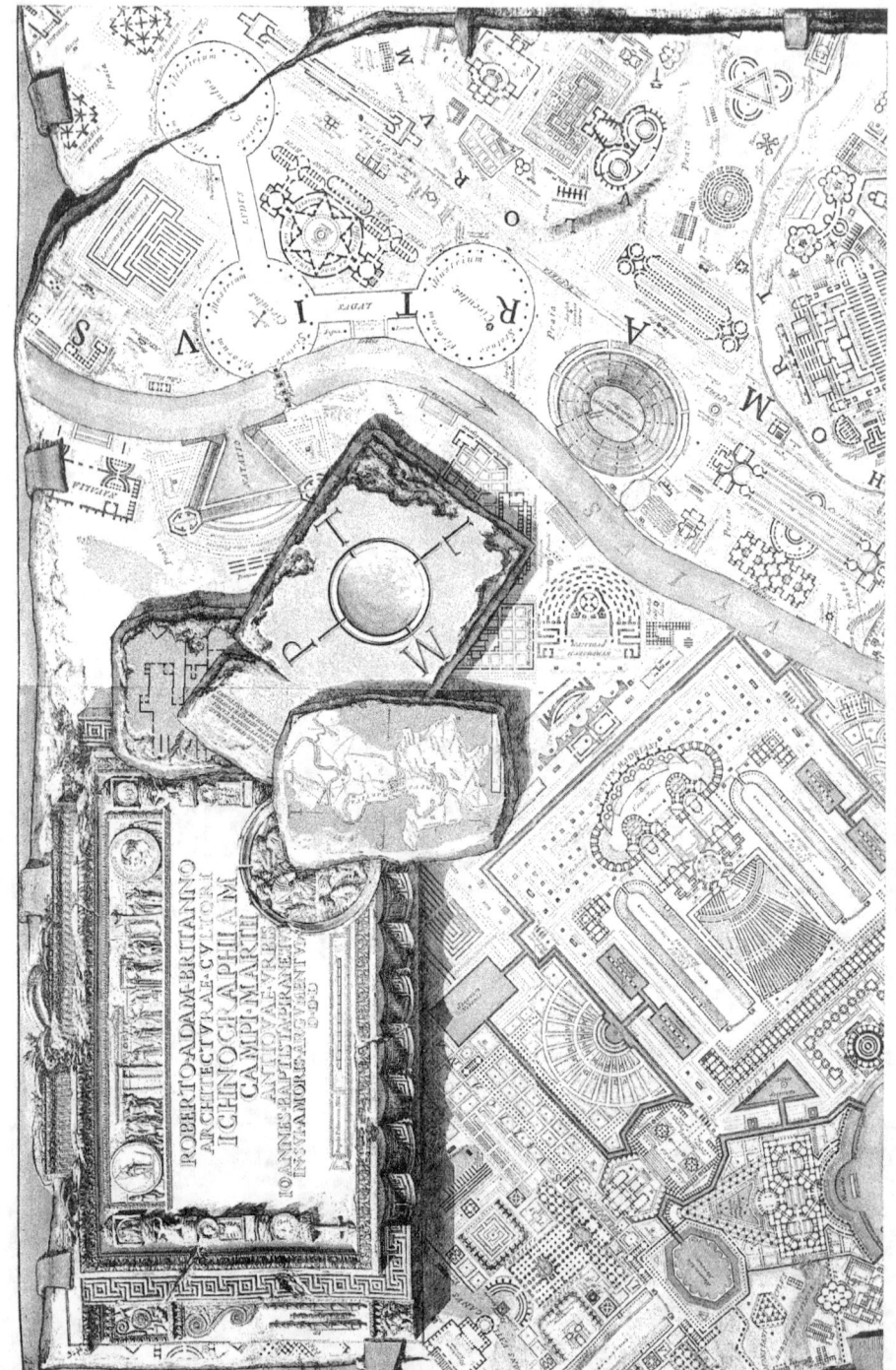

FIG. 184—ROME. PIRANESI'S CAMPUS MARTIUS, UPPER PART

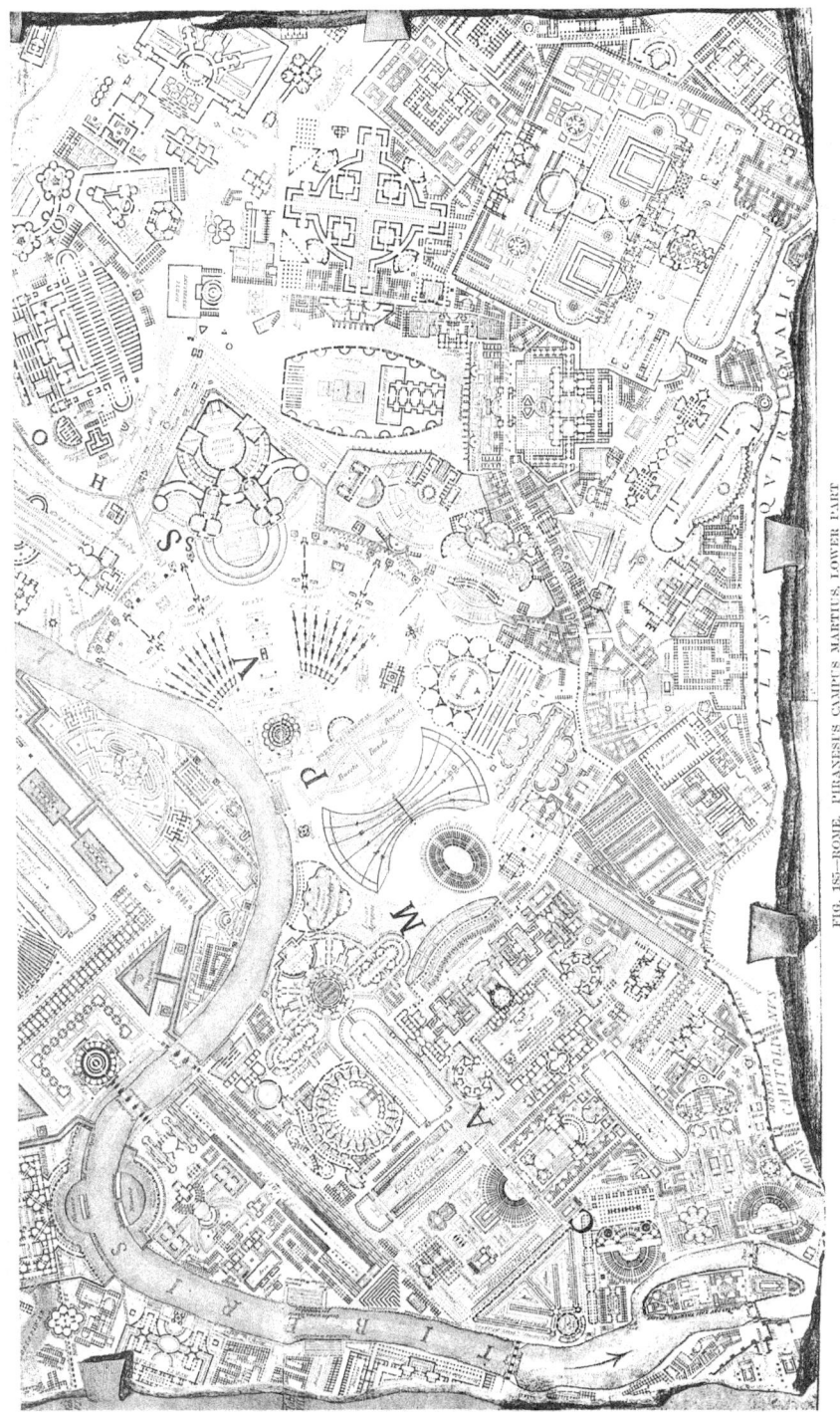

FIG. 18.—ROME. PIRANESI'S CAMPUS MARTIUS, LOWER PART

FIG. 186—PIRANESI'S RECONSTRUCTION OF THE CAMPUS
MARTIUS

A visualization of part of Piranesi's imaginative plan of the lower
areas of Rome (Figs. 184-85). The tower-like building across the Tiber
is just recognizable as the Tomb of Hadrian. Piranesi signs himself
"Fellow of the Royal Society of Antiquaries of London." His plan (Fig.
184) was dedicated to Robert Adam.

FIG. 187—PIRANESI'S RECONSTRUCTION OF A ROMAN FORUM

"A forum of ancient Rome surrounded by porticos with loggias,
some connecting with the imperial palace and others with the prisons.
This forum is surrounded with magnificent flights of steps among which
are fountains and sculptured horses, serving as ornaments to the area."

While Vitruvius can thus be seen at work securing
perspective effects and axial relations for his buildings,
the fora he describes seem to have been so completely
framed by the colonnades that their area could have been
designed practically independent of the buildings rising
behind the colonnades. So uniform was the effect which
such colonnades gave to a forum, making it appear as a
large room, that Vitruvius considered a forum as a building like a theater or a basilica and he discusses their de-

sign together in one chapter. Such a forum is a large
hall without a ceiling. Along the sides statues were
placed in great numbers, keeping the center free. Even
the entrances were bridged over by the colonnades. For
special purposes the forum was actually closed entirely.
And the square shape which Vitruvius mentions as typical for the Greek fora suggests that the four walls of the
forum were in perfect equilibrium and that the artist
had no desire to give special emphasis to one of the walls,
as he could have done by the elongation of the plaza or
by some other intricacy of design, if one of the walls had
been formed by the façade of a prominent public building which deserved special recognition in the plan of the
plaza.

The situation was different in the case of the new
forum in Pompeii, which was probably built before the
time of Vitruvius. (Fig. 19). This new forum — there
is also an old irregularly shaped one — is a wonderful
example of a plaza developed as a setting for one public
building. After entering the forum one is involuntarily
attracted by a monumental stairway which on one of
the short sides breaks the even scheme of colonnades surrounding the plaza. These stairs lead up to the terrace
of the Temple of Jupiter which effectively dominates the
harmonious plaza designed for its setting. It is to this
temple alone that prominence is given; the uniform
scheme of colonnades which insure the harmonious effect of the plaza is carried in front of all the other public
buildings assembled into this civic center. Triumphal
arches close the breaks in the wall of the plaza between
temple and colonnades.

According to Vitruvius, colonnades, one-storied with
the Greeks, two-storied with the Romans, were a feature
essential to every forum. The importance of colonnades,
as an element in the setting of public buildings and in
street design will be specially dealt with in a later chapter. In the Roman forum the colonnade and arches provided an effective screen against undesirable outside aspects, as private buildings were kept low by tradition and
by primitive technique; the larger public buildings, facing the forum behind the colonnades could be seen but
were not inharmonious. One high building looming close
into view would of course have changed the effect of
the design and detracted from the interest which was
meant to be concentrated upon one or two single buildings. The Romans, however, built no skyscrapers nor
towers nor high buildings of any kind. The tower from
which Shakespeare's Brutus heard the clock strike was
as much the invention of a later time as was the clock,
and while it was long supposed that the Roman Septizo-
nium was a building of seven stories it actually had only
three. Skyscrapers may overpower the fine buildings
which were meant to dominate Independence Square in
Philadelphia, but the plaza of antiquity was not thus
threatened.

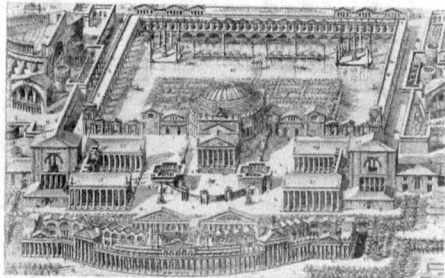

FIG. 188—PIRANESI'S RECONSTRUCTION OF THE VICINITY OF
THE PANTHEON

Temple settings, similar to the one achieved in the forum of Pompeii, were evidently much admired and therefore developed into a type gradually refined upon. In the astounding array of fora built by the Roman emperors one finds the Forum Transitorium of Nerva (Figs. 177-9) designed on a very similar plan, except that the emperor's statue was placed in the middle of the plaza. Covent Garden in London (Fig. 11), which is now filled up by the market structure, was Inigo Jones's development of the same classic conception of setting a temple by a forecourt specially designed for it. That this method was dear to Palladio, Inigo Jones's great master, may be gathered from his reconstruction of the temple of Antoninus and Faustina (Figs. 180-81) for which he designed a forum wider and shorter than the Forum Transitorium but otherwise very similar, and of which, he claims, parts were standing and demolished in his presence. As Palladio seems to have been mistaken in the matter of this forum, his reconstruction gains the value of an original design for a forum as a temple setting. Many similar temples have been and are being built in America to serve as banks or churches and it is certainly interesting to know how Palladio, who had such a deep influence on traditional architecture in America, thought that such temples should be set.

In his reconstruction of the temple of Mars Ultor (Fig. 182) Palladio mentions the forum that formed its setting "and made it much more admirable". But in reconstructing this forum Palladio does not go so far as modern research has proved justifiable. Christopher Wren has made his own reconstruction (Fig. 183) and has written an interesting paper on this forum. Modern investigation, vindicating the great English architect, has reconstructed (Fig. 189) between the Forum Transitorium and the Forum of Trajan, the admirable Forum of Augustus as a setting for this temple of Mars Ultor. Some reconstructors of this forum show two triumphal arches set symmetrically on each side of the temple on axis with two exedras outside the colonnades. The introduction of these exedras, suggesting in a remote way the transepts of a medieval church is the first step toward that wonderful intricacy of plaza design which blossoms forth in the large forum group of Trajan, the palaces of the emperors and Hadrian's villa, and celebrates its orgies in the Campus Martius of which Piranesi's reconstruction (Figs. 184-8) is perhaps not too fanciful. Nowadays it truly takes an American who has seen the great American world's fairs and is capable of combining in his mind their marvellous colonnaded expanses, to form an approximate idea of what this Campus Martius may have looked like.

The Forum Trajanum (Figs. 189-90) and the large temple group of Heliopolis (Baalbek) (Figs. 191-2) built about fifty years later, stand in a class by themselves as the highest climax in civic art of which antiquity was capable.

The imperial fora of Rome include many other variations of the idea of setting a temple, an important type being the placing of the temple in the center of a court. (Citadel and Temple of Juno Moneta, Forum of Julius Caesar, Temple of Venus and Rome, Forum of Vespasian). Viollet-le-Duc, in reconstructing ancient temple settings (Figs. 193-4), considers this central location as typically Roman. When placed in the center, the temple was put in the position which in the Forum of Nerva and in others was given to the imperial statue, and stood there, a precious shrine, just like a statue to be seen from all sides and protected from all sides by the surrounding porticos. The idea of the monument in the center of a court was to have a great future in the aspirations of the early Renaissance.

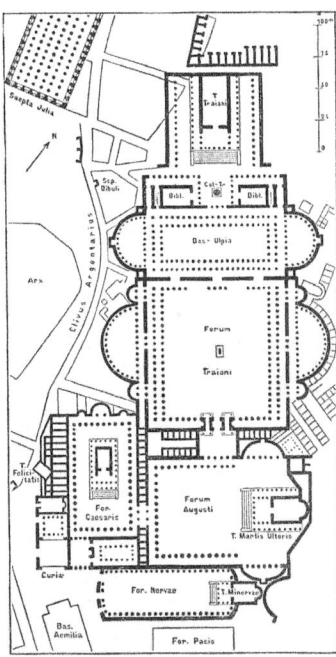

FIG. 189—ROME. PLAN OF IMPERIAL FORA

The principal axis is over twelve hundred feet long and Trajan's Forum covers about the area of a city block. The arches flanking the temple of Mars Ultor (which are mentioned in the text) are not included in this restoration (From Borrmann.)

FIG. 190—ROME. TRAJAN'S COLUMN FROM THE COURT OF THE TEMPLE OF TRAJAN.

(Reconstruction by Buehlmann.)

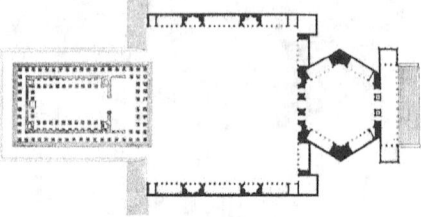

FIG. 191—HELIOPOLIS (BAALBEK), PLAN OF ACROPOLIS

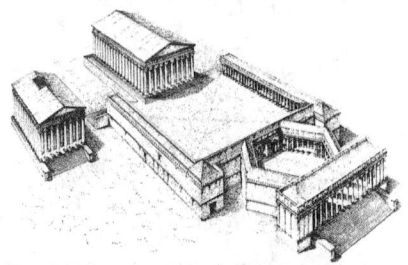

FIG. 192—HELIOPOLIS (BAALBEK). RECONSTRUCTION OF
ACROPOLIS

The main temple group on the Acropolis built 138-217 A. D. The
large temple of Jupiter was raised upon a stylobate 44 feet above the
natural level, and 23 feet above the forecourt. This court, about 350
feet square, was surrounded by colonnades and niches and had the
altar in the center. The altar court was preceded by an hexagonal
forecourt, 150 feet in diameter, surrounded by single or perhaps double
colonnades. In front of the hexagonal court were the Propylaea up to
which led a great staircase. All the work was of the best taste and
workmanship. To illustrate the great size of the buildings it may be
mentioned that the columns of the large temple measured over 60
feet compared with the 34½ feet of the Parthenon columns, and that
stones 70 feet long were raised 26 feet above natural level. (From H.
Frauberger.)

FIG. 193—AGRIGENTUM. TEMPLE OF JUNO LUCINA

"The great platform, which was built upon the rock, towards the
east, still remains, but the temple is an utter ruin." From Viollet-le-
Duc.)

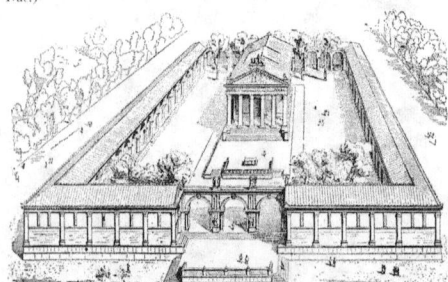

FIG. 194—ROME. TYPICAL TEMPLE SETTING OF THE IMPERIAL
EPOCH

A reconstruction by Viollet-le-Duc, who says: "In modern times we
cheapen the sites of our monuments, or, if we undertake to isolate
them, we surround them with blank deserts which belittle them, affording no introduction and no architectural preparation or contrasts;
we think we have answered the last requirements of good taste if we
surround our monument with an iron fence upon a low wall."

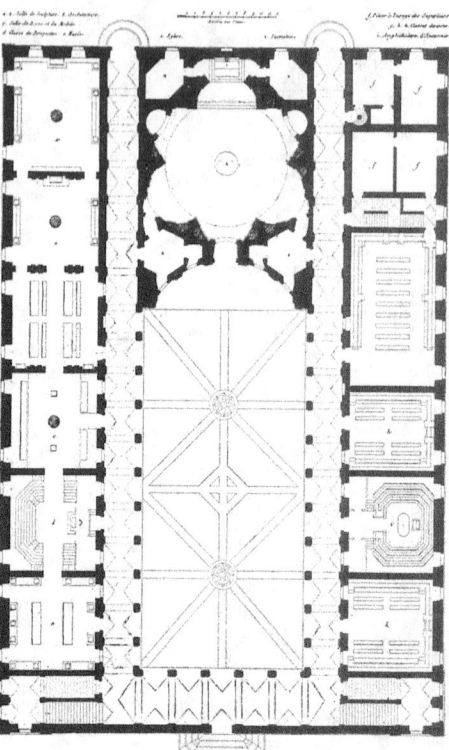

FIG. 196—ROME. UNIVERSITA DELLA SAPIENZA. PLAN

FIG. 197—ROME. UNIVERSITA AND CHURCH OF ST. IVO
(From Konrad Escher.)

FIG. 198—ROME. UNIVERSITA DELLA SAPIENZA. VIEW OF COURT

The two lower stories of the court were designed by Giacomo della Porta. The third story, almost a hundred years later, is the work of Borromini who also designed the Baroque church (1660), which displeased Letarouilly so much that he purposely selected his views so as not to show it (Fig 198). Modern critics appreciate the brilliant transition from the solemn "gravity" of the court to the lightness of the agitated dome. The lower part of the church façade is handled as the fourth wall of the court quite independent of the church plan, giving by its concavity an orientation to the court and tranforming it into a forecourt of the church. The third story is set back on all sides except the entrance side and is therefore strongly subdued for the observer standing on the ground floor. Both views (Figs. 197-98) are taken from the second floor, which it is important to remember in judging the whole effect. The dome is (not only actually but also when seen perspectively) disengaged from the walls of the forecourt and rises in nervous verticality to the spiral whirl of its lantern. (From Letarouilly.)

Renaissance Courts and Plazas

The classic conception of plazas developed as harmonious settings for public buildings has become one of the fundamentals of civic art. Andrea Palladio defines the role of the plazas in civic art as follows:

" . . . . ample places are left in cities, ... that there the people assemble to walk, to discourse, and bargain in; they afford also a great ornament, when at the head of a street, a beautiful and spacious place is found, from which the prospect of some beautiful fabric is seen,

and especially of some temple. But as it is of advantage, that there may be piazze dispersed through the city, so it is much more necessary, magnificent, and honorable, that there be one principal, which truly may be called public. These principal piazze ought to be made of such bigness, as the multitude of the citizens shall require, that it may not be small for their conveniency and use, or that, through the small number of people, they may not seem uninhabited. In sea-port towns they must be

FIG. 199—ROME. COURT OF THE CONVENT OF ST. EUSEBIO
(From Letarouilly)

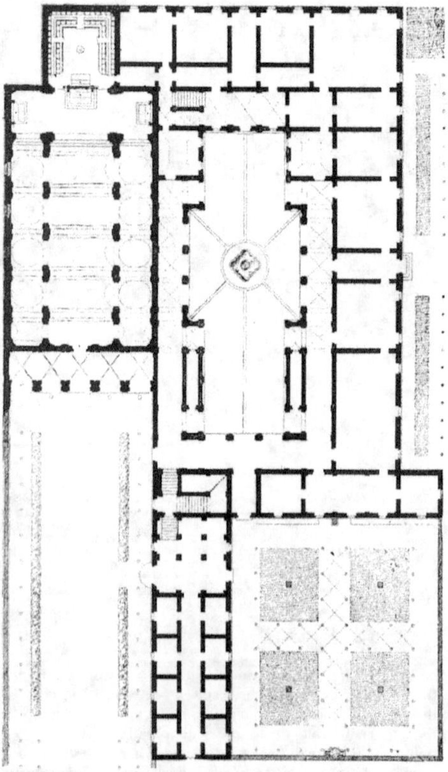

made near the port; and in inland cities they must be made in the middle of them, that they may be convenient for every part of the city.

"Portico's, such as the antients used, ought to be made around the piazze, as broad as their columns are high; the use of which is to avoid the rain, snow, and every injury of the air and sun. But all the edifices that are made around a piazza, ought not to be (according to Alberti) higher than the third part of the breadth of the piazza, nor lower than the sixth. And to the portico's one is to ascend by steps, which must be made as high as the fifth part of the length of the columns.

"Arches give a very great ornament to piazze that are made at the head of streets, that is, in the entrance into the piazza. . . . .

"But, returning to the principal piazza, the palace of the prince or of the signory (as it happens either to be a principality or a republic) ought to be joined thereto, so ought the mint, the public treasury and the prisons. . . . . . Besides the treasury and the prisons, the curia should be joined to the piazza, which is the place where the senate meets to consult on affairs of the state. . . . . . On the part facing the warmest region of the heaven, on one side of the piazza, the basilica must be made, that is the place where justice is administered, whither great part of the people and men of business resort. . . . ."

Palladio follows here the instructions of Vitruvius. Figs. 172 and 187 give Piranesi's interpretation of the same ideas.

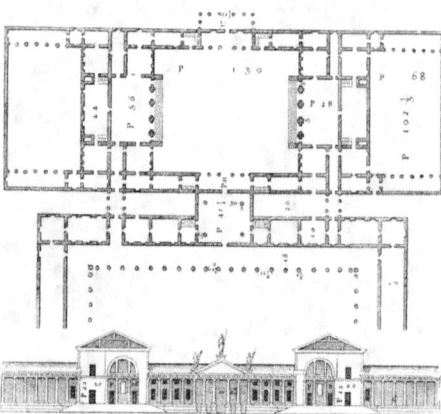

FIG. 201—PALLADIO. VILLA AT QUINTO

This villa is arranged around a central court. The entrance is through the loggia at the top of the plan. The central court was connected (by an atrium of four columns) with the large farm court.

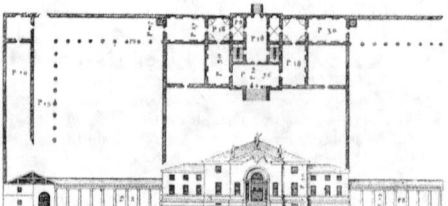

FIG. 202—PALLADIO. VILLA AT POGLIANO

The various courts are shown only in part; the entrance court in the middle, the service court at the left and the garden at the right.

FIG. 200—ROME. CHURCH AND CONVENT OF ST. EUSEBIO

The plan shows the cross-shaped layout of the court of the convent, also the long forecourt planted with trees and hedges separating the church from the highway. This group may have been built by Carlo Fontana about 1711. (From Letarouilly.)

VUE DU FOND DE LA COUR PRISE DU VESTIBULE D'ENTREE.

FIG. 203 (VIEW) AND FIG. 204 (PLAN)—ROME. CURIA
INNOCENTIA OR PALAZZO DI MONTE CITORIO

The court was begun by Bernini in 1650 and finished by Carlo Fontana about 1711. In 1871 it was roofed over to provide the new hall
of the Italian Parliament. The court in its old condition was flanked
on the square side by the three-storied wings of the palace. On the
round side it was framed by a double curved wall screening the stables
and service quarters. The outer wall was high, carrying the motive
from the palace wings around the whole court. The inner wall was
low with an opening in the middle affording a perspective of the
fountain scheme in the center of the outer wall. The public roadway
passed between the two walls. (From Letarouilly.)

According to Leon Battista Alberti, who to Palladio
is an authority almost equal to his master Vitruvius, the
size of a plaza should be so related to the size of the
buildings that the breadth of the plaza in front of a building should not be less than three times nor more than six
times the height of the building. These dimensions date
from the very beginning of the Renaissance and express
the craving for spaciousness animating the younger generation of artists eager to shake off the fetters of Gothic
proportions. In contrast to the very narrow streets of
an old city, with buildings many times higher than the
width of the streets, a plaza no larger than the height
of the buildings facing it may appear wide. But the early
Renaissance plaza of Pienza (Figs. 160-1) (1460) which is
still built on such narrow proportions, gives more the
feeling of a pleasant recess than of a plaza and is indeed
hardly larger than the court of the adjoining Palazzo Piccolomini. The arcaded courts of many Italian palaces
perfect this type, the most famous being perhaps the
square court of the Palazzo Farnese with sides equal to
the height of the surrounding walls (Fig. 157). An oblong
example is the court of the Sapienza in Rome which later
was transformed into the forecourt of one of the most

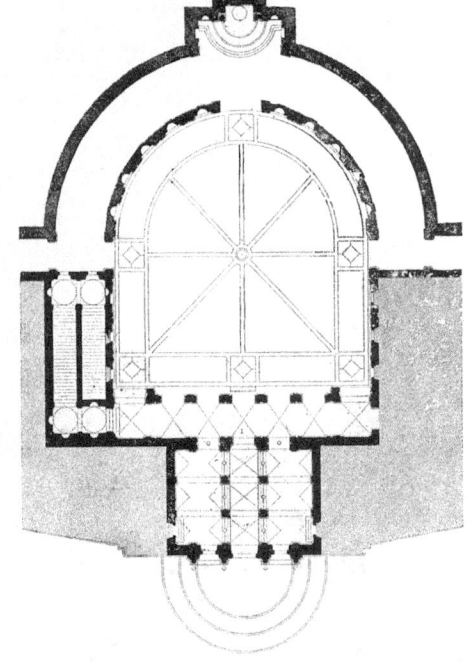

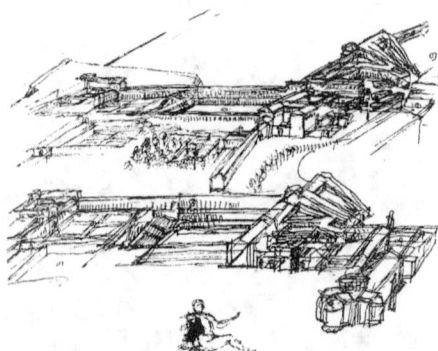

lively church façades of the Baroque period (Figs. 196-8), and the court of the Convent of S. Eusebio (Figs. 199, 200) is designed on a cross-shaped plan. Still richer shape was given by Bernini to the court of the Palazzo di Monte Citorio (Figs. 203-4) the dimensions of which (120 feet wide) suffice even for the requirements of a modern plaza.

The increase in the size of these courts illustrates how the Renaissance moved away from Gothic narrowness to the architectural mastery of larger and larger open areas, private or public. Palladio after endorsing the large dimensions asked for by Master Alberti gave to his reconstruction of a typical Roman forum the proportion of 1¾ by 2½ times the height of the adjoining buildings (Fig. 174) and the courts he designed for his country houses (Figs. 201-2) are sometimes relatively even larger, and partake of the repose of a small well-framed forum.

The first effort to create a similar effect on a big scale was made by the popes in Rome. One of the great events of the Roman high Renaissance is Bramante's bold undertaking to connect the palaces of the Vatican by long wings thus creating a scheme of courts stretching over 1000 feet and mastering irregular ground (Figs. 205-9). This ambition of the popes was soon to be outdone by the French kings who started upon the enormous scheme of connecting the Louvre and the Tuileries, which involved the creation of courts, 4000 feet in combined length (Figs. 210-3). In both cases closed areas were created

FIG. 205—ROME. THREE DRAWINGS ATTRIBUTED TO BRAMANTE

The upper one may be a study for the transformation of the Borgo. In the background is perhaps St. Peter's as conceived by Bramante (Fig. 243). The other drawings are sketches of the entire development proposed for the Belvedere and the Vatican. (From de Geymüller.)

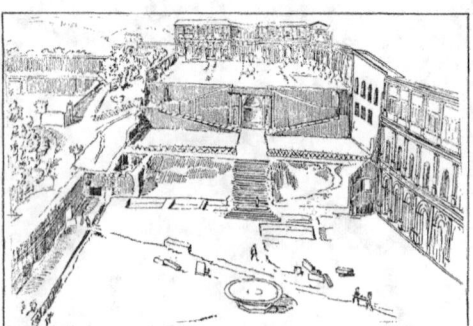

FIG. 206—ROME. VIEW OF THE COURT OF THE BELVEDERE

Showing condition at the time of Bramante's death in 1514. (After an old drawing published by Letarouilly.)

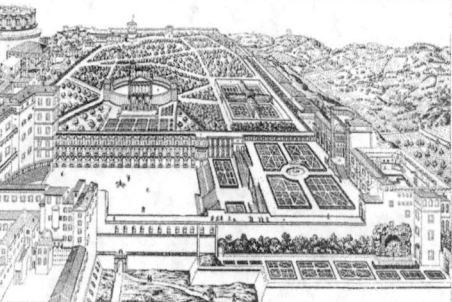

FIG. 208—ROME. COURT OF THE BELVEDERE ABOUT 1565.

In the upper left corner one sees the drum of the unfinished dome of St. Peter's; in the left middle background the Villa Pia (N); at the right the large niche, marked M. (From Letarouilly.)

FIG. 207—ROME. VIEW OF THE COURT OF THE BELVEDERE

From an engraving by H. Clivens in 1585. (From Letarouilly.)

FIG. 209—ROME. A TOURNAMENT IN THE COURT OF THE BELVEDERE

The incomplete dome of St. Peter's appears in the upper right corner. (From de Geymüller.)

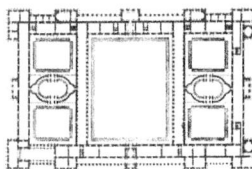

FIG. 210—PARIS. DE L'ORME'S PLAN FOR THE TUILERIES
Begun 1564. Length 925 feet. (From Durand.)

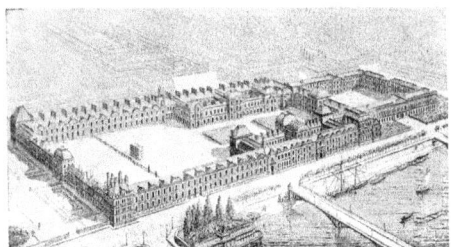

FIG. 211—PARIS. THE LOUVRE AND THE TUILERIES IN 1855
(From de Guilhermy.)

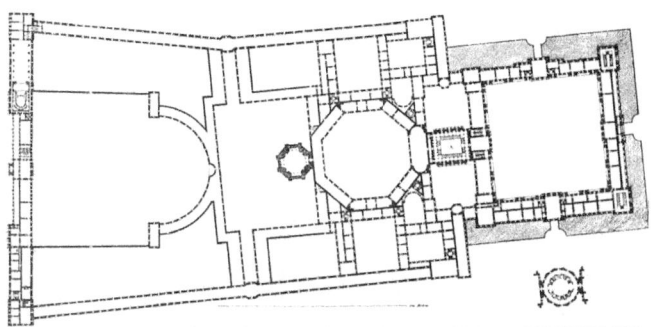

FIG. 212—PARIS. PERRAULT'S DESIGN FOR THE CONNECTING BUILDINGS BETWEEN THE
TUILERIES AND THE LOUVRE
For elevation see Fig. 221. The scale is 200 meters. Same scale as Figs. 210 and 213. (From Durand.)

FIG. 214—LONDON. PALACE OF WHITEHALL

As designed by Inigo Jones, 1619. After an engraving by T. M.
Müller, 1749. (From W. J. Loftie.)

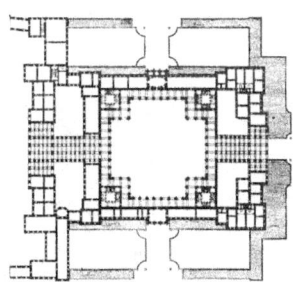

FIG. 213—PARIS. BERNINI'S PROPOSAL FOR THE DEVELOP-
MENT OF THE OLD LOUVRE

Same scale as Fig. 212. For elevation and section see Figs. 222 and
223. (From Durand.)

FIG. 215—BERLIN. SECOND COURT OF THE ROYAL CASTLE
By Andreas Schlüter, 1699. (From W. Pinder.)

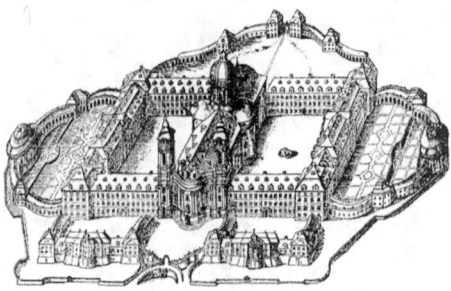

FIG. 216—WEINGARTEN MONASTERY, 1723

The choir, for the accommodation of the monks, was made as long
as the nave, bringing the crossing in the middle of the church. It was
thus easy to have balanced courts at both sides. Outside this central
group is a series of forecourts, partly terraced. (From W. Pinder.)

which suggested Roman fora even to the extent of furnishing suitable sites for gladiatorial exhibits. The accompanying illustration (Fig. 209) shows a tournament in
the court of the Belvedere, and "carrousel" which has
given, up to the present day, the name to the outer court
of the Louvre, is only another term for tournament.

Not satisfied with the sizes they could give to their
courts and plazas the designers of the Renaissance found
another way to give a feeling of expanse. It has been
shown how the public plaza in Pienza (Fig. 160) was designed to command fine views into the lower country. The
court of the adjoining Palazzo Piccolomini opened through
doors towards the garden to the south thus gaining the
same view as the plaza. For the court of the Palazzo
Farnese Michelangelo proposed to develop an axis across
the Tiber connecting the Palazzo Farnese with the gardens of the Villa Farnesina. The courts of the Palazzo
Negroni (Fig. 217-8) and of the Palazzo di Monte Citorio
(Figs. 203-4) show, on very much smaller scale, the effect
of such schemes of axiation reaching beyond the limits
of the plaza proper. It is as if the designers had inserted
windows into the walls of their plazas from which well-
framed views can be enjoyed, or as if they had decorated
the walls of their plazas with paintings of beautiful landscapes.

The Size of Renaissance Plazas

If one makes a study of the plazas which in the progress of the Renaissance movement have become the
most famous documentations of civic art, one finds a continuous recurrence of widths and breadths of plazas corresponding to one, two and three times the height of the
building or monument of which the plaza is the setting.
Modern investigation (H. Maertens) has determined that
these particular proportions to the height have a peculiar
meaning. It appears that the human eye is so organized as best to see the detail of an object if separated
from it by a distance equal to just about the largest
dimension (height or width) of the object. If the object is a building, height rather than breadth is of pre-
dominant importance because so far as breadth is concerned (in the case of buildings broader than high)
the onlooker is apt to make use of his freedom of movement and of choosing various points of view parallel to
the building. If the distance from the building becomes
so great that the width of the building can be embraced
without straining the eyes or moving the head, a good
relation between width of building and its distance from
the observer may become important, as will be seen further on in discussing the Place de la Concorde. A distance between observer and building equal to about the
height of the building is identical with his seeing the
building within an angle of 45 degrees. This angle is

FIG. 217—ROME. COURT OF PALAZZO NEGRONI

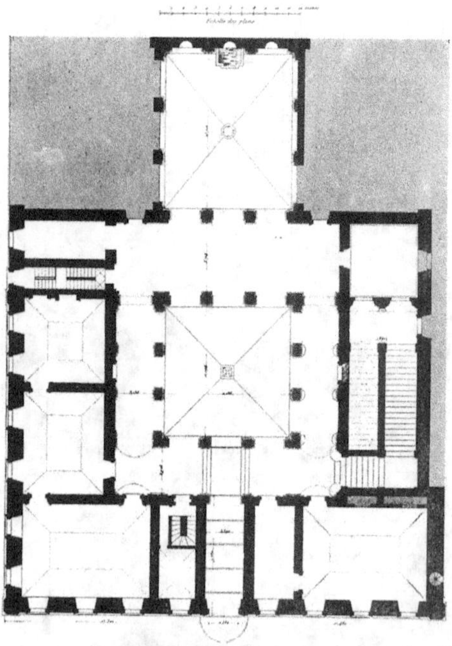

FIG. 218—ROME. PALAZZO NEGRONI

The most interesting feature of the Palazzo Negroni (built by Bartolomeo Ammanati in 1564) is the way in which an extraordinary effect
of spaciousness, almost a garden vista, was secured within so small an
area. The little cortile, eleven meters square, is walled on the side
toward the service court (the hatched areas are stables, etc.) only by
a loggia carrying a terrace. On axis, in the far wall of the service
court, is a fountain. By these means the central court was kept from
being dark and confined. Similar devices were used in the Palazzo
Farnese (Fig. 157) and the Palazzo Piccolomini at Pienza (Fig. 160).
(From Letarouilly, who, especially in the view of the court, represents
the original rather than the existing conditions.)

measured between two lines drawn (1) from the eye to
the horizon and (2) from the eye to the top of the building (either cornice line or top of balustrade, sometimes
even to the top of statues that may be placed closely
enough upon the balustrade to give the effect of a continuation of the wall).

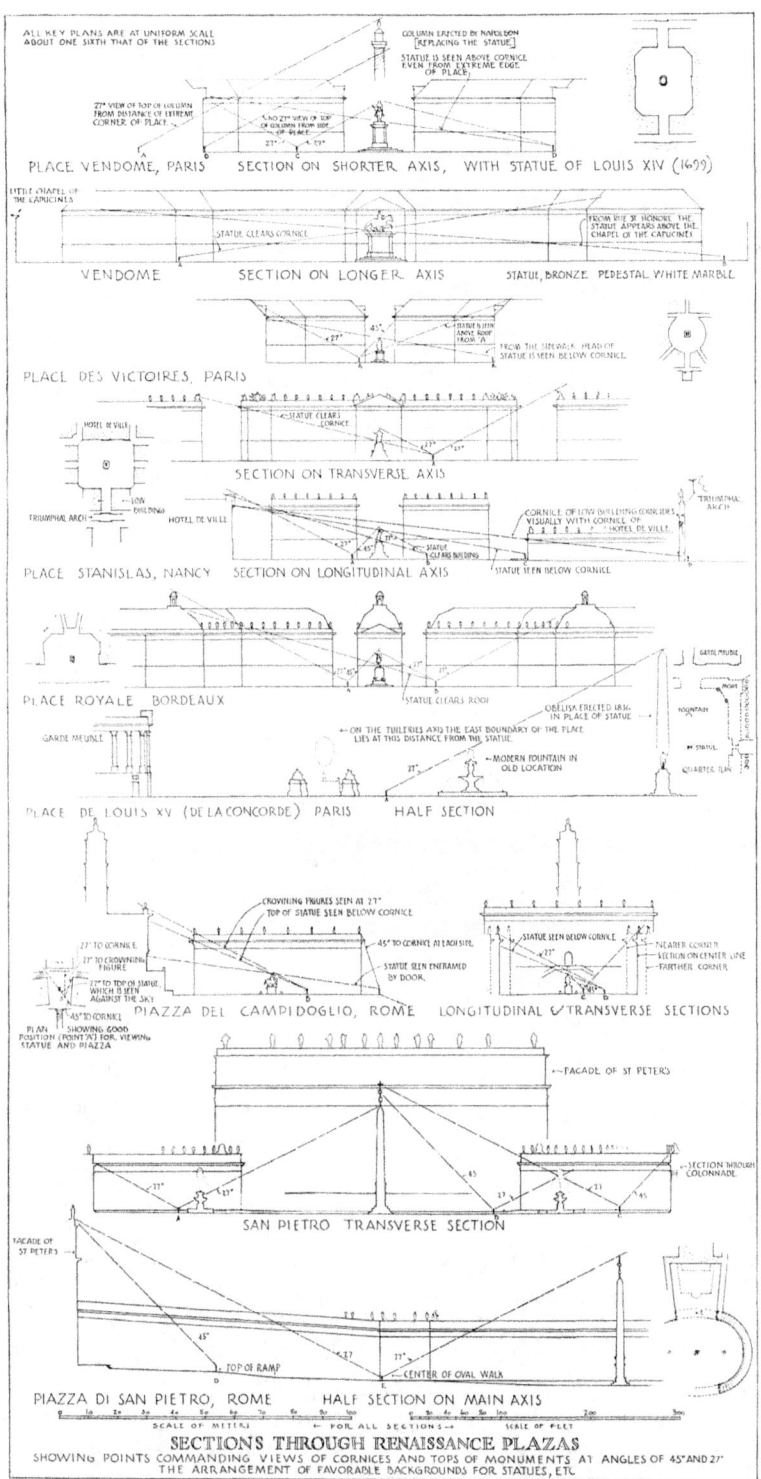

SECTIONS THROUGH RENAISSANCE PLAZAS

SHOWING POINTS COMMANDING VIEWS OF CORNICES AND TOPS OF MONUMENTS AT ANGLES OF 45° AND 27°
THE ARRANGEMENT OF FAVORABLE BACKGROUNDS FOR STATUES, ETC

FIG. 219

In order to see at its best a building as a whole (i. e. leaving aside the detailing) the observer should be separated from the building by a distance equalling about twice its height, which means he should see it at an angle of 27 degrees. In this latter case the building will fill the entire field of vision of an observer who holds his head motionless. If the observer wants to see more than just the one building, if for instance he wants to see this building as a part of a group, say a civic center group, he should see it at an angle of about 18 degrees, which means he should be separated from the building by a distance equal to about three times its height. If thus placed the observer, although losing many effects of the detailing, will still get a good view of the building as a whole, and his field of vision will be large enough to include considerable parts of the objects surrounding the building, say adjoining buildings of the group, colonnades, trees or vistas, which all may or may not be pleasing or designed to be pleasing and to heighten the effect of the building. Yet this distance of three times the height between observer and building is not too great to prevent the building, if the observer keeps it in the center of his field of vision, from dominating the picture presented to the eye. If the distance between the observer and building increases further, that is if the angle between the top of the building and line of sight to the horizon becomes less than 18 degrees, the building begins to lose its predominance in the field of vision, it merges into one silhouette with the neighborhood and distinguishes itself from its surroundings only if its roof line offers some surprising contrast of height against the neighboring buildings. A plaza larger than three times the height of the surrounding buildings is therefore in danger of being of imperfect value as a setting for monumental buildings (Fig. 220). Views of important buildings from distances of more than three times their height are important therefore, not in the design of plazas, but in street design, and will be discussed in the chapter on the design of streets. Even if a building can boast of unusual superiority in height above its neighborhood, and more so if it cannot, its predominance in a setting has to depend largely on the qualities of its design, detail, and material. All these features are likely to become blurred as the distance between observer and building increases beyond three times the height of the building and the desirable proportions of the plaza designed to set off the building are thereby indicated. This proportion becomes still more

definite as there exist quite definite desiderata regarding the relations between the height of a building and its possible width, relations about which Sir Christopher Wren has expressed himself very explicitly. General rules, similar to those regarding the size of plazas, are, of course, of a somewhat delicate character. While it may be perfectly safe for almost everybody to follow them, exceptions will often be made by great artists who are able to set their own law. An important exception in the matter of plaza dimensions may be effected by the use of long porticos. Wren, one of the greatest masters of civic art, has pointed out that the ordinary rules of architectural proportion do not apply to long porticos. While for ordinary façades he lays down the rule: "Fronts require a proportion of the breadth to the height: higher than three times the breadth is indecent and as ill to be above three times as broad as high," he adds: "From this rule I except obelisks, pyramids, columns, such as Trajan's etc. which seem rather single things than compositions. I except also long porticos, though seen direct, where the eye wandering over the same members infinitely repeated, and not easily finding the bounds, makes no comparison of them with the height." In fact, he believes a portico can never be too long: "form a portico the longer the more beautiful, ad infinitum". If one accepts Wren's rule that it is "ill to be above three times as broad as high" and has previously accepted the optical rule that a building seen at a less angle than 18 degrees (equal to a distance of three times the height) loses its value as a dominating feature in the design, one has a fairly definite idea of the limits of the forecourt, which it is dangerous to exceed. The proportions of the plaza will change further if the most important points from which the architect wants his main building to be seen do not lie at the circumference of the plaza but somewhat inside of the plaza; this latter case may arise, if an important street or walk passes through the plaza (as for instance Unter den Linden passes through the Opera plaza in Berlin (Figs. 396-9) or if a plaza is designed, like the plaza in front of St. Peter's in Rome, as a great hall of assembly in front of the building justifying the assumption that the best views of the building would be obtained from inside, instead of from the borders of, the plaza. In such cases it is advantageous to accentuate that area of the plaza which may be considered the most favored and from which one gains the best view of the principal building, by placing there minor monuments (fountains, statues, obelisks), which again will be seen to best advantage from the outer confines of the plaza (compare the cross section of Renaissance plazas, Fig. 219). By such minor monuments a very large plaza can be subdivided. The long Piazza Navona in Rome (Fig. 28) receives its peculiar rhythm from the location of its three fountains.

If one follows Wren in his attitude towards porticos and if one uses such porticos as a frame for a plaza, a set of proportions somewhat different from those contemplated so far might be introduced. Furthermore, the façades of quite large buildings can be made to partake of the even rhythm of porticos and to appear like huge porticos if seen from far away. One of the classical examples is Perrault's famous Louvre colonnade (Fig. 221), in which the designer pulled together the second and third stories to make them appear as one. He did this against severe opposition and with the avowed purpose of making his façade appear big, if seen from across the river. In his design for the Capitol, Michelangelo had, for the first time in the Renaissance, used the colossal order (the work of "a mason of genius", not of an architect, as Garnier characterized it in spite of his admiring it and partly copying it in the Loggia of the Opéra). The

FIG. 221—PERRAULT'S DESIGN FOR THE EAST FRONT OF THE LOUVRE
Showing the niches and statues in place of windows. (From Durand.)

FIG. 222—BERNINI'S DESIGN FOR THE EAST FRONT OF THE LOUVRE
Same scale as Fig. 221 (From Durand.)

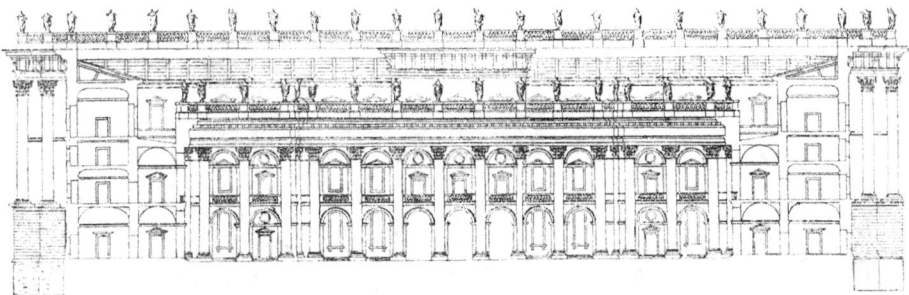

FIG. 223—BERNINI'S DESIGN FOR THE LOUVRE. SECTION
For plan see Fig. 213. (From Durand.)

FIG. 224—WEST FRONT OF THE LOUVRE IN 1660
A typical French palace front before the time of Perrault's boldly
simplified colonnade. After a contemporary drawing. (From Babeau.)

Capitol buildings could be seen from the lower level for a distance of about 800 feet of sloping ground, the stairs of the Cordonnata up to the higher level being about 30 feet high. Perrault, whose Louvre façade stood at the same elevation as the spectator and was to be seen from across the river (it is 1100 feet to the monument of Henry IV on the Pont Neuf), had to do more than Michelangelo to get a satisfactory effect. He followed Michelangelo in using the colossal order, but in addition suppressed the windows of his third story and pushed back those of the second story sufficiently to have them almost disappear behind columns (the original design provided niches with statues instead of the windows in the second story; the whole façade was an enormous piece of decoration built for perspective effect independent of what would happen behind it). Perrault thus succeeded perfectly in giving the appearance of one huge story standing on a podium sufficiently high to prevent an effect of sinking into the ground when seen from long distances. As it was unavoidable that the façade would be seen at a long distance by anybody crossing the Pont Neuf, while its continuation along the river (later carried out by continuing with pilasters Perrault's columnar motive) would even mainly have to be seen from across the river, this was certainly making intelligent use of the colossal order and signified

FIG. 225—PARIS. PLACE DE LA CONCORDE AND MADELEINE

FIGS. 226-229—PARIS. PLACE DE LA CONCORDE

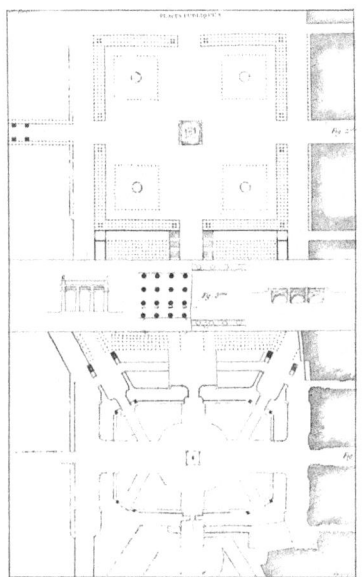

FIG. 230—PARIS. PLACE DE LA CONCORDE.
DURAND'S PLAN CONTRASTED WITH
GABRIEL'S

After the completion of the Place de la Concorde
with its approaches, Durand, the author of the well
known "Parallèle," claimed that a much better result
could have been achieved for less money if instead
of the moats (with expensive retaining walls and
bridges crossing them) by which Gabriel reduced the
area of the oversized plaza, a scheme of colonnades had
been built around the plaza. In fact, Durand was
commissioned to build a colonnade of temporary
character on the side of the Tuileries gardens for
one of the celebrations of the Revolution. The effect
of such colonnades around the whole plaza might
have been good as strengthening the intermediate
member between the plaza and Gabriel's façades,
thereby giving more architectural strength to the
plaza which at present is rather a "campus" than a
plaza.

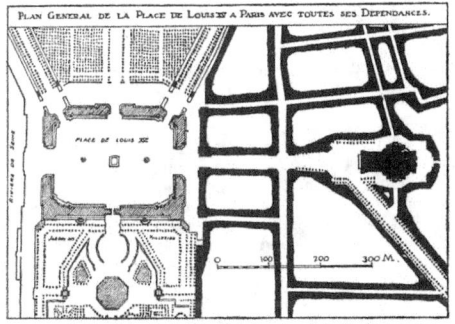

Original design for the Place de la Concorde and the Place de la Madeleine,
made by the architect Gabriel about the year 1753.

FIG. 233—(From Raymond Unwin.)

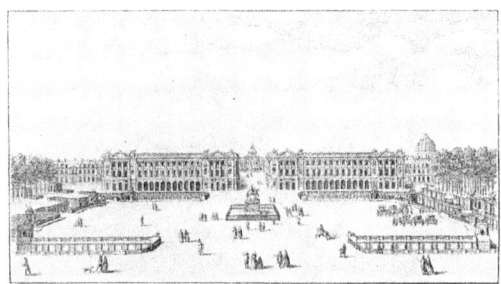

FIG. 231—PARIS. PLACE DE
LOUIS XV

This view (from Patte) shows
the Place de la Concorde as first
built, and the Madeleine with a
dome, as then planned.

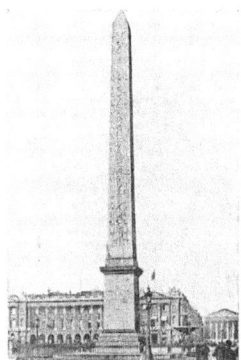

FIG. 232—PARIS. PLACE DE LA
CONCORDE

The obelisk occupies the site of
the original equestrian monument
which was less than one third as
high.

the victory of the Italian Baroque of Michelangelo, Palladio, and Bernini (Figs. 222-3). While the elder Blondel
like the rest of his contemporaries of the French Academy
never forgave Perrault (who like Michelangelo was not
a trained architect) for thus neglecting the strict French
canons of architecture and for making concessions to what
might be called the broader point of view of civic art, to-
day in looking at Perrault's colonnade — as it appears to us —
it seems incredible that for so long
a time it should have been considered by the architects of
the Academy as the starting point for all licentiousness
of "Rococo" art.

Perrault's departure convinced the succeeding designers of plazas. Mansard followed Perrault and used
colossal orders for Place Vendôme (Figs. 328-31) and
Place des Victoires (Figs. 326-7), but in view of the comparatively moderate size of these plazas did not find it necessary to push the windows back to disappear behind
the colossal order. Perrault was further vindicated when
during the period of Louis XV (often identified with Rococo) the two great competitions were held for the king's
monument and for the plaza which was considered, together with the buildings framing it, as the necessary
setting of an important monument. Gabriel's design (Figs.
225-34) was the biggest with the single exception of Patte's gigantic projet, (Fig. 375). Gabriel's plaza, more

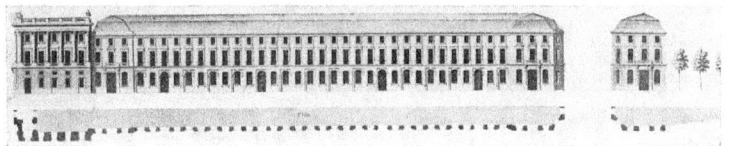

FIG. 234—PARIS. RUE ROYALE
Plan and elevation of Gabriel's design for the buildings lining the approach to the Madeleine. (From Patte.)

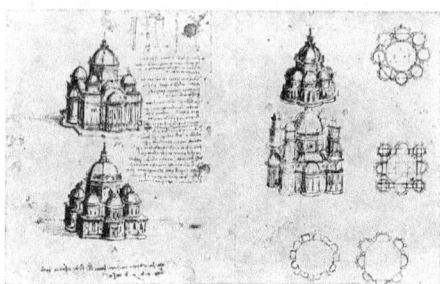

FIG. 235—STUDIES BY LEONARDO DA VINCI

Two sheets from Leonardo's sketchbook, containing studies for four-way symmetrical strongly centered buildings.

Leonardo is here playing variations upon one of the favorite architectural themes of his age—the building whose axis, so to speak, is a point and not a line. Most classical buildings were bi-symmetrical. The searching designers of the Renaissance were haunted by visions of a higher order of symmetry in which the plan could be folded not once merely but twice or four times, until the building seemed to radiate from a point. In part, doubtless, they were seeking the purest and strongest expression of the structural and esthetic principle of the dome; in part it was an almost transcendental desire for the superhuman perfection of the crystal, of pure mathematics, of astronomy. These sketches of Leonardo's do not bother themselves with street frontages or with doors; they obey a higher law than man's convenience. Such a building, obviously, can only maintain its perfect equilibrium when its surroundings are uniform and equidistant. It must stand in the center of a plaza the outline of which is an enlargement of the plan of the building.

FIG. 238—IDEAL CITY

This drawing attributed to Fra Giocondo (about 1500) shows an entire city radiating from a single "central building." The drawing was later copied by Du Cerceau who brought from Italy many suggestions of great importance to the development of the French Renaissance. (From de Geymüller.)

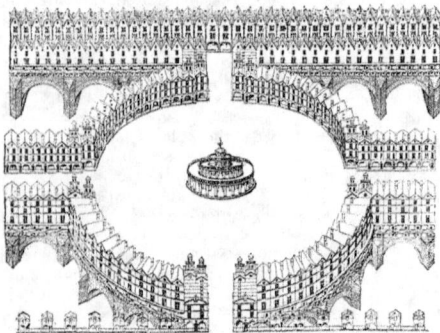

FIG. 239—PARIS. DRAWING BY DU CERCEAU

Scheme for a circular plaza with a central building designed for the point of the island, in connection with the Pont Neuf. See Fig. 322. (From de Geymüller.)

than five times as large as Place Vendôme and more than ten times as large as Place des Victoires, required all available means of giving a big scale to the buildings framing it. The colossal order with the windows behind it set sufficiently far back to obscure their human size, was therefore used by Gabriel, who thus succeeded in

FIG. 236—IDEAL TEMPLE SETTING

FIG. 237—A REMINISCENCE OF BRAMANTE'S MODEL FOR ST. PETER'S

Figs. 236-37 are drawings by a Flemish artist which were used by Du Cerceau. (From de Geymüller.)

giving to his two large buildings on the plaza the appearance of two very large colonnades standing on strong podiums. Another means of giving scale to his plaza was the introduction of intermediary members upon the plaza. He cut down upon the size of the plaza by surrounding its central area by large moats (about 60 feet wide and 12 feet deep) held by retaining walls and balustrades with eight little pavilions at the corners carrying seated and heavily draped statues on their tops (the plans originally called for groups of figures). These pavilions to the top of the statue measure 25 to 85 feet for the façades framing the plaza on the north side. Later, under Napoleon III the plaza was changed, evidently to its disadvantage. The moats were filled and the inner balustrades were taken away; the area of the plaza, which the designer wanted reduced, was thus increased. If in Gabriel's time one stood at the south end of the plaza, which means at the inner balustrade, one saw the buildings framing the northern confines of the plaza at a distance of 930 feet. This distance is so great that the usual relation between the height of the building and its distance from the observer loses interest, compared with the relation between the distance and the largest dimension of the building, in this case a length of the individual colonnades of 310 feet each. In other words while the distance of 930 feet between observer and building is more than eleven times the height it is not more than three times the breadth of these long colonnades which together (including the width of Rue Royale) measure about 700 feet. By the various methods mentioned the designer of the plaza succeeded — not in giving the feeling of triumphant architectural strength that one enjoys in such plazas as the Campidoglio, St. Peter, and, abstracting the modern column, Vendôme, — but in giving one the satisfaction of finding oneself in a pleasantly framed landscape. As a prominent contemporary of Gabriel, M. A. Laugier, expressed it: "Surrounded by gardens and groves, the plaza gives one only the feeling of a beautiful promenade in the midst of a smiling countryside, whence one observes several distant palaces". To give charm to the "distant palaces" of his composition Gabriel meant to go a step beyond what he or Laugier actually saw executed. He prepared an interesting vista between his two colonnades up Rue Royale and meant to have it dominated by a high dome at the end of this street (Fig. 231). This is a typical example of a well framed perspective picture, in this case a view into a strongly terminated street, being made part of the wall of a plaza. The design of the street view was excellent; it has been well preserved and must be discussed more fully in the chapter on street design.

On the whole the experience with the Place de la Concorde shows the extreme care that has to be taken when it comes to designing very large plazas, for instance in connection with modern civic centers. The American architect has of course the possibility of mastering even such large plazas as Concorde or larger ones, by the use of skyscrapers to frame the plaza. This possibility of which surprisingly little use has yet been made, will be discussed more fully in the chapter on architectural grouping in America.

Buildings Standing Within Plazas

A very effective means of overcoming the difficulties resulting in plaza design from excessive size is to place a large monumental building in the center of the plaza. If one side of the plaza is open the monument would stand in the center of the semicircle formed by the surrounding buildings. A monumental building thus placed belongs somewhat in a class with the monuments, fountains, and especially statues, which were set so beautifully in the center or in other striking locations within the plazas of antiquity or of the seventeenth and eighteenth centuries: jewels wonderfully shrined. If the building in the center is large, the plaza in the midst of which it stands is practically subdivided into a group of plazas laid in front of the various elevations of the central building.

In ancient Rome the Citadel and Temple of Juno Moneta, the Forum of Julius Caesar, the Temple of Venus and Rome and the Forum of Vespasian represented temples set in the center of courts (Fig. 240A). The Renaissance movement, as expressed by its leaders, Brunelleschi, Leonardo da Vinci (Fig. 235) and Bramante, valued most highly the conception of a building so designed and so perfectly balanced as to be fit and worthy for a location in the center of a plaza; such a building was considered as the ideal expression of complete symmetry. For the convenience of the following discussion a building belonging in this category will be called a "central building" and for the sake of clearness it might be mentioned that Bramante's design for St. Peter's (Fig. 242) and Palladio's design for the Villa Rotonda (see also Figs. 251-64) are perfect representatives of the "central building" type. As American contributions to this type might be mentioned buildings such as Jefferson's Monticello, the libraries of the Universities of Virginia and Columbia, Hunt's administration building of the Chicago fair, and Cass Gilbert's Festival Hall in the center of the St. Louis Fair.

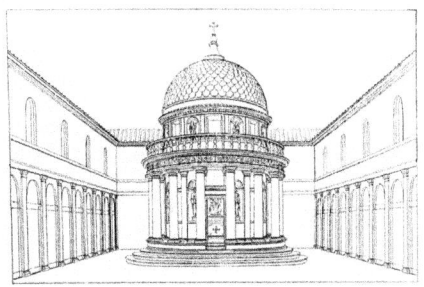

FIG. 241—THE TEMPIETTO AND SETTING, AS BUILT
(From J. A. Coussin.)

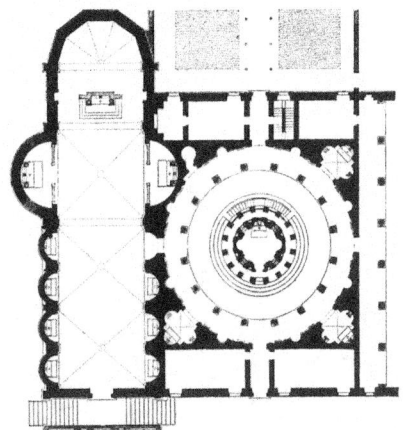

FIG. 240—ROME. BRAMANTE'S DESIGN FOR THE SETTING OF THE TEMPIETTO AT SAN PIETRO IN MONTORIO

The little temple is set in the center of a circular court of twice the diameter of the temple. The arcade around the court has the same number of columns as has the temple. The problem of the curved façade is interesting. (Compare Fig. 252.) To this project of Bramante's the following words by Wren might well be applied: "In this Court we have an Example of circular Walls; and certainly no Enclosure looks so gracefully as the circular; 'tis the Circle that equally bounds the Eye, and is every where uniform to itself." Plan from Serlio (Letarouilly).

FIG. 240A—PALLADIO. RESTORATION OF A TEMPLE ON THE VIA APPIA

The circular sepulchral temple of Romulus, part of the Circus of Maxentius, was built in the fourth century. Though the round temple has a radiating plan the extension at one side gives the whole building a definite orientation and makes reasonable the oblong shape of the court.

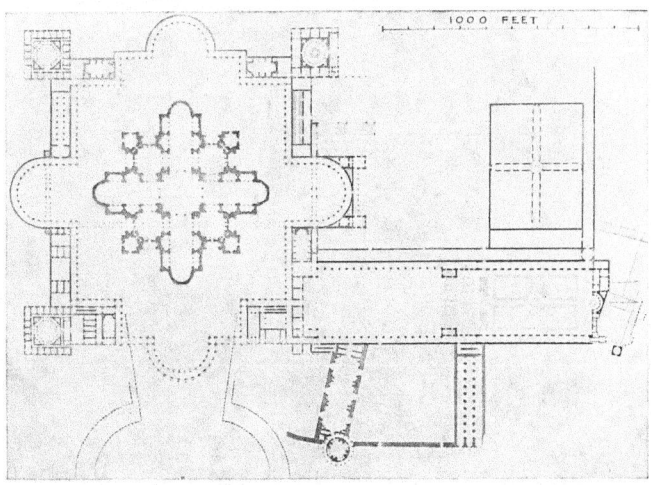

1000 FEET

FIG. 242—BRAMANTE'S PLANS FOR ST. PETER'S AND THE VATICAN

A combination of Bramante's plans for the church, the piazza in which it was to be centered and for the court of the Belvedere, with part of Bernini's plaza shown in dotted lines. (From de Geymüller.)

FIG. 243—ROME.

An early scheme for the setting of St. Peter's shown in a fresco painting made about 1495. Compare Fig. 205. (From de Geymüller.)

This interesting medley of classical and medieval forms must not be taken as an architect's design. The artist has taken the usual painter's liberties with the architecture, but the essential idea of the fresco—a forecourt surrounded by a high and thick architecturally membered wall—must be accepted as the expression of a definite architectural concept of the time. The great flanking arches form an effective motive which is not incapable of modern application.

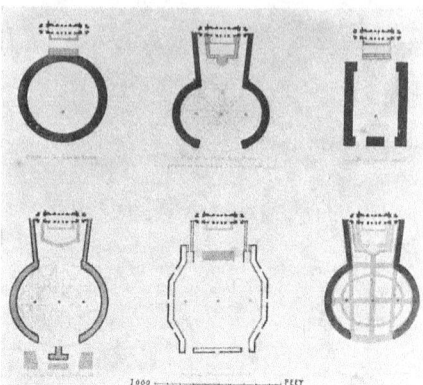

FIG. 245—ST. PETER'S, ROME. VARIOUS PLANS FOR THE PIAZZA

The obelisk and one fountain (not, however, in its present location—it was moved and the other was built to balance it) were "given" elements in the design. Rainaldi's study and two of Bernini's place the entrances to the plaza off center, so that the visitor's first view would give him a more definite impression of the great distance from the obelisk to the church and would also avoid a view in which the obelisk would appear to split the façade in the middle. (From Letarouilly.)

Bramante's St. Peter's, as the most perfect building of Christendom, was to realize this sublime dream of the great epoch. The pioneer of the French Renaissance, Du Cerceau, brought back from his visit to Italy drawings like his Templum Salomonis (Fig. 236) and Templum Cereris (Fig. 237) the latter of which shows a replica of Bramante's dome project with a flanking tower at each of the four corners, while the former shows the framing features that were considered appropriate to a prominent temple centrally located. Serlio has preserved the plan of the circular frame Bramante had planned for his Tempietto (Fig. 240) and Geymueller's studies led to the reconstruction of Bramante's intentions for the closed plaza in the center of which his great church of St. Peter was to stand (Fig. 242). The "central building" in this latter case was not circular, as was the Tempietto, but was a Greek cross in plan with the corners filled in by smaller circular chapels and the surrounding court was based on a design echoing the shape of the "central building", giving apsidal recognition to the branches of the Greek cross. A colonnade surrounded the entire court. There were minor colonnades connecting the pope's palace with the church and affording convenient circulation, but they must be thought of as sufficiently subsidiary not to interfere with the expanse of the plaza between the higher en-

FIG. 244—ST. PETER'S, ROME. MICHELANGELO'S GREEK CROSS WITH THE PLAZA SURROUNDING IT

The church was built as here shown and so stood until the change to the Latin Cross plan. The surrounding plaza was never built. Reconstruction by Aiker. (From Ostendorf.)

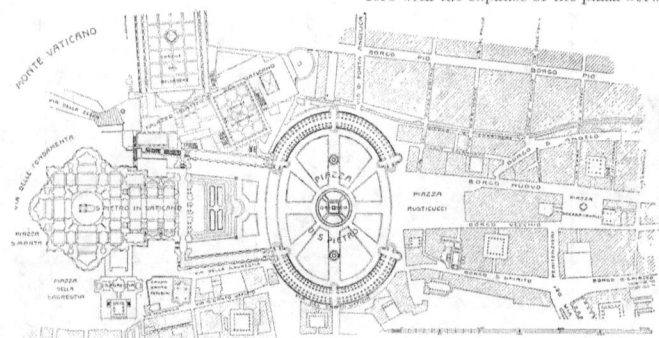

FIG. 246—ROME. VICINITY OF ST. PETER'S
Showing conditions in 1908. (Plan by Th. Hofmann.)

FIG. 247—ST. PETER'S, ROME. BERNINI'S PLAZA

In the perspective the fountains are shown rather too large. The
section brings out the concavity of the floor of the plaza. For other
sections see Fig. 219. (From Letarouilly.)

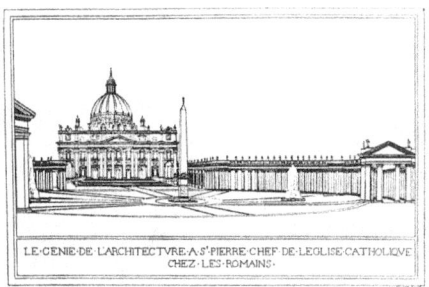

FIG. 248—ST. PETER'S ROME. PIAZZA DI S. PIETRO FROM
PIAZZA RUSTICUCCI

closing walls. The American student might visualize
them by remembering the low passages that connect Jefferson's Monticello with the servants' quarters.

After Bramante's death, his "central building" based
upon the Greek cross was threatened in pitched battle
by the adherents of the Latin cross, which was better
suited to the historic requirements of the Catholic Cult.
But against Raphael and San Gallo, who were induced to
make concessions to the cult requirements, prevailed
the spirit of Bramante, Peruzzi, and Michelangelo, and
the latter completed the work on the Greek cross plan.
Thus St. Peter's stood for forty years as the great "central building" par excellence (Fig. 244), when Maderna
at the pope's bidding added the long nave and his
much disputed façade. Afterwards Bernini transformed
what Bramante had meant to be a plaza surrounding the

FIG. 249—ST. PETER'S ROME. THE PIAZZA FROM THE CUPOLA
OF ST. PETER'S. (Courtesy of the Chicago Plan Commission.)

The obelisk is not exactly on the axis of the church, an error probably due to Domenico Fontana's acceptance, when he moved the obelisk,
in 1586, of a stake set by his predecessors as the true location. Only
after the extension of the nave and the completion of the dome of St.
Peter's was the error noticed. The obelisk is as high as a ten-story
building, but the breadth of the area in which it stands and the great
height of the façade and colonnade make it difficult to appreciate its
real size.

FIG. 250—ST. PETER'S, ROME. AIR VIEW OF BORGO, CHURCH, AND VATICAN
(From the City Planning Exhibition, 1910.)

FIG. 251—TRIEST. CHURCH OF S. ANTONIO

A "central building" with an entrance portico dominating a water court. (From P. Klopfer.)

FIG. 253—TURIN. CHIESA DELLA GRAN MADRE DI DIO

An old drawing (from an anonymous book of "Veduta Pittoriche") showing the originally planned formal setting. The situation of the church is somewhat similar to the Chamber of Deputies in Paris. It stands at the end of the bridge which connects it with the large Piazza Vittorio Emanuele on the other side of the Po.

This and the Triest church are "central buildings" structurally and internally. Externally they are oriented by the special treatment of one side.

FIG. 252—PARIS. STREET ENCIRCLING THE OLD GRAIN MARKET

A unified street-front on a curving plan as a setting for a "central building." The radial streets and parts of the circular street have been widened, thus destroying the continuity of the circular wall and the impression that the street is definitely a part of the design of the grain market. (From Commission Municipale du Vieux-Paris, 1911.)

FIG. 254—PARIS. AIR VIEW OF THE PLACE DE L'ETOILE

This view demonstrates the interrupted character of the "wall" of the area. The decorations, being practically continuous, bring out the circular plan of the plaza much more clearly. For plan and Camille Martin's criticism see Fig. 79 and p. 19.

FIG. 255—STOCKHOLM. KATARINA CHURCH

Silhouette view of design shown in Fig. 256. The designers put the emphasis upon protecting the silhouette of the church which dominates the sky line of Stockholm. Thus the buildings in the neighborhood of the church are kept low in order to let the domed building loom up without competition. (From a model, City Planning Exhibition, 1910.)

FIG. 256—STOCKHOLM. KATARINA CHURCH AND NEIGHBORHOOD.

The church is a "central building" centered on one side of a court which is framed by low buildings. The street layout represents the winning plan in a competition for the planning of this difficult hillside area and shows a gridiron plan broken where it touches steep ground. The streets are fitted to the grades without the use of curved building-lines.

By Cyrillus Johansson, architect, and R. Sandstrom and F. Eggert, engineers. (From City Planning Exhibition, 1910.)

FIG. 257—A CIRCULAR CENTRAL BUILDING IN A SQUARE

From a painting by Luciano da Laurana in The Palazzo Ducale, Urbino. (From T. P. Hofmann).

FIG. 259—CIRCULAR CENTRAL BUILDING IN CIRCULAR PLAZA

Perspective accompanying the plan below.

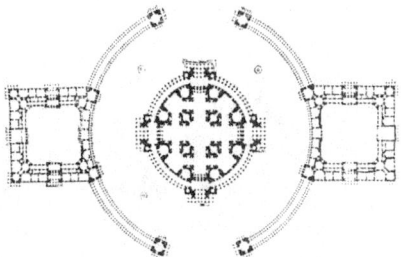

FIG. 258—A SQUARE ARCADED BUILDING ADAPTED TO OCCUPY THE CENTER OF A CROSS-SHAPED PLAZA

(From a drawing by Vignola in the Uffizi).

FIG. 260—CIRCULAR CENTRAL BUILDING IN CIRCULAR PLAZA

With palaces for the archbishop and the canons. Projet by M. J. Peyre (1765), who also designed the Odéon in Paris and completed the palace in Coblenz; Fig. 134. (From Peyre.)

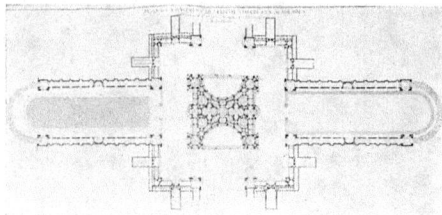

FIG. 261—CENTRAL BUILDING SET IN A CAMPUS

This design of Peyre's is intended for an educational institution in an ideal setting. (From Peyre, 1765; see Figs. 259-60).

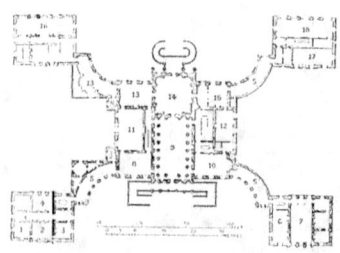

FIG. 262—KEDLESTONE

A central building on a plan representing a development over the one shown in Fig. 261. Plan from Vitruvius Britannicus (Swarbrick).

FIG. 263—VIENNA. CENTRAL BUILDING IN A SQUARE COURT OPEN ON TWO SIDES

A projet by Otto Wagner (1912) for the development of a new section of Vienna. Wagner was the leader of the secessionist movement in Europe, his position corresponding somewhat to Louis Sullivan's in America. This projet of Wagner's (like the design of W. B. Griffin for Canberra (Fig. 1635) and the highly formal plans for American colleges built in the Gothic style) proves that the great principles of civic planning are little affected by details of form.

FIG. 264—A CENTRAL BUILDING OUTSIDE OF A COURT

This round monument was designed by Wilhelm Kreis to stand at the edge of a plateau and to be seen in silhouette from below at long distances. The building was therefore pushed forward upon a support of retaining walls, while the court instead of surrounding the building, was put further back upon the plateau, thus not interfering with the silhouette. (From Deutsche Bauzeitung, 1912).

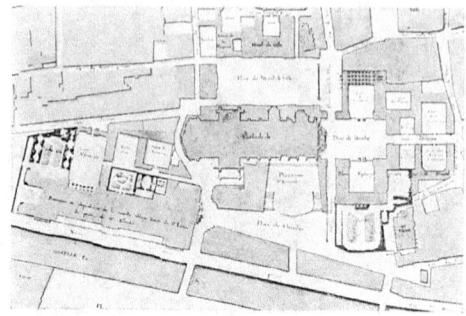

FIG. 265—METZ. CATHEDRAL AND SETTING AS DESIGNED BY J. F. BLONDEL, 1768.

Blondel's plan, of which the essential features were executed, gave the Gothic Cathedral an entourage of well designed plazas and partly screened the irregularities of the Gothic elevations. As a result of the Gothic revival and the "freeing" of the cathedral this fine setting was in large part destroyed in the nineteenth century by the successive efforts of Frenchmen and Germans. (From Paul Tornow).

church into a plaza laid in front of the church, thus giving additional emphasis to Maderna's long arm of the Latin cross (Figs. 245-50).

For the most part the possibilities of the radially symmetrical "central building" remained undeveloped in Europe. Some buildings have been constructed which attain that ideal more or less perfectly (Figs. 151-55), especially in park settings (see the discussion of park design). Many plans, indeed, were made (Figs. 256-64), but the strictly architectural development of the type has not been carried to its highest point. America has a place in the history of the idea, notably for the work of Jefferson. It is interesting to remember that his library at the University of Virginia has experienced architectural vicissitudes in part parallel to the fate of St. Peter's, for the original round building was made a very long one and so remained until fire and McKim, Mead, and White restored Jefferson's plan.

Churches Fronting on Plazas

After the transformation of St. Peter's the victory of the Latin cross, and the forecourt plaza suggested by it, over the Greek cross plan with a surrounding plaza was so complete in all Italy and in the rest of Europe, that Camillo Sitte in his otherwise so penetrating book on civic art mentions the possibilities of the monument in the center of a symmetrical plaza in only one rather unimportant instance. He recognized and condemned the nuisance which in his time the routine city-planners were continually making of the "central building" idea by placing in the center of plazas churches designed on the Latin Cross plan or other buildings which far from being fit for central locations would have been placed much more successfully near the side of plazas in situations for which Gothic and Renaissance art have created so many admirable precedents. The type of arrangement Camillo Sitte so heartily disapproved of is illustrated by Fig. 34-40, B and what he proposed are arrangements typified in Fig. 142E. The courts marked "d" and "f" in this latter plan are small courts not wider than the building is high and therefore little affected by the irregular shape which a church built on the Latin Cross plan exhibits on its long sides. In the

FIG. 266—ROUEN. PARVIS OF THE CATHEDRAL

In order to show the parvis the blocks of houses in the foreground were omitted from this engraving, made during the first half of the nineteenth century. (From C. Enlart).

FIG. 267—LOUVAIN. PLACE DU PARVIS

The west façade of the church has so strong an entrance feature in the center that the narrow approach on axis, which is not frequently found with Gothic churches, is very appropriate here. Part of the redesign for the inner city by Joseph Stübben.

FIG. 268—FLORENCE. PIAZZA DEL DUOMO

The plaza, which forms the setting for the Cathedral of S. Maria del Fiore with the Baptistry on the axis of the main entrance, was regraded, enlarged and straightened out in the years 1339-49 for esthetic reasons.

Modern clearing has made the area west of the baptistry larger than the area between it and the cathedral. This change has impaired the "feeling" of the group, making the baptistry seem to precede the cathedral in a general movement toward the west, whereas the old spacing, with the baptistry closely supported behind, must have given the baptistry its own movement and orientation toward the east, producing a better balance and for the baptistry a more dignified place in the group.

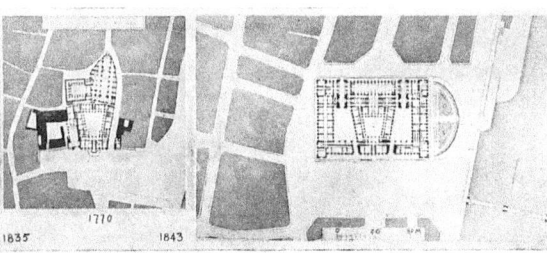

FIG. 269—PARIS. PLACE DE LA GREVE, 1770, 1835, 1843

These three plans show the deterioration of the frame of the Place de la Grève now called the Place de l'Hôtel de Ville. Since 1843 the opening of the wide Rue de Rivoli north of the city hall (to the left of it in the plan) has further contributed to leaving the city hall in an unrelated position. The building shown in the plan of 1843 was burned during the Commune in 1871. (From Victor Calliat.)

FIG. 270—PARIS. PLACE DE LA GREVE

The old popular center of Paris, facing the Seine, with pillory, city hall, and church of Saint Jean back of it, was a closely framed and partly arcaded plaza. As the plan dated 1770 (in center of Fig. 269) shows, the façade of the city hall was made to carry over one of the streets entering the plaza. The church of St. Jean back of the city hall was closely imbedded in buildings. The court of the city hall formed the parvis of the church. (From M. F. de Guilhermy.)

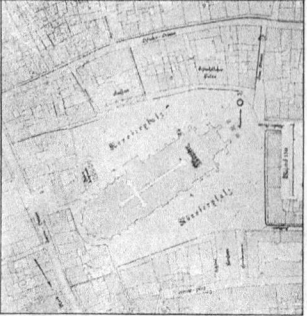

FIG. 273—FREIBURG. CATHEDRAL AND
SETTING

A typical Gothic setting. The church on
account of its eastern orientation stands diagonally to the closely framed plaza and to the
street plan to which it is tied by narrow
lanes only.

FIG. 274—FREIBURG

FIGS. 271, 272—FREIBURG

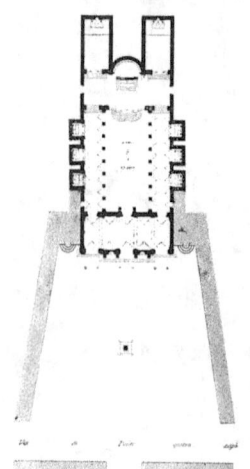

FIG. 275—ROME. FORECOURT
PLAZA OF S. BARTOLOMEO

ELEVATION DES TROIS CHAPELLES CI-DESSOUS

FIG. 276 ELEVATION AND FIG. 277 PLAN—ROME.
CHAPELS OF SSS. ANDREA, BARBARA,
AND SILVIA

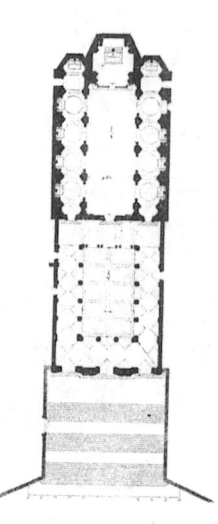

FIG. 278—ROME. CHURCH OF
S. GREGORIO

FIG. 279—ROME. PIAZZA AND CHURCH OF BARTOLOMEO.

The church of S. Gregorio was built in the eighth century and rebuilt in the
eighteenth. The fine arcaded forecourt and its façade and the great flight of
steps were built about 1630. The function of the court was perhaps in part to
bring the new façade forward, nearer to the plazza and the highway. (Figs.
275-279 are from Letarouilly.)

There is almost a touch of Baroque in the plan of the three chapels, though
they date from the sixth century. The detailing of the exteriors has been affected by early seventeenth century restorations. "There is nothing remarkable
about these little buildings," says Letarouilly, "unless it be their picturesque
disposition, due to the way they are grouped and connected. . . . The façades,
taken separately, do not merit attention, but taken together they form a piquant
group." The superior height of the central chapel is an important part of the
design. (From Letarouilly.)

Although the buildings at the sides of the plaza of S. Bartolomeo all' Isola,
(those at the right were razed when the Tiber was widened) are as high as the
church, the lower connecting elements enable the façade to maintain its dominance.

The church façade in the hospital group by Ernest Flagg (see Fig. 280A, on
the opposite page) has a setting somewhat like that of S. Bartolomeo. A difference between the two is the greater breadth and height given to the flanking
members immediately to the right and left of the façade in St. Margaret's Hospital. The Roman setting is probably more advantageous to the impressiveness
of the church.

FIG. 280—ROME. SANTA MARIA MAGGIORE

The Piazza dell' Esquilino terminates the Via Sistina, one of the streets laid out by Fontana for Sixtus V, who also started the Renaissance casing of the ancient basilica. The obelisk is on the axis of the street but not on the axis of the church which is at a slight angle with the street axis. This variation reduces the number of points from which the obelisk is seen against the center of the apsis. The fact that the doors stand at each side, as they must at this end of the church, causes the approaching spectator to branch off from the axial line and brings him where he will get pleasant groupings of the apsis, the obelisk, and one of the domes. (From Letarouilly.)

crowded cities of old, little of these façades could be seen; to throw them open to the eye in their entirety is often detrimental to the impression of the church. It has been tried by Renaissance designers (for instance in Salzburg, see detail plan Fig. 48CC and town plan Fig. 973), but the result is unsatisfactory.

A typical effort of an eighteenth century designer to overcome the informal appearance of the side elevations of a cathedral in order to make them suitable for framing plazas is illustrated by Blondel's plan for the vicinity of the cathedral in Metz (Fig. 265).

Sitte's proposal is really nothing but a suitable modernization of the settings evolved by former periods,

FIG. 281—ROME. PIAZZA S. MARIA DELLA PACE

This piazza, one of the few in Rome designed as a unit, was built by P. da Cortona about the middle of the seventeenth century. The narrow site forced some clever adjustments. The wing walls, buttresses for the octagon dome, conceal the neighboring houses, and frame the façade, and, being set well back, add a bit more space to the little plaza.

FIG. 280A—PITTSBURGH, PA. ST. MARGARET'S HOSPITAL

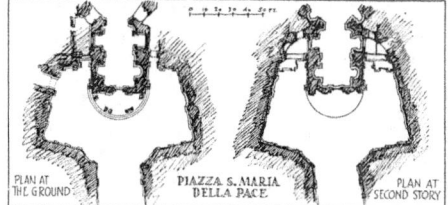

FIG. 281A—ROME. PIAZZA S. M. DELLA PACE

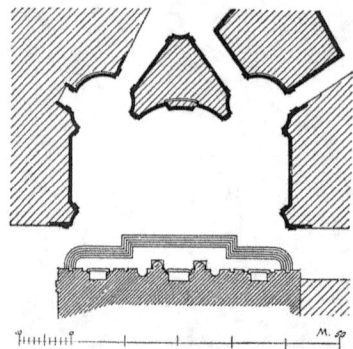

FIG. 282—ROME. PIAZZA S. IGNAZIO

Dates from the early eighteenth century. The uniform façades being fairly high, the various segmental sections have a rather meager vertical proportion. The cornice line is interesting but the total effect would be much stronger if the shape were reiterated by strongly contrasted lines in the pavement. (From Brinckmann).

FIG. 283—PARIS. DU CERCEAU, FACADE FOR ST. EUSTACHE

A translation into Renaissance forms of a Gothic church façade and parvis. The concentration of the parvis upon the portal probably magnifies the scale of the whole. Many details of this drawing are paralleled in the sketch, Fig. 236.

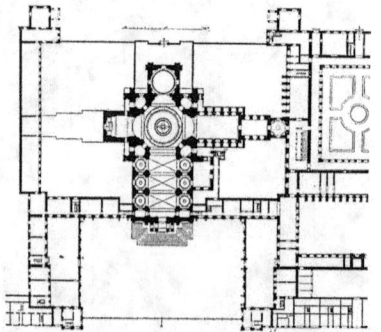

FIG. 284—PARIS. CHURCH OF VAL DE GRACE

Started in 1645 by François Mansart. The forecourt is separated from two service courts by a wall with niches and columns, making an intermediate step between the large court and the higher ranges of buildings back of the service courts. Only a part of this plan was executed. The street which approaches the church on axis spreads with a quarter-circle at each side, to "respond" to the forecourt.

as a short review of some of the methods of locating churches in Gothic and Renaissance times will demonstrate. While it has practically become a rule to-day to copy the architectural detail of the churches of former periods, the historic methods of setting them have fallen into oblivion and during many decades architects were well satisfied, in America to line their churches up indiscriminately along the highway with commercial or residential structures, or, as in Europe, to drop them rather inconsiderately into plazas often of dubious shape.

In the preceding chapter many examples were shown of how the difficulties of setting the unsymmetrical exteriors of churches were mastered. The builders of old times did their utmost to let the crystalline symmetry of the plans of their cathedrals penetrate into the crowded masses surrounding the churches. There is good reason to believe that many of the early Christian churches were free standing, giving room for processions around the church, and that most of them had forecourts and preserved them long into Romanesque and even Gothic times (Figs. 266-7). It is probably for their garden-like features that these forecourts were called "paradise" which term was later corrupted into "parvis". The baptistries on axis with the main entrances to the cathedrals of Florence (Fig. 268) and Pisa (Fig. 22) are reminders of the symmetrical layout of such old forecourts. In Gothic times, under the pressure of a growing population held in by fortifications expensive to enlarge, the free spaces surrounding the churches were more and more crowded upon and often it was only their being used either as cemeteries or covered with cloisters that prevented the churches from being built in entirely (Figs. 269-70). What ever was left was gradually transformed into the manifold plazas, often highly informal in plan but as a rule closed in, courtlike, and wonderfully restful in contrast to the restless church exteriors developing slowly and unsymmetrically through centuries with their changing styles. The irregularity in the plan of these plazas was necessarily increased by the strict adherence to the orientation of the apse required by the tradition of the cult, which often located the church entirely out of plan-relation to the surrounding streets (Figs. 271-4). The artists of the Renaissance made a great but unsuccessful effort to introduce a church type completely symmetrical, the "central building", instead of the long Gothic nave, but after the transformation of St. Peter's into a church of the Gesu type, they confined themselves, as far as the setting of their churches was concerned, to regularizing and systematizing the work of the Gothic builders upon a broader and less crowded basis. Bernini's Piazza in front of St. Peter's is the Gothic parvis in a Renaissance apotheosis. All Renaissance church settings try to live up to the same idea under more or less crowded conditions and many other public buildings are set in the same way (Figs. 275-94). If new churches or public buildings were built in old cities the forecourts often shrunk to smaller and smaller proportions and in extreme cases nothing was left but a symmetrical frame of the façade by some recognition on both sides of the public building. Under such circumstances the church, instead of being the main feature of a plaza, becomes a feature of street design and its setting will be dealt with in the chapter on streets.

The crowding from which the setting of old monumental buildings had to suffer under the rapid change of conditions surrounding them is drastically illustrated by the church of St. Charles Borromeus, Vienna, the resetting of which has kept many architects thinking since its situation was rendered unsatisfactory by the razing of the old city ramparts, the covering of the river, the change of lines of traffic, the building of a railroad and the imminent danger of high buildings in the neighborhood. (Figs. 294-301).

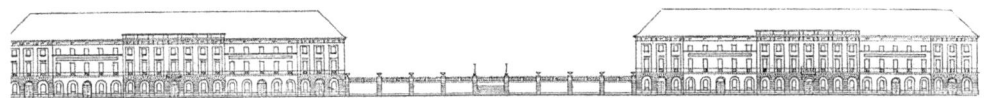

FIG. 285—PLAINE ST. PIERRE. ELEVATION OF SIDE OPPOSITE CHURCH

FIG. 286—PLAINE ST. PIERRE. VIEW TOWARD COURT
Note the arches closing the wall of the court.

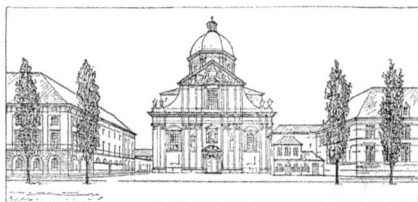

FIG. 288—PLAINE ST. PIERRE. THE CHURCH

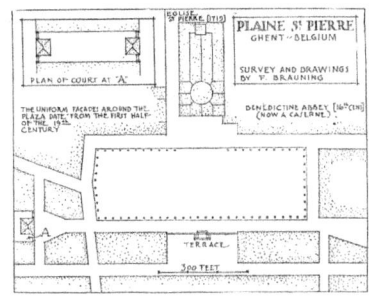

FIG. 287—GHENT. PLAINE ST. PIERRE

This fine plaza is a late flowering of Renaissance good taste. It was designed (perhaps by Roelandt) in connection with a reclamation scheme; the dignified buildings shown in Fig. 285 are rows of residences built with unified façades. The central area of the plaza is in gravel. (From "Der Staedtebau", 1918, with additions to the plan by the authors.)

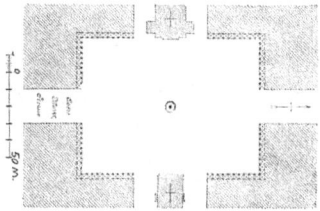

FIG. 289—LUDWIGSBURG. MARKET DEVELOPED AS FORE-COURT FOR TWO CHURCHES

The market place is surrounded by two-story houses. The churches are over two and a half times as high, and the contrast adds much to the impressiveness of the churches. The arcade arches are wider and less numerous than they are shown. (From Brinckmann.)

FIG. 290—CARLSRUHE. PROTESTANT CHURCH FACING THE MARKET PLACE

The church, which has no transepts, is centered on the tower in the rear and flanked by two courts which are separated from the market by double arches and framed by uniform buildings lower than the church. The portico of the church faces the entrance of the city hall; see plan of plaza Fig. 1000. Design of church and plaza by Weinbrenner, between 1801 and 1825. (From P. Klopfer.)

FIG. 291—PETROGRAD. COLONNADES OF KASAN CATHEDRAL

The façade of the Cathedral, built about 1800 by Wovonichin, is flanked by great colonnades which create a monumental setting somewhat resembling the Piazza del Plebiscito in Naples (Fig. 111), built some twenty years later.

FIG. 292—PARIS. ECOLE DE MEDECINE
The court which is the setting of the portico in front of the theater shaped auditorium is separated from the street by a colonnaded member. Built 1769-86 by J. Gondouin. (From J. A. Coussin).

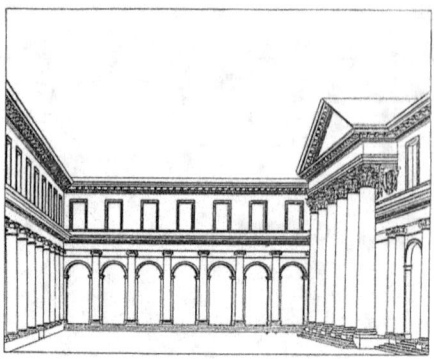

FIG. 293—PARIS. ECOLE DE MEDECINE
View of court.

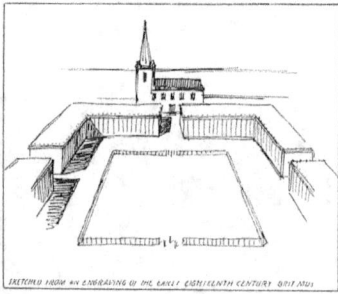

FIG. 293A—LONDON. ST. JAMES' SQUARE

FIG. 294—VIENNA. CHURCH OF ST. CHARLES BORROMEUS BEFORE THE COVERING OF THE WIEN RIVER

The church (built 1715-23 by Fischer von Erlach) dominating the valley of the little Wien river by a dome 240 feet high, has a strong Baroque setting between two columns and two lower bell towers, arched beneath for open passageways and long masses of comparatively low, uniformly roofed buildings. The whole was inspired by S. Agnese, on Piazza Navona, Rome.

FIG. 295—VIENNA. ST. CHARLES CHURCH AFTER THE COVERING OF THE WIEN RIVER

Through the covering of the river the church was made to face a plaza of more than ten acres, for which it was not designed and to which it stood in an awkward relation.

FIG. 296—VIENNA. FULL-SIZE MODEL OF OTTO WAGNER'S PROPOSED MUNICIPAL MUSEUM FACING ST. CHARLES CHURCH

Erected to demonstrate that a thoroughly modern building could, if it had a quiet outline, become a suitable setting for the Baroque church.

FIG. 297—VIENNA. FORECOURT FOR ST. CHARLES CHURCH
(A proposal by Friedrich Ohmann.)

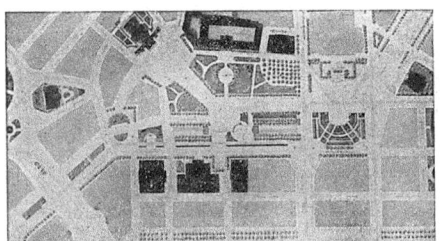
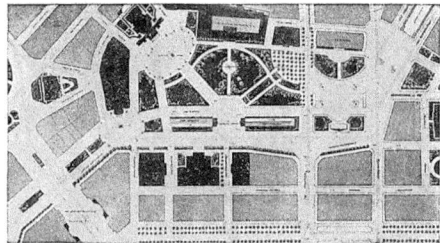
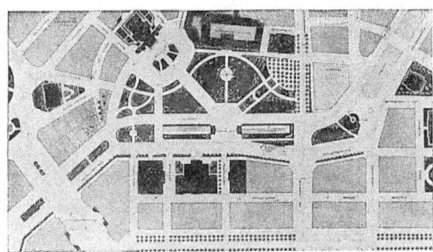
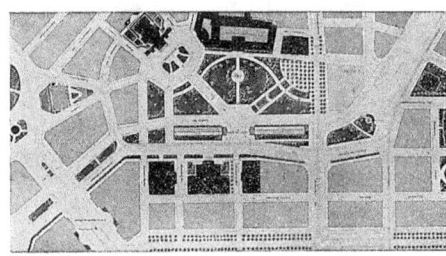

FIGS. 298-301—VIENNA. AREA IN FRONT OF ST. CHARLES CHURCH
Four studies for the redesign of the plaza by Mayreder, Stuebben, Simony, and Goldemund; typical German plans of about two decades ago.

FIG. 302—CHURCHES AND PLAZAS FROM A TRAVEL SKETCHBOOK

FIG. 303—PARIS.   PLACE DE L'OPÉRA

FIG. 304—PARIS.   OPERA, SIDE ELEVATION

The irregular elevation Garnier gave to the sides of his Opéra makes them unsuited to dominate well designed plazas.

The fine façade is flanked by lower members which do not agreeably unfold as they would if they came forward. Instead, they recede and crowd into each other, and what Garnier said about the unfortunate site (étroit par devant, étroit par derrière, et s'élargit en ventre au milieu) is true also of the building. In a good setting (take for instance the marble court of Versailles, Fig. 132, or the setting proposed for the Church of the Invalides, Fig. 305) one feels the central member as forming the background, secure and unquestionable. The façade of the Opéra, on the contrary, is felt to be artificially pulled forward, producing an uneasy effect of the real building standing further back somewhere in plane with the stage loft and side wings. If, to avoid the disturbing aspect of the side members, one recedes far enough to lose them, the high houses on both sides compete with the Opéra.

Theaters and Theater Plazas

The unsuitability of a central location for a building of non-central or unsymmetrical type is not confined to churches but is shared equally by the modern theater, the exterior appearance of which on account of the high loft required by modern stages somewhat suggests the shape of a church with a long nave and a tower over the crossing. The difficulty is well illustrated by the fate of the Paris Opéra, regarding the setting of which its architect Garnier has used the bitter words quoted at the beginning of the previous chapter. Garnier's indictment of Haussmann's planning was certainly well justified but the architect himself is not entirely without blame in this matter. In fact, both Garnier and Haussmann in a certain sense did exactly the same thing in connection with the Opéra: both were successful as long as they followed good precedent and failed where they abandoned it. In setting the main façade of the Opéra, Haussmann tried to follow eighteenth century precedent as exemplified in the location of the Panthéon at the head of Rue Soufflot or of the Madeleine at the head of Rue Royale. This following of the eighteenth century precedent is the part of Haussmann's work of which Camillo Sitte approved. But Haussmann disregarded the precedents by making his street of approach much longer than Rue Royale or Rue Soufflot (originally Rue Soufflot was even shorter than

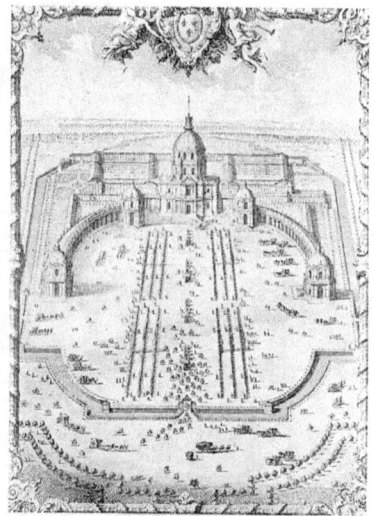

FIG. 305—PARIS, CHURCH OF THE INVALIDES

Project for the setting of the main façades (From J. F. Félibien, 1706). The height of the central building is not crushed by tall buildings but is contrasted against low colonnades. The pavilions in the foreground seem high, they being twice the size of the colonnades. They are repeated in the background and thus furnish a scale by which the spectator can estimate the height of the dome.

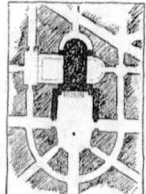 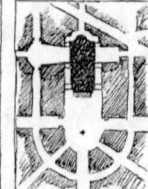 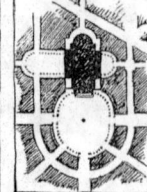

FIG. 307—THREE STUDIES
Compare Figs. 18, 111, 216, 306, and 308-19.

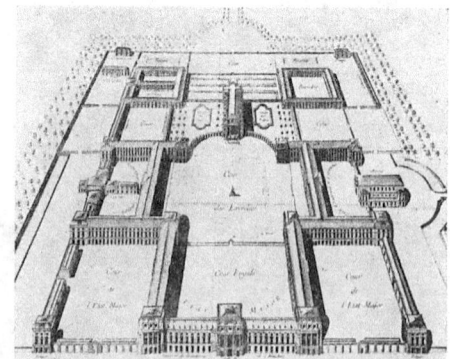

FIG. 306—PARIS.   PROJECT FOR SETTING THE CHURCH OF THE INVALIDES BY THE BUILDING OF THE MILITARY SCHOOL

The church was originally (1670-78) planned without Mansart's central building. The long nave of the original church was planned to be set in a scheme of oblong courts echoing the general mass of the church. (From Brinckmann.)

FIG. 308—LISBON. PLAZA OF DOM PEDRO IV

The symmetrical development of the side elevation of the theater without scenery loft made it possible to center a plaza on it. The group was built after the earthquake of 1755. (From a drawing by Franz Herding.)

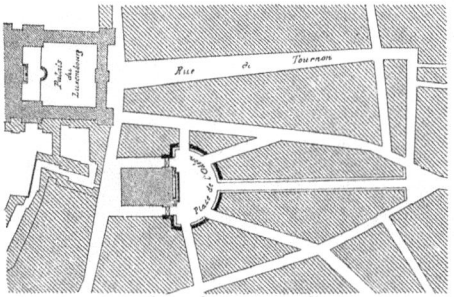

FIG. 309—PARIS. PLACE DE L'ODEON AND RUE DE TOURNON

The Place de l'Odéon is a semicircular plaza built about 1782 with uniform façades as a forecourt to the theater. The side elevations of the theater are not featured. This plan also shows the spreading Rue de Tournon of which Fig. 655 is a view. (From Brinckmann.)

to-day; Fig. 355 shows the old condition). He lined it with houses that are higher — this Garnier resented especially — than is advantageous considering the height of the Opéra. Nevertheless, if seen from a point near enough to prevent the high houses from perspectively dwarfing the Opéra, the setting, measured by the low modern standards, is unusually good, and one has to take a second look to realize why Garnier was so sorely grieved (see caption to Fig. 303) and why this setting is so inferior to its opportunities.

Everything Garnier says against the setting of the other three sides convinces upon first glance. However Garnier forgets that the side elevations of the Opéra are especially unsuitable for a monumental setting (Fig. 304). The Madeleine similarly located shows on its sides the even rows of its stately peristyle; the cross-shaped Panthéon has streets only, not plazas, on its sides.

In connection with the side elevations of the Opéra it seems that not all the blame can be fastened on Haussmann's site "bellying out in the middle". Good prec-

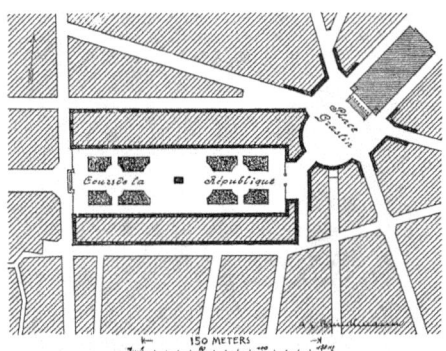

FIG. 310—NANTES. PLACE GRASLIN AND COURS DE LA REPUBLIQUE

Place Graslin, built as forecourt to a theater on a plan somewhat similar to the Place de l'Odéon, is lined by uniform houses, the upper stories of which continue the lines of the frieze of the theater façade. This group of plazas was built by Crucy, 1785. (From Brinckmann.)

FIG. 313—MADRID. PLAZA DE ORIENTE (BELOW)

When Napoleon's brother was made king of Spain he razed several convents, a church, and five hundred houses to create in front of the royal palace the Plaza de Oriente, the largest plaza in Madrid. (See Fig. 389 for an earlier scheme.) The theater is set between a square plaza and an oval court formed partly of curved house façades, partly of trees. (From Gurlitt.)

FIG. 311—NANTES. COURS DE LA REPUBLIQUE
View looking east. (Drawing by Franz Herding)

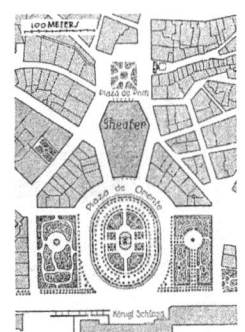

FIG. 312—NANTES. PLACE GRASLIN
View looking north. See plan above. (Drawing by Franz Herding.)

FIG. 314—STUTTGART. THE NEW THEATER PLAZA

The building of two theaters north of the royal palace (see plan Fig. 412) was made the starting point of a plaza design. Of the many proposals the one by Max Littmann shown in Figs. 314-15 is partly executed. Figs. 316-17A were interesting alternatives.

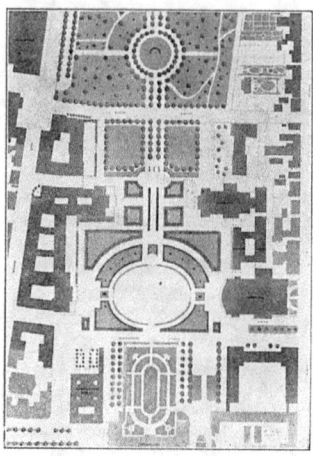

FIG. 315—STUTTGART. PLAN GOING WITH FIG. 314

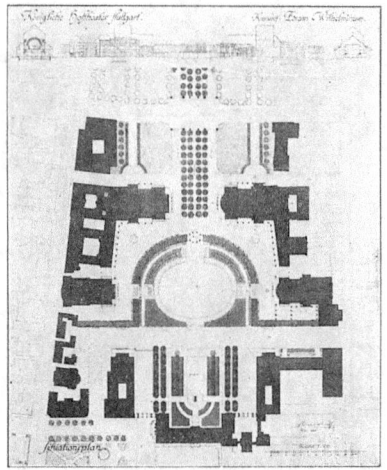

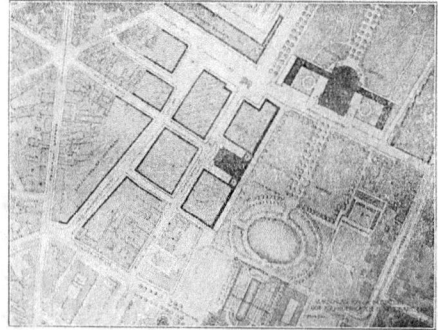

FIG. 316—STUTTGART. ALTERNATIVE TO PLAN SHOWN IN FIG. 315

By Theodor Fischer.

FIG. 317—STUTTGART. ALTERNATIVE TO PLAN SHOWN IN FIG. 315

This alternative proposes a perfectly symmetrical arrangement of two small and two large theaters. From the low buildings of the palace the height of the plaza walls is to rise to the two small theaters and reach its climax in the two large theaters, the high scenery lofts of which form the effective accentuations of the corners of the plaza. In view of the large number of theaters which in every large city are thrown together without pleasant correlation into a very small central district such a grouping of theater sites is a farsighted plan of great promise. Fig. 317A gives a view of the first two theaters. The design of plaza and theaters is by Bruno Schmitz.

FIG. 317A—STUTTGART. VIEW GOING WITH PLAN FIG. 317

The first two theaters of the group of four. The large one to the left, the small one to the right, both to be duplicated on the other side.

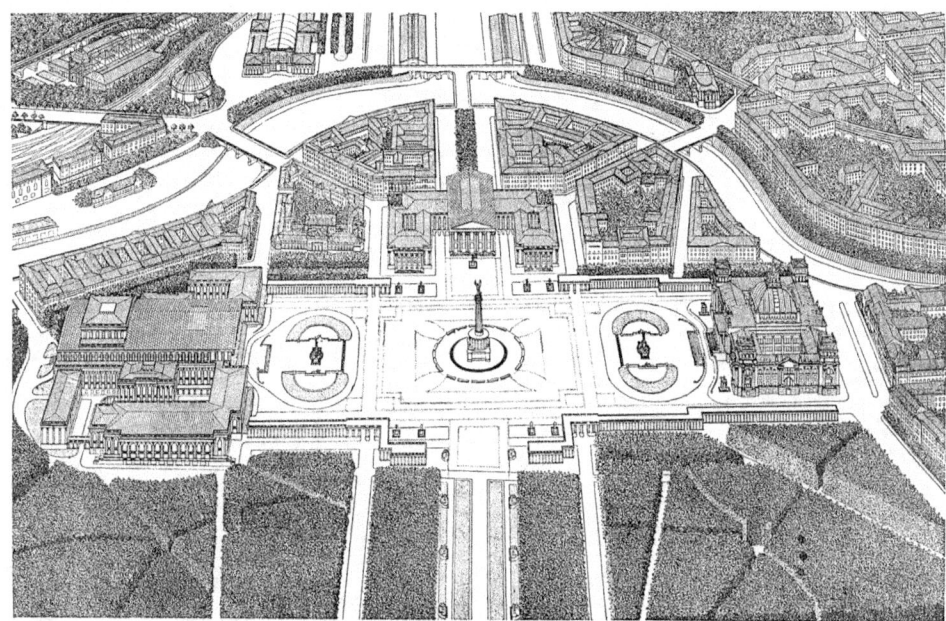

FIG. 318—BERLIN. PROJECT FOR NEW OPERA HOUSE TO FACE PARLIAMENT BUILDING

Designed by Otto March in 1912, this scheme represents one of the finest proposals for reducing the size of the Koenigsplatz. The street coming in on axis through the Tiergarten is the Sieges Allee. To the right stands Wallot's Parliament; to the left the proposed opera house; in the background another proposed building.

edent requires balanced appearance for every elevation of a building which is to be seen in full. This applies
also to the side elevations of theaters. Thus Victor
Louis's famous theater for Bordeaux (built 1788) was
harmoniously developed on all sides; and one of its side
elevations becomes a harmonious part of the wide Cours
du Chapeau Rouge. Soufflot's Grand Théâtre in Lyons
was similarly developed. The theater of Donna Maria in
Lisbon (Fig. 308) and the old Opera House in Berlin
(Figs. 396-97) show the opera building after the addition
of the modern stage loft) are eighteenth century cases
where the side façade of a big theater is the dominating
feature of a very large plaza. The stage requirements of
previous centuries made it easy to develop a theater with
symmetrical elevations on all sides. Nevertheless theaters were seldom made to stand entirely free. The oldest
theaters were parts of castles. The Comédie Française,
successor to Molière's theater, stands at the other end
of the Avenue de l'Opéra and is still a part of the Palais
Royale group (Fig. 13). Gabriel built an opera house
as a part of the palace of Versailles and there was another one in the Tuileries. Other theaters were built in
as a part of ordinary building blocks. Even free standing theaters were put in positions typified by the situation of the Odéon in Paris (Fig. 309), the Grand Théâtre
in Nantes (Fig. 310-2) or the theater facing the castle in
Madrid (Fig. 313). But such precedent was abandoned by
both Haussmann and Garnier; Haussmann tried to develop plazas at the sides of the Opèra and Garnier gave to
the sides unsymmetrical elevations. Instead of one harmonious mass—which, with an opera house, to satisfy the
expressionist, might express musical harmony if mere
beauty is not enough for a building to express — three
heterogeneous masses are put together and "give frank
and suitable expression" — to use the terms of an ad-
mirer of "functionalism"—to three different purposes:
foyer, auditorium and stage. This is not the place to

decide whether or not functionalism at the expense of exterior harmony is necessary or desirable. The fact is
that Garnier was not satisfied with eighteenth century
tradition but was influenced by the modern theatrical
movement which made Semper (who began his theater
building career in 1838) and Richard Wagner go back to
the Greek theater (with stage and auditorium entirely
separated). This development led to the very interesting,
but — especially as far as the "expressive" exterior is
concerned — certainly not beautiful theater in Bayreuth.
This functionalism introduced into the building of theaters put their side elevations into the situation of those
of Christian churches having high towers, long nave,
transepts and apse, the unbalanced aspect of which, before the nineteenth century, was as a rule made inconspicuous.

FIG. 319—BERLIN. PROJECT FOR NEW OPERA HOUSE

From the design by Eberstadt, Moehring, and Petersen premiated
in the competition of 1910 for a plan for Greater Berlin.

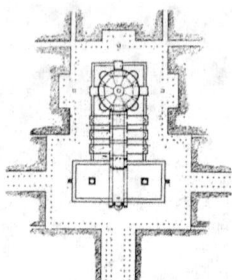

FIG. 319A—PLAN FOR A CHURCH SETTING

This plan creates an arcaded parvis in front of the main facade and gives recognition by returns in the street walls to those other features of the church which can stand a balanced setting. The center of the main facade and the two independent campaniles placed in the parvis area are the vista points of the avenues of approach. This scheme would be equally applicable to the setting of a large theater, the scenery loft taking the place of the dome. (Design by K. M. Heigelin, 1830.)

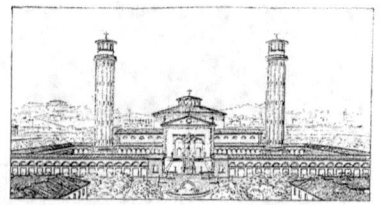

FIG. 319B—VIEW GOING WITH PLAN FIG. 319A

To-day, for fire protection, theaters should not be built otherwise than free-standing and as modern requirements necessitate very high spaces above the stage, the appearance of the theater will be thrown out of balance unless the high roof over the stage is continued over the entire building as was contemplated in the official plans for the new Grand Opera house for Berlin just before the war. Under special circumstances it may be possible to place the high stage in the center of the theater instead of at one end. In the majority of cases it will be possible to step back with the high part of the stage from the side wall of the theater thus preserving the entity in the plane of the side elevation and making it possible to develop a symmetrical plaza of not too great depth (about one and one half times the height of the main cornice line of the theater) without interference from the unsymmetrical feature of the stage.

If none of these or similar expedients is resorted to the side elevations of the theater will be unsymmetrical and therefore fitted to form walls of plazas only if they could be duplicated, as Wren has proposed to duplicate churches in order that their towers facing each other across the street would give a symmetrical aspect to the street.

A symmetrical arrangement of two theaters was proposed for Stuttgart (Fig. 317), where much thought was given to the grouping of two theaters and other public buildings.

A large number of valuable studies for the location of a large modern opera house were produced just before the war as plans for the new building in Berlin. The late Otto March, a leader in city planning thought, left the important proposal illustrated in Fig. 318.

In speaking of the setting of theaters, Perrault's reconstruction of a garden behind the theater for entr'acte promenades (illustrated in the chapter on park design) should be mentioned.

FIG. 320—PARIS IN 1615. PLAN BY MATHIEU MERIAN

FIG. 321—PARIS. PLACE ROYALE (PLACE DES VOSGES)

The plaza is 460 feet square (see plan Fig. 79E). The two buildings facing each other and rising above the uniform roof line are the pavilions of the king and queen. Built in 1605 by Henry IV, the plaza and the residences facing it soon became the center of fashionable life. See Fig. 325. (From an engraving by Israel Silvestre, 1652.)

The Royal Plazas of France

A monumental building placed, not as a part of one of the walls of a plaza, but as a self-contained unit in the center or in some other important point of a plaza has much in common with a statue or other sculptural monument which is especially honored by a first rate setting. This is especially true if the monumental building is to be lower than the frame, as has been suggested for modern American conditions by the late D. H. Burnham.

The development of monumental settings around statues started early; the Forum Transitorium in Rome with Nerva's statue in the middle, the setting Michelangelo designed as a frame for the statue of Marcus Aurelius on the Campidoglio have previously been mentioned as classic prototypes. In France the progress from the early Renaissance designs for the triangular Place Dauphine (Figs. 322-24) and the joyous Place des Vosges (Figs. 321, 325) to the majesty of Hardouin Mansart's Place des Victoires (Figs. 326-7) and Place Vendôme (Figs. 328-31) and the final diffusion of the Place de la Concorde (Figs. 225-34), reached what may be the climax conceivable for such architectural settings in the design for the group of plazas in Nancy (Figs. 344-51). The designers of the eighteenth century in carrying on the great tradition are overwhelmingly rich in creative suggestions. In Bordeaux, Valenciennes, Rennes, Nancy, Reims, Rouen, and in other cities, plazas were created as splendid settings for statues of the "beloved" Louis XV of France (Figs. 332-43), and besides the plans which were executed a wonderful sheaf of valuable "projets" has been preserved to us.

When in 1748 the merchants of Paris received permission to honor their king by erecting a statue, their initiative led to a great outburst of civic designing on a comprehensive scale involving large reclamation schemes. It must be remembered in this connection that Paris for several hundred years preceding 1700 had been the largest city of the world. While London, which surpassed it soon afterwards, had benefited from the terrific lessons of fire and plague (1665,'66) and decentralized housing to a degree up to that time unknown, Paris persisted within its old limits, and a slum problem of serious proportions resulted (see discussion of the transformations of Paris). To relieve the congestion within the fortifications was a prominent motive with the civic designers of 1748, and the placing of the king's statue was considered in connection with very large schemes for rebuilding parts of the city. The ideas about the replan-ning of old cities, as one finds them in the literature of that period, contain much of permanent practical and esthetic value. Gabriel, the designer of the royal plaza in Bordeaux and of the Place de la Concorde, revised the engineer's plans for the rebuilding of Rennes after the fire of 1720 along gridiron lines interrupted by interestingly grouped plazas (Fig. 339). The younger Blondel, a great theoretician and designer, made good plans for the redesigning of the central part of Strasbourg (Fig. 354) and for surrounding of the cathedral of Metz with a group of small plazas (Fig. 265).

The outburst of plaza design connected with the erection of the monument for Louis XV in Paris can be studied in the wonderfully illustrated book written by Pierre Patte (1723-1814), architect of the duke of Zweibruecken, and published in Paris 1765, under the title: "Monumens érigés en France à la gloire de Louis XV". This collection of plans is so important and of such fundamental value that it seems surprising how little it was appreciated or even known, until Robert Bruck recently (in 1908) emphasized its importance. Many esthetic blunders in modern city planning would have been avoided if the great body of French thought represented in Patte's book had found more serious students among civic designers.

Besides a description of the plazas that had been created in the provinces in honor of Louis XV, the book gives the results of the two competitions for the monument, in Paris, which were held in 1748 and 1753 and which deserve close attention.

Fig. 355 reproduces the large engraving giving the plan of Paris on which Patte has entered the locations of the various proposals for placing the statue. The proposals are described in detail in the captions going with the larger scale plans (Figs. 356-71) of the individual proposals. Even the most ambitious of the schemes described are outdone by the project given by Patte (upper right corner of Fig. 355; see also bird's-eye view, Fig. 375) comprising the reclamation, union, and comprehensive architectural treatment of the entire areas of the two Seine islands and the large areas west of them on both sides of the river. The grand river scheme had worthy followers, although on a smaller scale, in the more recent schemes for the London harbor (Fig. 377) and various schemes for an island in the Charles River, Boston, (Fig. 373). As to the esthetic effect of setting monumental buildings upon islands to be seen at great distances

FIG. 323.—PARIS. PONT NEUF AND PLACE DAUPHINE IN 1739

Portion of Turgot's plan shown in full in Fig. 353. In the left foreground Perrault's Louvre is unfinished and still faced by houses; also houses in front of S. Germain l'Auxerrois and in the court of the Louvre. On the other side of the river the College of the Four Nations (Palais Mazarin, now "Institut").

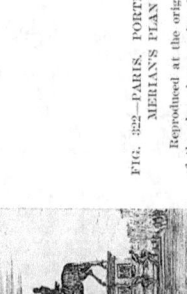

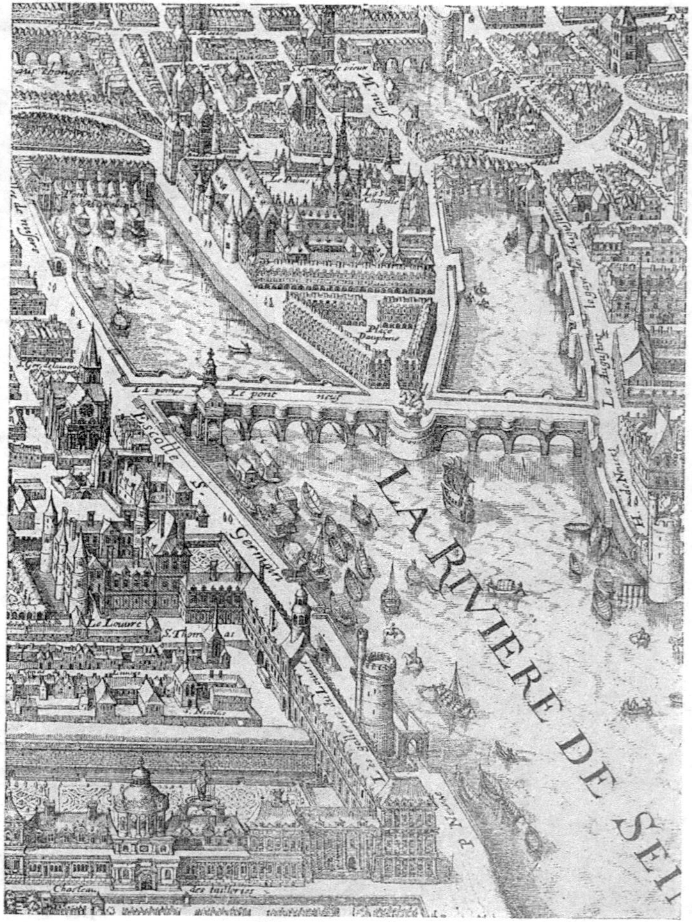

FIG. 322.—PARIS. PORTION OF MERIAN'S PLAN

Reproduced at the original size of the plan shown reduced in Fig. 320. In the foreground the Tuileries; in the center the triangular Place Dauphine with the equestrian statue of Henri IV on the Pont Neuf facing it. It was for this point that Du Cerceau's plaza shown in Fig. 329 was intended.

FIG. 324.—PARIS. PLACE DAUPHINE

From an engraving by Israel Silvestre, 1652

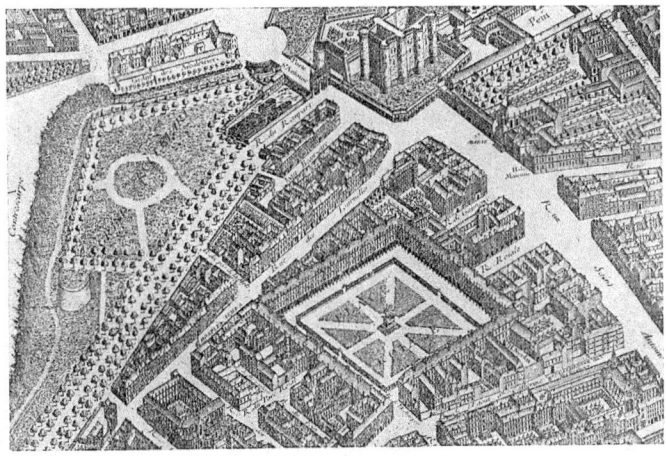

FIG. 325—PARIS. PLACE ROYALE (PLACE DES VOSGES)

Portion (at full size) of Turgot's plan of Paris of 1739 (see Fig. 353) showing the Place Royale completely closed in except at one corner, the main entrance being through the arch under the Pavillon du Roi on axis of the statue. At the top of the picture (center) is the Bastille of revolutionary fame. At the left the four tree-rows of Colbert's new boulevards. The large area marked "Grand Boulevart" is an old bastion showing the old sense of the word boulevard or "bulwark".

the illusive shortening of distance caused by looking across water would have been a favorable factor. To form an idea of the amount of pitiless clearing required for the execution of Patte's colossal scheme one must compare it with the five reclamation schemes made by other designers for the same district as given on the same sheet (Fig. 355) and realize that it was even proposed to wipe out monuments like Mazarin's Palace of the Four Nations.

But there was no danger for Mazarin's palace nor even for the church of St. Germain l'Auxerrois, built in the despised Gothic style. Since the rising of the Fronde against Louis XIV the French kings, much to the worry of great statesmen like Colbert, had lost all interest in the unmanageable city of Paris and had concentrated their interest upon the creation of the garden city of Versailles.

Servandoni's proposal of locating the new plaza which the merchants wanted to build for Louis XV outside the fortified area pleased the king much better than the idea of getting involved in a large reclamation scheme inside the built-up city, with the housing difficulties that unavoidably would result from the razing of large slum districts. He therefore gave, as a present to the city, the free territory west of the Tuileries gardens for the plaza. A new competition brought 28 plans for the development of the area. Gabriel's plan was accepted and in large part executed.

While the Place de la Concorde partook more of the landscaped character of a large American campus, the most wonderful of the plazas built in honor of King Louis, that of Nancy (Figs. 344-51), was an architectural creation in the strongest sense of the word. Much more than an ordinary plaza, it represented a group of plazas comprising the square with the centrally located monument of the King and what might be considered as two forecourts to this main plaza; the long "Carrière" with its clipped trees and the oval colonnaded area in front of the Palace which faces the City Hall at the other end of the long composition. This long procession of plazas has something of the character of the Forum Trajanum

or the sacred precinct of Heliopolis, and represents one of the climaxes of which civic art is capable.

Appreciation of these great creations in France and of the theoretical discussion going with them and following them (Figs. 380-87) was no small factor contributing to the development of similar aspirations all over France. In Belgium, Spain, Denmark, England, Germany, and Russia, and elsewhere, wonderful work was achieved. As the cities of the Middle Ages had vied with each other in the building of cathedrals, the cities of the seventeenth and eighteenth centuries, under the intelligent guidance of their often highly cultivated rulers, tried to surpass each other in the creation of plazas as wonderful settings for their public buildings, the castles often taking the place of the modern city hall. Figs. 388-411 give some of the numberless fine schemes of this period; many others can be found in other chapters of the book. To show them all would fill many volumes.

After the French Revolution the artistic value of these creations rapidly diminished (Figs. 412-4; 416-9). Often an uninspired geometrical arrangement of buildings (Fig. 418) seems all that the declining period was capable of until in the second half of the nineteenth century the new urbanism awakened to the study of the great precedents and gradually rediscovered the secrets of the lost tradition. While for decades public buildings had been built without taste and foresight, and often even without order (Fig. 419), the way was found again to orderly relation and often charming compositions. In means and taste and especially in will the modern many-headed political organizations do not always favorably compare with the centralized initiative of previous ages and the recognition which even large public buildings, if built in crowded districts, find in the street plan, is often feeble and confined to expedients (Fig. 424). In laying out new districts, however, and where in old districts sufficiently large areas become free by favorable circumstances (abandonment of fortifications, etc.) bolder and bolder methods are used (Figs. 425-38), promising a new climax of civic art which may some day surpass the achievement of previous ages, if not in originality, at least in size.

FIG. 326—PARIS. PLACE DES VICTOIRES AND APPROACH

Portion (at full size) of Turgot's plan of Paris of 1739 (Fig. 353) showing the Place des Victoires
(see plan Fig. 327) which is much distorted by the engraver's desire to show the street areas.

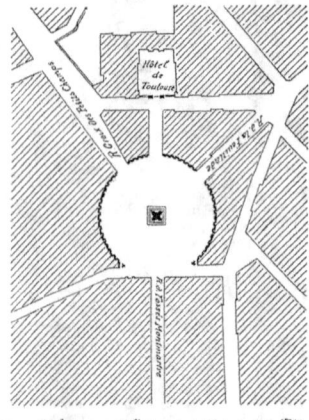

FIG. 327—PARIS. PLACE DES VICTOIRES

Designed by Hardouin Mansart in 1679. The
statue of the king is the center of the four radiating
streets. For cross section see Fig. 219. The plaza
has severely suffered by rebuilding of façades and
street widening. (From Brinckmann.)

FIG. 328—PARIS. PLACE VENDOME (PLACE DE LOUIS LE GRAND)

The plaza, started about 1680 as one of the most ambitious civic center projects
of all times, was intended as the execution of Cardinal Richelieu's great plan for a
forum of arts and sciences. The royal library, the academies, the mint, and a hotel
for ambassadors were to be grouped around a monument for Louis XIV. The plan,
a large square (see Fig. 330), was designed by Hardouin Mansart. The execution of
the original project was abandoned for lack of funds but also in recognition of the
advantage a smaller plaza would have as a setting for the excellent equestrian statue
which Girardon meanwhile had completed. Mansart made a new plan for a smaller
and octagonal plaza. The monument and most of the façades (without houses behind
them) were erected about 1699. The library remained unfinished for forty years;
the remainder of the land behind the façades was sold by the foot. The plaza soon
became the center of the neighborhood and an important factor in shaping its street
plan. Later street corrections have destroyed essential parts of the plaza enclosure
by lengthening the two short streets of access.   (From an old engraving.)

FIG. 329—PARIS. COLONNE VENDOME

In 1806 a column about thrice the height of the original monument
was erected in the plaza, the monument having been destroyed during
the Revolution. There can be little doubt that the beautiful plaza was
seriously harmed by the change. If seen, not from the plaza, but from
a distance in one of the approach streets, the column appears well set
between the four corners of the plaza entrance, as shown in this view.
(From a painting in the Carnavalet Museum dated 1835.)

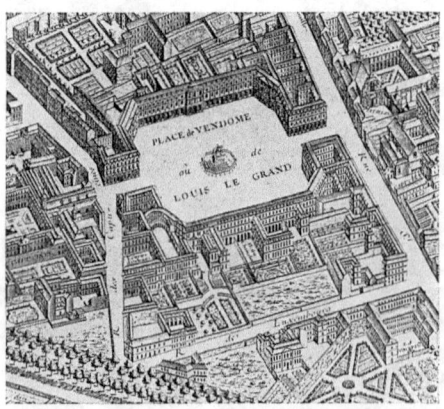

FIG. 330—PARIS. PLACE VENDOME IN 1739

Portion of Turgot's plan (see Fig. 353). This view of Place Vendôme shows in the upper right corner of the plaza what was left of
the constructions built in carrying out the original design on a square
plan.

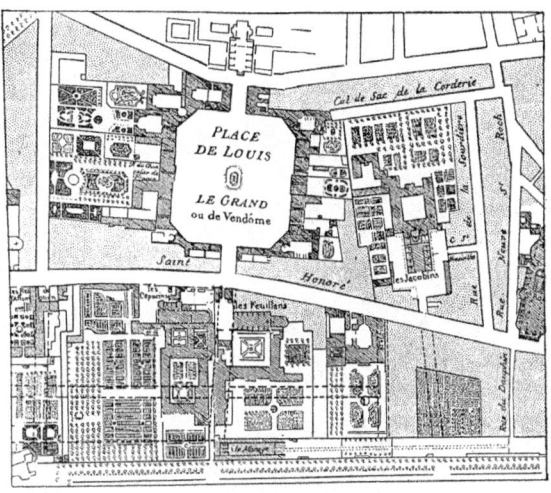

FIG. 331—PARIS. PLACE VENDOME IN 1772
From the plan of Jaillot.

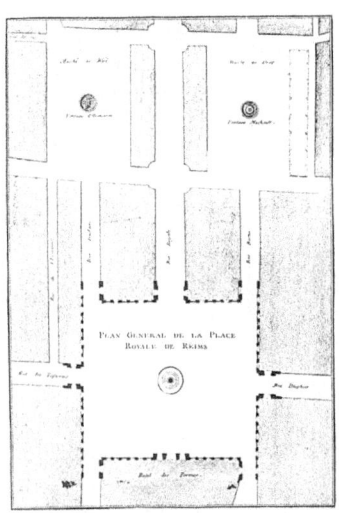

FIG. 332—REIMS. PLACE ROYALE AND MARKET
PLACES
From Patte. See Fig. 333.

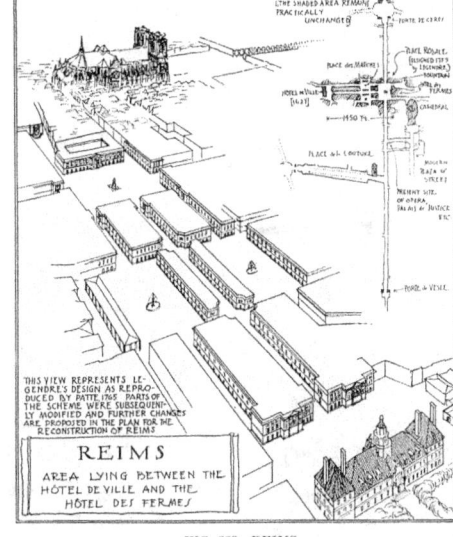

REIMS
AREA LYING BETWEEN THE
HÔTEL DE VILLE AND THE
HÔTEL DES FERMES

FIG. 333—REIMS.

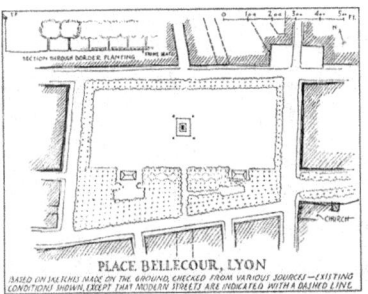

PLACE BELLECOUR, LYON

FIG. 334, PLAN; FIG. 334A, VIEW
—LYONS. PLACE BELLECOUR

Designed 1728 by Robert de
Cotte. The uniform buildings proposed by him were executed only on
the two narrow sides. The plaza
gains much strength by heavy tree
planting on the sides. One of the
sides (left of the picture) is made
rectangular by insertion of a triangle
of trees, a scheme which would be
effective in many cases where in
American cities radial streets cutting into a gridiron leave unsightly
triangles. Guadet says that "the
immensity of the Place Bellecour
does not permit one to feel the
symmetry of its opposite walls." If
the whole area had been walled uniformly this criticism would probably not have been made.

FIG. 335—RENNES. RUE NATIONALE

View looking east showing uniform façades framing the axis and the set-back of the old Palais de Justice to the left. See plan Fig. 339. (Drawing by Franz Herding.)

FIG. 337—RENNES. PLACE DU PALAIS DE JUSTICE

View showing the palace to the right and uniform façades framing it. The façades, originally inspired by Gabriel, were not completed before the end of the nineteenth century. See Fig. 339. (Drawing by Franz Herding.)

FIG. 338—RENNES. RUE DE BRILHAC

Looking west and past Gabriel's City Hall to the left. (Drawing by Franz Herding.) See Fig. 339.

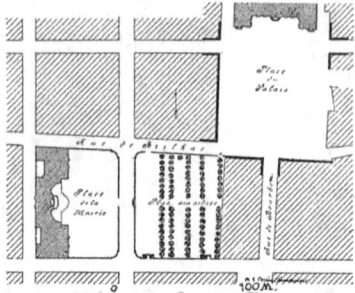

FIG. 336—RENNES. THE ROYAL PLAZAS IN 1826

FIG. 336A—RENNES.

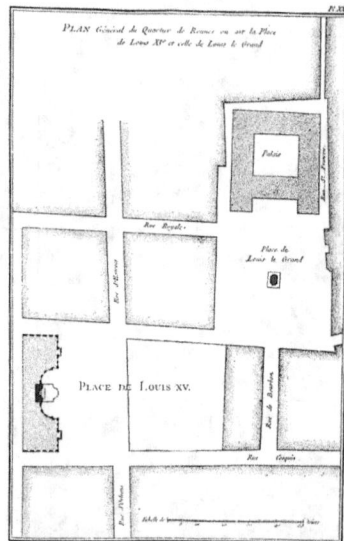

FIG. 339—RENNES. THE TWO ROYAL PLAZAS

(From Patte, 1765.) The heart of Rennes burned down in 1720 and the reconstruction was supervised by Gabriel, who later designed the Place de la Concorde. The design is specially interesting for American conditions because it largely fits into a gridiron. The old Palais de Justice, by Debrosse, 1618-54, (see Fig. 337), survived the fire. The new street plan lets it stand back a little to give it a more secure setting. The new building for the city hall (Mairie, see Fig. 336) is set still further back. In front of it is a court surrounded by balustrades. On the other side of the street a similar area is balustraded off and planted with trees in the back which, as Brinckmann suggests, may have been a temporary indication of another building by which Gabriel hoped to face the Mairie. A theater was later built there. The Mairie itself is divided into halves with separate roofs, with the tower in the middle and the monument of the king against the wall in the center.

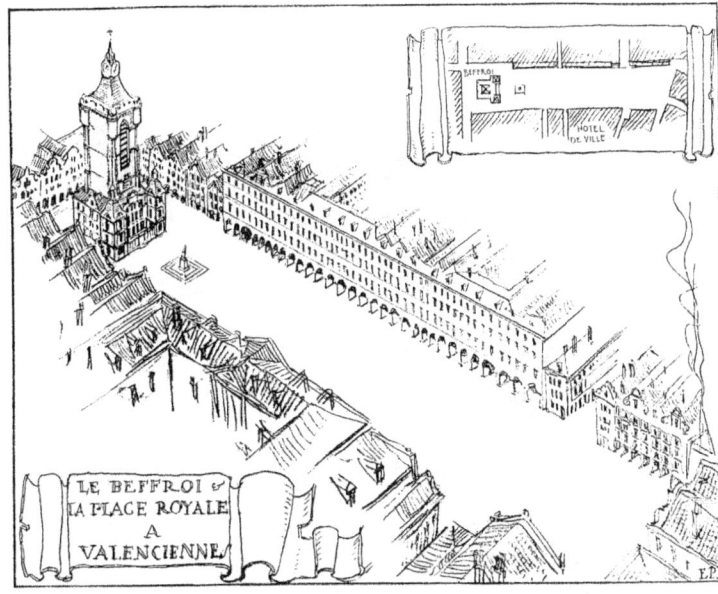

FIG. 340—VALENCIENNES. PLACE ROYALE

A birdseye-view based upon material published by Patte, 1765. A long row of Gothic houses have been pulled together into a unified façade bridging over the narrow entrance streets. The beffroi stands free at the end of the plaza.

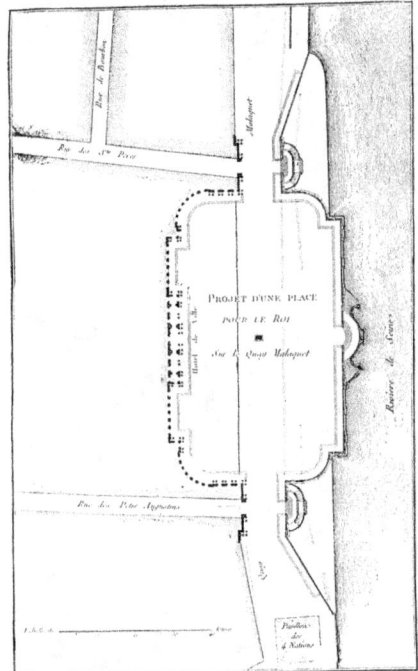

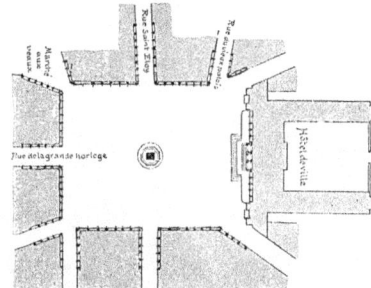

FIG. 342—ROUEN. PLAZA OF LOUIS XV

(From Patte.) The plaza has been destroyed by later street corrections.

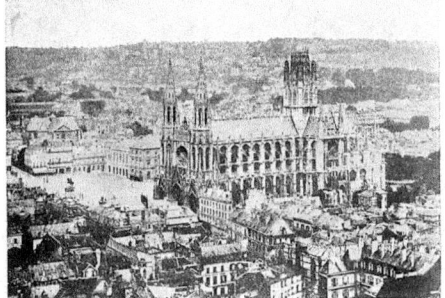

FIG. 341—PARIS. PROJECT FOR A PLAZA WITH MONUMENT OF LOUIS XV

A competition plan contemporaneous with the other French designs here illustrated. For elevation see Fig. 372.

FIG. 343—ROUEN. CHURCH OF SAINT OUEN
Seen from tower of cathedral.

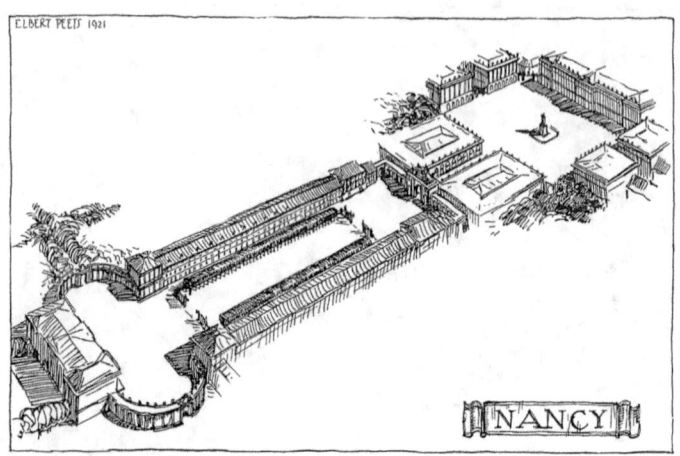

FIG. 344—NANCY. HEMICYCLE, PLACE DE LA CARRIERE, AND PLACE STANISLAS

FIG. 345—NANCY. GRILLE IN PLACE DE LA
CARRIERE

FIG. 346—NANCY. PLACE DE LA CARRIERE

FIG. 347—NANCY

Above, view from city hall looking north or northeast; below, view of one corner of Place Stanislas.

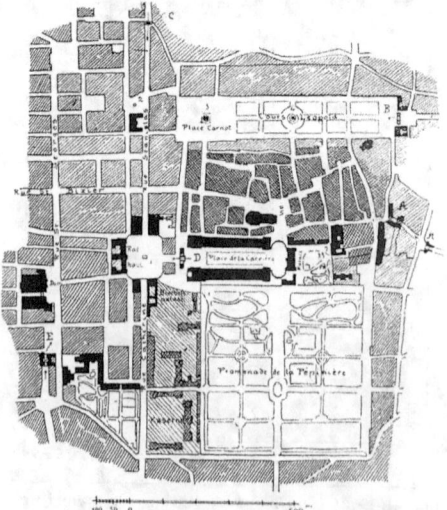

FIG. 348—NANCY. CENTRAL PART OF CITY
(From Stuebben.)

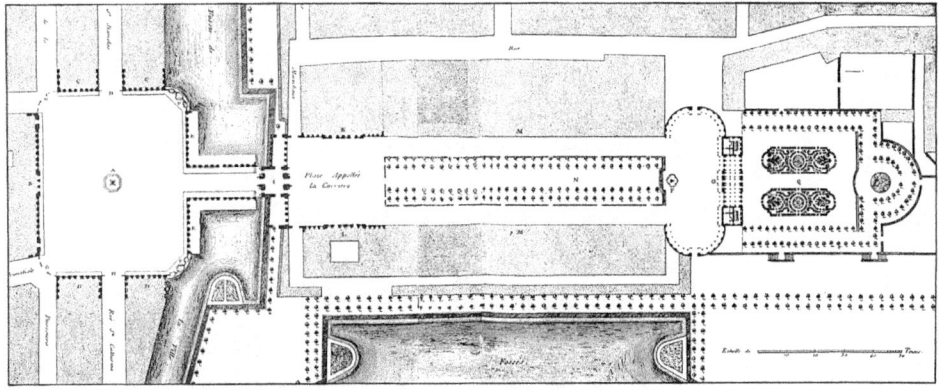

FIG. 349—NANCY. PLAZAS OF STANISLAS LESCZINSKI

The large square, the Place Royale, now the Place Stanislas, is dominated by the Hôtel de Ville "B". Beyond the triumphal arch "I" is a small open area flanked by two courthouses. The mall "N" leads to the Hemicycle de la Carrière and the ducal palace.

This plan, from Patte, is still substantially correct. The short street running from the Place Stanislas to the triumphal arch was built a trifle narrower than here shown. The fountain "P" in the lower end of the Carrière was not built, nor the steps near it. The curved wing walls of the palace were built with the columns closer to the wall and were carried around in front of the corner buildings (at the ends of the rows "M"). These corner buildings are part of the monumental construction and should be shown on the plan in black. The moats have been filled and the arcades "E" have become the façades of shops, as was doubtless intended from the first, it being probably by an error that the strips back of the arcades in the plan were not stippled. The corner fountains are now seen against trees, which is probably an improvement on the original plan.

FIG. 350—NANCY. FACADE OF THE HOTEL DE VILLE
Showing also the iron gates which close the corners of the square. (From Patte.)

FIG. 350A—NANCY. NORTH ELEVATION OF PLACE STANISLAS
The triumphal arch is set back half the width of the square. At the right hand side gates leading to the Pépinière have been substituted for the smaller units of the fountain. (From Patte.)

FIG. 351—NANCY. HEMICYLE DE LA CARRIERE

This suite of plazas in Nancy, constituting perhaps the most perfectly finished creation of civic art in the world, as well as one of the most varied and dramatic, was built by Stanislaus Lesczinski, Duke of Lorraine and King of Poland, in the middle of the eighteenth century, mainly from designs by the architect Héré, in whose honor a bronze statue has been erected at the east end of the triumphal arch. The axis of the design had been fixed by the ducal palace ("O" in the plan above) already built by Mansart.

The distinctive feature of the design, the sequence of varied but harmonious areas, was suggested or facilitated by the conditions of the site. It was natural to put the largest open area in the new land outside the walls and to constrict the plan where the axis crossed the moat. The resulting succession of areas is very pleasantly proportioned and modulated. The visitor's "processional" ought to begin at the Porte Stanislas. During his progress through Rue Stanislas he will see before him the heavy lead-colored statue of Stanislas (it might well be gilded or of marble, from this view) which he sees in profile, a sign that he is on a cross axis. The existence of a special area around the statue is expressed by gate posts of iron grille. Coming out into the large square he feels it at once as part of a larger composition, expressed by the lowness of the buildings on one side and the triumphal arch which towers above them. The narrow little Rue Héré again contracts, so to speak, the visitor's space-perception and gives it the pleasure of another expansion as he comes from under the arch into the open end of the Carrière. Then comes the charming garden-like promenade with its iron gate-posts recalling the iron-work around the great square. The simple house-fronts of the Carrière end in two more monumental pavilions, between which lies a little rectangular area serving as introduction to the perfectly proportioned area in front of the ducal palace, which, with its strong curved wing-walls, brings the flow of space to repose and the scansion of the metric sequence of plazas to its final accent.

If the scheme has any fault it is in the large square, where the four buildings bounding the square on the east and west sides are a bit high for their width. The iron grilles, whose function is to spread these buildings at the ground, do not, beautiful as of themselves they are, have quite enough architectural body to perform that function. And the two southerly corners are by no means perfect. Here again the iron posts help, but they seem to express the idea of the closed corner rather than actually to effect the enclosure.

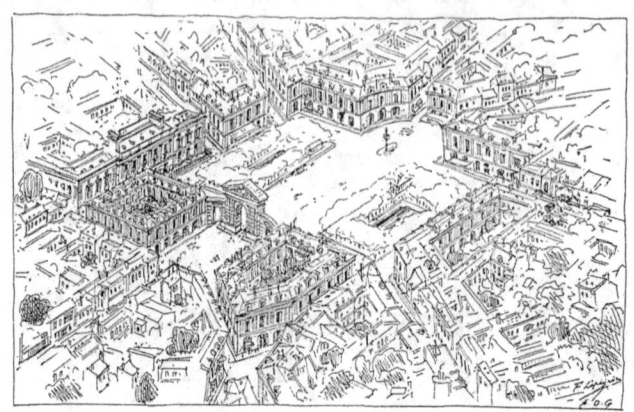

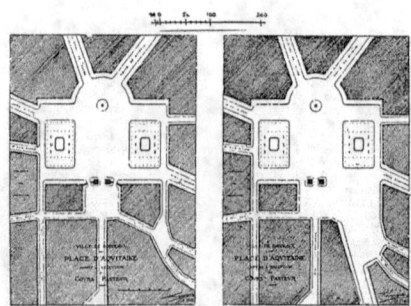

FIGS. 352 (A, B, C, D, AND E)—BORDEAUX. PLACE D'AQUITAINE

This late Baroque plaza was built as a forecourt to one of the important city gates. As part of a modern street-opening operation one of the buildings flanking the gate was removed. The ugly spot thus created in the plan suggests the ugliness of the present condition of the plaza itself. Throughout Europe, from Piccadilly Circus to the Piazza Navona, the same destructive cutting of the walls of old plazas has taken place or is provided for in official plans. And too frequently it is from these modern mutilated remnants of the old open places that American students of city planning take their inspiration.

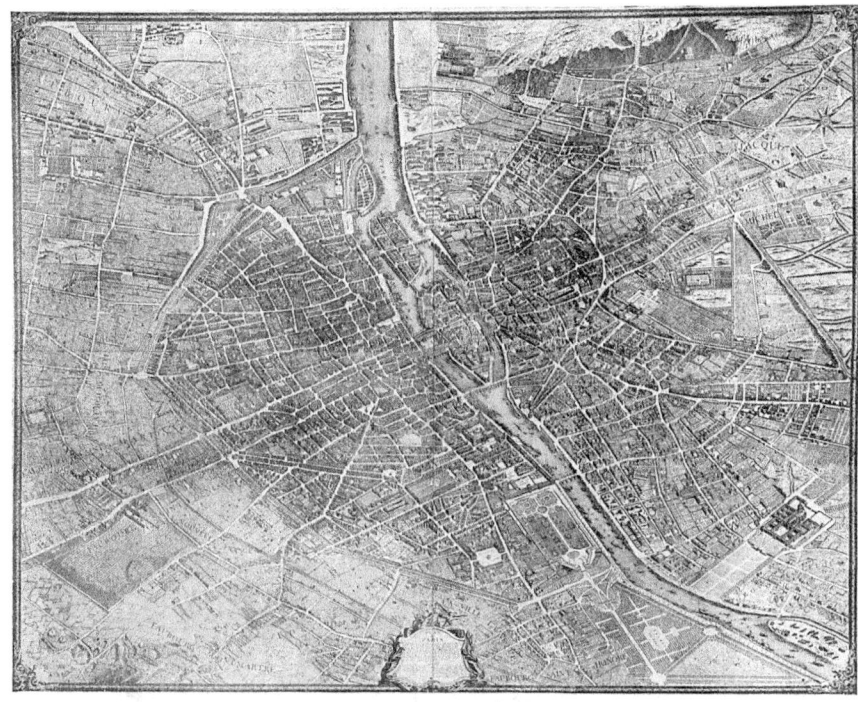

FIG. 353—PARIS. TURGOT'S PLAN, 1739
A reproduction, at greatly reduced scale, of the plan of which Figs. 323, 325, 326, and 330 are details shown at full size.

FIG. 354—STRASBOURG. BLONDEL'S PLAN FOR THE REALIGNMENT OF STREETS, 1768

FIG. 354A—STRASBOURG. SKETCHES VISUALIZING PARTS OF BLONDEL'S PLAN

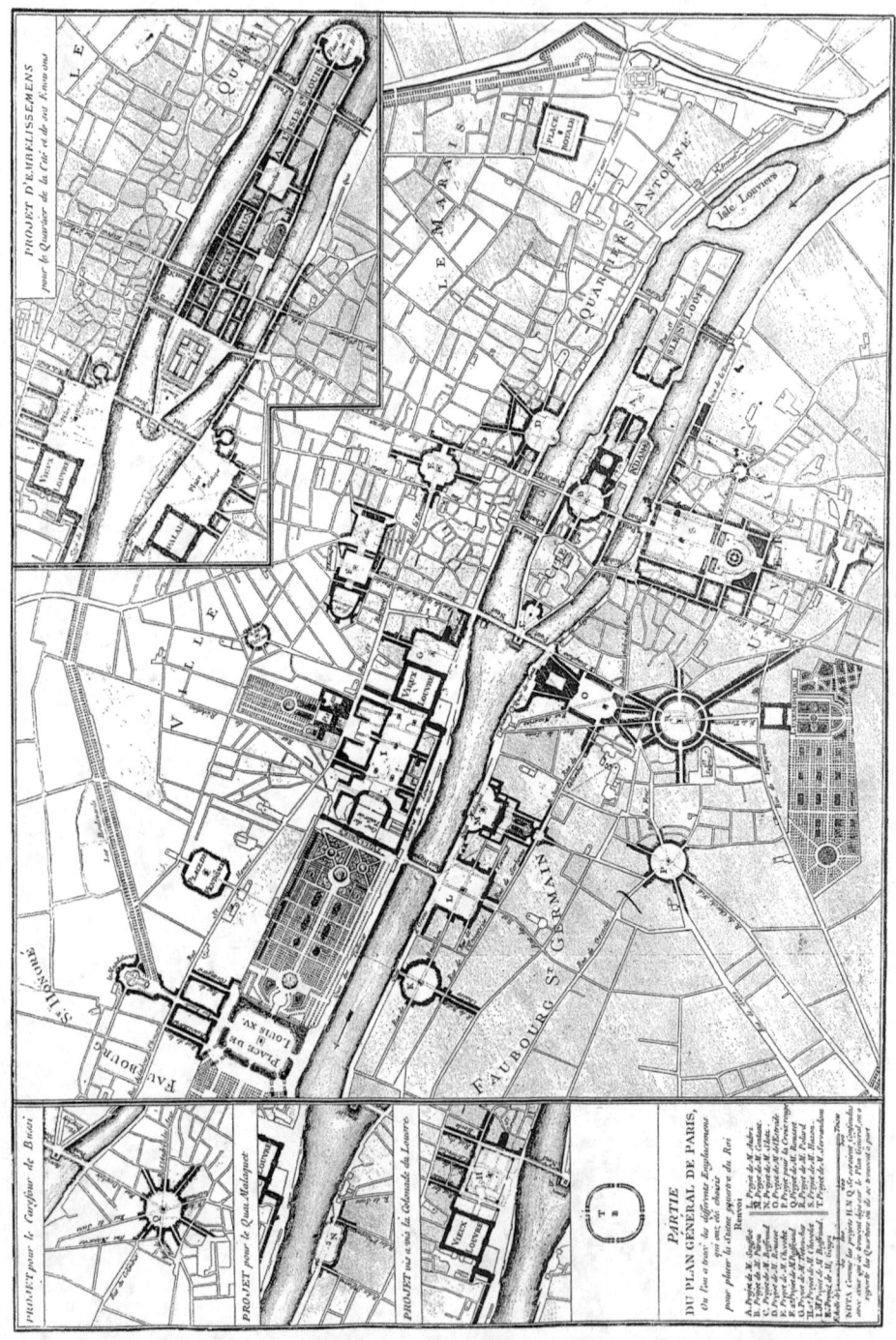

FIG. 355—COMPETITION OF 1748 FOR THE PLACING OF A STATUE OF LOUIS XV: KEY PLAN OF PARIS SHOWING PROPOSED
LOCATIONS OF THE VARIOUS PROJETS.   (FROM PATTE)

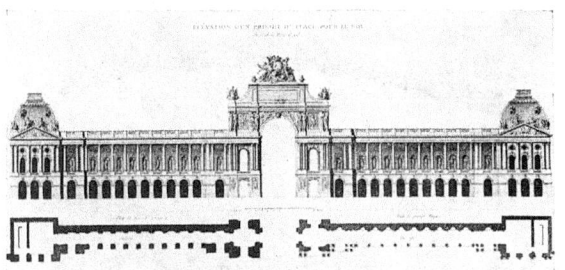

FIG. 356—PLAZA FOR LOUIS XV: PLAN AND ELEVATION OF PROJET BY AUBRI

Aubri's projet (see "L" on the key plan) proposed a square plaza on the axis of the Pont Royal. The side of the plaza facing the bridge was to be closed by two arcades connected by a triumphal arch. Over the arcades were Corinthian colonnades with statues and reliefs giving the history of the king's government. The other two sides of the plaza were formed by four palaces.

The book by Pierre Patte from which this and most of the illustrations on pages 78 to 82 are reproduced was published in Paris in 1765 under the title "Monumens érigé en France à la gloire de Louis XV." Its contents relate mainly to the competitions of 1748 and 1753, which preceded the construction of the present Place de la Concorde.

NOTES ON FIG. 355

These notes relate to those projects submitted in the competition of 1748 for the placing of a monument to Louis XV which are not illustrated and explained on the three following pages. The letters refer to Patte's large key plan of Paris.

Projet "A" was designed by Soufflot, the architect of the Panthéon. It aimed at a new regulation of the Seine channels by combining the two Seine islands, thus increasing the water flow in the southern channel and thereby improving navigation and helping the watermills and pumping stations west of the Petit Pont. Upon the area gained by filling between the two old islands a square plaza was to be located framed on two sides by the new embankments, on the two other sides by noblemen's palaces and—adjoining the Cathedral of Nôtre-Dame—by the residence of the archbishop. The king's monument was to stand on axis of the straight street St. Louis resulting from a previous rebuilding operation. This straight street was to be continued west in a straight line to the important north-south artery St. Jaques-St. Martin, thus connecting the two schemes intimately with the main traffic system and incidently largely rebuilding the congested "Cité." The large general plan also shows the surroundings of the Panthéon as contemplated by Soufflot.

Projet "E" by Chevolet planned as a bold connection between two main north and south arteries, a plaza of about the size of Place Vendôme closed towards the east by a palace for the governor of Paris with the monument in the center and on the axes of three streets.

Projet "H", by the same designer, contains features which may have influenced the finally executed design by Gabriel. It contemplates clearing a large area in front of Perrault's Louvre colonnade. The Gothic church of St. Germain l'Auxerrois (still standing to-day) was to be replaced by a church in the center of the east side of the plaza thus gained. The large territory was to be surrounded by balustrades with small pavilions at the corners supporting statuary. The northern façade of the plaza was to be formed by new buildings for the mint and the storage of salt (the taxation of salt was a revenue of the crown).

Projet "G" by Destouches was designed for the same territory in front of the Louvre façade; the smaller clearing contemplated by this projet saves the old church and is practically identical with the clearing actually effected a century later by Haussmann. Perrault's façade was to be one of the three sides of a plaza closed toward the water by an iron grille; the southern elevation of the Louvre was to be duplicated by the city hall east of this plaza reaching as far as the Pont Neuf and creating a balanced composition of great strength. The plaza was to be further developed by a return on the other side of the river.

Projet "K" by Goupi contemplates a civic center (buildings for the various departments of government) to balance, on the left side of the river, the Place Vendôme built for the previous king on the right side. The two plazas were to be connected by the opening of a vista across the gardens of the Tuileries, so that the two royal monuments could be seen at the same time.

Projet "O" by de l'Estrade provides for a large composition on the left bank immediately southwest of Pont Neuf. A city hall of keystone shape with square court in the center was to face the river to the north and the king's plaza to the south. The king's plaza was to be square (stores along the sides) with a semicircular bay toward the south containing a large fountain scheme; the monument to stand in the center of the semicircle, at the point of radiation of six streets.

Projet "P" is so located as to make the monument the point of radiation of six existing streets. This means that no expensive openings of new streets would have been required. It is interesting however in contrast to the modest minimum requirements modern architects are not to be satisfied with to see what long stretches of the old streets it was proposed to rebuild, to make them harmonious approaches to the new plaza.

Projet "S" by Hazon is one of the largest, representing the reclamation of a congested district of the old metropolis, the territory sloping towards the river immediately south of the Petit Pont. On the southern

and highest part of the very large area is a theater-shaped plaza with a circular Doric temple of glory. Separated from the semicircular plaza by a triumphal arch is situated, toward the river, a large forum surrounded by four-storied colonnades with pavilions at the corners. The king's monument in the center takes the shape of a large rock upon which the king drives a quadriga towards the temple of glory up the hill; columns and fountains are not spared.

Projet "T" by Servandoni (architect of St. Sulpice) contemplates a circular plaza (diameter 645') for some undefined location outside of the fortifications. The plaza is surrounded by a Doric and superimposed Ionic order with a terrace on the top. Of the eight entrances, four were treated with triumphal arches ornamented like the colonnades with statues and reliefs relating to the national history. The whole composition was thought of as an amphitheater for popular celebrations.

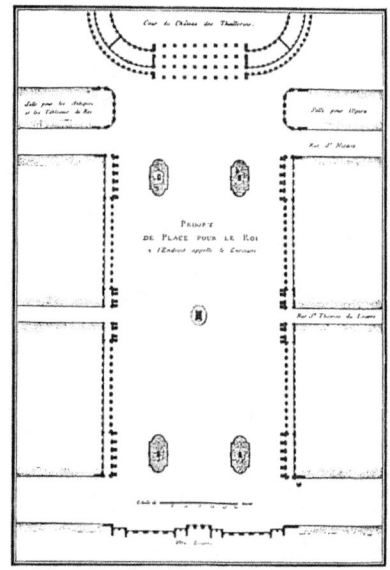

FIG. 357—PLAZA FOR LOUIS XV: PLAN OF PROJET BY BOFFRAND.

This projet (one of three) by Boffrand was a redesign of the area between the old Louvre and the Tuileries, an area for which there had been and were to be made many other studies. Boffrand suggested a large court east of the Tuileries (see "I" on the key plan) separated from the rest of the composition by a four-storied colonnade and flanked by an opera house and a museum of fine arts. The very large oblong plaza between the Louvre and the forecourts of the Tuileries, with the king's monument in the center and four fountains near the corners, was to be framed by the usual three-storied buildings with arcades on the ground floor and a colossal order above them. One street crossing the plaza was axiated on the king's monument in the plaza and on the entrance to the Palais Royal outside. The entrances of this street into the plaza were bridged by triumphal arches.

FIG. 358—PLAZA FOR LOUIS XV: PARTIAL SECTION OF PROJET BY BOFFRAND

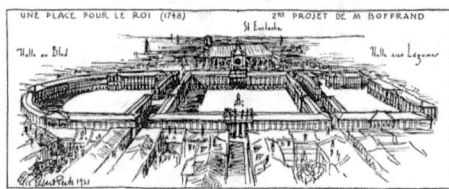

FIG. 359—SKETCH VISUALIZING BOFFRAND'S SCHEME

Boffrand's projet (one of three by him) for a plaza in the market quarter (see "F" on the key plan) was a triple forum reclaiming one of the worst slums of Paris. The easternmost of the three plazas was a square opened up by three main avenues, as it was meant to serve as general public market; at the western end of the composition a semicircular plaza surrounded by large warehouses, easily accessible for heavy teaming but also easily locked, was to serve as grain market. In the center the forum of the king with the monument In the center was to face the transept of the church of St. Eustache. The important street coming from the Pont Neuf was axiated on the monument.

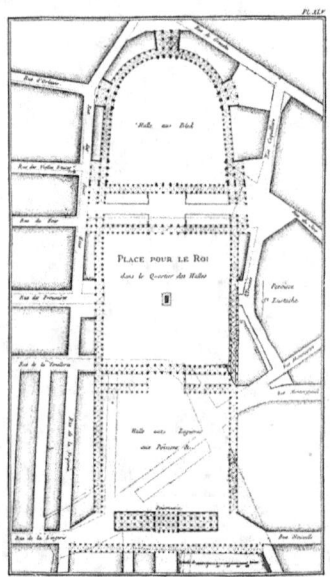

FIG. 360—PLAZA FOR LOUIS XV: PLAN OF PROJET BY BOFFRAND

PLAN ET ELEVATION

FIG. 361—PLAZA FOR LOUIS XV: PROJET BY PITROU

Pitrou's projet (see "B" on the key plan, Fig. 355) contemplated the rebuilding of the "city" island on an even more ambitious scale by reclaiming a large part of the congested areas for the building of the city hall grouped around two large courts with a large circular forecourt in addition. The circular forecourt would have had practical and esthetic advantages in connection with the processions to the cathedral of Nôtre-Dame and together with the old palace of Justice historically connected with this neighborhood, a civic center, dedicated to religion, justice and municipal purposes would have been created. The construction of the city hall was to be connected with an ambitious scheme for a covered harbor north of it.

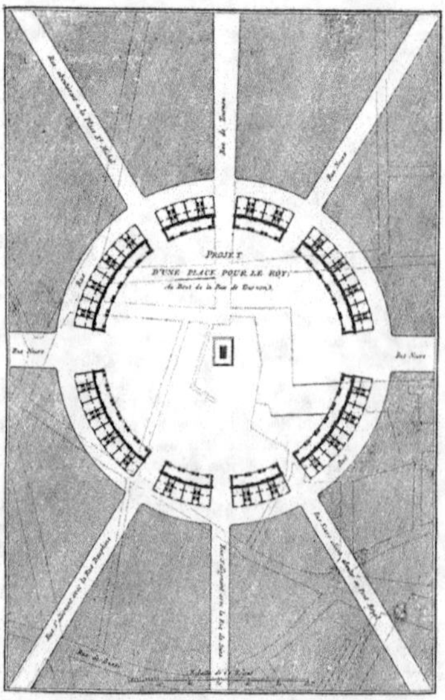

FIG. 362—PLAZA FOR LOUIS XV: PLAN OF PROJET BY POLARD

Polard's projet (See "R" on the key plan) was the largest circular scheme submitted in the competition. The eight streets which radiated from the plaza were new openings or straightenings to connect with important points, such as the Pont Royal, the Pont Neuf, and the central pavilion of the Luxemburg. The plaza was to be surrounded by a uniform scheme of high colonnades, backed by small houses with shops in the ground floor.

FIG. 363—PLAZA FOR LOUIS XV: ELEVATION OF PROJET BY ROUSSET

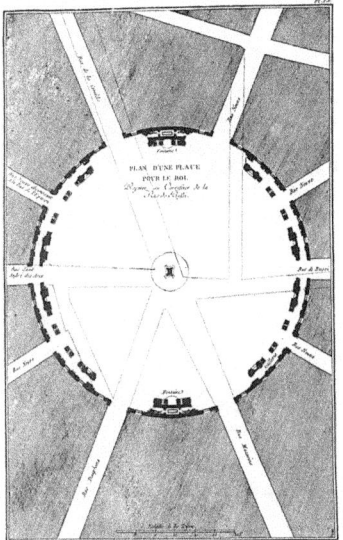

FIG. 364—PLAZA FOR LOUIS XV: PLAN OF
PROJET BY ROUSSET

Rousset's projet for a circular plaza (see "Q" on the key plan) represented a comprehensive reclamation scheme for a congested district. The plaza was to have a diameter of 460 feet and with the royal monument in the form of an obelisk as the center of ten radiating streets, five of these streets being new openings connecting the new plaza with all parts of town and creating by unusual devices interesting points of vista at considerable distances. The plaza itself was to have a wall the design of which was inspired by the Louvre colonnade. The continuity of the wall was preserved by permitting only the four main streets (of the ten which entered the plaza) to break the wall, the others entering the plaza through arched openings. The effect of the two main streets was to subdivide the wall into four parts, two large units, each with a triumphal arch in the center, and two small ones the sites of large wall fountains. This arrangement produced a definite axiation of the plaza. These fountains opposite the entrances, the concentrated power of the area surrounded by the curved walls, and the considerable length of these walls as compared with the width of the four open streets, were calculated to strongly arrest the eye within the plaza. There was therefore no danger that upon entering the plaza one's eye would wander beyond its area as it is apt to in modern creations where the gaps torn in the wall of the plaza by wide streets are unpleasantly conspicuous.

Boffrand's projet illustrated below (also see "C" on the key plan) provided for a column in a plaza at the lower point of the island of the Cité, a center of traffic and a site dear to French civic designers. Immediately west of this point, Du Cerceau had proposed a circular plaza (Fig. 239). Henri IV had built the triangular Place Dauphine faced by his monument (Figs. 322-24). Boffrand planned to wipe out the early Renaissance buildings of the Place Dauphine for a creation in the taste of his own epoch, with the statue of Louis XV 21 feet high on a high column in front of a tall triumphal arch facing the equestrian statue of the "good" king Henri IV. The triumphal arch was to be flanked by three-storied buildings with goldsmiths' shops (this was their quarter) in the ground floor.

FIG. 364A—SKETCH VISUALIZING
ROUSSET'S SCHEME

FIG. 365—SKETCH VISUALIZING
BOFFRAND'S SCHEME.

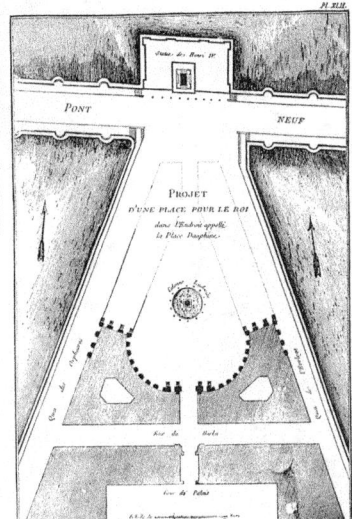

FIG. 367—PLAZA FOR LOUIS XV: PLAN OF
PROJET BY BOFFRAND.

FIG. 366—PLAZA FOR LOUIS XV: ELEVATION OF PROJET BY BOFFRAND

FIG. 368—PLACE ROYALE, BORDEAUX: ELEVATION

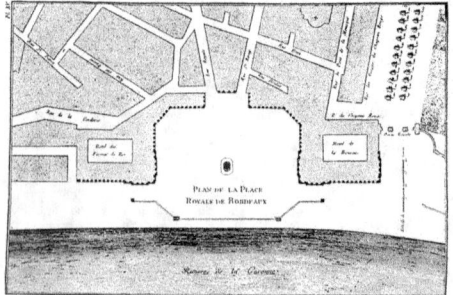

FIG. 370—PLACE ROYALE, BORDEAUX: PLAN

FIG. 369—PLACE ROYALE, (NOW PLACE DE LA BOURSE),
BORDEAUX: A MODERN VIEW

Of the plans submitted in the competition for "une place
pour le roi" in 1748, about half chose sites along the Seine.
Several of them (projet by Contant, Fig. 371, which is "M" on
the key plan, Fig. 355; projet by Slotz, Fig. 372 and "N" on
the key plan; and Rousset's semicircular projet, "D" on the key
plan) were plazas facing the water somewhat on the style of
the plaza actually built for Louis XV at Bordeaux. In all
these projets the statue was to stand near the water, in front
of a semicircular frame of three-storied buildings clearly indicating a movement toward the water or, conceivably, from
the water toward the center of the plaza. How the appreciation
of these finer artistic intentions has died out in the nineteenth
century is illustrated by the circular (and thus not oriented)
monument which in Bordeaux has taken the place of the
equestrian statue of the king with its definite orientation expressing what may be called the movement of the plaza. The
modern change of the boundary of the plaza toward the water
has helped further to make the present circular fountain quite
adverse to the design as expressed in the framing buildings
and the situation.

Contant's projet is more interesting than that of Slotz and
than the Place de la Bourse in Bordeaux because it gives
towards the south an interesting setting to the proposed city
hall by a series of closed courts and approaches. The elevation towards the water was centered on the galleries of the
Louvre on the other side of the river thus uniting the Louvre
and the new plaza into one huge composition astride the river.
The sculptural development of the new plaza towards the water
was accordingly very rich.

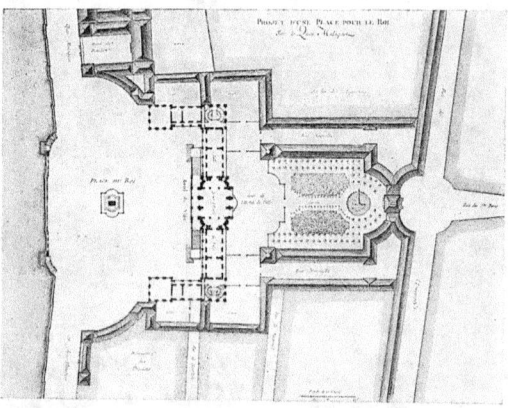

FIG. 371—PLAZA FOR LOUIS XV: PLAN OF PROJET BY CONTANT

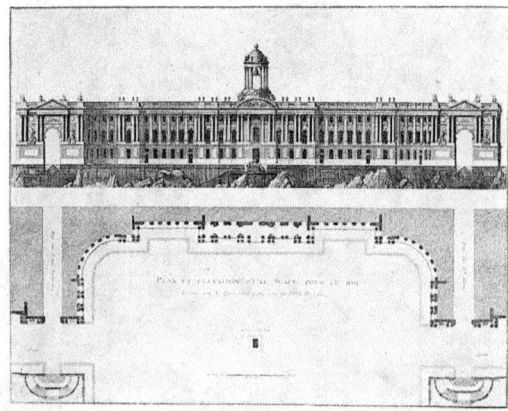

FIG. 372—PLAZA FOR LOUIS XV: PLAN AND ELEVATION
OF PROJET BY SLOTZ

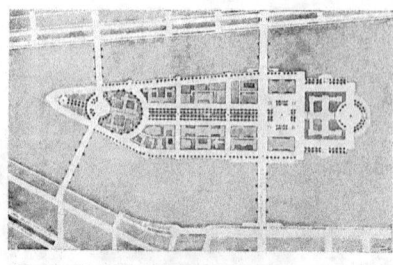

FIG. 373—BOSTON, PROJECT FOR AN ISLAND IN THE
CHARLES RIVER BASIN

This design by Ralph Adams Cram shares some of the
fine qualities of Patte's project for the replanning of the
islands of the Seine. (See key plan, Fig. 375.)

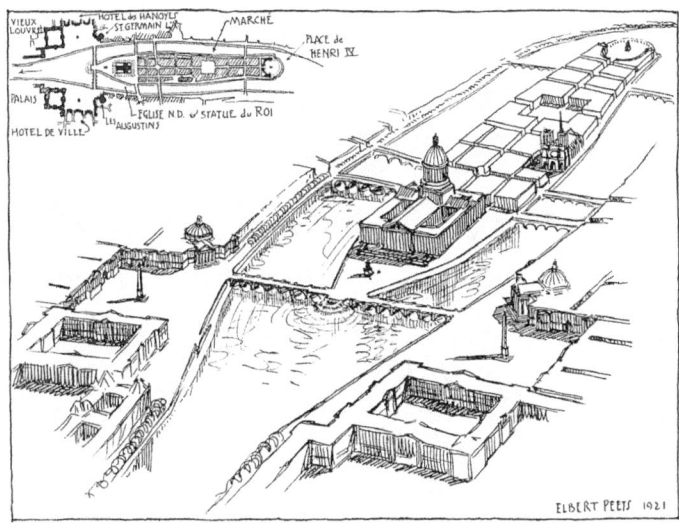

FIG. 375—PLAZA FOR LOUIS XV: SKETCH VISUALIZING PATTE'S SCHEME

See insertion in key plan, Fig. 355. Patte's plan provides for the erection of a huge cathedral near the point of the cité, where the Palais de Justice stands. The king's statue, in front of the cathedral, looks out on a vast area, the river and two symmetrical plazas. Back of the cathedral the streets of the cité are straightened, a great square market place is created by filling the channel between the islands, and the statue of Henri IV has as its new setting a plaza at the point of the Isle St. Louis.

FIG. 376—PARIS. THE ISLANDS OF THE CITE AND ST. LOUIS

This air view shows the present condition of the region for which so many plans have been made and in which so many changes have taken place. At the point of the island is the Place Dauphine, or what is left of it, and beyond it the Palais de Justice, the Sainte Chapelle, and Nôtre-Dame. At the left, on the right bank of the Seine, are the Place du Châtelet and the Place de l'Hôtel de Ville.

FIG. 377—LONDON. PROJECT FOR THE IMPROVEMENT OF THE PORT OF LONDON

George Dance's ambitious plan to redesign the harbor upon a spacious and at the same time beautiful plan. Part of an engraving by William Daniel, 1802. The design shares with Patte's (Fig. 375) the idea of two fora with obelisks facing each other on opposite shores of the river. (From Reginald Blomfield.)

FIG. 378—A DESIGN BY PIRANESI

"A magnificent bridge with loggias" and flanking arches, made the setting for an equestrian monument to a Roman emperor. The statue stands under the central arch of the superstructure.

FIG. 380—(See opposite page.)

Durand, the author of the "Parallèle d'Architecture" and under the First Empire and for many years afterwards professor of architecture at Paris, always put great emphasis upon the necessity of relating buildings to each other to create ensembles. The proposal shown here has great logical qualities. If executed the effect would depend largely upon the protection of the corners from undesirable outside features appearing above the colonnades. If walls of high trees could be arranged outside, the effect of the sunken court in the center could be very strong.

FIG. 381—(See opposite page.)

This plan, dated 1784, like Figs. 382-84, belongs to a collection published in Paris at the very beginning of the French Revolution under the title "Muséum de la Nouvelle Architecture Française", which contains probably the first documents for the student's competitions which have gradually become such an important part of the educational scheme followed by the École des Beaux-Arts. The value of the four students' designs shown in Figs. 381-84 is partly geometrical only, but the plans are interesting because they show the great French tradition of plaza design carried to its last geometrical consequences. The projet for a hospital shown in Fig. 381 centers a four-way symmetrical building in a court about 900 feet square framed by pavilions and colonnades on three sides and open to the water on the fourth side. See program given in caption to Fig. 382.

FIG. 382—(See opposite page.)

This design was premiated in the competition in which the projet shown in Fig. 381 received the second prize. The program was: "The Academy proposes as problem for grand prix a hospital situated upon an island, the shore of which offers a port protected by piers; it must be composed of several buildings which are intended to receive and to lodge the sailors who arrive at different dates and must be distinguished according to the state of their health, and the maladies of which they are suspected. Other buildings for the garrison, the general staff, the sick rooms and the chapel, several residences for the ministers and physicians, for the pharmacy, kitchens, and servants; finally, extensive storerooms. All the buildings must be surrounded by large plantings and separated gardens. The main building should contain halls and covered promenades, several dormitories and quarters for persons of distinction. The area to be covered should be 200 toises (1200 feet) square, not including the small port."

FIG. 383—(See opposite page.)

The program read: "The Academy proposes a residence for a noble lord, situated in a park. In the center of the principal pavilion smaller ones are to be provided for the favorites of the prince. There are to be a hall for spectacles, a dance-hall, a concert-hall and others." There is quite a resemblance between this plan (about 1785) and the plan of Carlsruhe in Silesia (laid out 1747, see Fig. 1011).

FIG. 379—LISBON. PRACA DO COMMERCIO

Laid out after the earthquake of 1755 as part of the Marquis of Pombal's large rebuilding scheme (see Fig. 308). The plaza unites a large number of administrative buildings. In the center of the long side facing the river is a high triumphal arch on axis with the monument of Joseph I in the center. The plaza resembles in plan the former Place Royale in Bordeaux, Figs. 368-70. The design of the plaza including the framing buildings is due to E. dos Santos Carvalho. (From a drawing by Franz Herding.)

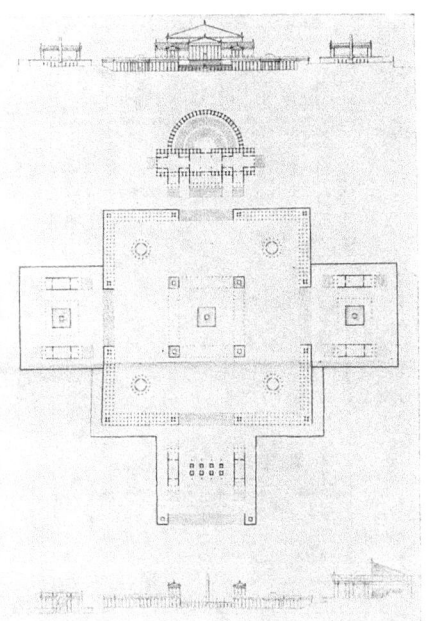

FIG. 380—DURAND'S PROPOSAL FOR A GROUP OF FOUR BUILD-
INGS FRAMING A FORUM
See caption on opposite page.

FIG. 382—PROJET FOR A HOSPITAL
See caption on opposite page.

FIG. 381—PROJET FOR A HOSPITAL
See caption on opposite page.

FIG. 383—PROJET FOR A COUNTRY RESIDENCE
See caption on opposite page.

FIG. 384—PROJET FOR A MENAGERIE

The program for this competition, held in 1783, read: "The Academy proposes as problem for its grand prix a menagerie enclosed by a park of the palace of the sovereign. The location shall be upon a square measuring 1800 feet on each side. The projet is to contain an amphitheater, 240 feet overall, with an open arena suitable for the combats of animals, with boxes and stepped seats for the spectators. The areas for the keeping of the animals shall be provided with courts sufficiently large for their needs; large birdhouses are an essential part of the scheme. There should be large galleries for the scientific collections; also a principal pavilion for the prince, services in the basements, several other small pavilions for the janitors, servants etc." In this projet the amphitheater is in the center of the large circle.

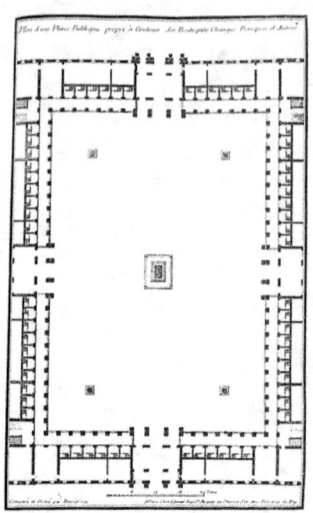

FIG. 385—"PLAN OF A PUBLIC SQUARE SUITED TO CONTAIN SHOPS, EXCHANGES, BANKS, ETC."

The plaza, measuring about 350 by 500 feet, is strongly enclosed, and the entrances, centered in the sides, are arched over. This plan and those shown in Figs. 386-87, all designed by Deneufforge, were published between 1757 and 1776 and thus antedate the work shown in Figs. 380-84.

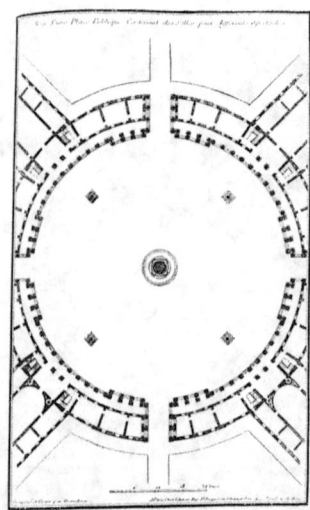

FIG. 386—"PLAN OF A PUBLIC PLACE CONTAINING HALLS FOR VARIOUS SPECTACLES"

Design by Deneufforge (see caption, Fig. 387). The halls, shown only in part, are distributed radially with entrances from the circular plaza. The street openings are made narrow in comparison with the arcaded quadrants, thus ensuring a strong effect of circular enclosure. Diameter about 420 feet.

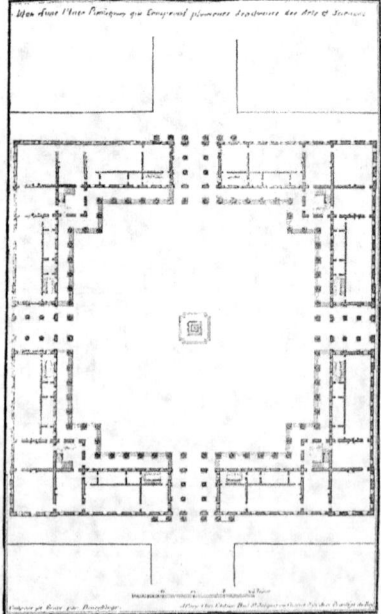

FIG. 387—"PLAN OF A PUBLIC PLAZA COMPRISING SEVERAL ACADEMIES OF THE ARTS AND SCIENCES"

A strongly framed plaza about 300 feet square with cut-in corners, in that respect resembling Bernini's plan for the court of the Louvre, Fig. 213, and Fontana's Convent of St. Eusebio, Fig. 199.

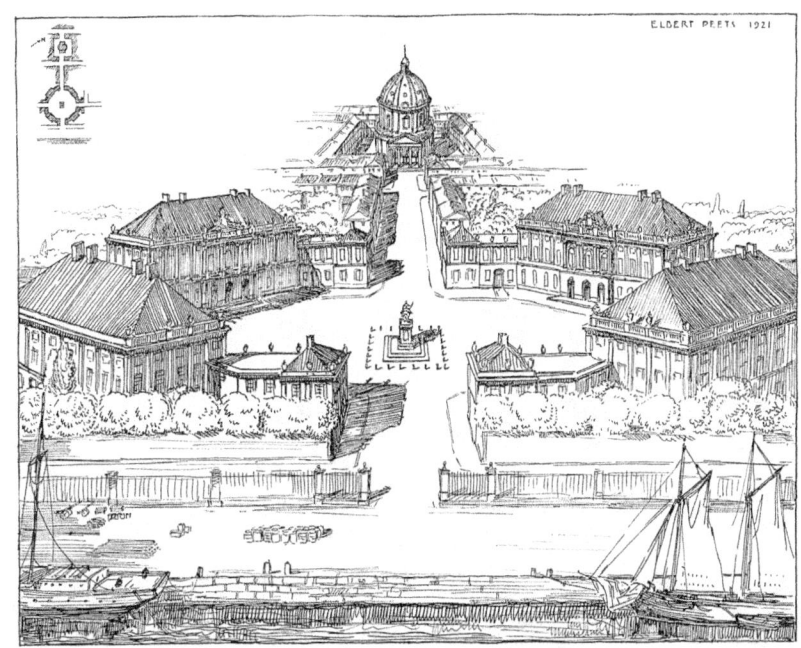

FIG. 388—COPENHAGEN. FREDER-IKSPLATZ (AMALIENBORG PLAZA)

The four palaces of similar design (by Eigtved) forming the walls of the plaza were built by four families to please their king, about 1796. The monument was erected in 1711. The four palaces together have now become the king's palace, the Amalienborg, of which the plaza forms the courtyard. In the court intersect the Amalien Street, which traverses the entire city and Frederiks Street which connects the domed "Marble Church" with the harbor. The church, begun in the eighteenth century but completed only recently, faces two strongly designed houses, which form the entrance feature to the church plaza.

FIG. 389 — COPENHAGEN. COLONNADE AT EN-TRANCE TO FRED-ERIKSPLATZ

This gate, closing the plaza at one side, was added to the original design in 1794. Designed by Harsdorf. (From Mebes and Behrendt.)

FIG. 390—FREDENSBORG PALACE (DENMARK). FORECOURT

Built about 1725. (From Mebes and Behrendt.)

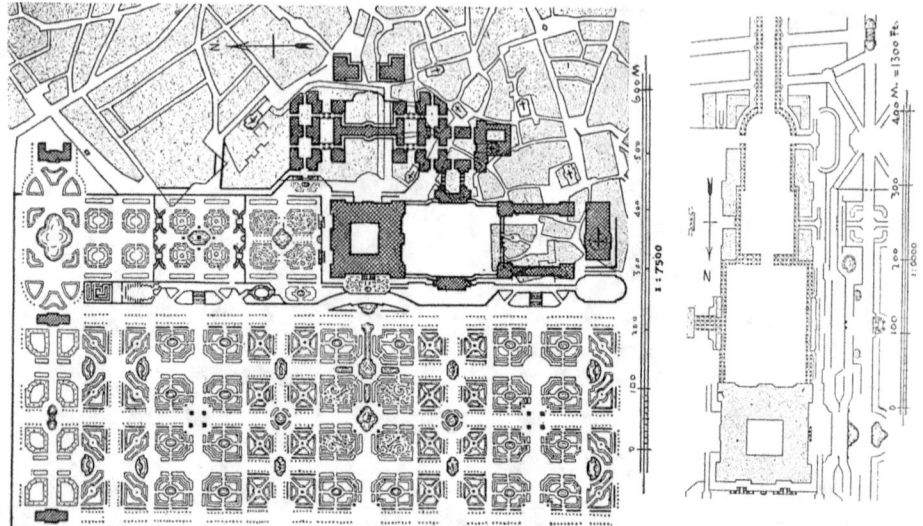

FIG. 391—MADRID. SACCHETTI'S PLAN OF 1738 FOR SETTING THE ROYAL PALACE

FIG. 392—MADRID. SACCHETTI'S PLAN OF 1757 FOR THE SETTING OF THE ROYAL PALACE

When Filippo Juvara was dying, in 1736, he proposed his great disciple Sacchetti as his successor in the work on the royal palace. The palace was erected (1738-64) according to plans by Juvara, Sacchetti, and Tizon. Sacchetti proposed a very ambitious setting, a comprehensive scheme of courts framed by administrative buildings and a cathedral. The axis of the courts was centered upon the transept of the cathedral. The cathedral, when built soon after 1805, was turned around, making this axis center upon the main entrance.

Figs. 391 and 392 are drawings by Oscar Jurgens who in 1910 discovered the original plans in the archives of the Spanish court. (From the Deutsche Bauzeitung 1919.)

A revision of the scheme of 1738. The cathedral is abandoned and the design which comprises only the part alongside the steep banks of the Manzanares river includes a bridge one hundred feet high crossing a side valley.

FIG. 393—BERLIN ABOUT 1645

From Merian's "Topography". This view shows the beginning of the transformation of the medieval town into a Renaissance city. The rows of lindens in the foreground are the beginning of the main western axis (Unter den Linden) which forms the backbone of the city plan. Perhaps the essential weakness of the plan lies in the fact that this axis had no orientation at right angles to the old Gothic castle, a defect which was not remedied when the new castle was erected about 1700.

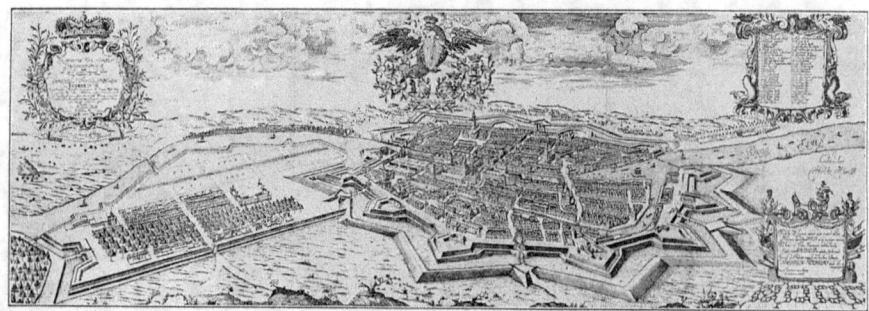

FIG. 394—BERLIN IN 1688

Showing to the left the new quarter (settled mainly by French immigrants) with the new street "Unter den Linden" leading through the center to the old castle from which it is separated by the new fortifications of the Vauban type.

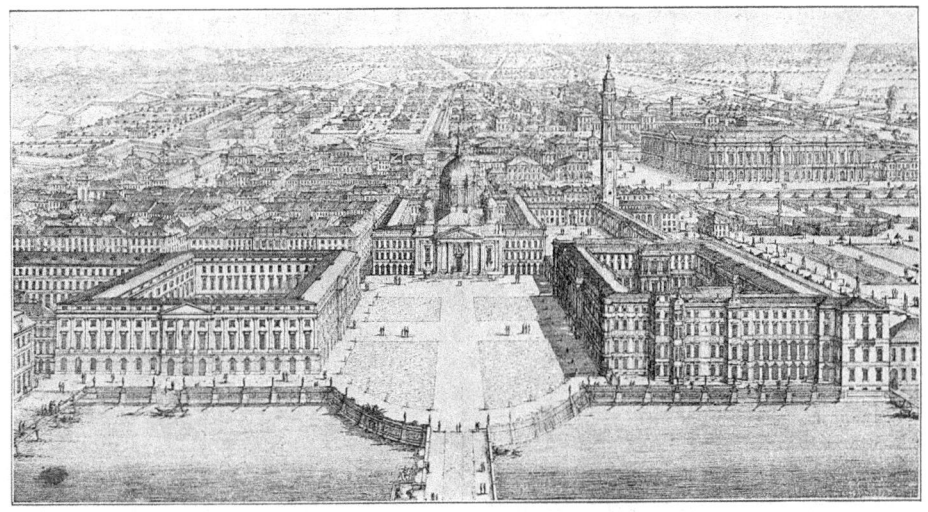

FIG. 395—BERLIN. SCHLUETER'S PROJECT FOR THE SURROUNDINGS OF THE ROYAL PALACE

The palace appears to the right. (See Fig. 215.) The bridge in the foreground (with the equestrian monument) and the arsenal in the back (to the right) is all that was realized of this project of 1700. The tower was started but being built on treacherous ground it fell, and with it went the designer's reputation. The large coachhouse (left foreground) was built about 1900 in substantially the shape proposed two hundred years before but was brought forward to the line of the bridge. This engraving pretends a right angle relation between Unter den Linden and the palace.

FIG. 396—BERLIN. OPERA PLAZA

FIG. 397—BERLIN. OPERA PLAZA LOOKING NORTH

The Opera Plaza (see number "2" in plan Fig. 398 which locates all the buildings) is one of the finest features of the "Unter den Linden" axis. It was built by Frederick the Great. The scenery loft over the opera house dates from the nineteenth century.

FIG. 398—BERLIN. KEY PLAN TO "UNTER DEN LINDEN" AXIS

Royal Berlin

1 Lustgarten
2 Opera Platz
3 Pariser Platz
4 Kongs Platz
5 Charlottenburger Chausée
6 Schloss Platz
7 Schlos
8 Zeughaus
9 Opera
10 University
11 Bibliothek
12 William I Pl.
13 Hedwigs Church
14 Crown Prince Palace
15 Commandant of Berlin
16 New Library
17 Cathedral
18 Altes Museum
19 National Gallery
20 Kaiser Friederich Museum
21 Kaiser William I Monument
22 Royal Stables
23 Parliament Building
24 Bismarck
25 Kurfürsten Brücke
26 Schloss Brücke
27
28 The Ra....y
.... Haupt....
Tiergarten

From a drawing by Patrick Abercrombie who in the "Town Planning Review" criticizes the scheme as follows:

Truly this colossal group of buildings is a fitting climax to the great approach, and not one of the wildest American dreams can excel the town-planning conception of it. As for Paris, you would have to walk over half its area to collect a like number of buildings to group round the Louvre, and you must turn a sharp corner across the Place de la Concorde to keep in the main traffic stream, and yet for sheer beauty there is no doubt that the Parisian entirely outshines the Berlin vista, not only because of its better design, but also by reason perhaps of its mere practical failings, to which must certainly be added its historical charm, the slight rise in the ground, too, is of immense value.... The larger scale of the Paris feature adds undoubtedly to its greater spectacular effect."

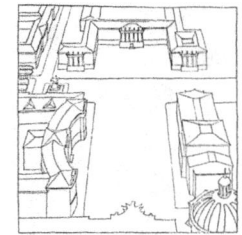

FIG. 399—BERLIN. OPERA PLAZA

Modern "landscaping" has badly interfered with the unity of the plaza. This sketch shows it as a unit.

FIG. 400—BERLIN. BRANDENBURG GATE

Looking west into the Tiergarten. The gate was designed by Langhaus in 1788.
(Courtesy of Chicago Plan Commission.)

FIG. 401—BRUSSELS. PLACE ROYALE
Part of a large scheme designed by Guimard in 1769

FIG. 402—CHARLOTTENBURG. FORECOURT OF THE ROYAL PALACE
Designed in 1696 by Andreas Schlueter.

FIG. 404—PETROGRAD. PLAZA OF THE
WINTER-PALACE, ENTRANCE GATE

The street entering the plaza in the center
of the semi-circle facing the palace is bridged
over by this double arch designed by Carlo
Rossi in 1819. (From a drawing by Franz
Herding.)

FIG. 403—BERLIN, GENDARMEN
MARKT

Probably the finest creation of Frederick
II consisted of the two domed towers of
which one is seen in the view (the other being directly back of the point from which the
photograph was taken) with the royal theater
between the two. All three buildings were
free-standing. The plaza was framed by fairly uniform low houses. The streets entering
the large plaza were to be bridged by arches
somewhat on the order of the ones shown
in Fig. 404 although more subdued; the
arches were never executed.

Figs. 707 and 708 show airplane view
and plan of the plaza; see also Fig. 1030.

FIG. 405—POTSDAM. THE "NEW PALACE" BUILT 1763-69

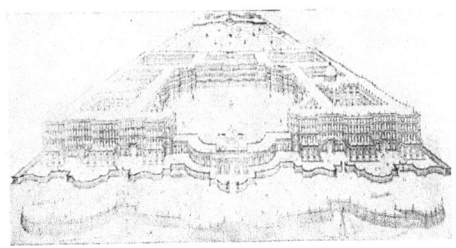

FIG. 406—DUSSELDORF. COUNT ALBERTI'S PROJECT FOR THE NEW PALACE

This scheme was not executed. (From Deutsche Bauzeitung.)

FIG. 407—LONDON. LINDSEY HOUSE, CHELSEA

A nobleman's country seat, acquired in 1750 by a German missionary society and developed into a scheme of courts framed by the residences of the brethren. (Figs. 407-08 from Waldemar Kuhn.)

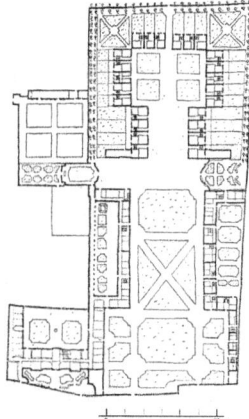

FIG. 408—LONDON. LINDSEY HOUSE

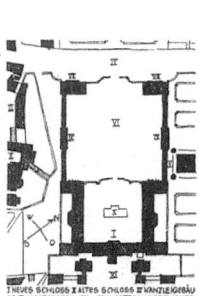

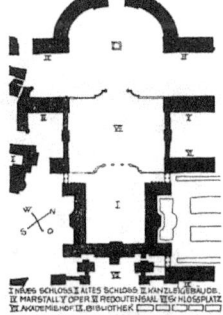

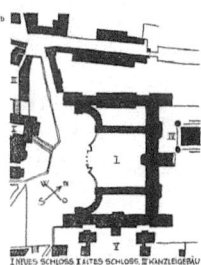

FIGS. 409-12—STUTTGART. DEVELOPMENT OF THE PALACE PLAZA

At the left, above, is the plan on which work was started in 1746 by Rettl; note location of Opera "VIII" to face guard-house "VII." The plan below is Balthasar Neumann's proposal to turn the axis of the composition. To the right, above, is Guêpiérre's return to the original axiation; note "V" Opera, "VI" Ballroom, "III" Archives. The fourth plan shows the plaza as finally left with tree rows taking the place of the unexecuted wings (see Fig. 412A).

FIG. 412A—STUTTGART. PALACE PLAZA

This view shows the plaza about 1865. The palace is at the left. To the right the somewhat oversized King's Building (a product of the mid-nineteenth century, used for commercial purposes) blocks the axis. (Figs. 409-412A from the magazine "Staedtebau.")

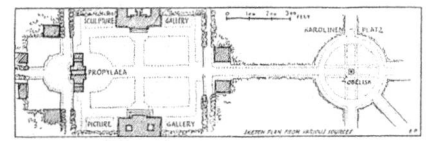

FIG. 413—MUNICH. PLAN OF PROPYLAEA GROUP

FIG. 414—MUNICH. PROPYLAEA AND SCULPTURE GALLERY
View going with Fig. 413. (Courtesy of the Chicago Plan Commission.)

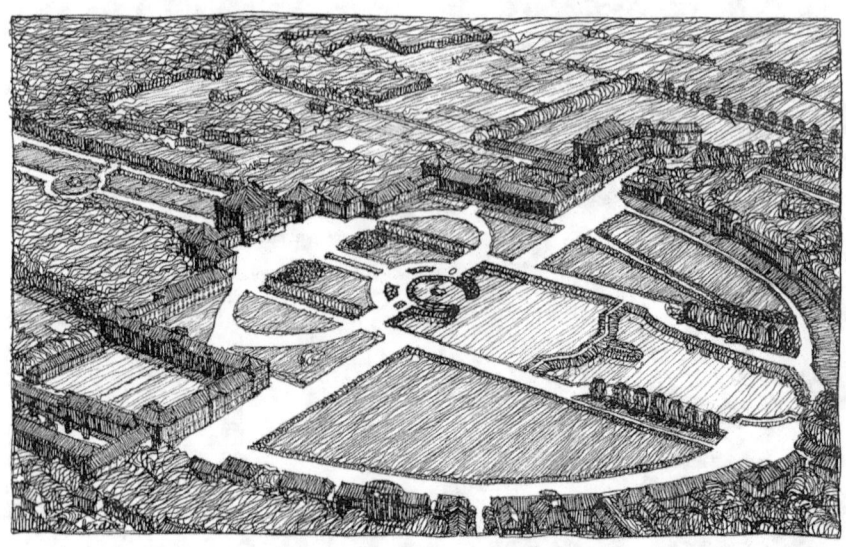

FIG. 415—MUNICH. ENTRANCE COURT TO THE NYMPHENBURG

Built 1663—1718 by Barelli, Viscardi, Zuccali, and Effner. Gardens designed by Girard, a disciple of Le Nôtre. There is a long canal, accompanied by quadruple allées, on axis of the main entrance. Thus a full axis view was not wanted, a case which has been compared with Bernini's sidewise entrances to the Piazza San Pietro in Rome. Approaching through one of the avenues one sees at its end a small framed picture which after one enters the forecourt suddenly broadens out. The contrast between the enclosed allée and the open forecourt makes the latter appear very large. The size of the central members of the palace appears large through being contrasted against the low members immediately to the right and left of it. The height of these low members corresponds again to the height of the other buildings one sees in the foreground immediately after entering the forecourt. As they frame the entire outer forecourt an optical scale is carried into the background from which the size of the main buildings can be appreciated. (From a drawing of Franz Herding, after a photograph published by Brinckmann.)

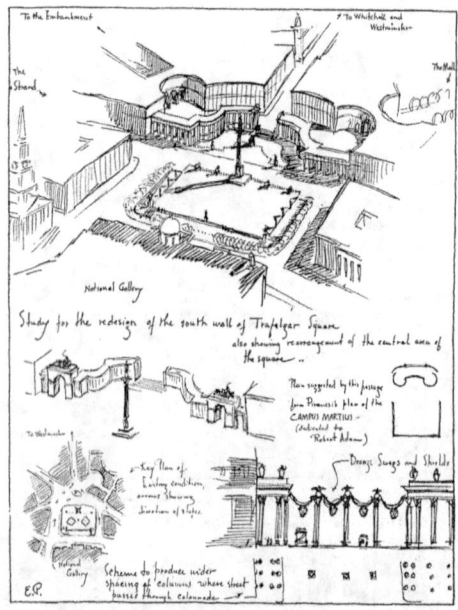

FIG. 417—LONDON. ADMIRALTY ARCH AND TRAFALGAR SQUARE

The square, which occupies the site of the "Royal Mews" or stables, was built in the thirties by Sir Charles Barry. The National Gallery, by Wilkins, and the Nelson Monument, by Baily, date from the same period. St. Martin's Church, by Gibbs, is a century older. The Admiralty Arch was built by Sir Aston Webb in 1910.

FIG. 416—LONDON. PAGE FROM TRAVEL SKETCH BOOK

FIG. 418—STRASBOURG. GROUP OF PUBLIC BUILDINGS BUILT 1884-1910

In the seventies a new city plan for Strasbourg was made which in many respects was superior to similar work done at that time but which was affected by the artistic disqualifications of the period. The plan of this forum is axiated on the single tower of the cathedral. Otherwise the design ranks somewhat with schemes like the one shown in Fig. 599.

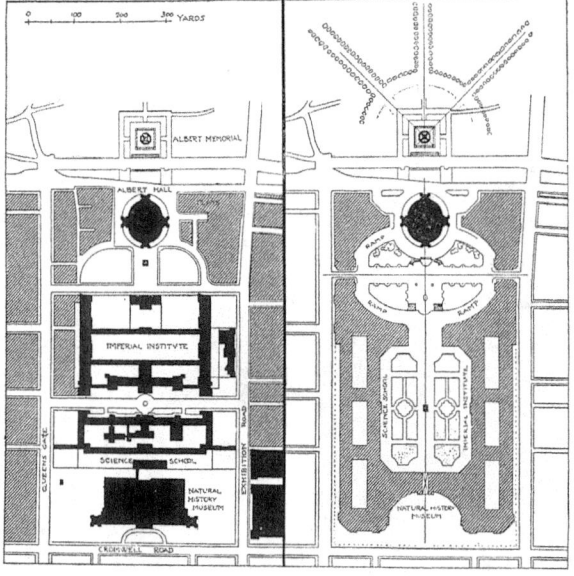

SOUTH KENSINGTON AS AT PRESENT LAID OUT

SOUTH KENSINGTON AS THE BUILDINGS MIGHT HAVE BEEN GROUPED

FIG. 419—LONDON. A CRITICAL SUGGESTION BY INIGO TRIGGS

In the proposed oval court the ground rises steeply and would have furnished an interesting problem in design.

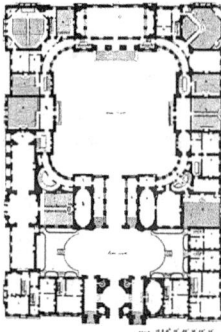

FIG. 420—EDINBURGH. PLAN OF UNIVERSITY AS DESIGNED BY ROBERT ADAM

On a much smaller scale this plan (only partially executed) illustrates a solution somewhat related to the one proposed in Fig. 419.

(From John Swarbrick.)

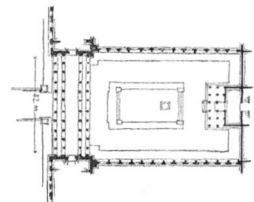

FIG. 421—BERLIN. COURT OF THE NEW MUSEUMS

This court measuring little more than one half acre is the center of the group of new museums that were designed by Messel for the "Museum-island" in the center of the city.

FIG. 422—BERLIN. VIEW GOING WITH FIG. 421

The colonnade separating the court from the water, bridge in the center.

FIG. 423—BERLIN. VIEW OF NEW CITY HALL
Going with Fig. 424.

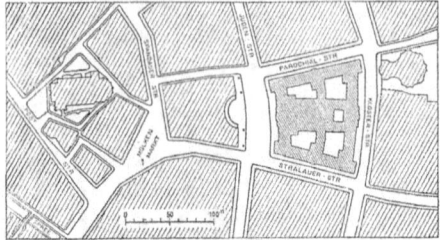

FIG. 424—BERLIN. PROPOSAL FOR THE SETTING OF THE NEW
CITY HALL

The new building stands in the oldest and most crowded section
of the city. The forecourt proposed by the designer, Ludwig Hoffmann,
had therefore to be of the smallest proportions. It must be remembered
however that a certain amount of dignity is secured to practically
every public building in European cities insofar as the building laws
do not permit high buildings. The limit in Berlin is five stories. (Figs.
423-24 from "Deutsche Bauzeitung" 1911.)

FIG. 425—ESSEN. THE MARKET PLACE IN MARGARETENHOEHE

Designed by Metzendorf. The views are of opposite sides of the
plaza.

FIG. 426—DESIGN FOR SCHOOL AND PLAYGROUND

FIG. 427—FRANKFORT. MODERN SCHOOL GROUP WITH PLAYGROUND
(From City Planning Exhibition, 1910.)

FIG. 428—MANNHEIM. FRIEDRICHSPLATZ

The view shows in the left foreground the circular site of the large water tower placed, about 1890, as terminal feature at the end of one of the central streets of the gridiron (Fig. 1051). The designer of the plaza, Bruno Schmitz, afterwards met this condition with his semicircular plan. Part of the façades have been built.

FIG. 429—SPANDAU. CITY HALL SQUARE.
Competition drawing by Emil Fader. (From "Staedtebau").

FIG. 430—BERLIN—HAVELSTRAND. SUBURBAN PLAZA ON THE LAKESHORE
Designed by Gessner and Schleh. (From "Staedtebau.")

FIG. 431—BERLIN—ZEHLENDORF. SEMICIRCULAR PLAZA
Designed by Schultze-Naumburg.

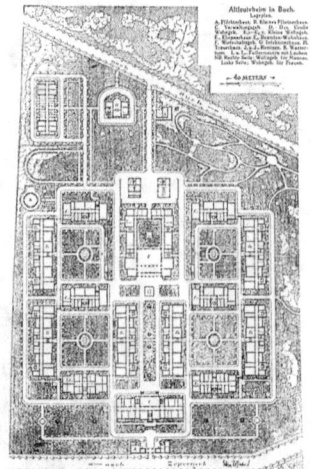

FIG. 433—BERLIN. OLD PEOPLE'S HOME
View (going with Fig. 432) from the little fountain in the center looking south.

FIG. 432—BERLIN. OLD PEOPLE'S HOME
The buildings of this municipal institution are grouped around four plazas. Design by Ludwig Hoffmann. (Figs. 432-33 from Wasmuth's Monatshefte.)

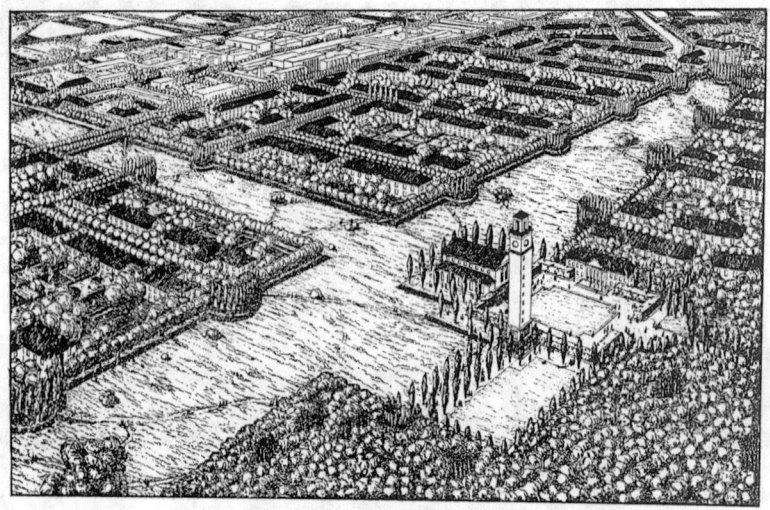

FIG. 434—BERLIN. DESIGN FOR SUBURBAN DEVELOPMENT
By Martin Wagner and Rudolf Wondracek.

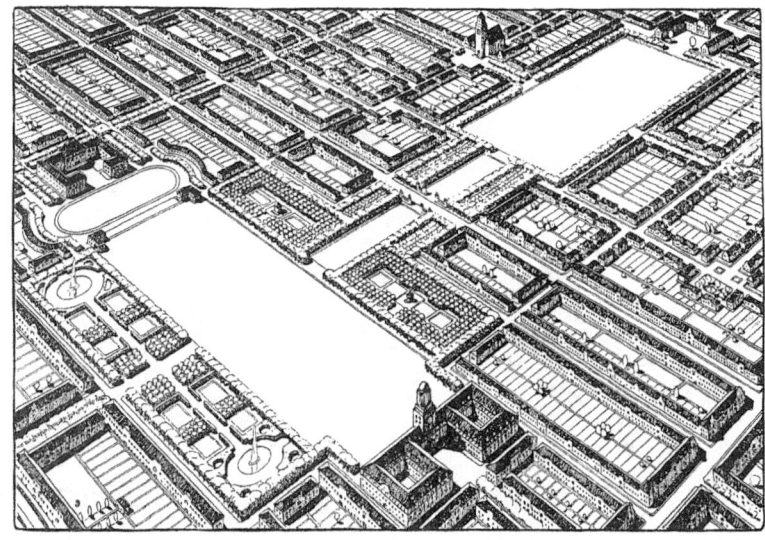

FIG. 435—SCHOOL, PLAYGROUND, AND PARK GROUPED IN DISTRICT OF INEXPENSIVE HOMES

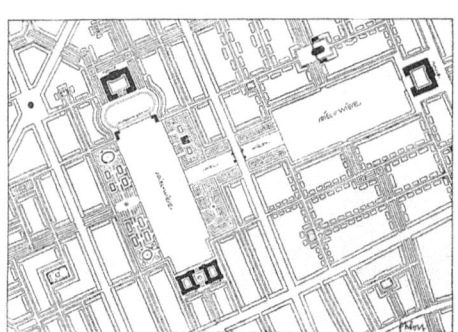

FIG. 436—PLAN GOING WITH FIG. 435
Designed by Paul Wolf.

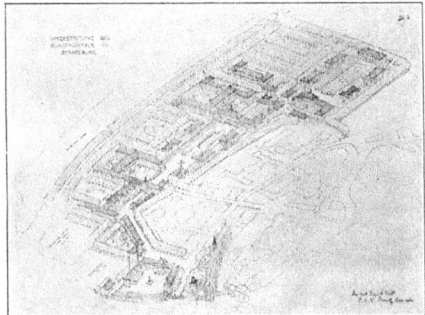

FIG. 437—STRASBOURG, EXTENSION OF MUNICIPAL HOSPITAL
The plan, designed by Paul Bonatz, covers 45 acres.

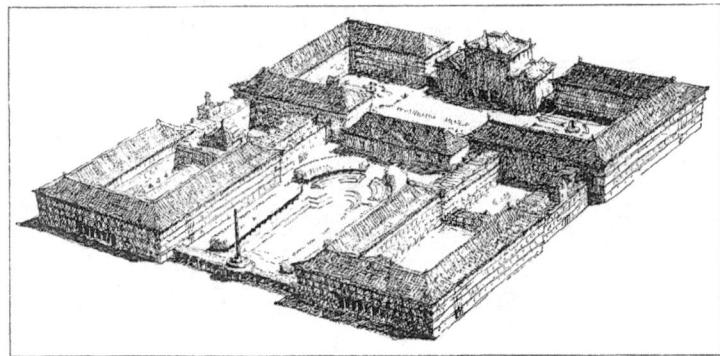

FIG. 438—DRESDEN. COMPETITION DRAWING FOR MUSEUM OF HYGIENE
Designed by Paul Bonatz and F. Scholer. (From "Wasmuth's Monatshefte" 1920.)

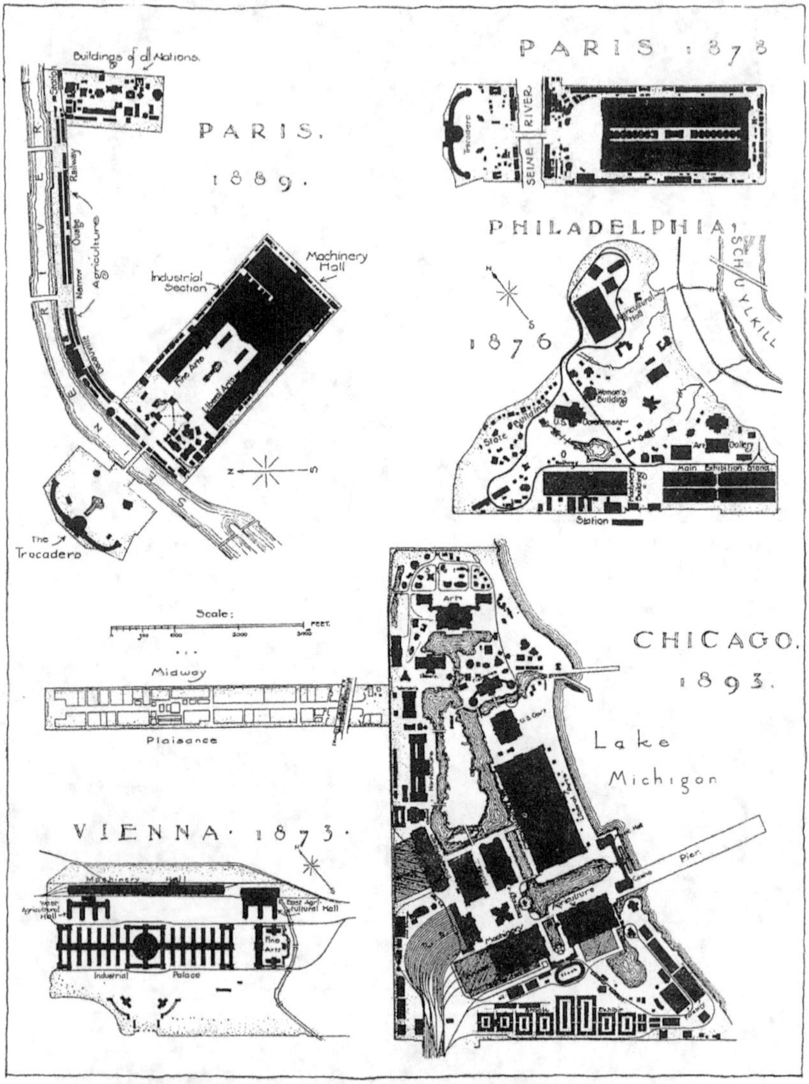

FIG. 441—FIVE WORLD'S FAIR PLANS (From the American Architect and Building News. 1893.)

HOWARD & GALLOWAY
SUPERVISING ARCHTS
OLMSTED BROS
LANDSCAPE ARCHTS

GROUND PLAN
ALASKA–YUKON–PACIFIC
EXPOSITION

FIG. 442—ALASKA-
YUKON-PACIFIC
EXPOSITION,
SEATTLE, 1910

(From Landscape
Architecture.)

FIG. 443—LOUIS-
IANA PURCHASE
EXPOSITION, ST.
LOUIS, 1904

(From the Archi-
tectural Review
1904.)
All plans on this
page are brought to
approximately the
same scale.

FIG. 444—PANAMA-PACIFIC INTERNATIONAL EXPOSITION, SAN FRANCISCO, 1915.

CHAPTER III

The Grouping of Buildings in America

To modern civic art America has made important contributions with her world's fairs, the evolution of the university campus, the civic center movement, and some features of her large restricted subdivisions for high grade and recently for inexpensive houses. Furthermore, since the introduction of the skyscraper and the conception of the park system idea, great promises of original civic design are held forth.

The World's Fairs

While the surprising developments in civic art which may be expected in America from the use and judicious grouping of skyscrapers can be fostered in practice only, the "world's fairs" have proven a fertile ground for experimental exercises with older motives. The growth from 1876, "when", to quote Ralph Adams Cram, "the Centennial in Philadelphia finally revealed us as, artistically speaking, the most savage of nations", to the two great Californian fairs of 1915, has been stupendous. The turning-point was Chicago. "Chicago was the first expression of American thought as a unity; one must start there", says Henry Adams, and it must be remembered that this recognition of the great fair as the birthday of modern civic art in America comes from the author of "Mont St. Michel and Chartres: a study of 13th century unity", an apotheosis of Gothic art edited by Ralph Adams Cram. Indeed the importance to America of '93 and the succeeding great fairs could hardly find truer appreciation than is given in the intuitive utterances of a man so highly cultivated and so highly esteemed by the architectural profession as Henry Adams, who was made an honorary member of the American Institute of Architects.

When it comes to judging the value of the world's fairs great caution is required, because the fairs, especially Chicago, had a far-reaching influence upon the relation of American architecture towards Classical and Renaissance precedent. One knows the attitude taken by men of the type of Russell Sturgis who in his letter to Peter B. Wight (Feb. 16th, 1897, published in the Architectural Record, Vol. 26, p. 127) speaks of "the accursed influence of the Chicago Exposition" and supposes "that the reason why M——, M—— & W—— and other such firms resort to this Roman style is because it must be so very easy to work in", "a most depressing and saddening symptom". On the other hand, the author of "Mont St. Michel and Chartres", though he was by no means blind to the shortcomings of the exposition of 1893, was nevertheless not only startled, but full of admiration. True, his criticism too is sharp, but, finally, like the majority of critics, he is fully conquered. "The first astonishment became greater every day", he says; "that the exposition should be a natural growth and product of the Northwest offered a step in evolution to startle Darwin; but that it should be anything else seemed an idea more startling still; and even granting it were not — admitting it to be a sort of industrial, speculative growth and product of the Beaux Arts artistically induced to pass the

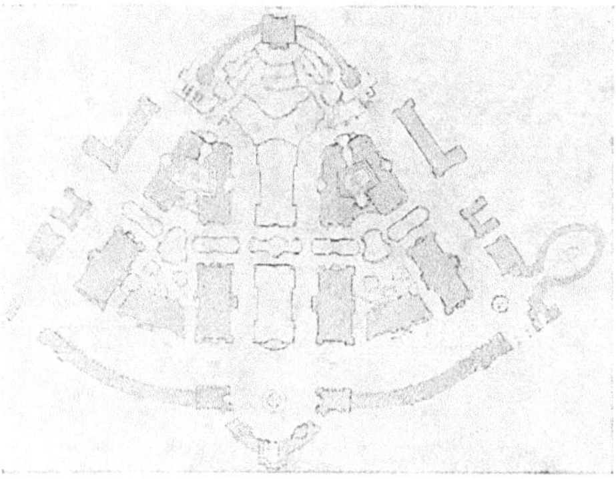

FIG. 445—ST. LOUIS. CASS GILBERT'S ORIGINAL PLAN FOR THE EXPOSITION
This sketch contemplated a terminal feature for the main axis and two large courts which were omitted in the final plan.

FIG. 446—SAN DIEGO. B. G. GOODHUE'S ORIGINAL PLAN FOR THE EXPOSITION, 1915.
Compare Fig. 451.

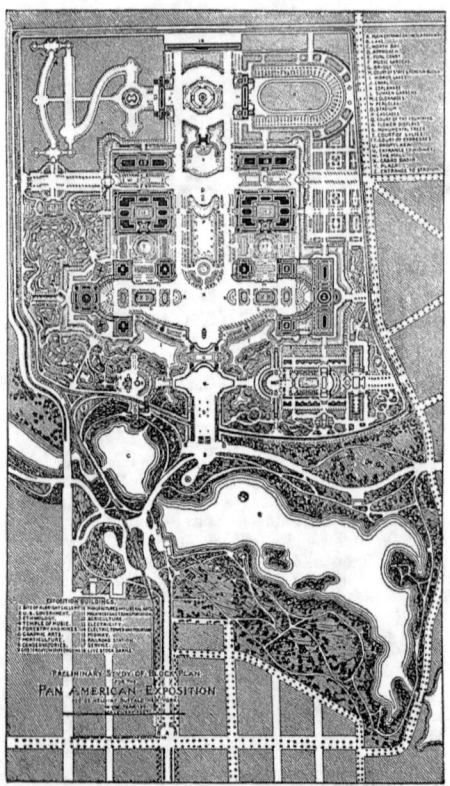

FIG. 447—BUFFALO. PAN-AMERICAN EXPOSITION, 1901.

(From the Architectural Record 1901.)

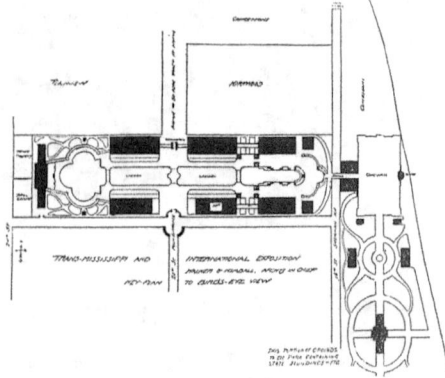

FIG. 448—OMAHA. TRANS-MISSISSIPPI AND INTERNATIONAL
EXPOSITION

Walker and Kimball, architects-in-chief. (From the Architectural
Review, 1898.)

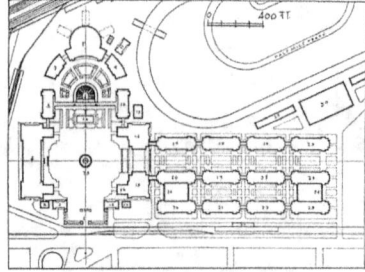

FIG. 450—SYRACUSE. NEW YORK STATE FAIR

Designed by Green and Wicks. (From the Brickbuilder, 1910.)

The plans on this page are all brought to approximately the same
scale (see graphic scale in Fig. 451). They are relatively twice as large
as those shown on page 98.

FIG. 449—SAN FRANCISCO. PANAMA-PACIFIC INTERNATIONAL EXPOSITION, 1915

Mr. Henry Anderson Lafler of San
Francisco has kindly furnished the following statement regarding the authorship of
this plan:

President C. C. Moore asked the San
Francisco Chapter, American Institute of
Architects, to select twelve architects from
whom he appointed Willis Polk (Chairman), John Galen Howard, Albert Pissis,
William Curlett and Clarence Ward. This
board dissolved and Polk, Ward, and
Faville were placed in charge as executive
committee.

Later the committee gave way to a commission composed of Polk, Faville, Kelham,
Mullgardt, Ward, Farquhar, McKim,
Mead, and White, Carrere and Hastings,
and Henry Bacon. Later Kelham became
chief of architecture.

The following is from "The City of
Domes," by John D. Barry: "At the first
meeting, President Moore explained that
at the St. Louis Exposition, according to
wide-expressed opinions, the buildings had
been too far apart. He favored maximum
of space with minimum of distance. The
architects first considered the conditions
they had to meet, climate and physical sur-
roundings. They were mainly influenced by wind, cold, rain. The result
was that for the protection of visitors they agreed to follow the "block
plan"...developed in many talks among the architects. Valuable suggestions came from Willis Polk and E. H. Bennett of Chicago, active in
the earlier consultations. The plan finally accepted was the joint work
of the entire commission."

From "The Jewel City" by Ben Macomber: "When San Francisco
had been before Congress asking national endorsement for the Exposition, the plans then presented, and on which the fight was won, were
prepared by Ernest Coxhead...These proposed a mass grouping of the
exposition structures around courts, and on the bay front. They were
afterwards amplified by Coxhead, and furnished the keynote of the
scheme finally carried out.

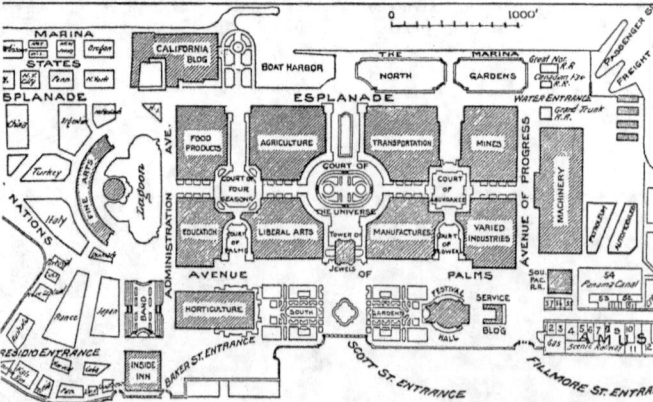

From the official history of the Exposition by Frank Morton Todd:
"Edward H. Bennett was appointed by the President on October 11th,
1911, to prepare a block plan. About 150 different plans and studies and
variations of plans were worked out, first and last, on the way to a conclusion....For the plan finally evolved, much praise is due Mr. Bennett.
His labors were great and valuable, and they produced abundance of
material. But ideas that have any vitality in them are prone to the
changes of evolution. During the conferences of the Architectural Commission, which was organized the following month, the elements involved were tried under all possible tests, and finally the members of
the Commission drew individual block plans and the ultimate result
was a composite of the best ideas of all of them."

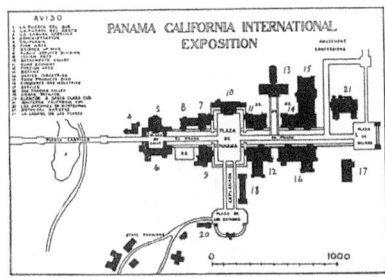

FIG. 451—SAN DIEGO, 1915

summer on the shore of Lake Michigan — could it be made to seem at home there? Was the American made to seem at home in it? Honestly, he had the air of enjoying it as though it were all his own; he felt it was good; he was proud of it; for the most part, he acted as though he had passed his life in landscape gardening and architectural decoration. . . . Critics had no trouble in criticizing the classicism, but all trading cities had always shown trader's taste, and, to the stern purist of religious faith, no art was thinner than Venetian Gothic. All trader's taste smelt of bric-a-brac; Chicago tried at least to give her taste a look of unity...... If the new American world could take this sharp and conscious twist towards ideals . . . . if the people of the Northwest actually knew what was good when they saw it, they would some day talk about Hunt and Richardson, La Farge and St. Gaudens, Burnham and McKim, and Stanford White when their politicians and millionaires were otherwise forgotten''. And Henry Adams's enthusiasm even grew, if possible, in view of the St. Louis fair of 1904. Of the Chicago fair he had said: "As a scenic display Paris had never approached it.'' But in St. Louis he exclaimed:

"The world had never witnessed so marvellous a phantasm; by night Arabia's crimson sands had never returned a glow half so astonishing, as one wandered among long lines of white palaces, exquisitely lighted by thousands upon thousands of electric candles, soft, rich, shadowy, palpable in their sensuous depths; all in deep silence, profound solitude, listening for a voice or a foot-fall or the plash of an oar, as though the Emir Mirza were displaying the beauties of the City of Brass, which could show nothing half so beautiful as this illumination, with its vast, white monumental solitude, bathed in the pure light of setting suns. One enjoyed it with iniquitous rapture, not because of exhibits but rather because of their want. Here was a paradox like the stellar universe. . . . . One saw here a third rate town of half-a-million people without history, education, unity or art, and with little capital — without even the element of natural interest except the river which it studiously ignored — but doing what London, Paris, or New York would have shrunk from attempting. This new social conglomerate, with no tie but its steam power and not much of that, threw away thirty or forty million dollars on a pageant as ephemeral as a stage flat.'' Surely Henry Adams's wonder

FIG. 452—CHICAGO. COURT OF HONOR

Looking east from Administration Building; for view in opposite direction, see Fig. 454 (Courtesy of the Chicago Plan Commission).

FIG. 453—CHICAGO. THE OLD FIELD MUSEUM

The fine arts building of the Exposition, designed by Charles B. Attwood. In spite of its dilapidated condition the old building and its wings form an effective group and create a fine plaza. The design is based on Besnard's Prix de Rome projet. (Photograph courtesy of Mr. E. S. Taylor. Copyright 1911 by A. C. McGregor.)

FIG. 454—CHICAGO, 1893. COURT OF HONOR

FIG. 455—PARIS, 1900. MONUMENTAL ENTRANCE
GATE

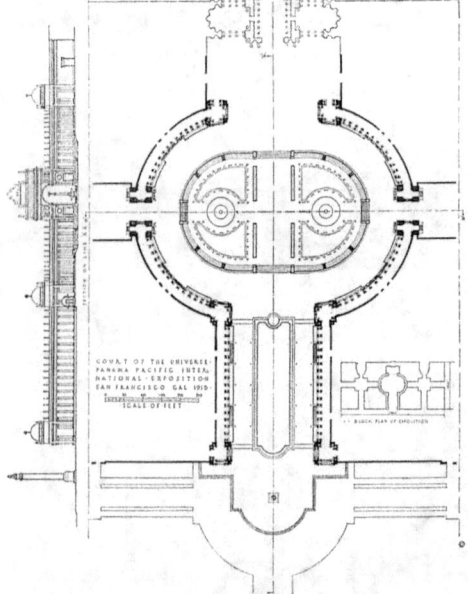

FIG. 459—SAN FRANCISCO, 1915. COURT OF THE UNIVERSE.
(From the Monograph of the work of McKim, Mead, and White.)

FIG. 456—PARIS, 1900. PALACE OF EDUCATION

FIG. 457—ST. LOUIS, 1904. VIEW FROM FESTIVAL HALL
NORTH EAST OVER THE GRAND BASIN.

FIG. 458—ST. LOUIS, 1904. FESTIVAL HALL AND TERRACE OF
STATES FROM THE NORTH EAST
(Figs. 457 and 458 from the Architectural Review, 1904.)

would have reached a third climax if he had had the privi-
lege of seeing the two Californian fairs of 1915 with their
new unheard-of color and lighting schemes and with their
architecture free from suspicion of being "a product of
the Beaux Arts artistically induced to pass the summer",
in America, but with roots firmly in the ground of traditional architecture suitable to the climate and the
historical antecedents of the state. If Henry Adams had
seen, after the fairs of 1915, the intelligent use the architects of the West and Southwest made of the lessons and
suggestions of the fairs, he probably would have joined
the optimists who feel that the American West upon the
basis furnished by the Spanish Colonial style, is about
to give an exhibition of architectural strength, perhaps

FIG. 460—SAN FRANCISCO, 1915. VIEW OF THE COURT OF THE UNIVERSE.

FIG. 461—SAN FRANCISCO, 1915. TOWER OF JEWELS AT NIGHT

Designed by Carrère and Hastings. This view shows the system of illumination by flood lighting. On the left is the south portal of the Palace of Liberal Arts designed by W. B. Faville.

FIG. 462—SAN FRANCISCO, 1915. PORTAL BETWEEN THE COURTS OF PALMS AND SEASONS

The Court of Four Seasons was designed by Henry Bacon; the Court of Palms and the "Italian Towers", one of which is shown in this view, by George W. Kelham.

FIG. 463—SAN FRANCISCO, 1915. AVENUE OF PALMS WITH SOUTH FACADE OF THE
"WALLED CITY"

On the right are the Spanish portal of the Palace of Varied Industries, two of the Italian Towers, and,
beyond, the Tower of Jewels. The use of massed foliage to relieve blank wall space is well shown.

FIG. 464—SAN FRANCISCO, 1915. PALACE OF FINE ARTS ILLUMINATED BY FLOOD LIGHTING
By B. R. Maybeck. Figs. 461-64 and 475 from Macomber's "Jewel City", John H. Williams, publisher.

FIG. 466—SAN FRANCISCO, 1915. COURT OF ABUNDANCE
Designed by Louis Christian Mullgardt.

FIG. 465 (AT THE LEFT)—SAN FRANCISCO, 1915. COURT OF FOUR SEASONS
Designed by Henry Bacon

FIG. 467—SAN DIEGO, 1915. APPROACH OVER THE PUENTE CABRILLO
Bertram Grosvenor Goodhue, Consulting and advisory architect.

FIG. 468—SAN DIEGO, 1915. VIEW OF EXPOSITION TAKEN FROM ACROSS THE CANYON
Cram, Goodhue and Ferguson, Architects; Bertram G. Goodhue, Consulting and advisory architect.

FIGS. 469-74—SAN DIEGO. 1915. SIX VIEWS

as permanent and almost as strong as the one given "in the town of Coutances," — whither Henry Adams went from St. Louis and where he says — "the people of Normandy had built towards the year 1250, an Exposition which architects still admired and tourists visited. . . ."

The amazing development expressed in the progress of the American fairs and their influence upon American architecture is largely a purely American product, created by American genius and administrative skill and American capital applied to the realization of dreams born in Europe. Russell Sturgis, therefore, may not be entirely wrong when he says, "all that I want to insist upon is that, according to my lights, it is not the influence of the Beaux Arts society or the Paris School at all, in no matter how remote a degree, which has given us the accursed influence of the Chicago Exposition and the resulting classical revival of our time". However, the step from the irresponsible dotting about of buildings in Philadelphia 1876 to the Court of Honor in Chicago '93 and the highly organized procession of courts in San Francisco, could not be thought of without the lesson of the intervening Paris Exposition of 1889. All the buildings of this Paris fair were conceived as a unit; the gates and roofs were organically joined as parts of the ensemble in a way that even San Francisco could not outdo in 1915. The development towards the water was even better in Paris in 1889, the Eiffel Tower between the Court of Honor and the river being at the same time the gigantic entrance, water gate, and triumphal exclamation mark of the exposition. The Trocadéro on the other side of the river in some respects foreshadowed Maybeck's finer Palace of Arts at San Francisco.

Important as the direct and positive influence of Paris '89 was for the planning conceptions of the American world's fairs, it was perhaps surpassed by the negative influence coming from Paris in 1900. The exposition of 1900 signified a disaster for the ambition of iron and steel, of "functionalism" and "art nouveau", which had promised so much at the Paris world's fair of 1889, with its victorious Eiffel Tower, and the disregard for which shown in the Chicago Fair had elicited much adverse criticism. If Chicago was criticized for shirking the duty of developing the new glass and iron functionalism, the designers of Paris 1900 tried their best to fulfil this duty and failed. Binet's "Monumental Entrance Gate" to the exposition and the Palace of Education by Sortais illustrated in Figs. 455-56 are only two of the many examples of discomforting developments of 1900. The world's fair of 1900 was not the only place where the new movement demonstrated the absurdity of forswearing precedent. While the world's fair grounds were an interesting, but rapidly vanishing, field for experimentation, the permanent buildings of Lavirotte and Schollkopf in Paris, of Delcoigne and Horta in Brussels, of Van Averbeke in Antwerp, of Van Goor and Cuypers in Holland, and many similar products in Germany are lasting monuments of what appears to-day as one of the most curious aberrations of taste. If one tries to analyze the strange sickening effect such buildings to-day give to the onlooker, one arrives at the conclusion, that in this hurricane of fitful new departures it is probably after all the historical motive emerging here and there unexpectedly in the whirlpool, which, however distorted it may be, gives one for moments at least something to cling to and prevents one's dizziness from turning into positive physical seasickness. Nothing could be more curious than to remember that there was a time when many highly cultivated people saw the salvation of architecture in these creations which to-day are apt to strike us as sheer craziness. One thing is surely demonstrated to the satisfaction of probably everyone: if the salvation of architecture depends upon abandoning precedent, this precedent must be abandoned very much more slowly and gently than was attempted in 1900. We must respect the old, however vigorously we must strive for the new. "An architect ought to be jealous of novelties" said Sir Christopher Wren; or, to quote the younger Blondel's safe advice given to the French architects in 1752, it is only in the field of temporary construction (as for instance the fairs) "that one should give free range to

FIG. 475—SAN FRANCISCO, 1915. THE PENNSYLVANIA
BUILDING
Designed by Henry Hornbostel.

one's genius and prefer the fire of one's inventiveness to the rules of precedent; but in all building for permanent purposes one must observe the rules of good manners and the proportions established by the ancients and moderns. Architecture which follows the fashions of the day deserves to become ridiculous just as one clothiers' fashion impresses us as ridiculous after it is once superseded by the fashion of the following season".

Many of the maniacs of 1900 to-day have learned this lesson and turned into conservative designers often ready to use classical detail.

Viewed historically the selection of "style" is, of course, not an arbitrary matter, left in the hands of individual architects; on the contrary, it evolves with the necessity of a natural event. The progress of this evolution is of the highest importance for all civic art, as "style" is the basis of harmony without which no strong civic art is possible. It was therefore a historic session of artists — "the most inspiring meeting of artists since the fifteenth century" St. Gaudens called it enthusiastically — in which the committee preparing the world's fair at Chicago agreed upon the use of classic motives and a uniform cornice line (60 ft.) around the Court of Honor. The esthetic result was so convincing that the question of whether or not modern architecture in America should follow precedent was decided by a landslide. The precedent accepted was the classic revival of the Italian Renaissance. A basis for future unity in American civic art was found.

The subsequent fairs until 1915 were important not so much for introducing variations of the effects arrived at in Chicago but because they brought home the great lesson to larger and larger multitudes of Americans.

In Buffalo 1901 (Fig. 447) a Spanish Colonial note and warmer coloring of the buildings was attempted, with much less success however than accompanied the same effort when it was made again in California where Spanish Colonial architecture had a traditional basis. In the California Fairs of 1915 (Figs. 459-75) the Spanish Colonial note in form and color had special significance because it represented acknowledgment of the mastery of local precedent, the traditional art of the state, the style conforming to local landscape and climate. The resulting influence upon the architectural development of the American West and Southwest as expressed in Goodhue's U. S. Naval Base (Figs. 477-9) and in developments like Tyrone (Figs. 480-7) or Ajo, (illustrated in chapter on city plans) as well as in numerous churches, schools, and private residences, are very fine and the only source of doubt may be the question whether modern conditions of mind and taste are sufficiently selfrespecting and stable to permit a continuous development forestalling the abrupt and disappointing shifts from style to style, like milliners' fashions, which some critics claim are the necessary expression of a degenerating period.

If the lesson of the Californian fairs can be taken seriously, the practical application to eastern conditions would be a sincere and progressive development of the traditional architecture of the Atlantic States, the American Colonial style. This development should be free to draw from all the sources from which the style is derived or to which it is akin comprising the wide field of Greek and Roman classicism, the Italian Renaissance and practically the entire post-Renaissance architecture of Europe and America, the whole forming a body of wonderful magnitude to the use of which the United States has a legitimate claim because it has made signal contributions to its development before 1840 and again since 1893. Within this enormous field of precedent an amount of freedom is possible which almost equals independence. The intelligent use, adaptation, and development of traditional forms makes constant demands upon originality and good judgment. Among the most important precedents set by Colonial architecture, one might well say, stands the ease with which the Colonial builders were ready to break away from precedent whenever it became necessary, and their ability to do so without violating the spirit of the style. Seen in this light even Gothic forms become possible for special purposes in modern architecture — which should be called synthetic rather than eclectic — because Gothic in certain respects stands in somewhat the same relation to Renaissance architecture as the archaic Doric forms stood to later Greek art, the older being severer and often bolder than the younger but without being necessarily contradictory in spirit. It is the study and the

FIG. 477—SAN DIEGO, U. S. MARINE CORPS BASE
Designed by Bertram G. Goodhue.

FIG. 478—SAN DIEGO. U. S. MARINE CORPS BASE
Bertram G. Goodhue, Consulting Architect.

The Marine Corps Base and the town of Tyrone are illustrated here to show the general applicability of the principles embodied in the plans of the California fairs.

FIG. 481—TYRONE, NEW MEXICO. INTERIOR OF OUT-DOOR
WAITING-ROOM

FIG. 479—SAN DIEGO. MARINE CORPS BASE.
ADMINISTRATION BUILDING
Bertram G. Goodhue, Consulting Architect.

FIG. 482—TYRONE, NEW MEXICO. SCHOOL HOUSE

FIG. 483—TYRONE, NEW MEXICO. STORE BUILDING TO THE RIGHT,
OUT-DOOR WAITING ROOM TO THE LEFT

FIG. 480—TYRONE, NEW MEXICO. PLAN.
Designed by Bertram Grosvenor Goodhue.

FIG. 484—TYRONE, NEW MEXICO.
PELTON HOUSE

These little houses show how the materials, and, with proper simplifications, the architectural style used in the public buildings can be employed in the most modest private houses, thus producing a feeling of unity throughout the town.

FIG. 485—TYRONE, NEW MEXICO.
SMALL HOUSE

FIG. 486—TYRONE, NEW MEXICO. BIRD'S-EYE VIEW LOOKING NORTH ACROSS THE PLAZA
Designed by Bertram Grosvenor Goodhue.

FIG. 487—TYRONE, NEW MEXICO. HOUSE FOR
AMERICAN WORKMAN

FIG. 487-A—BOSTON. HARVARD MEDICAL SCHOOL
Designed by Shepley, Rutan, and Coolidge. (Courtesy of Professor
Harold C. Ernst.) For plan see Fig. 488.

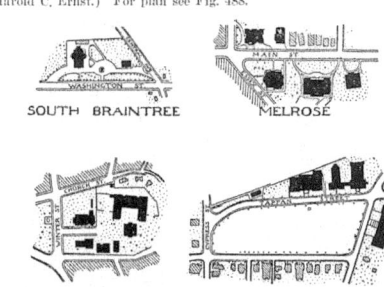

SOUTH BRAINTREE

MELROSE

MEETING HOUSE HILL
DORCHESTER

BROOKLINE
PLAYGROUND

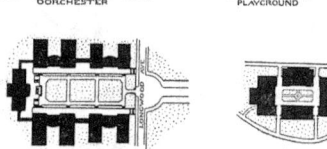

HARVARD MEDICAL
SCHOOL

NORMAL AND LATIN
SCHOOLS
BOSTON

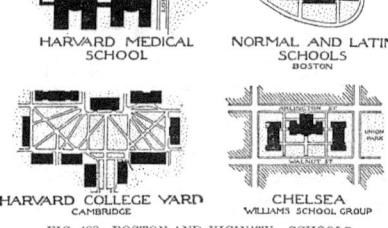

HARVARD COLLEGE YARD
CAMBRIDGE

CHELSEA
WILLIAMS SCHOOL GROUP

FIG. 488—BOSTON AND VICINITY. SCHOOLS
AND CIVIC CENTERS.

From A. A. Shurtleff's report to the Metropolitan Improvements Commission, 1909.

cultivation of the great spirit of the Colonial style in its
broadest aspects, therefore, that must be considered as
an important duty of everybody who has to do with
designing in America. Nevertheless, the future architecture of America might be spoken of, not so much as
a development from the Colonial style, but as a new syn-
thesis in which the Colonial is to be so important a part
that the whole should not contain anything incapable of
blending harmoniously with this important component.

As this matter of harmony of style is of paramount
importance in any consideration of civic art it may be
worth while to draw an analogy between the modern attitude towards the use of old and new forms and the
development of ancient architecture in the Roman empire. It was left to the Roman architects to finally realize
some of the finest possibilities inherent in the forms
originally conceived in Greece and developed in the Hellenistic kingdoms. As ensembles the Forum Trajannm
and Heliopolis represent a climax. At the same time the
Roman architects consummately blended the Greek
forms with newly acquired ones, as arch and dome, and
creations like the Pantheon and the Thermes surpass
Greek standards without violating them. In the same way
it may be hoped that modern America will finally fully
realize the dreams of the Renaissance and happily blend
the inherited forms with the newly conquered materials
and with the new forms made possible by them.
Thus compositions may be designed and executed that
combine the qualities of St. Peter's Plaza, of Versailles,
of Nancy, of Wren's London and of Carlsruhe, with the
giant's pride expressing itself in steel and reinforced concrete and in the hundredstoried public building dominating the axis of great "parksystems." The American fairs
justify optimism.

FIG. 489—CAMBRIDGE MASS. ENTRANCE TO HARVARD YARD
To the left Harvard Hall; to the right Massachusetts Hall. Entrance gate designed by McKim, Mead and White. (From the Monograph of the work of McKim, Mead and White.)

The Development of the American College Campus

The appreciation of the existing achievements of Colonial architecture in America was no small factor in the development of civic art. While the great American fairs revealed the superior qualities of regular design, even to the blind, the convincing presence of the historic buildings, public meeting places, stately mansions, and entire sections of old towns still lined with harmonious houses, was quietly at work.

The development of the American campus starting from a traditional basis is a contribution the United States has made to the classic revival which in importance may well compare with the world's fairs.

The first campus of Harvard University framed by Harvard Hall, Massachusetts Hall, and old Stoughton Hall, was a simple group in the Georgian style not planned for organic extension (Figs. 488-89). The burning of old Stoughton made possible the formation of a large open quadrangle, the "old yard", with its axis at right angles to the axis of the first group. The original axis, however, was recognized by Bulfinch when he built University Hall at the east side of the yard. The effect achieved was an orderly lining up of buildings in the same style without other refinement of general plan, much of the charm depending upon a liberal planting of fine elms.

When Thomas Jefferson made the plan for the University of Virginia (Figs. 492-95) his design, more ambitious than Harvard's, aimed at the effect of a closed forum laid out as a forecourt to the Rotunda (Library). The teachers' residences were connected by the colonnades framing the court, and with the members called "west range" and "east range" an outer frame was created for the gardens which represent subsidiary formal units parallel to the main campus. Towards the south the composition was left open, giving the possibility of enlargement. After Jefferson's time the Rotunda was transformed into a very long building by extensions towards the north, which however were destroyed by the fire of 1901. Traditional American art and the modern classic revival joined hands harmoniously when McKim, Mead, and White were called for the restoration. The closing of the court at the south end and the restoration of the library as a rotunda were their work.

The element of unification furnished by Jefferson's colonnades and arcades and much of what is best in Jef-

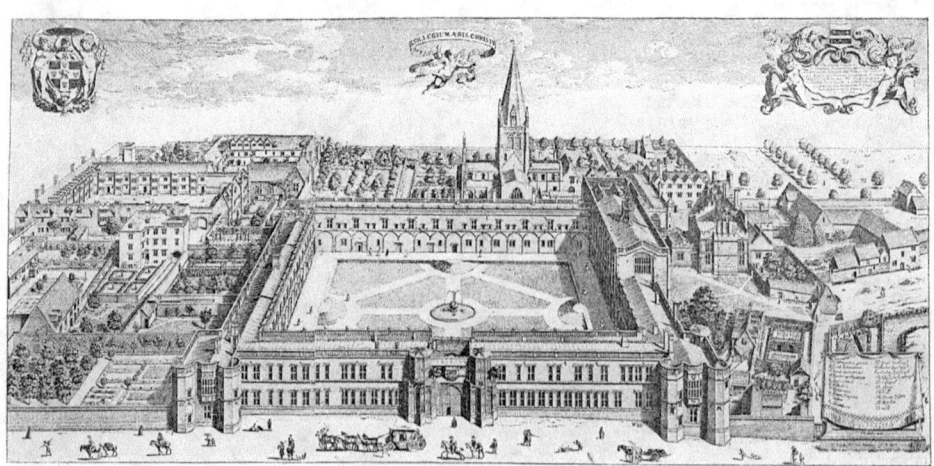

FIG. 490—OXFORD, CHRIST CHURCH
Founded by Cardinal Wolsey about 1525. The main quadrangle is the largest in Oxford. (From an engraving by D. Loggan.)

ferson's design is taken up in the plans for Sweet Briar College by Cram, Goodhue, and Ferguson, a truly American campus (Figs. 496-7), the whole constituting what may appear a design more pleasing, lighter and freer than Jefferson's work.

When Frederick Law Olmsted Sr. was called to Berkeley, California, in 1865, he designed a plan for the State University (Fig. 501) in which he grouped the buildings along a mall or "tapis vert" sloping down the hill and shooting at the sunset beyond the Golden Gate. The buildings placed upon an artificial plateau at the head of the mall were to overlook an informal park. Though there is just a touch of formality in the setting of the buildings, Olmsted specifically expressed himself against formal design for the college buildings. Following the romantic tendencies of his time, he wanted to "adopt a picturesque rather than a formal and perfectly symmetrical arrangement" and he saw in the latter "a cause of great inconvenience and perplexity". The neighborhood of the college grounds Olmsted laid out for an informal placing of refined residences and his description of the charms of highly refined home life which he hoped would find its place there is truly inspiring. It happens that in Berkeley and its neighborhood a very charming and quite individual type of cottage architecture developed under the influence of Maybeck (the designer of the Fine Arts Palace 1915) and others. These wooden houses are so characteristic a part of the frame surrounding the university that they deserve illustration (Figs. 498-500). They show what fine capacity for informal design was at work in this neighborhood making the failure of the Olmsted plan for an informal campus even more conclusive. The college buildings during the following decades were placed in accordance with Olmsted's suggestions (Fig. 509).

About thirty years after the date of Olmsted's design the University required considerable enlargement. It was then that Olmsted's informal plan, unlike Jefferson's much older formal plan for Virginia, failed to prove its eternal youth, the innate quality of great works of art. America, under the spell of the Chicago Fair, had awakened to new architectural thought, and Olmsted's plan of 1865 was abandoned.

One may well assume that Olmsted himself had abandoned the theory that informal design is the most suitable for the campus of a large educational institution. Indeed in 1886 he had been called upon to make a design for the magnificently large grounds of Leland Stanford University (about 35 miles south of Berkeley) and had himself produced a thoroughly formal plan (Fig. 491). Regarding the formal feature he said in his report: "The central buildings of the University are to stand in the midst of the plain. . . . This has been determined by the founders chiefly in order that no topographical difficulties need ever stand in the way of setting their buildings as they may, in the future, one after another, be found desirable, in eligible orderly and symmetrical relation and connection with those earlier provided." Olmsted thus repudiates his former contention that "symmetrical arrangement" is "a cause of great inconvenience and perplexity". Olmsted's conversion gains further interest through the fact that the formal buildings erected upon his symmetrical layout were designed by Shepley, Rutan and Coolidge, the heirs to Richardson's practice and ideals, the same Richardson with whom Olmsted had repeatedly been associated in the informal setting of Romanesque designs. The buildings for Leland Stanford, Romanesque as they unquestionably are, were meant from the beginning to have in them a touch of Spanish Colonial design, — and a very light touch it now seems, in the light of modern enthusiastic use of the Spanish forms.

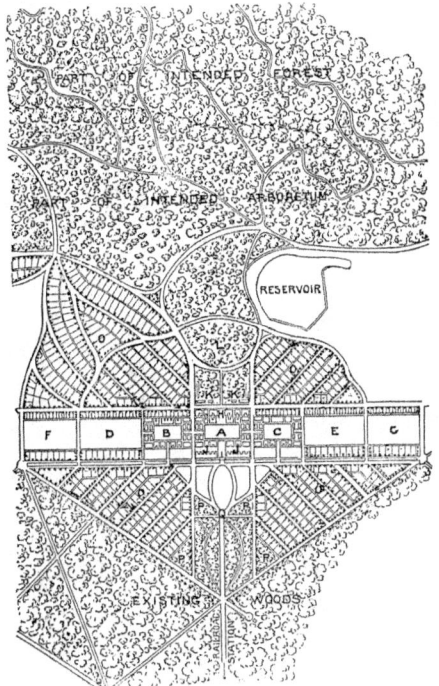

Plan of the Leland Stanford, Jr., University.

A: The central quadrangle, with buildings now partly under construction. **B C:** Sites for adjoining quadrangles, with proposed buildings. **D E F G:** Four blocks of land of form and extent corresponding to the above, to be held in reserve as sites for additional quadrangles and proposed buildings. **H:** Site for University Church. **I:** Site for Memorial Arch. **J:** Sites for University Libraries and Museums. **K:** Site for buildings of Industrial Department of the University, now partly under construction. **L:** Site for University Botanic Garden. **O O O O:** Four districts laid out in building lots suitable for detached dwellings and domestic gardens, with public ways giving direct communication between them and the University central buildings. **P P P P:** Sites for a Kinder Garten, a Primary School, an Advanced School and a School of Industry and Physical Training. **Q R:** A direct Avenue between the central quadrangle and a proposed station of the Southern Pacific Railroad, with bordering groves and promenades. Space is allowed in the wheel way for a double track street railway.

FIG. 491—LELAND STANFORD, JR., UNIVERSITY, PALO ALTO. PLAN BY F. L. OLMSTED, SR.

(From *Garden and Forest*, 1888.)

The new popularity of architectural art in America led to the calling of two international competitions for a new plan for the State University in Berkeley. They were held in Antwerp, 1898, and in San Francisco, 1899, and brought about a sweeping victory for formal design. Against Russell Sturgis's contention that it was not the influence of the Ecole des Beaux-Arts "in no matter how remote a way" which brought about the classic revival, it is interesting to see that the eleven premiated designs of the first competition all came from Beaux-Arts students, not excepting even the German-Swiss and Austrian prize winners. The winning design by E. Benard showed two powerful courts located on the main axis and on the cross axis. The finally executed design (Figs. 502-8) by John Galen Howard shows to some extent the return to the system of "detached structures, each designed by itself" as suggested by the elder Olmsted, but these detached structures are grouped upon a strong system of axes. Parallel to the main axis, shooting again at the Golden Gate, runs a side axis at the head of which stands the campanile, 303 feet high, which also terminates the main cross-axis. Further ties uniting these detached buildings are to be found in the general similarity of style, material, and color, and mainly in the foliage which in California is largely permanent.

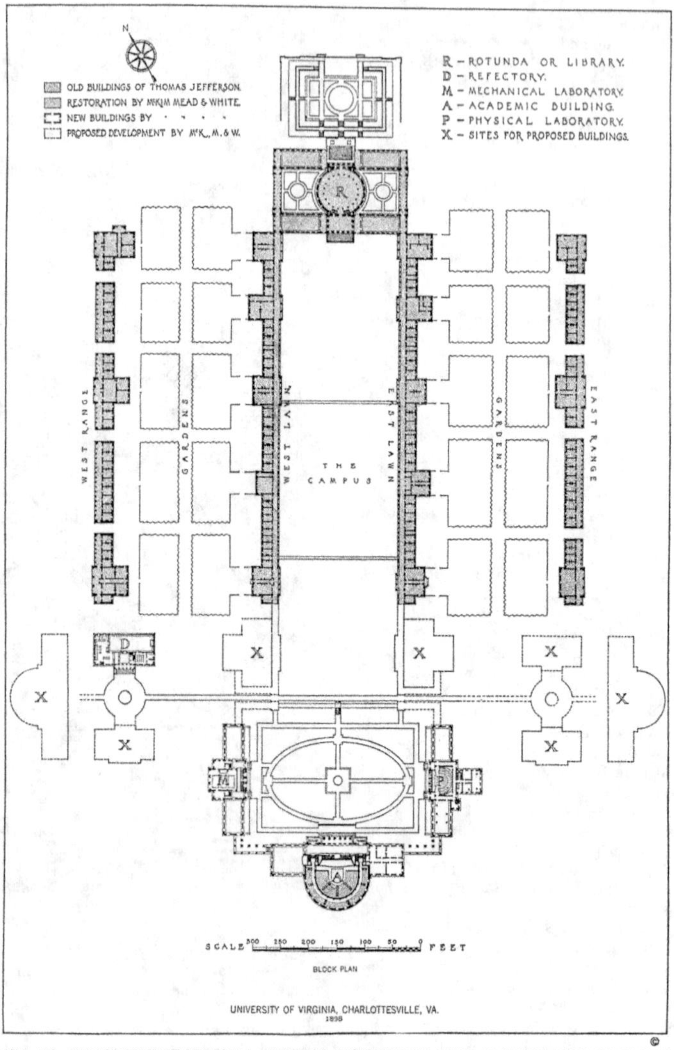

N

OLD BUILDINGS OF THOMAS JEFFERSON.
RESTORATION BY McKIM MEAD & WHITE.
NEW BUILDINGS BY " " "
PROPOSED DEVELOPMENT BY McK., M. & W.

R – ROTUNDA OR LIBRARY.
D – REFECTORY.
M – MECHANICAL LABORATORY.
A – ACADEMIC BUILDING.
P – PHYSICAL LABORATORY.
X – SITES FOR PROPOSED BUILDINGS.

R

WEST RANGE   GARDENS   WEST LAWN   THE CAMPUS   EAST LAWN   GARDENS   EAST RANGE

D

X   X   X
X   X
X   X   X

A

A

SCALE 500 250 200 150 100 50 0 FEET

BLOCK PLAN

UNIVERSITY OF VIRGINIA, CHARLOTTESVILLE, VA.
1898

FIG. 492—UNIVERSITY OF VIRGINIA. THOMAS JEFFERSON'S PLAN AS DEVELOPED BY McKIM
MEAD AND WHITE
(From the Monograph of the work of McKim, Mead, and White.)

FIG. 493—UNIVERSITY OF VIRGINIA. TERRACE NORTH OF
THE LIBRARY

A stronger tie welding college buildings into one unit was conceived by McKim, Mead, and White in their design for Columbia University (Figs. 510-3). The whole group of buildings stands upon a continuous strong podium of light stone over which, and stepped back from it, the many-storied buildings rise detached, in graceful masses of red brick and white stone. The esthetic value of this uniting podium is considerable and the price paid for it — all the rooms in the podium must have walls three feet thick — is hardly too great. The esthetic value of this uniting element, however, is felt mainly from the outside. When inside the campus, one sees the enclosing buildings simply as detached structures and the outlook between them, into the wilderness of New York apartments, is often disappointing (Fig. 513C). Between the individual buildings small courts are formed which present satisfactory or unsatisfactory aspects according to the point of view and angle at which they are seen.

FIG. 494—UNIVERSITY OF VIRGINIA. THE CAMPUS, LOOKING NORTH
(From Coffin and Holden.)

FIG. 495—UNIVERSITY OF VIRGINIA. THE CAMPUS WITH LIBRARY IN THE FORE-
GROUND

Sometimes the corners of one building harmoniously connect with the next, sometimes they unpleasantly cut across windows and ornaments (Fig. 513B). Here again the physical connection between the buildings which the podium gives to the observer standing outside the group (say for instance on Broadway) is missing.

The buildings north of 116th Street form a wonderful frame around the "central building", the library, from which one steps down to the fine forecourt formed by the buildings south of 116th Street (at present used as the athletic field).

In New York University (Figs. 514-16) another library suggesting a "central building" in the sense of the Renaissance is flanked by two subsidiary buildings and held together by a scheme of colonnades. The libraries of both Columbia and New York Universities are given

FIG. 496—SWEET BRIAR COLLEGE. DESIGNED BY CRAM GOODHUE AND FERGUSON
(Figs. 496-97 by courtesy of Miss Susan Marshall, Secretary to the President of Sweet Briar College.)

strong exteriors avoiding the round Pantheon type followed in Jefferson's Rotunda which slightly suggests a gas tank.

In Baltimore, one of the centers of traditional art in America, and adjoining old Homewood, one of the finest Colonial groups still standing, the new campus of Johns Hopkins University (Figs. 522-5) has been planned with great respect for the best lessons of the past and without sacrifice of modern practical requirements. Under the force of topographical conditions Homewood was made a side feature in the frame of the outer court, to be matched on the other side by a new building of similar outline; this may be slightly irreverent, especially as the new grading is not favorable for the old mansion. But every-

thing connected with the campus shows so much taste, moderation, and sincerity that even the architect of Homewood ought to be satisfied.

For the Massachusetts Institute of Technology (Figs. 517-20) a forum of great strength has been developed facing the Charles River. Here no traditional American detail has been used, but the design being based upon the same classic forms from which the American Colonial is derived by ancient lineage, shows an Americanization of its own by using classic forms with an austerity that suggests steel and concrete.

Some recent designs for the grounds of colleges and similar institutions have abandoned both American tradition and the classic forms from which American tra-

FIG. 497—SWEET BRIAR COLLEGE. VIRGINIA. DESIGNED BY CRAM GOODHUE AND FERGUSON

FIG. 498—BERKELEY. SHINGLED HOUSES AS DEVELOPED BY B. R. MAYBECK AND HIS FOLLOWERS

dition is derived and have selected Gothic and Elizabethan forms instead, which have no roots in the traditional art of this continent. However the Gothic or semi-Gothic forms in many cases are applied only to the detail and do not interfere with the plan at large, which on the contrary follows the requirements of spaciousness and even of symmetry which make for so much in the enjoyment of architecture. The use of the forms of Gothic, or the hybrid styles that followed the Gothic, upon plans of Renaissance character is not necessarily contradictory as much of the so-called picturesqueness, i. e. sinuosity, of old Gothic plans was caused by conditions of crowding and lack of space which should not prevail on the American campus. It is therefore not surprising that modern designers in Gothic have produced plans for college grounds with or without Gothic structural detail but perfectly balanced and axiated according to the best modern ideas.

The plan for the Rice Institute in Houston (Figs. 534-37) combines a balanced plan with Byzantine detail, while the plan for the development of the University of Colorado (Figs. 538-40) is a prompt confirmation of the value of the Californian world's fairs.

One of the reasons which the elder Olmsted gave against the use of formal design in connection with college grounds seems quite strong. He said that "a picturesque rather than a formal and perfectly symmetrical arrangement would allow any enlargement or modification of the general plan of building adopted for the college which may in the future be found desirable", which is another way for saying that it is comparatively simple to ramble along informally, while to make an elastic formal plan is by no means an easy matter. The stupendous development of modern colleges is apt to break down the frame of a formal scheme however ambitiously it may have been conceived. It is not in the spirit of a great composition to have annexes attached to it which do not stand in close axial relation to the scheme. It would therefore be desirable if in a group the plan of each one of the individual buildings were designed in such a way as to allow for an organic extension as soon as the need arises. These individual extensions should not disturb the general plan but should contribute to its completion and enhance the appearance of the whole. If planned for in advance, a campus composed of a small number of individual buildings tied together only by foliage or light colonnades can gradually be transformed into a scheme of physically connected buildings grouped around courts which stand in axial relation to each other with all the perspective refinement connected therewith. One scheme of courts can be surrounded by a second chain of courts without losing interrelation, balance, and symmetry.

(Text continued on page 127.)

FIG. 499—BERKELEY. THE FACULTY CLUB ON THE UNIVERSITY CAMPUS

Designed by B. R. Maybeck.

FIGS. 500 and 500A—BERKELEY. A PRIVATE SCHOOL HOUSE

Designed by B. R. Maybeck.

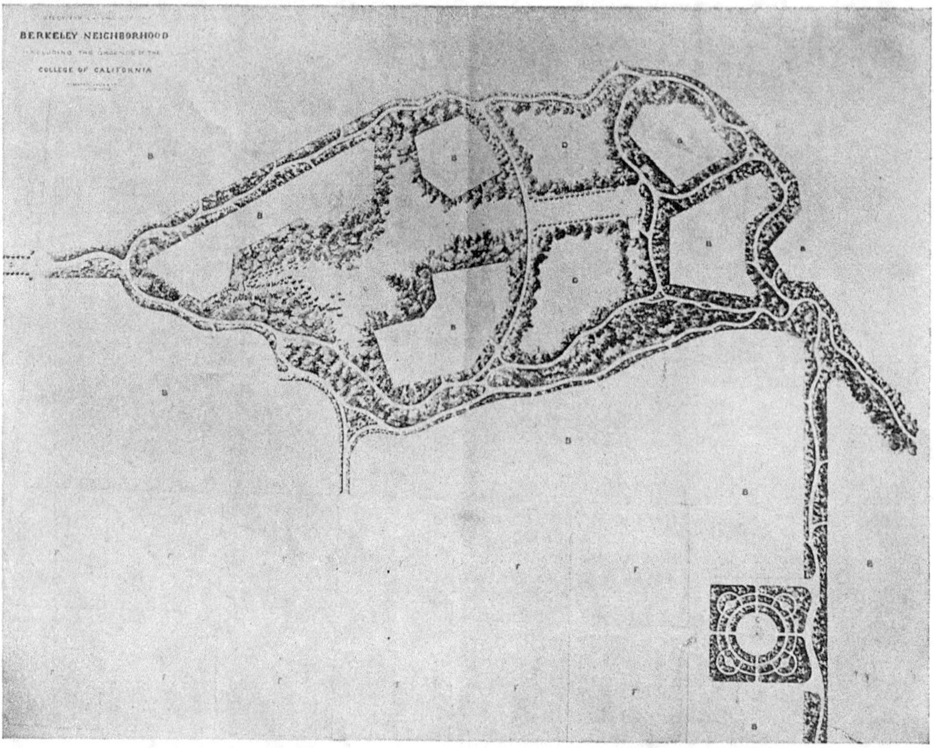

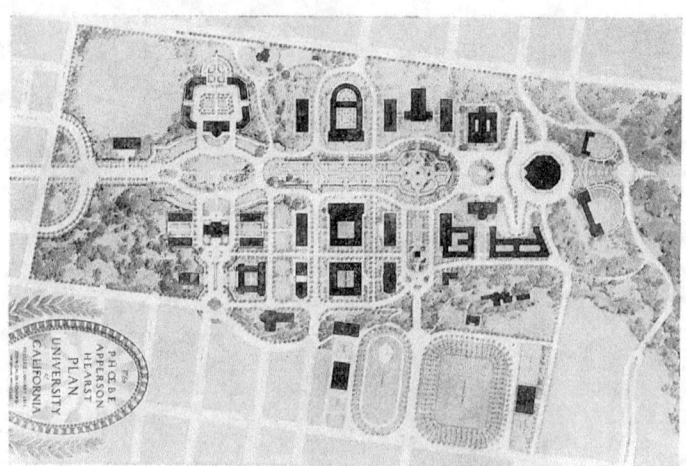

FIG. 501—BERKELEY. FREDERICK LAW OLMSTED'S "STUDY FOR LAYING OUT OF THE BERKELEY NEIGHBORHOOD, INCLUDING
THE GROUNDS OF THE COLLEGE OF CALIFORNIA. OLMSTED VAUX & CO., LANDSCAPE ARCHITECTS"

(From the report of 1866.) The top of the plan is north. The rectangular blocks, "F,F, F, Village Lots", are 600 feet square, which furnishes
a scale for the map. Key: A—Site for College Buildings (Olmsted figured on three buildings) ; B—Grounds for Residences ; C—Public Grounds ;
D—Grounds reserved for College purposes ; E—Public Garden ; F—Berkeley Village Lots ; G—Avenue to the landing.

FIG. 502—BERKELEY. GENERAL PLAN OF THE UNIVERSITY OF CALIFORNIA

By John Galen Howard. This plan is the outcome of two international competitions. In the first, judged
at Antwerp in 1898, 105 plans were submitted. The eleven premiated architects entered a second competition judged at San Francisco in 1899. Five prizes, ranging from one to five thousand dollars, were awarded; the first prize went to Emile Benard of Paris. His drawings formed the basis upon which, since 1902,
Professor Howard has developed the plan of the University.

FIG. 503—BERKELEY. UNIVERSITY OF CALIFORNIA. HUMANITIES GROUP

FIG. 504—CAMPANILE ESPLANADE

FIG. 505—THE AGRICULTURAL GROUP

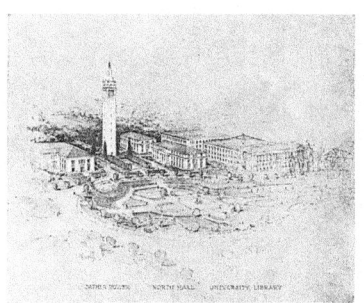

FIG. 506—LIBRARY ANNEX

BERKELEY. THE UNIVERSITY OF CALIFORNIA

The drawing above, of the humanities group, is an elevation looking east. The Campanile is in the center. The individual buildings are brought into composition by planting and balustrades and by harmonious roof lines. The two small units on the right side are connected by a colonnade.

Fig. 504 represents a design made by Professor Howard for the esplanade from which the Sather tower rises. It is substantially the plan which was executed.

The agricultural group, being on the more level ground at the lower part of the campus, could enclose a larger area than was practicable in the other groups.

The rendered drawing of the stadium, a concrete structure seating 40,000, represents it as seen from the campanile.

The so-called library annex, a new classroom building, is built around an auditorium seating a thousand people.

The Sather tower or campanile, which is shown with its setting in Fig. 508, is 303 feet high, 34 feet square at the base and 30 feet 6 inches at the top. It is of steel-frame construction faced with granite.

The view below, taken looking west, shows the original buildings put up before the inception of the Phoebe Apperson Hearst plan.

FIG. 507—STADIUM

FIG. 508—VICINITY OF CAMPANILE

FIG. 509—BERKELEY. OLD VIEW OF THE TOWN AND CAMPUS

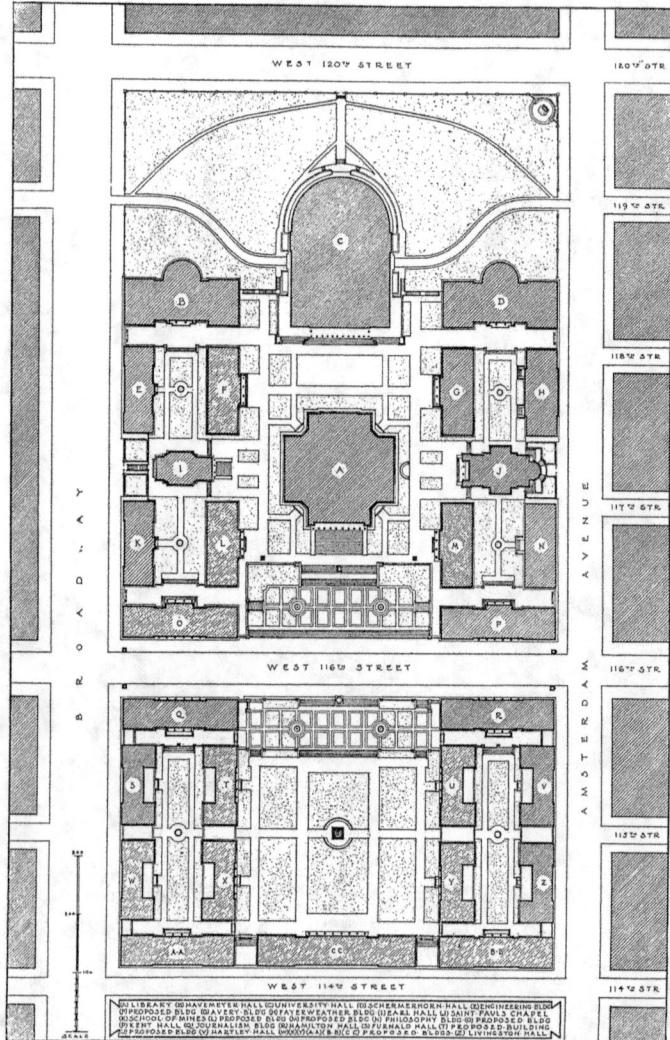

FIG. 510—NEW YORK. GENERAL PLAN OF COLUMBIA UNIVERSITY

By McKim, Mead, and White. The library, "A", stands in the center of a plateau formed by levelling the top of a hill. All the surrounding streets are well below the plateau, especially West 120th which is some thirty or forty feet below the central campus. The buildings stand on a high podium, as shown in Fig. 513A. (From the Monograph of the work of McKim, Mead, and White.)

FIG. 511—NEW YORK. THE LIBRARY OF COLUMBIA UNIVERSITY
Designed by McKim, Mead, and White.

FIG. 512—NEW YORK. TERRACE IN FRONT OF THE LIBRARY OF COLUMBIA UNIVERSITY

FIGS. 513A, B, AND C—NEW YORK. THREE VIEWS OF COLUMBIA UNIVERSITY
See text, p. 112.

FIG. 514—NEW YORK. LIBRARY OF NEW YORK UNIVERSITY, WITH ONE OF THE FLANKING
BUILDINGS

Designed by McKim, Mead, and White.

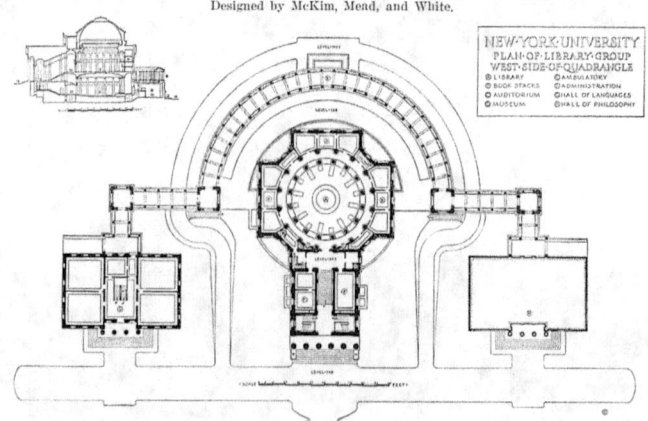

FIG. 515—NEW YORK UNIVERSITY. PLAN OF LIBRARY GROUP.

In the "ambulatory", which supports the library on the Hudson side, is the so-called "Hall of Fame".
The buildings are of yellow brick and grey stone. (Figs. 514 and 515 are from the Monograph of the work
of McKim, Mead, and White.)

FIG. 516—NEW YORK. LIBRARY OF NEW YORK UNIVERSITY

FIG. 517—CAMBRIDGE. MODEL OF NEW DORMITORY GROUP
AT M. I. T.

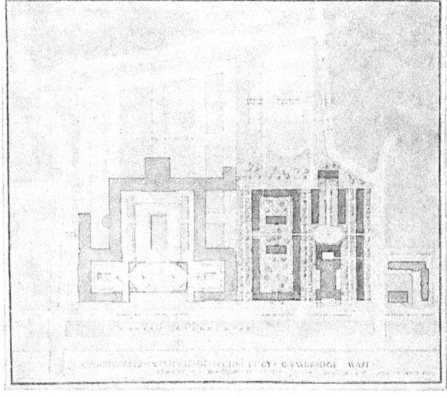

FIG. 518—CAMBRIDGE. GENERAL PLAN OF THE MASSACHU-
SETTS INSTITUTE OF TECHNOLOGY.

Designed by Welles Bosworth.

FIG. 519—CAMBRIDGE. THE FLANKING COURTS
OF THE M. I. T. BUILDINGS
From a drawing by Birch Burdette Long.

FIG. 520—CAMBRIDGE. THE NEW M. I. T. BUILDINGS FROM
THE BOSTON SIDE OF THE CHARLES RIVER BASIN

FIG. 521—BELVOIR, VA. MODEL OF NEW ENGINEER SCHOOL AND POST AND COLLEGE OF MILITARY RESEARCH
On the Potomac River, below Washington. Designed by Welles Bosworth. architect, and Eric Kebbon, Major, Engineer
Corps, U. S. A.

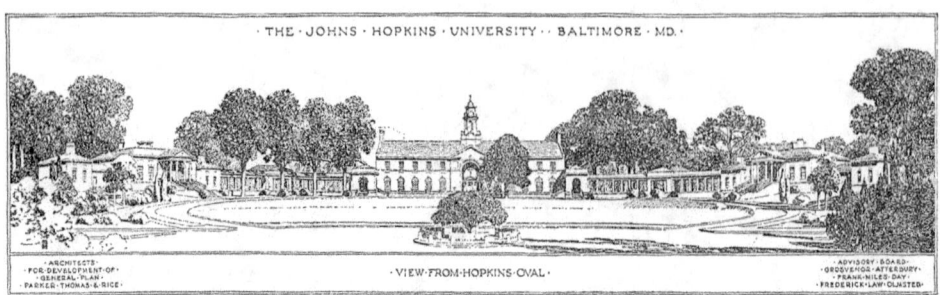

FIG. 522—BALTIMORE. JOHNS HOPKINS UNIVERSITY. HOPKINS OVAL

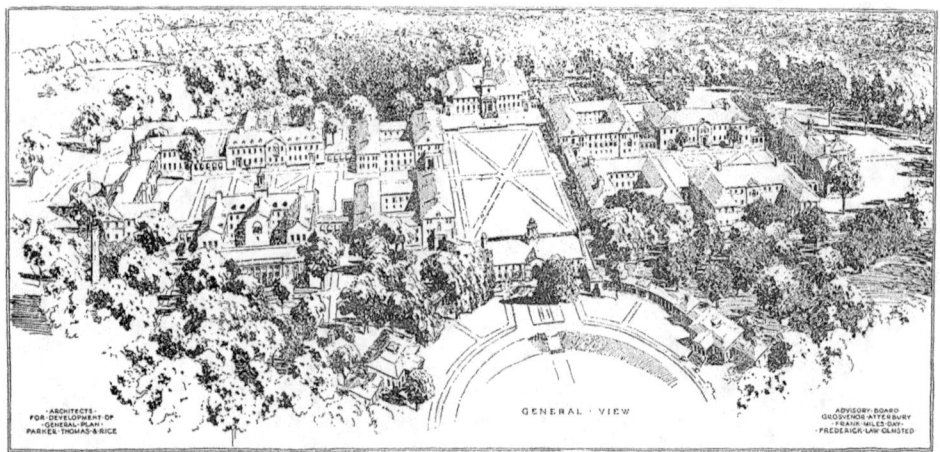

FIG. 523—BALTIMORE. JOHNS HOPKINS UNIVERSITY. GENERAL VIEW

FIG. 524—BALTIMORE. JOHNS HOPKINS UNIVERSITY. GILMAN HALL
Designed by Parker, Thomas, and Rice. (From the Brickbuilder.)

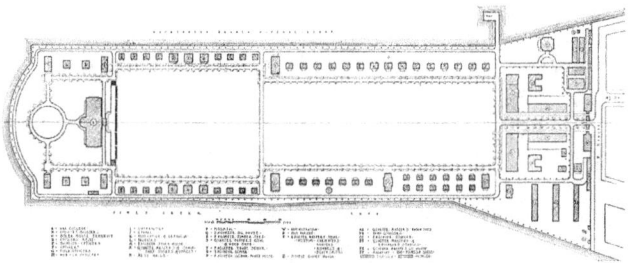

FIG. 525—BALTIMORE. HOMEWOOD

The fine old Colonial mansion standing in the new grounds of the Johns Hopkins University furnished the keynote of the entire architectural development and was incorporated into the scheme by being made one of the flanking pavilions of the gateway group. (From Coffin and Holden.)

FIG. 526—WASHINGTON. ARMY WAR COLLEGE AND ENGINEERS' POST

(From the Monograph of the work of McKim, Mead, and White.)

FIG. 527—PITTSBURGH. WESTERN UNIVERSITY OF PENNSYLVANIA

A competition design by Palmer and Hornbostel. For plan see Fig. 528.

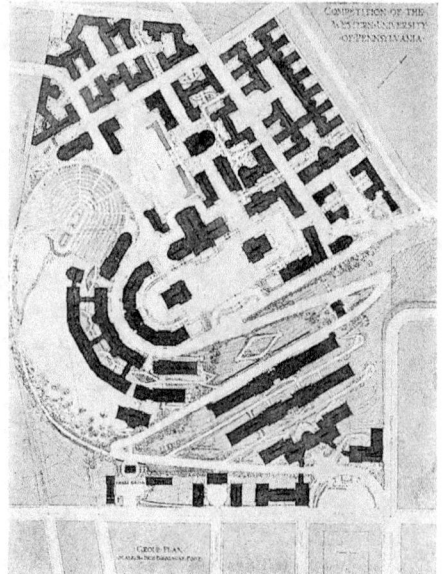

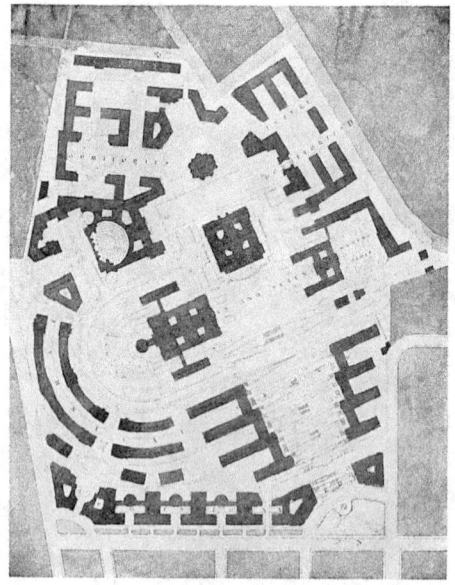

FIG. 528—PITTSBURGH. WESTERN UNIVERSITY OF
PENNSYLVANIA

A competition plan by Palmer and Hornbostel. For elevation see
Fig. 527.

FIG. 529—PITTSBURGH. WESTERN UNIVERSITY OF
PENNSYLVANIA

A competition plan by Guy Lowell. For elevation see Fig. 530.

FIG. 530—PITTSBURGH. WESTERN UNIVERSITY OF PENNSYLVANIA

A competition design by Guy Lowell. For plan see Fig. 529.

FIG. 531—MINNEAPOLIS. UNIVERSITY OF MINNESOTA

Designed by Cass Gilbert.

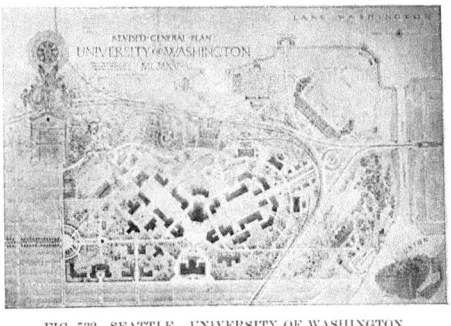

FIG. 532—SEATTLE. UNIVERSITY OF WASHINGTON

Designed by C. H. Bebb and C. F. Gould. This plan is interesting for the many points at which the city street plan is recognized and for its detailed adaptation to the difficulties and to the opportunities of the site. The southern group is axiated on Mt. Rainier. This motive, as well as the topography and the location of existing buildings, suggested the daring parti embodied in the angular relation of the principal groups.

FIG. 533—PORTLAND. PLAN OF REED COLLEGE

FIG. 533A—PORTLAND. BIRD'S-EYE VIEW OF REED COLLEGE

Designed by Doyle, Patterson, and Beach.

FIG. 534—HOUSTON. RICE INSTITUTE

Designed by Cram, Goodhue, and Ferguson. The connecting arcades and the formal avenues of trees which show but lightly in the plan, are an essential part of the design.

FIGS. 535, 536, 537—HOUSTON. RICE INSTITUTE

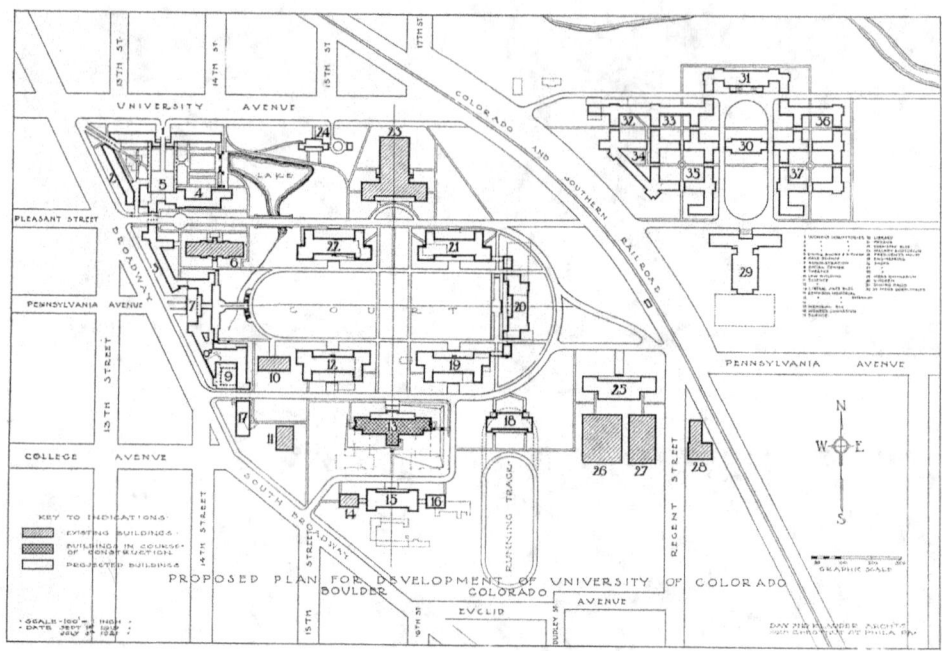

FIG. 538—BOULDER. UNIVERSITY OF COLORADO
Designed by Day and Klauder.

FIG. 539—BOULDER. UNIVERSITY OF COLORADO
Court of women's dormitory group, number 4 on the plan above.

FIG. 540—BOULDER. UNIVERSITY OF COLORADO
Terrace in front of administration building, number 7 on the plan above.

(Text continued from page 115.)

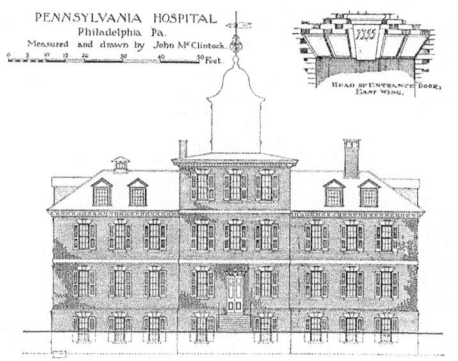

FIG. 541—PHILADELPHIA. PENNSYLVANIA HOSPITAL.
EAST WING

Everything that has been said about the design of college grounds applies of course to the design of other institutions, schools, asylums, barracks, hospitals (Figs. 541-59), and even prisons. As an example of organic extension of a formal design we have a fine Colonial precedent in the east wing of the Pennsylvania Hospital in Philadelphia (Figs. 541-43), built in 1755, and gradually added to until one of the finest groups of Colonial architecture was achieved, multiplying the capacity of the hospital without destroying the harmony and balance of a great plan. That it would be perfectly possible to multiply the capacity of such a group over and over again, may be judged from the plan of the Burke Foundation Hospital for Convalescents, White Plains, N. Y. (Figs. 544-46), where a group about equal in size to the Pennsylvania Hospital forms one side of a court which itself is the center of an institution many times larger.

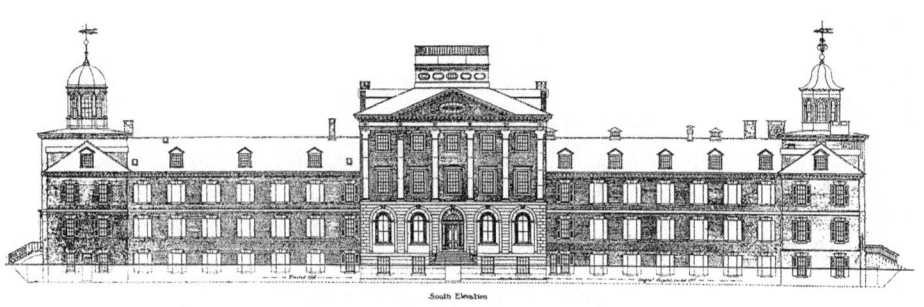

FIG. 542—PHILADELPHIA. PENNSYLVANIA HOSPITAL. SOUTH ELEVATION

FIG. 543—PHILADELPHIA. PENNSYLVANIA HOSPITAL. VIEW OF SOUTH FRONT

The east wing was built first and was duplicated at the west end when the large E-shaped plan was made. Figs. 541-43 are from Ware's "Georgian Period."

FIG. 544—WHITE PLAINS. BURKE FOUNDATION HOSPITAL FOR CONVALESCENTS
A corner of the central court.

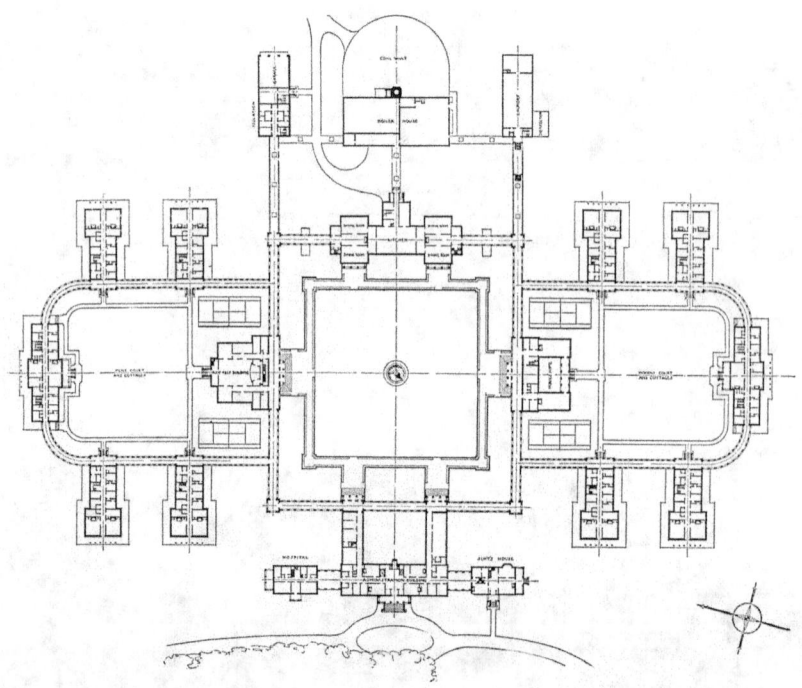

FIG. 545—WHITE PLAINS. BURKE FOUNDATION HOSPITAL FOR CONVALESCENTS
Figs. 544-46 are from the monograph of the work of McKim, Mead, and White.

FIG. 546—WHITE PLAINS. BURKE FOUNDATION HOSPITAL FOR CONVALESCENTS

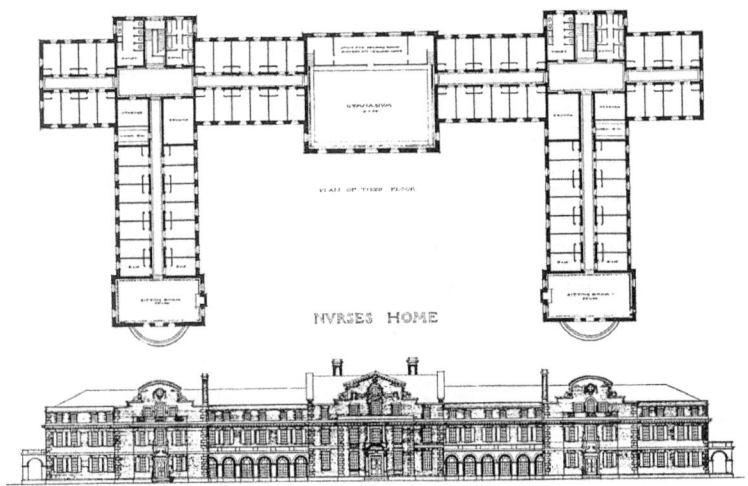

FIGS. 547-48—WASHINGTON. PLAN AND ELEVATION. NURSES' HOME, HOSPITAL FOR THE DISTRICT OF COLUMBIA

Designed by Frank Miles Day and Brother. (From the Brickbuilder, 1902.)

FIGS. 549-50—BOSTON. EVANS GALLERY AND GENERAL PLAN, BOSTON MUSEUM OF FINE ARTS

Designed by Guy Lowell. The view of the new Evans wing is a graphic demonstration of the incongruity of setting which is likely to result when an architect does not have control over the vicinity of his building. Nothing could well be more dissonant with the firm refinement of the building than is the soft scrambled vegetation along the pond-shore, completely negating that expression of firm support which is the first essential of a monumental setting.

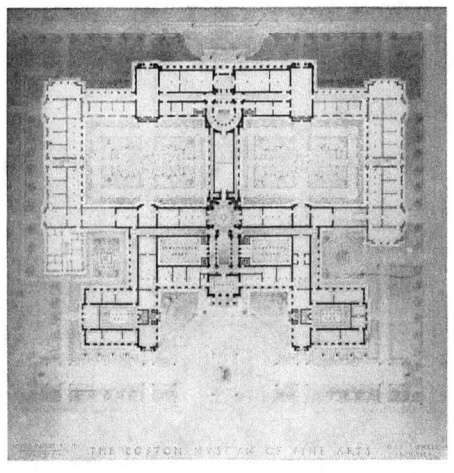

FIG. 551—CAMBRIDGE. HARVARD FRESHMAN DORMITORIES. GORE HALL

FIG. 552—CAMBRIDGE. GORE HALL

FIG. 553—CAMBRIDGE. SMITH HALLS

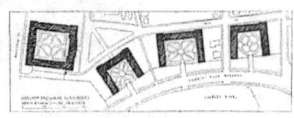

FIG. 554—CAMBRIDGE. KEY PLAN
OF THE HARVARD FRESHMAN
DORMITORIES

This group, which is illustrated in Figs. 551-
53 and 556, was designed by Shepley, Rutan,
and Coolidge. Smith Halls make up the
quad at the left side of the plan; Gore Hall is
the second from the right.

FIG. 555—CHINO, CALIF. GRAMMAR SCHOOL.   Designed by Withey and Davis.

FIG. 556—CAMBRIDGE. THE QUADRANGLE OF SMITH HALLS

FIG. 556A—LOS ANGELES. OCCIDENTAL COLLEGE. By Myron Hunt.

FIG. 557—OAKLAND. EMERSON SCHOOL   Designed by John J. Donovan and John Galen Howard.

FIG. 558—PASADENA. POLYTECHNIC ELEMENTARY SCHOOL   Designed by Myron Hunt and Elmer Grey.

FIG. 559—ALBANY. NEW YORK STATE NORMAL SCHOOL
Albert R. Ross, architect; George L. Heins and Franklin B. Ware, state architects.

FIG. 560—PHILADELPHIA. INDEPENDENCE HALL FROM THE SQUARE

FIG. 561—PHILADELPHIA. INDEPENDENCE HALL. CHESTNUT STREET FRONT

FIG. 562—PHILADELPHIA, INDEPENDENCE HALL

FIG. 563—INDEPEN-
DENCE HALL

(Figs. 560-63 from
Ware's "Georgian Pe-
riod.")

American Civic Centers

The group of buildings developed in connection with Independence Hall (Figs. 560-63) is another example of the capacity for extension which may inhere in a formal design. This group could with advantage be extended considerably by continuing the subsidiary buildings around the entire Independence Square thereby creating a framed plaza and at least some visual protection against the rapid changes which are transforming the old frame of the plaza from low Colonial residences of a rather uniform appearance into overpowering and diverging masses of huge business structures.

Achievements like the Independence Hall group, the University of Virginia, or the Pennsylvania Hospital should have furnished fine precedents for the dignified design and grouping of public buildings. The most unassuming American farm group (Figs. 565-9), reflecting in its simplicity the qualities of the Colonial period, has a truly civic stateliness. But it took time before the significance of the great Colonial precedent was fully appreciated, and the American movement for "civic centers" got its first impetus from the success of the world's fairs. The Exposition of 1893 is largely responsible for the revision of the plan of Washington by the Burnham commission. It also brought about the revision and extension of the plan for Manila (Fig. 1036), enriching it with a proposal for a civic center and several other groups of public buildings laid out around courts following the victorious ideas of 1893.

The same ideas, the ephemeral realization of which had vanished with the destruction of the Chicago Fair, found permanent expression in the civic center group of Cleveland (Figs. 586-7). The main body of thought ruling the design of the group plan for the public buildings of Cleveland, as well as of other plans inspired by it, is well expressed in the words of the Board of Supervision for Public Buildings and Grounds quoted in the caption to Fig. 586.

Following similar ideas civic centers were designed for many American cities, some of the finest of which are illustrated in these pages. Some, like the one originally proposed for Denver (Figs. 607-8), remain unexecuted, while others such as the fine group in Springfield, Mass. (Fig. 593), and the much more ambitious plaza in San Francisco (Fig. 592), are realized or well under way. In some instances, as in the first proposal for St. Louis, (Fig. 590), the achievement of the plan is largely geometrical, while in cases like the proposal for Seattle (Fig. 581) the effort to apply the new ideas produced singular results.

More recently and especially since the success of the Californian fairs civic designers have returned to the appreciation of local traditional art in the development of public groups but except in educational and hospital buildings the use of the Georgian in the east and the Spanish Colonial in the west is only slowly making headway when it comes to the design of groups of considerable size.

All the groups of public buildings mentioned so far avoid high buildings except in the shape of ornamental domes and towers, following also in this respect the example of the world's fairs, the Beaux-Arts teachings and the European examples which were back of the design of the fairs. The three-storied building was practically standard height for all European plazas. This standard had its justification not only in esthetic intentions and in technical limitations before the time of steel construction and elevators but also in the court etiquette of pre-revolutionary times according to which the king was housed in the second story and wanted nobody above his head. It was considered as a matter of course that the remainder of a castle or its setting could not be higher than the central abode of the king. As every gentleman and especially every nouveau-riche carefully imitated the example set by the king, two high stories for the main buildings, corresponding to three ordinary stories or less in the subsidiary buildings, became a generally accepted height for monumental purposes except the churches. The Colonial builders in America built under the same technical conditions and fine compositions such as the Independence Hall, Washington's Mount Vernon, the University of Virginia, and the United States Capitol could not be anything but low buildings.

However much the modern designer of plazas and civic centers can learn from eighteenth century precedent, his problem is curiously complicated by the possibilities — for good and evil — of the newly evolved manystoried building and by new social ideas. Modern city planners in America have suggested sticking to the height accepted in Europe in civic center design. Facing the disorder resulting from uncontrolled skyscraper building the school of city planners headed by the late Daniel H. Burnham proposed to distinguish public buildings of monumental character not by making them high, but by making

The Old Rochester Market; now destroyed.

FIG. 564—ROCHESTER. THE OLD MARKET

(From Ware's "Georgian Period.")

FIG. 565—LOCUST VALLEY, L. I. FARM BUILDINGS OF
GLENN STEWART, ESQ.

Designed by Alfred Hopkins.

FIG. 566—EAST NORWICH. CAMPBELL FARM GROUP

See plan below.

FIG. 567—EAST NORWICH. CAMPBELL FARM GROUP

See plan below.

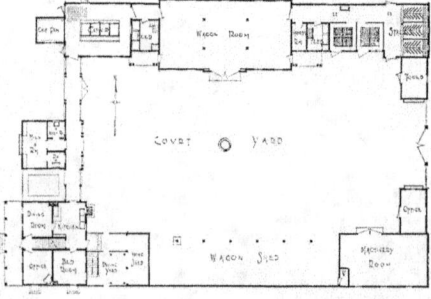

Lay-out of Farm Group for O. A. Campbell, Esq., at East Norwich, L. I.

FIG. 568

Designed by James W. O'Connor. (From the Architectural
Review, 1920.)

them low. They suggest letting a public building of
monumental character be surrounded by commercial
buildings, rising much higher than the monumental building. They are satisfied to let such public buildings as
demand the ordinary accommodations of an office building be absorbed into the mass of high commercial down-
town buildings, and believe that there will be left enough
public buildings which "are still obeying in their expression the tendency to more formal and architectural
lines"; these "cannot vie in vertical mass with commercial buildings and must, by reason of their function, find
distinction by strength of design in contrast to their
surroundings" from which evidently not much strength
of design is expected. The monumental buildings would
stand independent, without physical connection with the
surrounding skyscrapers, which are to act as a frame.

This idea, which properly developed may have a great
future, finds expression in the design for the Grant Park
group in Chicago ("Plaza on Michigan Avenue") where
buildings of the low "monumental" two-stories-and-attic
type, (Marshall Field Museum, Art Institute, and Library) are grouped in front of an array of twenty-story skyscrapers along the west side of Michigan Avenue. The
design made by the same artists for the Civic Center of
Chicago (Figs. 579-80) follows a different idea. As it is
proposed to locate this Civic Center about a mile away
from the lake, and thus well outside the present business district, it is surrounded by a uniform frame of only
moderately high skyscrapers. The minor buildings of
the civic group keep well below the frame afforded by the
commercial buildings and seek "distinction by strength
of design in contrast to their surroundings", while the
main building of the group, a dome high as St. Peter's,
rises well above everything and therefore is to find distinction not only by strength of design but also by domination of outline. The idea of achieving domination of
outline by a skyscraper for office purposes instead of a
purely ornamental dome is not accepted, evidently on the
assumption that such a skyscraper is not a worthy object
of central location.

The open area in front of the high domed building
may be calculated to measure over fourteen acres. As
design and height of the domed building invite a comparison with St. Peter's in Rome it may be interesting to
remember that the oval area (Piazza obliqua) in front of
St. Peter's measures a little less than five acres, to
which another three acres are added by the "Piazza
retta" (the keystone-shaped area in front of the church),
which means that the open area in front of the proposed
Chicago dome is almost twice the size of the Piazza of
St. Peter's. In comparing these sizes it ought to be
further remembered however that the Roman plaza is
closely framed and that the width of the Piazza retta does
not exceed the width of the church façade, which is specially broadened out. The plaza proposed in front of the
Chicago dome is not enclosed but to its large area wide
expanses are added by eight wide radial streets coming
in from all sides and by a mall on axis about 300 feet wide;
also there are great openings on both sides of the façade.

It is doubtful whether areas of such magnitude and
so loosely framed can be esthetically dominated by placing on one side a domed structure even if it should grow
to what looks at present like a maximum size, the height
of St. Peter's in Rome. It seems probable that esthetic
domination of such an enormous expanse could be secured
with less difficulty if, first, the frame were tightened;
second, if the main building were put in the center instead of at one side; and third, if instead of the ornamental
dome from 300 to 500 feet high a beautiful and useful
office tower of about twice the height were introduced. St.
Peter's measures 470 feet, a hundred feet less than the
New York Municipal Building (to top of figure), while
the national capitol measures only 307 feet from the es-

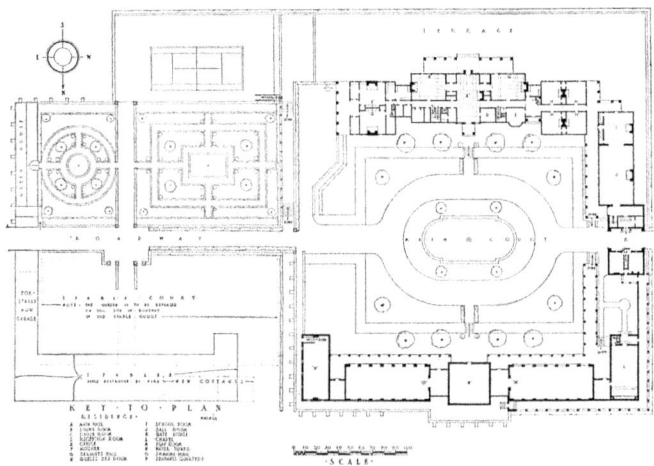

FIG. 569—WHEATLEY HILLS, L. I. ESTATE OF E. D. MORGAN
(From the Monograph of the work of McKim, Mead, and White.)

planade to the top of the crowning figure. The domed state capitol in Madison measures only 300 feet (cost $7,200,000, without furnishings; its office space is given as 180,000 square feet exclusive of corridors and storage room). The New York Municipal Building is stated to measure 539 feet (cost $12,000,000, office space 648,000 square feet), Woolworth Building 793 feet (cost $14,000,000, office space 40 acres), the City Hall in Oakland, Calif., 334 feet (cost of building $1,893,688, office space 90,000 square feet).

All will depend, it seems, on whether towers can be made as beautiful as domes. Everyone will have to admit that achievements like the Municipal Building in New York (see Frontispiece), the spire of the Woolworth Building (Fig. 617), the Boston Customhouse (500 feet high; Fig. 589), the City Hall in Oakland (Fig. 591), and proposals like those for the Nebraska capitol (Fig. 603) and others are very promising. A clever designer may even be able to find ways in which middle-sized cities can start with a tower planned so that tiers of additional stories could be added subsequently with a considerable increase of impressiveness. Sufficient office space would be assured for all future needs.

The designer of a civic center would of course be specially anxious to have the façades of the skyscrapers forming part of his scheme detailed in such a way as to make their members, from the largest colonnade to the smallest mullion, esthetically effective for the spectator standing at various distances, be it in the court of honor or in the approaches. It is beyond the field assigned to this book, but would be very interesting, to go into a discussion of the optical and esthetic problems involved. But a word may be permitted about one of the most important methods of esthetically organizing the huge masses for the manipulation of which the American architect is setting the precedent, this method being the grouping of windows and the spaces between them into large, easily recognizable and impressive units. The grouping of windows is less difficult to-day than it was in the time of Michelangelo, Perrault, and Gabriel, who had to hide them behind colonnades or block them entirely. To-day groups of windows can be raised into the air far away from the over-critical eye, and steel construction and dark material introduced for subsidiary floors make disturbing horizontal members inconspicuous next to strongly visible vertical members. It is esthetically possible especially in the upper stories of a building of great height,

to have, not only two, but three or more stories merge into one and have them appear as one order, one arcade or what appears from below like a loggia. Such grouping of windows however has been condemned as unjustifiable because of its being inexpressive of the interior arrangement of the building. No doubt the facilities of modern building materials are apt to be abused by the indiscriminate designer. As he places rooms not only in the space above the capitals but also underneath the base, he finds that the height of his columns is limited only by the veto of the real estate man who objects to obscuring too much window area by increasing beyond seven feet the diameter of the enormous shafts which can serve at best for ventilation purposes or possibly as smoke conductors or for holding washrooms; though the client who accepts the columns as something unavoidable prefers the rooms in the frieze and in the podium because

FIG. 570—BALTIMORE. LAFAYETTE MONUMENT IN WASHINGTON PLACE SOUTH

Part of a design by Carrere and Hastings for revision of the approaches to the late Colonial monument to Washington. The ground rises towards the monument in each part of the cross-shaped "square." There is a limitation upon the height of abutting buildings, but, as the drawing demonstrates, a mere limitation is not a successful way to produce uniformity. (From the American Architect, 1918.)

FIG. 571—NEW YORK. APARTMENT HOUSE
An example of the horizontal subdivision of a high building, a principle capable of varied use in plaza and street design. (From the Monograph of the work of McKim, Mead, and White.)

they are better lighted. Frederick the Great, who was himself responsible for some of the fine designs produced under his reign, on principle objected against columns being placed in front of rooms to be used for habitation or work as he disliked "the feeling of being behind the bars of a cage". There have recently been raised, in front of rooms for office use, colonnades of twice the height of Perrault's Louvre colonnade and in situations where they are to be seen at best from the other side of a medium wide street, i. e. only at a distance equal to their height or even less. The attempt to tuck away five or more office floors behind this gigantic screen of columns is thus made close to one's eyes and produces the unpleasant effect of big motive and small motive contradicting each other. As a result the first appears as a sham and the second as a makeshift.

In condemning such grotesqueness however, emphasis must be placed purely on the esthetic and practical side and not on the failure of "expressiveness". It is interesting to note how the term has changed under which the objections against the grouping of windows into impressive units have been made. While Perrault's critics, representing the conservative French Academy, objected in the name of precedent, to-day the critics opposing the decoration of façades by motives not directly expressive of the interior distribution and size of rooms like to think of themselves as progressives and decry as academical the artist who holds different ideas.

To accept such an argument would be equivalent to asserting that it is unjustifiable to give harmony to a plaza or a street by pulling together, horizontally, different structures to appear as members of one façade as it was done for instance at the Place Vendôme in Paris (Figs. 328-31) where the façades were originally constructed independently and the land behind them afterwards sold by the foot to such persons as were willing to

build and guarantee the preservation of the façades. Robert Adam's design for Fitzroy Square, London, (Fig. 576) and many similar examples show unified façades.

It will be worth while to follow a little more closely the line of argument in favor of "structural expressiveness" as applied to horizontal grouping, because a highly important principle affecting plaza and street design vertically and horizontally is affected. In his design for Fitzroy Square, Robert Adam, having the control over the whole length, used different houses with separate entrances to make up one long balanced façade. The brothers Adam, as their own speculation, developed the long Adelphi Terrace (Figs. 377-8) (named after them, "adelphi" meaning "brothers"), and, of course, developed it as one balanced design irrespective of the fact that behind this harmonious façade are distributed many different apartments, the tenants of which may be anything but in harmony with each other. The street of Muenster (Fig. 734) which John Ruskin—who surely believed in sincerity and expressiveness — praised so highly, and many similar streets in medieval and Renaissance times, were built up by individuals independent of each other but having enough civic sense, i. e. common tradition, harmonious inclination and sense of solidarity to use the same motive and produce, taken altogether, a harmonious façade to which in a certain sense one can apply Wren's description of a portico: "The longer the more beautiful". Similar cases of harmonious street development are illustrated by the two examples from Baltimore shown in Figs. 572-3 and by many others shown in the chapter on streets. In street design, as long as no approach to a public building and its setting has to be thought of, a mere general harmony of the façades may be entirely satisfactory especially because the walls of a street are not seen at right angles, but only from the other side of the street, which means mainly at very sharp angles. But when it comes to the architectural development of a wide plaza and the framing of a prominent building it becomes desirable to group the units into rhythmical members of the visible ensemble, for instance by giving stronger development to the corners and centers of blocks. The justification of this grouping simply lies in the fact that it is more beautiful. This grouping of houses into units may or may not be expressive of the immediate workaday attitude of mind of the people living and working behind the unified façades, but it strongly expresses that same civic pride which makes them willing to put on their best clothes, march in parades, advertise the city and, — if necessary — make sacrifices for worthy causes. If these façades are not entirely expressive of the smaller needs of their owners they are expressive of their location near an important building and of their own important functions in the civic center scheme.

If it is thus justifiable and necessary to organize low façades horizontally to give them their due place in a beautiful ensemble, it is hard to see why it should not be equally justifiable to organize high façades vertically, subdividing rhythmically into pleasing parts of a beautiful scheme what otherwise would be interminable walls perforated by monotonous rows of similar office windows. In the Greek temple very tall columns, suitable for long distance views, were used at the outside, where they were likely to be seen from afar; while two superimposed orders of small columns were used inside, where inspection from nearby and economy of space was to be provided for. In a similar way a skyscraper has to express its size and esthetic purpose in a different way on the outside from what is practical and esthetic for interior purposes. It is interesting to remember in this connection that Michelangelo's introduction of the colossal order into modern architecture was not the only concession this great architect made to civic art. He also designed the beautiful cornice which crowns so successfully Palazzo Farnese. This cornice is much larger than

FIGS. 572, 573—BALTIMORE

Two examples of pairs of houses unified by architectural treatment, in one case by perfect symmetry and in the other by harmony of style and by the carrying through of horizontal members.

FIG. 574—LONDON. ADELPHI BUILDINGS. THE UPPER TERRACE ALONG THE THAMES

FIG. 575—LONDON. SCHEME FOR REBUILDING LINCOLN'S INN, BY ROBERT ADAM

Lincoln's Inn is one of the groups of buildings where members of the legal profession live or have their offices. The grounds bound one side of the large square, Lincoln's Inn Fields. Adam planned to make the square a huge forecourt for the new buildings of the Inn. If he had carried through the whole plan, including the treatment of the buildings around the square and the design of the square itself he would certainly have made a spectacularly fine thing of it. The modeling of the Inn façade had to be very emphatic in order to distinguish it from the other sides of the square.

FIG. 576—LONDON. FITZROY SQUARE

A row of private houses, designed by Robert Adam.

FIGS. 577-78—LONDON. THE ADELPHI BUILDINGS FROM THE THAMES

The brothers Adam designed and built this row of houses as a commercial venture. The houses fronted on a terrace (see Fig. 574) which was built over an arcaded wharf back of which were warehouses and from which streets led to the Strand. In the long façade each separate house is three windows wide. The Adelphi buildings were destroyed when the Victoria Embankment was built, but very similar river-front treatments can be seen in various European cities. (From the Works of Architecture of Robert and James Adam.)

FIG. 580—CHICAGO. THE CIVIC CENTER

the one which Sangallo, the designer of the remainder of the Palace had conceived. It is a cornice crowning not the upper story only but measuring over eleven feet, that is, three times the height of the string-courses and is proportioned to the development of the piazza in front of the palace (Fig. 158). In a similar way Michelangelo also went beyond Bramante when designing the finally executed dome for St. Peter's. Keeping in mind that the dome would be seen at entirely different angles from the interior than from the exterior, he gave different shapes to the interior and exterior shells, stilting the latter high enough to overcome the unavoidable perspective diminution.

The exterior of a building is part of the street or of the plaza it faces and has to submit to their esthetic and optical laws, and these laws are determined much less by the interior requirements of the building than by the

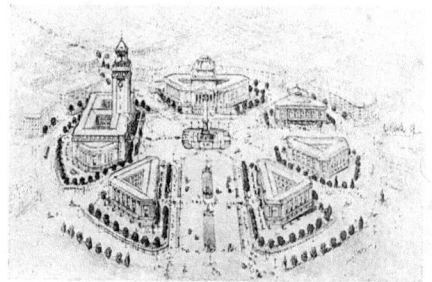

FIG. 579—CHICAGO. PLAN OF CIVIC CENTER
AND GRANT PARK

From the "Plan of Chicago" prepared under the direction of the Chicago Commercial Club by Daniel H. Burnham and Edward H. Bennett.

FIG. 581—A CIVIC CENTER PROPOSAL

The ultimate result of the application of the principle that a civic center is a magnified street-intersection and that the buildings can be fitted into any odd shapes which the streets happen to leave.

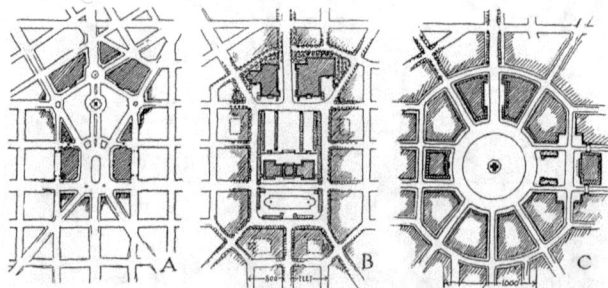

FIGS. 582-84—THREE CIVIC CENTERS

Sketch A is from a proposal recently submitted to an American city, providing for a civic group and several new streets, all but one of the radials being proposed. This plan exhibits all the difficulties which arise when diagonals are laid upon a grid without adjustments in the gridiron streets and shows how those difficulties are emphasized by the effort to set a group of monumental buildings around such an intersection. Sketches B and C suggest ways of avoiding these difficulties by reducing the number of acute angles and by creating fewer and more widely separated traffic breaks. In each case a large traffic circuit is indicated, to relieve the inner circuit. The circular plaza was suggested by the eighteenth century French plans shown on p. 78 and the following pages.

FIG. 585—CIVIC CENTER ON A RADIAL

The gridiron street plan has been adjusted to the radial avenue. Some of the intercepted streets are given terminal features. The group is definitely related to the avenue without interrupting it, and it is protected from inharmonious neighbors by including the four contact points in the design.

FIG. 586—CLEVELAND. CIVIC CENTER

Designed by Burnham, Carrere, and Brunner, the "Group Plan Commission" of 1902, who, in their report, stated the basic principle of their work in the following passage:

"It needs no argument to prove that in such a composition as this, uniformity of architecture is of first importance, and that the highest type of beauty can only be assured by the use of one sort of architecture. This was the lesson taught by the Court of Honor of the World's Fair of 1893, in Chicago; a lesson which has deeply impressed itself on the minds of the people of the entire country, and which is bearing much good fruit.

"The Commission recommends that the designs of all the buildings of this group plan should be derived from the historic motives of the classic architecture of Rome; that one material should be used throughout and that a uniform scale of architecture should be maintained in their design. The cornice line of the principal buildings should be uniform in height, and the general mass and height of all the buildings on the east and west of the Mall should be the same; in fact, these buildings should be of the same design and as uniform as possible.

"It must be remembered that the architectural value of these buildings does not alone lie in their immediate effect upon the beholder, but much more in their permanent influence on all building operations of the city. An example of order, system and reserve, such as is possible here, will be for Cleveland what the Court of Honor of '93 was for the entire country, and the influence will be felt in all subsequent building operations, both public and private.

"Your Commission believes that all the buildings erected by the city should have a distinguishing character; that there is not a gain, but a distinct loss in allowing the use of unrelated styles, or no styles, in schools, fire, police and hospital buildings; that it would be much better to hold the designing within certain lines for these buildings, and that uniform architecture be maintained for each function, which shall make

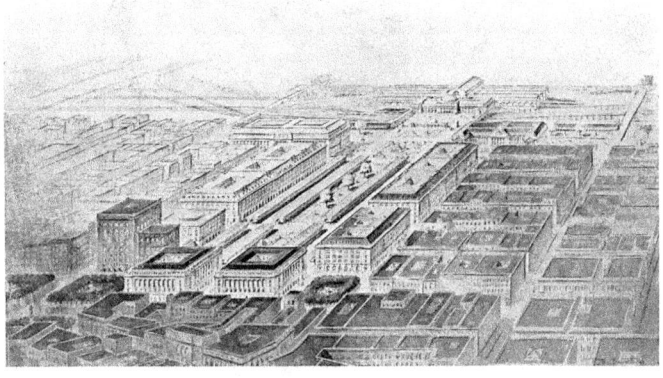

it recognizable at first glance. The jumble of buildings that surround us in our new cities contributes nothing valuable to life; on the contrary, it sadly disturbs our peacefulness and destroys that repose within us which is the true basis of all contentment. Let the public authorities, therefore, set an example of simplicity and uniformity, not necessarily producing monotony, but on the contrary resulting in beautiful designs entirely harmonious with each other."

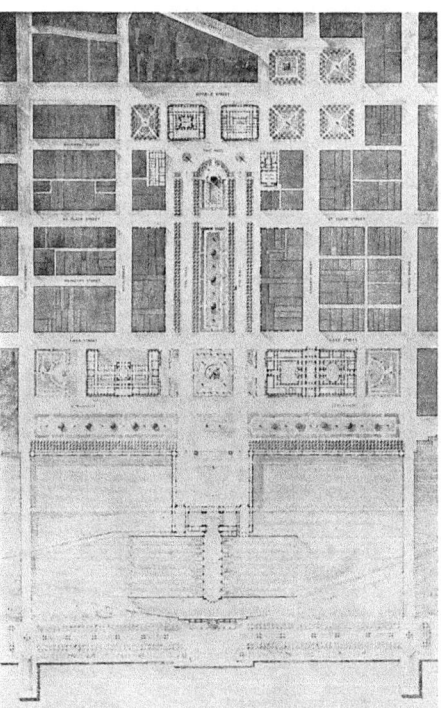

FIG. 587—CLEVELAND. PLAN OF CIVIC CENTER

FIG. 588—SPOTLESS-TOWN. CIVIC CENTER

Though it is with reluctance that one ventures to criticize a plan so optimistically sent forth, it might be suggested that if the drive to the town hall had been put at the rear, a more dignified "footing" for the hall could have been arranged and better provisions for traffic and parking. The quiet breadth of the common is the best feature of the plan, which is from an article by Albert Kelsey in the "town hall series", Brickbuilder, 1902.

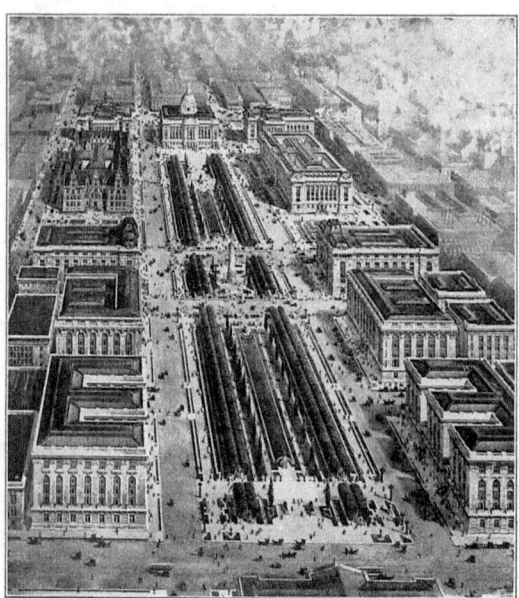

FIG. 590—ST. LOUIS. CIVIC CENTER
Designed by J. L. Mauran, Wm. S. Eames, and A. B. Groves.

FIG. 589—BOSTON. CUSTOM HOUSE

Designed by Peabody and Stearns. The old Custom House serves as the base for the new tower, five hundred feet high. The building is the conspicuous feature in the view of Boston as one comes into the harbor. (Photograph by A. H. Folsom.)

size of the street or plaza and by the relations of reciprocity established between major and minor buildings in the immediate neighborhood.

The height of the central building of a civic group is a determining factor not only in the design for the plaza immediately in front of the building, but it also determines the distances from which the central building can be a satisfactory point of vista in street design. These important aspects will be touched upon in the chapter on streets.

Whatever attitude one may take to the question of whether the central building should or should not be an office tower, the study of the finest settings created in great periods for great buildings compels the conclusion that the frame of a plaza needs no less attention than the monumental building for which the plaza is meant to be the setting. This is as true when the monument is to stand in the plaza as when it is to be part of the framing members of the plaza. As the result of such a study (for which there is ample material in this book)

FIG. 591—OAKLAND. THE CITY HALL.
Designed by Palmer, Hornbostel, and Jones.

one might conclude that, when it comes to schemes of importance, it is essential that the architect's clients secure for him control over the buildings surrounding the monuments (especially public buildings) the impressiveness of which is meant to be a value to the community. The control can result from either giving public character to the buildings surrounding the civic center plaza, or by finding some way to subject the height and design of the private or commercial structures surrounding the civic center group to restrictions which make a harmonious development obligatory. The most divergent procedures to reach similar ends have been followed in Paris and in innumerable European cities. Either the façades were erected, as in the case of Place Vendôme, without houses behind them and sold afterwards by the running foot, or sample houses were built or sample plans furnished which in definite locations were to be followed. It is only a question of time when similar expedients will be made possible in America after it has once been understood that it is essential to do so in order to secure the full value of the large investment connected with monumental building. It is naive to assume that "such things can be done in Europe but not in America" or that such things met any less resistance in Europe than they are apt to meet in America. As a humorous example one may refer to the considerable amount of ill will encountered in Berlin, when in the eighteenth century her rulers monumentalized the main streets of the capital by forcibly, and at their own expense, replacing old and inharmonious by new and harmonious houses having one additional story. The owners of the property presented with new houses as free gifts felt terribly abused. One might surmise that a similar Prussian method would find more appreciation with American business men; at any rate a financial contribution made by the city or state to private owners building in the immediate neighborhood of public buildings would go far toward inducing them to submit to a harmonious scheme for the architecture around the civic center. In other cases the city or a public spirited organization of interested citizens could buy the necessary land and resell it with such restrictions

FIG. 592—SAN FRANCISCO. CIVIC CENTER

Designed in 1912 by John Galen Howard, Frederick H. Meyer, and John Reid, Jr. This plan
has the virtue of not trying to cover too large an area, seeking instead to master as completely as possible the space it marks out. The inclusion of the four corner buildings in the architectural control was a step in advance.

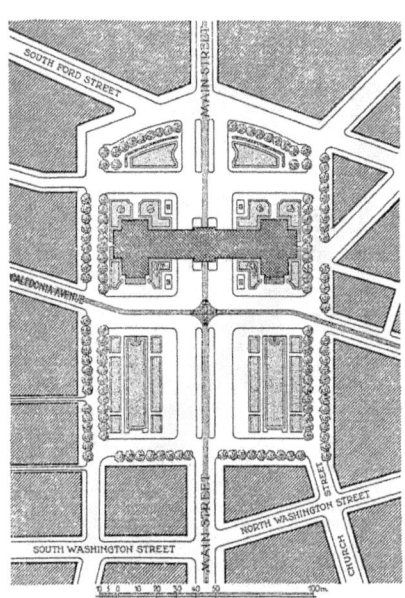

FIG. 594—ROCHESTER. PLAN OF PROPOSED CIVIC
CENTER

Designed by A. W. Brunner, F. L. Olmsted, and B. J.
Arnold. (From Gurlitt.)

FIG. 593—SPRINGFIELD, MASS. CIVIC CENTER
Designed by Pell and Corbett.

FIG. 595—ROCHESTER. PROPOSED CIVIC CENTER

as to guarantee suitable development. Many other methods are conceivable.

Unfortunately the American architect had generally to be satisfied to consider the piece of land given him as the location of a public building as something independent of the rest of the world. How much this is the case one can easily realize by looking at the numerous cases of projects for important buildings published without accompanying plans showing the definite relation between these monumental buildings and the buildings surrounding them; nothing indicates clearly for what situation the new building is designed, whether in order to be effective it requires a frame of five-story or of ten-story buildings. At best some "landscaping" is done around the building and even this is often of a casual or informal type. The assumption to which the architect evidently resigns himself is that his monument will be surrounded by the usual mixture of one story bank buildings, two-story tax-payers, ten-story to twenty-story office buildings and perhaps a few Gothic churches. Only gradually it is being recognized that a prominent building must either be large enough with its various wings, pavilions, and spacious inner courts to produce its own setting, at least for the most important features in the center (as for instance the Columbia Library is so firmly set by the other University buildings surrounding it) or it must control the archi-

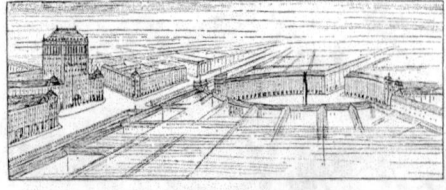

FIG. 598—BERLIN. PROPOSAL FOR A TOWER BUILDING

This is one of a large number of recent suggestions for the construction of tall buildings in Berlin. The designs are of course based upon American skyscrapers, with adaptations, especially in the treatment of the roofs, in the direction of German tradition. If a limited number of tower buildings are built they may well be a decided artistic asset to the now flat and uniform city. (From P. Wittig.)

tecture of a not inconsiderable area in the neighborhood. To think of a building independently of its situation is the death of civic art.

The design submitted by the firm of McKim, Mead, and White at the recent competition for the Nebraska capitol (Fig. 600) is an interesting effort to use the surrounding private buildings as a suitable setting for the capitol, while the design by Magonigle (Figs. 601-02) conceives of a group of public buildings sufficiently large to include a closed plaza in the center as a suitable setting for each of the surrounding buildings. (See also Fig. 599). The author of the winning design of the competition (Fig. 603), appreciating the practical and political difficulties which to-day are still in the way of every effort towards harmony, relied for effect—not upon the usual "monumental" building — but upon a tower high enough to hold its own, for some time at least, even against very uneven company. Yet even with skyscrapers as monumental central buildings, control of the neighborhood is highly desirable. This is by no means only a matter of good morals, though one should not disregard the criticism which has been directed by advocates of better building laws against the narrow and necessarily badly lighted courts in the office buildings shown by the heartless renderer of the perspective view of the proposed civic group for Cleveland (Fig. 586). The matter of building laws has also, of course, far-reaching esthetic bearings.

In this connection there is for the dignity of American civic centers and their approaches much to be hoped for from the successful development of the zoning movement, because zoning means the fixing of districts (of various sizes, often not more than a few blocks or streets) for each of which the most suitable maximum height and other characteristics of the type of buildings to be erected are determined by law. In Europe, especially in Germany where the zoning of cities has been carried to an extreme, zoning, with exclusion of buildings higher than five to seven stories, has produced very uniform sky lines but also great monotony. Energetic efforts are being made at present to break this monotony by skillful and sufficiently regulated use of skyscrapers.

In the United States on the other hand where the limitation of building heights has remained in its infancy skyscraper building has not only produced the wildest possible skylines but also very unsatisfactory conditions as far as air and sunlight are concerned. The zoning ordinance for New York, although it represents one of the most far-reaching city planning measures of all time, has come too late; the heights which had to be permitted for future building upon the highly capitalized land, together with the large amount of damage done before the ordinance came into existence, represent untold evil. So far as the esthetics are concerned the stepping back of the upper stories required by the ordinance promises very picturesque effects for future New York. If this picturesqueness could be domesticated and made to serve a large scheme embracing plazas and approaches to them, effects of unheard-of power could be achieved.

The idea of zoning represents a desire to abandon the wildcat individualism which is sure to transform every city block into a heterogeneous monstrosity. What zoning is supposed to do for the entire city must be supplemented by comprehensive plans for units at least the size of a city block, a necessity which may be demonstrated by the juxtaposition of four illustrations of two modern city blocks occupied by hotels (Figs. 609-10, 613, 615).

The esthetic control of larger areas should be contemplated when it comes to the setting of the civic centers of a city. The civic designer can conceive of a monumental building, say for instance of the domed type, surrounded by buildings which (like some of the constructions surrounding Grand Central Station in New York,

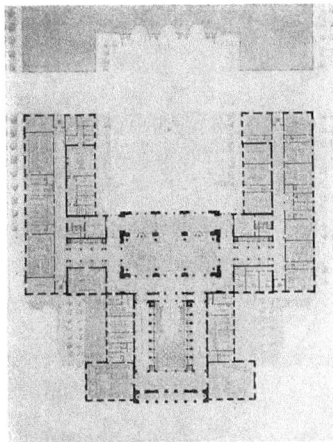

FIG. 599—NEW YORK. PLAN SUBMITTED IN
COMPETITION FOR THE NEW YORK
COURT HOUSE, 1913

By Carrere and Hastings. The plan is interesting
because it is very orderly and yet closely adapted to
an irregular plot of ground. The light-court is thrown
open and, along with the essential "respond" across
the street, forms a large plaza in ideal relation to the
main hall of the building.

FIG. 600—LINCOLN. NEBRASKA CAPITOL COMPETITION
Plot plan, submitted in the final stage, by McKim, Mead, and White.

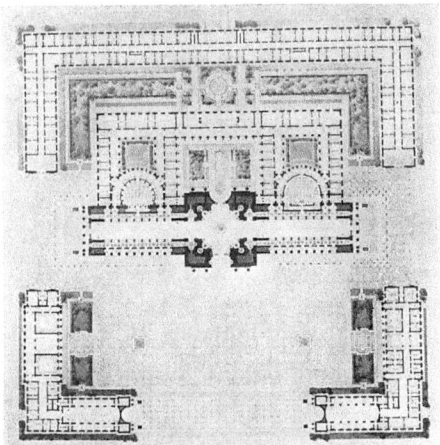

FIG. 603—LINCOLN. NEBRASKA CAPITOL COMPETITION

The winning design, submitted by B. G. Goodhue. The site consists
of four city blocks at the intersection of two important avenues. Mr.
Goodhue's plan is a cross within a square, 360 feet over all. The designs submitted by McKim, Mead, and White and by H. Van Buren
Magonigle fill pretty nearly the entire site, which is 720 feet square.
All of these designs show a remarkable independence of state capitol
traditions. The official and popular approval with which that freedom
has been received is perhaps due to the educational effect of the California fairs, which demonstrated the beauty of enclosed courts and
the superiority of a spreading "system" of buildings over a single isolated monument. (Figs. 600-603 from the Architectural Review, 1920.)

FIG. 601—LINCOLN. NEBRASKA CAPITOL COMPETITION

Main floor plan, submitted in the final stage, by H. Van Buren
Magonigle.

FIG. 602—LINCOLN. NEBRASKA CAPITOL COMPETITION
Principal elevation, design submitted by H. Van Buren Magonigle.

FIG. 604—OLYMPIA. WASHINGTON STATE CAPITOL COMPETITION
Elevation of the project by Howells and Stokes, of which Fig. 605 is the plan.

FIG. 605—OLYMPIA. WASHINGTON STATE CAPITOL
COMPETITION

Plan awarded second prize, designed by Howells and Stokes. (Figs.
604-606 from the American Architect, 1911.)

FIG. 606—OLYMPIA. WASHINGTON STATE CAPITOL
COMPETITION
Accepted design, by Wilder and White.

FIG. 607—DENVER. CIVIC CENTER
The plan of 1912, designed by Arnold W. Brunner and Frederick
Law Olmsted. (Figs. 607 and 608 from the Town Planning Review,
1913.)

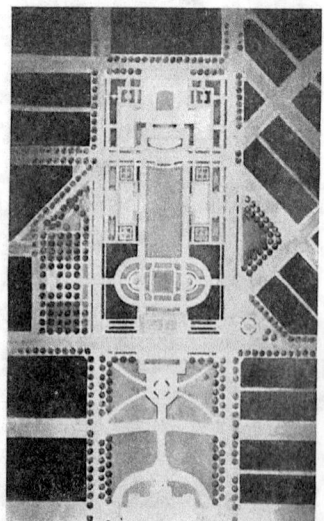

FIG. 608—DENVER. CIVIC CENTER

FIG. 609—OAKLAND. ENTRANCE COURT OF
HOTEL OAKLAND

Designed by Bliss and Faville. This is an excellent
example of modern planning without the use of dark and
ill-ventilated "light-courts." The hotel is two or three
blocks away from the principal business street, an economy in the cost of the site which made possible the liberal
planning. The court, above the first story, is much
deeper than it is shown in the block-plan below.

FIG. 610—OAKLAND. HOTEL OAKLAND. 14TH
STREET FRONT.

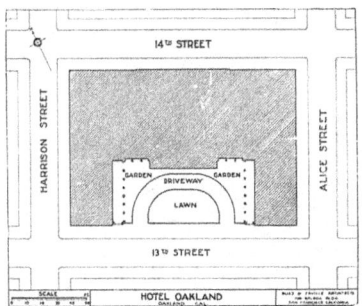

FIG. 613—OAKLAND. HOTEL OAKLAND. PLAN

FIG. 614—ZURICH. APPROACH TO CITY HALL.

A two-level scheme embodying some of the features incorporated in the civic center
study, Fig. 624. The new Zurich city hall had to be built in an area of traffic congestion
and topographic difficulty. The problem was solved by devising a system of bridges and
two-level passageways which permitted the civic group to be carried right over several
traffic streets. (From Staedtebau, 1915.)

FIG. 611—NEW YORK. PARK-MADISON BUILDING

Designed by Warren and Wetmore. A type of planning, induced by
the New York zoning law, which assures good light permanently to
every office, and to the street.

FIG. 612—SIENA.

The towers of medieval Siena suggest the ideal use
of skyscrapers,—spaced well apart and small in section.
They do not shade each other and they do not unduly
darken the streets and low buildings.

FIG. 615—SAN FRANCISCO. REAR OF A
FASHIONABLE HOTEL

An example of the unwise planning of high buildings.
The narrower light courts, quite insufficient at best, will
be extremely undesirable when a similar building is built
near by. The solution lies in the direction of free-
standing towers or of ample cut-in courts such as are
now becoming common in New York.

SCALE ⊢ 10 20 30 40 50 60 70 80 90 100 ⊢ FEET

THE MUNICIPAL BUILDING, NEW YORK CITY
WEST ELEVATION

FIG. 616.—(From the Monograph of the work of McKim, Mead, and White.) See frontispiece.

FIG. 617—NEW YORK.   COLONNADE OF THE MUNICIPAL BUILDING

Fig. 611 gives an instance) rise from the street line only a limited number of stories, and are then stepped back, and carried up with high shafts of less ornamental exterior. The daring effects thus produced would suggest San Grimiano and Siena (Fig. 612).

An attempt to visualize some of the various possibilities in modern civic design has been made in the plans shown in Figs. 618-33. The more simple use of the skyscraper in connection with lower buildings would be the surrounding or preceding it by simple courts formed by low buildings. The recent proposal to place a skyscraper in front of Belle-Alliance plaza in Berlin (Fig. 598) is a daring combination of a creation of the eighteenth century with an entirely modern product. The high building would correspond in the design to the Madeleine in relation to the Place de la Concorde.

One can conceive of civic centers surrounded by an amphitheater produced by areas of low construction in the immediate neighborhood and of higher and still higher buildings at regulated distances. Thus very interesting plazas of a terraced type — introducing a new dimension so to speak—unknown to European precedent, could concentrate the interest upon a civic building soaring from a low point in the center.

The intelligent use of the skyscraper in civic design will be America's most valuable contribution to civic art.

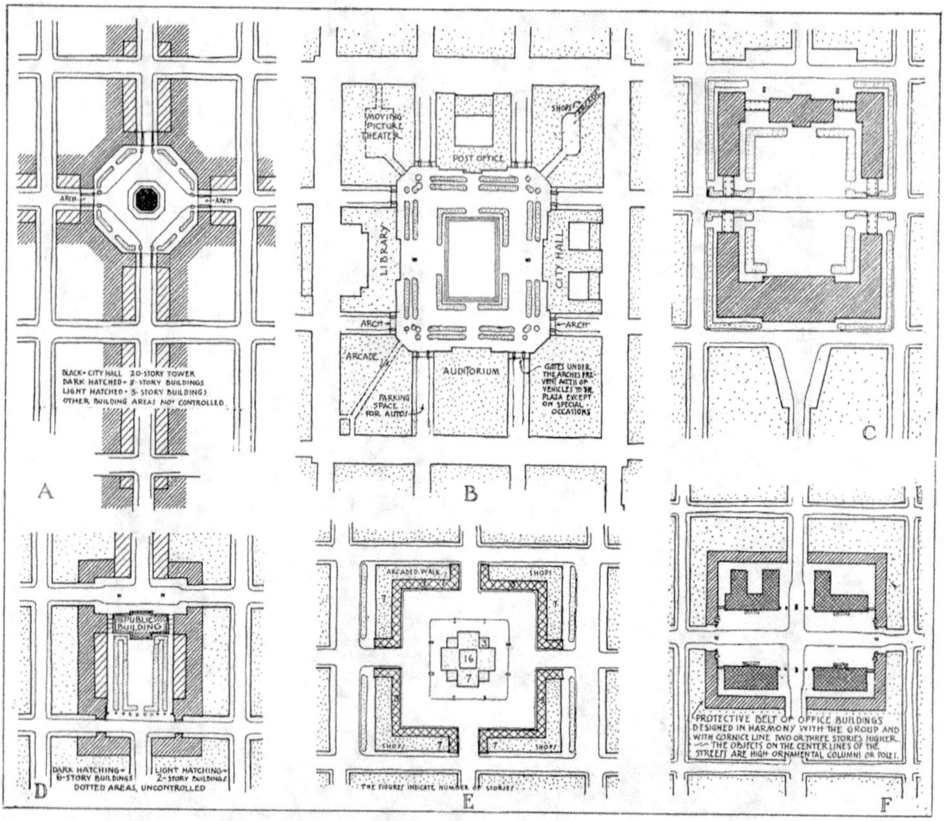

FIGS. 618-23—SIX PLANS FOR CIVIC CENTER GROUPS

These studies, by the authors, illustrate the adaptation of various Renaissance motives to modern conditions and gridiron street plans. For visualizations of these plans see Figs. 626-31.

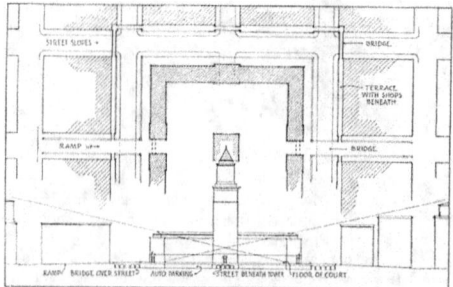

FIG. 624—CIVIC CENTER GROUP SURROUNDED BY A TRAFFIC CIRCLE AT A LOWER LEVEL

Regarding the two-level idea compare Fig. 614 . The intention is to raise the entire civic group upon a higher level surrounded by terraces. Since the interior court would be protected from traffic and by restricting buildings outside to heights below the lines of vision, the esthetic unit would remain uninterfered with. All traffic would stay on the lower level; the area under the civic group is reserved as parking space. The elevators of the tower would connect with the street beneath the tower and the court.

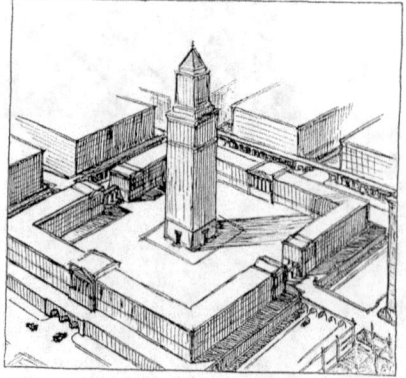

FIG. 625—CIVIC CENTER GROUP

View going with plan Fig. 624.

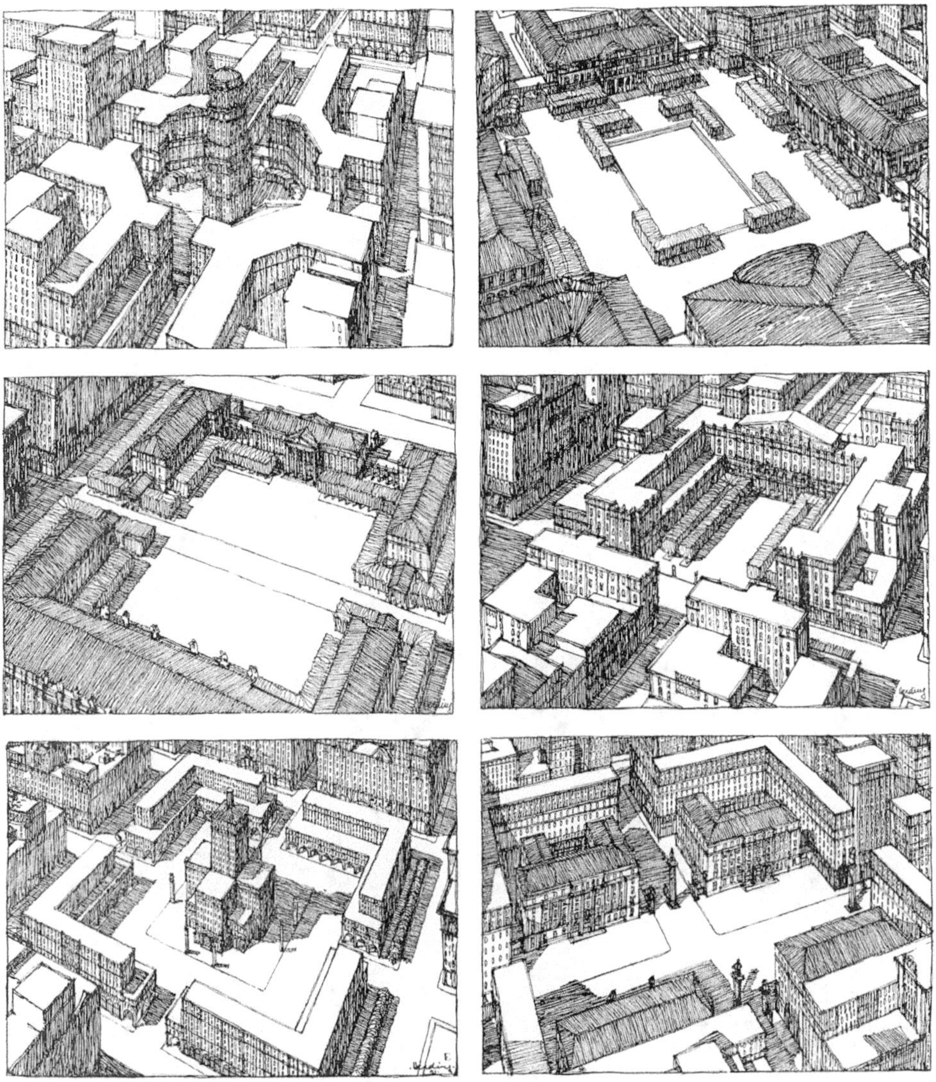

FIGS. 626-31—SIX CIVIC CENTER GROUPS

Bird's-eye views developed from the plans, Figs. 618-23. (From drawings by Franz Herding.)

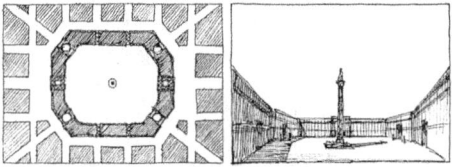

FIGS. 632-33—PLAN AND SKETCH FOR CIVIC GROUP

The buildings fronting on the small oblong forecourt plazas would have to be simple and uniform, thus subduing the little left-over blocks at the ends of the plazas. Or these blocks might be the sites of specially designed pavilions, which would have to be high enough to conceal the buildings back of them on the diagonal streets.

FIG. 636—SAN FRANCISCO. MARKET STREET

The impressive Spreckels Building dominates the vistas from O'Farrell, Kearney, and Third Streets. An effective contrast is produced by the lowness of the neighboring buildings.

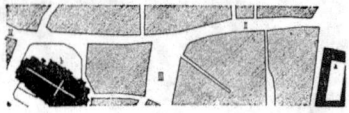

BRUGES

a. Halles. I. Grand'Place. III. Place Stevin.
b. Cathédrale Saint-Sauveur. II. Rue des Pierres. IV. Rue du Sablon.

FIG. 638—BRUGES

The cathedral appears on axis of a part of Rue des Pierres. See Fig. 638B. (Figs. 638-38B were added by Camille Martin to his translation of Camillo Sitte's book on civic art.)

FIG. 637—BOSTON. STREET SCENE

The Minot Building (Parker, Thomas, and Rice, architects) and adjoining buildings, showing a suggestion of uniform lower cornice lines. (From the American Architect, 1912.)

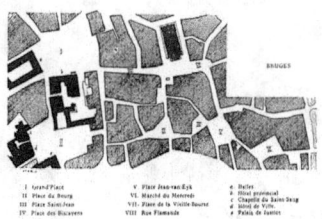

FIG. 638A—BRUGES. SECTION OF THE OLD CITY

Showing how closely the streets of medieval towns were related to plazas.

FIG. 638B—BRUGES
See Fig. 638.

FIG. 639—LUEBECK

FIG. 640—LANDSHUT. ST. MARTIN'S
CHURCH (From Theodore Fischer.)

FIG. 634—STREET VIEW ATTRIBUTED TO BRAMANTE

Colonnades on both sides; church on axis, seen through gate; two balancing towers to the right and left. (From Muentz.)

CHAPTER IV

Architectural Street Design

"There is indeed a charm and sacredness in street architecture which must be wanting to even that of the temple: it is a little thing for men to unite in the forms of a religious service, but it is much for them to unite, like true brethren, in the arts and offices of their daily lives". These words by John Ruskin describe an attitude towards street architecture which one does not find very often in modern America. There are, however, still fine old streets to be found in those sections of the country which were settled before 1850. There a quaint

FIG. 635—BOSTON STREET NEAR BEACON HILL

Figs. 636 to 640 are on p. 150.

harmony lives, an echo of a worthy period of building (Fig. 635). Sometimes in new streets a powerful new rhythm announces itself; for instance where skyscrapers happen to spring up at intervals over an otherwise low street (Figs. 636-37).

The artist sees in a street mainly its potentiality of being, like a plaza, a beautifully framed area with effective perspectives. It has been mentioned before how Camillo Sitte insisted that every street be an artistic unit. Such a unit was easily created in a medieval city or in the ideal city described by Palladio, where, "the principal streets ought to be so comparted that they may be straight and lead from the gates of the city in a direct line to the greatest and principal piazza. . . . . . Between the said principal piazza and any of the gates you please there ought to be one or more piazzas made somewhat less than the aforesaid principal piazza. . . . . The other streets especially the more noble of them, ought also to be made, not only to lead to the principal piazza, but also to the most remarkable temples, palaces, porticos, and other public fabrics".

The street unit therefore consisted of a houselined area between two terminal features, city gate and central plaza. What such streets looked like in plan may be gathered from the ideal plans by Vasari il Giovane, Scamozzi or Speckle (Figs. 983-87) or from the plans of little cities like Richelieu (Figs. 972, 974-75). The view of the king's Venery near Turin (Fig. 699) illustrates the appearance of such a street. The views of St. Francis Wood (Figs. 682-3) show an American application of

FIG. 641—ULM. OLD HOUSES AND CATHEDRAL SPIRE
From a drawing by John Ruskin.

the same principle. The strong Gothic and Renaissance gates with their deep shadowed arches formed effective terminating features on the one side and the plaza with some prominent public building was the objective on the other side.

The effective placing of terminal features is an important part of street design. In medieval cities which as a rule are supposed to have "grown" without a preconceived plan, it is almost uncanny how many times the curving streets manage to secure in their axis line, over the roofs of the low houses, glimpses of the highest monuments which often do not even stand in the same street from which the view is enjoyed (Figs. 638-42). The effect continually recurring in these cities of street views being terminated by a kink in the street is still appropriate to-day with otherwise straight streets, when one has to deal with minor streets, often even for purely practical reasons, because by such breaks of the straight line sharp intersections and awkward angles can be avoided. (See Wren's plan for London, Fig. 1028, also Sitte's recommendation Fig. 48P and collection of street intersections Fig. 728).

A Gothic church, with the deep shadows of its exterior, with the deep undercuttings of its gates and galleries, with the asymmetrical appearance of its side elevations and with the graceful curve of its apse and

FIG. 642—BOSTON. STATE HOUSE TERMINATING STREET VIEW

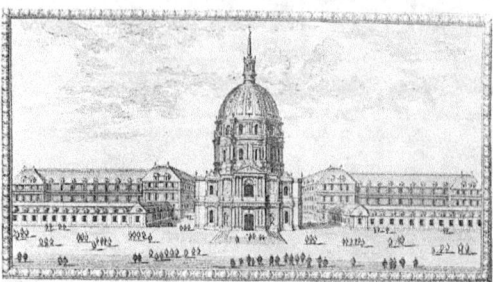

FIG. 645—PARIS. ST. LOUIS DES INVALIDES
(From J. F. Félibien, 1706). See Fig. 305.

FIG. 643—PARIS. AVENUE DE L'OPERA LOOKING TOWARD THE LOUVRE

FIG. 644—PARIS. AVENUE DE L'OPERA LOOKING TOWARD OPERA   Compare Fig. 304.

FIG. 646—LONDON. ST. PAUL'S CATHEDRAL
From an old photograph showing the dominance of the church over the surrounding buildings.

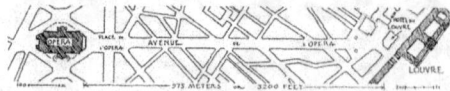

FIG. 644A—PARIS. AVENUE DE L'OPERA. PLAN

chapels, is peculiarly fit to be seen at an angle as it will be seen if it stands at the point where a street curves. The advantage of symmetry is seldom lost in these views as few Gothic churches, even in their front elevations, ever achieved symmetry however much their original designers had hoped for it and because modern designers of Gothic work as a rule accept the lack of symmetry as a virtue.

It seems that the Baroque designers, after the interlude of the pure Renaissance period with its preference for axial views of façades designed in a single plane, greatly enjoyed side views of their churches which, highly symmetrical as they were, rivalled in undercuttings and other fancifulness those of the late Gothic. The symmetry of these Baroque buildings being developed to the last possible limit, their designers did not want it to appear too obviously. The slightly sidewise entrances which Bernini planned for St. Peter's (see his studies Fig. 245) by closing the center are therefore in the opinion of as consummate a critic as Woelflin not accidentally caused by the existence of old buildings, but furnished, more than an unqualified axial approach could have done, that first sidewise aspect of a highly symmetrical setting which Bernini wanted in order to give a more intense en-

FIG. 647—PARIS. L'INSTITUT. FORMERLY MAZARIN'S PALACE
Designed by Levau, 1661. (From A. Maquet.)

FIG. 648—TURIN. THE SUPERGA
Designed by Juvara, 1718. (From Brinckmann.)

FIG. 649—PARIS. RUE SOUFFLOT
FIG. 650—PARIS. HOTEL DES INVALIDES AND PONT ALEXANDRE III

FIG. 651—PARIS. ECOLE DE DROIT.
Facing the Panthéon and Rue Soufflot. (From Brinckmann.)

FIG. 652—ROME. THE AMERICAN ACADEMY
Designed by McKim, Mead, and White. (From the Monograph.)

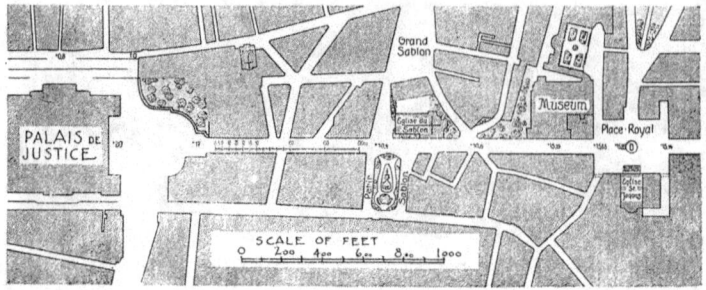

FIG. 654—BRUSSELS

For elevations showing profile of street see plan. (From Camillo Sitte.)

FIG. 653—BRUSSELS. RUE DE LA REGENCE

Plan (with elevation figures) going with Figs. 654 and 401. (From Gurlitt.)

joyment of this symmetry and invite the longing to advance and explore the mystery of the unrevealed. Similar effects were produced by the relation of the Piazza Navona to Bernini's church S. Agnese (Fig. 28) or by the sidewise flights of the Scala di Spagna (Fig. 685) or the off-center entrance-drives of Nymphenburg (Fig. 415) where an ornamental canal occupies the center of the grand avenue. It may be by a similar reasoning that one has to interpret for instance the location of the obelisk close to and on axis of the apse of Santa Maria Maggiore (Fig. 280) which otherwise would be hard to appreciate.

Slightly sidewise views of monumental buildings can be enjoyed also—and are in fact unavoidable—for the pedestrian on the sidewalk of a modern wide street, wherever such a monumental building stands as terminal feature on the axis of a street.

In designing such streets with terminal features one can again learn much from study of precedent. A consideration of typical examples will prove that during the best periods the direct shots at big buildings were not nearly so long as the nineteenth century designers thought it was wise to make them. It has already been pointed out that the street which lay originally in front of the Panthéon was less than half the length of the Rue Soufflot familiar to us (Fig. 355). The street design by Gabriel as a suitable shot at the Madeleine is one third the length Haussmann gave to the avenue shooting at Garnier's Opéra. Reference has already been made to the investigations carried out by Maertens who establishes three times the height of a building (corresponding to an angle of eighteen degrees) as about the maximum distance from which a prominent building is felt as a strong dominant feature of the view. Maertens points out that the building begins to merge into a silhouette effect with the neighborhood as this distance increases, unless

its roof line offers some surprising contrast of height against the structures in the neighborhood, whether they stand behind, beside, or in front of the building, which is meant to form the terminal feature. The effect resulting from high buildings standing behind the object to be looked at may be illustrated by the following examples. If in Paris one looks at the Hôtel du Louvre from the northern end of the Avenue de l'Opéra, the hotel, which closes the southern end of the avenue, in spite of its considerable mass, merges into a unit with the strong roof of the Louvre back of it (Fig. 643). A similar case of a large building losing its identity is the huge mass of the Berlin castle; if seen by an observer standing some distance back Unter den Linden the prominent feature is not the castle — for the setting of which the design was made — but the tower of the city hall which stands back of the castle and for which the castle appears to be something of substructure. A similar awkward effect is produced by the wonderful dome of the Hôtel des Invalides if seen from the northern end of the Place de la Concorde (i. e. about 4700 feet distant, Fig. 229); it appears behind the Chambre des Députés and the two

FIG. 656—VICENZA. THE STAGE OF PALLADIO'S TEATRO OLIMPICO

Through the Roman "scenae frons" views are opened into streets of tapering width representing constructed architectural perspectives. Built 1580. (From P. Klopfer.)

FIG. 655—PARIS. RUE DE TOURNON

Widening toward the Palace of the Luxembourg. For plan see Fig. 309. (From a drawing by Franz Herding.)

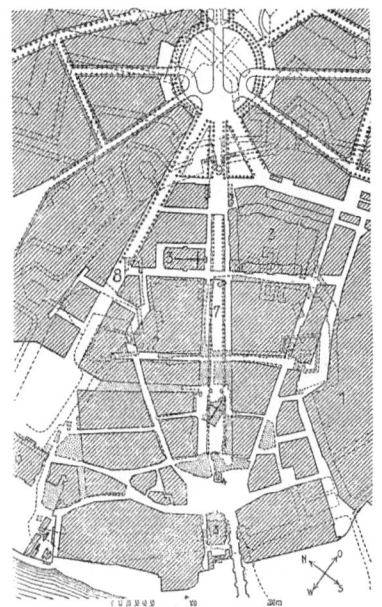

FIG. 659—ST. PAUL, MINN. REVISED PLAN FOR CAPITOL
APPROACH

Designed by Cass Gilbert. (From The Park International, 1921.)

FIG. 657—DRESDEN. NEUSTADT
(From Gurlitt.)

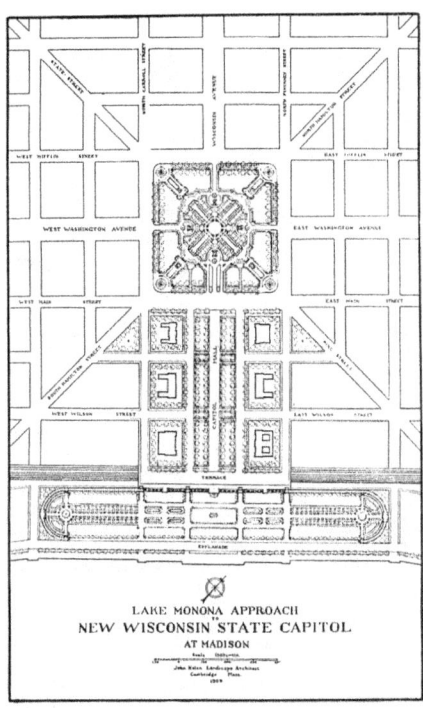

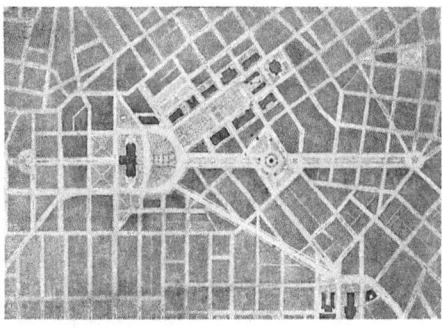

FIG. 658—ST. PAUL, MINNESOTA. "ORIGINAL IDEAL GROUP
PLAN"

Designed by Cass Gilbert.

FIG. 660—MADISON. PLAN OF ESPLANADE AND CAPITOL
MALL

Designed by John Nolen. Compare Figs. 661-63.

FIG. 661—MADISON. ESPLANADE AND CAPITOL MALL

From John Nolen's proposal for the replanning of Madison. Compare Figs 660 and 662-63.

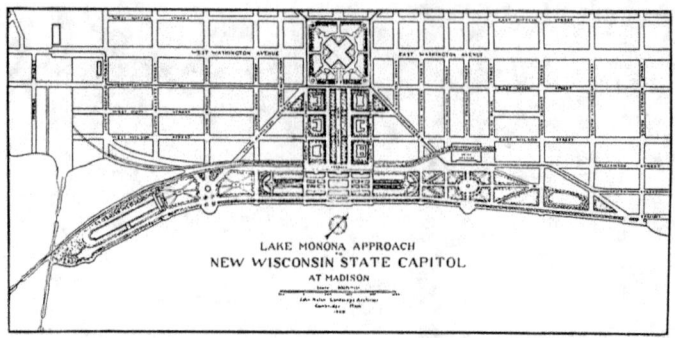

SECTION OF LAKE MONONA APPROACH TO NEW WISCONSIN STATE CAPITOL

FIGS. 662-63—MADISON. PLAN AND SECTION ACCOMPANYING FIGS. 660-61.

silhouettes merge in a way which disturbs the design of each. One may question if the effect would not be even less pleasant if the two buildings appeared to be on axis.

An example of the way a terminal building loses its value when there are high buildings at the side and in the foreground is furnished by the large opera house in Paris, at the northern end of the Avenue de l'Opéra. Seen from the southern end of the street (Fig. 644) it is near being swallowed up perspectively by the apartment houses on both sides of the avenue, above which much to the disgust of Charles Garnier its low half-dome and scenery loft rise only moderately.

Individual buildings are seen to advantage at such long distances only if they tower high above an otherwise unbroken skyline. A good example to the point is the dome of the Invalides seen from the Pont Alexandre III. The silhouette which presents itself is pure and easily interpreted and the high dome contrasts against long horizontals (compare Fig. 650 with Fig. 649). Thus cathedral towers are often seen to advantage from long distances as soaring high over their cities. Wren's St. Paul's was seen that way (Fig. 646) before modern building swamped it. Mazarin's "Institut" (Fig. 647) can still be enjoyed that way. On the other hand even so powerful a dome as the national capitol in Washington, if seen from the other end of Pennsylvania Avenue (at a distance of about 7000 feet) loses much of its impressiveness because it has to compete against high structures in the foreground which are enlarged by perspective.

This perspective danger is guarded against in the case of the Madeleine on axis of the Rue Royale (Figs. 225-32). As this is a most successful setting it is worth while to analyze the situation carefully. Rue Royale, including the big church terminating it was designed by Gabriel as a part of his comprehensive plan for his royal plaza, to-day called Place de la Concorde. Gabriel was thus fortunate enough to be in charge of the façades lining Rue Royale, and of course he took great care not only to keep them low but also to make them in every other respect suitable as an approach and setting to the ter-

minal building, the Madeleine. It is natural that Gabriel wanted the Madeleine to appear powerful and large to the spectator standing upon the Place de la Concorde who should feel the church as being an essential part in the frame of the plaza. The original plan conceived the Madeleine as a climax to the whole composition with a dome about 170 feet high. The design of the church was by Constant and is reproduced by Patte. The portico in front of this temple was to be about forty percent higher than Gabriel's colonnades; a very wise precaution. Since the portico was to be seen from the Place de la Concorde flanked on both sides by Gabriel's colonnades, which stood 1000 feet nearer to the spectator, perspective diminution had to be guarded against. In addition to the forty percent increase given by the architect came the dome rising above the portico and bringing the whole structure to more than twice the height of Gabriel's colonnades. The façades of the houses on the Rue Royale, as can be seen in Fig. 234, were kept another 10 feet below the cornice line of the Madeleine. When the Madeleine, almost half a century after Gabriel had made his plans, was finally built a perfect Corinthian temple (designed by Vignon) was erected in place of the proposed domed church. But even this much lower building still found a respectable setting under the conditions so carefully prepared by Gabriel. The columns of the peristyle are considerable higher than those used by Gabriel for the colonnades facing the Place de la Concorde and the dark shadows between the columns appear entirely unbroken by windows back of them, which would have been apt to introduce an undesirable scale. The transition from the plaza to the Madeleine is made by the uniform façades of the Rue Royale. These street façades are designed without the colossal order, they do not need it because they can be seen at right angles from across the street only. By omission of the colossal order the small scale of ordinary windows is introduced again, well suited to let the church look large by contrast. Furthermore all lines of cornices and window frames guide the eye of the observer standing in the Place de la Concorde

FIG. 664—ARCHED CITY GATE

FIG. 665—TRIPLE ARCH CITY GATE

Figs. 664 and 665 are drawings by Robert Atkinson, from Mawson.

FIG. 666—PARIS. PORTE SAINT DENIS

One of the city gates which were an important part of Colbert's program for the development of Paris laid down in the plan of 1665 (Fig. 1024 shows this plan and the other gates). The gate, designed by the elder Blondel, is a masterpiece of calculated proportion.

Divers Passages faits sur le naturel, par Israel Silvestre. Avec privil du Roy 1650.

FIG. 667—MONUMENTAL GATE

FIG. 668—COLOGNE. SETTING OF A DOMED TOWER

Part of Fritz Schumacher's design for the old area of fortifications.

FIG. 669—BROOKLYN, N. Y. U. S. ARMY SUPPLY BASE

Walks and galleries carried on arches across streets. Designed by Cass Gilbert. (From the American Architect, 1919.)

FIG. 670—MILAN. A CITY GATE

FIG. 671—BOROUGH OF BOLTON

FIG. 672—BOROUGH OF BOLTON

Figs. 671 and 672 are taken in opposite directions. Designed by Thomas H. Mawson.

FIG. 674—ESSEN. MARGARETENHOEHE

Same view as Fig. 673 taken after construction from under the entrance gate structure (see Figs. 675-76). Built about 1910 by Metzendorf. The church on axis is still missing. (Courtesy of Mr. Richard Philipp.)

FIG. 673—ESSEN. MARGARETENHOEHE

This new street is developed in the vernacular style found in that region. There are gardens behind the houses.

in such a way as to make it easy for him to transfer the scale from the buildings of Gabriel in the foreground to Vignon's peristyle at the end of Rue Royale. This facility of actually scaling the great size of the Madeleine which otherwise would be apt to suffer from perspective diminution, helps to make up for the absence of the dome which would have been a more effective means of dominating the vista.

The play of the lines of cornices and window frames of Rue Royale which works so perfectly guiding the eye from façades in the Place de la Concorde back to the façade of the Madeleine, facilitating the comparison of their sizes deserves close attention. It is desirable to contrast a high building which has only few, or like the Madeleine only one — but very high — story against a lower building of many stories, provided the many storied low buildings are, like the houses of the Rue Royale, preceded and also followed by high buildings of few stories. If the high building with few stories stands in the foreground against a lower building with many stories in the background, the actual small size of the stories in the low building is apt to appear unreal and as being an effect of perspective diminution with the result that one unjustly thinks of the nearby monumental building as being low because it has "only" few stories, regardless of the fact that these stories actually are much higher than those of the low building in the background. An example to the point is the Superga in Turin (Fig. 648) where a fine dome over an order of classic simplicity is seen in front of the six-storied monastery with which it is connected. This monastery keeps its six stories below the cornice line of the church the fenestration of which suggests two stories. This juxtaposition of six-story and two-story buildings under the same cornice line is a doubtful achievement as long as the six-storied buildings are confined to the background, but are missing in the foreground. Without such a reassertion of the small scale in the foreground the church appears dwarfed by the multiplicity of the six-storied building behind it.

The very fine setting of the church of Nôtre Dame, Versailles, at the end of a short street, similar to the settings of the vanished chapel of the Capuchins which was a part of the original design of Place Vendôme, Paris, (Figs. 328-31 and 219) and of the church that belongs to the Amalienborg Plaza in Copenhagen (Fig 388) should be mentioned here. They all demonstrate how short a direct shot at a church must be in order to be fully effective in revealing the quality not only of the silhouette but also of the façade. The recent design of a church setting in connection with the razing of the fortifications of Cologne (Fig. 668) is a modern example of a well dimensioned straight street leading to a church. Regarding the length of the street leading to St. Peter's, Rome, as it seems to have been proposed by Bramante (Fig. 205) it must be kept in mind that this street had for an objective not the cathedral itself but the gate (Fig. 243) leading to the forecourt of St. Peter's with the dome appearing over the gate structure. The effect wanted therefore was more in the character of a prelude, which was to be followed by the full revelation of the cathedral after one had passed through the gateway.

Much less satisfactory than the approach to the Madeleine is the setting of Soufflot's Panthéon as it developed during the last century. (Figs. 649, 651 and plan Fig. 355). The Panthéon with its main body (main cornice line about 80 feet above ground) almost equals the height of the apartment houses (about 90 feet including mansard roof) framing the vista, and the dome towers more than three times as high (height with crowning figure about 290 feet). In spite of its great height and mass the Panthéon is too refined and elegant a composition to suc-

FIG. 675—ESSEN. MARGARETENHOEHE
Bridge on axis of main entrance. Designed by Metzendorf.

FIG. 676—ESSEN. MARGARETENHOEHE
Figs. 675-76 illustrate parts of one of the largest executed schemes of well designed housing enterprise in Germany. Compare Fig. 425.

FIG. 678—GENOA. PIAZZA NUOVA
The Palazzo Ducale, a building of the thirteenth century remodelled in the sixteenth and eighteenth centuries effectively terminates the narrow Pollajuoli street coming in at a slight angle.

FIG. 679—BERLIN. LEIPZIGER PLATZ
This gate plaza was laid out as a part of the great Renaissance enlargement which nearly doubled the area of the city in 1688. The gate houses, of which Fig. 680 gives a larger view, can barely be distinguished, flanking the nearer entrance to the plaza. For plan see Fig. 1039.

FIG. 681—PARIS. PLACE DU TRONE
The columns of Phillipe-Auguste stand in the Place du Trône which lies between the Cours Vincennes and the star-plaza called the Place de la Nation, the whole forming a civic gate of great impressiveness.

FIG. 680—BERLIN. THE GATE TO THE LEIPZIGER PLATZ
This view shows Schinkel's charming little temples (built 1823) from outside the plaza.

FIG. 682—SAN FRANCISCO. ST. FRANCIS WOOD

A residential district designed by Olmsted Brothers; the fountain by
H. H. Gutterson. The entrance is below, at the break in grade, the
road in the distance not being part of the design.

FIG. 684—ROME. PIAZZA DELLA TRINITA DE' MONTI

An engraving by Sylvestre showing the site before the building of
the Scala di Spagna; see Figs. 685-86.

FIG. 685—ROME. THE SCALA DI SPAGNA

Built 1721 by Specchi and de Sanctis, this terminal feature of the
Via de' Condotti transforms a steep hillside into an effective setting
and support for the church of Trinita de' Monti. The relation between
the stairs and the lower stories of the houses on both sides is hardly
satisfactory.

FIG. 680—BRUSSELS. COLONNE DU CONGRES

The column, which terminates a long avenue, stands on a terrace at
a sharp break in grade and is visible from most of the lower part of
the city. Built about 1850 from designs by Poelaert, architect of the
Palais de Justice.

FIG. 683—SAN FRANCISCO. ST. FRANCIS WOOD

One of two shelters at the entrance, designed by John Galen Howard.

cessfully compete against the clumsy masses of apartment houses seven stories high (including the roofs
which are developed as living quarters). The long distance of more than three times the height of the dome
and of more than ten times the height of the main cornice line of the building makes matters worse. We know
exactly what the architect of the Panthéon considered
as a good setting for this monument because he himself
designed the Faculté de Droit (Fig. 651) adjoining the
Panthéon which was copied by Hittorf on the opposite
side of the street when a district city hall was needed in
the nineteenth century. These buildings are three stories
high and greater height is harmful to even as high a
dome as the Panthéon.

It is not sufficient that the cornice lines of the buildings lining the approaches to a domed building be kept
below the drum of the dome, although this means something at least. In order to get a fully satisfactory effect
the buildings lining the approach must be kept so low
that even the play of perspective cannot make them rise
beyond the cornice line of the building for which they
are to act as a setting. Otherwise drum and dome will
not soar with their full majesty. The same applies to
any building which is meant to appear high.

An interesting little demonstration of how to guard
against perspective distortion has been made in the design for the American Academy in Rome; the cornices of
the two detached studios were wisely kept more than a
yard below the cornice of the pair attached to the main

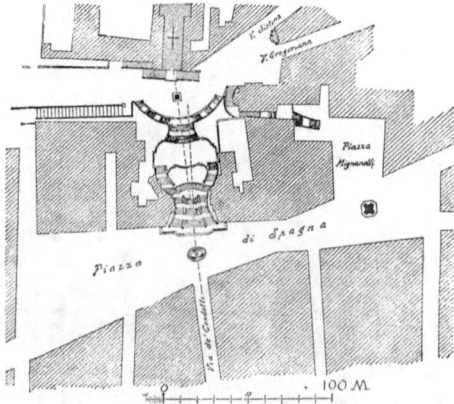

FIG. 686—ROME. PIAZZA AND SCALA DI SPAGNA

The plan shows how the axis of the street strikes the center of
the church façade, though not at right angles to it. (From Brinckmann.)

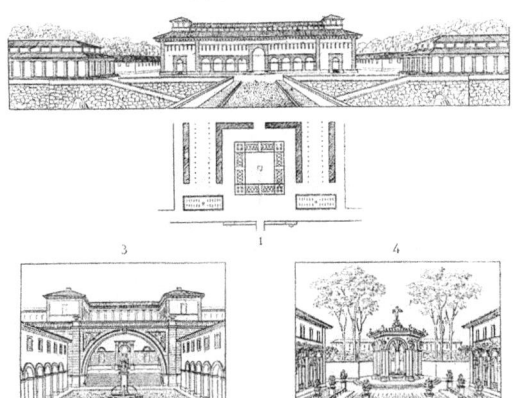

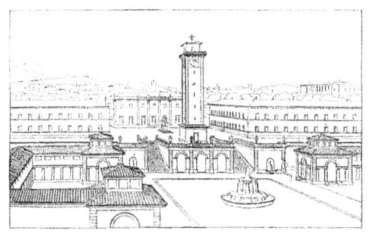

FIG. 693—STREET TERMINATION. MARKET ON LOWER
LEVEL. MUNICIPAL GROUP ON UPPER LEVEL

From K. M. Heigelin's architectural handbook published
1828-32 and stating in a very modern way many requirements
of harmonious street and formal garden designs. From the
same source are Figs. 690-92, 319A, and 319B.

FIG. 693—STREET TERMINATION. MARKET ON LOWER
ARCH AND PAVILION

FIG. 694—KOENIGSBURG. VIEW OF CHURCH FROM THE
STATION SQUARE
Designed by Former. (From Staedtebau 1916.)

FIG. 695—NAUHEIM
The large group near the center of the plan is the great bathing
establishment of which Fig. 696 is a detail.

FIG. 697—METZ. RUE DE LA GARE WITH MODERN TERMINA-
TION

FIG. 696—NAUHEIM
The porches arched over the sidewalks help to mark the transition
from street to garden court, and also to supplement the boundary walls
of the court.

FIG. 69S—NEW YORK.   WASHINGTON MEWS STUDIOS
A street unit resulting from an alteration of old city houses. Designed by Maynicke and Franke.
(From Architecture, 1918).

building (Fig. 652). This is on a small scale a repetition
of what Gabriel did in keeping his colonnades lower than
the Madeleine.

The Rue de la Regence in Brussels (Figs. 653-54)
makes a comparatively good composition with the dome
and entrance of the Palais de Justice in so far as the
buildings on both sides are either comparatively low or
have a low member strongly developed, which can act
as term of comparison. The concave profile of the street
in front of the Palais is also an important factor in
making the view impressive, provided the view is enjoyed from the high point and not taken from a point in
front of the highpoint as in Fig. 654.

The Rue de Tournon in Paris (Fig. 655, for plan see
Fig. 309) widens towards the Palais du Luxembourg,
making the small dome appear even smaller.   But as

FIG. 699—TURIN. LA VENERIE ROYALE
Under this title Thomas H. Mawson in his book on Civic Art reproduces this charming street ensemble.

this dome is not the all-important feature of the palace
the broadening is to be mainly understood as a welcome
uncovering of the wide façade of the palace since it
well could face a broad plaza. While a gradual widening of a street makes it appear shorter than it actually
is, a gradual narrowing down of the street width and a
gradual rise in the profile of the street make it appear
longer. Against such an apparently lengthened street
the building at the end of it impresses one as higher than
it is because it is not diminished as much perspectively
as the eye expects comparing it with the apparent length
of the street. There is no reason why such an optical
illusion should not be used to give additional value to a
monumental building. Palladio's stage streets are designed this way (Fig. 656). Also the Scala Regia in the
Vatican gradually narrows as it rises and there can
hardly be any doubt that Bernini's hand was not forced
by lack of space but that the artist was well aware of the
optical effect he wanted. In the eighteenth century the
Hauptstrasse in Dresden Neu-stadt (Fig. 657) was designed this way and produces a fine effect. Perhaps Cass
Gilbert in his latest scheme for the approach toward the
capitol in St. Paul had an effect of this kind in mind
(Fig. 659). On a small scale the same effect was tried
and carried out in Washington Highlands (Fig. 1158)
where the main approach to the hill called Mt. Vernon
narrows down from one hundred feet to fifty-six feet and
has a concave profile in addition. The effect is very satisfactory; the diminution might well have been made
stronger, without danger of freakish appearance.

A fine design for an approach was made by John Nolen
for the capitol at Madison (Figs. 660-3).   The ground
rises and the length of the approach is short enough to
guard against the emaciation of the terminal effect. The
buildings on both sides were planned to be low but would
not have been of much importance as the vista would
have been practically reserved to the central mall. One

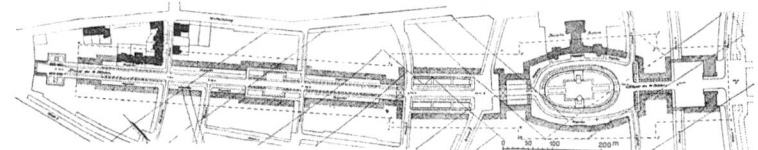

FIG. 700—LEIPZIG. STREET OF THE EIGHTEENTH OF OCTOBER

This modern street consisting of strongly marked units has recently been made the basis of an architectural competition for designs of harmonious façades. (From Deutsche Bauzeitung, 1915.)

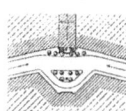

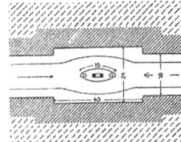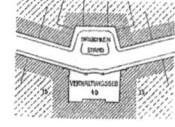

FIG. 701—DEVICES FOR MAKING BREAKS AT THE HIGH POINTS OF CONVEX STREETS
(From Gurlitt.)

FIG. 702—BRUSSELS. PLACE DES MARTYRS
The "place" is just off the busy Rue Neuve, and the monument terminates the street which connects them. (From P. Klopfer.)

FIG.703—TOURS. BRIDGE OVER THE LOIRE WITH ENTRANCE TO RUE NATIONALE BETWEEN SYMMETRICALLY DESIGNED CORNER HOUSES.
(From a drawing by Franz Herding.)

FIG. 704—ROME. PIAZZA DELLE TERME

FIG. 707—BERLIN. GENDARMEN-MARKT
The two domed churches by Von Goutard, 1780; the theater (1818) Schinkel. See Figs. 403, 708, and 1030.

FIG. 705—ORLEANS. BRIDGE OVER THE LOIRE WITH DESIGNED ENTRANCE TO RUE ROYALE
(From a drawing by Franz Herding.)

FIG. 706—LONDON. THE GREENWICH HOSPITAL
Looking toward the water. For plan and other views see Figs. 3 and following. (From W. J. Loftie.)

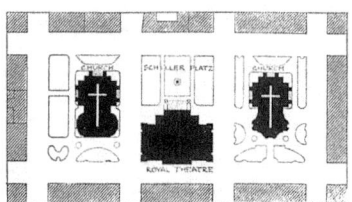

FIG. 708—BERLIN. GENDARMEN-MARKT
Compare Figs. 403, 707, and 1030. (From Inigo Triggs.)

FIG. 709—HAMPSTEAD. CENTRAL SQUARE

St. Jude's Church, the Free Church (on left) and the Vicarage (on right), from the south. Designed by E. L. Lutyens. See Figs. 710-11.

FIG. 710—HAMPSTEAD. HOUSES FRAMING CENTRAL SQUARE

Designed by E. L. Lutyens. (From the Architectural Review, 1912.)

may question whether the use of a diminution would not be desirable also for a mall similar to the one proposed, making the two streets which parallel the mall converge towards the capitol, thereby giving them the benefit of the terminal vista which they miss if they lie parallel.

If a building of the height of the Panthéon, towering two hundred ninety feet requires a setting by houses of only three stories, while six and seven stories actually prove to be too high for the situation, the difficulty of course becomes still greater, when it comes to the setting of civic buildings in the United States with apartment and office buildings many times higher than those the Panthéon or any civic building in Paris had ever to contend with. It has been mentioned in discussing the design of plazas in America that the national capitol measures only three hundred and seven feet, and is thus about fifty feet lower than the twenty-five story Times building in New York.

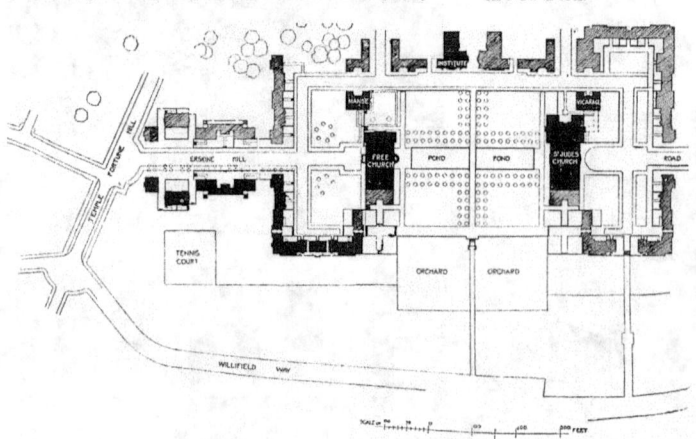

FIG. 711—HAMPSTEAD. CENTRAL SQUARE

Designed by E. L. Lutyens. (From Lawrence Weaver.)

FIG. 712—BOSTON. STREET VISTA

Christ Church, "Old North," built 1723.

People are willing to spend many millions to produce a monumental building, the value of which in large part is avowedly not practical but ideal; and then the same people are equally satisfied to largely destroy the ideal — and main — value of the investment by permitting an unsuitable neighborhood to crowd in upon it. If it comes to setting a monumental building of the conventional type, even if it has a high dome, the broken skyline of an American street, with continuous variations of height from one to twenty-five stories, is impractical. Compared to it the unsatisfactory setting of the Paris Panthéon may appear almost perfect; but the American architect, when he is called upon to advise regarding first rate settings of monumental buildings constructed for important municipal, state, or national purposes, will remember that better settings are possible and that Soufflot's own conception was indeed very different.

With the knowledge of satisfactory settings which today can easily be gathered it is simply a question of means in the hands of our gifted designers to produce satisfactory results. If they cannot be given the control of the approaches they should not be asked to design "monumental" buildings. As in the case of plaza design the very tall skyscraper would again appear to be the logical way out. If the community cannot control the approaches the only way to give distinction to public buildings would be to make them the tallest in the maze of skyscrapers.

It is not only the value of the building that becomes emaciated if its architectural strength is meant to spread over too long an approach. The walls of such a street, also, if treated harmoniously as they should be, are apt to become monotonous if the same harmony is continued for too great a distance. A long straight street therefore must be subdivided into units of design. Changes in the cross section and width of the street offer important means of interpunctuating a street. The plan of the new street of the 18th of October in Leipsic (Fig. 700) illustrates this idea. In boulevard design changes of cross section at points of curvature are frequently used. A stronger method of dividing a street into units of design is the insertion of plazas. Palladio required: "Between the said principal piazza and any of the gates you please there ought to be one or more piazzas made somewhat less than the aforesaid principal piazza." Since the time of the Renaissance with its love for spaciousness plazas have been connected also with the entrance gates of cities. (Figs. 664-70.) With the growth of population these gate plazas have been surrounded by the built-up town and

FIG. 713—COSEL. CHURCH TERMINATING A STREET

The Garrison Church, built by Langhaus 1787, seems large in comparison with the one story houses at the right, but only of moderate size if compared with the two story houses, and is quite dwarfed by the three story houses in the foreground. (From Staedtebau, 1920.)

FIG. 714—CHARLESTON, S. C. ST. MICHAEL'S CHURCH

The porch is brought over the sidewalk; see plan Fig. 715 and view Fig. 718. (From Ware's "Georgian Period.")

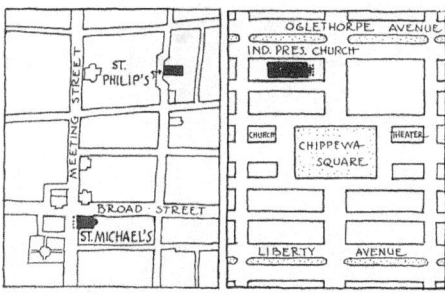

FIG. 715—CHARLESTON, S. C. ST. MICHAEL'S AND ST. PHILIP'S

See Figs. 714, 718-19. (Courtesy of Mr. J. H. Dingle, City Engineer.)

FIG. 716—SAVANNAH, GA. INDEPENDENT PRESBYTERIAN CHURCH

See view and plan Figs. 720 and 1069. (Courtesy of Mr. W. O'D. Rockwell, City Engineer.)

FIG. 718—CHARLESTON, S. C.   ST. MICHAEL'S CHURCH

The Church built 1760 and attributed to Gibbs, dominates an important street intersection. Compare
Figs. 714-15.   (From Crane and Soderholtz.)

form just that kind of interpunctuation of the street
asked for by Palladio. Figs. 664-81 and 728 show a number of such plazas and other effective street terminations
or interpunctuations. The introduction of gate features
into street design, as it has become an established practice with American real estate developers, is a welcome
modern means of street interpunctuation (Figs. 682-3).
The development of steep hillsides as street terminations deserves special attention in the American city,

where, as in San Francisco, the rigid gridiron often produces steep street endings (Figs. 684-9, 693).

Somewhat akin to the insertion of plazas is the judicious treatment of corners at street intersections as a
method of giving rhythm to a street. The corners can
be cut back rectangularly or in quadrants or brought out
over sidewalks (Figs. 694-6). They can be emphasized
by towers or even more effectively by areas kept low.
It is specially desirable to thus give architectural re-

FIG. 710—CHARLESTON, S. C. ST. PHILIP'S CHURCH
The church, built in 1837 as a copy of an older one destroyed by fire, is brought forward into the street;
the tower appears almost on the street axis. See plan Fig. 715. (From Crane and Soderholtz.)

cognition to a high point of a street, as the buildings seen behind the high point appear half buried (Fig. 701). To get the full effect in all these cases it is necessary of course, that opposite houses be treated harmoniously if not symmetrically (Figs. 702-5). The arranging of symmetrical door entrances opposite each other, as frequently found effective in the narrow streets of Genoa, the symmetrical opposition of front courts enlarging the street on both sides into the body of the houseblocks, also the simple opposition of higher features, such as gables and towers on both sides of the street, are means of accentuating the rhythm of the street which can be applied in the middle of the block.

The symmetrical arrangement of churches on both sides of the street is a motive dating from the Renaissance. While in the Middle Ages the idea of the unique-

FIG. 720—SAVANNAH. INDEPENDENT PRESBYTERIAN CHURCH

The church, which was built in 1819, occupies one of the several
public lots which were "granted by the crown" when the city was laid
out. See plans, Fig. 716 and Fig. 1069. (From Crane and Soderholtz.)

ness and absolute predominance of the temple of God
was prevalent, the increase in the size of cities and the
freedom of religion that came in the time after the Renaissance made it possible for the civic designer to group
churches and let their domes or steeples become balancing features similar to the obelisks which in their Egyp-
tian home always appeared as twin features, framing the
processional road towards the sanctuary. The twin domes
of Piazza del Popolo in Rome (Figs. 988-91), the domed
towers of the Greenwich Hospital and of the Gendarmen-
Markt in Berlin are illustrations (Figs. 706-8, see also
Figs. 3-6). The bold accentuation of the Central Square
of Hampstead (Figs. 709-10) by two churches is entirely
in keeping with this Renaissance idea.

When Wren replanned London after the fire he had
to transform a very crowded Gothic town into a Renaissance city. Very little room was available for plazas.
Churchyards, cemeteries and gardens that still existed
in the old town were to be put outside the city limits.
So far as forecourts of churches were concerned he therefore confined himself to the large triangular plaza in
front of St. Paul's. For the other churches, of which
many scores had to be rebuilt, he abandoned the traditional orientation and brought the tower and main
façade well forward into the street, making the best of
it as an object of vista. This is the way he expresses
himself:

"As to the Situation of the Churches, I should propose
they be brought as forward as possible into the larger
and more open Streets, not in obscure Lanes, nor where
Coaches will be much obstructed in the Passage. Nor

are we, I think, too nicely to observe East or West, in
Position, unless it falls out properly: Such Fronts as
happen to lie most open in View should be adorn'd with
Porticos, both for beauty and Convenience; which, together with handsome Spires, or Lanterns, rising in good
Proportion above the neighboring Houses (of which I
have given several Examples in the City of different
Forms) may be of sufficient Ornamentation to the Town,
without a great Expence for enriching the outward Walls
of the Churches, in which Plainness and Duration ought
principally, if not wholly, to be studied. When a Parish
is divided, I suppose it may be thought sufficient, if the
Mother-church has a Tower large enough for a good Ring
of Bells, & the other Churches smaller Towers for two
or three Bells; because great Towers, & lofty Steeples,
are sometimes more than half the Charge of the Church."

Wren's recommendations became a living part of the
Georgian traditions of Colonial architecture in America.
The situations of many Colonial churches form wonderful
demonstrations of the wisdom of Wren's recommendations. Among the most striking examples are St. Philip's
church and St. Michael's church in Charleston, S. C.
(Figs. 714-9; see also Figs. 720-2). It was left for the
period of international decline of civic art to locate
churches without recognition of any kind among buildings closely adjoining them, or to visually smash even
their steeples by building much higher skyscrapers in the
immediate neighborhood. Under such conditions a
church is not benefited even by a location at the head of
a street. The famous location of Trinity Church at the
head of Wall Street may be strangely picturesque, but
the somewhat grotesque effect of the Liliputian church
steeple surrounded by the giants of Wall Street would
hardly have appeared dignified to the original builders
of the religious edifice.

The development of the Georgian and Colonial
churches with only one tower as a part of the main façade
made them suitable objects to act as points of street-vista,
much more so than the double and often unsymmetrical
towers of the Gothic churches (Fig. 672). The prominent feature of a church façade brought close to the sidewalk is also suitable for the accentuation of a curve in
the street (Figs. 725 and 728) or for giving emphasis
to a site on a slope (Figs. 474-75) or a water course (Figs.
726-7). In a straight level street however a single
steeple or other prominent feature on one side of the
street destroys the balance. St. Philip's Church, Charleston, is brought so far forward that the tower almost appears on the street axis (Figs. 715, 719; see also Fig. 728)
and St. Michael's Church and other Colonial churches
dominate the narrow streets so powerfully that one may
become reconciled to the picturesque effect. Speaking
generally, however, and applying the highest standards,
one might wish that no strong emphasis be given one side
of an ordinary straight street on level ground without
significance. Such justifying significance would lie, for
instance, in the coming in of one or more strong cross
axes, of which the steeple or other prominent feature
should be felt as the objective. Or, the large building
placed asymmetrically on one side of the street could announce the insertion into the street system of a plaza or
forecourt of some kind, which, lying on the other side
of the main street, would be felt as balancing the tall
building by its expanse. Where no such justification
of one-sided emphasis is given, it would be well to do
away with the asymmetry by following a suggestion of
Wren's, who proposed in his plan for London to group
in some instances churches from adjoining parishes in
order to secure a symmetrical arrangement of towers
facing each other across the street (Fig. 1028). This fine
solution should be used also in grouping churches of
different creeds, which to-day so often antagonize each

other in appearance. Litchfield's design for Yorkship Village (Figs. 1160-5) promises great success in this respect.

In a way similar to the grouping of steeples on both sides of a street, other features could with great advantage to the appearance be handled symmetrically, especially the little forecourts or other recognitions given to façades which under crowded conditions are all that is left as a setting (Figs. 729-33).

The areas between the points of termination or interpunctuation of a street require harmonious development along the building lines. It is the harmony between these buildings that John Ruskin calls "the great concerted music of the streets of a city", "a sublimity . . . capable of exciting almost the deepest emotion that art can ever strike from the bosoms of men". The example of Muenster (Fig. 734), of which a drawing by Ruskin's own hand accompanies his remarks about "the street scenery of continental towns", shows that absolute similarity of the individual houses is by no means required. It is enough for one strong motive in the lower stories to pull the buildings together, and to develop the rest of them in the same spirit, however individual that may be.

The amount of individuality in the development of adjoining houses found in old streets is often considerable and quite in contradiction to the feeling of harmony that they produce in spite of many dissimilarities (Figs. 740-1). The secret of this harmony lies in many different features some of which are always prevalent, be it similarity of story heights, window sizes, or sizes of openings. The Guild Clubhouse shown in the foreground of Fig. 742 is of the sixteenth century, and thus three hundred years younger than the "Staple House", the last of the three gables, which is a grain elevator. And yet there is no doubt about the harmony between these buildings. Such a general feeling of harmony was achieved more easily during the slow growth of previous ages. After it was once established it was often able to withstand the infringements of modern times (Fig. 737) for quite a while.

If once the harmony of street architecture has been destroyed by the rapid and often revolutionary changes connected with modern city building, or if in new cities it does not spring up spontaneously as an expression of a refined civic conscience, it is necessary to produce it by modern methods. In discussing the surrounding of public monuments by harmonious private buildings a good deal has been said that applies equally well to the development of harmonious streets. Numberless streets in European cities have been developed, though on a smaller scale, upon the same principles that were sweepingly applied at quite a late date in the Rue de Rivoli in Paris (Figs. 746-7). When there was no legal obligation to stick to a certain house type the moral obligation or mere tradition was equally strong (Figs. 738-9 and 743-9). Mere intelligent cooperation between individuals, the friendly joining of hands between neighboring houses, was common and is again developing more and more in Europe and America (Figs. 572-8, 750-3). The extensions of Harvard Club in New York, though of course part of the same building, might, as far as appearance is concerned, be quoted as examples to the point (Figs. 755-6). There are examples where under less favorable circumstances a somewhat artificial unity has been achieved by giving to houses of otherwise quite different features at least a uniform main cornice. Fig. 771 shows an example, about the propriety of which one might be in doubt if it were not that the two houses thus united represent a much more satisfactory appearance than the jungle of houses back of them in the same picture.

The subject of developing large real estate operations according to a uniform artistic design has been referred to in a previous chapter (see Figs. 574, 576-8).

FIG. 721—PHILADELPHIA, CHRIST CHURCH.

Designed by Dr. John Kearsley, 1720, and completed about 1750. (From Ware's "Georgian Period.")

Some of the finest work in this field has been done in the English city of Bath (Figs. 767-70). England with her large estates is especially rich in good examples (Figs. 765, 772). Practically everywhere in big modern cities one is apt to find entire streets developed by the same financial concern. Though large sections of Riverside Drive in New York built up by one company were evidently developed with the intention of carefully avoiding harmony and continuity, real estate enterprise today is more apt to produce streets like those shown in Figs. 773-5 where several motives are carried through the block, such as cornice lines, similar front gardens, fences, and similar roof material, or like the houses shown in Fig. 776 built on higher ground, a uniform retaining wall serving as bases for the houses. Some of the best products of real estate enterprises in America are found in Roland Park, Baltimore, where one of the streets, for example, was developed from the design of Charles Platt (Fig. 777) and where many harmonious groups were developed (Figs. 1135-8).

Uniformity can be exaggerated when carried to an extreme. The example often quoted in Europe is the city of Mannheim (Figs. 1051-6) which to Europeans long appeared unique because it was built entirely on the gridiron plan. Its appearance, which was praised by Goethe, has sometimes been criticized as being monotonous because all its houses were so to speak under one roof. One of the popular treatises on building published at the

FIG. 722—NEW YORK. ST. JOHN'S CHAPEL, VARICK STREET

The church, built 1803-06 by McComb, is set in an open space between two symmetrical houses, the first of the adjacent rows. The severity of their side walls is probably due to the influence of standardized party-wall construction.

FIG. 723—BOSTON. STREET TERM-
INATED BY THE ARCH UNDER
THE STATEHOUSE

FIG. 724—BOSTON. PARK STREET
CHURCH FROM THE COMMON

FIG. 725—BERLIN. OSKAR PLATZ

Proposal to improve a bad street intersection by
introducing a church. From Brix and Genzmer's
premiated design for the city plan of Greater Berlin.

FIG. 726—LILLE. PALAIS DE JUSTICE

The portico dominates the view from the quays around the canal
and from an important bridge.

FIG. 727—NICE. EGLISE DU PORT

The church and the flanking colonnaded buildings stand at the head
of the large rectangular port.

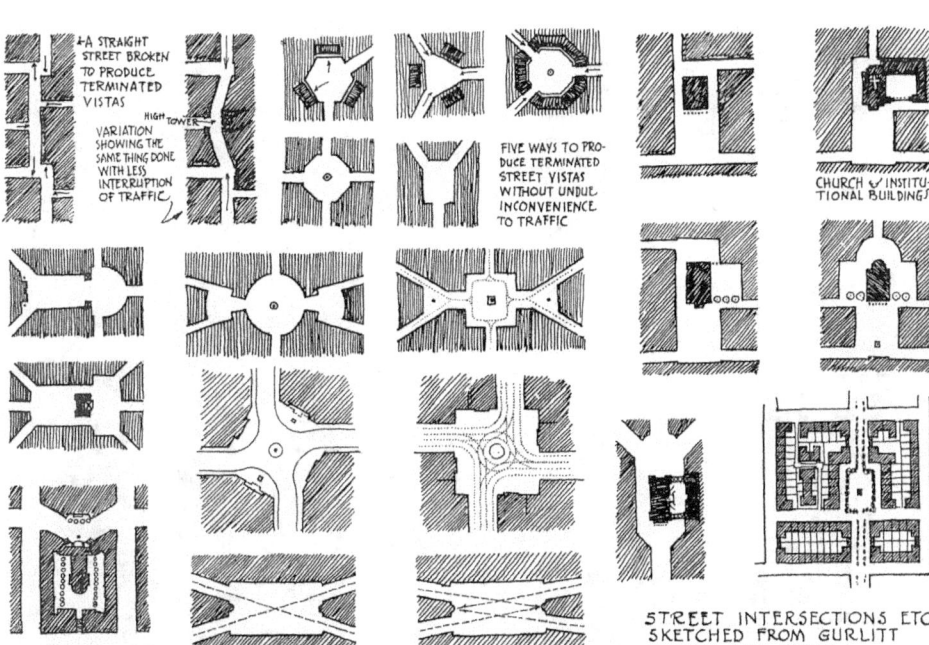

FIG. 728

FIG. 729—PARIS. CHAPEL IN RUE JEAN GOUJON

Designed by M. Glibert. (From the Architectural Review, 1902.)

end of the eighteenth century for the use of the "carpenter architect" in small cities of Germany, reasoned that cities should not look like one huge building but should be an aggregate of many regular buildings which were likely to please by being individually different and setting each other off advantageously. As very small spaces between houses are neither beautiful nor useful, while larger distances are apt to make the individual houses stick out like lonesome teeth, an arrangement is recommended of which Fig. 763 gives as good an idea as could be secured by making a reduced reproduction from a large folded copper engraving. The idea is to have a balanced grouping of symmetrical detached houses, with even cornice lines, connected by gateways with verandas over them. These gateways, which practically were to serve as portecochères and entrances to the courtyards behind, had the esthetic function of tying the houses together and of framing each façade by two lower members. The idea which was thus naively expressed for the consumption of contractors in small cities is excellent and has an august precedent. The setting off of the main member by side members, as found in Palladio's Villa for Francesco Pisano (Fig. 758), inspired the design for a mansion by Colen Campbell, author of Vitruvius Britannicus, for Lord Perceval, of which he says "two covered arches that joined the offices to the house are disposed to receive coaches for conveniency in wet weather." Robert Adam's "Stratford House" (Fig 783), his Royal Society of Arts in London (Fig. 751A) and especially the fine "Crescent" shown in Fig. 757 are models of the rhythmical juxtaposition of high and low in street design.

Fig. 778 shows the rhythmical development of a street facing a park by the repetition of small forecourts through which the benefit of the park is brought into a much larger number of rooms than would otherwise be possible.

Much good work is being done in the reclamation of entire city blocks and often much larger areas of old sections of towns that needed design. The design of

FIG. 730—MUNICH. ADDITION TO UNIVERSITY

Designed by G. Bestelmeyer. (From Wasmuth's Monatshefte, 1918.)

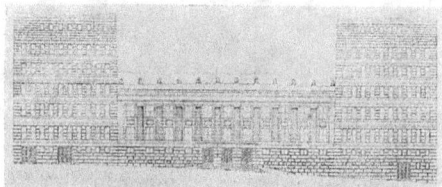

FIG. 731—WASHINGTON, D. C. PROPOSAL FOR GERMAN EMBASSY

A colonnade set between two high members. Design by Hans Poelzig. (From Wasmuth's Monatshefte, 1919.)

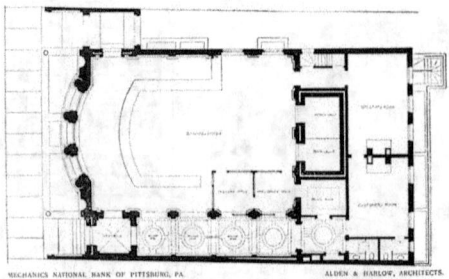

MECHANICS NATIONAL BANK OF PITTSBURG, PA.   ALDEN & HARLOW, ARCHITECTS.

FIG. 732—PLAN GOING WITH FIG. 733

FIG. 733—PITTSBURGH, PA. MECHANICS NATIONAL BANK

Designed by Alden and Harlow. See plan Fig. 732. (From the Architectural Review, 1905.)

FIG. 734—MUENSTER. ARCADED STREET

From a drawing by John Ruskin.

FIG. 735—FRANKFORT. ROEMERBERG

Medieval buildings, on the left hand, surrounded by harmonious
modern façades, to the right. For plan see Fig. 736. (From Deutsche
Bauzeitung, 1910.)

FIG. 737—STEYR, AUSTRIA. MAIN STREET

From a drawing by Otto Buenz.

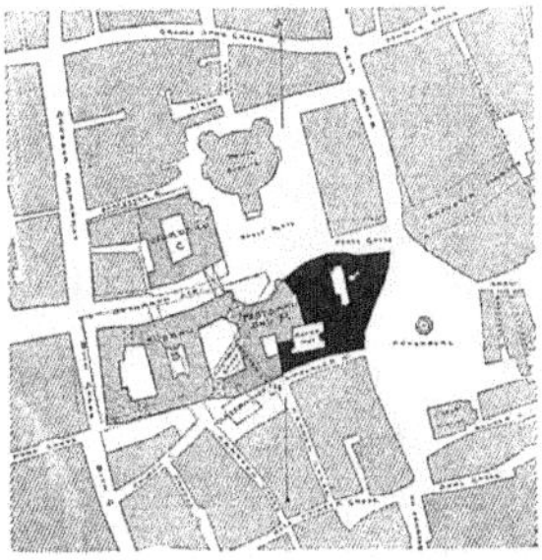

FIG. 736—PLAN GOING WITH FIG. 735

FIG. 738—HAMBURG. ESPLANADE

Compare Figs. 572-73, showing similar buildings in Baltimore.

FIG. 739—GENOA. VIA NUOVA (GARIBALDI)

The street of sixteenth century palaces that made Rubens turn to
the study of architecture.

FIG. 741A—BOSTON. TWO COLONIAL SQUARES
(From Shurtleff.)

FIGS. 740, 741—MUNICH. MEDIEVAL STREET ARCHITECTURE
Drawn from a wooden model of the city of Munich made by Jacob Sandtner in 1571.

FIG. 742—GHENT

Harmonious façades built at different periods. The Staple house, the farthest of the three gabled buildings, was built in the thirteenth century; the Guildhouse, which is the nearest, in the sixteenth.

FIG. 743—BOSTON. LOUISBURG SQUARE
Typical Colonial street-architecture, the houses thoroughly unified by their common material, scale, and style.

the street façades in many reclamation schemes was left to individual enterprise, producing sometimes esthetic results far inferior to the appearance of the previous slums. Often the work was handled on a large scale, good street design being enforced as an incidental advantage that should result from so costly a scheme. Among the many examples that could be mentioned, the reclamation of the oldest part of Stuttgart and the reclamation recently effected upon land owned by the Prince of Wales in London may be referred to (see Figs. 764-6 and captions). In both cases a large area of old houses had to be pulled down, many of which had architectural merit. In both cases also the architects succeeded in translating into their own new houses the spirit of the old. The esthetic problem in reclamation schemes is sorely complicated by the economic problem of high land values suggesting very intensive use of land. This problem exists even where no buildings have to be pulled down but where the proximity of high buildings has driven up land values to so high a point that artistic achievement is interfered with and becomes possible only if combined with shrewd calculation. West Hill Place, Boston, (Figs. 784, 787) is an interesting example and Figs. 785, 788-90 show other examples where the design for areas of one or more blocks made or promises valuable contributions to the harmonious appearance of the street although it had to cope with difficult conditions.

FIG. 744—JAPANESE STREET OF SHOPS
From a print by Hiroshige.

FIG. 745—FORST. STREET FACADES
Official designs for the town hall and private houses around the market place in the German town of Forst, used in the rebuilding of the town in 1748. (From Kuhn.)

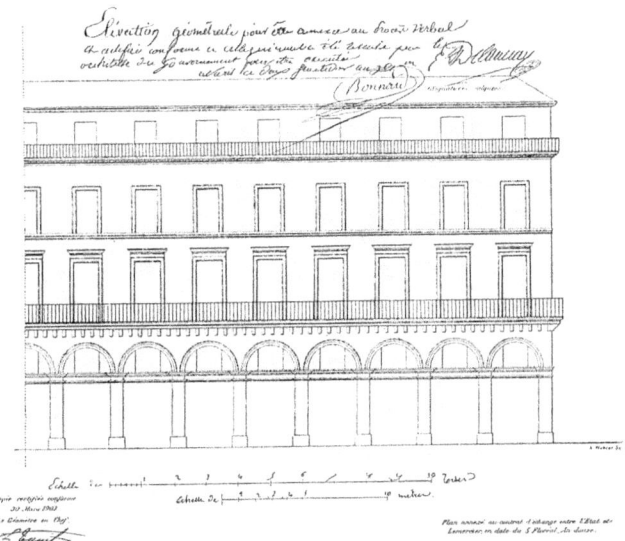

FIG. 746—PARIS. RUE DE RIVOLI

The official design for the houses on the Rue de Rivoli, which has remained in force since the time of Napoleon I. (From Stuebben.)

FIG. 747—PARIS. RUE DE RIVOLI AND THE TUILERIES GARDENS

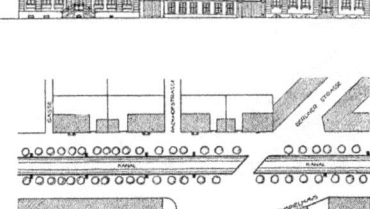

FIG. 748—POTSDAM. UNIFORM HOUSES

Official building designs, eighteenth century. (Figs. 748 and 749 from Otto Zieler.)

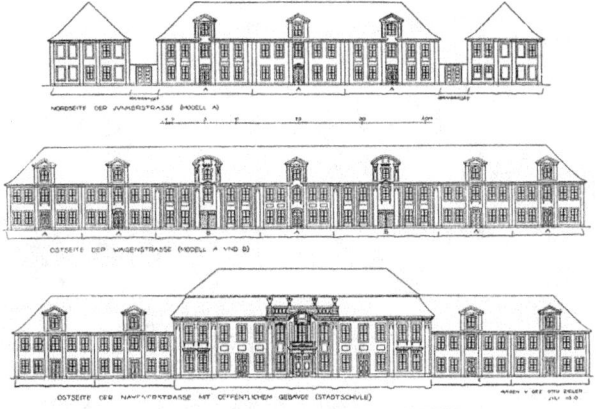

FIG. 749—POTSDAM. THE "DUTCH QUARTER"

Harmonious street façades designed 1737 by the Hollander Baumann.

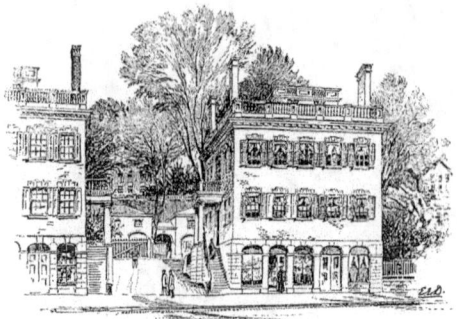

A couple of Residences with Stores under on South Main St built about 30 years ago.

Yard and Stabling to the above

FIGS. 750-51—PROVDENCE, R .I.

Esthetic cooperation; façades and yards.

FIG. 752—LONDON. GEORGIAN DOORWAYS IN QUEEN'S SQUARE

A unification of what would otherwise be competing elements. (From Ware's "Georgian Period," as are also Figs. 750-51.)

FIG. 751A—LONDON. ROYAL SOCIETY OF ARTS

In this design Robert Adam used a monumental motive but simplified it so completely that it harmonizes perfectly with the almost penurious facades which flank it.

FIG. 753—RICHELIEU. COMBINED COURTYARD OF TWO RESIDENCES

The two stable buildings are developed to frame the entrance into the garden. Compare Figs. 972, 974-75. (From the American Architect, 1902.)

FIG. 754—LONDON. OLD PALACE TERRACE, RICHMOND

A row of harmonious, but not absolutely uniform, houses. (From R. R. Phillips.)

FIGS. 755-56—NEW YORK. HARVARD CLUB. 44th STREET FACADE AND 45th STREET FACADE

An example of the architectural unification of street-fronts in spite of variations in height of buildings and in width of lots. (From the Monograph of the work of McKim, Mead, and White.)

FIG. 757—LONDON. THE "PARAGON"

Designed by followers of Robert Adam. From S. C. Ramsey, who makes the following interesting comments: "The paragon at Blackheath, London, built in the closing years of the eighteenth century, shows what a striking effect can be obtained when series of houses of moderate size are unified under one scheme. The treatment of the different blocks linked up with the Doric arcades is most original, preserving as it does the continuity of the design, whilst indicating the individuality of the separate house. The detail throughout, though delicate in execution, is extremely masculine and direct. The paragon was originally built with the idea of providing accommodation for naval officers stationed at Greenwich, or for those who had retired from the service; and this, no doubt, was partially responsible for the suggestion of a uniform treatment for their residences."

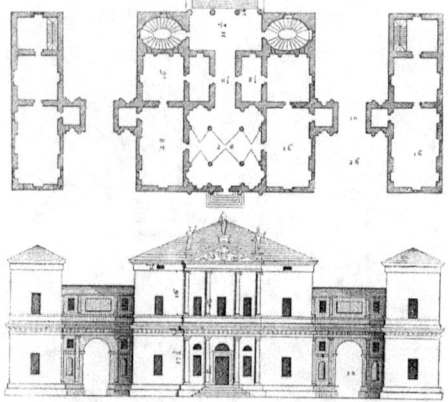

FIG. 758—PALLADIO'S VILLA FOR FRANCESCO PISANO

A group of buildings unified by connecting arches. See Fig. 763 for an eighteenth century application of this principle to an entire street.

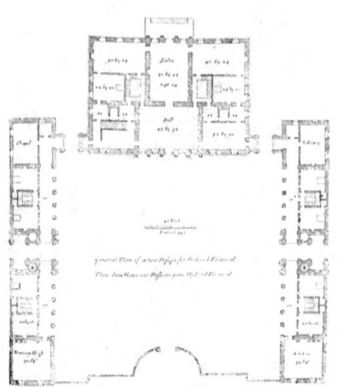

FIG. 759—HOUSE FOR LORD PERCIVAL. PLAN

FIG. 761—POTSDAM. CITY HALL, 1753

FIG. 760—HOUSE FOR LORD PERCIVAL. ELEVATION

This design by Colen Campbell applies Palladio's principle (Fig. 758) to a larger group, unifying the group while still maintaining the dominance of the central building.

FIG. 762—POTSDAM. EXTENSIONS TO THE CITY HALL

This design by Landsberg, premiated in a competition, sets the old city hall (Fig. 761) between two symmetrical wings, one of which would bridge over a street entering the market place. (From Staedtebau, 1914.)

FIG. 763—DESIGN FOR A UNIFIED STREET

From a German handbook for carpenters and masons, published about 1800. The buildings are unified horizontally, which is the important thing in a street-perspective. Arches are used much as they are in Figs. 758 and 760.

FIG. 764—STUTTGART. TRANSFORMATION OF THE INNER CITY

The central part of the old city having sunk into a disreputable condition the pulling down and rebuilding of the district was handled as one operation and completed by 1910. In view of the high real estate values the streets were only slightly widened and straightened out, and the architectural character of the district, sanctioned by historical associations, was preserved. Design by Hengerer, Mehlin, and Reissing.

FIG. 765—LONDON. COURTENAY SQUARE. KENNINGTON

This illustration and the succeeding one are characteristic views of the large housing project recently carried out on the estates of the Prince of Wales, south of the Thames. The workingmen's houses around the square and the "middle class flats" on Chester Street were designed by Adshead and Ramsey, in close conformity to the local style which was developed in the first half of the last century. The brick is yellow-brown and hoods and lattices are bronze-green. The design of the interior area of the square, paved with gravel and planted with lindens in straight rows, is a great improvement upon the ordinary London square which is fenced in and usable only by the abutters. (Figs. 765 and 766 from the Brickbuilder, 1920.)

FIG. 766—LONDON. CHESTER STREET, KENNINGTON

FIG. 767—BATH. THE CIRCUS

FIG. 768—BATH. NORFOLK CRESCENT

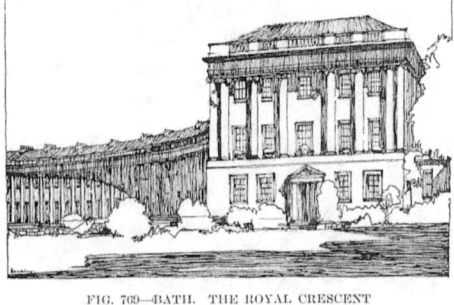

FIG. 769—BATH. THE ROYAL CRESCENT

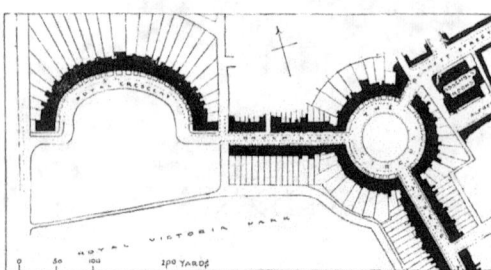

FIG. 770—BATH. PLAN OF ROYAL CRESCENT AND CIRCUS

The town of Bath grew rapidly during the eighteenth century. An entire section in the northern part of the town was laid out in 1725 by John Wood. The buildings around the Circus were designed by Wood himself shortly before his death in 1754. The Royal Crescent was built by Wood's son about twenty years later. Both of these units were planned on a liberal scale, the Circus being over three hundred feet in diameter and the Crescent nearly five hundred. The arrangement of the Circus, with three radial streets instead of the ordinary four, makes it a stronger feature in the street plan because its walls stop the streets, thus making the Circus the objective and crowning feature of each of the streets and not merely an incident in their course.

The "new town," Edinburgh, was laid out in 1767.

Figs. 767-69 are drawings by Franz Herding after photographs from Brinckmann. Fig. 770 is from Triggs and Fig. 772 from Unwin.

The houses illustrated in Fig. 771 are given a certain unity by the rough-and-ready method of giving them the same cornice, regardless of the fact that no other horizontal lines carry through. Yet the result justifies the expedient, probably on account of the uniformity of materials and of architectural details in the two parts. Designed by Peters and Rice.

FIG. 771—BOSTON. HOUSES ON BAY STATE ROAD

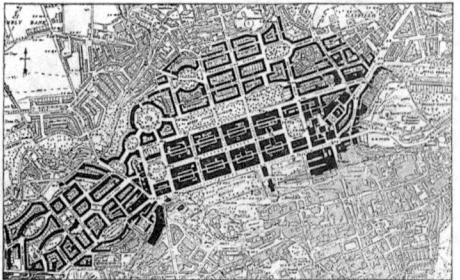

FIG. 772—EDINBURGH. THE "NEW TOWN"

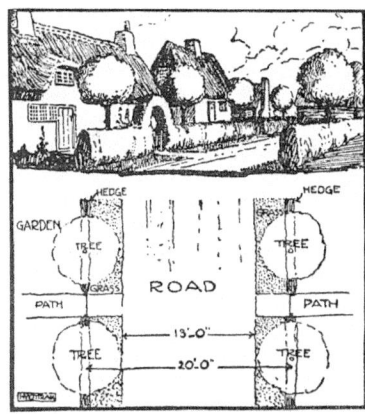 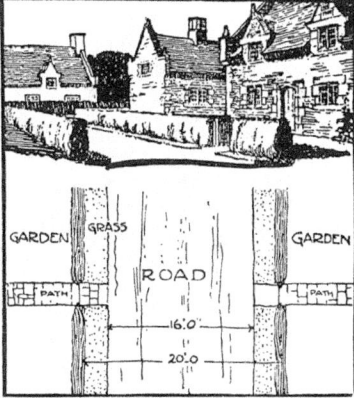

FIGS. 773, 774—ENGLISH GARDEN CITY STREETS

Light-traffic roadways designed by Raymond Unwin for use at Letchworth and Hampstead. The street is unified, even when the houses are not, by uniform continuous hedges.

FIG. 775—BERLIN, STREET OF APARTMENTS

Designed by M. Wagner. (From Migge.)

FIG. 776—STREET IN A GERMAN GARDEN CITY

Sloping street given unity by a continuous retaining wall. Designed by Herman Muthesius. (Courtesy of Mr. Richard Philipp.)

FIG. 777—BALTIMORE, STREET IN ROLAND PARK

In accordance with suggestions made by C. A. Platt, this street was made a unified design by building uniform retaining walls and by giving all the houses the same color. Mr. Platt is not accountable for the convex profile of the street.

FIG. 778— HANOVER, BENNIGSEN STREET

The municipal government by holding large areas of land and by municipal ordinances has secured considerable control over street façades. It held a competition for the design of the new Bennigsen Street and this bird's-eye view was part of the premiated projet by Siebrecht and Usadel.

FIG. 779—LONDON. REGENT QUADRANT

As originally built by Nash. The colonnades were later removed because they shaded the shops too much.

FIG. 780—LONDON. WATERLOO PLACE

The fine terminal feature of Lower Regent Street, designed by John Nash. Just back of the point from which the photograph was taken are the Duke of York Column and the broad steps which lead down to the Mall and St. James' Park. The buildings have in part been rebuilt and made higher but the uniformity is ultimately to be restored.

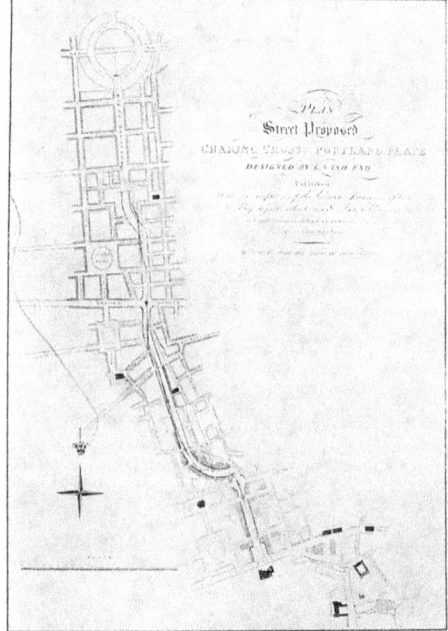

FIG. 781—LONDON. PLAN OF REGENT STREET

Laid out in 1813 by John Nash and largely built up from his designs.

FIG. 783—LONDON. STRATFORD HOUSE

Designed by Robert Adam. This, like Figs. 758-60, is an example of the unification of a group by the use of connecting members. The large entrance court is virtually a public plaza forming a setting for the principal façade.

FIG. 782—LONDON. REGENT QUADRANT

Premiated design, by Richardson and Gill, in the "Builder's" competition for a scheme for the rebuilding of the quadrant.

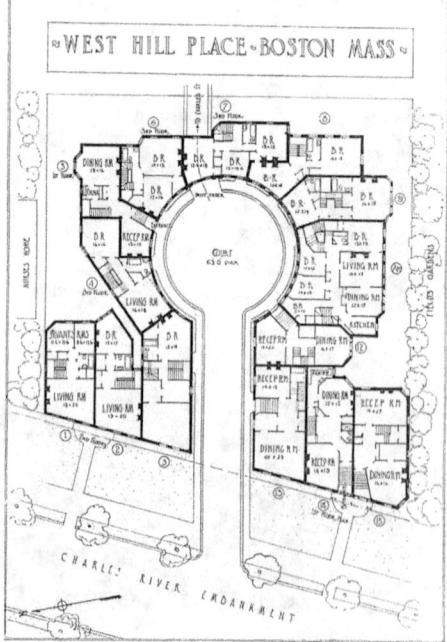

FIG. 784—BOSTON. WEST HILL PLACE

A unified group of houses and apartments, designed by Coolidge and Carlson. See Fig. 787.

FIG. 785—BERLIN. INTERIOR COURT IN A GROUP OF APARTMENT HOUSES

Part of the large scheme of harmoniously designed apartment houses of which the next figure is a plan. This is a view of the long court parallel to Rubens-strasse.

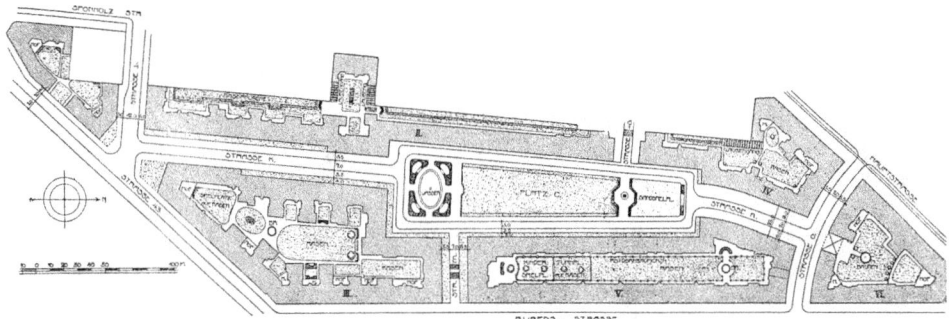

FIG. 786—BERLIN. GROUP OF APARTMENT HOUSES

The Cecilien Gardens, Schoeneberg, an area of about twenty-five acres built up with apartment houses of uniform architecture. Designed by Paul Wolf.

FIG. 787—BOSTON. WEST HILL PLACE
Designed by Coolidge and Carlson.

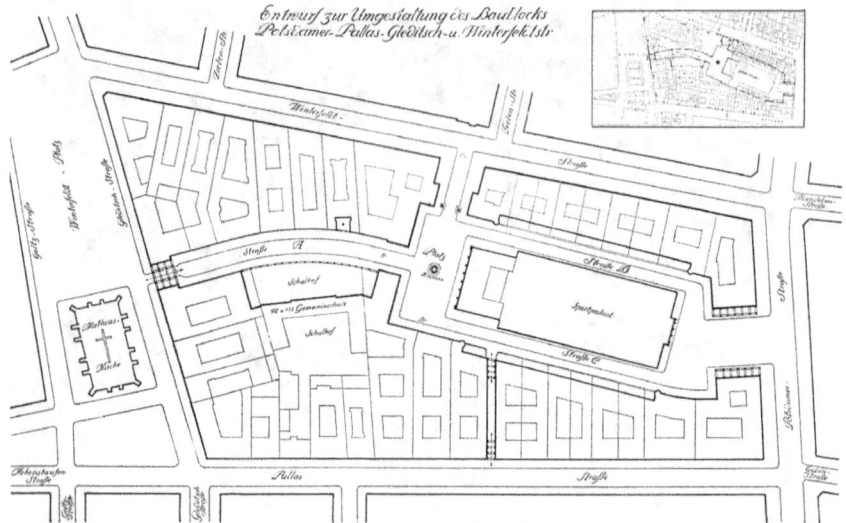

FIG. 788—BERLIN. REDESIGN OF A CITY BLOCK. (See caption, Fig. 789.)

FIG. 789—BERLIN. REDESIGN OF A CITY BLOCK

FIG. 790—BERLIN. UNIFIED STREET FACADES. (See Fig. 796.)

The problem involved in Figs. 788 and 789 is one which is common in American cities, especially where blocks are unduly large. A large public recreation building required an economical site in the midst of a crowded neighborhood. This solution gives the building a detached situation, with harmonious architectural surroundings, without occupying valuable street frontage and without reducing the housing accommodations. A similar use could be made of the large block-interiors of Washington, where the "alley slum" problem is so acute.

The perspective, which shows the plaza in front of the "sport palace," is taken from the point "B" in the plan. Designed by Brodfuehrer and Bardenheuer.

Figs. 788-90 and 796 are from Staedtebau.

FIG. 791—SCHEME TO UNIFY A BLOCK OF OFFICE
BUILDINGS

This sketch was made as a study in the direction of giving at least some elements of unity to a city block. The block, which houses three large banks, is at the side of a river where it is seen as a whole and not merely as part of a street perspective. The most conspicuous building in the block is a huge office building with its unattractive light court and ugly blank walls. Through the middle of the block runs an excellently designed bank building of the temple type. The third bank is housed in a very picturesque old office building, built in the days when roofs were still the mode. This building terminates an important street-vista, but it is not profitable and the owners determined to replace it with a one-story "monumental" bank building. This seemed an opportunity to shape the entire block into some sort of harmony. The most obvious difficulty was the complete unlikeness of the fixed elements—the huge office building and the pedimented bank. The scheme here illustrated sought to reconcile these elements by giving the new building two cornice heights, the monumental part of the building taking up the lines of the nearer neighbor and the higher part reproducing the upper stories of the skyscraper office building. To strengthen this last element of likeness two tower-like additions are suggested for the existing building, which could have windows on all three sides since permanent light would be assured.

The study was still early in the scratch-sketch stage, however, when it was decided not to sacrifice the picturesque old office building.

FIG. 793—NEW YORK. INSTITUTIONAL CHURCH

A design, by Hoppin and Koen which might be used to form an opening in a gridiron street plan, as shown in the insert (upper right hand corner) which has been added. (From the Brickbuilder, 1911.)

FIG. 792—"BANK BLOCK".

Present appearance on the street side. The sketch and inserted view, Fig. 791, show the side toward the river.

FIGS. 794—BERLIN-NEUKOELLN

The site for the buildings shown in Fig. 795.

FIG. 795—BERLIN-NEUKOELLN

School building, designed (by Kiehl) to hide the ugly party walls of the neighboring tenement houses. Compare Figs. 791-92.

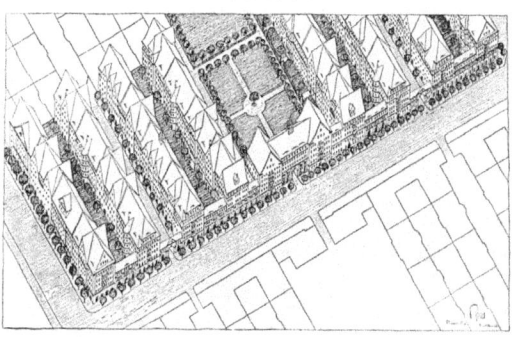

FIG. 796—BERLIN-NEUKOELLN. UNIFIED STREET FACADES

Figs. 796 and 790 are isometric perspectives of schemes for groups of tenements in a congested suburb of Berlin. Fig. 790 is by W. and P. Kind, and Fig. 796 by Kiehl, former City Architect and first supervising city planner for Berlin. Both proposals, besides attaining architectural harmony, secure a maximum of light and air for the tenements by eliminating courts and wings and by developing as garden courts the land saved by the elimination of superfluous streets.

FIG. 797—NEW YORK. MADISON SQUARE GARDEN

FIG. 798—FLORENCE. LOGGIA DEI LANZI

FIG. 799—HAMBURG. ARCADE ON THE ALSTER

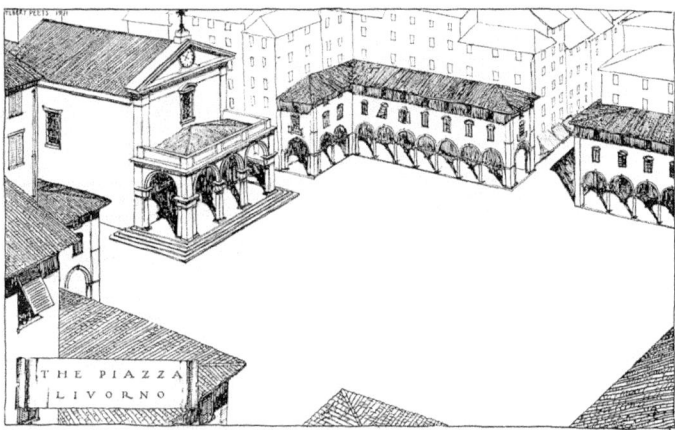

FIG. 800—LEGHORN. PIAZZA VITTORIO EMANUELE
This plaza dates from about the year 1600. The façade of the church is ascribed to Inigo Jones, who
made a long stay in Leghorn during his first Italian journey.

Street Arcades and Colonnades

The great problem in street architecture is the difficulty of combining the large amount of individuality required by the difference of taste and practical needs of the individual house owners with the necessary element of harmony and even unity without which a street turns into a disagreeable hodge-podge of contradictory assertions. The classic way out of this difficulty was the introduction of colonnades or arcades in the ground story, a motive strong enough to tie the different buildings together without depriving them of the possibility of individual development in the upper stories. It has been pointed out before how Greek and Roman forums can hardly be thought of without surrounding colonnades, and almost the same can be said of the streets of Hellenistic and Roman antiquity. Most of the conceptions of plazas inspired by Roman precedent, as for instance the designs of Palladio, Inigo Jones and many others, consider the colonnades as a necessary requisite. The student of civic art repeatedly encounters the recommendation of arcades and colonnades as an essential part of street design. Many Italian cities had arcades along their streets dating from Romanesque and Gothic times and the ideal street of the Renaissance, as one finds it for instance in the old drawing attributed to Bramante (Fig. 634), has arcades or colonnades.

It was for military reasons, which influenced city planning during the Renaissance as much as under Napoleon III, that in most cities the arcades were done away with as giving the people too good a chance to defend themselves against their autocratic rulers. The city of Bologna, where the arcades have been preserved in most of the streets, is often praised for the beautiful effect they give.

When Lorenzo di Medici asked for advice on beautifying the central plaza of Florence, Michelangelo recommended carrying the arcades of the Loggia dei Lanzi around the entire plaza (Fig. 798). In northern cities all during the Middle Ages and the Renaissance the idea of colonnades was revived wherever special effort towards the city beautiful was made. Sir Christopher Wren designed a plan and elevation for a "Gallery of Communication" "consisting of a long Portico of Doric Columns on the Bank of the Thames, extending from Whitehall to Westminster", a distance of 2000 feet.

In the nineteenth century, Regent Quadrant, one of the shopping centers of London, was provided with a scheme of colonnades according to the designs of Nash, and in Paris the arcades of the Palais Royale (Fig. 13), and later of the Rue de Rivoli (Fig. 821), long contained the most desirable shops. The great value of the street arcade does not consist solely in furnishing a sufficiently strong element to tie the individual buildings together esthetically without interfering with an individual development of the upper stories, but it consists also in the charm and feeling of security enjoyed by the pedestrian. Sheltered from rain and sun without being deprived of fresh air, he walks through the street as if it were a unit and a homogeneous member in the makeup of the city. With the growing difficulty of parking machines in the busy down-town districts of big cities, covered arcades in the north should be only a question of time, as their introduction could transform an entire down-town district into a huge store, a bazaar like those of Bagdad and Damascus.

The disadvantage of colonnades, which deprive the rooms behind to some extent of direct sunlight, can be met under modern conditions by giving sufficient height to the colonnades, by introducing light from above the colonnades or from the rear of the building, and especially by the consideration that modern stores, especially department stores, more and more depend upon artificial lighting. Modern stores close up their show windows to such an extent that sun-light if admitted at all, enters only through the upper part and this could conceivably lie above the colonnade (Figs. 846-7). It must be remembered that most sections of the United States, so far as sunlight is concerned, range not with European countries north of the Alps, but with Italy and the other Mediterranean countries which are the home of the colonnades. The greater rainfall in the United States adds to the desirability of colonnades in shopping streets.

The colonnade or arcade is such a joyous element of architectural design that one may almost be sure to find it wherever some happy and graceful effect is achieved. The examples in America belong to buildings often cited as the finest achievements of American architecture (Figs. 797, 825, 831). The introduction of arcades in the American South promises to make rapid progress after the fine

FIG. 801—HONOLULU

Drawings by Louis Christian Mullgardt for the proposed Honolulu "Commercial Civic Center." The streets are unified by carrying through strong horizontal members. (From the Mid-Pacific Magazine, 1918.)

examples of the world's fair at San Diego. Developments like the one shown in Fig. 812, showing a building in Houston, Texas, or the arcades around the plaza in Ajo, Arizona, are very promising. The commercially successful development in front of the Hotel Maryland. Pasadena, (Fig. 848), though not exactly an arcade, is interesting for its double sidewalk. The inner one, covered by a pergola, is faced by the busy stores, while the outer sidewalk serves unimpeded pedestrian traffic. Fig. 847 shows an application of the same idea to more northerly conditions, light being admitted from above the pergola, thus making possible a dense cover of foliage over the pergola.

The esthetic advantage of continuous covered colonnades, tying the street together and yet permitting above them an irregular individual development, may be appreciated to a certain degree from the unifying effect achieved by structures like the colonnade framing the Piazza del Plebiscito in Naples (Fig. 111) or "The Gateway" of Minneapolis. This building shows how a plaza can be given a harmonious aspect if it is separated by a strong demarcation line from the unbridled commercial developments behind the colonnade. The Gateway of the Nation, proposed for New York, illustrates the same idea on a gigantic scale.

Even without the application of continuous covered arcades, a somewhat similar effect could be secured by carrying through a strong cornice line with continuous uniform development underneath and individual free development above. A proposal to this effect was made in connection with the development of land surrounding the Grand Central terminal in New York. Although this plan was not adhered to it led to some interestingly developed buildings (Fig. 611). A committee of architects made a similar proposal for an organization of Chicago property owners in connection with the exten-

sion of Michigan Avenue (Fig. 803). In this case three strong horizontal lines are carried through.

A practical problem of a similar kind offered itself recently in Milwaukee, where the replacing of an old landmark, the fine Pabst Building, by a modern structure was for some time considered. This was felt to be an opportunity to give a little more harmonious treatment to the entire block, which at present exhibits a remarkable maze of heterogeneous motives (Figs. 791-92). The necessity of handling districts of at least block size as an architectural unit has been emphasized before in connection with the illustrations Figs. 572-78 and 738-49.

Mr. Granger in his book on McKim suggested that the business section of Fifth Avenue, New York, should be lined uniformly by a continuation of McKim's Gorham Building. This proposal, even bolder than Michelangelo's suggestion of surrounding the central plaza of Florence with the continuation of the Loggia dei Lanzi, would certainly produce a very striking result, provided of course that monotony were avoided by sufficient interpunctuation of important intersections with east and west streets. With a similar purpose the designer of the Court of Abundance at San Francisco (Fig. 466) is working on a commercial center for Honolulu (Fig. 801), and proposes a nearly uniform ground story brought well in front of the general wall plane.

Smaller cities, the main business streets of which have not reached the climax of development of Fifth Avenue, should seriously strive for the development of a successful type of business building to give harmony at least to some sections. If the adoption of an entire building as ruling type cannot be agreed upon, the adoption of a lower member at least, corresponding, for instance, to the arcaded lower stories of the Gorham Building, should be contemplated. By such farsighted action the main business section of the thriving cities of the Middle West

FIG. 802—NEW YORK. ARCADE OF THE GORHAM BUILDING

(From the Monograph of the work of McKim, Mead and White.)

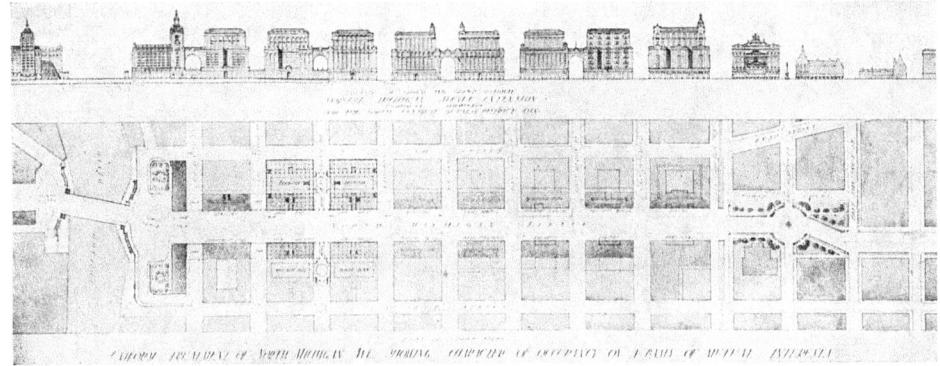

FIG. 803—CHICAGO. PROPOSAL FOR THE UNIFORM TREATMENT OF NORTH MICHIGAN AVENUE

Designed by A. N. Rebori for the North Central Association, Chicago. (From the American Architect, 1918.)

FIG. 805—CREFELD

An effect of unity produced by uniform planting, inspired by the Avenue de l'Observatoire. The trees here, and the trees and river parapets in Fig. 804, serve as unifying elements just as do the uniform lower stories of buildings in Figs. 803 and 806.

FIG. 804—MILWAUKEE

A proposal, by A. C. Clas, to give uniform treatment to the banks of a river.

FIG. 806—CHICAGO. NEW UNION STATION

Designed by Graham, Anderson, Probst, and White. The large office buildings, though of different heights, are surrounded by uniform monumental colonnades projecting well out from the principal masses of the buildings. These colonnades will have a strong unifying effect; much more so, from the central plaza, than may appear from this view.

FIG. 807—SPALATO. CATHEDRAL PLAZA

The arches remain from an ancient basilica. (From a drawing by Niemann.)

FIG. 808—EPHESUS. COLONNADED STREET

(From a restoration by Niemann.) The four columns mark the intersection of two principal streets.

FIG. 809—CARLSRUHE. OLD HOMES AND ARCADED WALKS AROUND THE SCHLOSSPLATZ

FIG. 810—GENOA. VIA VENTI SETTEMBRE

A modern street. The large arch at the left is the carriage entrance to the court of a hotel. The bridge in the distance carries an important avenue.

could become architecturally superior to that of New York, just as in antiquity the younger cities of the Roman empire developed finer forums than the old congested forums of Rome.

Perhaps the most popular means of giving a fine element of harmony to a street is the planting of trees. If the street is wide enough and the nurseryman's preference for specimen trees does not interfere with fairly close planting, it is possible to secure effects much akin to those of street arcades built of stone which, according to Sir Christopher Wren, are only substitutes for trees. The attempt to go into the large subject of allée planting will not be made here, important as it is in civic design. Two examples only may be referred to, showing the fine formal park effect which can be achieved even in densely built up streets, the most remarkable being the Koenigstrasse in Duesseldorf where means have been found to secure the effect of a great formal garden axis in the main business street of a city with a population of four hundred thousand people.

As a new type of arcaded street the two-level roadway has made its appearance in the modern city and promises to become very important. One of the first and most successful was built in Berlin, 1878-82, as a four-track elevated steam railroad, including suburban traffic, through the very center and entire length of the city. This bold development deserves special mention as one of the most important contributions to modern city planning. This scheme, which has been copied in Tokio and has been much under discussion for the new city plan for Chicago, combines efficiency with great saving of land enabling the inner city to avoid being strangled by the large areas required for terminal stations. The designer of the scheme had hoped to flank the elevated railroads with wide tree-planted roadways at the street level.

This idea has received new importance through the development of the automobile. Modern street designers must give serious attention to the design of two-level streets affording an unimpeded field to high locomotion. Many suggestions for such designs can be gathered from existing elevated railroads. (See Figs. 841-44.) The modern development of beautiful two-level highways should afford the thrill one has in driving through Fifth Avenue without the delays caused by cross-town traffic.

FIG. 811—DESIGN ATTRIBUTED TO BRAMANTE

This sketch might be construed to suggest a two-level street, with an upper sidewalk carried by arches over the lower.

FIG. 812—HOUSTON. ARCADES OF THE TEXAS COM-
PANY BUILDING

Designed by Warren and Wetmore.

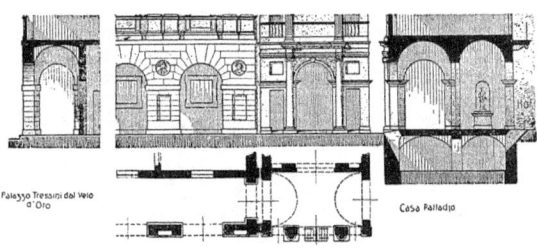

FIG. 813—VICENZA. STREET ARCADES BY PALLADIO

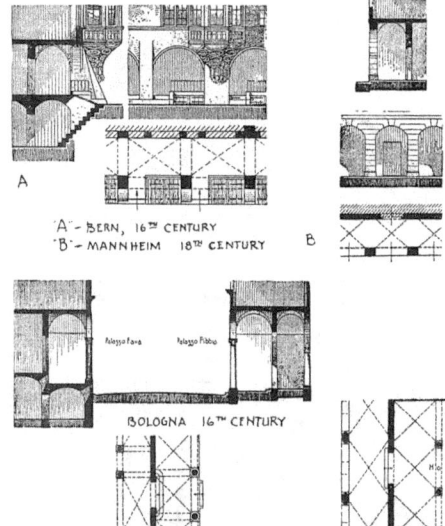

'A'—BERN, 16TH CENTURY
'B'—MANNHEIM 18TH CENTURY

BOLOGNA 16TH CENTURY

FIG. 814—BERN; FIG. 815—MANNHEIM; FIG. 816—BOLOGNA.
PLANS AND SECTIONS OF STREET ARCADES
(Figs. 814-16 and 817-21 are from Gurlitt.)

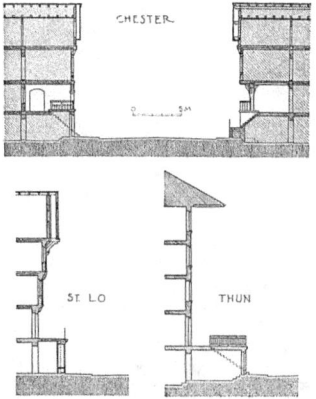

CHESTER

ST. LO   THUN

FIG. 817—CHESTER; FIG. 818—ST. LO;
FIG. 819—THUN. COVERED SIDE-
WALKS ABOVE STREET GRADE

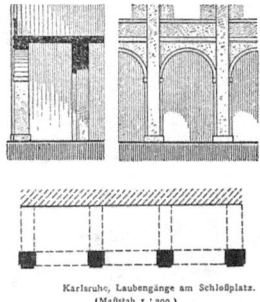

Karlsruhe, Laubengänge am Schloßplatz.
(Maßstab 1 : 200.)

FIG. 820—CARLSRUHE. ARCADED
WALK ON THE SCHLOSSPLATZ

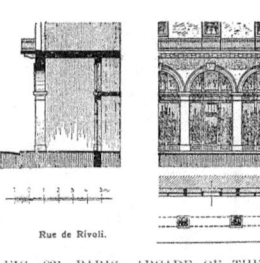

Rue de Rivoli.

FIG. 821—PARIS. ARCADE OF THE
RUE DE RIVOLI

FIG. 822—PALMYRA. STREET COL-
ONNADES AND ARCH

The arch stands at the bend in the street.
(From Wood.)

FIG. 823—CHARLEVILLE, MARKET PLACE

Built early in the seventeenth century, contemporane-
ously with the Place des Vosges, which it resembles.
(Drawing by Franz Herding.)

FIG. 824—BATH, COLONNADES

Bath street was rebuilt with colonnaded sidewalks by
Baldwin about 1790. The little Rue des Colonnes, near the
Paris Bourse, is quite similarly treated. (Drawing by Franz
Herding.)

FIG. 825—BOSTON, COURT OF THE PUBLIC LIBRARY

(From the Monograph of the work of McKim, Mead, and White.)

FIG. 826—FLORENCE, PIAZZA DI SS. ANNUNZIATA AND
LOGGIA DEGLI INNOCENTI

(From Burckhardt.)

FIG. 827—COLOGNE, WERKBUND EXPOSITION, 1914, ARCAD-
ED SHOPPING STREET

Designed by Oswin Hempel. (From Wasmuth's Monatshefte.)

FIGS. 828, 829—AJO, ARIZONA.   ARCADES AROUND THE PLAZA

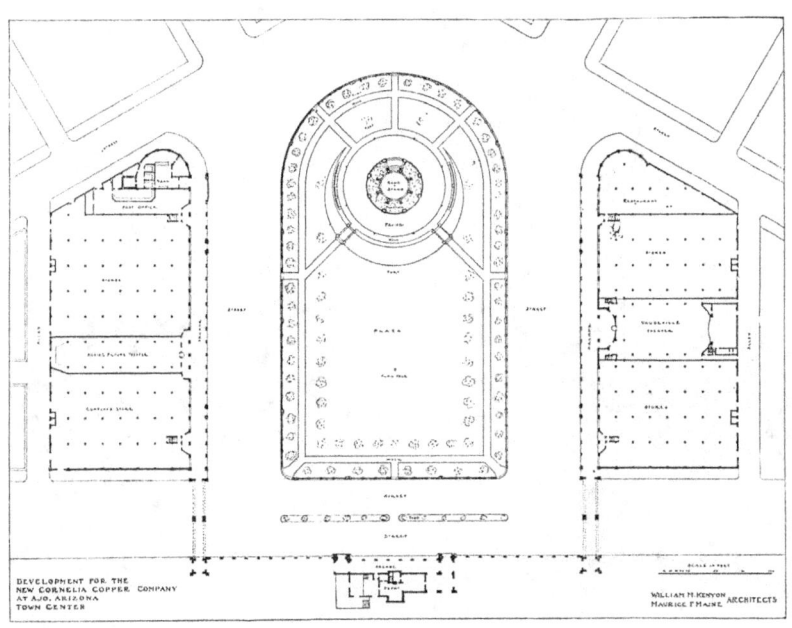

FIG. 830—AJO, ARIZONA.   PLAN OF TOWN CENTER

Designed by William M. Kenyon and Maurice F. Maine.   (Figs. 828-30 from Architecture, 1919.)

FIG. 831—NEW YORK. HERALD BUILDING

The design follows closely the Palazzo del Consiglio in Verona.   (From the Monograph of the work of McKim, Mead, and White.)

FIG. 832—NEW YORK. COURTYARD OF APARTMENT HOUSES ON PARK AVENUE

Designed by Warren and Wetmore. See Figs. 833, 834.

FIG. 833—NEW YORK. COURTYARD OF APARTMENT HOUSES ON PARK AVENUE

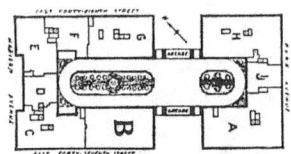

FIG. 834—PLAN OF PARK AVENUE APARTMENTS

Plan of the apartment houses and court illustrated in Figs. 832, 833. Designed by Warren and Wetmore. The arcades extend around the court and with the arches, which serve as porte-cocheres, make a very convenient means of access to the apartments. (Figs. 832-34 are from Architecture, 1918.)

FIG. 835—BERLIN. COURT OF A LARGE HOTEL

A general scheme much like that of the apartment house court illustrated above, though more use is made of planting. (From Migge.)

FIG. 836—DUESSELDORF. COLONNADED COURT IN THE PROJECTED EXPOSITION OF 1915

A very large exposition of industry and art had been projected by the city of Duesseldorf for 1915. The block plan and most of the buildings were designed by William Kreis in a very restrained manner based upon various classical and Renaissance styles. The building at the end of the court here illustrated was to house the exhibition of interior decoration. It is an interesting evidence of the universality of architectural motives that the designs illustrated in this book which most closely resemble this drawing by Kreis are a street in Ephesus (Fig. 808) and Jefferson's University of Virginia. (From Wasmuth's Monatshefte, 1915.)

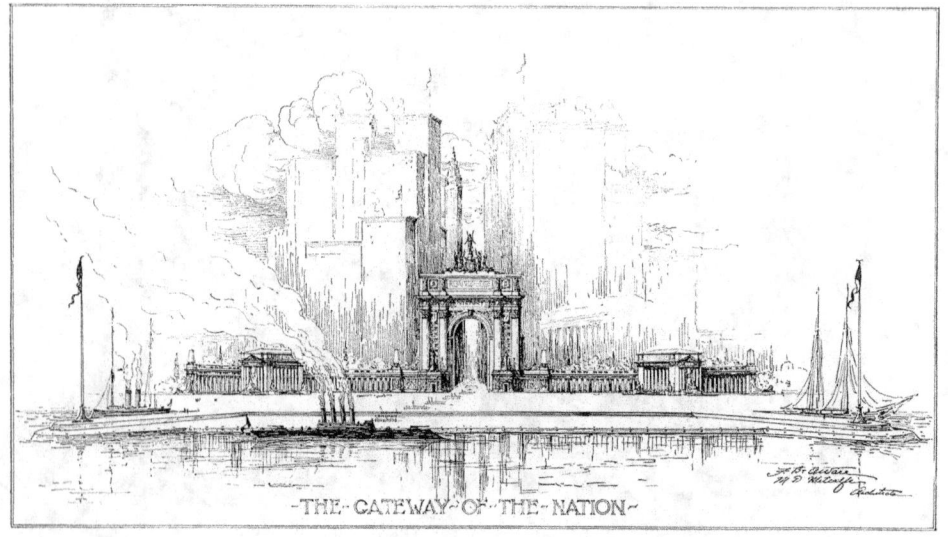

FIG. 837—NEW YORK. STUDY FOR A "GATEWAY OF THE NATION"
By F. B. and A. Ware and M. D. Metcalfe. For plan see Fig. 840.

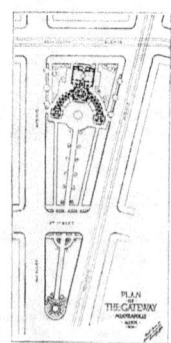

FIGS. 838, 839—MINNEAPOLIS. THE GATEWAY
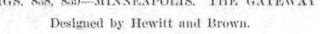
Designed by Hewitt and Brown.

FIG. 841—BOSTON. ELEVATED RAILWAY CROSSING THE ARBORWAY AT FOREST HILLS

FIG. 842—BERLIN. WALK UNDER BALLASTED ELEVATED

FIG. 840—NEW YORK. STUDY FOR
A "GATEWAY OF THE NATION"

See Fig. 837

FIG. 844 (RIGHT)—FOREST HILLS
GARDENS. ELEVATED STATION

Designed by Grosvenor Atterbury and
Olmsted Brothers.

FIG. 843—NEW YORK. PENNSYL-
VANIA STATION

A suggestion for a colonnaded two-
level street. (From the Monograph of the
work of McKim, Mead, and White.

FIG. 845—PARIS. PONT DE PASSY WITH ELEVATED TRACKS OF THE "METRO"

FIG. 846—MADISON. CIVIC CENTER AT LAKE FOREST

(See caption, Fig. 847.)

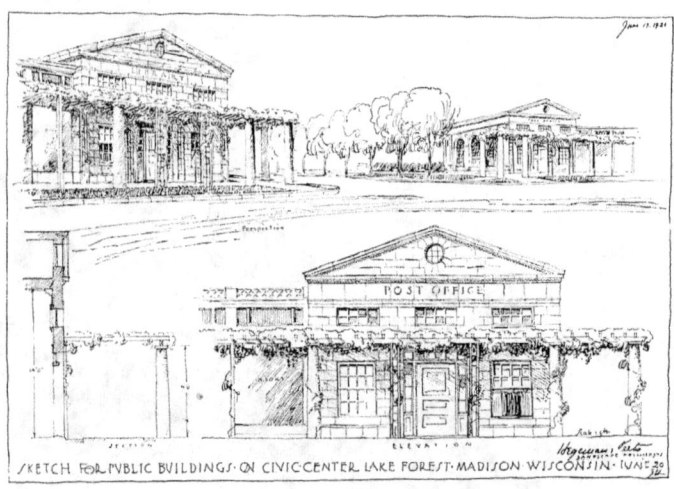

FIG. 847—MADISON. CIVIC CENTER AT LAKE FOREST

The objective in these studies was to fix upon some means of immediately economically and definitely marking out the shape of the large round plaza in such a way that shops and small public buildings could be built later without breaking the uniformity of the frame. It was therefore determined to build a high pergola and, when buildings were put up behind it, to light them from clerestory windows just above it.

FIG. 848—PASADENA

A pergola is here used somewhat as suggested for Lake Forest, but here there are two sidewalks. Since the shops have no windows above the pergola a heavy growth of vines is not permitted. The windows are illuminated at night by lamps on the pergola posts.

FIG. 849—DUESSELDORF

The garden treatment of a business street is here carried even further than in Figs. 846-48. The canal and the rows of luxuriant trees, with a shopping street on one side and residences on the other, penetrate the heart of the city.

FIG. 850—PIRANESI. ENGRAVING OF RUINS AND HEDGES IN THE GARDENS OF THE BARBERINI ON MONTE ALBANO

(From Piranesi's Antichità d'Albano, Rome, 1764.)

CHAPTER V

Garden Art as Civic Art

The business of the architect is often thought to be confined to the design of the house proper. Taken in a higher sense however, architecture is civic art, i. e., the master art which coordinates the other arts. It is only by chance that the names of such distinguished architects as Raphael, Christopher Wren and Thomas Jefferson or, to mention at random two modern examples, Platt and Lutyens, are more intimately connected with gardening or city planning than are the names of other designers of note. For the architect in the higher sense of the word, the conception of a building independent of its surroundings is impossible. For him every building is part of a street, a plaza, a garden, a park, a city. There are no exceptions, unless it be the abode of the cave dweller or the hut of the pioneer, which are beyond the scope of civic art. To conceive a building in connection with its surroundings and to mold both so that each determines the other is architecture in the full sense of the word; it is civic art.

In the field of garden and park design, more than in the other civic arts of America, the developments outside the field of classic and Renaissance art are of but slight interest. Renaissance planning, from Raphael to Robert Adam, was based on Roman work as described by Vitruvius and as it survived in such examples as the Roman fora and thermae and Hadrian's Villa. But speaking generally, the modern garden came into existence with the period of the Renaissance, and represents in a sense the influence on civic art of the highly cultivated women of the Italian courts. The house, set free from the crowded fortified city, could expand into the lighter element of greenery. The strongly axiated plans of Renaissance summer houses and palaces radiated their o r g a n i c strength into the environment and the results were such garden plans as Raphael's Villa Madama and Michelangelo's conception of throwing the axis of the Palazzo Farnese across the Tiber into the gardens of the Villa Farnesina. The idea of far reaching axiation was appreciated and taken back to France by Du Cerceau and others whose sketch-books are full of bold renderings of the new idea. It reached a mightly development in France almost faster than in its Italian home. The great Cardinal de Richelieu contrived for his own benefit to raze the fortifications of Paris in front of his new palace in order to push out with a garden axis of an unheard of fancy (Fig. 13 shows what is left of this garden). When he repeated this wonder in his provincial birthplace on an even bigger scale (Figs. 972, 974-75), as it appeared to his contemporaries, complicating it by inserting a new city into the scheme, the modern garden was acclimatized north of the Alps. The vitality given to it by Le Nôtre and by hosts of artists inspired by him was sufficiently strong to radiate all over Europe and even across the ocean where it molded not only the national capital of the United States but a continuously growing number of garden schemes that send their organizing axes through American landscapes.

FIG. 851—VERSAILLES. FOUNTAIN OF THE OBELISK

"There are two hundred and thirty-one jets which form a great sheaf rising to a height of fifty feet." (From Le Pautre, 1716.)

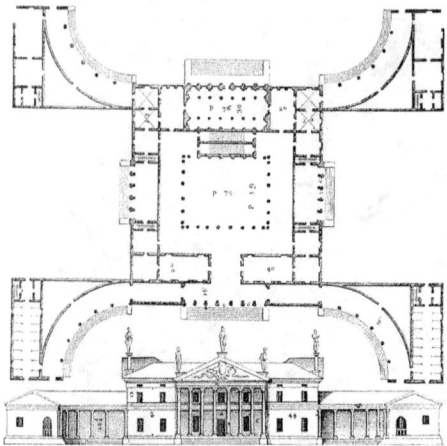

FIG. 852—PALLADIO. VILLA FOR LEONARDO MOCENICO

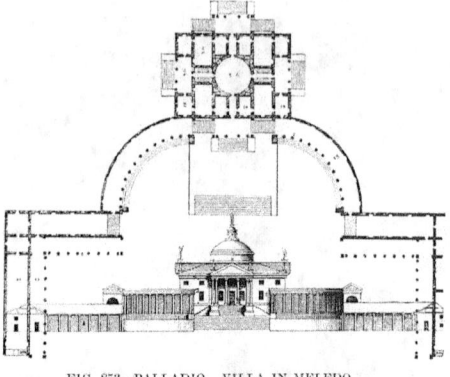

FIG. 853—PALLADIO. VILLA IN MELEDO

These Palladian villas are typical examples of the very formal designs, very carefully "supported" and thoroughly tied in place by spreading members taking firm hold upon the site, which made such an appeal to the intellectual period of the late Renaissance. Such a design is eminently suited to control large areas of land. Compare the plan of Kedleston, Fig. 262, and other English plans on pages 4 and 5.

One can conceive of a garden as a unit independent of a house. The closely hedged "salons" in the bosquets of the formal garden as illustrated by Le Pautre's engraving (Fig. 851) and the Garden of Weld, Brookline, belong to this class. (These and the following examples are quoted at random as they happen to illustrate the argument). In this case the garden will be beautiful in the degree that it is a well balanced design. In most cases, however, the garden will not be an independent unit but will be closely related to one or more buildings. The beauty of the garden will depend on the manner in which it expresses and continues the ideas controlling the plan of the building or of the group. The discussion of the garden plan cannot but include the discussion of the house plan, and the garden plan, in turn, in the ideal city, should be related to the city plan.

The small Italian villa built on a square plan and set in the center of a square garden is a suitable combination. Palladio gives equal development to the four elevations: "because every front has a beautiful prospect, there are four loggias" . . . , loggia meaning a colonnaded temple front (Figs. 853 and 855). To have practically four façades, "four fronts", is the essential idea underlying the plan of the famous Villa Rotonda. It is a "central building", centrally located, the high ambition of the Renaissance (Figs. 235-264) transferred into garden surroundings. In such a garden Thomas Jefferson wanted to realize his Monticello when he placed the service connections underground (Fig. 870 A). The Grosse Garten at Dresden well expresses the equal value of the four elevations of the castle in the center (Figs. 867-69).

When it comes to large palaces however, the con-venience of the service is apt to enforce a "back court with offices" on one of the four sides. If a house is located on a lake, a water course, a hillside or close to a street, there are further inducements to concentrate upon one axis, turning the face of the house and garden to the sides which offer easy development or deserve special recognition. Such a double, instead of a quadruple, face is given to Palladio's villa for Leonardo Mocenico (Fig. 852). "Four colonnades, which like arms tend to the circumference, seem to receive those that come near the house". One pair of arms frames the river view, the other that of the garden. At the other pair of sides are square service courts for stable and kitchen. This amounts to a sacrifice of the cross axis, a wise sacrifice if the views from the side of the house are unimportant or blocked, as is ordinarily the case under crowded city conditions. In such a case the type of the "Bryce House" is a wonderful solution (Fig. 891); for similar solutions see Figs. 898 and 901. Still further limitations of space produce the simple row house which even in its most inexpensive shape should still have its organic little garden (Figs. 900, 905, 907). If more room is available, a number of buildings can be grouped, uniting their small gardens into a common forecourt of satisfactory size as illustrated by many developments in Roland Park, Baltimore, and in the various English garden cities (see Fig. 906 and many illustrations in the sixth chapter).

If plenty of room is available for the location of house and garden and if the views are good on all sides a plan very similar to the "central building" plan can receive an orientation, towards the main highway for instance, by an arrangement similar to the one made by Palladio

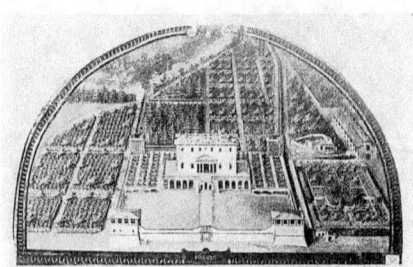

FIG. 854—FLORENCE. VILLA MEDICI IN POGGIO A CAJANO
Built by Sangallo for Lorenzo the Magnificent.

FIG. 855—PALLADIO. VILLA AT MELEDO
Reconstruction by Burger. It hardly seems possible that a terrace supporting the house on its three free sides was not at least intended.

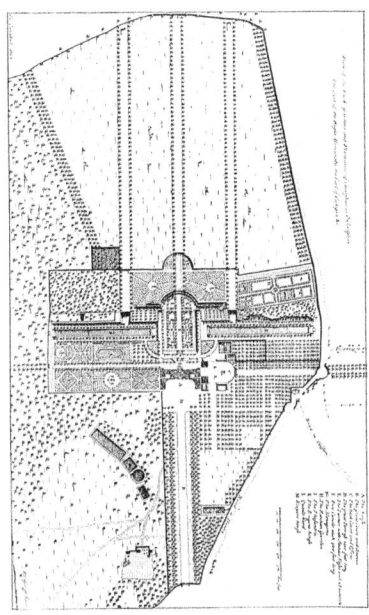

FIG. 856—CAVERSHAM, OXFORDSHIRE
From Campbell's Vitruvius Britannicus

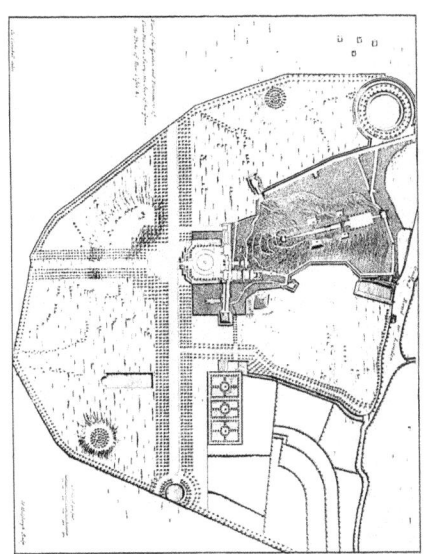

FIG. 857—CLARE MONT, SURREY
From Campbell's Vitruvius Britannicus

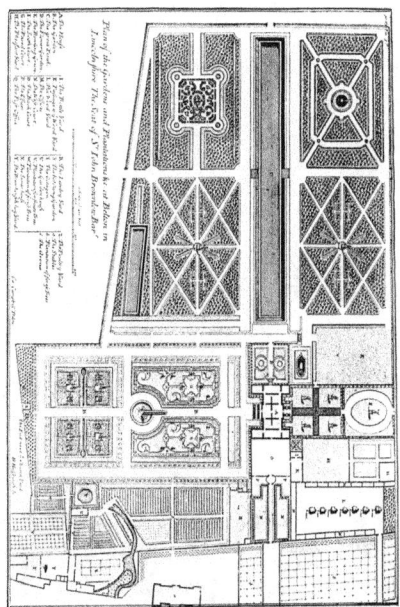

FIG. 858—BELTON, LINCOLNSHIRE
From Campbell's Vitruvius Britannicus

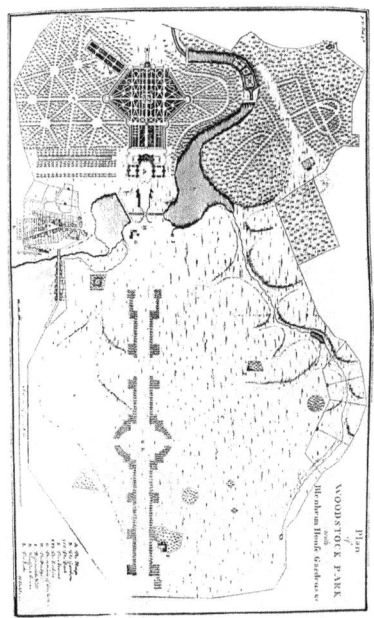

FIG. 859—WOODSTOCK PARK (BLENHEIM PALACE),
OXFORDSHIRE
From Campbell's Vitruvius Britannicus

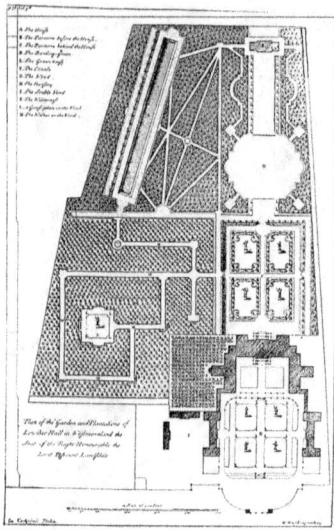

FIG. 860—LOWTHER HALL, WESTMORELAND
From Campbell's Vitruvius Britannicus

in the case of his villa in Meledo (Figs. 853 and 855). It
lies upon the summit of a hill; the main axis is accentuated
without sacrifice of the crossaxis. "The situation is very
beautiful because it is upon a hill, which is washed by an
agreeable little river, in the middle of a very spacious
plain and near to a well frequented road". All axes are
kept free, but special emphasis is given to one side: the
main vista is especially framed by colonnades, to which
some of the services are attached.

The idea of the Villa in Meledo is developed further
in places like Stansted or Ragly (Figs. 892 and 909; both
cases with undue neglect of the cross axis of the garden),
Schoenbrunn (Figs. 893-95), and especially well in George
Washington's Mount Vernon (Figs. 862-66) and many
other colonial seats, such as Rosewell (Fig. 870) and
"Tryon's Palace" (Fig. 901). In Mount Vernon the
service buildings are grouped along a secondary cross
axis and between them fine vistas open to the north and
to the south. One of the most beautiful arrangements
is represented by Marly (Fig. 888) where the central
building has a hill axis on one side, an emphasized water
axis on the opposite side and fine buildings to close the
vistas on the cross axis. What corresponds to the service
features of the previously named seats is represented
at Marly by a charming group of cavalier residences
along the richly developed water axis. The outline of a
plan for a civic center, the nucleus of a fine city plan, is
evident. The underlying idea is similar to the plan of
Shirley Mansion in Maryland (Fig. 871), though much
more richly developed.

With increasing ambitions, the main buildings which
form the basis of these garden schemes rise to the proportion of veritable mountains in the landscape with
watersheds, so to speak, in two directions only, as is
dramatically illustrated in the airplane view of Versailles
(Fig. 873). The idea of developing the four sides equally
is abandoned as the designers are fascinated by the triumphal procession of one very long axis through interminable distances. All resources were employed to give
strong preponderance to this idea. The full-fledged development from horizon to horizon became an economic
undertaking of such gigantic proportions that concentration upon one such axis was almost a necessity.

FIG. 862—VIRGINIA BUILDING AT THE SAN FRANCISCO
FAIR, 1915
An exact replica of Mount Vernon.

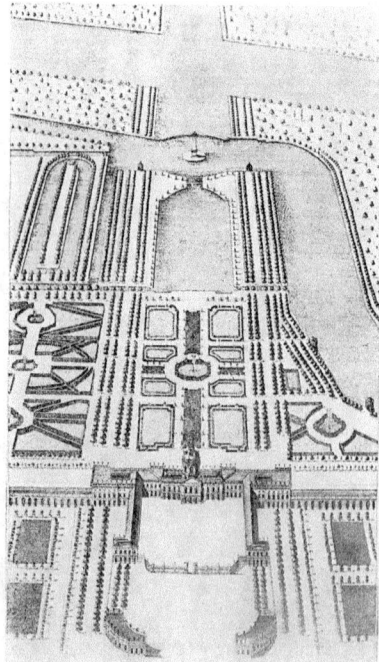

FIG. 861—BERLIN, CHARLOTTENBURG CASTLE

A design for the park, made about 1704, in the same French
style that was used in contemporary English designs.

FIG. 863—MOUNT VERNON, WEST FRONT

Mount Vernon, home of George Washington, is on the Potomac River,
sixteen miles south of the city of Washington. The house which was
built in 1743, measures thirty by ninety-six feet. The disposition of
the buildings is perfectly formal, as are the plans of the gardens, but
the entrance drive, though symmetrical, clearly shows the influence of
the "landscape school" then flourishing in England.

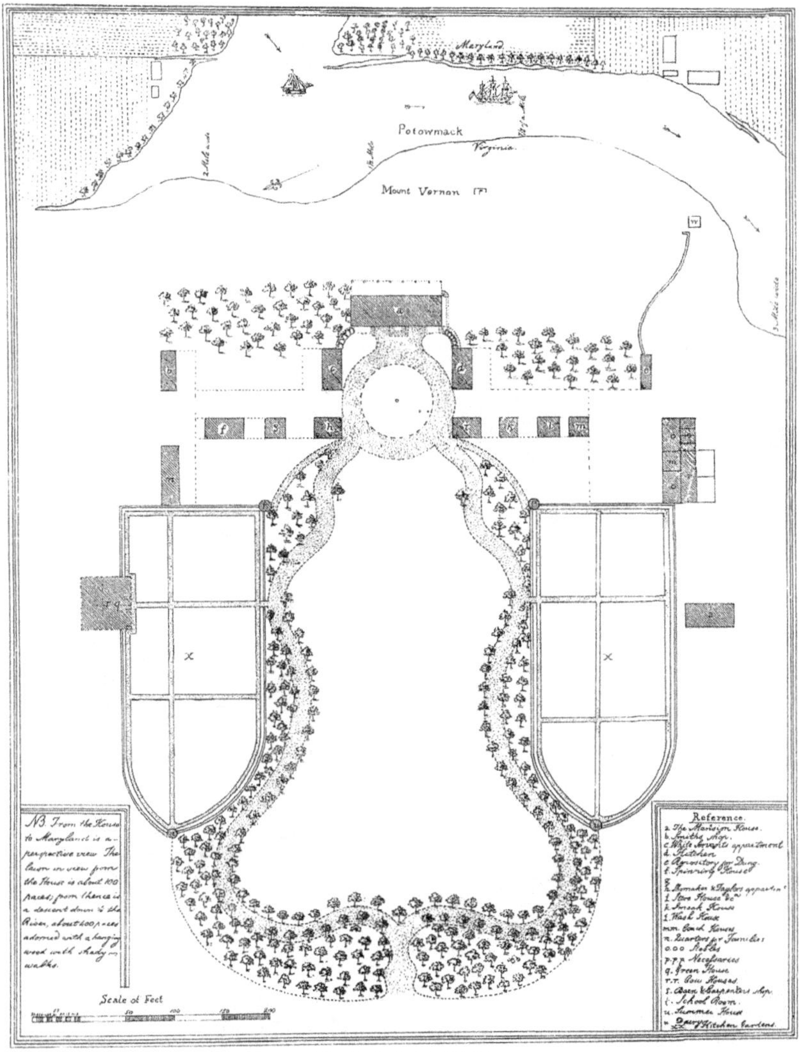

FIG. 864—MOUNT VERNON
(From Ware's "Georgian Period.")

FIG. 865—MOUNT VERNON
A suggestion for a clubhouse or shelter in an American park.

FIG. 866—MOUNT VERNON. ARCADED WALK

FIG. 867, 868—DRESDEN. GROSSER GARTEN. ENTRANCE AVENUE
AND PALACE

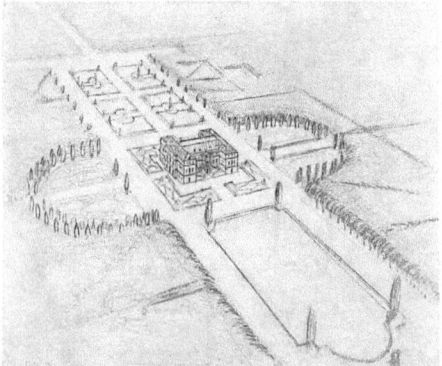

FIG. 869—DRESDEN. GROSSER GARTEN. VICINITY OF THE
PALACE

The "Grosse Garten", one of the most beautiful public parks in
Europe, occupies a rectangle of absolutely flat land a thousand meters
wide and two thousand long. The original plan was formal but various
parts of it have been "landscaped", one being the quartered parterre
(restored in this sketch) which occupied the north-west arm of the
cross-shaped court in which the palace stands.

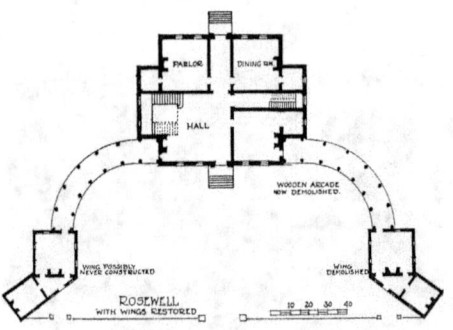

FIG. 870—ROSEWELL

The discovery and exploration of the secrets of perspective fired the imagination of the artists of the Renaissance and drawing, painting, the interior design of
churches and palaces, the design of plazas, streets, cities
and especially of gardens all fell under the spell of perspective magic. It is interesting in this connection to re-
call that parallel to this discovery of perspective appears
in science the new conception of the infinite, upon which
modern mathematics is based, and it seems as if art were
trying to explore the newly conceived infinite space. As
painting from Leonardo to Rembrandt discovers the
secret of representing the fine graduations of atmosphere
into immeasurable distances, civic design celebrates its
highest triumph in the development of axes of great
length.

To develop such axes, to plant them firmly upon a
strong architectural basis, to strengthen and graduate
their vanishing into the distance and to scale them by
counter axes, to accentuate them by fountains, cascades,
tapis verts, and sheets of water of various shapes and levels, to parallel and frame them strongly with buildings,
colonnades, statues, hedges, bosquets and mighty tree-
rows, to transform the intricacy thus achieved into quiet
areas of "salons" and open but strongly framed étoiles,
to relate these axes to important features of the landscape
letting them gain power as they roll down the hillsides
and,—as a climax,—to let the highly concentrated might
of these shots into space appear interminable and uninter-
rupted: this is the ambition of numberless designers. Its

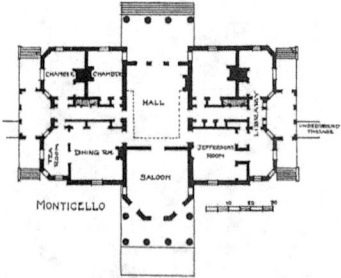

FIG. 870A—MONTICELLO

Designed by Thomas Jefferson shortly before the Revolution. The
plan, a product of the Palladian influence, resembles the Dresden palace
(Fig. 869) in its suitability to lie at the intersection of two axes and
thus to dominate a design covering a large area.

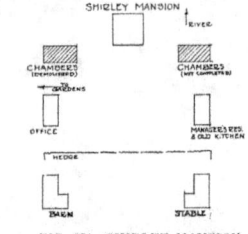

FIG. 871—SHIRLEY MANSION

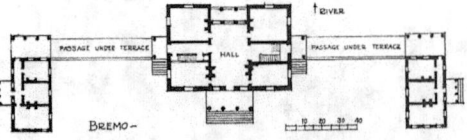

FIG. 872—BREMO

Figs. 870-72, from Coffin and Holden, are typical Southern Colonial
mansion groups. The plans derive directly from Palladio. Compare
Rosewell with the Villa at Meledo, Fig. 853.

FIG. 873—VERSAILLES.

FIG. 875—VERSAILLES

For plan see Fig. 994.

realization requires the close correlation between the master art of architecture and the arts serving it and it may be called the sublime triumph of architecture. In this sense the main western axis of Versailles may be called the unsurpassable climax of modern art; its endless perspective into unlimited space, opening like a magic window into infinity, ministers to such a deep longing of the heart, that its contemplation almost partakes of the character of a sacrament.

The enjoyment of the marvels of perspective is not limited to designs giving the endless perspective, though

this is no doubt its most wonderful climax. Instead of the opening into space, a feature of the type of the Arc de Triomphe in Paris or the Gloriette in Schoenbrunn may furnish the climax to the perspective axis. But without a strongly developed axis a modern civic design of any consequence is as inconceivable as a fine cathedral without altar and apse, or a Gothic town without the spires of a cathedral.

Here one encounters an amusing contrast: While in feudal times the sunk ha-ha fence had to be an almost unavoidable requisite of the formal gardener bent upon

FIG. 876—NEW YORK. THE TERRACE IN CENTRAL PARK
"C. Vaux, architect; J. W. Mould, assistant."

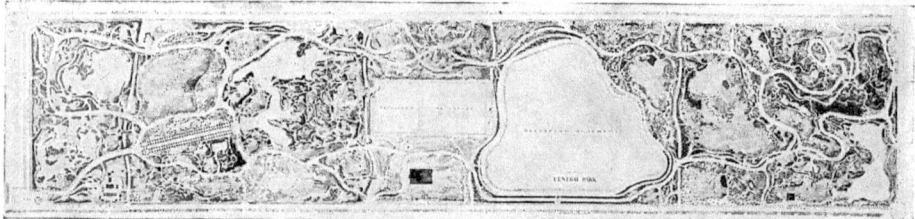

FIG. 877—NEW YORK. GENERAL PLAN OF CENTRAL PARK

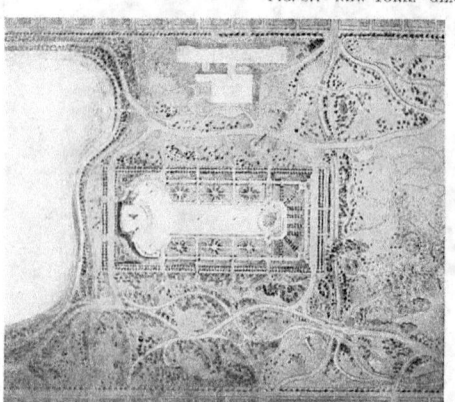

FIG. 878—NEW YORK. PROPOSED FORMAL GARDEN ON SITE
OF RESERVOIR
Designed by Carrere and Hastings.

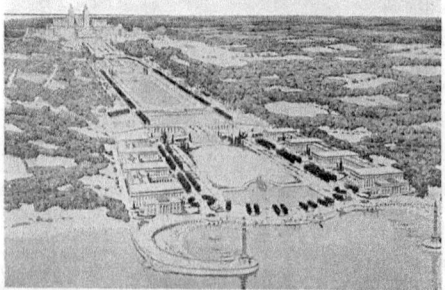

FIG. 879—NEW YORK. THE "NEW VERSAILLES"
A proposed apartment hotel colony, designed by Carrere and
Hastings.

the development of long axes, to-day every American
city built on flat land on the customary gridiron plan
could be thrilled by the view of an unbroken perspective
at the end of every street. The wonderful when vulgar-
ized is little appreciated. That the finest effect of civic
art should be carelessly thrown away at the end of each
city street petering out aimlessly amongst neglected surroundings seems almost a sacrilege. It is not hard to
understand why in this, as in every other field, the ro-
manticism of the early nineteenth century was sick of
formal art, which had become flat and meaningless.

The great movement for parks in American cities,
which began in this period and was guided by men of
such note as F. L. Olmsted, reacted strongly and very
properly against the degenerate formal art then practiced.
But instead of superseding bad by good formal art, or
better, instead of superseding bad art by good, the idea
of "informal" art was heralded as the antidote. As a
result of the park constructions of the nineteenth century
in America, which, so far as size and expense are concerned, rival or surpass the work of European feudalism,
make no attempt to continue the great tradition although
George Washington himself had done his best to ac-
climatize it in the United States. The great mall conception west of the National Capitol was neglected and
superseded by "informal" gardening which strikes the
modern student as very inferior to the original plan
which has since been restored.

Central Park in New York (Figs. 876-78), which com-
pares in size with the parks of Versailles and both Trian-
ons combined, "is different from most English parks,"
as Baedeker's guide ably puts it, "by having a large
number of small picturesque scenes instead of the broad
expanses of turf and large groups of trees". This type
of development was encouraged by a very difficult topography. A wonderful amount of loving genius was employed to paint these "picturesque little scenes", which
unfortunately, under the heavy wear of the population
of the largest city in the world, could not but lose the effect of untouched nature the designers meant to achieve.
Every relation between the park and the plan of the city
is carefully avoided. Not only are the cross traffic roads

FIG. 880—HAMBURG. ENTRANCE TO THE NEW CITY PARK
For plan see Fig. 882.

FIG. 881—HAMBURG. RESTAURANT IN THE NEW CITY PARK
For plan see Fig. 882.

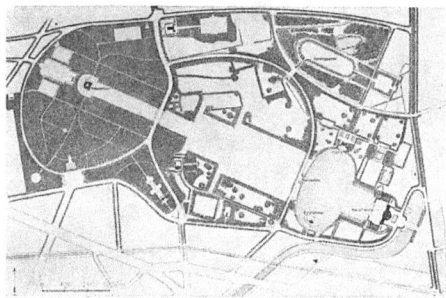

FIG. 882—HAMBURG. NEW CITY PARK
F. Schumacher, architect. See views above.

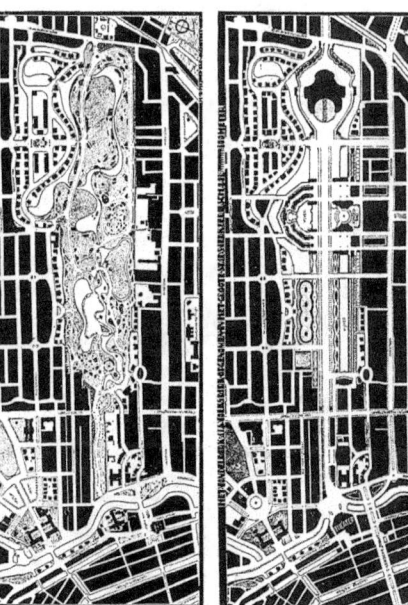

FIG. 883—NANCY. PLACE D'ALLIANCE

This charming little square is but little known, perhaps because it is overshadowed by the famous Place Stanislaus, a block away. For location plan see Fig. 348.

FIGS. 884-85—AMSTERDAM. VONDEL PARK

A scheme (by H. T. Wijdefeld) for the redesign of a park. Quite aside from any question as to the detailed merits of the new plan, the contrast of style is very striking.

FIG. 886—HAMPTON COURT. THE LONG POND
(From Mawson.)

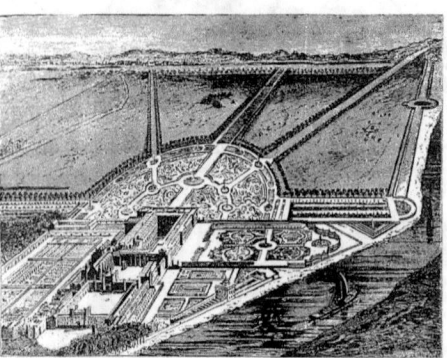

FIG. 887—HAMPTON COURT

The little gardens along the Thames date from the sixteenth
century; the canal was dug and the long linden avenues were planted
about 1662; the gardens around Wren's addition to the palace were
laid out about a quarter of a century later and have since undergone
many changes.

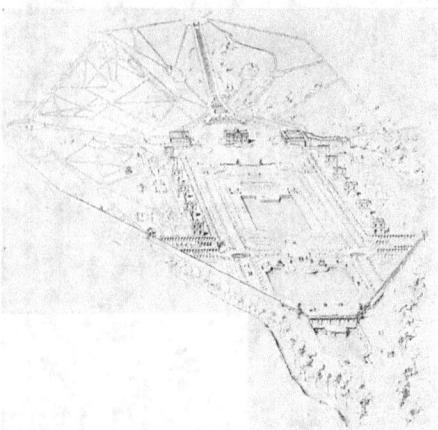

FIG. 888—MARLY-LE-ROI

The chateau and gardens at Marly were built for Louis XIV about
1680 by Mansart Le Brun and Le Nôtre.
Marly is an hour's walk north-east of Versailles. Only a few
vestiges of the buildings remain, but the strongly modeled ground-form
and the balanced masses of foliage still make of the site a very beautiful park. The sunk garden is now a pasture flanked by rows of huge
elms and lindens. The lowest pool still remains and the villagers still
water their horses there. The plan of Marly has influenced many
modern designs, among them the scheme shown in Fig. 879.

through the park sunk and cleverly hidden, which is commendable, but the main entrances to the park are almost
treated in a similar way by roads winding casually from
the corners. There is no suggestion of stateliness or axiation. In the interior of the park one finds the formal
feature of "the mall", but it is short, connecting to the
southeast with a winding road and terminating at the
opposite end in a vista over an informally framed sheet
of water. To see this one has either to cross a main line
of vehicular traffic or go down through a tunnel. The
visual axiation upon a little water tower is hardly to be
taken seriously. The design of the architectural feature
terminating the mall (Fig. 876) is equally handicapped
by the period of its conception and justifies the lack of
interest which the people of that time took in formal art
as they understood it.

While the great awakening following Chicago, 1893,
restored the formal plan of the Washington Mall, through
the work of the commission of 1902, the situation of Central Park has changed little. The entrances to the park
from Columbus Circle and especially from the newly developed Plaza at the southeastern corner of the park
have been formalized so far as their location permits,
and the construction of the new water supply system for
New York has made possible the plan of transforming
the southern of the two old reservoirs which lie in the
park into a formal sunken garden of considerable size
(34 acres), according to the plan of Thomas Hastings (Fig.
878). The war interfered with the realization of this project. Since the general park plan does not recognize the
reservoir except by an informal walk around it, the introduction of a formal garden into the area of the reservoir, however desirable such a note of architectural
strength would be, could not change the general character
of the park. The large Metropolitan Museum of Art,
which lies immediately east of the proposed formal gard-
en, is an architectural mass of such size that, if properly
placed, it could well have become the basis of a main
north-south garden axis rivalling Versailles in proportions. As things are, it turns its back on the park so
distinctly that the designer of the proposed formal development of the reservoir did not attempt any relation
between the Museum and the new formal garden.

There was a time when many fine formal parks were
destroyed in order to be Repton-ized. There is now coming a time when "informal" parks will be redesigned.
A redesign of Central Park, like the one proposed under
somewhat similar circumstances for the Vondel Park in
Amsterdam (Figs. 884-85), would be timely in connection
with the dying out of the fine old trees which still give so
much charm, regardless of design, to this large park in
the heart of New York.

If a garden or a park cannot benefit from being part
of the larger scheme of the city plan, it must strive to
shut out the elements of disorder surrounding it by a
strong screen (of trees, walls, colonnade) in order to
develop within itself as a microcosm the laws of balance
and symmetry which are the essentials of art. This
means a definite break with the conception that gardens,
parks or residential developments should be laid out on
the pretense that they are a piece of untouched nature or
something that has "just grown" in a happy, haphazard,
unrestrained way. A movement toward recognition of
formal principles in the design of open spaces has gained
impetus since 1890. In America (Figs. 938-43, 947-48)
and England this movement has mainly affected private
gardens, while in Germany the public park has been
equally benefited (Figs. 880-82, 923-37).

Cemetery design has perhaps seen the most serious
desolation suffered by any field of civic art. In the ceme-

FIG. 891—ANNAPOLIS. THE BRYCE HOUSE

The Bryce house is one of several Colonial houses of similar plan in Annapolis. The plan creates a very strongly bounded garden forecourt as a setting for the house. Such a group is ideally suited to terminate a street or to form one side of an open area. (From Elwell.)

tery, where all should meet on common ground, where beauty and harmony should rule and order be strictly enforced, ruthless individualism in the development of individual graves and wild informality of road design have produced the most unpleasant results. The example of the old cemeteries of colonial times (Fig. 971), with the noble simplicity of the tombstones, is in keeping with the Renaissance examples of fine cemeteries (Figs. 956, 959-61, 968-69), some of which are today the object of esthetic pilgrimages. Modern cemetery designers, as for instance in London (West London Cemetery), Vienna (Fig. 955) and Munich, have made remarkable efforts to return to the strong architectural frames one finds in the Campo Santo of Genoa or Pisa.

Since the advocates of informal garden design sought encouragement from the example of Japanese gardeners it may be interesting to give here three views from a cemetery in Tokio (Figs. 962-67) which show an almost puritan simplicity and are well in keeping with the dignity of the temple settings which in Japan and other parts of Asia are customary for buildings of state and religion.

The designer of cemeteries will not lose sight of a precious set of observations regarding cemetery designs made by Sir Christopher Wren when he proposed the relocation of cemeteries from the crowded interior of old London into outlying quarters. These recommendations picture a design of noble simplicity worthy to serve as a model. Wren, after proposing an area of about two acres as a suitable cemetery unit continues: "This (piece

of ground of two acres) being enclosed with a strong brick Wall, and having a Walk round, and two cross Walks, decently planted with Yewtrees, the four Quarters may serve four Parishes, where the Dead need not be disturbed at the Pleasure of the Sexton, or piled four or five upon one another, or Bones thrown out to gain Room. In these Places beautiful Monuments may be erected; but yet the Dimensions should be regulated by an Architect, and not left to the Fancy of every Mason; for thus the Rich, with large Marble Tombs, would shoulder out the Poor; when a Pyramid, a good Bust, or Statue on a proper Pedestal, will take up little Room in the Quarters, and be properer than Figures lying on Marble Beds: The Walls will contain Escutchions and Memorials for the Dead, and the Area good Air and Walks for the Living. It may be considered further, that if the Cemeteries be thus thrown into the Fields, they will bound the excessive Growth of the City with a graceful Border, which is now encircled with Scavengers Dung-stalls."

Wren takes for granted that the cemetery will be divided into "quarters" in accordance with the traditional Christian symbolism. A related idea, that the foot of the grave should lie to the east, is still occasionally met with. We moderns smile at these quaint old fancies, but it was perhaps just such interminglings of superstition and esthetic feeling which gave stability to the folk-art of the ages of faith and produced the unquestioning dignity and homely order which are now so wanting in popular art.

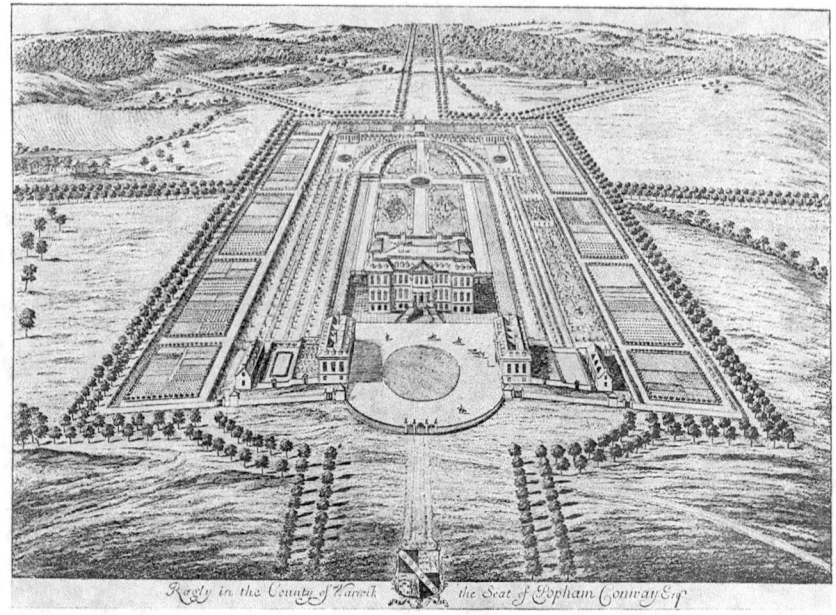

FIG. 892—RAGLY, WARWICKSHIRE

The house was built in 1698. Engraving by Kip, 1707. (From Macartney.)

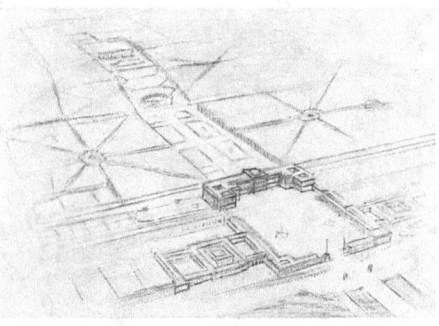

FIG. 893—VIENNA. BIRDSEYE SKETCH OF SCHOENBRUNN

FIG. 895—VIENNA. PALACE AND GARDENS OF THE BELVEDERE

The gardens were designed early in the eighteenth century by Fischer von Erlach and the French "garden engineer" Girard; the palace, by von Hildebrand, is somewhat older. The Belvedere lies inside modern Vienna and the upper terraces command a fine view of the old city. (From Dohme.)

FIG. 894—VIENNA. ENTRANCE COURT OF THE PALACE, SCHOENBRUNN

The palace was begun by Fischer von Erlach in 1696; the gardens were built in the middle of the eighteenth century from the plans of the French architect Le Blond. The gardens include botanical and zoological collections and now form one of the most popular Viennese parks. (From Sitte.)

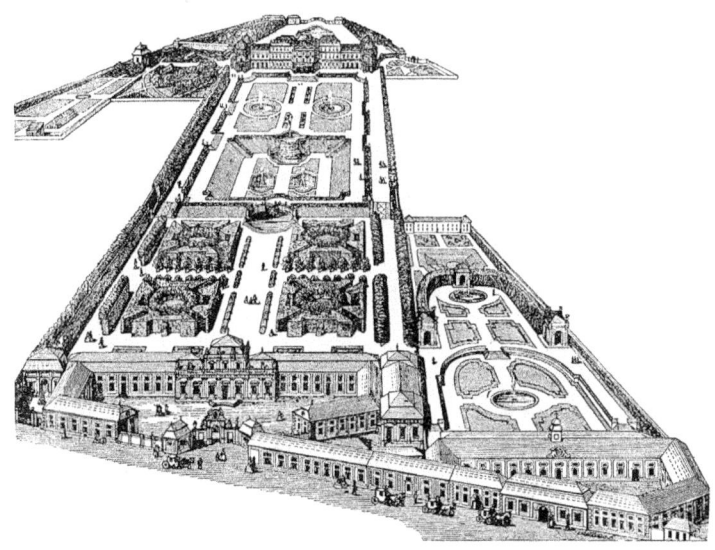

FIG. 896—VIENNA. GENERAL VIEW OF THE BELVEDERE GARDENS

This view shows all of the Belvedere gardens but omits the botanic garden and the Schwartzenberg garden, which lie to the left and right, respectively, of the Belvedere. The "lower Belvedere" and the stables and guardhouse are cleverly planned to fill in the irregular area between the gardens and the "Rennweg."

FIG. 897—CASERTA

The palace was built for the king of Naples by Vanvitelli in 1752. The oval range of stables was not built, this drawing being in part based upon Vanvitelli's plan, as reproduced by Gromort. The garden axis is two miles long.

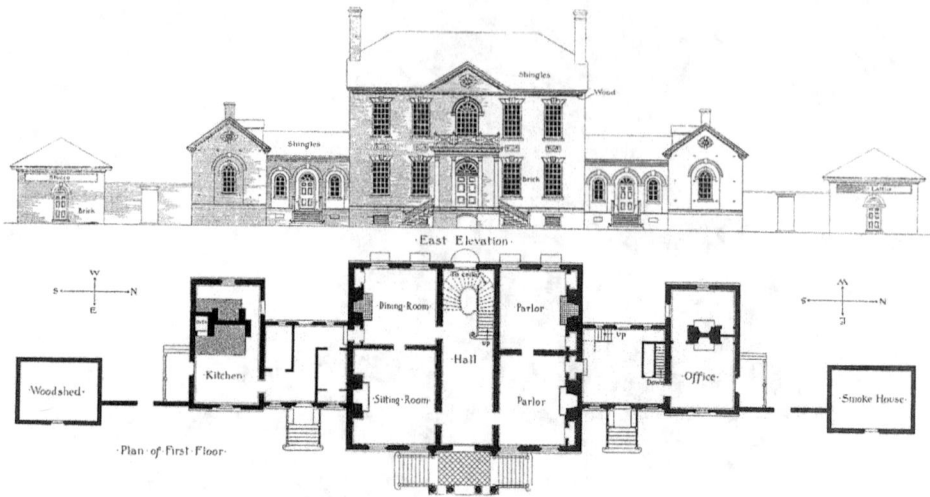

FIG. 898—"WOODLAWN," VIRGINIA

Designed by Dr. William Thornton. (Figs. 898 and 899 from Ware's Georgian Period.)

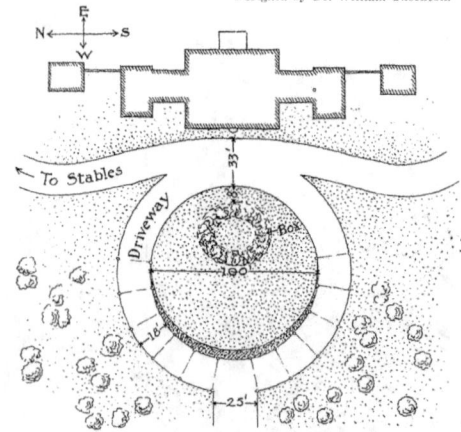

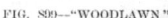

FIG. 899—"WOODLAWN"

FIG. 900—ESSEN. REAR YARDS OF HOUSES AT ALFREDSHOF

These gardens are so designed as to give each owner a definite area while at the same time preserving the openness and unity of the entire court. For plan see Fig. 1124. Designed by R. Schmohl. (From Wasmuth's Monatshefte, 1921.)

Rear View: Tryon's Palace, Wilmington, N. C.

FIG. 901—WILMINGTON, N. C. "TRYONS PALACE"

A quaintly detailed but dignified domestic group employing outlying pavilions to spread and support the house and to give it a grip on a large area of ground. Without the cottages and connecting colonnades the central building would be bleak and unrelated to the site.

FIG. 902—CHARLOTTESVILLE, UNIVERSITY OF VIRGINIA

FIG. 903—ST. MARTINS, PA. PHILADELPHIA CRICKET CLUB

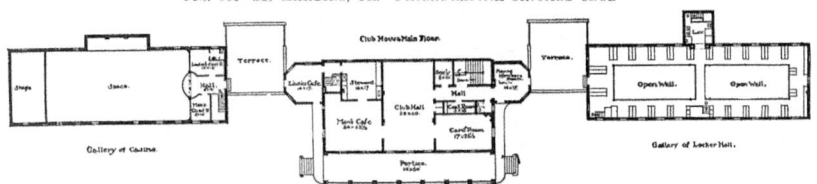

FIG. 904—ST. MARTINS, PA. PHILADELPHIA CRICKET CLUB
Designed by G. T. Pearson. (From the American Architect, 1912.)

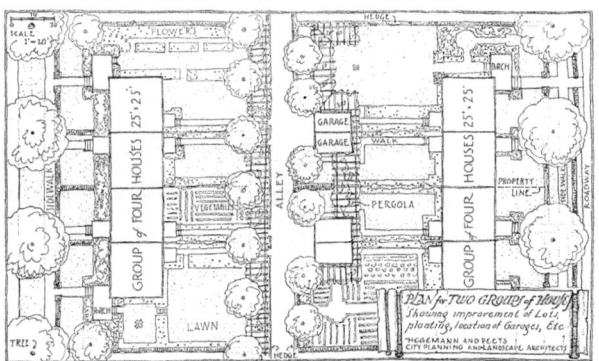

FIG. 905—GROUPED HOUSES AND YARDS WITH AND WITHOUT GARAGES

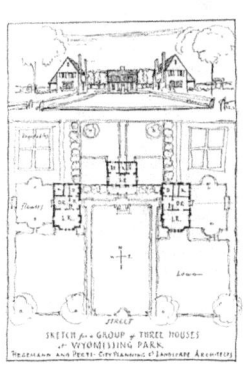

FIG. 906.

FIG. 907—GROUPED HOUSES AND YARDS WITH AND WITHOUT GARAGES

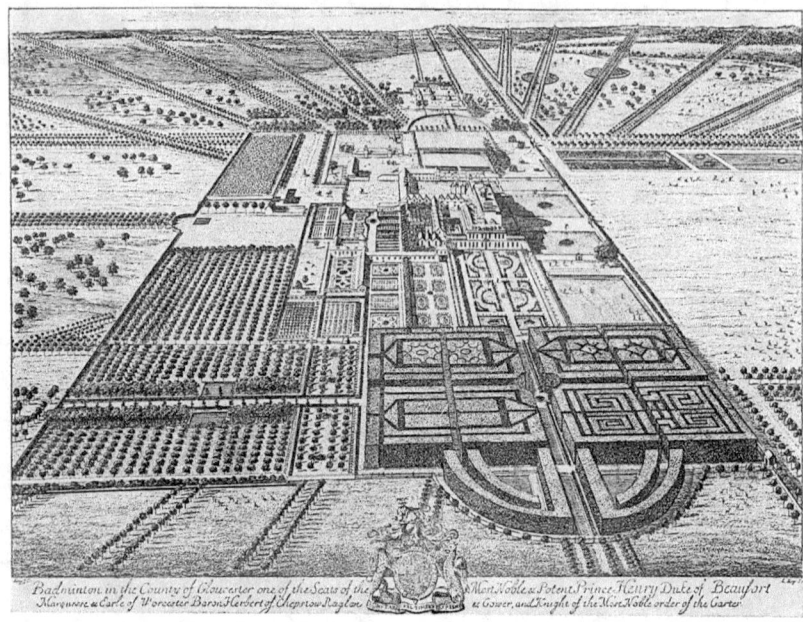

FIG. 908—BADMINTON, GLOUCESTERSHIRE

Built in 1682; one of the most important English applications of the French style of gardening. The avenues radiating from the house are aimed at church steeples and other similar objectives. (From Macartney's reproduction of Kip's engraving.)

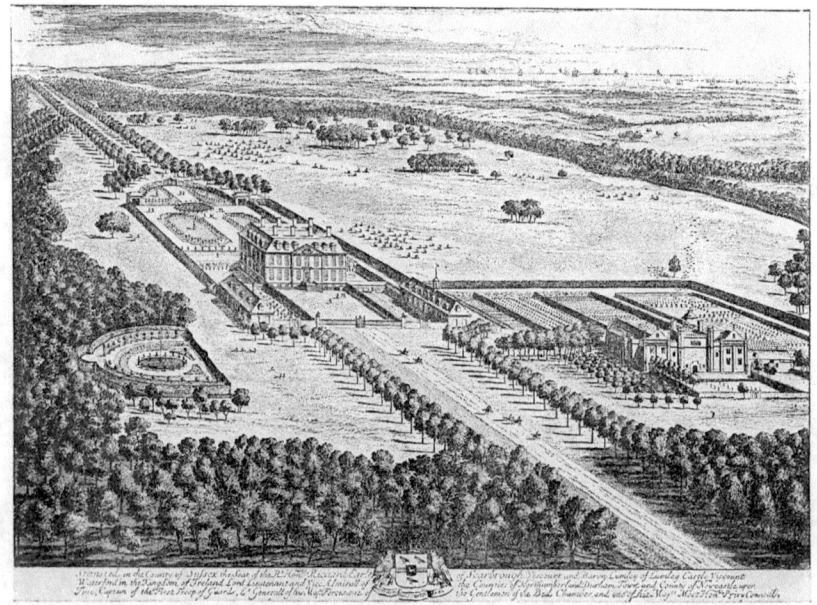

FIG. 909—STANSTED HOUSE, SUSSEX

The larger house was built in 1687, possibly by Wren. (Engraving by Kip, from Macartney.)

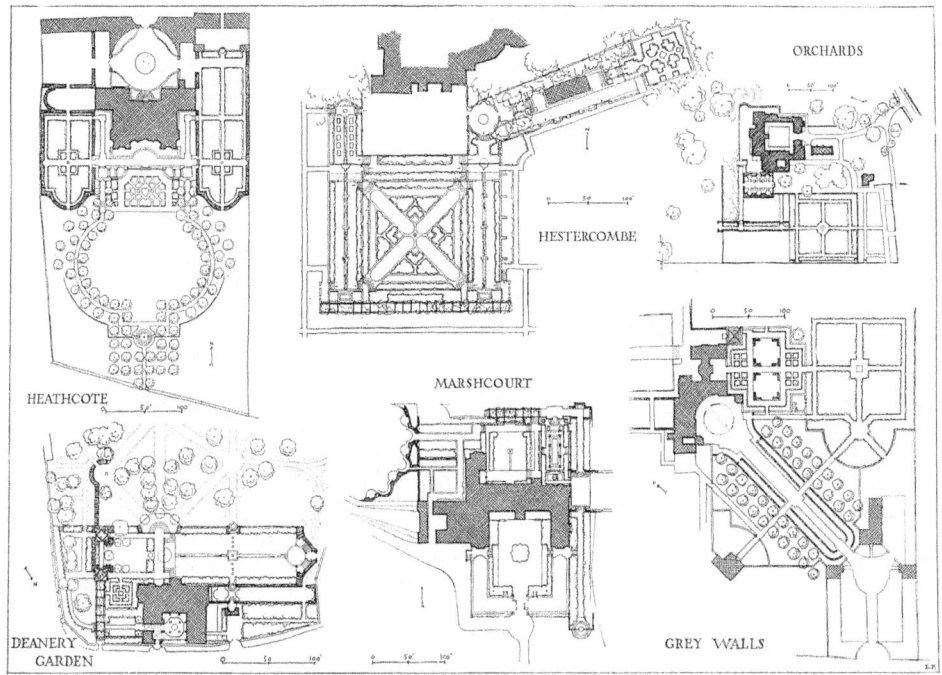

ORCHARDS

HESTERCOMBE

HEATHCOTE

MARSHCOURT

GREY WALLS

DEANERY GARDEN

FIG. 910—GARDENS DESIGNED BY E. L. LUTYENS

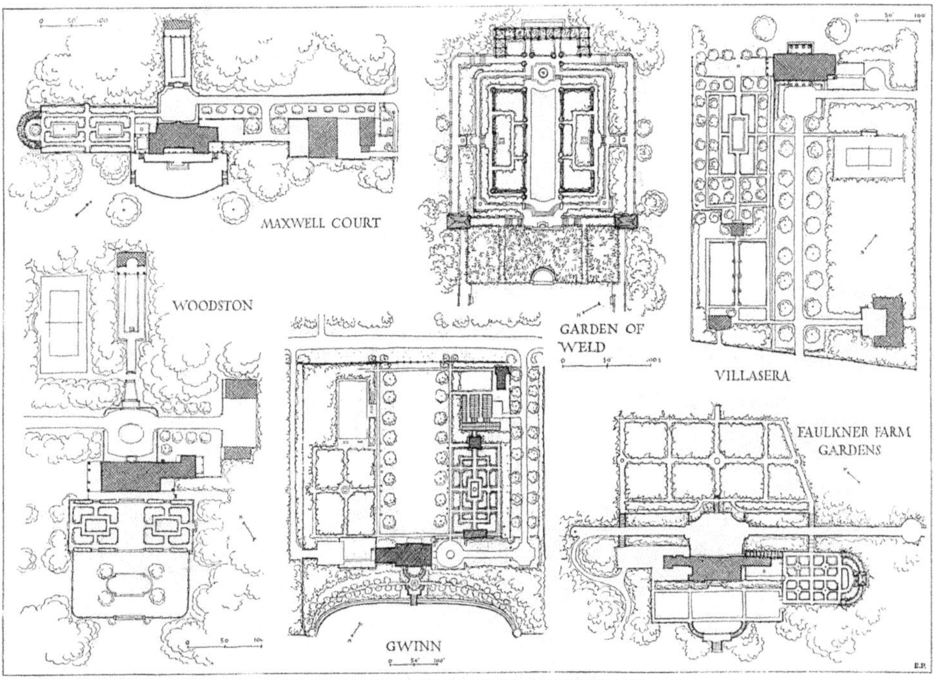

MAXWELL COURT

WOODSTON

GARDEN OF WELD

VILLASERA

FAULKNER FARM GARDENS

GWINN

FIG. 911—GARDENS DESIGNED BY CHARLES PLATT

These sketches from plans by Lutyens and Platt are reproduced to illustrate well developed personal styles of garden design which could be employed with equal success in the planning of public parks and even of residential districts.

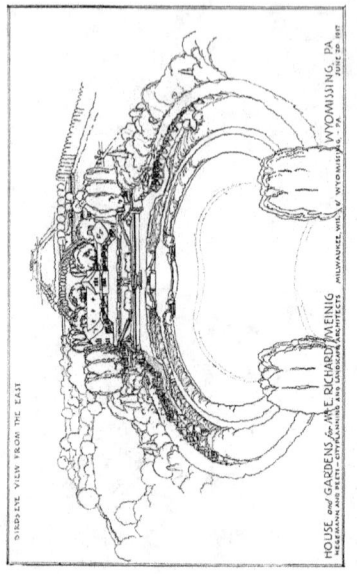

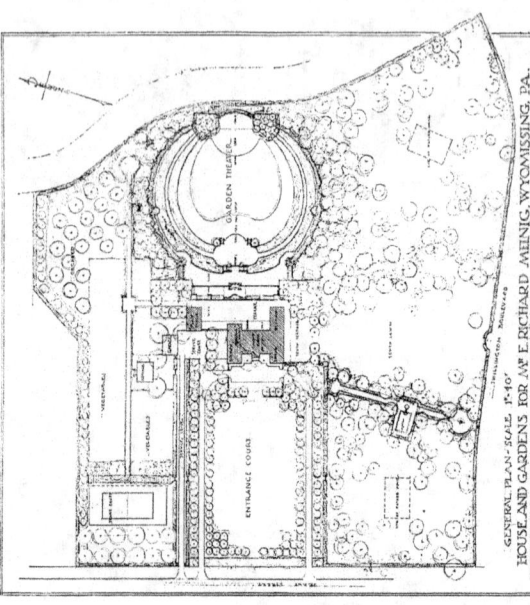

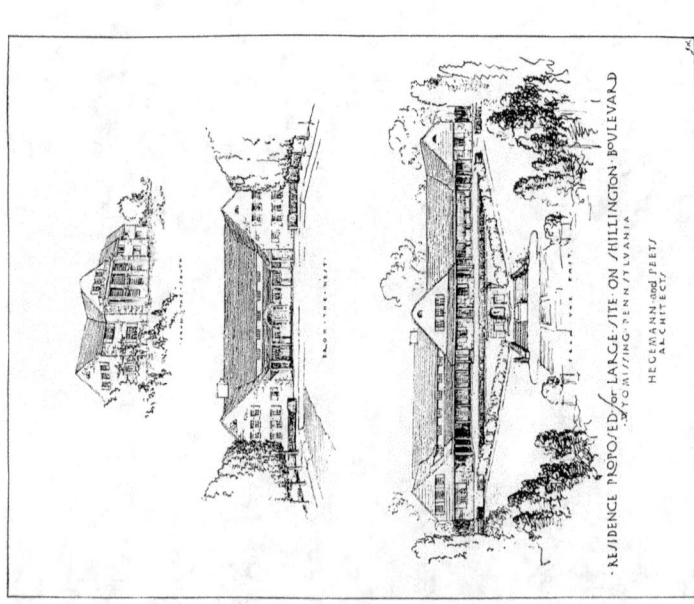

FIGS. 912, 913—STUDIES FOR HOUSE AND
GARDENS AT WYOMISSING

The objective in this design was to produce a house-plan closely related to the site and one from which strong axes could be drawn out in three directions and thus control and unify the entire estate. The entrance court and the theater-shaped garden were both strongly individualized geometrically, but the axes of these two areas were thirty-five feet apart, and the house-plan had to be adapted to that condition. The axes were not restricted to the central merely of the façades but were carried deep into the house; only in this way can a garden-plan be made the natural expansion of the house-plan.

The entrance court was built as here shown, but the garden theater has been "landscaped" into the semblance of an alpine meadow.

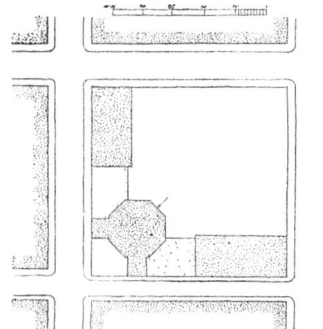

FIG. 914—BUILDINGS ON A SMALL SITE

The buildings are concentrated at the very limits
of the site so that the free area may be consolidated.

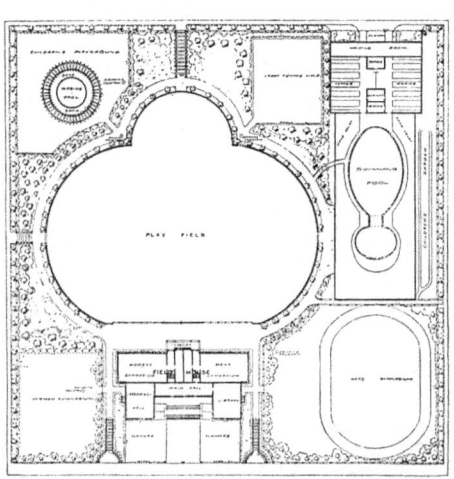

FIG. 915—CARLSRUHE. A SMALL GARDEN PLAZA

For the architectural development of this plaza see Fig. 1002.

FIG. 916—CHICAGO. PLAYGROUND IN THE WEST PARK
DISTRICT

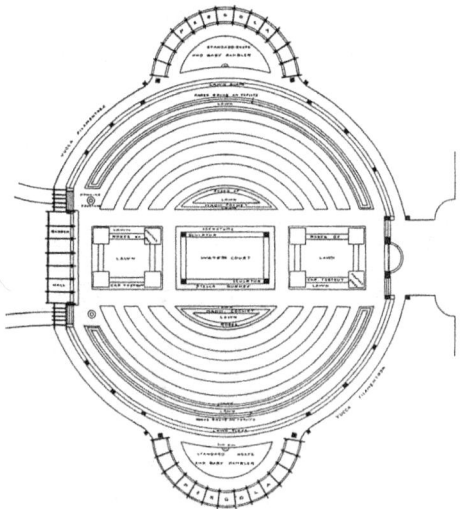

FIG. 917—CHICAGO. ROSE GARDEN IN HUMBOLDT PARK

Figs. 916 and 917 designed by Jens Jensen.

FIG. 918—SHEBOYGAN. THREE STREET-ENDS IN LAKE FRONT PARK

Extracts from the general plan for the park. These street-ends command views of the park and the lake.

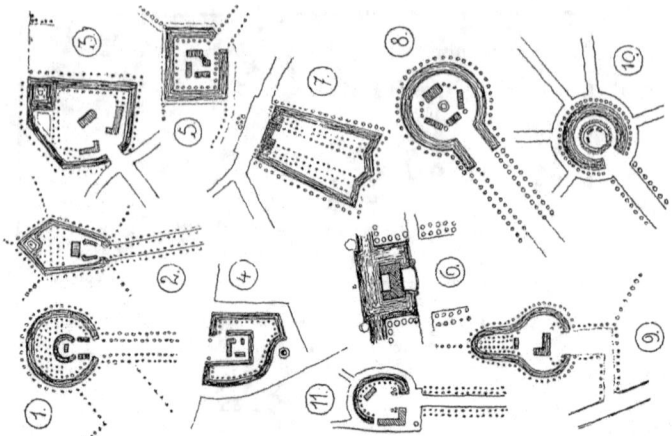

FIG. 919—FLEMISH FARMS AND CASTLES

Formal layouts employing moats and avenues of trees as the setting of small chateaus. Numbers 1, 2, 3, and 4 are near Bruges; 5, Callebeek, near Antwerp; 6, chateau between Tourcoing and Lille; 7, Bremenstraet, near Antwerp; 8, at Dronkaerd, near Menin; 9, "Le Vintage," near Roncq; 10, "Calvair"; 11, farm near Courtrai. (From Staedtebau, 1917.)

FIG. 920—NIMES. JARDIN DE LA FONTAINE
(From the American Architect, 1912.)

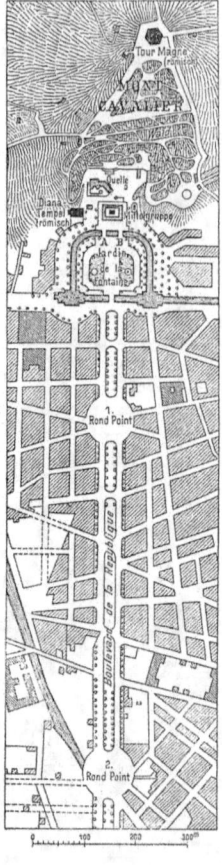

Nimes. Jardin de la Fontaine.

FIG. 921—NIMES
(From Gurlitt.)

A PUBLIC BUILDING IN A PARK.

FIG. 922—BUILDING IN A PARK

The central building of the group exists. It is separated from the nearby avenue by an informal pond. This study suggests the construction of wings which will orient the building toward the avenue and indicates a more orderly arrangement of the intervening area.

FIG. 923—BERLIN. PROPOSED GROUP OF HOUSES AT HAVELSTRAND

A drawing submitted in the competition for the treatment of the banks of the Havel River. (From Staedtebau, 1914.)

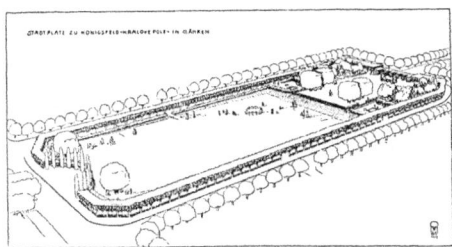

FIG. 924—KOENIGSFELD-KRALOVE POLE. TOWN PARK
Designed by Leberecht Migge. (From Migge.)

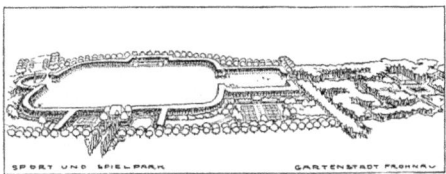

FIG. 926—BERLIN-FROHNAU. RECREATION PARK
Designed by Ludwig Lesser. (From Migge.)

FIG. 928—WOHLDORF. PARK
Designed by Leberecht Migge. (From Migge.)

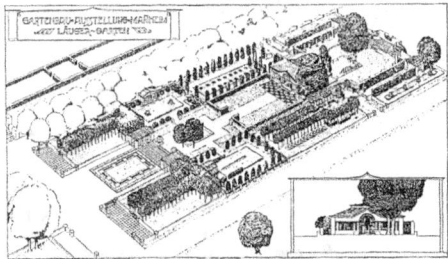

FIG. 929—MANNHEIM. GARDEN EXHIBITION
(From the Architectural Review, 1908.)

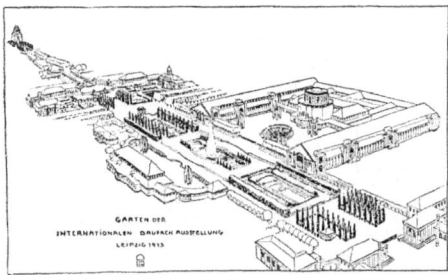

FIG. 930—LEIPSIC. GARDENS OF THE INTERNATIONAL
ARCHITECTURAL EXHIBITION, 1913
Designed by Leberecht Migge. (From Migge.)

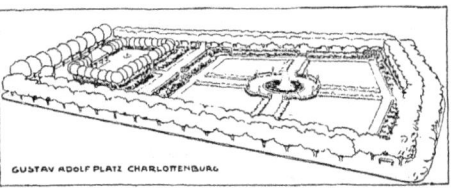

FIG. 925—CHARLOTTENBURG. GUSTAV-ADOLF PLATZ
Designed by E. Barth. (From Migge.)

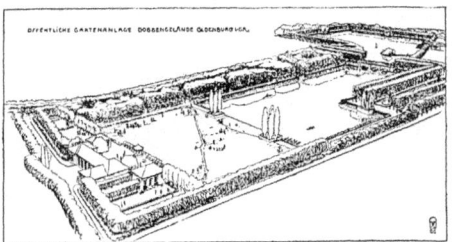

FIG. 927—DORBENGELÄNDE. PUBLIC GARDEN
Designed by Leberecht Migge. (From Migge.)

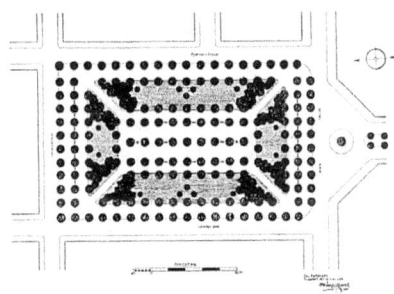

FIG. 931—DUESSELDORF. LESSINGPLATZ

Figs. 931 to 935 are a series of plans by W. von Engelhardt for small city squares showing the development of style, 1900 to 1912. Fig. 931, dated 1900, shows the last traces of informal design, not yet completely cast aside.

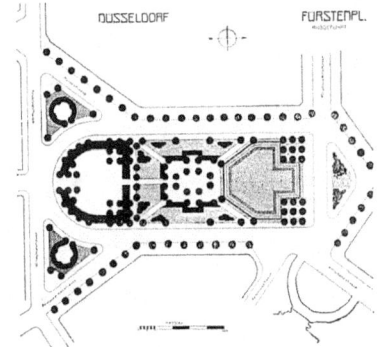

FIG. 932—DUESSELDORF. FUERSTENPLATZ

Compare Fig. 931. In this plan, made in 1906, the area is too much subdivided and diagonals are still used.

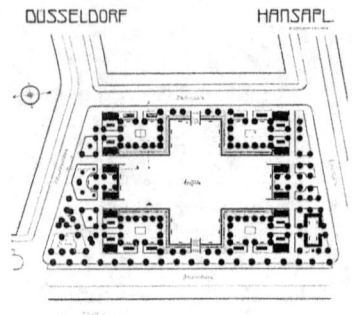

FIG. 933.—DUESSELDORF. HANSAPLATZ

Compare Fig. 931. This plan, dated 1908, is simpler and more successfully unified than its predecessors.

FIG. 934.—DUESSELDORF. BRESLAUER PLATZ

Compare Fig. 931. This design, made in 1912, provides a single large play area surrounded by hedges.

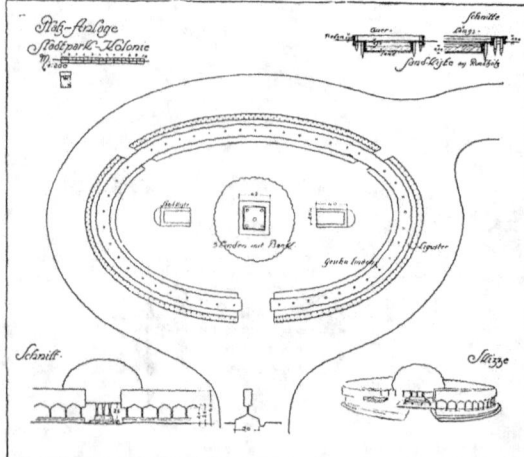

FIG. 936—SMALL PLAYGROUND

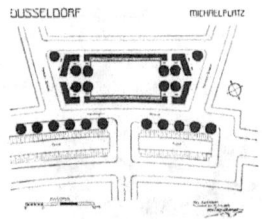

FIG. 935—DUESSELDORF. MICHAELPLATZ

Designed (as were Figs. 931-34) by W. von Engelhardt. This plan, made in 1912, is very simple and economical of space.

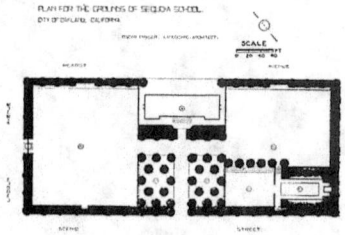

FIG. 938—OAKLAND. SEQUOIA SCHOOL

A school playground designed by Oscar Prager. A—School; B and D—Boys' and girls' playgrounds; C—Small children; E—Basketball; F—Garden.

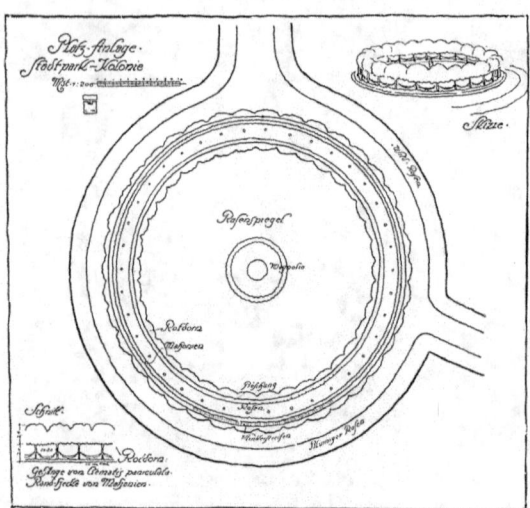

FIG. 937—SMALL CIRCULAR GARDEN
Designed by Leberecht Migge.

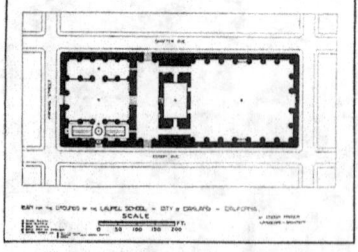

FIG. 939—OAKLAND. LAUREL SCHOOL
Grounds designed by Oscar Prager.

FIG. 940—NEW YORK. HUDSON PARK
Designed by Carrere and Hastings. (From Robinson.)

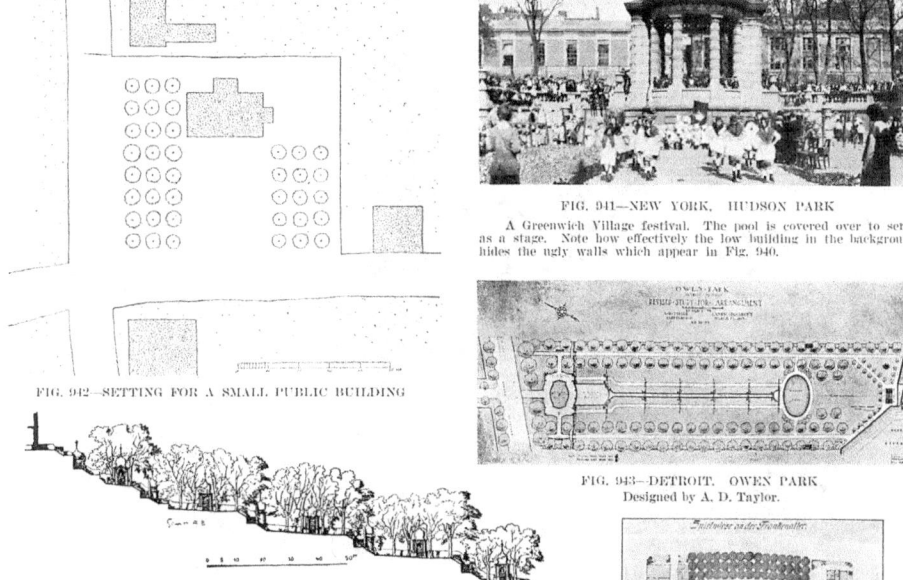

FIG. 941—NEW YORK. HUDSON PARK

A Greenwich Village festival. The pool is covered over to serve as a stage. Note how effectively the low building in the background hides the ugly walls which appear in Fig. 940.

FIG. 942—SETTING FOR A SMALL PUBLIC BUILDING

FIG. 943—DETROIT. OWEN PARK
Designed by A. D. Taylor.

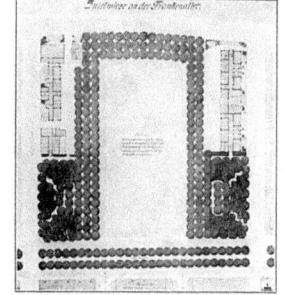

FIG. 944—WUERZBURG. ASCENT TO THE NIKOLASBERG CHAPEL
A very effective garden-like arrangement of the fourteen "stations."

FIG. 945—FRANKFORT. PLAYGROUND
The large playlawn, an area of three and a half acres, lies between two schoolhouses.

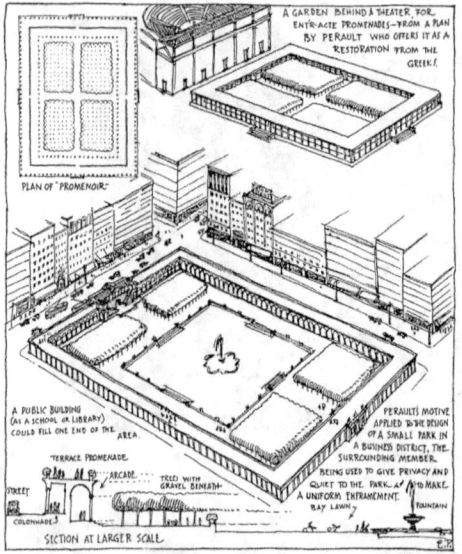

FIG. 946—STUDY FOR THE TREATMENT OF A CITY SQUARE

FIG. 947—HOBOKEN. PAVILION IN HUDSON COUNTY PARK
By Arthur Ware. (Figs. 947-48 from the American Architect, 1912.)

FIG. 949—PADUA. PRATO DELLA VALLE

The Prato is now called the Piazza Vittorio Emanuele. In the midst of the huge roughly triangular area was built, in the eighteenth century, an oval canal spanned by four bridges and bordered by eighty-two heroic statues of Paduan worthies, which, though of slight interest individually, form together a novel and spirited garden-like composition. As old engravings do not show trees and the present planting looks less than half a century old, it was probably intended to have none, perhaps out of consideration for the spectators of the annual horse-races, which races probably suggested the oval plan of the canal. On purely esthetic grounds, considering the extreme irregularity of the surrounding walls of the Prato, it would perhaps have been better to have planted a heavy avenue of trees just outside the canal, thus forming of the island an open plaza.

FIG. 948—HOBOKEN. COUNTY PARK

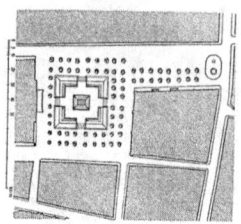

FIG. 951—HEIDELBERG
LUDWIGSPLATZ
(From Gurlitt.)

FIG. 950—PADUA. BIRDSEYE SKETCH OF THE PRATO

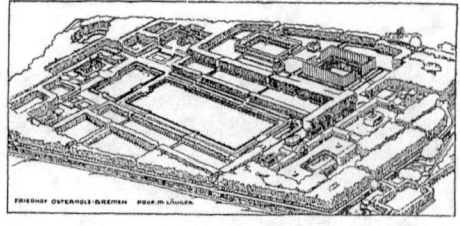

FIG. 952—BREMEN. OSTERHOLZ CEMETERY
A proposal by M. Läuger. (From Migge.)

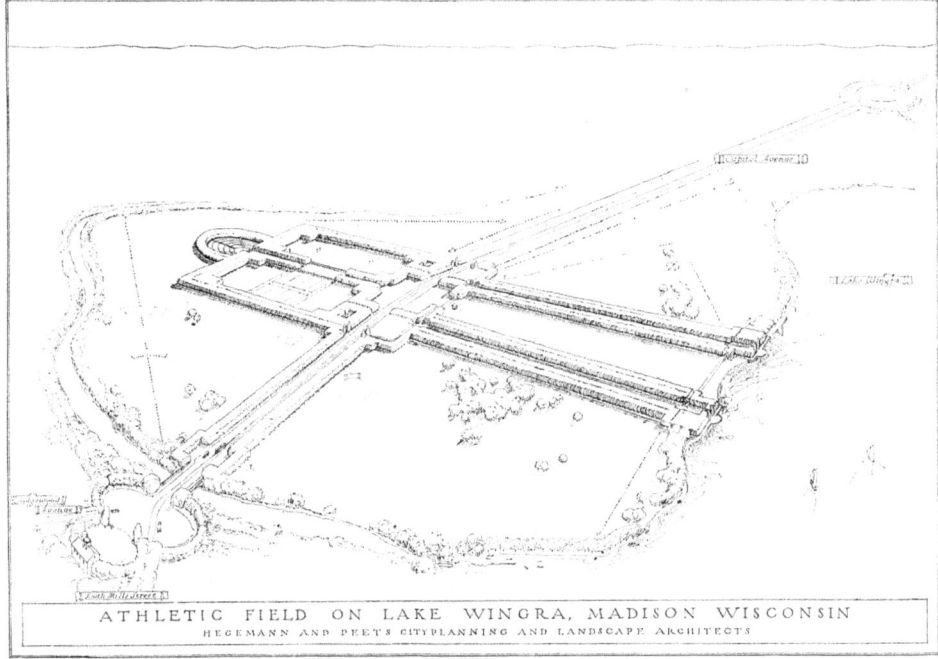

ATHLETIC FIELD ON LAKE WINGRA, MADISON WISCONSIN
HEGEMANN AND PEETS CITY PLANNING AND LANDSCAPE ARCHITECTS

FIG. 953—MADISON. ATHLETIC FIELD

The mall, from Capitol Avenue to the lake is a thousand feet long. The site is a flat reclaimed marsh and it is proposed to do the entire planting with willows. In addition to the ordinary track and field sports a large open-air theater is provided for, as well as a nine-hole golf course.

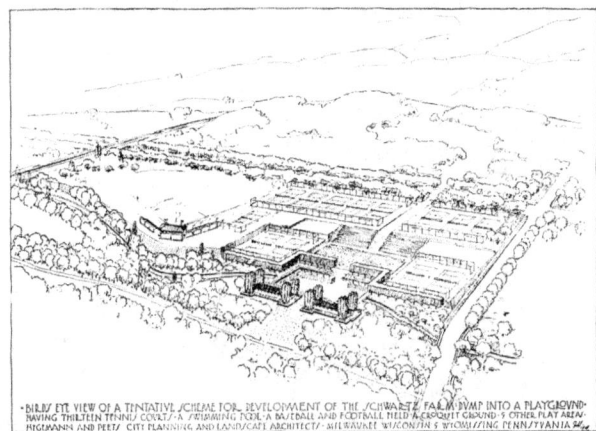

FIG. 954—WYOMISSING, PA. PROPOSED PLAYGROUND

FIG. 955—VIENNA. MUNICIPAL CEMETERY

FIG. 956—GENOA. CAMPO SANTO
The buildings were started in 1807.

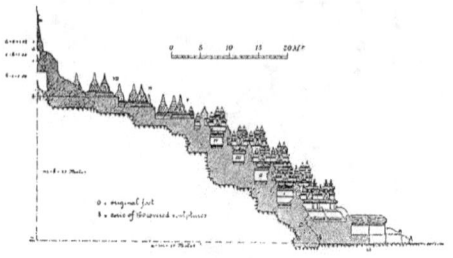

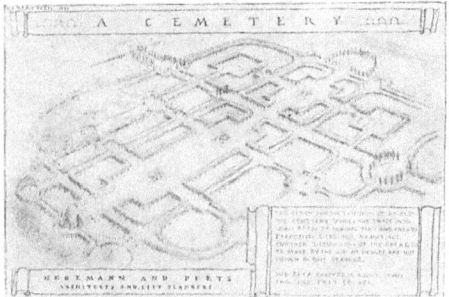

FIG. 957—DESIGN FOR A CEMETERY

FIG. 958—JAVA. THE BOROBUDUR

This monument, built about the year 800, originally a tomb, later
became a place of worship. The Borobudur (the name means "numberless Buddhas") contains 505 statues and about 2,000 reliefs. As a
problem in design, therefore, the practical requirements were not unlike those which confront the designer of a modern cemetery. The
perfect unity here attained is a challenge to us, to find some way to
make our cemeteries look less like a romantic mid-Victorian park which
has been devastated by a hail of marble fragments.

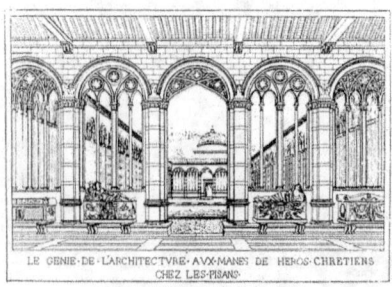

LE·GENIE·DE·L'ARCHITECTVRE·AVX·MANES·DE·HEROS·CHRETIENS
CHEZ LES·PISANS·

FIG. 959—PISA. CAMPO SANTO

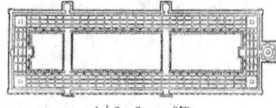

FIG. 960—PISA. PLAN OF THE CAMPO
SANTO

Built in the thirteenth century. (Figs. 959
and 960 are from Coussin.)

FIG. 961 (LEFT)—HERRNHUT. CEMETERY

The burial ground of the original chapter of
the German religious order of Herrnhut. The
home of an English branch of the brotherhood
has been illustrated in Figs. 407 and 408. No
headstones are used in this cemetery, the
graves being marked by uniform horizontal
slabs. The quaint rows of clipped lindens create
a feeling of unaffected simplicity and order
which is surely more appropriate to "God's acre"
than is the pretentiousness of the modern lavish-
ly "naturalistic" American cemetery.

FIGS. 962-67—TOKIO. CEMETERY AND TEMPLE GROUNDS

In the upper row are three views of a Japanese cemetery, showing its striking resemblance to a European formal garden. The pictures in the lower row illustrate the formal setting of a temple.

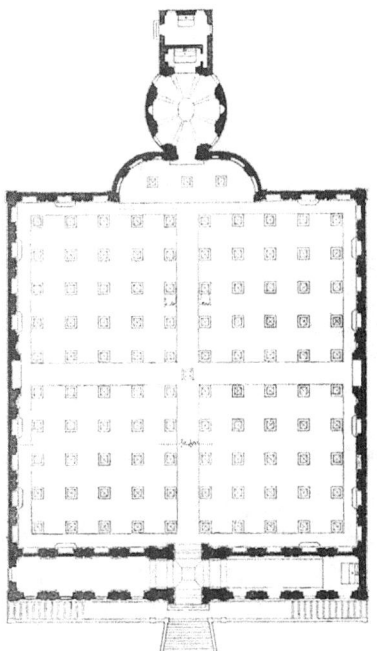

FIG. 968—ROME. CIMITERO DI SAN SPIRITO
(Figs. 968 and 969 from Letarouilly.)

FIG. 969—ROME—CIMITERO DI SAN SPIRITO

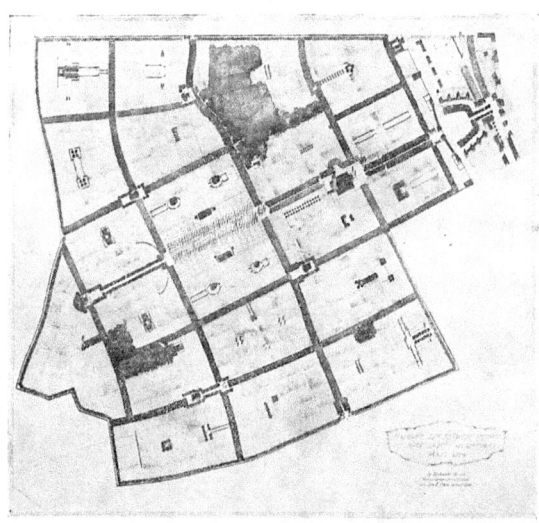

FIG. 970—BERLIN (STAHNSDORF). UNION CEMETERY
A project by Hans Bernoulli.

FIG. 971—BOSTON. OLD GRANARY BURYING GROUND

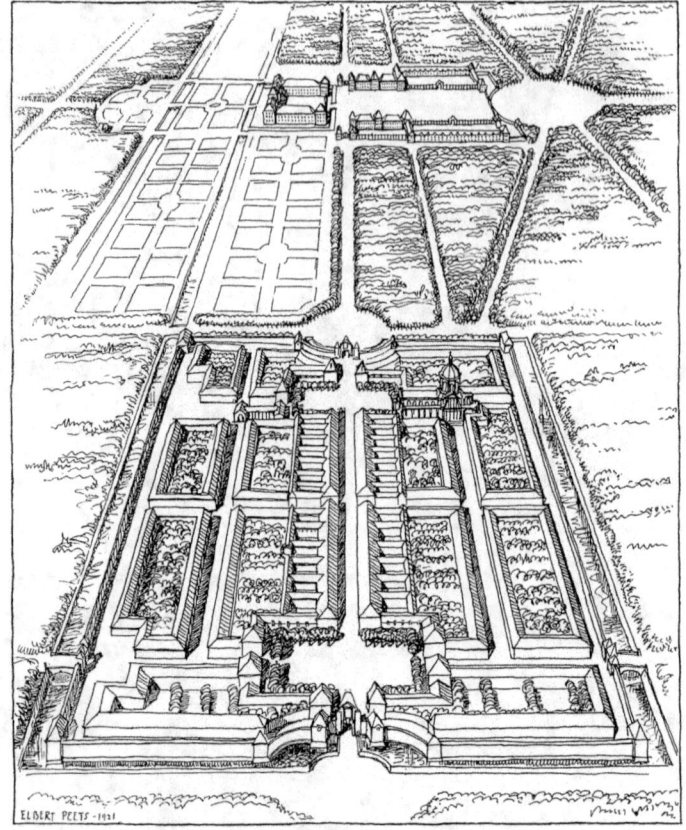

FIG. 972—RICHELIEU

Richelieu is near Chinon, 120 miles south-east of Paris. The château and town were built by Cardinal Richelieu. The work was begun in 1629 by Lemercier, architect of the Palais Royal. This diagrammatic bird's-eye view is based upon plans and views published by the American Architect, 1902 (see Fig. 975), by Simpson, 1911, and recently by Stuebben and Brinckmann. No picture of the church being available, Lemercier's church of the Sorbonne was borrowed for the occasion. The park has been much changed; only in the plan of 1634 does the diagonal avenue which is in line with the church dome continue up to the walls of the town.

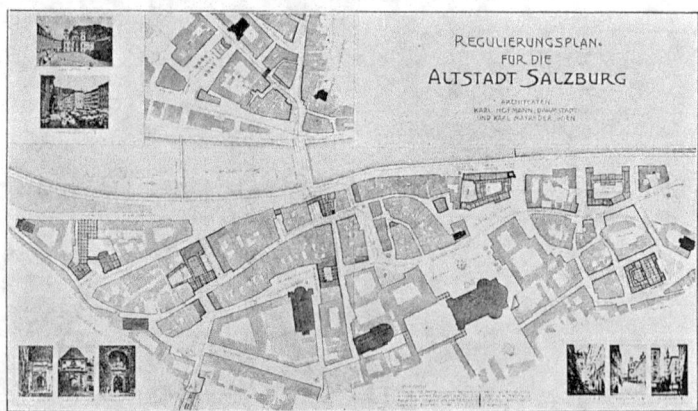

FIG. 973—SALZBURG

The plan of old Salzburg is medieval with Renaissance insertions. This drawing indicates a number of suggested changes, all conceived in the modern eclectic spirit, equally sensitive to the value of medieval and of Renaissance work, and thus in contrast to the attitude of the Renaissance designers who had confidence enough in their own taste to brush aside the Gothic maze at every opportunity.

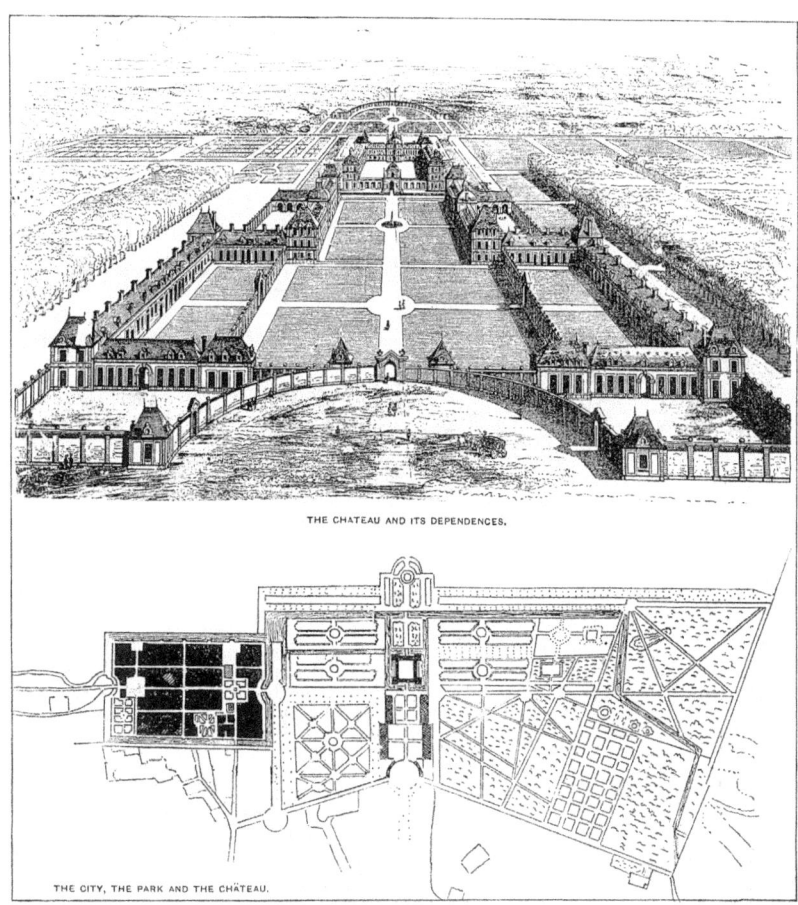

THE CHATEAU AND ITS DEPENDENCES.

THE CITY, THE PARK AND THE CHÂTEAU.

FIGS. 974-75—RICHELIEU
(From the American Architect, 1902.)

CHAPTER VI

City Plans as Unified Designs

The boldest conception of civic art makes it embrace not merely individual groups of buildings with their approaches and gardens but even entire cities. It is one thing to distribute fine groups of public buildings over the area of a city and to connect them effectively. It is a much more difficult thing to relate the entire city to such a scheme. Still, if the city to be planned is small, the difficulty has proved not insurmountable. Small cities, as for instance the town of Richelieu (Figs. 972, 974-75), may have the charm of a finished creation; but when the architect's ambition is to organize into a consistent work of art the place where tens of thousands, hundreds of thousands, or millions of people live, work, and seek recreation, the problem becomes gigantic. Modern industry, transportation, and other technical achievements, instead of facilitating the solution, have immensely complicated it. The

problem, far from remaining purely a matter of good design, becomes so involved in an intricate maze of closely related problems, especially of transportation, real estate operations, and taxation, that its solution requires a combination of talent, artistic, engineering, economic, legal, diplomatic, and executive, that is almost too much to hope for. So far the problem has not been solved and its solution may be the great ideal of civic art left for American genius to realize.

It would, however, indicate forgetfulness of the sore fate of great ambitions if the American city planner should too optimistically hope for a transformation of such large cities as New York and Chicago from their present state into "cities beautiful". Undue optimism in this respect may best be guarded against by a short retrospect. It is not the object of this book to go into all the

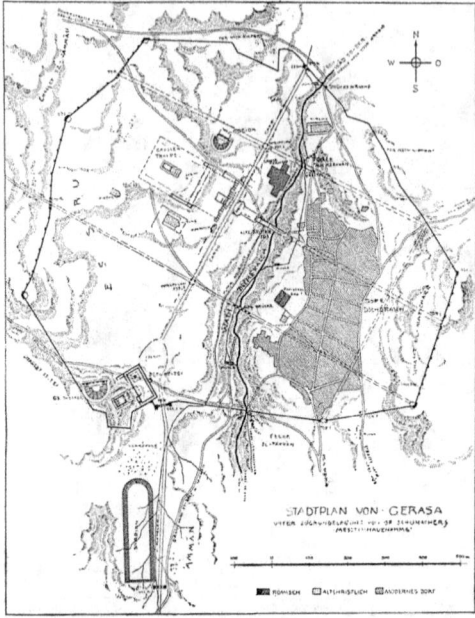

FIG. 976—GERASA

Survey by the German Baalbek expedition. For other ancient town plans see Fig. 168A.

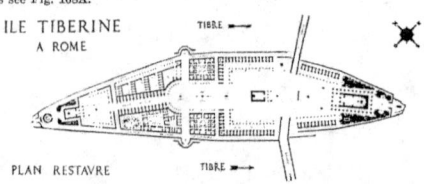

FIG. 977—ROME. ISLAND IN THE TIBER
(Restoration by Patouilla.)

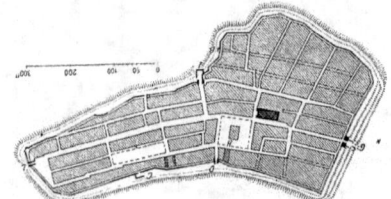

FIG. 978—MONSEGUR
Founded in 1265. Compare Fig. 977. (From Brinckmann.)

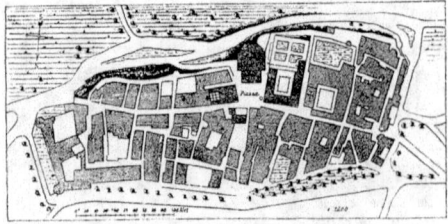

FIG. 979—PIENZA

Partly rebuilt by Pius II, 1458. For plan and view of the piazza see Figs. 160 and 161. (From Mayreder.)

intricacies in which the architect may be involved when he attempts to draw plans for large cities. Nevertheless, a few bits of history may help to warn him of some of the snares awaiting skilled but unsophisticated designers.

Of the enormous amount of material which could be studied to advantage by the American city planner, the contrast between the experience of larger cities, as Rome, Paris, London, Berlin, and the history of such smaller cities as Versailles and Carlsruhe is specially illuminating. Each of these examples may be called a wonderful achievement or an amazing failure, according to the angle from which one looks at them. They are typical cases which illustrate in various modifications the fate of all European city planning and go far toward proving that old builtup cities are like hardened sinners with little chance of reformation.

Rome

The popes of the Renaissance found Rome a huge old city. They mightily attacked the task of replanning it, without, however, achieving more than to hang a gorgeous Renaissance cloak upon a medieval skeleton. This gorgeous Renaissance drapery was a quite new invention little influenced by conceptions resuscitated from antiquity or traditions inherited from the Middle Ages.

The ancients had planned streets for artistic effects only to a limited extent and in cases little known to the Renaissance, as for instance at Gerasa (Fig. 976) or Antinoë, where the main avenues terminate in civic centers. On the whole the city plans of antiquity, outside of the magnificent civic centers, were controlled, like those of Gothic times, by practical factors and the limited space of crowded towns. Many old towns, like old Boston, followed the traditional "cowpaths" and the accidents of irregular sites. In laying out new towns on flat land the use of the gridiron seems from time immemorial to have been the rough and ready method almost always used. Modern civic art, as applied to the city plan at large, begins with a desire to make the gridiron street plan serve artistic purposes and to deviate from it in order to secure better settings for important buildings. The growth of medieval cities was confined into areas hemmed in by water, mountains, or fortifications. The inevitable encroachments of houses upon street areas and the formation of crooked streets resulted even in cities which, like Florence, had originally (in Roman times) been laid out on straight lines.

It may be repeated with new emphasis that there is no evidence confirming the suggestion that the medieval townsmen purposely made their streets crooked for the sake of "picturesqueness" or as "informal" art. Whenever the medieval designer had an unhampered opportunity to lay out streets he used straight lines. Hundreds of colony towns were laid out in the Middle Ages on gridiron plans similar to that of Montpazier (Fig. 982). When the ground was rolling, the medieval designer made concessions to topography as for instance in the case of Monségur (Fig. 978), where the gridiron is broken to conform to the site, just as the Roman designer was sometimes obliged to break his straight lines (Fig. 977). Such practical concessions give no justification to the romantic contention of the nineteenth century that men who delighted in designing the crystalline and strongly axiated cathedral plans or schemes as those in Figs. 980-81 had a liking for the labyrinths of their crowded old cities or for the tortuous stage settings of the romantic novel.

Into the picturesqueness of the Gothic street-chaos the Renaissance brought a powerful desire for order, largely dictated by esthetic considerations. Florence set the pace, beginning in 1339 to straighten and regrade the

FIG. 980—PARIS. CHATEAU OF VINCENNES

A typical example of medieval planning, commenced in 1337 and completed forty years later. (From an engraving by Israel Silvestre.)

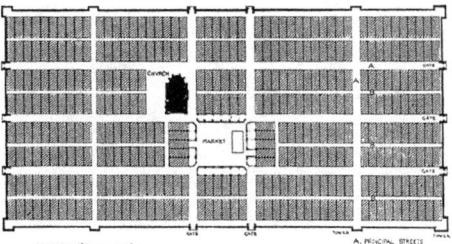

MONTPAZIER

FIG. 982—MONTPAZIER

Laid out in 1284; one of a score of similarly planned towns founded by the English in southern France in the thirteenth century. (From Triggs.)

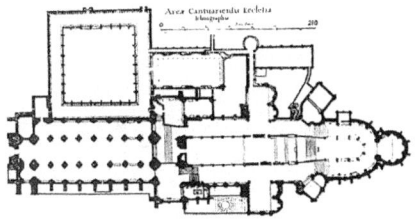

FIG. 981—CANTERBURY CATHEDRAL

A typical Gothic group. Many of the units are formal in plan but, except along the main axis, the principle of axiation is not employed to relate the different units.

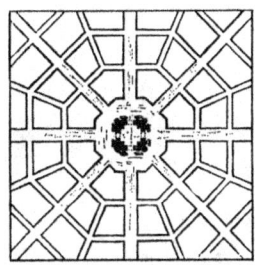

FIG. 983—THEORETICAL TOWN PLAN

"Modified from an ideal town plan by Roland Levirloys, Paris, 1700." Compare Wren's plan for London, Fig. 1028. (From Unwin.)

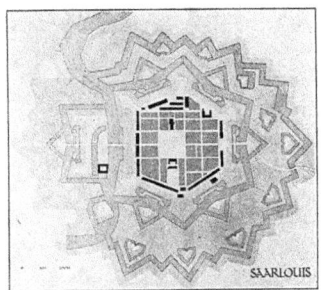

FIG. 984—SAARLOUIS

Planned by the great military engineer, Vauban, in the latter part of the seventeenth century.

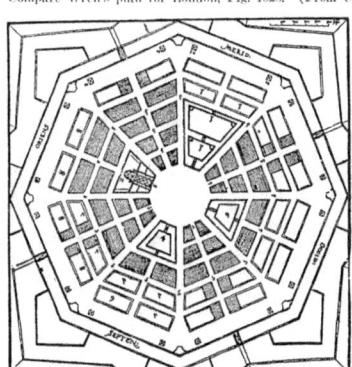

FIG. 985—IDEAL TOWN PLAN BY SPECKLE, 1608

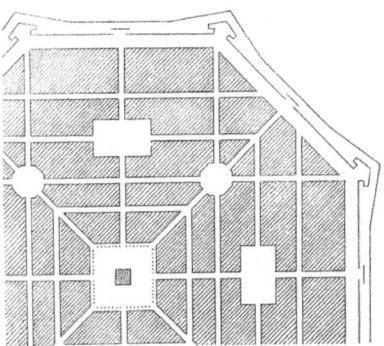

FIG. 986—IDEAL TOWN PLAN BY VASARI IL GIOVANE, 1598

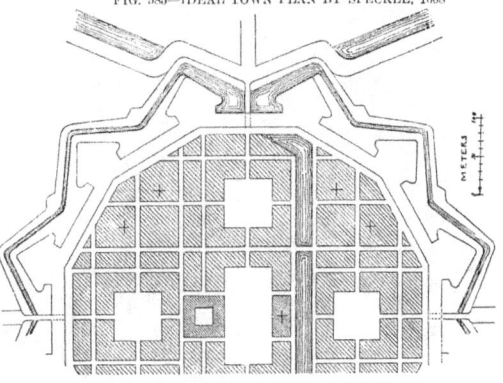

FIG. 987—IDEAL TOWN PLAN BY SCAMOZZI, 1615

(Figs. 985-87 from Brinckmann.)

FIG. 988—ROME. PIAZZA DEL POPOLO

FIG. 989—ROME. PIAZZA DEL POPOLO
View from the Pincian hill, showing the modern street which connects the piazza with the new district across the Tiber.

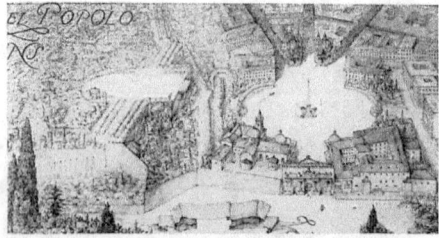

FIGS. 990, 991— ROME. PIAZZA DEL POPOLO

Extracts from two drawing made by Ernest Farnum Lewis, Fellow in Architecture of the American Academy in Rome, 1908-1911. The complete set of drawings was reproduced in Landscape Architecture, April, 1914.

streets around the cathedral for purely esthetic reasons. Soon important cities like Bologna, Ferrara, Milan and others vied with one another in the realization of ambitious schemes for the re-alignment of streets and the reconstruction of abutting houses. Siena appointed the first commission for the settlement of problems of street esthetics. But all this was outdone in Rome (Fig. 992), where the popes by gigantic efforts carried on through generations penetrated the enormous ancient and medieval conglomeration of houses (much of which was standing deserted as dead masonry, an amazing quarry) with a magnificent exhibition of great art. The popes, only in part following old highways, connected by straight streets the sacred landmarks of Rome, the objectives of pilgrims from all Christendom. Henceforth the old monuments, Santa Maria Maggiore (Fig. 280), the Lateran, the Campidoglio (Figs. 162-64), and St. Peter's (Figs. 242-50), appeared restored, rebuilt, and placed in new and surprising settings, visible from afar at the end of straight approaches, as inspirations to the tired wanderer. All Rome, to its pilgrims arriving at the Porta del Popolo (Figs. 988-91), was opened up by the three avenues spreading out from the wonderful plaza inside the gate. This motive of a threefold opening concentrating three long vistas into one point of departure has become a familiar feature in plans influenced by Renaissance precedent.

The replanning work of the great popes had to make headway against a heavy handicap of historical and physical conditions. How splendidly they were able to overcome topographic difficulties may be appreciated by comparing the steep street terminations in Rome ennobled by fine schemes of stairs like the Cordonnata (Figs. 162-63) and the Scala di Spagna (Figs. 684-86 and 993), with innumerable street endings offering similar problems in American cities, notably in San Francisco.

Versailles and Carlsruhe

The example of Rome having early demonstrated the practical difficulties which obstruct the realization of the Renaissance city planning ideals in an old congested city, it is not surprising that the French kings preferred the fields and forests of Versailles for their greatest city planning efforts.

It was in the plans for new cities like Versailles (Figs. 994-97, 132-33, 873-75), built on virgin land and covering only a comparatively small area, that the new ideas were worked out. The design of these cities, as they became more numerous during the seventeenth and eighteenth centuries, was often influenced at the outset by considerations of military defence (Figs. 984-87). But with the increasing reliance upon large armies the Renaissance city planners became as independent of strategic laws as are their modern followers in America. They gave themselves entirely to the evolution of city plans which were to harmonize with the buildings and gardens they and their fellow architects designed. The might of the Renaissance house-plan, which previously had radiated into garden and countryside, henceforth swept entire towns and organized them as settings in harmony with all other features of Renaissance art. In Versailles the highly developed organism of the civic center, consisting of palace and garden and sheltering every conceivable form of refined social activities, radiated its lines of vista as city streets to the east and as park avenues and water gardens to the west.

The diagonal street introduced and emphasized as a basic esthetic feature by the designers of the Piazza del Popolo (Figs. 988-91), possesses charm and convenient directness; it has, however, the disadvantage of frequent-

FIG. 992—ROME IN THE SEVENTEENTH CENTURY
(From the Town Planning Review, 1914.)

The first great city planning creation of the Renaissance was the extension or replanning of Rome during the papacy of Sixtus V, 1585-1590. Professor Patrick Abercrombie has very interestingly discussed the Sixtine plan in an article on the era of architectural town planning in The Town Planning Review, October, 1914. "It was at Rome," he says, "that the new function of the city street was evolved, emancipated from being mere access to building plot on the one hand and urban extension of national highway on the other. To Pope Sixtus V and his architect, Domenico Fontana, belong the merit of the first use of the independent main city street. It will be remembered that Mediaeval and early Renaissance Rome grew up on the low-lying Campus Martius and the quarter beyond the Tiber where St. Peter's stands, the reason being that with the destruction of the high-level aqueducts, the hills and the area of the Fora were cut off from water supplies. Sixtus V by his Aqua Felice made the healthful high lands once more habitable, and Fontana set himself to open up the vast area of deserted Rome which was thus available for building. For this purpose he constructed a series of bold straight streets which had connection with neither building plots nor outside country roads. But, though uninhabited, this tract of ancient Rome was dotted with great basilicas erected on holy spots, such as St. Maria Maggiore, St. John Lateran, and S. Croce in Gerusalemme. By a stroke of original genius Fontana decided to punctuate his straight roads with these mighty monuments, and where a church was not handy to create a monument or an obelisk to take its place. Where several of these streets met on a monument, a traffic place was naturally formed. So was evolved the vista or straight avenue leading directly up to a monument, which at once invested the system of straight roads with an architectural

FIG. 993—ROME, SCALA DI SPAGNA   Drawing by Franz Herding.

quality. The vista . . . is the conversion of a road from a purely utilitarian purpose to one of the highest artistic glory."

Fontana's streets can easily be traced on the map above.

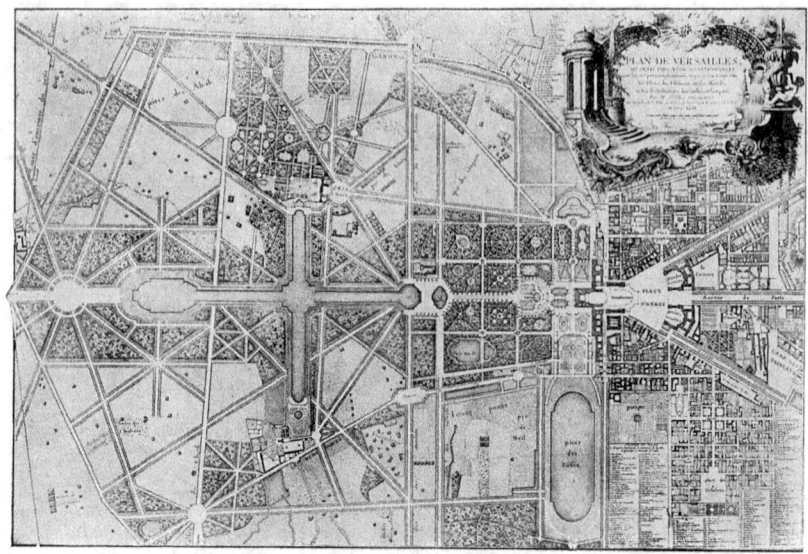

FIG. 994—VERSAILLES
Plan made by Abbé Delagrive in 1746.

FIG. 995—VERSAILLES. MARKET PLACE

This market is shown in the plan above, about an inch and a quarter from the lower right hand corner. The scheme of the market, low buildings surrounded by high ones, suggested the study for a civic center shown in Figs. 623 ("F"), and 631.

FIG. 996—VERSAILLES. TWO PLAZAS

The buildings in the market place are modern—and ugly. The original design is shown in the plan above, just below the cartouche.

THE ODD SIDES OF THE OCTAGON (AS SIDE "A")
ARE TOO LONG   THE WALL "B"
SHOULD BE AT LEAST
EQUAL TO "A"

THE CHURCH IS WELL RELATED TO
THE "PLACE." THEY SEEM PARTS OF
THE SAME DESIGN   THE DISTANCE
APART IS JUST RIGHT.

FIG. 997—VERSAILLES. PLACE HOCHE

Formerly the Place Dauphine; situated just north of the Place d'Armes. The criticism entered on the plan would probably not hold good for the original layout, in which there were only eight houses, one at each street corner.

ly cutting other streets of the city at angles which easily become artistically and practically unsatisfactory. The value of the many plans which followed the Roman precedent of diagonals depends to a considerable extent upon the degree in which the difficulty of awkward street corners is avoided or overcome by the genius of the architect designing the facades at the critical intersection.

In Carlsruhe, founded 1715, the idea of radiation from one center had been carried much further than in Versailles. Carlsruhe represents a valuable realization of the Renaissance schemes of grouping cities entirely around a central building (Figs. 998-1006, 290). In Carlsruhe, which is conceived as an open garden city, three quadrants of the area opened up by radial avenues were reserved for park and forest while originally only about one quarter was given to the building of houses. Interwoven into the motive of radiation from the main center is the radiation from the city gates. In spite of these various systems of diagonals intersecting each other, the sharp corners, which occasionally appear in the plan of Versailles at the intersections between diagonal avenues and rectangular streets and which severely damage L'Enfant's plan for Washington, are surprisingly well avoided.

The designers of the plan of Carlsruhe rival Sir Christopher Wren in avoiding sharp, unsightly corners. Corners which threaten to be dangerous are cut or rounded off and the difficulty is often further mitigated by special architectural treatment (Fig. 1003). One may grant, however, that the last word in this matter of corner treatments has not yet been said. The solutions in Carlsruhe may represent the best attainable under the circumstances but their architectural design and the little triangular areas which result are satisfactory only if considered as a rather unimportant part of the whole and as a necessary concession to the importance of carrying out a bigger scheme. They would not be designed independently and considered as independent units they may well shock sensitive observers (see p. 18). By careful study and combination of the methods used by the different designers for avoiding unpleasant corners in the plans of London,

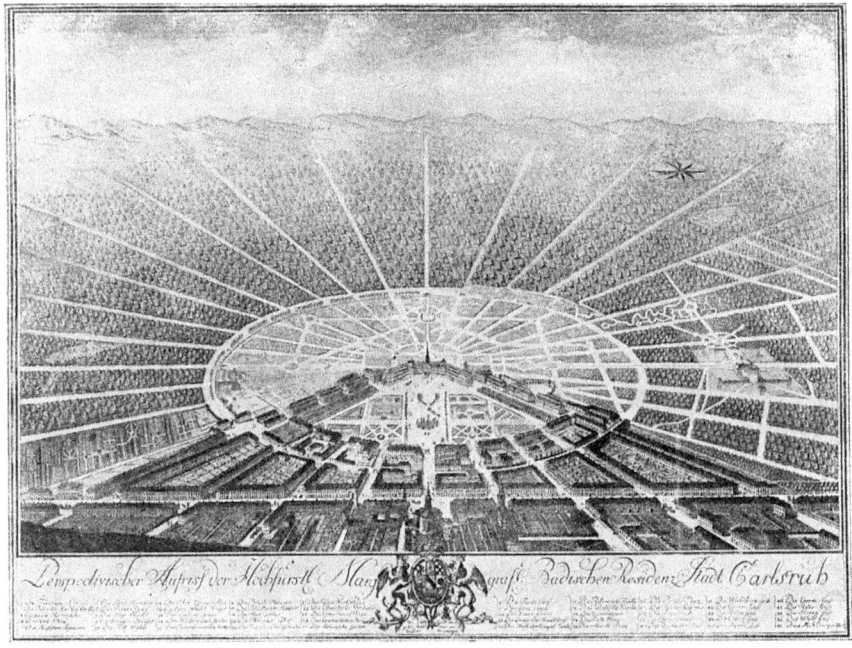

FIG. 908—CARLSRUHE

This view shows the city and the park as they appeared in the eighteenth century. The palace and its appendages were begun in 1712 from designs by Markgraf Karl-Wilhelm and the architects Bagnetti, Retti, and von Batzendorf. There were originally thirty-two radials of which nine were streets of the town. Later, under the influence of English landscape gardening, much of the formal park was destroyed. The church shown at the lower edge of the engraving, on the main axis, was not built, and the axis has never been effectively terminated.

Versailles, Carlsruhe and other cities, it may be possible to eliminate them still further without going to the other extreme of abandoning the beauty and convenience of the straight diagonal street and the artistic centralization it allows.

A word about the later developments in cities like Versailles and Carlsruhe, which were started so auspiciously, may be of interest. Neither city was flooded by the sudden overpopulation that has made good work impossible in the great capitals. Carlsruhe has the larger growth of the two. A hundred years after its founding the plan had to be enlarged. The great architectural tradition out of which the plan was born was still sufficiently strong to insure the finest appreciation of the capabilities and requirements of the original plan, and the design of important buildings then erected (Fig. 290) fortunately lay in the same hands (Weinbrenner's) as did the design of additions to the city plan. Though much damage was done during the nineteenth century, creditable work was achieved and when, early in the twentieth century, the reorganization of the railroad areas offered great opportunities for monumental creations, a great effort was made to profit by the lessons of the newly awakened civic art (Figs. 1001 and 1004-6). Much of the fine original architecture of the town is preserved to-day and much of the new work has been made to fit in harmoniously with the old. Even under these comparatively favorable conditions the contrast between the old sections and most of the work done in the second part of the nineteenth century is disheartening. The same is true in Versailles, but as the cities are comparatively small the damage covers a limited area which could in course of time be restored. Unfortunately this is not true of cities like Paris or Berlin with populations of several million people, where immense

FIG. 999—CARLSRUHE. MARKET PLACE AND FORECOURT OF THE PALACE.

For plans of both plazas see Fig. 1000; for plan and view of the church in the foreground see Fig. 290; for characteristic old houses see Fig. 809.

areas are covered with modern dreariness or even with monstrosities and where real estate values have leaped so high that neither fire nor plague nor earthquake, neither wise pope nor brutal Haussmann would seem capable of repairing the esthetic damage that has been done.

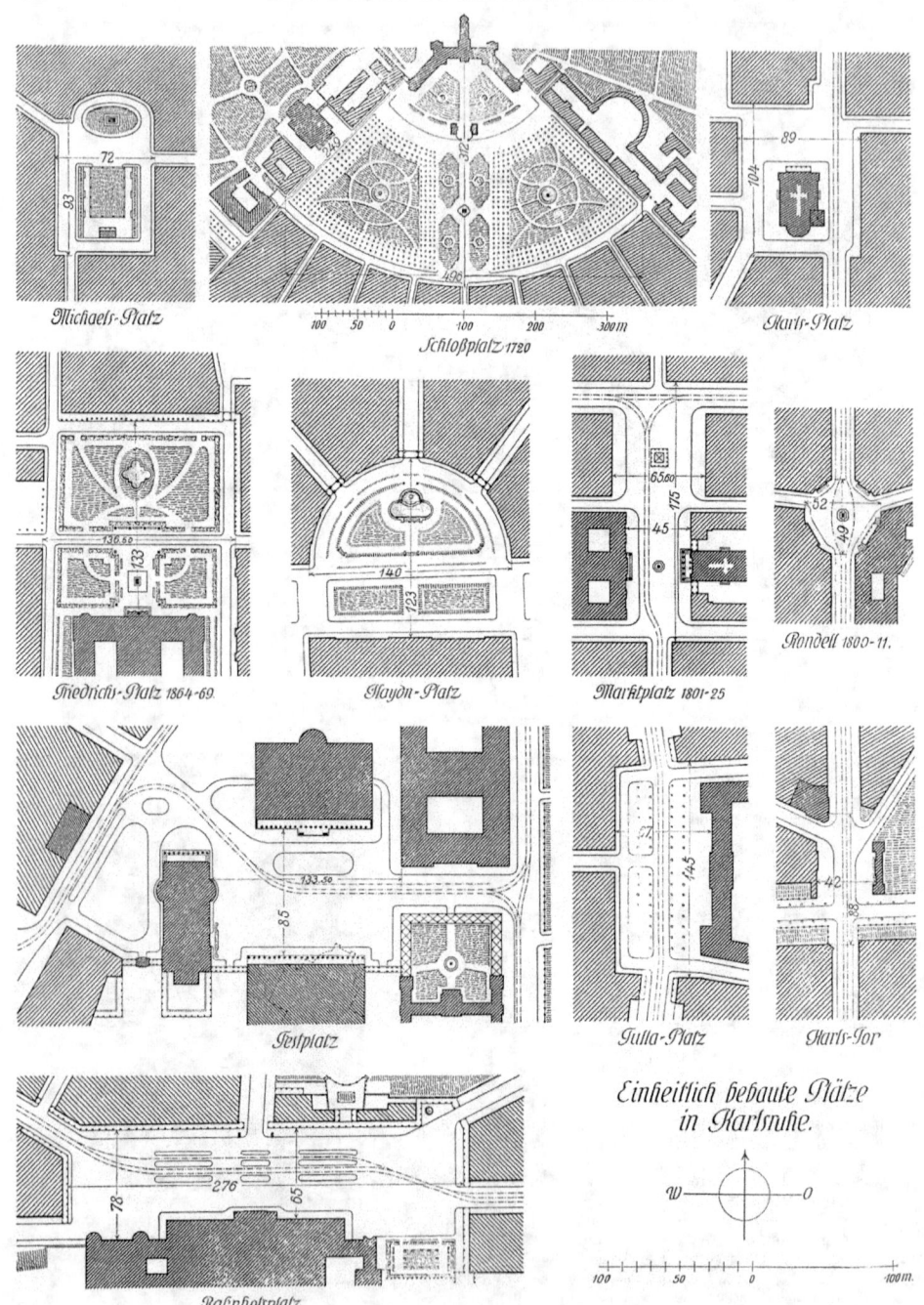

FIG. 1000—CARLSRUHE. PLAZAS.
Those for which no date is given are modern. (From Staedtebau, 1917.)

FIG. 1001—CARLSRUHE. TULLA PLATZ

For plan see Fig. 1000. The large building is a school. (Figs. 1001 to 1006 from Staedtebau, 1917.)

FIG. 1002—CARLSRUHE. HAYDN PLATZ

See plan, Fig. 1000, and details of gardening, Fig. 915.

FIG. 1003—CARLSRUHE. KARLS-TOR

One of the old city gate-plazas which suffers for want of uniformity of architecture. The houses on the angular street-corners (see plan, Fig. 1000), though roughly similar, are not symmetrical in location because the streets do not spread at equal angles.

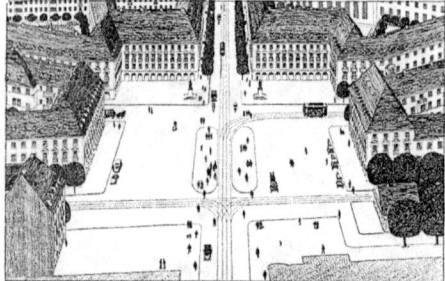

FIG. 1004—CARLSRUHE. (See Fig. 1005.)

FIG. 1006—CARLSRUHE. (See Fig. 1005.)

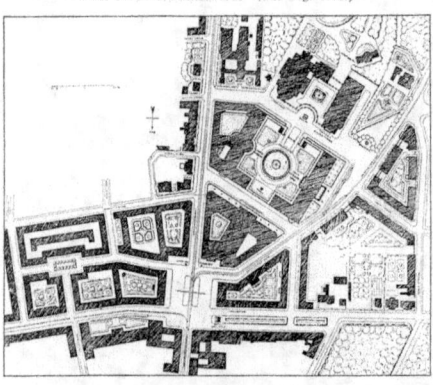

FIG. 1005—CARLSRUHE

Figs. 1004-06 illustrate a scheme (by Moser) for the subdivision of a tract freed by the removal of the railroad station. Only part of this undertaking and following a different scheme, has been carried through. See plan of Festplatz, Fig. 1000.

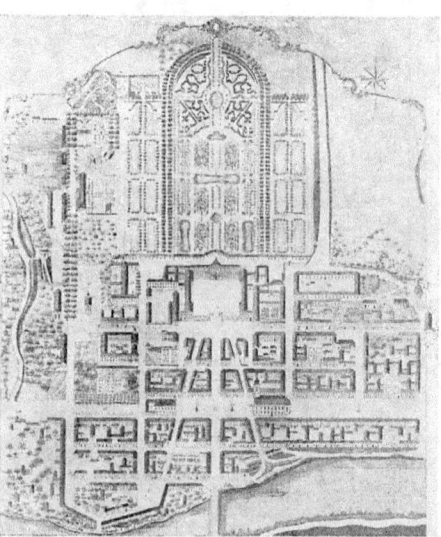

FIG. 1007 (ABOVE); FIG. 1008 (LEFT)—RASTATT

Rastatt was built at the end of the seventeenth century. The plan is obviously influenced by that of Versailles. The principal plaza, two blocks from the castle forecourt, has a separate identity as part of the town and yet is near enough to the castle to be felt as part of its setting. This method of giving importance to a building by creating an expansion of the axis street as a sort of out-post forecourt is common in Renaissance planning, as at Versailles (Place Hoche, Fig. 997), Copenhagen (Fig. 388), Carlsruhe (Fig. 998), and Oranienbaum (Fig. 1661). The main axial street terminates in a plaza on the other side of the river.

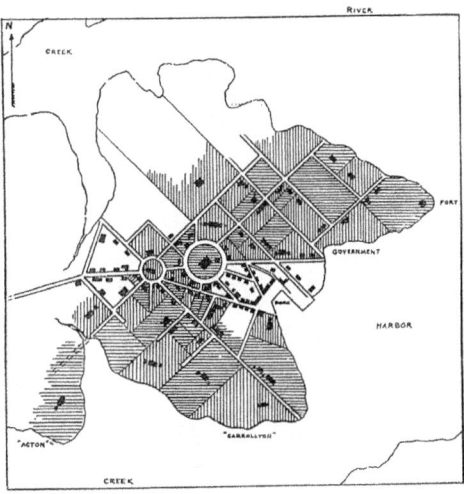

FIG. 1009—ANNAPOLIS

Probably the first American radial plan, laid out at the end of the seventeenth century.

FIG. 1010—ANNAPOLIS. THE STATE HOUSE FROM ONE
OF THE RADIAL STREETS

FIG. 1011—CARLSRUHE IN SILESIA

Laid out in 1747. The palace is at the center, surrounded by a circle of residences for members of the court. The church and cemetery are a short distance away on one of the rays. (From Richard Konwiarz.)

FIG. 1013—LUDWIGSLUST. HOTEL WEIMAR
See plans on p. 239.

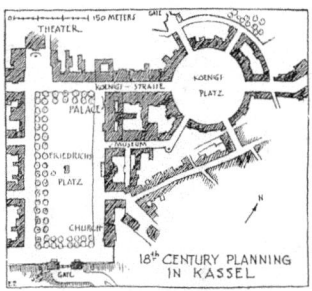

FIG. 1012—CASSEL. OBERNEUSTADT

Many French Huguenots settled in Cassel, and the "Upper New Town," designed by Simon du Ry, was part of the resulting growth. It is worth noting that the four narrow radials from the round plaza are all of the same length, and that each is interestingly terminated.

FIG. 1013A—LUDWIGSLUST. SCHLOSS-STRASSE
See plans on p. 239.

FIG. 1015—LUDWIGSLUST. SCHLOSS-STRASSE

FIG. 1017—LUDWIGSLUST. THE CASCADE

obvious touch is the use of the cascade, which falls toward the ducal palace, to take up the difference of level between the palace forecourt and the area surrounding the pool. A difference of level in that direction is pretty certainly regrettable, but the cascade is probably the way to make the best of it. As a terminal feature for this axis it was intended to raise a tower over the church, which would surely have improved the view shown in Fig. 1022. It is not easy to see what motives the position of Schloss-strasse, unless it was intended to erect a monument of some sort in front of the palace at the intersection of the axes. (Illustrations from Otto Zieler's article in Staedtebau, 1919.)

FIG. 1014—LUDWIGSLUST. RESIDENCE OF THE PRINCE

FIG. 1016—LUDWIGSLUST. GROUP OF HOUSES

Ludwigslust, one of the most modest but most charming of the definitely planned towns of the late Renaissance, was built by the dukes of Mecklenburg during the latter part of the eighteenth century. The architectural style is surprisingly like the contemporary building in England and America. The groups shown in Figs. 1014 and 1016, if set a little farther from the street, would not look out of place in the suburbs of Boston or Philadelphia. Many fine qualities in the plan are instantly recognizable—the rhythmic articulation of Schloss-strasse, for example, and the spacious dignity of the main axis. A less

FIG. 1018—LUDWIGSLUST. SCHLOSS OR DUCAL PALACE

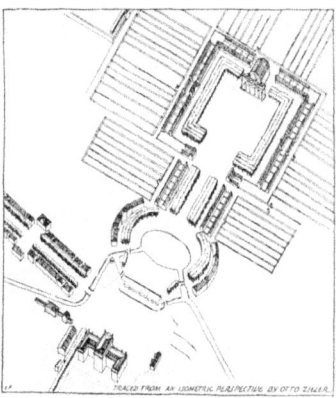

FIG. 1019—LUDWIGSLUST

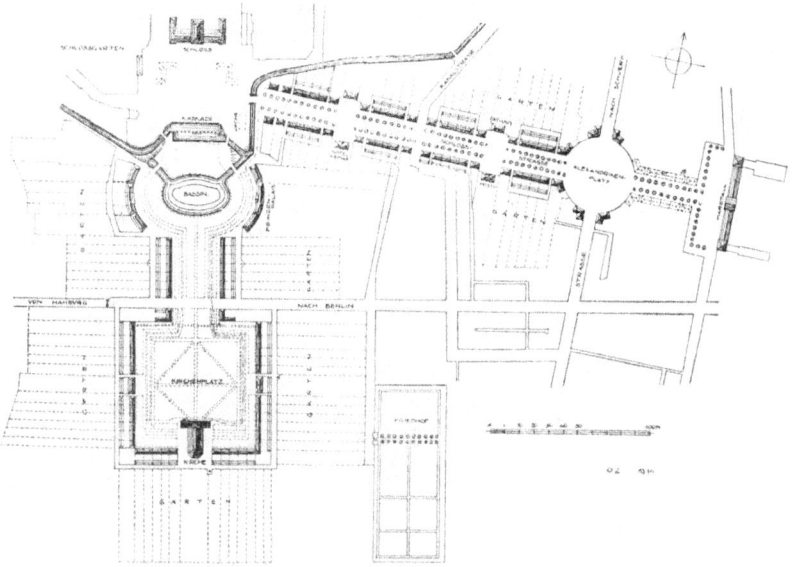

FIG. 1020—LUDWIGSLUST. PLAN OF THE TOWN
See caption on opposite page.

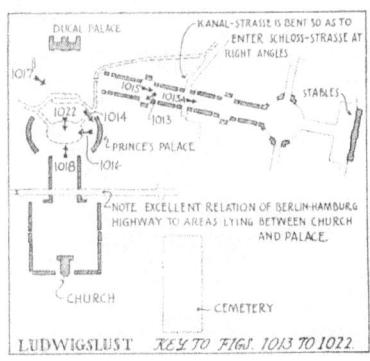

FIG. 1021—LUDWIGSLUST. KEY TO VIEWS

FIG. 1022—LUDWIGSLUST. VIEW TOWARD THE CHURCH

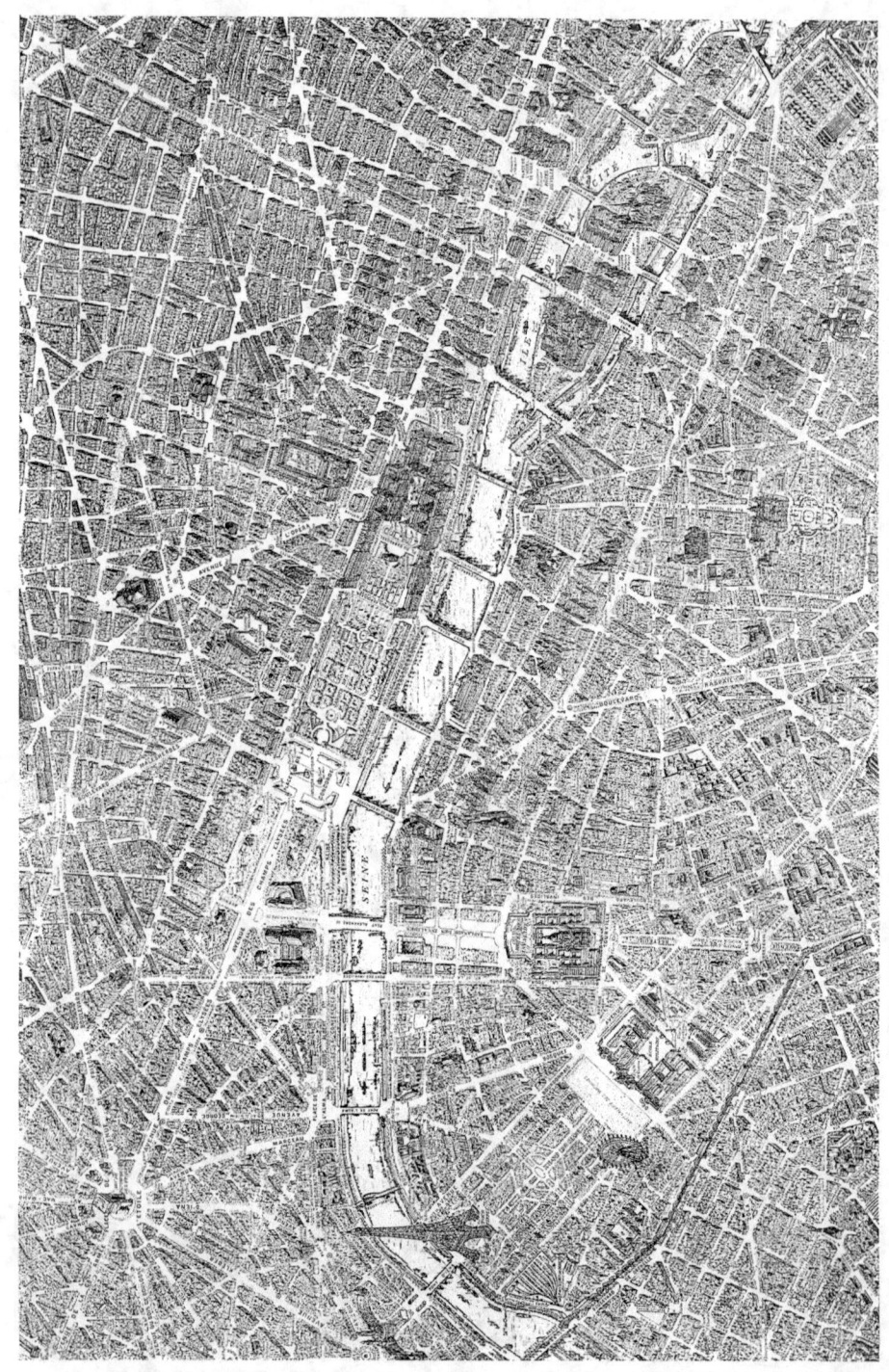

FIG. 1022, 1023.—PARIS, 1921. From the large "Plan de Paris à Vol d'Oiseau" published by Ed. Blondel la Rougery, Paris.

FIG. 1024—PARIS. PLAN BY BULLET AND BLONDEL, 1665.

This plan shows the building program agreed upon by Colbert and the merchants of Paris, especially the new city gates and the promenades or boulevards built on the site of the fortifications. Outside these limits building was prohibited.

Paris

No city is mentioned more often in matters of city planning than Paris. In Paris as in Rome memorable effort was made to realize the city planning ideals of the Renaissance in a large built-up city. "The city is so big and the houses are so high that it looks as if two or three cities had been piled on top of each other, and there are so many people that there is no empty space. All streets, one might say, are paved with people and they bump into each other as in a continuous procession," wrote the royal engineer Gomboust in 1652 on his plan of Paris. Indeed until about the middle of the eighteenth century, when it was surpassed by London, Paris was the most populous city of the world. According to somewhat inaccurate statements found in current city planning literature, the development of this unparalleled conglomeration followed a consistent plan. This plan, which is supposed to have covered the transformation of the built-up districts and the developments of the outlying lands. is said to have been executed in due course of time until finally an almost perfect city appeared as an accomplished fact.

In reality the development was not so simple. The number of errors current regarding the often quoted example of Paris is so large that it is worth while to clear the point by a historical note on the plan of this city so familiar to most architects. Very soon after the courageous efforts of King Henry IV to beautify parts of the city (Figs. 321-25, 1033), the monarchs abandoned the task of remaking the oversized old city which had sided against them during the revolt of the nobility in 1652. They turned their attention to the more promising new city of Versailles, where the great esthetic ideals of the Renaissance could be realized on virgin soil.

What was done in the built-up districts of Paris, creations like the plazas Vendôme, Victoires, and Concorde, was done almost against the will of the monarchs these

plazas were supposed to honor. The gigantic project of the Louvre-Tuileries combination, with the accompanying garden axis to the west, was officially abandoned in 1717 (Fig. 323). In the outlying districts the activity of the kings since Richelieu's great city enlargement of 1633 (Fig. 13 shows a part of it) was limited to prohibiting by a long series of draconic laws every extension of the city beyond certain narrow limits. Even inside the city limits building was interfered with. These extraordinary edicts, in force from 1638 to 1784, were intended to stop the growth of the city. This was not because of the city fortifications which the kings had no reason to cherish since they themselves had to beleaguer their capital in 1652. There were sanitary reasons and the not unimportant fiscal convenience of collecting at a clearly defined limit the heavy taxes (octroi) on food entering the city. But the most important reason was the difficulty of policing the huge disorderly conglomeration. After 1652 the kings looked with fear at the sinister growth of Paris and history has proved that their fear was justified. Since the growth of the enormous population could not be stopped entirely, building actually went on, depending on a large system of graft or favoritism by which, with the help of conniving officials, the strict prohibitions were evaded. Inside the city limits new houses were crowded into every available corner and new stories piled upon the already over-built land. All building beyond the city limits and outside of the law went on entirely without plan or alignments. The results were chaotic.

So far as one could speak of a preconceived plan for Paris as an ensemble, the plan of 1665 (Fig. 1024) may be called the record of a number of proposals, for the execution of which an understanding between the merchants of Paris and Colbert, the last great minister who held the beauty of the capital at heart, was reached in 1675. This contract covered the transformation of the old bulwarks of the city into new boulevards with tree-planted

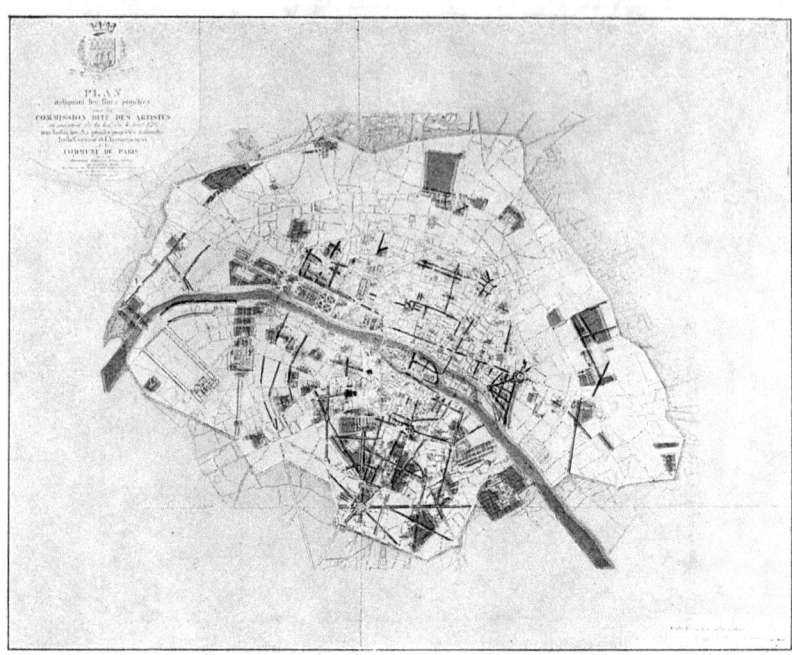

FIG. 1025—PARIS, PLAN OF THE COMMISSION OF ARTISTS, 1793

Showing the improvements recommended by the commission of experts appointed after the Revolution. See text below.

promenades, the building of quais along the river and especially the new ornamental city gates (Fig. 666, the four gates are also shown in the views inserted in the plan of 1665, Fig. 1024), which meant much to the great Colbert. This contract, however, like many subsequent agreements of a similar character, had another very important bearing. It represented a bargain between the royal government and the real estate interests inside of the old city. One of the results of this bargain was the rigid enforcement of the prohibition of building outside the city limits. The interests of house and city ground rent, which under the crowded conditions of Paris for the first time showed their full power, went hand in hand with the interests that wanted to limit the expansion of the city. Thus an unparalleled concentration of the city was accomplished in a way similar to that supposed to have been achieved by the loop interests in modern Chicago. The plan of 1665 therefore is not so much a plan for the extension as for the limitation of the growth of the city. Even within the boulevard lines, which are seen there to encircle the city, no new street could legitimately be built. While the kings, according to Voltaire's hasty estimate, spent for the beautification of Versailles, so much money that one fifth of it would have sufficed to make all Paris as beautiful as the Tuileries and Palais Royal, the old capital was allowed to sink deeper and deeper into a condition of unexampled overcrowding, the effects of which can hardly be overrated in accounting for the horrors of the revolutionary convulsions.

On the eve of the revolution the king consented to a preposterous legalization of the enormous amount of haphazard building that had gone on outside the official city limits, and the circle within which food could not enter without paying octroi was increased from 1760 acres to 8425 acres. The revolutionary government confiscated the city land holdings of the king, the nobles and the clergy, the owners of practically all the remaining garden land in the city, and charged a new body, the so-called Commission of Artists consisting mainly of architects and engineers, with making a plan for the subdivision of the large areas. Proposals for better communications, more markets and the sanitation of slum districts were also left to the commission. Something of the spirit which had animated the projects of 1748 (Figs. 355-72) was called to life again and, as no dominating artistic problem stood in the foreground as it did in 1748, expressed itself in over a hundred projects, mostly of a practical nature and for the entire town, for the opening of the streets and plazas. All were correlated and entered upon the new city map by Verniquet, a magnificent piece of surveying that had just been completed. The plan thus created was lost in the burning of the city hall but has been reconstructed from the minutes of the commission (Fig. 1025).

Notable among the proposals of the Commission of Artists were those for the opening of long straight streets. The importance of such streets was at once appreciated by Napoleon I, who had won his throne by taking a novel attitude in the difficult matter of policing the big city. The hapless Louis XVI had observed the attitude of respect mingled with commiseration for "the people" typical of gentlemen of the prerevolutionary age who had fallen under the influence of Voltaire and Rousseau, and he therefore stopped his soldiers from shooting "the people"

KEY TO COLORS, FIG. 1026

Fig. 1026 is a detail, almost full size, from the plan by Napoleon III reproduced in Fig. 1027. The streets left white, without border color, existed when Napoleon III began his work. Those in white with red borders are new streets completed by Napoleon before 1867. Those shown in black were proposed cuttings, and of these the ones bordered with red were under way in 1867. Tree plantings then complete are indicated by green lines; planting contemplated, by green dots. Areas cross-hatched in red had been set aside for public buildings.

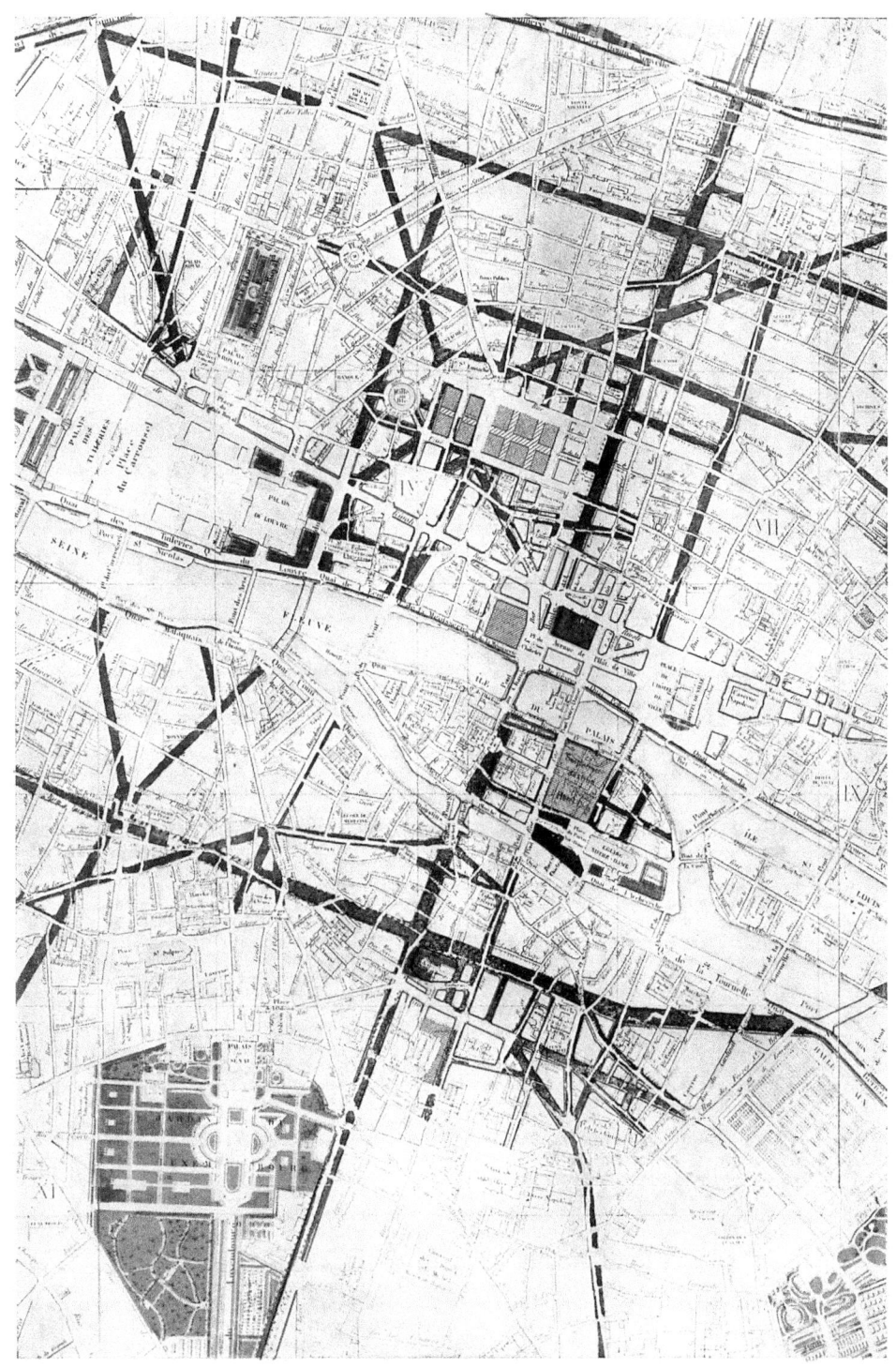

FIG. 1026—PARIS, 1867. (See key to colors on opposite page.)

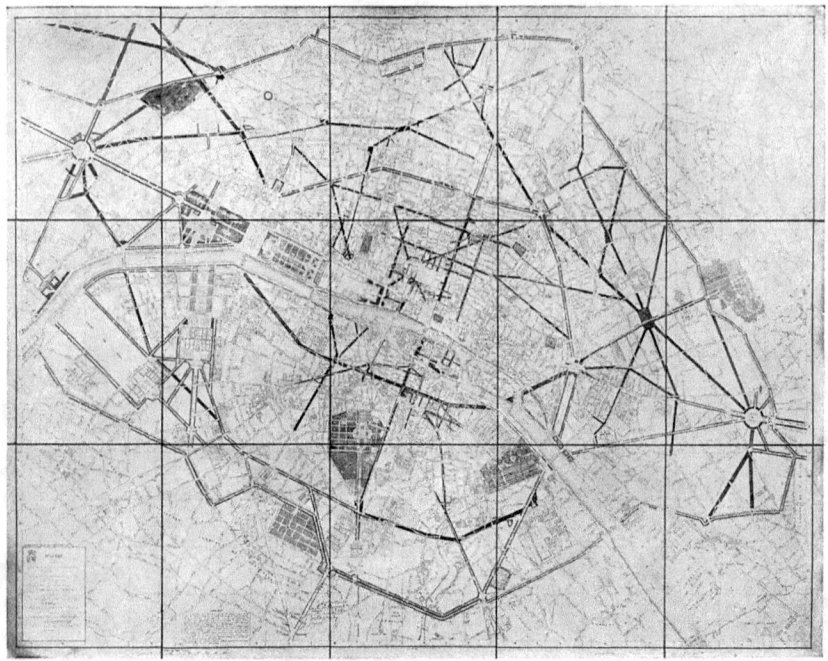

FIG. 1027—PARIS, 1867

At the beginning of his reign Napoleon III personally designed a plan for the transformation of Paris. In 1867 a plan was prepared to show the status of the work, indicating what had been completed, what had been started, and what it was planned to do. Of this map three copies were made for presentation to royal visitors, only one of which, in the royal library at Berlin, is now known to exist. The original was burned during the Commune. Fig. 1026 is a reproduction, at full size, of part of this map.

down. Napoleon I, himself a son of the Revolution had less respect for "the people" calling them "canaille", (which might be translated by "rabble from the slums") and let his cannon play on them. This successful departure gave him practical appreciation of the disadvantage at which his guns were placed by the tortuousness of the old street labyrinth and he unhesitatingly began to carry out the proposals made by the Commission of Artists. He began with the strategically important Rue de Rivoli, giving it the unprecedented width of 76 feet. Following the plan of the Artists he completed the smaller streets of Castiglione and de la Paix, with a connection through Place Vendôme, the streets Mondovi, Mont Tabor, Cambon, Daunout, Avenue de l'Observatoire, and three new sections of the quais along the river. He did much for the ornamentation of the city. He built Rue d'Ulm towards the Panthéon and lengthened Rue Soufflot. He built the forecourt to St. Sulpice (Fig. 149), started the Temple of Glory (Madeleine), built the Arch of Triumph on the Etoile Plaza, and erected the huge column on the Place Vendôme.

But in spite of this great activity Waterloo came long before the proposals of the Commission of Artists or even the Rue de Rivoli were completed. During the years following Napoleon's fall until the advent of Napoleon III, the Restoration proceeded very slowly with street opening operations, although some narrow streets were widened. But the period is memorable for an unexpected development of great importance which changed, accidentally as it were, the center and thereby the entire aspect of the street plan of Paris. Balzac has written a spirited description of the shifting of the center of Paris. In the

Middle Ages it was at the Place de la Grève (Figs. 269-70). In 1500 it was in the Rue St. Antoine. By 1600 it was at the Place Royale (des Vosges, Figs. 321 and 325) and by 1700 it was at the Pont Neuf (Figs. 322-24). In 1800 it was at the Palais Royal (Fig. 13). After 1800 the center of life moved to the "Grands Boulevards" between the Faubourg du Temple and the Madeleine. This piece of the promenades, planted outside the city almost 200 years earlier, was suddenly discovered to lie in the heart of the street labyrinth that developed along the planless lines of accident. Here was a piece of tree-planted street of good width that had been chosen by the society life of Europe as a charming new setting. Fortunes in real estate operations were made overnight by those who grasped the new situation.

Even less planning foresight than may be claimed for the astounding development of the boulevards was shown in the location of the railroads which entered the city after 1842. That the importance of bringing the railroads to the heart of the city, as done in London and Berlin, was not appreciated in Paris where land values were so much higher, is not so surprising as is the location of the railroad terminals in inaccessible places, requiring street openings immediately afterwards, a lack of foresight which was evident even to contemporary critics.

The advent of Napoleon III brought no change of attitude in the important matter of railroad location. Napoleon required security at all costs for his usurping government. During the street fighting of 1848 regiments of soldiers had been beleaguered for two days in their barracks without possibility of relief as there were no convenient streets of access. No wonder Napoleon III eagerly resumed the street-opening operations which had been interrupted by Waterloo. In Napoleon's service Haussmann made it his supreme object to "slash the belly of the center of revolutions." He succeeded by his unique street engineering activities (Figs. 1026-27) for which, taken all in all, half a billion dollars was expended during the reign of Napoleon III alone, while the completion of the work since 1870 has probably consumed as much more. Much of Haussmann's work coincided in a general way with suggestions made more than half a century earlier by the Commission of Artists, but a great deal was of less fortunate inspiration. It was, of course, impossible for Haussmann to cut through large sections of old Paris as he did without having to make numberless decisions affecting the setting of old and the construction of new monumental buildings. The most important decision in this respect was the setting of the new Opéra (Figs. 16, 17, 303-04), referred to in the first chapter of this book where Charles Garnier's bitter criticism of Haussmann's work is quoted.

Aside from immense benefits derived from Haussmann's new sewer system, gas lighting scheme, tree-planting and facilitated circulation in the city, Haussmann's work deserves credit from an esthetic point of view for the many new streets developed with harmonious façades of refined design, often with uniform cornice lines. The pulling down and rebuilding of large areas lay in the hands of individual companies and an easy basis for harmonious street design was thus secured. The high land values, further raised by Haussmann's great investments, unfortunately often enforced or excused building heights which, as in the case of the Opéra, were harmful to the monumental buildings in the neighborhood. The outstanding example of uniform street façades is the developing of Rue de Rivoli as a scheme of continuous arcades in connection with the completion of the old plan of combining the Louvre and the Tuileries. The credit for the final execution of this gigantic plan also goes to the two Napoleonic administrations.

So far as esthetic city planning is concerned, be it in connection with the Opéra or the Etoile, with the mutilation of the Place des Victoires or of the Luxembourg gardens, or with the informally developed small and large parks, Haussmann's work has little value. His "street systems" may have furnished good connections between the various barracks but they do not form an artistic organism. To give him credit, as is sometimes done, for all the wonderful achievements of previous centuries that escaped his destructive hands would be unjustified. The most serious criticism of Haussmann's work must be directed not against his disqualifications as a designer, for he was not an artist, but against his failure to relieve the inhuman over-crowding of the congested old city. Congestion is by no means a problem only of social policy, but largely also of civic beauty and design. The realization of the city planning ideals of the Renaissance, which include spaciousness and grace, is impossible on land which is so highly capitalized that it enforces development of endless districts filled with overcrowded six story tenement houses without gardens. From such grim districts there is no graceful transition possible to the great schemes of civic beauty which fire the imagination of the designer. And the population of the hapless tenement house areas is ill prepared for active support of such great schemes. Haussmann's policy of making great investments in the already over-built and overcapitalized areas resulted in the doubling of real estate values, which may have been enjoyable for the landowners but which had largely to be paid for by increased crowding in the already congested city. The over-populated city needed decentralization which, as London has proved, would, have been possible by the intelligent use of rapid transit and by opening up of large tracts of land outside the city. The railroads, the efficient instrument of a decentralizing policy, were kept out of the city and the concentration in the congested area was intensified. The plan of the Commission of Artists, however bold its ideas on new means of communication may have been when made at the end of the eighteenth century for a city of 600,000 people, was hopelessly antiquated after the introduction of railroads by which a population of several millons actually was fed in the same narrow center of congestion.

The Paris failure of city planning was not isolated but repeated in one form or another in practically every large city of the world, especially in the large tenement-house cities of continental Europe. The failure in city planning stands in relation to the size of their population. The outlying quarters of Paris therefore look much like those of Berlin and the conditions of crowding in the two cities are equally severe.

London

Overconcentration, one of the most serious defects of city planning in the continental cities, was avoided in London. Fortunately the example of London, not of Paris, Berlin, Vienna or Petrograd, has so far been followed in America, with the exception of important sections of New York and San Francisco.

In London the advent of the Renaissance found a populous old city, but it was almost swept out of existence by the great fire and the plague of 1666 and 1667. Wren's majestic plan for rebuilding the city (Figs. 1028-29) offered the opportunity of realizing on a large scale the esthetic aspirations of the Renaissance at a time when the movement was virile, but the plan was not executed. One of the greatest opportunities in all history went by unheeded. But an entirely novel thing happened instead. The two successive catastrophes induced large masses of London's population to move their living quarters from the old city, which was gradually turned into a place of work only. This separation of working and living quarters gave rise to the suburbs, garden cities which at their best could have been a hundred scale the democratic little editions of Versailles. But their development, unguided by comprehensive city planning intelligence, was promiscuous and the young crop of Renaissance ideals was in constant danger of being swamped by the flood of cheap building that tried to keep pace with the sudden growth of the city. The new suburbs soon turned into another maze of poorly related conglomerations, producing on an immensely extended area, with two story houses and cheap land, a condition which was more bearable than that of old Paris with her six story tenements, but which in spite of many fine oases was scarcely superior to the plight of the outlying quarters of continental capitals. Among these oases are many fine plazas of the Georgian period (see Figs. 574-78, 757, 779-82, especially garden suburbs like Hampstead). The greatest service London has rendered to the cause of city planning is her having demonstrated that a big city, even the biggest city of the world, can be planned for without resorting to the wholesale building of huge tenements, as in Paris or Berlin, provided that intelligent use is made of vehicular traffic in all its forms. This is the lesson so many American cities (always excepting of course the crowded peninsulas of New York and San Francisco) seem to have learned from London. Most of them, not having reached the million mark, are still comparatively small and it remains for them to demonstrate that the type of the spread-out city (the London type against the piled-up type of Paris) can hold its own under the stress of growth. A warning example in this respect is furnished by Berlin.

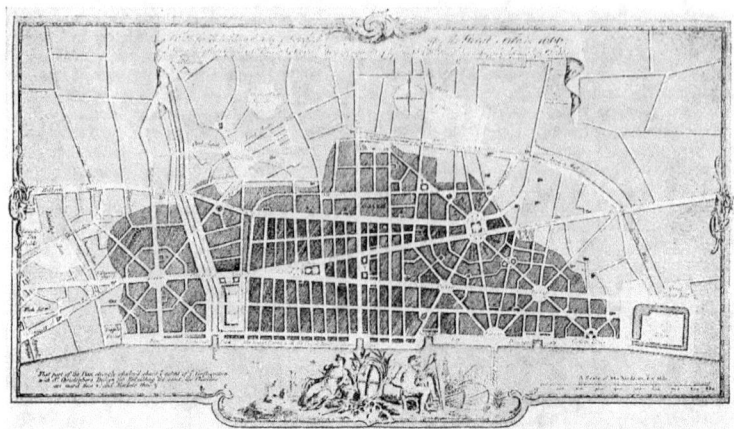

FIG. 1628—LONDON. WREN'S PLAN FOR REBUILDING, 1666

From an eighteenth century engraving of the plan, reproduced by Robinson.

The best explanation of the plan is the one in the "Parentalia", an account of the life and work of Sir Christopher Wren, published by his son:

". . . Dr. Wren (pursuant to the royal Commands) immediately after the Fire, took an exact Survey of the whole Area and Confines of the Burning, having traced over, with great Trouble and Hazard, the great Plain of Ashes and Ruins; and designed a Plan or Model of a new City, in which the Deformity and Inconveniences of the old Town were remedied, by the inlarging the Streets and Lanes, and carrying them as near parallel to one another as might be; avoiding, if compatible with greater Conveniences, all acute Angles; by seating all the parochial Churches conspicuous and insular; by forming the most publick Places into large Piazzas, the Centers of eight Ways; by uniting the Halls of the twelve chief Companies, into one regular Square annexed to Guild-hall; by making a commodious Key on the whole Bank of the River, from Blackfriars to the Tower.

"Moreover, in contriving the general Plan, the following Particulars were chiefly consider'd and propos'd.

"The Streets to be of three Magnitudes; the three principal leading straight through the City, and one or two Cross-streets to be at least 90 Feet wide; others 60 Feet; & Lanes about 30 Feet, excluding all narrow dark Alleys without Thorough-fares, and Courts.

"The Exchange to stand free in the Middle of a Piazza, and to be, as it were, the Nave or Center of the Town, from whence the 60 Feet Streets, as so many Rays, should proceed to all principal Parts of the City: the Building to be contriv'd after the Form of the Roman Forum, with double Porticos.

"Many Streets also to radiate upon the Bridge. The Streets of the first and second Magnitude to be carried on as straight as possible, and to center into four or five Piazzas.

"The Key or open Wharf on the Bank of the Thames, to be spa-cious and convenient, without any Interruptions; with some large Docks for Barges deep loaden.

"The Canal to be cut up Bridewell, 120 Feet wide, with Sasses at Holborn Bridge, and at the Mouth to cleanse it of all Filth; & Stores for Coal on each Side.

"The Churches to be design'd according to the best Forms for Capa-city and Hearing, adorn'd with useful Porticos, and lofty ornamental Towers and Steeples, in the greatest Parishes. All Church-yards, Gar-dens, & unnecessary Vacuities; and all Trades that use great Fires, or yield noisome Smells, to be placed out of the Town.

"The Model or Plan form'd on these Principles, delineated by Dr. Wren, and is thus explain'd.

"From that Part of Fleet-Street which remain'd unburnt, about St. Dunstan's Church, a straight Street of 90 Feet wide, crosses the Valley, passing by the South Side of Ludgate Prison, and thence in a direct Line ends gracefully in a Piazza at Tower-hill; but before it descends into the Valley where now the great Sewer (Fleet-ditch) runs, about the once Middle of Fleet-street, it opens into a round Piazza, the Center of eight Ways, . . .

"Passing Forward we cross the Valley, once sullied with an offensive Sewer, now to be beautified with a useful Canal, passable by as many Bridges as Streets that cross it.—Leaving Ludgate Prison on the left Side of the Street, (instead of which Gate, was design'd a triumphal Arch to the Founder of the New City, King Charles the Second.) This great Street presently divides into another as large, which carries the Eye and Passage to the South-front of the Exchange, (which we leave as yet for a second Journey) and before these two Streets spreading at acute Angles, can be clear of one another, they form a triangular Piazza, the Basis of which is filled by the cathedral Church of St. Paul.

"But leaving St. Paul's on the left, we proceed as our first Way led us towards the Tower, the Way being all along adorn'd with parochial Churches.

"We return again to Ludgate, and leaving St. Paul's on the right Hand, pass the other great Branch to the Royal-exchange, seated in the Place where it was before, but free from Buildings, in the Middle of a Piazza included between two great Streets; the one from Ludgate leading to the South-front, & another from Holborn, over the Canal to Newgate, and thence straight to the North-front of the Exchange.

"The Practicability of this whole Scheme, without Loss to any Man, or Infringement of any Property, was at that Time demonstrated, & all Material Objections fully weigh'd, and answered: the only, &, as it happened, insurmountable Difficulty remaining, was the obstinate Averseness of great Part of the Citizens."

FIG. 1029—LONDON

This sketch, based on Wren's plan for the rebuilding of London in 1666, pretends to no accuracy of detail. It gives only a diagram-matic indication of what may have Wren's intention. The three pairs of churches are shown on the older reproductions of Wren's plan but are frequently omitted from modern redraughtings.

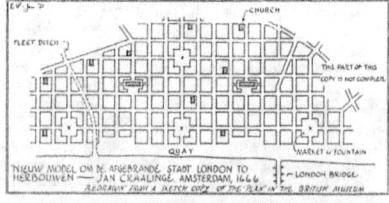

FIG. 1629A—LONDON, CRAALINGE'S PLAN

This plan was inserted in one of the numerous contemporary engraved views and maps showing the extent of the Great Fire. One must suspect that it is by an error of the engraver that one of the two large buildings is shown a block off the axis on which it apparently ought to be.

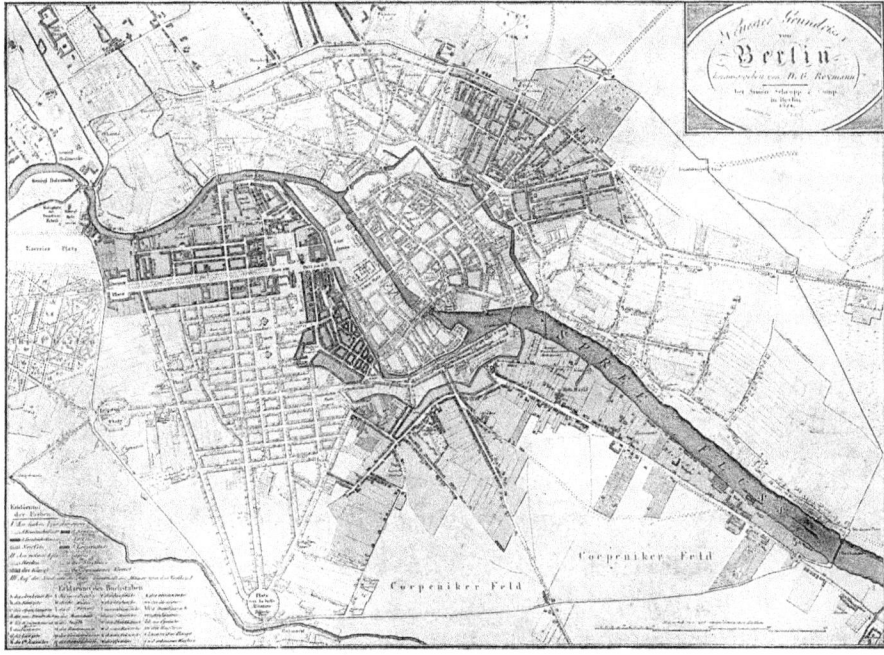

FIG. 1030—BERLIN, 1824

For the aspect of Berlin in the seventeenth century see Figs. 393-95. Unter den Linden and most of the nearby gridiron streets date from that period. In 1721 Frederick William I extended Friedrichstrasse and built the three gate plazas. This work has been appraised by Professor Abercrombie in the following words: "The boldness of this area of enclosure and the length of Friedrichstrasse make this epoch noteworthy. A real piece of Town Planning originality . . . .was the idea of placing, just inside the three principal entrances to the ceremonial town, large open spaces. The extremely pleasant effect of entering from the open country through a narrow gateway, and finding oneself, instead of a street, in a large airy enclosed space, may still be judged in the Pariserplatz."

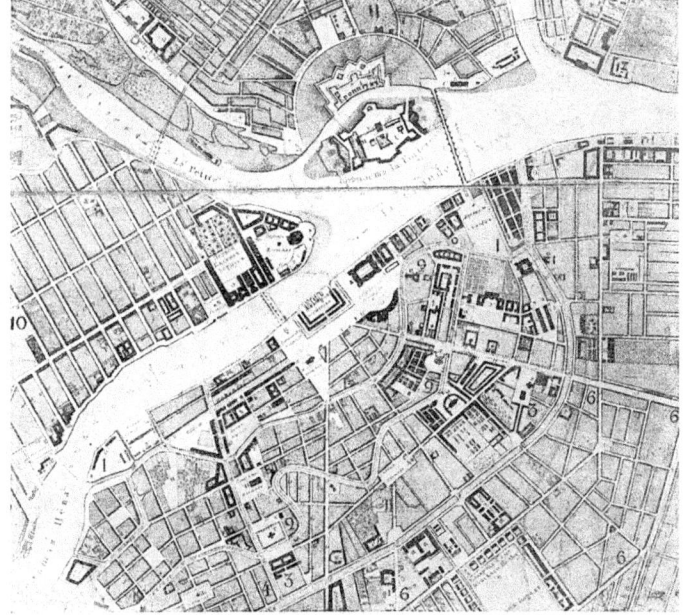

FIG. 1031—PETROGRAD, 1830. (From Brinckmann.)

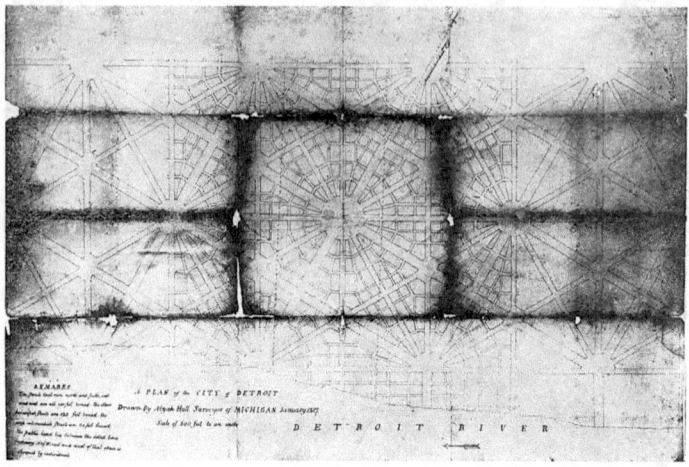

FIG. 1032—DETROIT. THE WOODWARD PLAN, 1807

Said to have been made by Judge A. B. Woodward who had been familiar with L'Enfant's work at Washington. Only a small part of this plan was executed; see Fig. 1034. (Courtesy of Mr. T. Glenn Phillips.)

Berlin

In Berlin the advent of the Renaissance found only an insignificant city. An intelligent succession of rulers, especially from 1648 to 1786, was thus in a position to apply the lessons learned in Rome, Versailles, and London, and to lay out and develop a city which, by 1825 (Fig. 1030), was probably as perfect a place for 200,000 people to live and work in as was possible under existing conditions of climate and social life. But even in this promising attempt toward civic order made under comparatively favorable conditions, the industrial and social revolution of the nineteenth century proved to be stronger than the Renaissance ideals which organized the original city plan. After the general stampede during the nineteenth century that swept people by tens and hundreds of thousands into the big cities, Berlin became, much like other big cities, a huge badly organized mass with a small and vanishing, though bravely defended, area of architectural dignity in the center and a number of sincere but often severely handicapped efforts toward good modern work in the outskirts.

Petrograd

To this sad list of city planning defeats must be added Petrograd, where another promising realization of the new city planning ideas was attempted by the czars of Russia, who had employed disciples of Le Nôtre for the development of their capital ever since 1716. Immediately after her accession to the throne in 1762 Catherine II called a noteworthy international competition for a plan to beautify St. Petersburg. The architect Patte, to whom we owe the great book on the royal plazas of France, has recorded in detail the conditions of this important competition; but what its outcome was is no longer known. The plan of Petrograd (Fig. 1031) has the typical Renaissance arrangement of three main arteries converging on a powerful public building (the Admiralty with a façade measuring 1250 feet) and shows by many plazas and boldly located public buildings that Renaissance thought influenced Russian civic art until late in the nineteenth century. But Petrograd, developing rapidly into a very large city, shared the fate of other large cities, as its sudden growth exceeded its capacity for good city planning.

Large new quarters were handed over to typical nineteenth century dreariness.

American Radial Plans

The use of the diagonal street and the idea of radial planning has inspired many city plans not only in Europe but in America. The most important of these plans is L'Enfant's design for Washington, to which a special chapter is devoted.

Boston, often cited as an example of growth without preconceived plan, presents in its old highways a surprisingly complete spider web scheme. Among the preconceived radial plans perhaps the oldest and best is the original plan for Annapolis (Figs. 1009-10) on rolling ground. Annapolis was laid out about 1694.

The other radial plans for American cities unfortunately date from a late period when, in Europe as well as in America, the essential requirements of artistic street design had been lost sight of. Evidently the city planners of this late period were not architects and had little feeling for the hardships arising for artists from sharp corners. They designed on paper what they called plazas but they had not the clear architect's conception of what the buildings around these would-be-plazas should look like. L'Enfant's plan for Washington is full of unfortunate angles and undesirable plazas and the so-called Woodward plan (Figs. 1032-34) for Detroit (1807) looks very much like the "playing with geometrical patterns" against which Camillo Sitte emphatically protested. While the plan for Washington is redeemed by the fine central mall scheme, the original plan for Detroit represents a monotonous repetition of the one idea of the star shaped plaza. It is hard to believe that the designer of the star motive plan had a conception of the architectural development of the many circular or semicircular plazas he proposes as otherwise he might have facilitated the task of the architect, without changing the street plan, by a different arrangement of the lot lines. There exists an old engraving (Fig. 1033) showing a starshaped plaza scheme of the early seventeenth century in Paris which demonstrates that good design is possible for star plazas concentrating a large number of radials. The picture presented stands in curious contrast to the chaotic skyscraper development around the Grand Circus in Detroit (Fig. 1034),

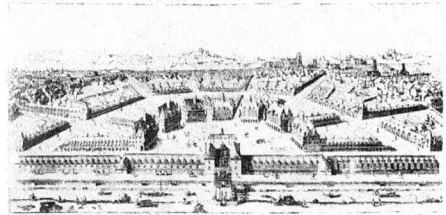

FIG. 1033—PARIS. "PLACE DE FRANCE"

One of the gate-plazas which Henri IV planned to build. (From an engraving by Claude Chastillon, 1610.)

FIG. 1034—DETROIT. GRAND CIRCUS

The plan is almost exactly the same as that of the "Place de France", being half of the star plaza in the center of the Woodward plan.

the only semicircle in the Woodward plan that was executed. A wise arrangement of the lots is found in the plan for Canberra (Fig. 1035) which in spite of its similarities to the Woodward plan is superior to it. The Canberra plan is interesting as a remarkable effort to adapt an ambitious geometrical scheme to the requirements of very complicated topography. It must be remembered, however, that the beauty of a plaza the design of which is based upon symmetry—especially the beauty of a star plaza— is established not merely by well shaped lots and harmonious buildings surrounding it, but that its character and artistic value will depend largely upon the views which open up along each of the streets entering upon the plaza. This aspect may seriously damage the intended symmetry of the plaza, a difficulty particularly hard to overcome upon a topographically irregular site like Canberra.

The plan for developing the new quarter of Gothenburg (Figs. 1130-31) shows a strong design for very irregular ground without the daring attempt to achieve geometrical perfection. The plan for Madison, Wisconsin (Fig. 1039), which is distinguished by a radial scheme concentrated upon the state capitol, seems to have been inspired by the fact that the quarter-section lines run diagonally to the requirements of the narrow site between two lakes. The superimposing of a radial scheme upon a rigid gridiron results in the regular recurrence of sharp corners along each of the radials. The central plaza (Figs. 1044 and 660-63), which would have been an ideal location for a central building in the full Renaissance sense, suffers from the undesirable sharp-angled blocks at the corners of the plaza. These sharp angles are elements of weakness just where strength is specially desirable. The plaza suffers further from the demoralized architecture and building heights of its circumferential walls. Fig. 1043 shows a number of suggestions which in a similar case might produce better results. The existing capitol, in many respects a fine architectural achievement, offers as point of vista for the most important, because widest, avenues, the rather unsatisfactory view into the corners of the cross formed by the building. Nothing but a central building, in the sense of the Renaissance architects, (see pp. 48-54 and Figs. 1040-42), offering first class views in the direction of the eight approaches would give satisfaction unless it be a series of entrance courts (as suggested in upper right corner, Fig. 1043) which might perhaps be formed by dense tree planting.

So far as the plan is concerned the difficulty of the sharp angles at the corners of the plaza is better coped with in the central feature in the plan of Indianapolis, but there again the undisciplined architecture destroys the value of the commendable design.

Rectangular Plans

The abandoning of the straight diagonal avenue was preferred to the irregular and often doubtful block shape by the seventeenth century schemes for Magdeburg and Mannheim, Philadelphia and Reading and many other seventeenth and eighteenth century cities in which effective setting of buildings was secured by less radical deviations from the rigid gridiron system. As these schemes are nearer to the routine accepted for the planning of American cities they are of special interest for the American civic designer. The not inconsiderable artistic value of the original scheme for Mannheim (Figs. 1051-56) depended, first, upon its enormous civic center, large enough to head almost one entire set of parallel streets; second, upon the open spaces, especially the long "Planken" which tie the city together in a direction opposite to the main axiation toward the castle; and third, upon the harmonious design of all the buildings, public and private, a harmony carefully planned for and enforced by methods mentioned elsewhere in this book (see pp. 174-75).

The weakness of the scheme of Mannheim became evident the moment it had to be enlarged. The choice had to be made between the introduction of the radial street or continuation of the gridiron. While the latter under favorable circumstances could have been handled by artists to avoid monotony, it would have been inconvenient under any circumstances. No city could be more interesting to study than Mannheim in the development of its plan (Fig. 1051). The first enlargement of the plan came in a bad period of civic art. It brought nothing but subdivision of the old fortification areas into long blocks carelessly appended to the original scheme. By the next enlargement (called "Oststadt") a geometrical scheme that was not a gridiron yet had neither artistic value nor organic connection with the old city was attached. The following enlargements in various directions, characterized by the avoidance of straight streets and regular design, show the influence of the misunderstood teachings of Camillo Sitte. In the next addition, "Garden Suburb, Mannheim" (not entered in general plan, see special plan Fig. 1062), the influence of the English gardening design is evident, the curved street becomes firmer and the plan partakes of the charm of geometrical design at its best, though its feeling is alien to the original Mannheim plan. In the latest addition (Fig. 1059) all these weaknesses are overcome. True to the spirit of old Mannheim, a firmly rectangular design is made to furnish effective sites for public buildings heading the streets and for well calculated open spaces as forecourts of the public buildings. Such a scheme if brought in organic relation to the plan of the main part of the city might well be called perfect.

There exists a close family relation between the original plan for Mannheim (1699) and the even older plan (1682) designed by William Penn for Philadelphia (Fig. 1078), the original plan for the city of Reading designed for the sons of William Penn (Fig. 1075), the original plan for the city of Savannah (1733) (Figs. 1069, 716, 720) and the original plan for the city of New Orleans (Figs. 1072-73). The similarity of these American plans to Mannheim consists in their providing settings, though

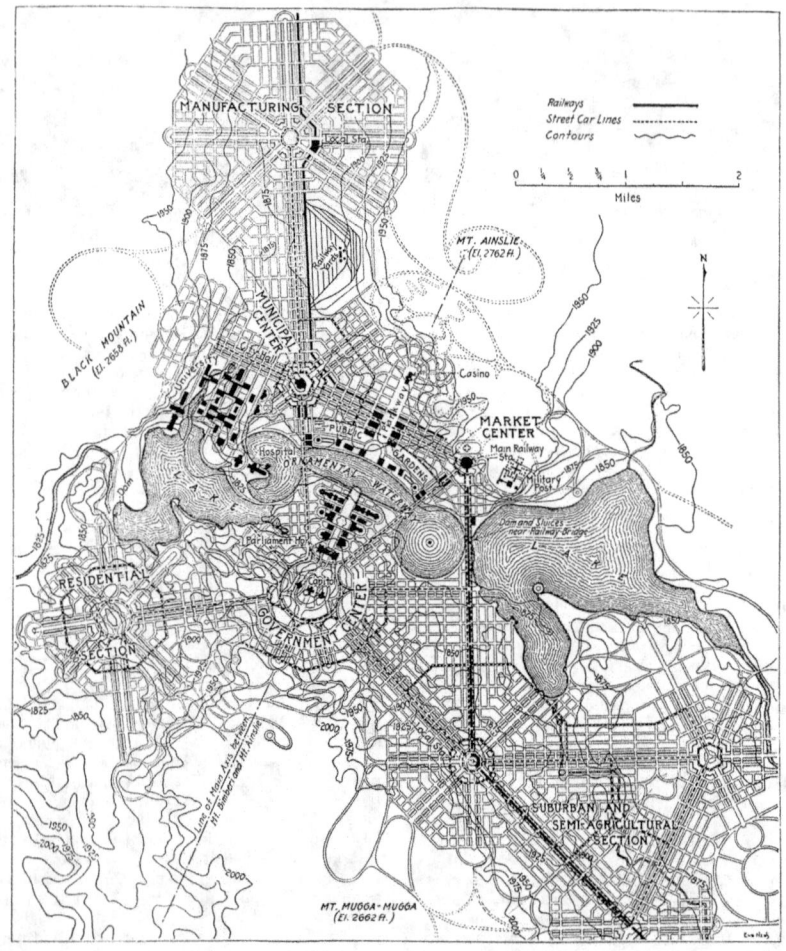

FIG. 1035—CANBERRA. PLAN FOR THE AUSTRALIAN CAPITAL

By Walter Burleigh Griffin; the premiated design in an international competition.

only to a limited extent, for public buildings by square plazas interrupting the gridiron. In extending the American cities this mitigation of the rigid gridiron was carelessly abandoned and a gridiron scheme, pure and simple, was made to cover very large areas. Philadelphia has sought the remedy for this calamity by the introduction of radial streets and by the introduction of the novel feature of a "perimeter of distribution" (Figs. 1076-77), which signifies a street designed as traffic circuit around the center of the city. On account of its great width and the further broadening given to some of its sections this perimeter affords an opportunity for worthy settings of prominent buildings. As the conception of the perimeter promises relief from traffic congestion it may become important for many cities.

While a large part of these proposals for the transformation of Philadelphia remains on paper (Fig. 1079), the very costly execution of the first link in this ambitious set of projects, the building of Fairmount Parkway (Figs. 1080-81, 1083-85), has demonstrated again how difficult

it is to cut radials through a gridiron. Bad building sites result unless quite a large area adjoining the new radial street is redesigned. In order to secure satisfactory results and sites capable of monumental buildings worthy of standing on what is intended as a show street of the city, it would have been necessary to acquire an area considerably wider than that required for the street and to redesign all street intersections. Such a design requires the breaking of the gridiron on lines followed by Wren (Fig. 1028) and indorsed by Camillo Sitte (Fig. 48P). Objectionable though the deviation of the gridiron streets from the straight course may be from a purely utilitarian point of view, this subjection of the minor streets to the more important radial avenue would have been one of those concessions to civic design without which a fine scheme is impossible. The superior importance of the radial street is indicated not only by its greater width but also by its forming the approach to a new important plaza, with one of the most prominent buildings of the city, the new museum, on the axis of the street.

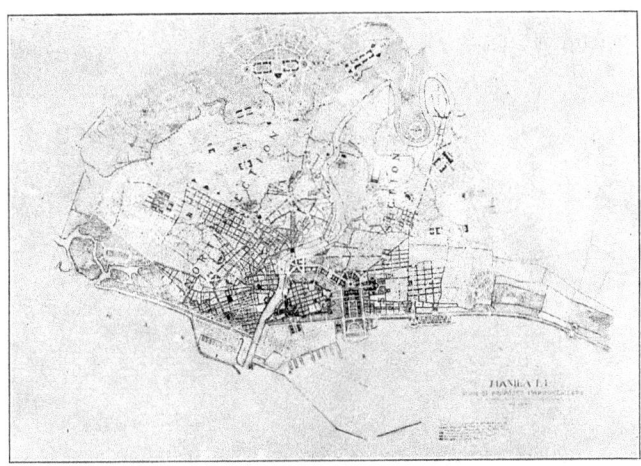

FIG. 1036—MANILA

Plan for the improvement and extension of the city, prepared in 1905 by D. H. Burnham and Pierce Anderson.

Town Extensions

Many of the difficulties in the way of the city planning architect, such as lack of space, interference by previous and successive unsatisfactory developments and high land values enforcing too intensive a development, are happily absent when the designer has the good fortune of finding virgin land to work on.

The value of working on virgin land is so great that attention should be called here to the immense advantage enjoyed by American city planning enterprises on account of the superior system of America's municipal taxation as compared with Europe's. So much undue praise has been given to new foreign systems of land taxation, especially to the German plan of taxing a small percentage of the unearned increment, that one often loses sight of the fact that the American system of taxing real property is an ideal toward which the European systems were slowly progressing. The essential feature of the American system is that it aims at assessing unbuilt land in or near the city at its potential value as building land and taxes it in a way which makes it very much harder in America than it is in most parts of Europe, especially in Germany before the war, to keep large tracts of land out of the market for speculative purposes for considerable lengths of time. As a result new land is constantly opened up and the essential basis for spacious residential developments (additions, subdivisions or "garden cities") is thus furnished Few Americans seem to appreciate fully these important facts.

The city planning architect should be free from the handicaps connected with building within an already developed district, particularly when inexpensive residences are planned for. The planning for inexpensive residences, which means the majority of the residences in each community, has long been badly neglected. Unsightliness and crowding have practically become the rule for the sheltering of the large populations brought together in the industrial cities since the early nineteenth century.

Planning for inexpensive residences has only recently been discovered as one of the most attractive fields for the civic designer. The purchasers of more expensive homes have as a rule an exaggerated idea of the amount of individuality which should be expressed in the place that is to house their quite commonplace existence; the results are often glaringly unsuitable juxtapositions of divergent ambitions. The inexpensive homes on the contrary often lend themselves more easily to harmonious design, to uniform material and color, to the grouping of single and row houses, and to effective rhythmical repetition.

England is the pioneer in this field, the great teacher of the world in all matters referring to residential and housing matters, palatial or inexpensive. Sir Christopher Wren not only designed Hampton Court but also the charming group of the Trinity Ground Almshouse (Fig. 1090). The great English tradition in residential matters, which had its American echo in the refinements of the Colonial residences, made its contribution to modern city planning in the development of the new garden cities like Letchworth and Hampstead (Figs. 1095-98), the influence of which has been very strong, especially in Germany, upon the housing activities of large employers and of municipalities, and recently in America in connection with war activities. Long before this wave of housing developments became effective America had produced, for more expensive residences, large and very interesting schemes on the order of Roland Park, Baltimore (Figs. 1154-57, 1161-62), and its imitations all over the country, where by means of private restrictions and protections laid upon large areas of land considerable tracts were developed with an unusual degree of harmony.

In the following pages a few illustrations have been brought together giving a general idea of some of the tendencies at work. To describe these in detail will not be attempted as they have been selected chiefly as demonstrations of ideas developed in this book.

It has been possible to give only a few pages to war housing developments, one of the most important bodies of work in city planning which this country has accomplished. In these layouts the older American ideal for suburban extensions, the imitation of the "rural" park, was pretty definitely abandoned and the European method, employing compact groups formally planned, was adopted instead. The reason was primarily economic but aesthetic motives surely played their part. It is to be hoped that this work will not be without permanent influence upon expensive suburban developments as well as upon industrial housing.

Plat of the Town of Madison

FIG. 1039—MADISON, WIS., ORIGINAL PLAT

The town was built substantially as here shown, except that the canal has been cut along the line of the river at the right hand side of the plan, and that Fulton and Franklin Avenues were not built. The designer made a serious practical mistake in not foreseeing that the diagonals would become the principal traffic courses and made them much too narrow. (From Nolen.)

FIG. 1040—CIRCULAR BUILDING

A study by Cass Gilbert for the Festival Hall at the St. Louis Fair, showing the type of plan which is adapted to stand at the center of a star of streets. (From the Architectural Review, 1904.)

FIG. 1041—NEW YORK COURT HOUSE

This drawing of Guy Lowell's project is from the "Sechs Bücher vom Bauen" by Ostendorf, who comments thus: "Whatever one may say of the details, one can but admire the extraordinary vision of architectural unity had by the individual who designed it and the nation which selected it."

FIG. 1042—DUBLIN, BANK OF IRELAND

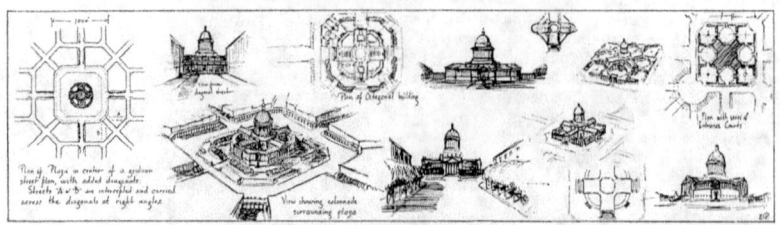

FIG. 1043—SHEET OF SKETCHES

Thumbnail studies bearing on the problem of the large public building located at the center of a star of eight radials.

FIG. 1044—MADISON, WISCONSIN STATE CAPITOL.

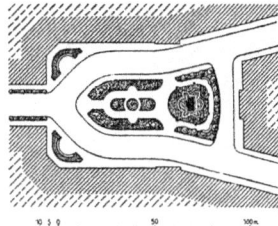

FIG. 1045—ACUTE STREET INTER-
SECTION

A solution, by Gurlitt, of the aesthetic
and practical difficulties of the sharply
forked street. The gardening is not incapable
of further study.

A demonstration of the difficulty involved in placing a public building in
the center of a gridiron with added diagonals. Perfect unity of mass is not
easy to attain in a large spreading design seen from many directions. In the
Madison capitol the arms of the cross have been drawn out much beyond the
power of the dome to control them. From this air view it is quite evident that
the opposite and not the adjacent wings are unified, and that each pair cuts the
other in half, in spite of the best intentions of the dome and its four little
assistants. One can imagine how the building would look if two adjacent
wings were removed, leaving only an L with the dome at the angle. Yet that
is exactly the composition offered the spectator from many points on the ground.
The intellectual assurance that two additional wings exist, unseen, on the other
side of the building, cannot remove the physical perception of the huge dome
crushing down the ends of the two unbalanced buildings. It is practically impossible to bring together, on equal terms, a monumental dome and an office
building. Either the offices must be reduced to secondary rank as the setting
for the dome (as in the Nebraska Capitol drawings on p. 143), or the office
must be suppressed entirely, the dome standing free (see Gilbert's sketch, Fig.
1040), or the offices themselves must be mastered by some such Titanic stroke
as shaped Lowell's design for the New York court house.

FIG. 1046—UGLY INTERSECTION OF DIAGONALS

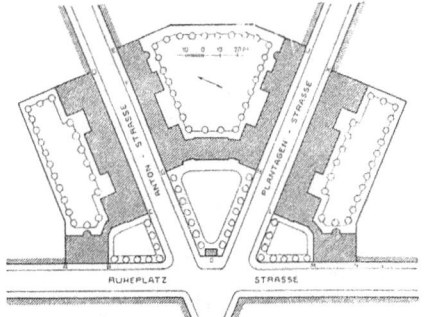

FIG. 1047—BERLIN. SCHOOL ON FLATIRON LOT

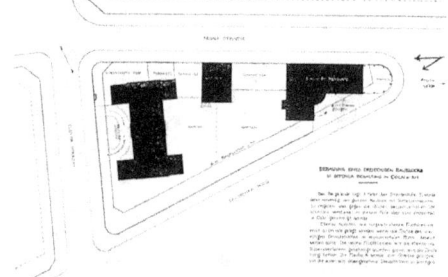

FIG. 1049—COLOGNE. TRIANGULAR BLOCK

FIG. 1048—BERLIN. SCHOOL ON FLATIRON LOT

By Ludwig Hoffmann. (From Wasmuth's Monatshefte.)

FIG. 1050—COLOGNE. TRIANGULAR BLOCK

Figs. 1049-50 represent a design by Paul Schultze-Naumburg for
a three-sided block of the kind so common in Washington. In consideration of the intelligent planning of the buildings the authorities
permitted slight encroachments on the building line.

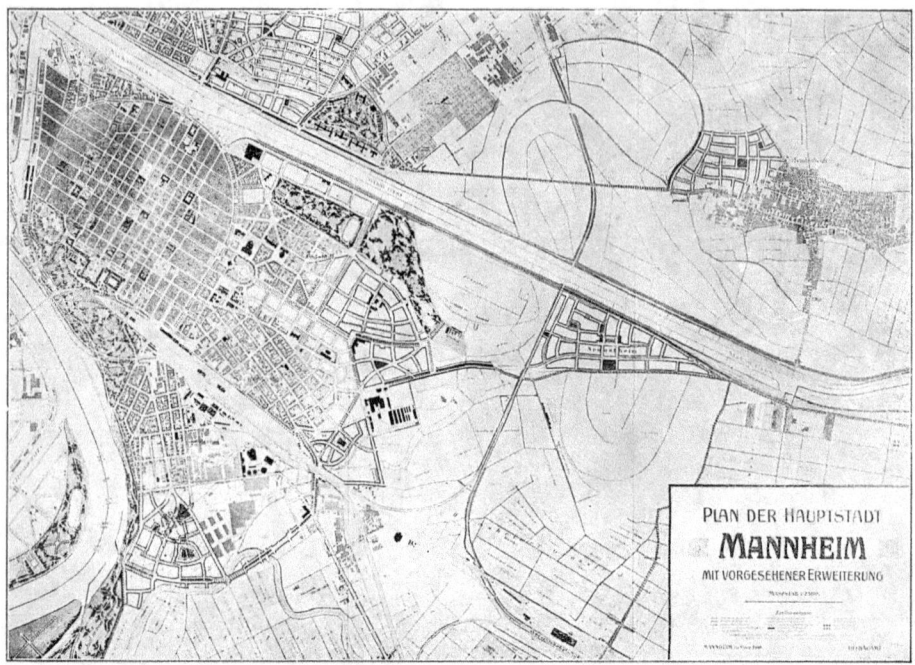

FIG. 1051—MANNHEIM. MODERN MAP OF THE CITY AND VICINITY SHOWING VARIOUS STAGES OF GROWTH

For a discussion of the different zones of expansion see the text, p. 248. For the most recent additions see Figs. 1059 and 1062. (Figs. 1051, 1053-54 and 1056 by courtesy City Plan Director Ehlgoetz of Mannheim.)

FIG. 1052—MANNHEIM. MARKET PLACE WITH CHURCH
AND COURTHOUSE

The market place occupies one block of the gridiron, marked G1 in the plan of 1799. The church and courthouse, which form, with the tower between them, such a picturesque group, were built in 1700, thus antedating Gabriel's similar design, at Rennes, shown in plan in Fig. 339. Some of the original buildings fronting on the square appear in this view, along with one modern intruder. This view and Fig. 1056 indicate the considerable degree of uniformity of façades which was attained through regulations and the exhibition of approved models of houses.

The other principal open place of the town, the Parade-platz (see Fig. 1053), which was first laid out as a setting for the guildhall, as shown in Fig. 1056, has in recent years been planted as a garden square with diagonal walks forming lines which destroy the relation of the area to the building. The adjacent "Planken", the wide cross-axis of the town, which originally had two roadways with a promenade between, has now a single wide pavement with trees at the curb. The Planken is continued at each end by a narrow street set over at one side in order that a building might be located on the axis of the mall.

Fig. 1053 represents the town substantially as it was replanned in 1699 after having been burned by the French.

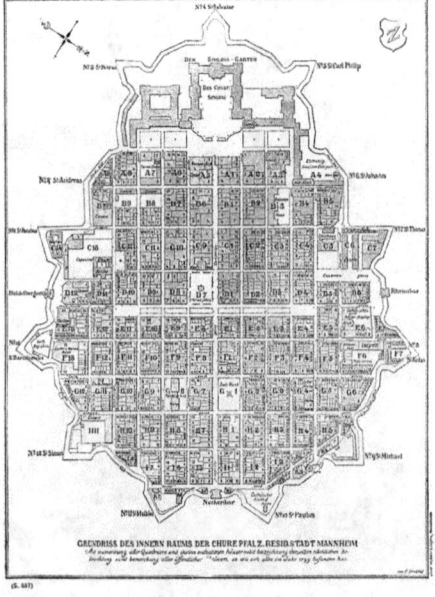

FIG. 1053—MANNHEIM IN 1799

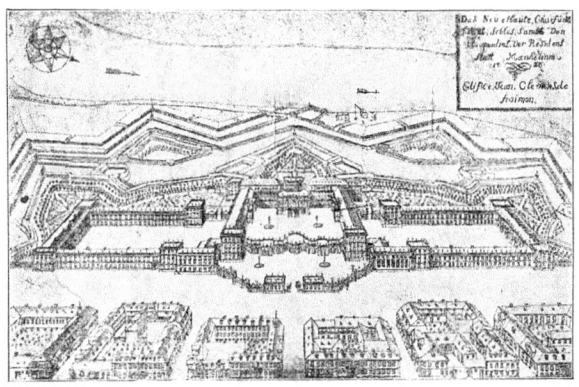

FIG. 1054—MANNHEIM. PALACE
Built about 1725 by Marot, Froimont, Bibiena, and Pigage.

FIG. 1055—MANNHEIM. JESUIT CHURCH

FIG. 1055A—LA ROCHE-SUR-YON
A military town founded by Napoleon. The hatching
emphasizes the skeleton of the design.

FIG. 1056—MANNHEIM. GUILDHALL AND PARADE-PLATZ

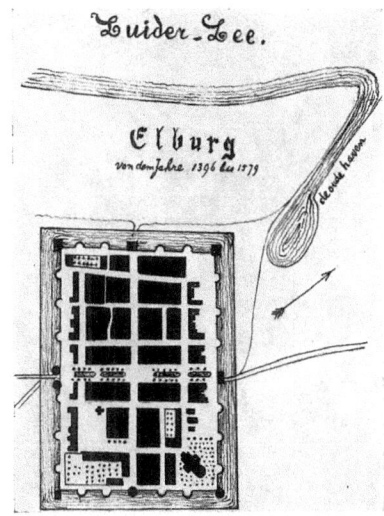

FIG. 1057—ELBURG

FIG. 1058—INDIANAPOLIS, 1821
Probably by Ralston, an assistant of L'Enfant.

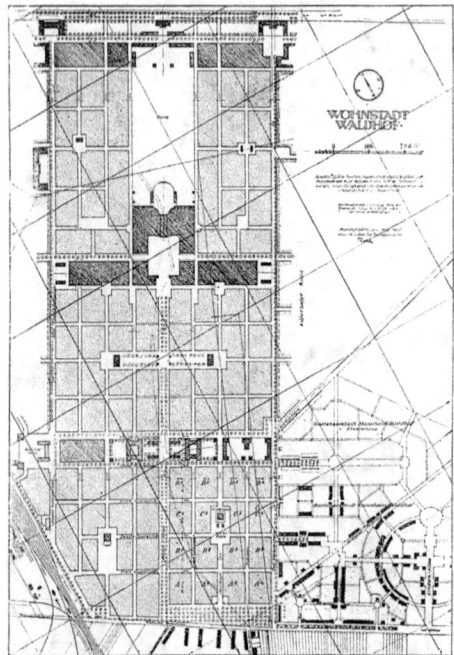

FIG. 1059—MANNHEIM. PLAN OF THE SUBURB WALDHOF

The latest addition to the city, designed by Carl Roth, 1920. The plan follows the old Mannheim plan in being a gridiron but with more frequent and more skilful variations from the checkerboard, especially in the handling of the open places. In this respect it seems to show the influence of such plans as the one by Scamozzi, Fig. 987. Compare also the plan of La Roche-sur-Yon on the previous page.

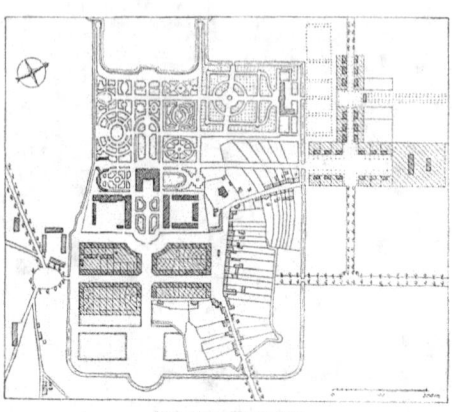

FIG. 1060—PFOERTEN

An industrial settlement of the middle of the eighteenth century, made to attract a population to the estate of the Counts de Bruehl. (From Kuhn.)

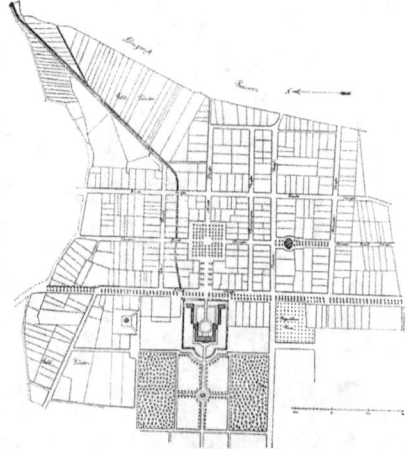

FIG. 1061—ORANIENBAUM

Planned about 1683. Except around the market place all houses have but one story, thus forming an easily dominated setting for the church and palace.

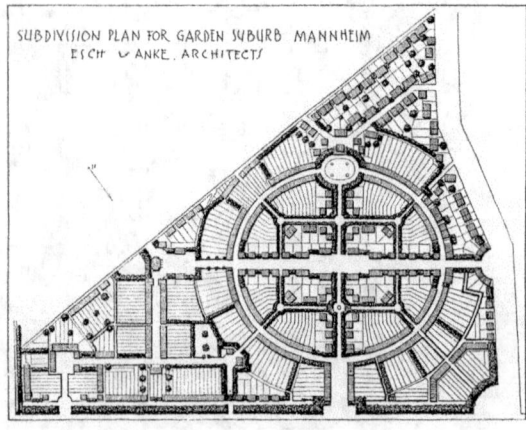

FIG. 1062—MANNHEIM

A suburb influenced by English garden city plans.

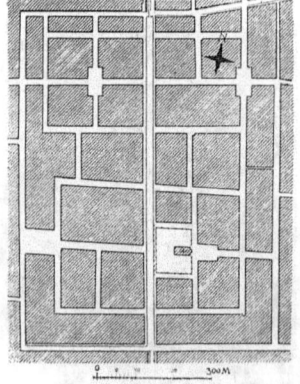

FIG. 1063—MAGDEBURG. NEUSTADT

Built by Napoleon. (From Gurlitt.)

FIG. 1064—TREMADOC

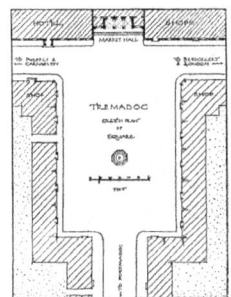

FIG. 1065—TREMADOC

A little town in the west of Wales, built in 1798. The view is taken from a high cliff just back of the market. (From the Town Planning Review, 1919.)

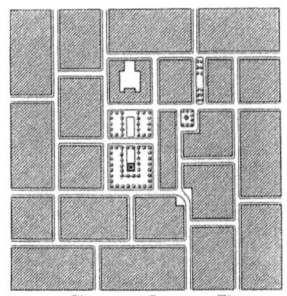

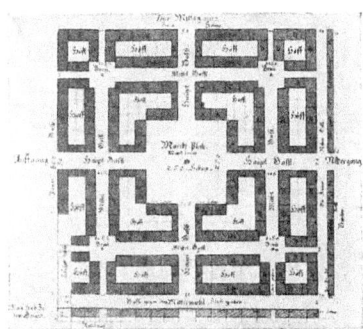

FIG. 1068—ANSBACH

A suburb planned for Huguenot immigrants in 1685. Settlers were supplied with sample plans of harmonious houses of sizes appropriate to the various types of site.

FIGS. 1066-67—STREET PLAN STUDIES

Both, but especially the lower one, show traces of the picturesque semi-formality which has prevailed in German city planning during the last two decades. Some very recent work such as Roth's Waldhof plan, Fig. 1059, is almost completely free from this stylized informality. (From Gurlitt.)

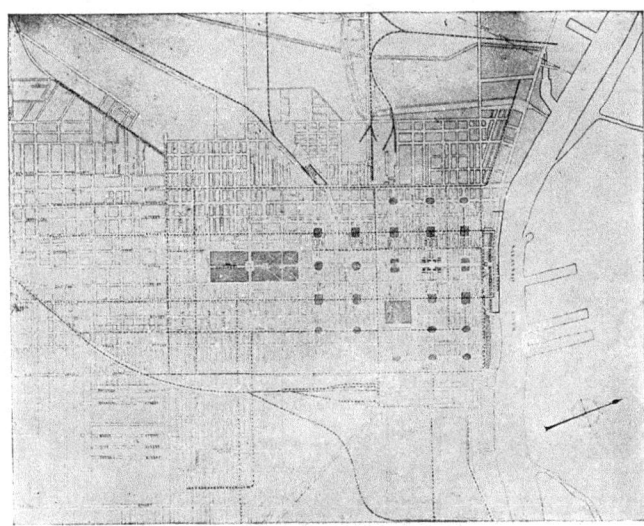

FIG. 1069—SAVANNAH

Said to have been planned by Governor John Oglethorpe, in 1733.

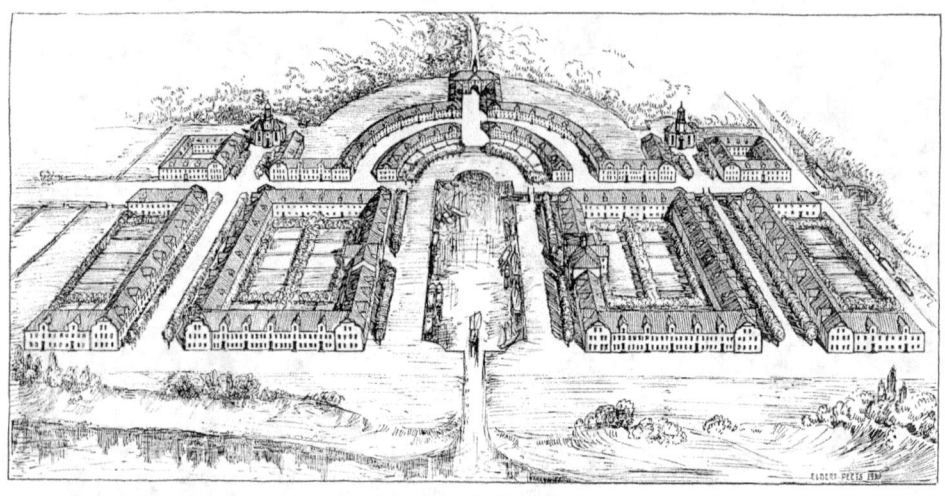

FIG. 1070—CARLSHAFEN

Carlshafen is a little town on the Weser River built as a commercial undertaking to serve as a port and transfer point where a canal joins the river. This imagined view follows the original plan of 1699. Many modifications were made in execution, as appears from the modern plan shown below. The ground rises sharply just back of the town and it was probably to avoid grading difficulties that the scheme was curtailed in that direction. It was apparently the intention, if growth required it, to duplicate this layout on the land lying to the left. The houses of the town are practically uniform, as they are here shown.

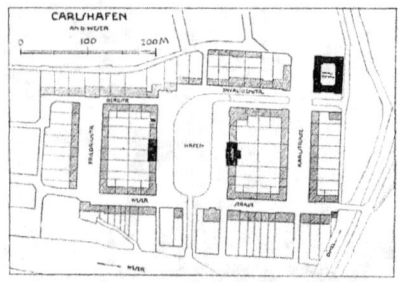

FIG. 1071—CARLSHAFEN, MODERN PLAN
(From Paul Wolf.)

FIG. 1072—NEW ORLEANS, PLACE D'ARMES
Now called Jackson Square.

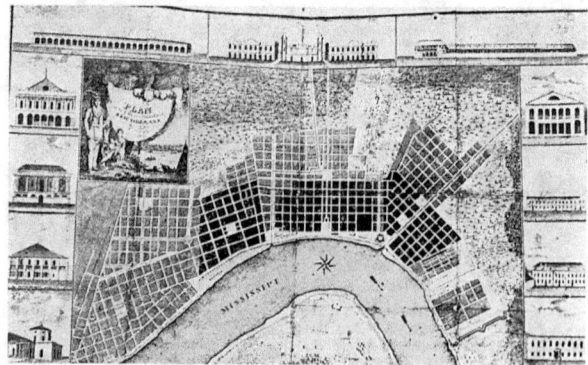

FIG. 1073—NEW ORLEANS

From a map made by J. Lanesse in 1815, reproduced by Moïse H. Goldstein in an article in "Architecture", New Orleans, 1906. The central area, measuring about twelve by six squares, was the original town planned by Sieur Blond de la Tour about 1720. The "place", now Jackson Square, of which Fig. 1072 is a view, is on the waterfront in the center of the old town. The buildings are subsequent to the fire of 1788. The plan displays a more intelligent and elastic use of the gridiron than do the plans of the later towns laid out by government surveyors.

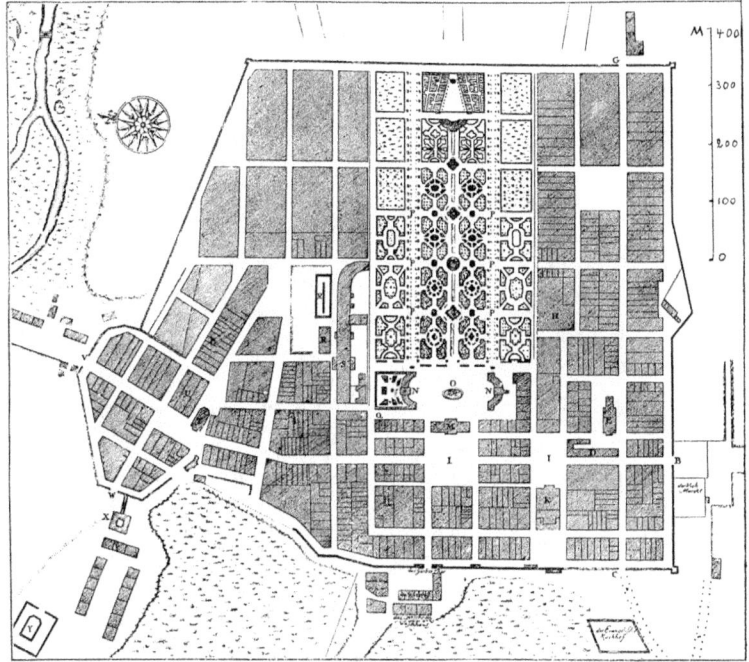

FIG. 1074—ERLANGEN

The area around the two squares marked "1" was laid out, in 1686, as an industrial suburb of the old town. So effective was the larger square that, some years later, it was chosen as the site of the Markgraf's palace, "M". An interesting feature of the Erlangen plan is that many pairs of houses at street corners are made higher than their neighbors and pulled slightly forward so as to enframe street vistas and accentuate axes. These are aptly called "Richt Haeuser", or "houses which indicate the direction". They often group effectively with the lower houses.

This plan of the town dates from about the year 1740.

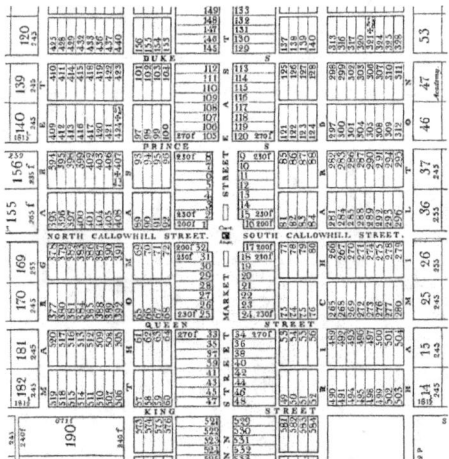

FIG. 1075—READING

Central part of the original plat of the city as laid out by Nicholas Scull, a surveyor in the service of the sons of William Penn, in 1748. In Colonial times Reading must have been an extremely attractive town, with its orderly streets and quaint rows of red brick houses. It still retains much of its old charm, though modern taste has little appreciation of the simple and dignified traditional street-architecture to which is due its characteristic and distinctive charm.

Penn Square, the fine central plaza of the town, is now an open paved area, the old courthouse and markets having long since been removed. It is to be hoped that the recent suggestion that Penn Square be adorned with central planting-strips, comfort stations, and so on, will not be effectuated. (The plan is reproduced by courtesy of Mr. E. B. Ulrich, City Engineer.)

FIG. 1076—THEORETICAL DIAGRAM OF A CENTRAL
TRAFFIC CIRCUIT

Henard's scheme, by which through traffic is enabled
to by-pass the central district. Philadelphia, when first
planning to use this idea (see next figure), proposed making
the circuit so small that rotary movement of traffic could
be enforced.

FIG. 1077—PHILADELPHIA. CENTRAL TRAFFIC
CIRCUIT AND APPROACHES

Proposed by the Bureau of Surveys of the city, which
claims for the plan that it "would greatly relieve traffic
conditions in the center of the city, would break up the
present tendency toward centralization and the intensi-
fication of the use of land for business purposes, would
enhance the value of property which is now stationary
or declining, would aid in the elimination of slum districts, and would add a feature of great distinction as
well as usefulness to the city." This proposal has had
to be much modified on account of the erection of new
buildings.

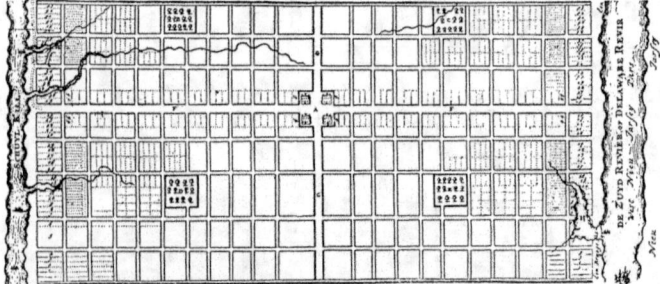

FIG. 1078—PHILADELPHIA. PENN'S PLAN, 1682

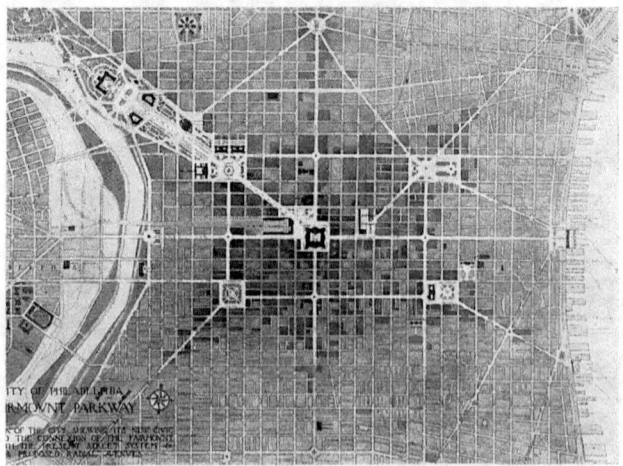

FIG. 1079—PHILADELPHIA. FAIRMOUNT PARKWAY AND PROPOSED RADIALS

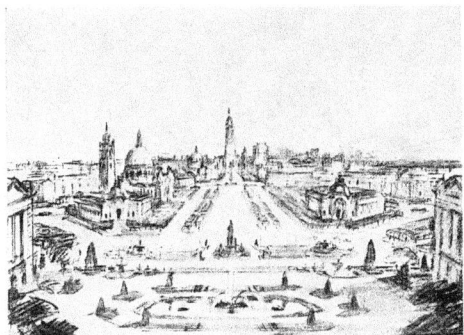

FIG. 1080—PHILADELPHIA. THE PARKWAY, LOOKING TOWARD
THE CITY HALL

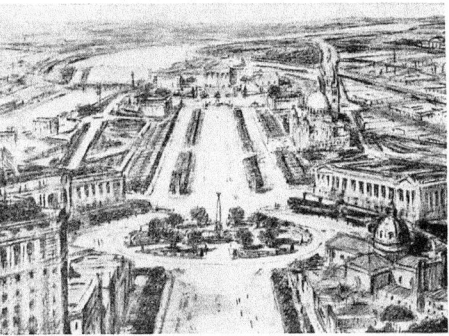

FIG. 1081—PHILADELPHIA. THE PARKWAY, LOOKING TOWARD
THE PARK

Figs. 1080 and 1081 are drawings by Jacques Gréber reproduced (as
also Figs. 1083-85) from "The Fairmount Parkway," published by the
Fairmount Park Art Association, 1919.

Fairmount Parkway is discussed in the text on p. 249. The two
plans below show the old and new plans for the Parkway. Fig. 1084,
at the right, is the plan recommended by Mayor Reyburn in 1908 and
incorporated in the city plan the following year. Fig. 1083 is the
revised plan made in 1917 by Jacques Gréber, the French architect and
city planner. M. Gréber obviously offers a better solution of the enorm-
ously difficult Logan Square problem, of which, probably, no perfect
solution is possible. He is wise to depend upon trees rather than upon
the random-shaped buildings which give a fictitious appearance of
order to the frame of the Parkway in the older plan. He has eliminated
some of the angular intersections but one must suppose that it was
with reluctance that he retained the complicated crossing in front of
the Episcopal cathedral. It is a little surprising that the diverging
avenues which flank the Parkway do not also shoot at the tower of the
city hall.

FIG. 1082—ATHENS. THE ACADEMY

A common type of museum block plan, cited here because of the
twin columns which suggest a means of interestingly terminating all
three vistas of a three-roadway avenue. Designed by von Hansen.
(From the Architectural Review, 1901.)

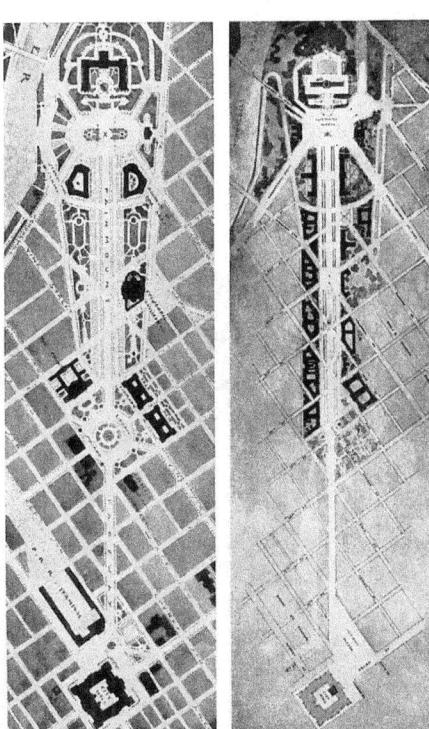

FIGS. 1083, 1084—PHILADELPHIA. FAIRMOUNT PARKWAY
Plans of 1917 and 1907. See caption above.

FIG. 1085—PHILADELPHIA. FAIRMOUNT PARKWAY
View from the city hall tower.

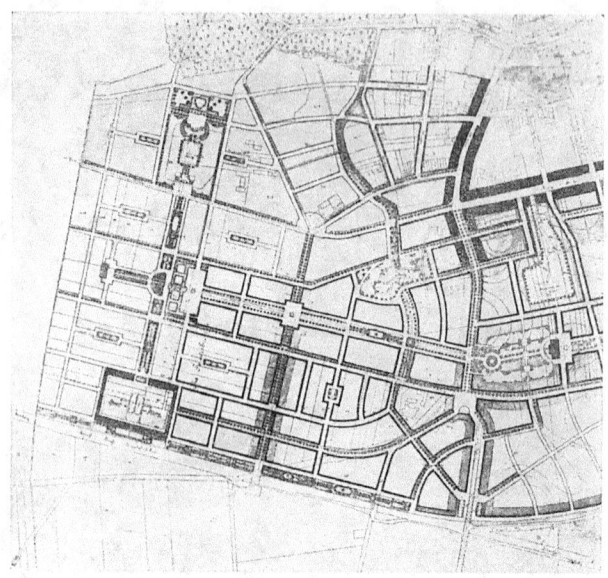

FIG. 1086—COETHEN.   PLAN FOR STREET LAYOUT AND GARDENS

Designed by A. E. Brinckmann. This plan, especially the left half of it, where the topography was favorable, is an excellent example of the formal designs now being made by intelligent students of Renaissance planning, among whom Brinckmann is an acknowledged leader.

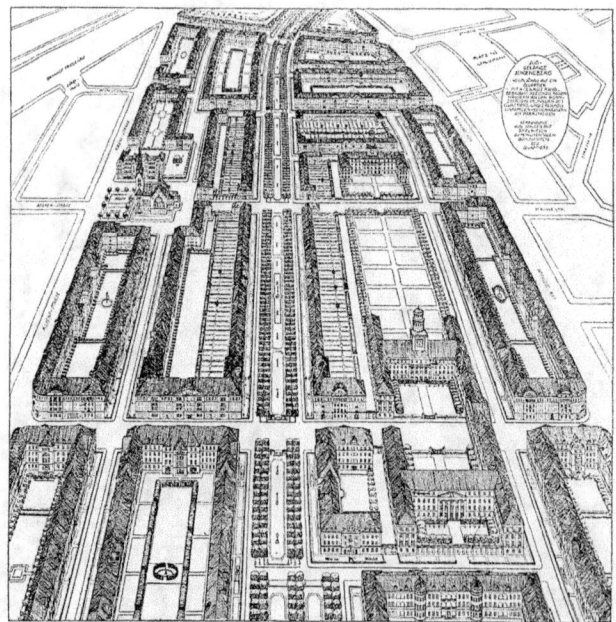

FIG. 1087—BERLIN.   RESIDENCE DISTRICT IN SCHOENEBERG

Designed by Paul Wolf. The inscription explains the design: "Bird's-eye view of a district surrounded by four-story buildings, with three-story row houses on the residence streets of the interior of the district, and two-story row houses along the parked street; the monumental dominance of the district effected by a correlation of schools and play lawns."

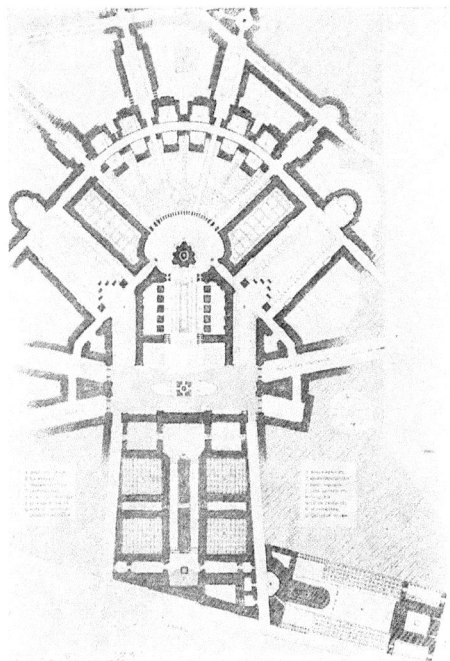

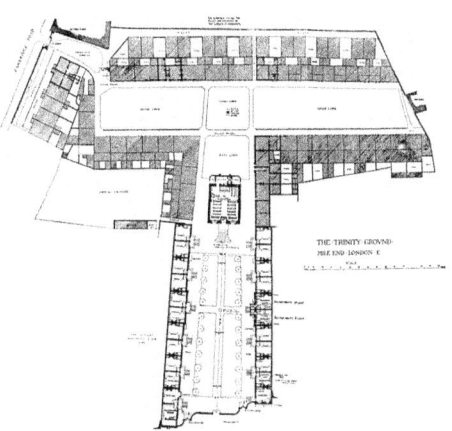

FIG. 1089—LONDON. THE TRINITY GROUND, MILE-END

An almshouse for the widows of seamen, designed by Wren. The long court back of the chapel is a later construction. This charming court might be followed closely in planning a group of apartments or row houses. It is, in fact, a miniature garden city. The Baroque plan of the fence is one of the most interesting touches in the design.

FIG. 1088—HANOVER. TETSTADT

Housing and shops of the Tet biscuit company, designed by Bernhard Hoetger. (From Wolf.)

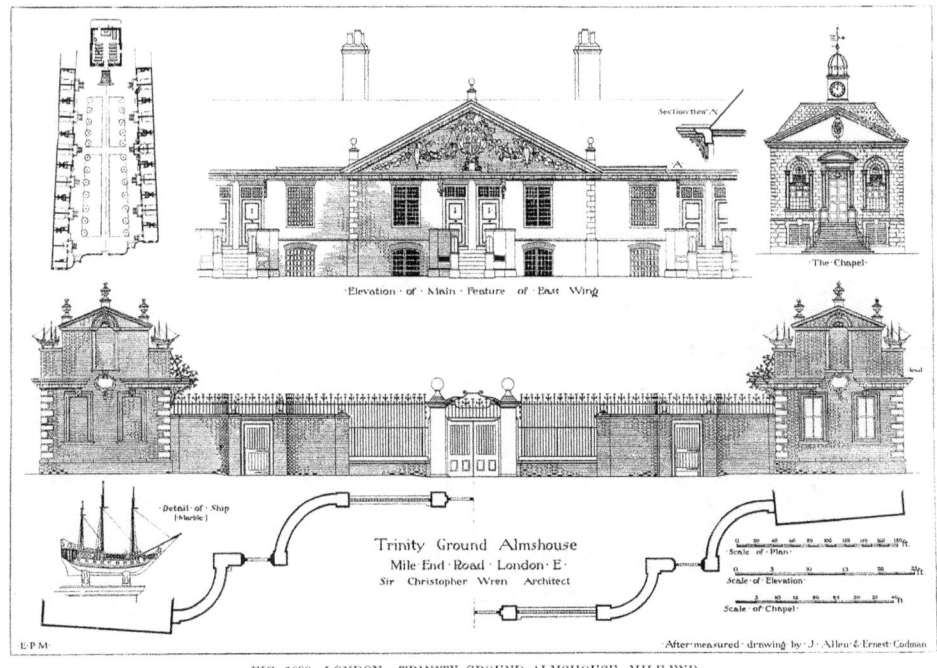

FIG. 1090—LONDON. TRINITY GROUND ALMSHOUSE, MILE-END

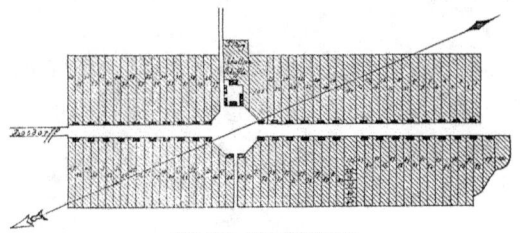

FIG. 1091—SCHOENWALDE

A village near Berlin, laid out in 1751. (From Kuhn.)

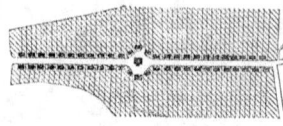

M 1 : 10 000

FIG. 1092—NEW LITTAU

A village near Berlin. The building at the expansion of the road is the church, so located as to bring the side windows on the street axes.

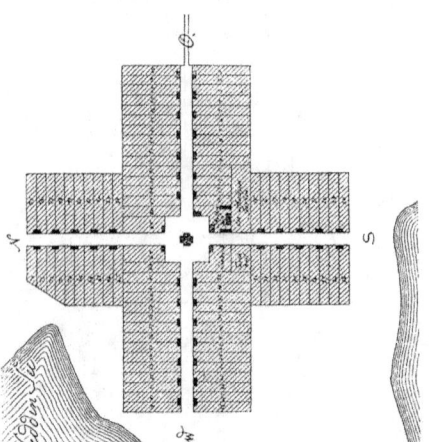

FIG. 1093—GOSEN

The church, which was not built, was to have stood at the center of the plan. Compare the central square of Reading, Fig. 1075, a contemporary plan.

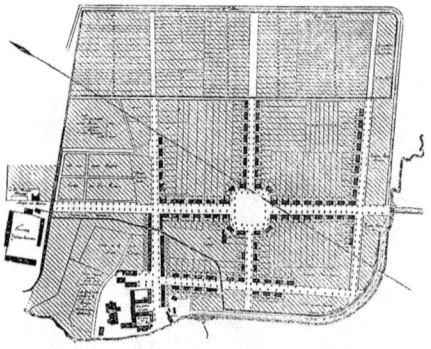

FIG. 1094—ZINNA

A mid-seventeenth century village for weavers, near Berlin.

These four plans of Prussian settlements are from Waldemar Kuhn's book on the town and village plans of the time of Frederick the Great. Kuhn also reproduces many pictures showing the present appearance of these prim and dignified little villages.

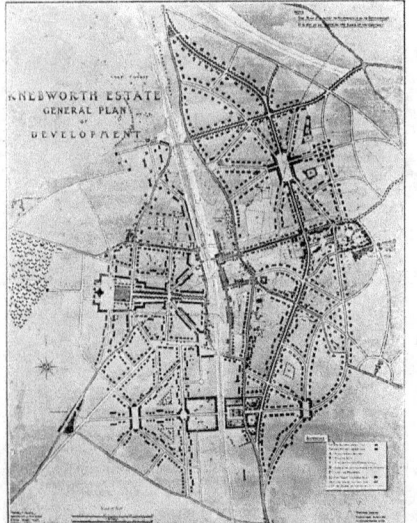

FIG. 1095—KNEBWORTH ESTATE

An English garden city designed by Thomas Adams and E. L. Lutyens.

FIG. 1096—LETCHWORTH

Designed by Barry Parker and Raymond Unwin.

FIG. 1097—A GROUP OF HOUSES

Designed by C. E. Mallows.

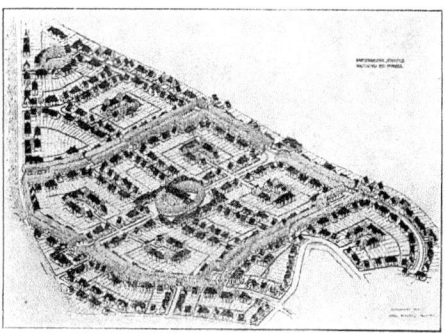

FIG. 1099—STRASBOURG. PROJECT FOR THE GARDEN SUBURB
STOCKFELD

The design, which was not executed, is by Karl Bonatz.

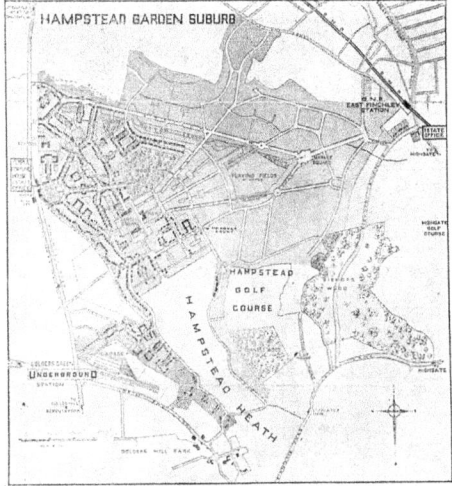

FIG. 1098—HAMPSTEAD

Designed by Barry Parker and Raymond Unwin. Hampstead is a
garden suburb of London, and is not, like Letchworth, a "Garden City"
where the people work as well as live.

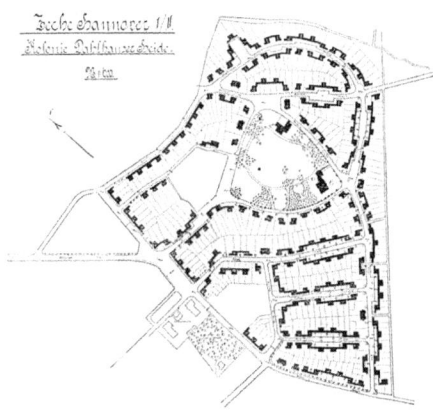

FIG. 1100—DAHLHAUSER HEIDE

Plan, by Schmohl, for a mining village.

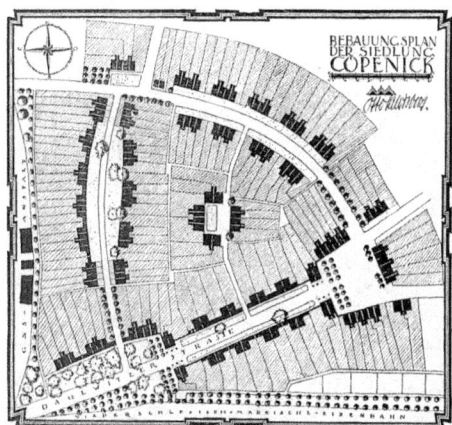

FIG. 1101—COEPENIK

FIG. 1102—COEPENIK

A suburb of Berlin designed by Otto Salvisberg; view in Dahl-
witzer-strasse.

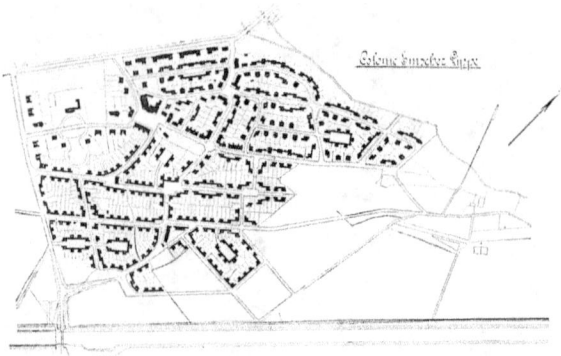

FIG. 1103—EMSCHER LIPPE

A garden suburb of Essen, designed by Schmohl.

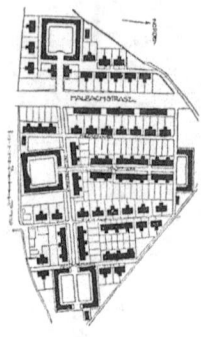

FIG. 1104—ESSEN, SMALL SUBDIVISION

By Schmohl. From Muthesius, who calls it a "barrack settlement".

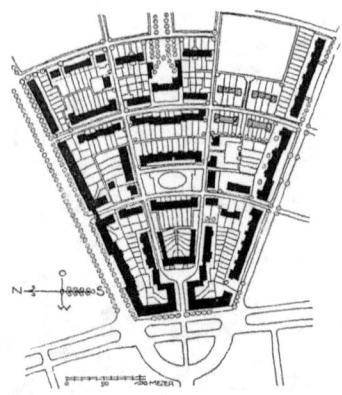

FIG. 1105—MARIENBRUNN

Built to house the laboratory employees of a large chemical works; designed by Salvisberg.

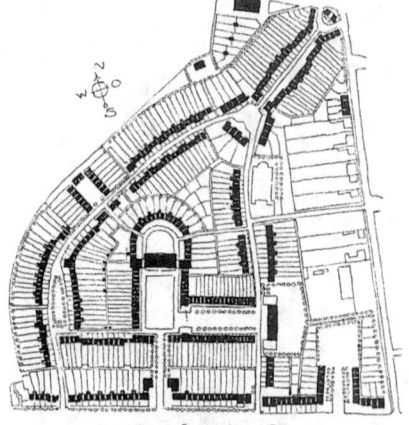

FIG. 1106—WITTENBERG, GARDEN SUBURB

A garden suburb of Leipsic, designed by Strobel. (From Muthesius.)

The four plans reproduced from Muthesius on this and the opposite page are typical of the semi-formal planning which is now so much used in Germany and also in England, for it is scarcely possible to distinguish the garden city plans of one country from those of the other. It is perhaps through the example of the English work, which has always been formal in its details and separate groups, that these German designers have in part abandoned the more picturesque, though rarely curvilinear, style which is associated with the names of Sitte and Henrici. Other German architects, armed with a love of the Renaissance which is strengthened by a healthful distaste for medieval picturesqueness, have gone back to the pure sources, the sixteenth century in Italy, the seventeenth and eighteenth in France, England, and Germany, and have produced plans which are not only formal in detail but are pulled together into large formal schemes. (As, for instance, Figs. 1059, 1086, and 435.)

FIG. 1107—LEIPSIC

A modern street axiated on the monument commemorating the battle of Leipsic.

FIG. 1108—LICHTENBERG, ROW HOUSES

In a garden suburb of Berlin, designed by Peter Behrens. (From Wasmuth's Monatshefte, 1921.)

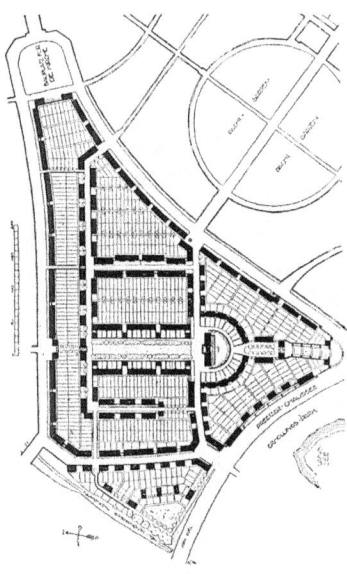

FIG. 1109—KIEL-GAARDEN

A housing scheme for Krupp workmen, designed by Schmohl. The central part of the plan is quite like the old town of Carlshafen, Fig. 1070. (From Muthesius.)

FIG. 1110—HALLE. GARDEN VILLAGE REIDEBURG

FIG. 1111—BERLICH. WESTPHALIAN MINING TOWN

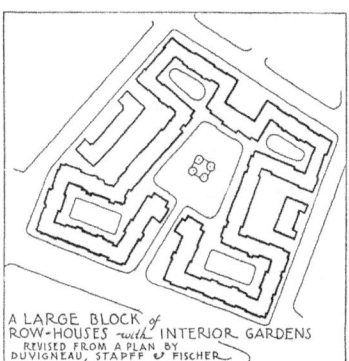

A LARGE BLOCK of ROW-HOUSES with INTERIOR GARDENS
REVISED FROM A PLAN BY DUVIGNEAU, STAPFF & FISCHER

FIG. 1109A

This plan makes intensive use of a large block without unreasonably restricting outlook and access.

Figs. 1110-12 are from Staedtebau, 1918; Figs. 1113-14 are from Wasmuth's Monatshefte. Reideburg was designed by Jordan, Berlich and Hassel by R. Wall, using local peasant styles, and Friesland by Jansen, who took a first prize in the competition for the plan of Greater Berlin.

FIG. 1112—HASSEL. WESTPHALIAN MINING TOWN

FIG. 1113—EMDEN. SUBURB FRIESLAND

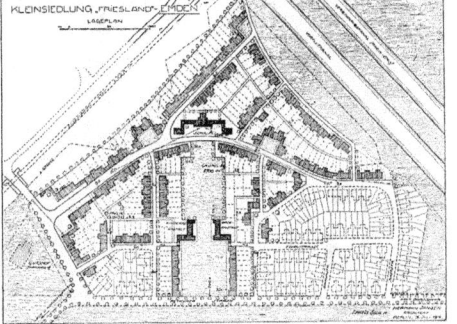

FIG. 1114—EMDEN. SUBURB FRIESLAND

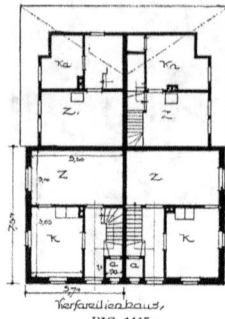

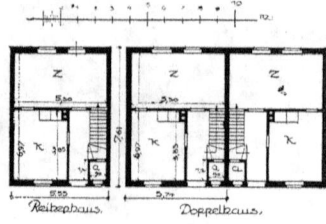

FIG. 1116—CHEAP HOUSES

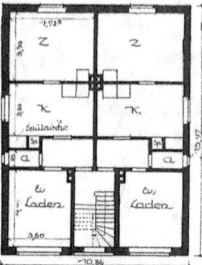

Figs. 1115-17 are representative plans of very cheap German cottages. Fig. 1115 is a four-family house with one family in each corner. Fig. 1116 shows a row-house unit and a double house, and Fig. 1117 a two-story house with two families on each floor. See Fig. 1120 for the lot dimensions and Figs. 1126-27 for plan and view showing use of these units.

FIG. 1115

FIG. 1117

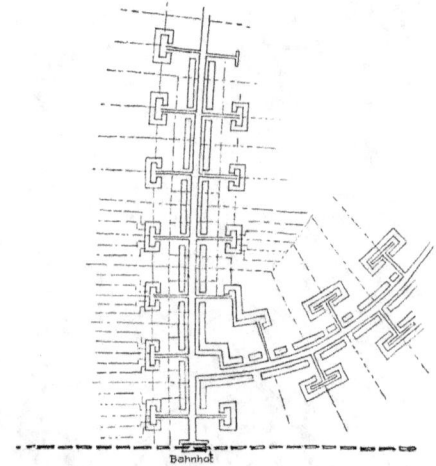

FIG. 1118—CHEAP HOUSES

A single rear-lot unit group from the general plan, Fig. 1119. The idea here is to economize on roads by making the blocks very deep, their interiors being occupied by groups of houses with a fan-like arrangement of gardens.

FIG. 1119—SCHEME FOR CHEAP HOUSING

See Fig. 1118 for detailed plan and Fig. 1123 for view of one of the units. (From competition designs by Leopold Stelten, published in Staedtebau, 1918.)

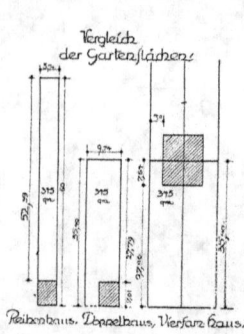

FIG. 1120

See also Figs 1115-17, above, and 1126-29, on page 270. All these drawings are from a design made by K. Erbs for a settlement in Lower Silesia. Fig. 1120 gives the sizes of lots used in the plan. (From Staedtebau, 1918.)

FIG. 1121—GROUP OF HOUSES

By Leopold Stelten. (From Staedtebau, 1916.)

FIG. 1122—CIRCULAR PLAZA

(From Willy Lange.)

FIG. 1123—INEXPENSIVE HOUSES ARRANGED AROUND A COURT

A view in one in the courts shown in the detailed and general plans, Figs. 1118 and 1119.

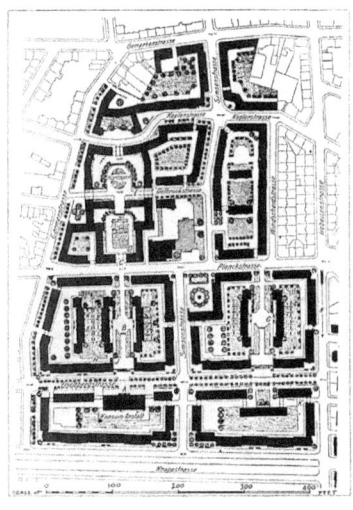

FIG. 1124 (PLAN); FIG. 1125 (VIEW)—ESSEN,
SUBURB ALFREDSHOF

Designed by Schmohl. The view is taken from in front of the "Konsum Anstalt" looking up toward the arch at "C". The arch itself is perhaps not quite beyond question, but the whole design seems to be an unusually successful effort to apply the principles of formal gardening to a compact group of inexpensive houses. The houses in the middle distance are the same whose rear gardens are shown in Fig. 900.

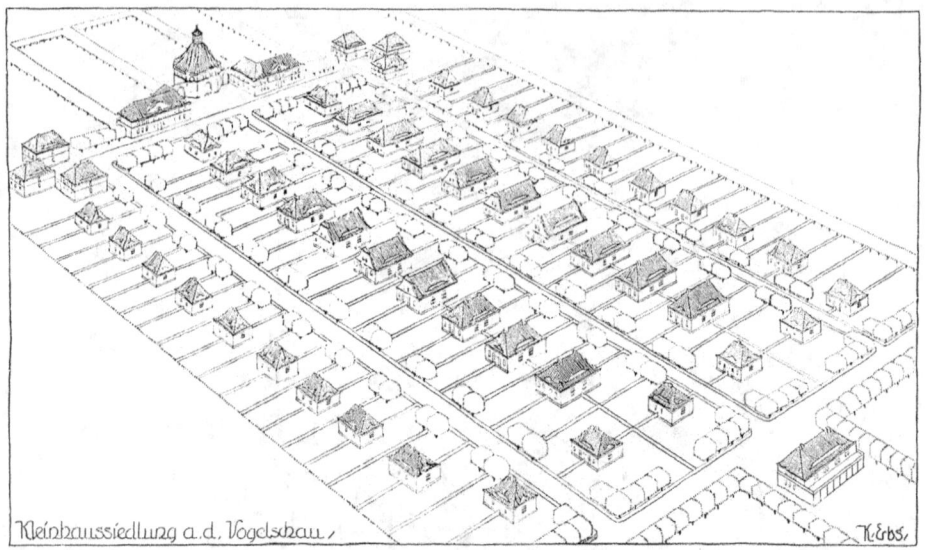

FIG. 1126—SETTLEMENT IN LOWER SILESIA

A unified layout of two-family and four-family houses. See plan below.

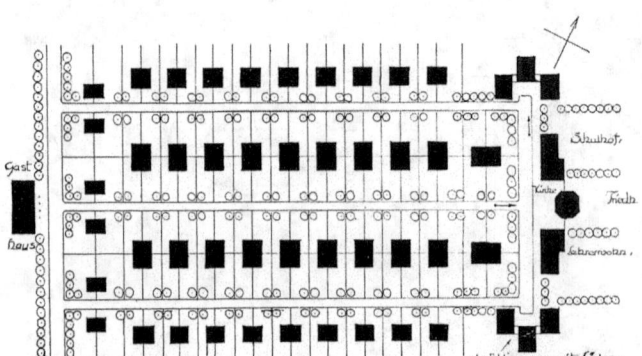

FIG. 1127—SETTLEMENT IN LOWER SILESIA

By K. Erbs. For details as to sizes of lots see Fig. 1120 and of houses, Figs. 1115-17.

FIG. 1128—SETTLEMENT IN LOWER SILESIA.
CHAPEL AND SCHOOL

FIG. 1129—SETTLEMENT IN LOWER SILESIA.
GROUP OF SHOPS

FIG. 1130—GOTHENBURG

Model of a suburb of the city, planned by A. Lilienberg, city engineer. This view of the model corresponds to the view from the point marked "I" on the plan below. The site is a rather steep hill. The designer has tried to secure the maximum amount of architectural formality which is consonant with economy and convenience. Lilienberg believes that when a hill is covered with buildings the tallest should be at the top of the hill. He thus produces a general effect of organization in a district even though an axial unification may be impossible.

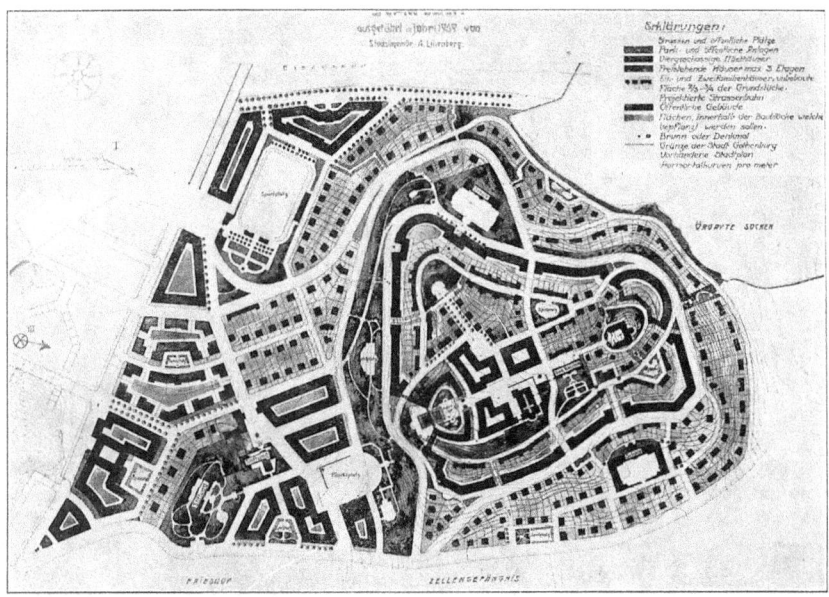

FIG. 1131—GOTHENBURG

Plan accompanying model shown in Fig. 1130.

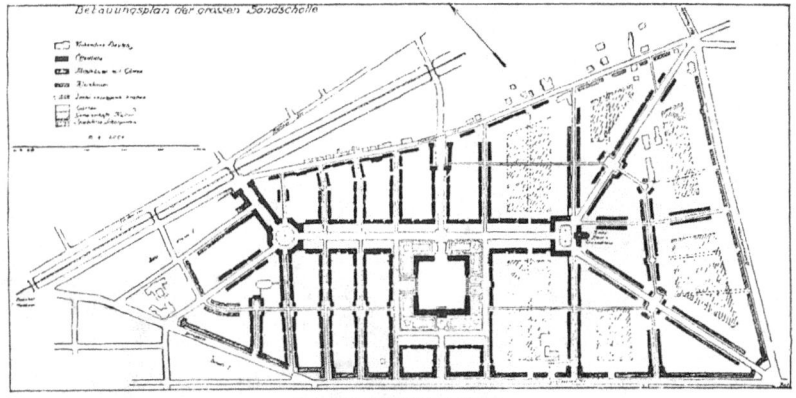

FIG. 1132—HOUSING SCHEME

A recent German competition plan by Bräuning.

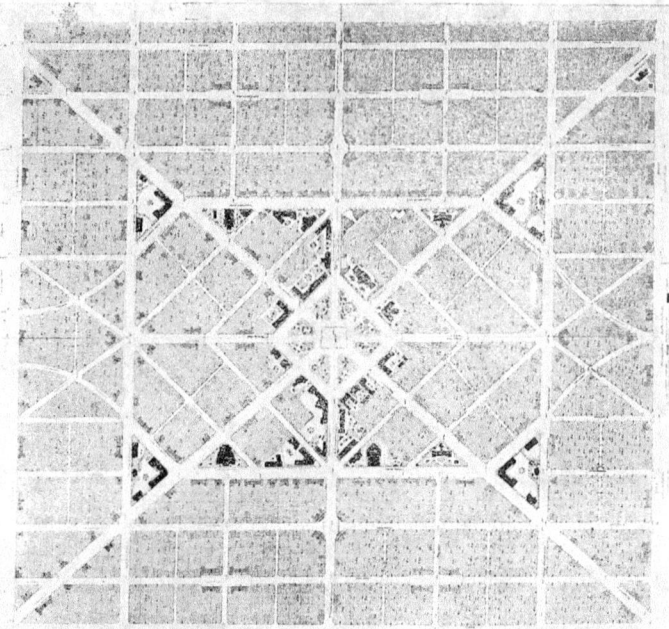

FIG. 1133—BUDAPEST. MUNICIPAL HOUSING SCHEME. 1909

FIG. 1134 (VIEW); FIG. 1135 (PLAN)—SAN FRANCISCO. GROUP OF
HOUSES IN ST. FRANCIS WOOD

Designed by L. C. Mullgardt. An intelligent planting plan (see for
instance Fig. 1164) would pull the buildings together and express the
formal shape of the area.

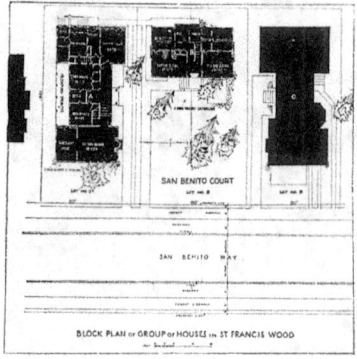

FIG. 1136—ST. MARTINS, PA. THE HALF MOON GROUP
Designed by Duhring, Okie, and Ziegler.

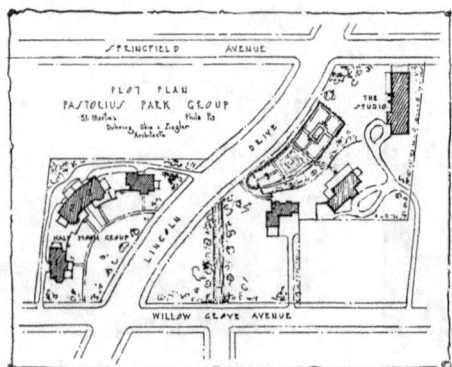

FIG. 1137—ST. MARTINS, PA. THE HALF MOON GROUP

FIGS. 1138, 1139—YORKSHIP VILLAGE. ALBEMARLE SQUARE AND NORTH COMMON
Houses for shipping workers near Camden, designed by Electus D. Litchfield. (Figs. 1138-43 from the Architectural Forum, 1918.)

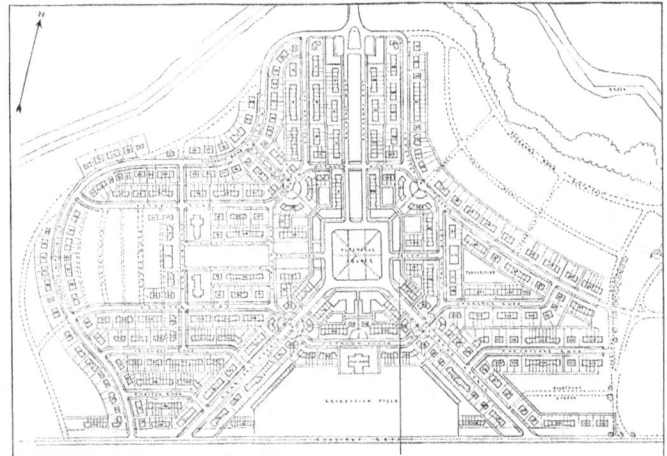

FIG. 1140—YORKSHIP VILLAGE. PLAN

Elevation of Nine-Family Group House Composed of Typical Units
FIG. 1141—YORKSHIP VILLAGE. TYPICAL HOUSES

Plans for External and Internal 45° Angle Houses
FIG. 1142—YORKSHIP VILLAGE.
ANGLE HOUSES

FIG. 1143—YORKSHIP VILLAGE. WASP ROAD

FIG. 1144—BRIDGEPORT. GRASSMERE DEVELOPMENT

R. Clipston Sturgis, architect; Skinner and Walker, associated architects. This is a view looking south along the shorter arm of Roanoke Avenue. (See the plan below.) The photograph by no means does justice to this very interesting plan, thanks to the inevitable rawness of a barely completed construction. The handling of wall-planes and ground areas is extremely effective. It is to be hoped that the street trees will be made to branch very high so as to leave the ground free and so as not to destroy the unity of the large area which opens up just beyond the pair of houses flanking the entrance to the street.

FIG. 1145—BRIDGEPORT. BLACK ROCK DEVELOPMENT

R. Clipston Sturgis, architect; Skinner and Walker, associated architects. For plan see Fig. 1148. This is a view looking up Rowsley Street.

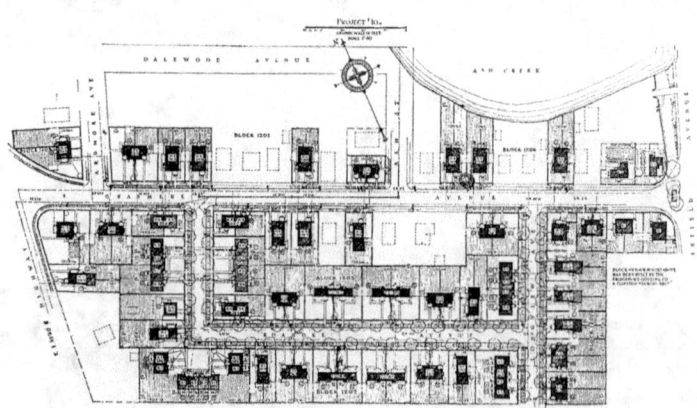

FIG. 1146—BRIDGEPORT. GRASSMERE DEVELOPMENT
See Fig. 1144 and caption.

FIG. 1147—BRIDGEPORT. BLACK ROCK DEVELOPMENT
Designed by R. Clipston Sturgis. See plan, Fig. 1148.

FIG. 1150—CLARKDALE, ARIZONA. GROUP OF HOUSES
Designed by Herding and Boyd.

FIG. 1151—CLARKDALE, ARIZONA. GROUP OF HOUSES
Designed by Herding and Boyd.

Plot Plan, Site 1, Black Rock Development

Plot Plan, Site 14, Connecticut Avenue Group

BRIDGEPORT

FIG. 1148—BLACK ROCK DEVELOPMENT

FIG. 1149—CONNECTICUT AVENUE GROUP

R. Clipston Sturgis, architect; Skinner and Walker, associated architects. For views in the Black Rock group see Figs. 1145 and 1147. (Figs. 1144-49 are from the Architectural Forum, 1919.)

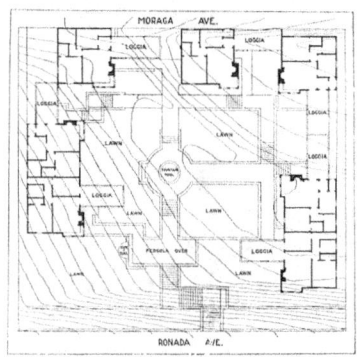

FIG. 1152—BERKELEY. RONADA COURT
A group of cottage apartments. See Fig. 1153.

FIG. 1153—BERKELEY. RONADA COURT

A compact group of small houses with common heating plant, janitor service, and the other conveniences of an apartment, and at the same time affording the advantages of a separate house, close to the ground. Similar groups, often on a very large scale, are now common in California cities.

FIG. 1154—BALTIMORE. MERRYMAN COURT IN ROLAND PARK

Designed by Howard Sill. The Baltimore tradition fortunately makes possible a greater degree of uniformity than would probably be acceptable in most American cities. For plan see Fig. 1161.

FIG. 1155—BALTIMORE. NORWOOD PLACE GROUP, GUILFORD

Designed by Edward L. Palmer, Jr. While not strongly formalized in plan this group is at least orderly. It has proved popular and profitable. For plan see Fig. 1162.

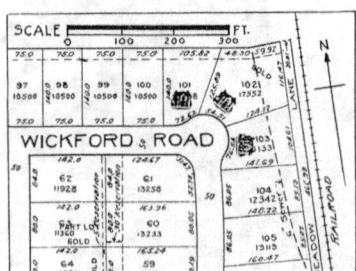

FIG. 1156—BALTIMORE. GROUP OF HOUSES IN
ROLAND PARK

FIG. 1157—BALTIMORE. GROUP OF HOUSES IN
ROLAND PARK

The group is an interesting use and emphasis of an "elbow" in the street. A low wall, with piers at the sidewalk and curb, helps to mark off the group as a special unit. The houses are harmonious without losing their separate identity.

FIG. 1158—ANN ARBOR. GROUP OF HOUSES IN SCOTTWOOD

Designed by Fiske Kimball. In spite of an irregular site and the commercial requirement that each house be "distinctive", this group has about it a pleasant feeling of friendly harmony, created by the general uniformity of scale and cornice height and by the essential, though not superficially obvious, likeness of architectural style. One of the houses, the nearest in the third picture of the upper tier, employs a motive often used by the pioneer settlers of the region.

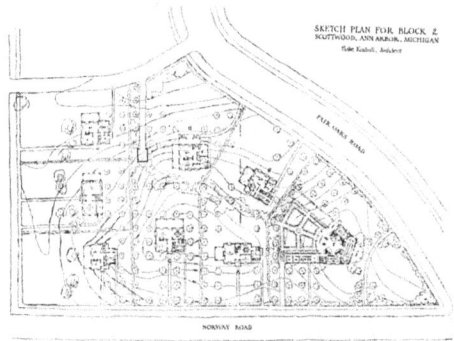

FIG. 1159—ANN ARBOR. GROUP OF HOUSES IN SCOTTWOOD

See views above. The locations of the houses and the plan of the house on the triangular lot were influenced by an enforced set-back line.

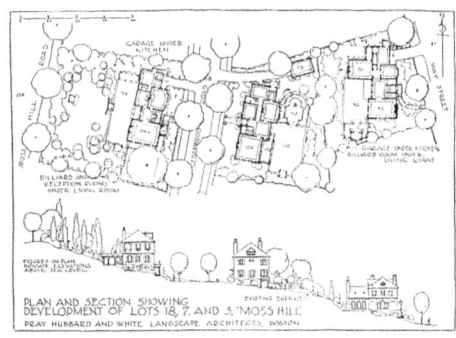

FIG. 1160—BOSTON, GROUP OF HOUSES AT MOSS HILL

Designed by Pray, Hubbard, and White. This is one of a series of studies for the harmonious development of a side-hill subdivision.

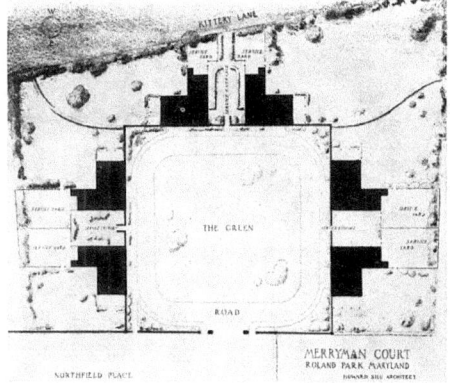

FIG. 1161—BALTIMORE, MERRYMAN COURT IN ROLAND PARK

See Fig. 1154

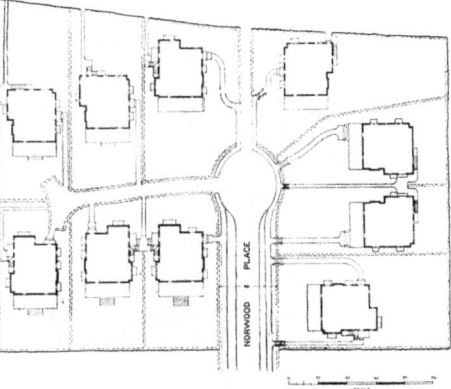

FIG. 1162—BALTIMORE, NORWOOD PLACE GROUP, GUILFORD

See Fig. 1155

FIG. 1163—ST. MARTINS, PA. LINDEN COURT.   See plan and caption below.

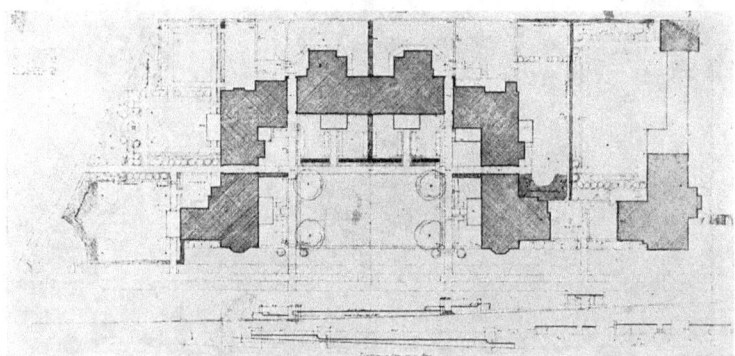

FIG. 1164—ST. MARTINS, PA. LINDEN COURT

Designed by Edmund B. Gilchrist. This group is interesting as an adaptation of a formal plan to sloping ground (Fig. 1167 shows how the cross-slope has been handled). The detached house at the right side is the house at the left in Fig. 1163. Built of both materials, it forms a transition from a brick group to one in stucco. The gardening, the approach walks, and the service entrances are handled with admirable formality and simplicity, as they are also in the neighboring group by Mr. McGoodwin, of which Fig. 1166 is a sketch plan.

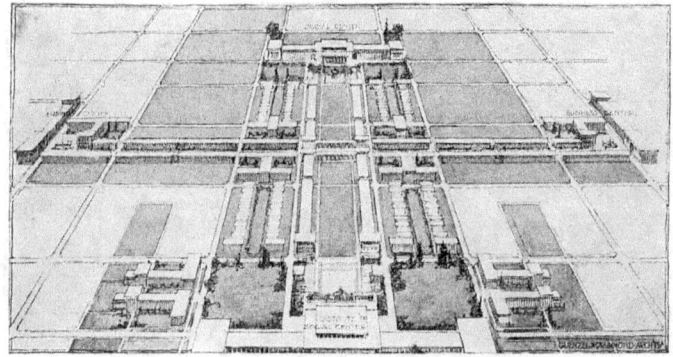

FIG. 1165—CHICAGO. "A TYPICAL QUARTER SECTION"

Submitted by Guenzel and Drummond in the City Club competition, 1913, for a plan for the subdivision of a typical quarter section in the outskirts of Chicago.

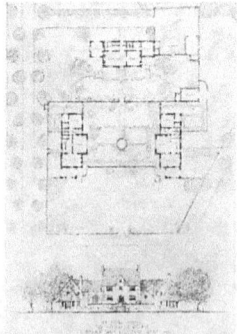

FIG. 1166—"COTSWOLD VILLAGE"

Designed by R. R. McGoodwin; one of the interesting groups which have been built at St. Martins.

FIG. 1167—ST. MARTINS, PA. LINDEN COURT
Designed by Edmund B. Gilchrist. (Figs. 1163, 1164, and 1167 are from the Architectural Forum, 1917.)

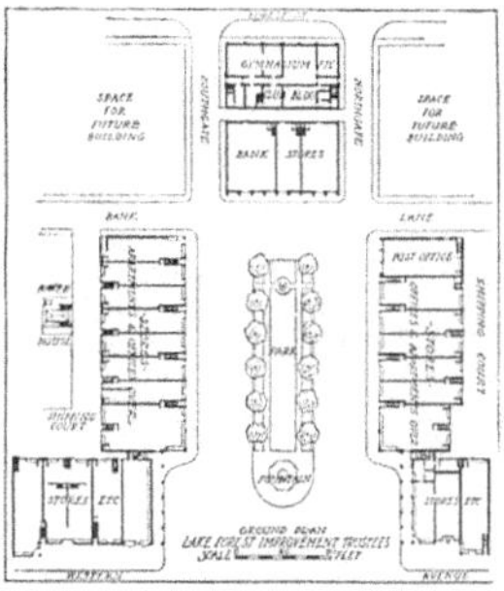

GROUND PLAN

FIG. 1168—LAKE FOREST. MARKET SQUARE
Designed by Howard Shaw. (From the Architectural Forum, 1917.)

STUDY FOR THE SUBDIVISION OF THE PABST FARM, WAUWATOSA WIS
WERNER HEGEMANN CITY PLANNING CONSULTANT
SCALE, 1 INCH EQUALS 100 FEET   16 FIFTH AVENUE, NEW YORK CITY   JUNE 1, 1916

FIG. 1169—MILWAUKEE. WASHINGTON HIGHLANDS

The straight street which dominates the design is a continuation of a straight city boulevard running out from a large park. This formal axis, which drops ten feet to its middle point and then rises twenty, both in straight grades, bridges over a creek valley developed as an informal cross-axis. Above the end of the straight street (which in execution was tapered from a hundred feet at the east end to fifty-six at the west) the axis is carried up a steep hill (Apple Croft, an orchard park) and terminates in a group of large houses at the high point of the tract, a hundred feet above the valley park. Access to this high ground is had by streets adapted as closely as possible to the difficult topography. The wide Washington Circle connects the northern part of the property with the main axis and provides a route at easy grade for those who wish to avoid the steep ascent of Mount Vernon Avenue. Two Tree Lane and Elm Plaza are motived by fine existing trees. The entire property is bounded by a hedge and hedges line the principal axis street. All entrances are marked by uniform entrance posts and varying plantings of hedges and clipped lindens. The construction work on the subdivision was completed in 1920.

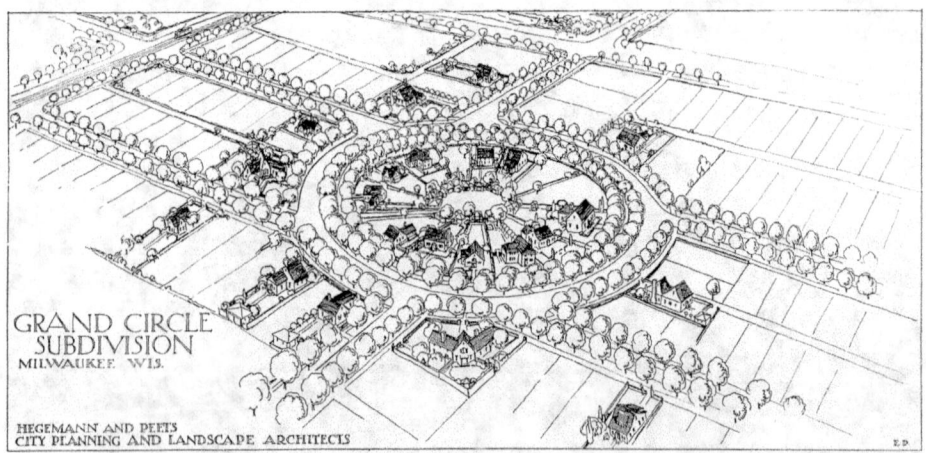

GRAND CIRCLE
SUBDIVISION
MILWAUKEE. WIS.

HEGEMANN AND PEETS
CITY PLANNING AND LANDSCAPE ARCHITECTS

FIG. 1170—MILWAUKEE. GRAND CIRCLE

An effort to insert a pleasant variation into an existing gridiron. The plan facilitated the creation of a garage court in the center of the round block, reached by a lane from the street. The assorted doll-houses are due in part to the fact that the drawing had to be appropriate for use as a newspaper advertisement.

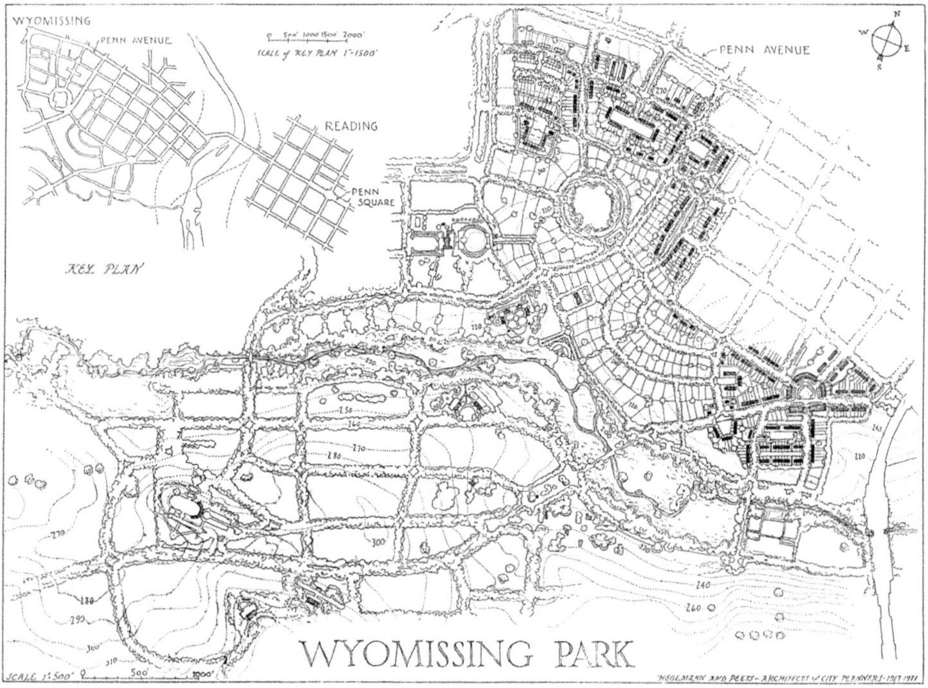

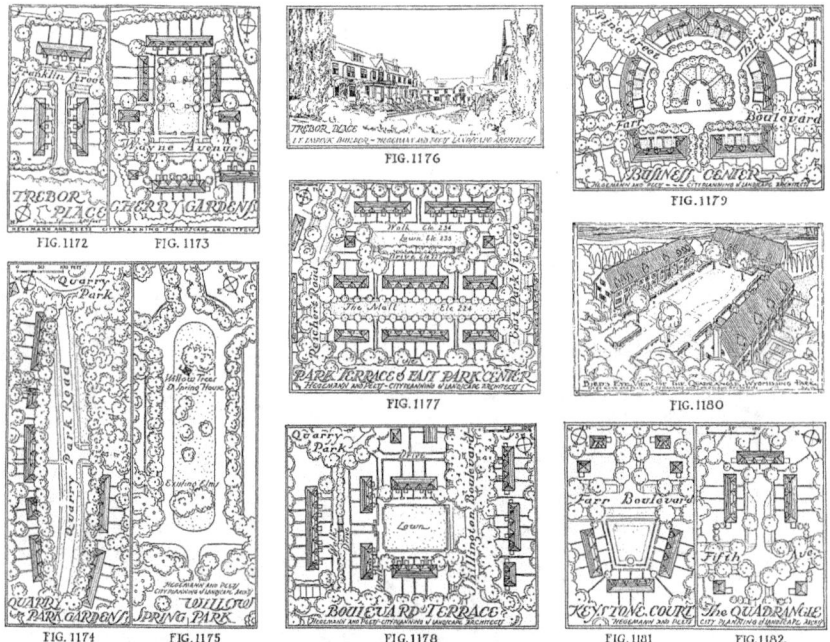

FIG. 1171—WYOMISSING, PA. GENERAL PLAN OF WYOMISSING PARK

FIG. 1172   FIG. 1173

FIG. 1176

FIG. 1179

FIG. 1177

FIG. 1180

FIG. 1174   FIG. 1175   FIG. 1178   FIG. 1181   FIG. 1182

FIGS. 1172-82—WYOMISSING. DETAILS FROM THE PLAN OF WYOMISSING PARK

FIG. 1183—WYOMISSING. HOLLAND SQUARE. See Figs. 1186-87.

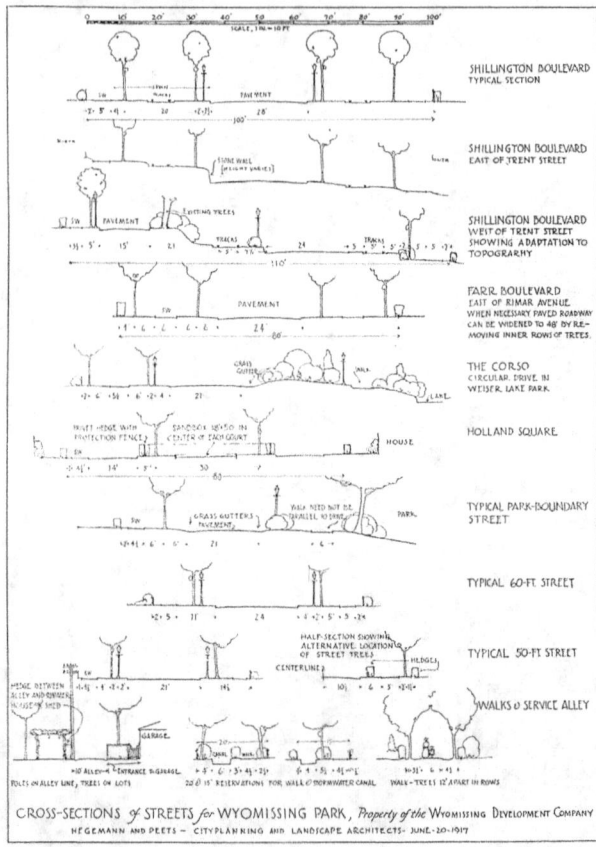

FIGS. 1184—WYOMISSING. STREET SECTIONS FOR WYOMISSING PARK

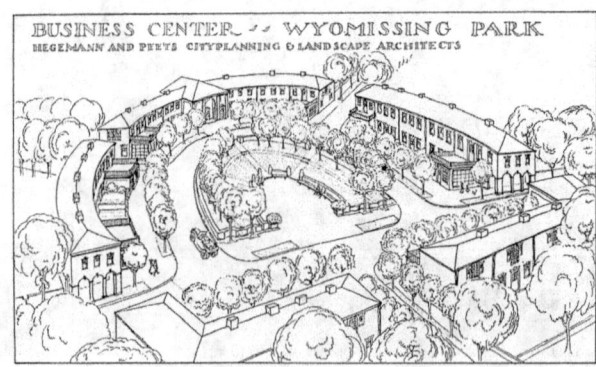

FIG. 1185—WYOMISSING. BUSINESS CENTER, WYOMISSING PARK

Wyomissing Park is a large land subdivision in Wyomissing, a suburb of Reading. (See the general plan, Fig. 1171.) In developing the plan the first principle fixed upon was to divide the tract roughly into three zones: the one nearest to the city and to the knitting mills in Wyomissing to be rather closely built up with grouped houses; the next, on the slopes toward Wyomissing creek, to be divided into fairly large lots for free-standing houses; the third, beyond the creek valley, to be divided into estates of various sizes. The building traditions of the region recognize the esthetic and economic value of row houses. It was therefore possible to plan the first zone mainly as a series of courts surrounded by rows of houses, in the style of the English garden cities. Two of these, Trebor Court and Holland Square, have been built and others are under way.

The Wyomissing Creek valley is a meadow fringed with elms, forming a pleasant natural park. The little lake in the northern part of the tract is the site of a mine from which iron was taken in colonial times.

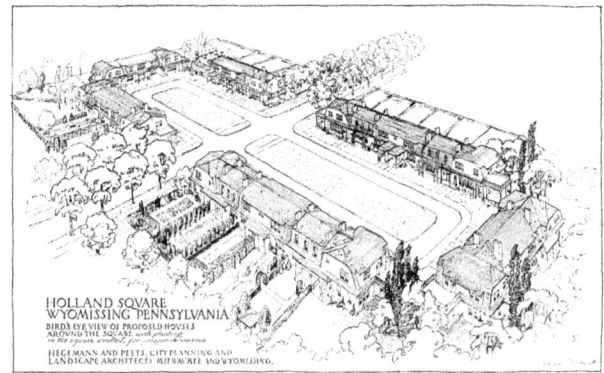

FIG. 1186—WYOMISSING. HOLLAND SQUARE

Comparison with Fig. 1183 will show that the suggestions embodied in this drawing were not followed very closely.

VIEW DOWN LAKE VIEW AVENUE, ACROSS HOLLAND SQUARE, WYOMISSING, showing PROPOSED HOUSES
HEGEMANN AND PEETS, CITY PLANNING AND LANDSCAPE ARCHITECTS, MILWAUKEE AND WYOMISSING NOV. 7 1917

FIG. 1187—WYOMISSING. LAKE VIEW AVENUE

Holland Square constitutes a rest or pause in this sharply descending straight street which ends at the shore of a little lake. See plan, Fig. 1171.

FIG. 1188—WYOMISSING

An old stone house in Wyomissing Park. The farm buildings of the region are usually of stone, and the town houses of red brick.

PROPOSED DEVELOPEMENT OF LAKEVIEW PLAZA WYOMISSING PENNSYLVANIA
HEGEMANN & PEETS CITY PLANNING & LANDSCAPE ARCHITECTS MILWAUKEE WISCONSIN & WYOMISSING

FIG. 1189—WYOMISSING. LAKE VIEW PLAZA
A study for the uppermost unit in Lake View Avenue

FIG. 1190—MADISON. VISTA
FROM THE HILL, LAKE FOREST

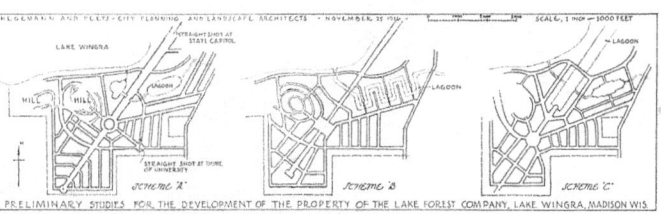

FIG. 1191—MADISON. STUDIES FOR THE PLAN OF LAKE FOREST
See Figs. 846 and 953 for other Lake Forest drawings.

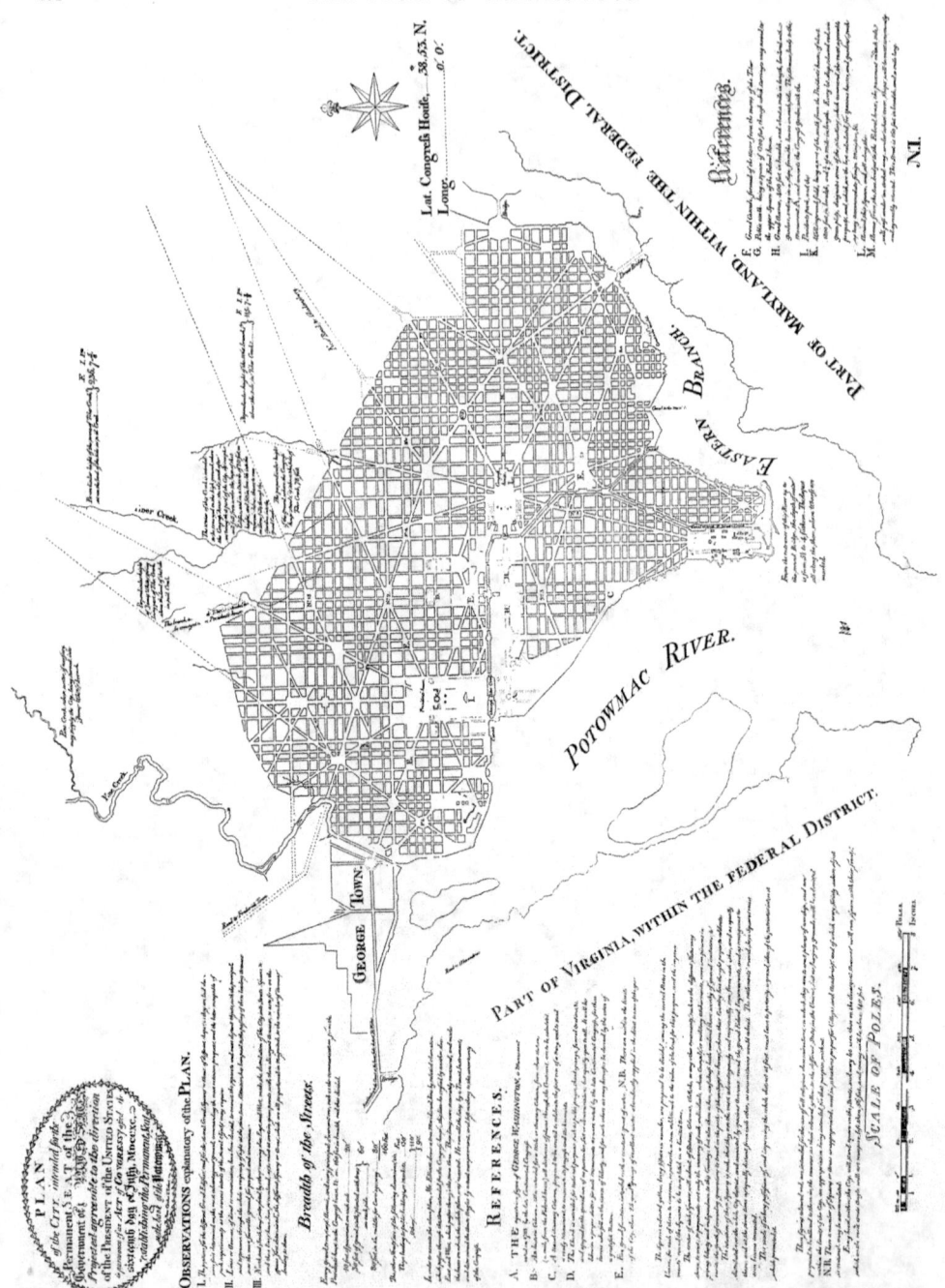

FIG. 1192—WASHINGTON. L'ENFANT'S PLAN

Reproduced from the copy made from the original in 1887. Nothing was included in the copy which could not be distinguished in the worn and faded original, which explains the imperfect indication in the vicinity of the mall and elsewhere. Some of these imperfections are due to the fact that this tracing does not reproduce the colors which were employed in the original. The plan was made by Peter Charles L'Enfant in 1791.

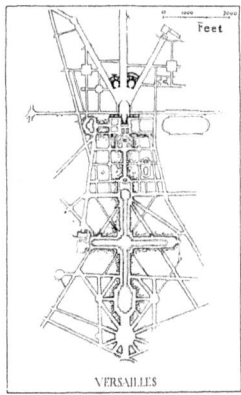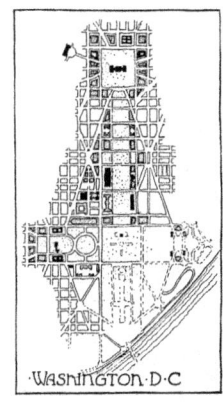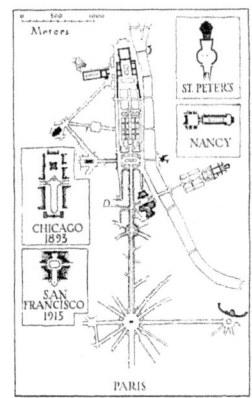

FIG. 1193

These plans, all drawn to the same scale, are intended to give an impression of the very liberal scale of the central part of the Washington plan, and especially of Capitol Square. The plan of Washington is lifted from an article by A. A. Shurtleff in the Architectural Review, 1910. It is from the plan proposed by the Commission in 1901.

CHAPTER VII

The Plan of Washington

In the preceding chapters the discussion has been of principles, confirmed and illustrated by examples. In these following pages civic art is approached in a different way: starting with an example, the city of Washington, the search will be for the principles of civic design which it illustrates, as a whole and in some of its details, whether by conformity to them or by variation from them. In a way this chapter will stand as a summary; to some degree, also, it will serve to show how the authors hope that the philosophy of design which this book has been meant to express will be put to use in creative and in critical city planning thought.

The city of Washington is chosen, not alone because it is truly a creation of civic art and not merely because it is so familiar and so near the national heart, but also because the plan of Washington is rapidly becoming established, in the current practice of American city planning, as an unquestioned ideal. It is undoubtedly through the influence of L'Enfant's plan that there is now a general acceptance of the idea that no gridiron plan can be good without added diagonals and that gridiron cities by cutting through a few radials can thus, as if by the touch of a fairy wand, attain city planning perfection. Assuredly, L'Enfant's plan is a great one and the best model in America, but no model should be accepted unappreciatively or uncritically, and in the growth of art there is no place for fetish worship.

The plan of Washington is a carefully considered design. In essence, it is a design of two axes with a strongly-marked intersection at right angles; on each of these axes is a building and each of these buildings is a focus upon which a cycle of avenues is drawn together. Then, for convenience, and to give a uniform texture to the whole area of the design, a plaid of gridiron streets is laid in as background. A few secondary diagonals cut across the plaid, but each of them is at least a servant to the

servant of the king—or of the queen. The plaid remains upon the plan a plaid, but for the true appreciation of the street plan of Washington the first essential is the clear recognition of the fact that Washington is not a gridiron city. Except when the gridiron streets lie upon important axes it is not important that they do form a gridiron—not important that they are long and straight and cross each other at right angles.

This conflict, which is so obvious in the printed plan, between the "avenues" which really form the design and the streets which open up the spaces not tapped by the dominant avenues, seems to have shown itself at the very conception of the plan. L'Enfant saw the value of the star of avenues which can make a monument the master of a great area or bring into the crowded city almost a prairie spaciousness; he saw that streets ought if possible to run straight from one center of traffic to another and that they ought to be related to the natural features of the site. Jefferson felt the dignity of a simple gridiron, the beauty of a straight street with equispaced openings cut at right angles and exactly opposite each other, and he knew the architectural convenience of rectangular building-plots. Whether the adopted plan was a compromise or an unfettered expression of L'Enfant's judgment we do not know. But whether the plan was a compromise between men or not it is certainly a compromise between ideas, for in it neither the method of placing streets individually and in groups where they will create the beauty of an organized articulated design, nor the method of distributing them uniformly in an orderly gridiron, has attained purity, nor has either realized the full value of its type. Wren, in drafting his plan for London, employed both the gridiron and the radial motives, but he knew that they could not both be used in the same area.

As a type, the plan of Washington has two general faults, both of them the result of the application of the radial and the gridiron types of street plan to the same area without sufficient interadjustment. The first of these

NOTE: This chapter is a partial record of a study made by Mr. Peets during a year's sojourn in Washington as a member of the Camp Planning Section of the Construction Division, during the war.

faults is that the radial and diagonal avenues have their identity, beauty and dignity sapped away by the constant intrusion, often at very acute angles, of the gridiron streets. These streets enter the avenues at irregular intervals, often bringing one of their own right-angled intersections so close to an avenue that the area of the intersection becomes an awkward enlargement of the avenue, and, even more often, marking out along the course of an avenue little triangular blocks which, being too small to build on, are freighted with clumps of trees and remain like undigested fragments of the primeval forest. Such thoroughfares may be convenient utilities, though sharp intersections are anathema to the traffic engineer, but they cannot be works of art as Pall Mall and Regent Street, the Via Nuova—yes, and Fifth Avenue—are works of art. To produce a coherent esthetic effect a street ought to be or to seem as orderly in design as a great cathedral, and surely no one would enjoy walking through a church whose nave-columns were spaced with grotesque irregularity, whose walls were at intervals broken out at heterogeneous angles or cut through entirely, whose transepts stood out on the bias from a lopsided crossing and whose choir terminated in a shrubbery bosquet.

Perhaps the best example to cite in this connection is Pennsylvania Avenue. Here, potentially, is a glorious street—broad, long but not too long, level or just sufficiently concave in profile, and at its end the largest dome in America. But, no matter how skillfully the buildings fronting on it may be designed, Pennsylvania Avenue, with its present ground plan, will never be a really monumental street, simply because it cuts across the east-west streets of the gridiron at an angle of about fifteen degrees. As a result, between Fourteenth Street and Sixth Street some six of the little left-over slivers are moored alongside the great avenue. More than a quarter of this stretch is taken up by street openings, about as much more by the little parklets, and less than half is built-up frontage. In other words, many more than half the buildings directly in sight at either hand, as one goes from Fourteenth Street to Sixth, stand at angles of fifteen or seventy five degrees with the avenue. Now a good street view is an orderly, concentrated, composition of planes. How can this part of Pennsylvania Avenue make a monumental effect, when half the planes which bound its volume of space cut into each other, now on one side and now on the other, at all sorts of unrelated angles? Above Sixth the street walls are much more continuous, but the official plan remedies this want of uniformity in the avenue by joining up the two sections of B Street, thus creating two more of the little triangles.

When a monumental building is to be built on Pennsylvania Avenue the authorities must decide between a building of true rectangular plan, placed at an angle with the avenue, and a building of unequal sides, conforming to the avenue building line. The old post office, the District Building, and the Southern Railway Building stand

square with the gridiron and hence at an angle with the avenue. A similar placing is planned for the Justice Building. Thus, at the south side of Pennsylvania, of the first five blocks east of the Treasury four will be occupied by buildings standing at an angle with the avenue and in three different planes. Particularly bad is the block between Twelfth and Thirteenth Streets. Here, where the workings of geometry have created an open parallelogram of which the avenue is a diagonal, the interruption to the spatial flow of the avenue is especially violent.

These difficulties anent the placing of buildings along Pennsylvania Avenue are not primarily due to lack of judgment on the part of individual architects. They are the inevitable result of the inelastic application of the gridiron street plan, of itself admirable, to situations for which it is not fitted. The gridiron streets which thus butcher Pennsylvania Avenue are, for the most part, not important streets. They could easily have been diverted and concentrated and brought into or across the Avenue at right angles. The areas now used in planted triangles and superfluous pavement at awkward intersections could have been concentrated into plazas forming worthy sites for public buildings and adding actual beauty to the avenue.

Such plazas are rare indeed in Washington, and that is the second of the two basic shortcomings of Washington as a type plan.

The map of Washington, to be sure, is dotted over with a variety of expanded street-intersections bearing such labels as "square" or "circle", but these are no more plazas in the architectural sense of the word than is a pile of stones a beautiful building. The idea that an open area is a virtue and a thing of beauty in itself, merely because it is so many square feet of space capable of growing grass or shrubs, that is an idea which one can sympathetically observe in a horse or a caterpillar, but it is entirely unworthy of us human beings, to whom has been given that ultimate sense which is sensitive to form, to art. It is no more definitive praise to say of a city "square" that it has a superficies of two acres than is it to say of a piece of sculpture that it weighs a ton. The shape, enframement, and development of the open area are just as vital to its value as a work of civic art as are silhouette and modelling to the beauty of a statue. There are people who think of architecture as a thing of façades and mouldings and textures, who do not feel the mass of a building and are not sensitive to rooms as shaped and proportioned volumes of space. The words "court", "plaza", and "square" can have little association with art in such minds; and yet the cult of the plaza, the feeling for enclosed space, like all the rest of art, is firmly rooted in the universal human desire for clarity, rhythm, and poise. Even the superficial madam chairman of the committee which planted the round bed in front of the court house with cannas and elephant-ears cannot but feel a genuine thrill of joy when, having traversed the dark and tortuous Merceria, she suddenly passes under an arch and steps out into Piazza San Marco. She will come back and plant more cannas (just as her male equivalent will continue to cite Thomas Circle as one of the beauty spots of Washington) but that is because she does not know why she enjoyed the Piazza San Marco and there is no tradition, no propaganda even, to help her to do the right thing without conscious cultural training.

The years of L'Enfant's boyhood in France were the heyday years of the plaza, when the "place" was as much an accepted part of architectural thought as is the skyscraper with us. But his training was not in architecture and he seems not to have brought to the design of the Washington plan any strong feeling for formal, enclosed, architectural areas. Perhaps he thought that such details would be worked out with the gradual execution of the plan, but it must be admitted that some of his "open spaces" at the intersections of streets and avenues seem inherently incapable of any possible hammering into esthetically effective shapes. The few simple and regular openings which appear in his plan were mostly lost in execution.

This absence of effective plazas, and even of the sites for plazas in L'Enfant's plan is, like the architectural imperfection of the radiating avenues, almost a necessary result of the superposition of the gridiron over the radials. The intersection of a number of streets is in general by no means an ideal location for a plaza but at least it is certain that if several streets have to be brought together their union must be contrived in some sort of orderly and dignified way. If you start with a checkerboard and lay upon it, not geometrically, but in conformity to actualities of the site or of the larger design, a system of diagonals, it is going to be mighty hard to fudge the intersections into any semblance of regularity. Take the just-mentioned Thomas Circle, for instance. It is at the intersection, at right angles, of Vermont and Massachusetts Avenues—also the intersection of M Street and Fourteenth Street. If this double intersection had produced an "étoile" with eight equispaced rays it might with inspiration have been made into a creditable composition. But these "avenues" do not happen to lie at forty-five degrees with the "streets", and the mechanical acceptance of the gridiron principle does not permit a "street" to be bent. So the rays, besides being of unequal width, are not equally spaced; the wall of the circle is made up of four small arcs and each of the wide spaces separating them is unequally split by knife-edge slivers of building-sites, neither in the circle nor out of it.

What makes it especially surprising that L'Enfant did not, in such a case as this, bend his gridiron streets and make them bisect the angles between the avenues, is that he did not insist upon perfect continuity in the gridiron streets. Not only are many of them interrupted by sites for monuments and buildings but a very considerable number (more in the executed plan than in L'Enfant's design) are broken at their intersection with such avenues as cut them at sharp angles. Thus L Street, where it meets Massachusetts Avenue at Eleventh Street N. W., is set over to the north rather more than its width, and at its intersection with New York Avenue at Fifth Street it is set back, approximately in line with the first section. But each section of the street is bounded by perfectly straight lines—there is no angle in the street line corresponding to the angle there normally is in the track of a vehicle which makes the shift over from one section of the street to the next. These breaks were apparently motivated by a perception of the inconvenience, even to coach traffic, of extremely acute street intersections, and perhaps also as a means of regulating the size of blocks. No esthetic motive is distinguishable. But they have the important negative value of showing that L'Enfant was not entirely adverse to the visual and linear interruption of the gridiron streets, if only the break could be made without a change of orientation. It is regrettable that this element of ductility in his attitude toward the east-west and north-south streets was not sufficiently enlarged to permit him, when circumstances required it, to break the streets by angles as well as by off-sets.

If one result of the generally uncompromising relation between the two street systems has been the destruction of the regularity of almost all of L'Enfant's avenue intersections, thus making an architectural treatment of them almost impossible, another result has been the practical impossibility of creating plazas in other situations. The avenues are the important highways as well as the dominant elements in the design of the street plan. A monumental plaza must almost necessarily relate itself to one of the avenues. But it is nearly impossible to find a practicable plaza site near an avenue, for there is not an avenue which has fronting upon it a single rectangular block,

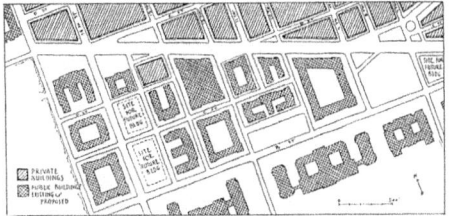

FIG. 1195—WASHINGTON. PART OF PENNSYLVANIA AVENUE

From the map of the "Mall and Vicinity" issued by the Public Buildings Commission in 1917. The original distinguishes between existing buildings, those proposed for immediate construction, and future expansions.

and there is not an avenue which is crossed at right angles by a single street. Given such conditions and given a public opinion which looks upon the closing of a street with almost fanatical abhorrence, what can be hoped for? Rarely in history has there been such an opportunity for architectural grouping on a grand scale as is offered by the building program proposed for the area between Pennsylvania Avenue and the Mall. Is not the plan as it now stands a sufficient proof of the inhibiting potency of the sacred system of gridiron streets?

If the thing L'Enfant produced had been no more than a type or texture of street arrangement his plan would be worthy of little attention. What makes his vision a work of true creative imagination, compelling our homage and repaying our closest study, is that it is articulated, organized, pulled strongly yet suavely together, into a single work of art of unparalleled magnitude. But that vision was one of unprecedented daring; its author, without experience himself and with almost no opportunity to learn from the experience of others, had the most limited means of foreseeing its effect in reality; it was formulated and put on paper in a very brief time; the control of its realization, a process in which numberless refinements would have been worked out, was taken from him; the greatest part of it was embodied in brick and stone during a period and by a society probably unequalled in paucity of artistic feeling. No greater hurt could be done to L'Enfant than to accept without question every detail of his plan and to acclaim as beautiful every part of the imperfect realization of it which the vicissitudes of history have assembled.

The plan of Washington is "organized" by the vertical relation of the great meridional and longitudinal axes on which lie the White House and the Capitol. In the plan this relation is obvious and effective; in the city itself it is not easy to say how definitely it is felt, nor is it easy to determine the degree to which the perception of this relation would be facilitated by such a clarified expression of the axes as L'Enfant intended or as is proposed in the present official plan. Obviously much depends on the treatment of the intersection of the axes, of which more presently. This integration by normality of axes is supplemented by a diagonal connection, Pennsylvania Avenue. But the function of Pennsylvania Avenue in the design is not a separate one. The avenue affords, as L'Enfant expressed it "reciprocity of sight", but plenty of buildings visible one from another create no effect of common design. As a working statement of the esthetic function of Pennsylvania Avenue in relation to the White House and Capitol—taking it for granted that L'Enfant intended the White House to project well into the view down the avenue and not to stand, as it does, at one side of its course—one might say that it is an opening affording, from one building, information not merely of the existence of the other, but especially of its orientation. If for instance one could stand on the west terrace of the Capitol and look down Pennsylvania Avenue and see the White House with sufficient clearness to detect its orientation, and if one could then turn and look down the Mall and see some conventional marker of intersecting axes, such as a fountain, a statue, or an obelisk, just a bit less distant than the White House, one's innate sense of geometry, abetted by the universal human desire to see order in the world, would at once create the conviction that the White House faced toward the statue, or whatever it might be, and that the two axes crossed at that point at right angles and were thus organized and unified. The result would be a three-dimensioned, spatial, architectural composition, whereas if there were no view down the Mall and if one could not discern the orientation of the White House one would have a pretty "vista" and nothing more —a two-dimensional, photographable picture.

Capitol Square

Of the plan's two organizing axes the more important is the east-west axis, which is dominated by the "Congress House." Besides standing at the head of the Mall the Capitol performs various city planning functions. By its height and mass it assumes the office of presiding over the whole city; it is the center of a star of avenues; it dominates the open area immediately around it. This last rôle of the Capitol is the one to which the least attention has been given, but it is not unimportant. The Capitol stands, in conformity to what might be called the American tradition, in the midst of a seventy-acre park, the "Capitol Grounds." Such a situation has advantages and disadvantages; perhaps the best way to shed light on the problem from various angles is to take the plan as it exists (perhaps to be credited to Washington or to the surveyor, Ellicott,—for L'Enfant, a circumstance which adds sympathy to our respect, could not agree with the commission he was serving and was dismissed soon after his plan was drafted) and compare it with L'Enfant's own version. It would seem that L'Enfant had in mind the common Renaissance motive (as at Versailles, for instance, or Carlsruhe) of a large building with the town on one side and a park on the other. One of the premises of his plan was that the business district of the city would lie east of the Capitol. Of Capitol Square he notes on his plan that "around this Square and all along the Avenue from the two bridges to the Federal House, the pavement (sidewalk, we now say) . . . will pass under an Arched way, under whose cover, Shops will be most conveniently and agreeably situated." To the west of the Capitol he intended having a cascade falling into a "reservoir", with three "fills" (whatever they may be) running to the "Grand Canal"; at each side, masses of trees. Quite naturally, this garden area is much wider than the shopping square. The resultant setting of the Capitol is strongly oriented; one might suspect, merely from an inspection of the plan, that the ground falls toward the west. But in execution this orientation was lost: the Capitol stands in the center of an area whose outline gives no hint that one side of it is some eighty feet higher than the other. The topography, certainly, is not favorable to the present program of edging the entire Capitol Grounds with public buildings. But even if the site were level and if the Capitol had been planned to stand in the center of a square, it would still be of doubtful wisdom to line the square with monumental buildings under the pretense of thereby creating an æsthetic ensemble. The area is certain always to be planted with trees; and even if "reciprocity of sight" were assured the breadth of the area is too great to permit any feeling of architectural interdependence between its sides. It is twice as wide as the

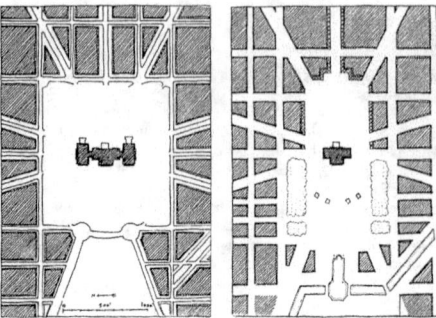

FIG. 1196—WASHINGTON. THE CAPITOL GROUNDS

At the left is the block plan as it stands, restored to symmetry by ignoring the Congressional Library; at the right is an enlargement of L'Enfant's plan, at the same scale, with street-arcades indicated in accordance with his note. Omitting from consideration the present great extent of the Capitol, but keeping in mind the fact that the Capitol stands at a sharp break in grade, it seems obvious the L'Enfant's plan is the superior in imagination, plasticity of design, and adaptability to the site.

Piazza S. Pietro, the Place de la Concorde, or the court of the Tuileries; take any of these, quadruple its area, plant it with an informal park, and how much architectural value would remain? Only enough to make a pretty rendered plan.

The situation of the House and Senate office buildings constitutes a sufficient proof of the difficulty of making a composite photograph of Central Park and the Place de la Concorde. Architecturally they are excellent buildings, barring the cigar store location of the entrances, but they can hardly be called an accomplishment in city planning. The streets on which they stand slope sharply across their principal façades, a condition always inimical to true monumental effect; they are so far apart, and the foliage of Capitol Square is so dense, that in summer one of them can hardly be seen from the other; the ground between them is convex in profile, in defiance of the primary law of the monumental relation of buildings to grounds and of pairs of buildings to each other. All of these difficulties could have been avoided much more easily if L'Enfant's less expansive square had been built. The sloping streets for instance would have lain back of the framing buildings, permitting the floor of the square itself to be perfectly flat.

The Mall

The "reference" to letter "H" on L'Enfant's plan runs "Grand Avenue, 400 feet in breadth, and about a mile in length, bordered with gardens, ending in a slope from the houses on each side." This was the inception of the "Mall" now recognized as the æsthetic backbone of the Washington plan. It would be interesting to work out in detail L'Enfant's visualization of the Mall. What, for instance, would these "Gardens" be like, and just what would the slopes be? There could hardly be a slope toward the avenue from the houses north of it because they, bordering the "Grand Canal", would certainly be lower than the avenue. And of the "houses" one would probably see the rear façades (or, more properly, the garden fronts) since these houses would face on the streets paralleling the avenue. It was perhaps on account of the topographic difficulties (for the ground is almost hilly at places, especially between Eighth and Fourteenth Streets) that the planting of the avenue was postponed, with the unfortunate results of the incorrect location of the Washington Monument, the railroad invasion, and the creation of a naturalistic park.

FIG. 1197—WASHINGTON. EAST END OF MALL
From the report of the Commission of 1901.

When Senator McMillan's commission (Burnham, McKim, St. Gaudens, and Olmsted) came on the ground in 1901 they rediscovered L'Enfant's "Grand Avenue" and saw that it was needed to pull together the Washington plan. Incidentally, they expanded the idea by making the avenue not merely an avenue of trees but of public buildings, and that is now the current understanding of the word "mall" in this country. L'Enfant, to be sure, had apparently intended (if one may judge from some reproductions of his plan) that there should be rows of houses about where the buildings are to stand, but red brick row-houses, separated from the avenue by gardens and slopes, would produce an effect quite unlike that of widely separated (they are at least two hundred feet apart) and strongly membered monumental constructions of granite and marble. One cannot but pray for the early completion of the new Mall so that the reality can be judged and not merely the plan. It must be confessed that the many published ululations of the conception are disquietingly general in statement. To be told that the buildings along the Mall will be "brought into harmonious and effective relation to each other" will not calm a questioning mind. Certainly, it is a grandiose composition and, in a large way, orderly, but will it hang together? A mile long, a thousand feet wide—was there ever such a group? Can it possibly be felt as a whole? That it will not be good if it can't be sensed as a whole seems certain. That the intention was to produce "effective" situations for individual public buildings seems most unlikely since it takes much more than a general atmosphere of monumentality to breathe architectural distinction into a building which is one of a dozen lined up like cars in an auto park. If the purpose was to create a sort of glorified avenue of sphinxes as an approach to the Capitol the separate buildings should have been severely subordinated, made uniform, and equally spaced, as were the courtiers' residences at Marly. But if these motives have influenced the design they must have done so secondarily, as an effort to utilize esthetic by-products. The Mall must be primarily what L'Enfant called it, a "Grand Avenue", an open way and a channel of space, a member of the Capitol organism extended to the point of union with a similar spatial extension of the White House. In this channel the longitudinal movement is all-important—what happens at either side is as irrelevant as is the interior treatment of the bosquets which flank the tapis vert and the canal at Versailles. Every lateral pull upon the attention will diminish the essential value of the Mall. In detailing the buildings facing on the avenue and in arranging their settings use should be made of every unifying device: uniform terraces and fences, hedges and clipped trees—everything that will tighten the bounding walls of the avenue, define its channel, and facilitate its flow.

A plea for simplicity and uniformity in the Mall buildings is not likely to profit much. We Americans are too prone to feel that nothing is monumental which is not of granite and in granite scale. We do not know that good taste and fine proportion are more effective than prodigal appropriations; we forget the modest little residences of teachers and avocats which form the beautiful Place de la Carrière in Nancy.

This effort to sketch a critical interrogation of the Washington Mall before it is built would perhaps be unwarranted if it were not that every big idea of this sort promptly generates a flock of little progeny the study of which cannot but make the judicious grieve that some contraceptive measure had not been employed. Cleveland made a "group plan"—the renderings were hardly dry when civic centers sprang up everywhere; Philadelphia started Fairmount Parkway, and straight-edges were laid diagonally across every gridiron plan in the country; the Washington Mall was heralded, and now the air is full of malls and rumors of malls. This doing things because they are done, and designing in terms of names written on a plan, the idea that a mall must be good just because it's a mall, is as deadly to artistic creation as it is paralyzing to intelligent thought.

The Monument

In L'Enfant's plan the intersection of the Capitol and White House axes, the western end of the Grand Avenue, was made the site of the proposed monument to Washington, then intended to be an equestrian statue. Instead of it there now stands (some one hundred and twenty feet south of the true intersection and three hundred and sixty feet east of it) Robert Mills's beautiful obelisk, one of the architectural glories of America. The new Washington plan provides a formal garden to the west of the monument, with a circular pool on the White House axis. The story of this one phase of the plan of the capital could be developed into an entire theory of city planning.

L'Enfant's approach to this delicate problem was probably guided by a memory or understanding of European precedents. Perhaps the nearest parallel was the intersection in the Place Louis XV (now de la Concorde) of the Tuileries axis with the Madeleine axis. This intersection was then marked by an equestrian monument about fifty feet high facing up the longer axis—that is, toward the Tuileries. The use of a statue to mark an intersection of axes was very common in France. A statue is an object large enough to attract attention and definitely to indicate a node in the axis, but not so large as to stop the view dead, and the capacity of the statue to indicate orientation is often useful in the expression of the direction of flow of the design and the relative importance of the axes.

But when, after some fifty years, work on the monument was finally begun its function in the city plan was ignored—the site itself was doubtless lost in deep woods. In addition to the statue, plans were made for a great temple, of which the obelisk was to be part. The site chosen was probably favored on account of its elevation above the river marsh, which, besides facilitating the laying of foundations, was a clear gain in height. It is unquestionably regrettable that the obelisk was not set on the axis of the Capitol because the fudging of the Mall axis will be easily discernible from various important points. The further question whether it is to be regretted that the Monument was not set on the White House axis, i. e., exactly at the intersection, would form an interesting topic for an architectural debate. In theory, certainly, the object marking the intersection of the axes ought to be in sight along each. It is the pin at the joint and it oughtn't to be anywhere else. The

FIG. 1198—WASHINGTON. THE MONUMENT

The sketch at the left suggests the view south from the White Lot as it will be after the realization of the present plan. In the other sketch the Monument is set on axis, where L'Enfant would have placed it. The proposed gardens at the intersection of the axes will be fine of themselves but they cannot, from this viewpoint, contend against the immense size of the Monument, which will always seem inorganically situated.

only possible doubt is whether the Monument, as it was built, would unpleasantly block, with its fifty-five feet of breadth, the view from the White House. If the mall or meadow running south from the White House were made very wide, say a thousand feet, the Monument would hide such a small part of the horizon that it would not be felt as cutting the view into halves. Such a situation would be admirably suited to emphasize the characteristic beauty of the obelisk. The apotheosis of verticality ought surely to be enthroned amidst a setting of horizontals.

An incidental regret—or, rather, a genuine tragedy—in relation to the incorrect location of the Monument is that, though supremely fitted to serve as the objective of long vistas, almost no street in Washington shoots directly at it. If L'Enfant had dreamt of any such prodigiously effective star-center he would surely have radiated additional avenues from the intersection of the axes. Whether one would want to have the Monument appear above the White House in the view south along Sixteenth Street may be open to question. The distant views, with the Monument soaring above the converging foliage of the street trees, would be fine, but from nearby one would probably wish for a light mist to intensify the atmospheric perspective and clearly separate the Monument from the White House.

The plan for the Mall prepared by the Commission of 1901 could not but vary in many ways from L'Enfant's plan, as we know it, if only because of the differences in practical conditions. The most important of these was the existence and location of the Washington Monument; another was the filling of the swamp below the Monument. This last change made possible a considerable extension of the Mall axis, an extension, by the way, which cannot from every viewpoint be considered as an integral part of the Mall. From the Capitol terrace it will be an effective continuation of the Mall, but from the floor of the Mall itself the extension will not be visible, for the Mall rises toward the south. It will be interesting to see how this will effect views from the Mall of the Lincoln Memorial, which is raised, for this reason, on a fifty-foot platform. It may be desirable to block the ground-view south along the Mall by introducing a low screen of some sort near the Monument. That would make of the Monument the unquestioned terminal feature of the eastern section of the Mall and, saving the spectator from imperfect glimpses of the Memorial and the intervening gardens, would give him a sudden and

dramatically comprehensive view of them as he passed through the screen and came out on to the high terrace on which the Monument will stand. That view will in any case be a fine one, for the gardens between the Monument and the Memorial promise to be very beautiful indeed.

The intersection of the axes, where L'Enfant intended an equestrian statue, is to be occupied by a large circular pool. The function of expressing the axial intersection, which could hardly be performed by a flat water surface, is transferred to the garden as a whole with its surrounding tree-masses which, by the clearing of the "Oval", will be brought into view from the White House. The plan of the garden is a Greek cross; the Monument, at the top of a flight of steps, like the Duke of York column in London, is in the eastern arm of the cross. The cross is bounded by a heavy band of trees. This band is arranged symmetrically on the north-south as well as on the east-west axis, in spite of the fact that the ground rises abruptly at the east side. One must suppose that Le Nôtre, innocent of the temptations of rendered show plans, would hardly have combined an asymmetrical section with a symmetrical plan.

The White House

The changes which have come to the passage in L'Enfant's plan represented by the Monument are hardly greater, though perhaps more conspicuous, than the changes which have come in the vicinity of the White House. L'Enfant's street plan has been followed very closely, but in the third dimension, if the expression may be used, his intentions have been forgotten and nullified. To him the White House appeared, perhaps, at the end of the north-south arm of the central axis scheme, as a fist gripping firmly the radiating reins which should hold in subjection all that part of the city. And we may be sure that as a son of France and the Renaissance he intended that dominance to be a real one, a concrete experience, and not merely an intellectual conception built up out of the spectator's knowledge of American history and government, his study of maps and guide books, and his messenger-boy familiarity with the names and beginnings and ends of streets. An esthetic unity based on such elements as these has the same sort of reality as had the heaven of Jurgen's grandmother, a reality which consists in its being believed in. In real flesh-and-blood

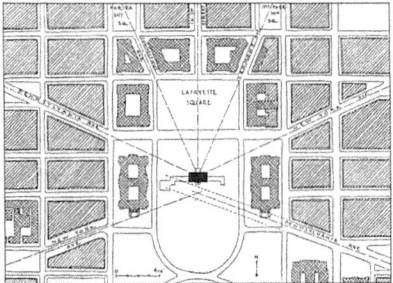

FIG. 1199—WASHINGTON. THE WHITE HOUSE

The buildings indicated by cross-hatching are either existing or proposed, according to the plan issued by the Public Buildings Commission in 1917. The center-lines of the radiating streets are shown, as well as the curb lines (which are also the tree lines) of Pennsylvania Avenue, which clear the White House, indicating that the vista would not be perfect even if the Treasury had not been built where it is.

This study by Cass Gilbert antedates the plan of the Commission of 1901. Its most interesting feature is the "New White House" on Meridian Hill. The plan is at a scale of about 4,000 feet to the inch; the graphic scale exaggerates dimensions about one seventh.

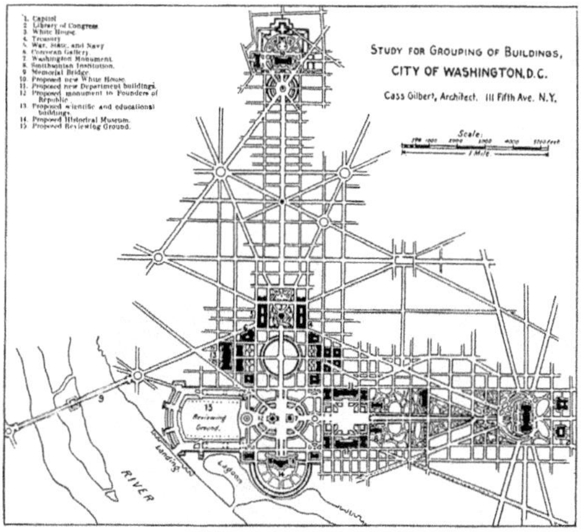

STUDY FOR GROUPING OF BUILDINGS,
CITY OF WASHINGTON, D.C.
Cass Gilbert, Architect. 111 Fifth Ave. N.Y.

FIG. 1200—WASHINGTON

city planning that won't do. The composition must be sensible to the senses and not merely knowable to the mind. Here you stand and there you look and that you see—and you like it, with the help of no diagram. If the White House is to dominate the region to the northwest, the White House must be visible from Connecticut Avenue; it is not enough that the people living around Dupont Circle should know that that thoroughfare is the shortest route to Keith's Theater and that one passes the White House on the way.

L'Enfant, then, made his "President's House" the center of radiation of seven broad avenues. These Avenues radiate; they also converge. Now, in general, streets are converged on a point to get two sorts of effect: there is a beauty in the view out from their intersection; there is another beauty in the vistas from the avenues in toward the building or monument which marks that intersection. The view out produces an impression of the extent and unity of the city and gives importance to the center of the star. If the avenues are symmetrically placed and if their intersection is architecturally well expressed, the whole composition may have a decided esthetic value, in addition to the intellectual satisfaction which comes from the perception of a convenient mechanically ordered arrangement of things. The three avenues which radiate to the south from the Piazza del Popolo in Rome make a very beautiful composition. But L'Enfant probably did not intend this views out from the center of the étoile to be commonly enjoyed by the public, but rather to serve the pleasure of the president himself and to impress his guests. We must not overestimate the democracy of those men and those times. L'Enfant and Washington may well have thought of that part of the city as a huge formal garden, the entourage of the "President's House." Indeed, to reconstruct L'Enfant's thought, we must constantly keep in mind not alone the French formal gardens but especially the great forests, St. Germain, Fontainebleau, Chantilly, with their arrow-straight roads and many-rayed stars. And it is quite likely that L'Enfant himself saw at Washington a closer realization of some phases of his plan than we can see now, for early accounts speak of the beauty of the newly cleared wide straight avenues with floors of grass and walls of primeval forest. Doubtless L'Enfant hoped to preserve much of this parklike effect, since all that part of the town was intended for the better

residences. The business district would be east and south of the Capitol, convenient to the river. Under these circumstances it was quite justifiable to make the president's residence a city planning feature, the center of a star of avenues. When the White House was a pioneer, the second largest of the few dozen structures in the town, and the streets of Washington were lanes cut through the forest, it was wise to play the fine building for all it was worth and to spread as far as possible its beauty and its solid promise of the urbanity to come. Today the streets are crowded with people and autos and street cars and are lined with tall buildings, many of them very ugly. These are not to an American the ideal surroundings of a home, which, after all, the White House is, and it should be a pleasant and comfortable one. It is not easy, therefore, to protest against the growth of trees and shrubs in the White House grounds and in Lafayette, McPherson, and Farragut Squares, though that growth has hidden the White House from the four avenues radiating to the north-east and north-west.

The two avenues which radiate to the south-east and south-west (Pennsylvania and New York) are also blocked, but by buildings instead of by trees, and no discussion of the Washington plan is complete without a bit of a dash of indignation thereanent. Assuredly one can but regret the failure to realize the popular conception of what ought to be the "Capitol-White House vista", but, which is also regrettable, the popular impression that the White House now lies on the extended centerline of Pennsylvania Avenue is not in harmony with fact. In truth, the White House stands so much to one side of the course of the avenue that the north curb and tree row could be carried through without a break. An engraving of about 1820 shows the roadway thus continued across the south front of the White House. Of course Pennsylvania Avenue is very wide and the White House would be visible for a considerable distance up the avenue, especially from the south sidewalk, but it is erroneous to suppose that the building of the Treasury destroyed a perfect creation of civic art. If it had not been built the avenue would indubitably now terminate in a heavy mass of trees, than which, as a street picture, the present arrangement is surely better. For the view of the Treasury from Pennsylvania Avenue is a fine one: to the left is undifferentiated foliage, but from the

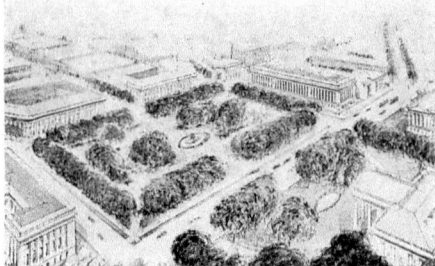

FIGS. 1201, 1202—WASHINGTON. PROPOSED TREATMENT OF LAFAYETTE SQUARE

Cass Gilbert's design for the buildings which will enframe Lafayette Square. The first section of the Treasury Annex, shown in the drawing at the right, has been completed. It will be noticed that in the bird's-eye view it was felt necessary to greatly exaggerate the size of the White House.

right juts out the robust mass of the granite building with its strong columns and cornice and mighty buttresses flanking the broad steps. Not to see the White House is a loss, a loss in sentiment and a loss, much more than sentimental, to the coherence of L'Enfant's geometrical composition, as we understand it. But that we do understand L'Enfant's intention cannot be asserted unreservedly. In his own "manuscript" plan the four northern radials and the one which is now lower New York Avenue come together pretty accurately at a single point, but Pennsylvania Avenue is deflected to the south, disquietingly like the way it was built. Since L'Enfant pretty surely thought of the President's House as a domed building it is improbable that he intended the northern suite of avenues to concentrate on the north façade and the southern pair on the south façade. L'Enfant's plan is quite inaccurately draughted—Pennsylvania Avenue is not even shown as a straight line. But to suggest that the incorrect—at least, the unexplainable—location of the principal diagonal avenue in Washington is due to the careless ruling of a line would be absurd. Ellicott, Washington, Jefferson and many others must have understood L'Enfant's purpose too well to permit of their being misled by a trivial error.

The theory that L'Enfant intended Pennsylvania Avenue to shoot at the White House has with it the authority of the Commission of 1901, which held that the closing, by the Treasury, of a "carefully planned vista of the White House" is "inconsistent with the fundamental principles" of L'Enfant's plan.

With this expression "fundamental principles" the Commission coupled an allusion to the "historic arteries representing the original states." That phrase might well have been extended to include Capitol Avenue and Sixteenth Street which are even more deeply fundamental than the radiating avenues of stately name. Sixteenth Street alone, of all the seven avenues radiating from the White House, commands a view of its objective. If only one was destined to be preserved the Fates have been kind in their choice, for the fact that Sixteenth Street is on the axis of the White House makes it incomparably more valuable than the diagonal avenues. A diagonal street may afford a view of a building but unless some architectural element in the building recognizes its existence the diagonal street does not become an organic part of the design of the building, as does a street on axis. Sixteenth Street is further fortunate in being a "street" of the gridiron, thus avoiding the unbalanced openings, the distressing unordered variations in width, the unimpressive flatiron buildings, and the triangular parklets, which mar all the "avenues." The two principal diagonal avenues crossing it do so at Scott Circle, a very interestingly designed little area. L'Enfant planned two other

open spaces intended to mark the importance of the street, but both were lost in execution.

Lafayette Square

The view of the White House from Sixteenth Street is across Lafayette Square. Anyone who has often enjoyed that view on pale misty mornings and bright snowy nights will read with a shock this passage from the report of the Commission of 1901: "The location of the building to contain the Executive offices is a more difficult matter; but the Commission are of the opinion that while temporary quarters may well be constructed in the grounds of the White House, a building sufficient in size to accommodate those offices may best be located in the center of Lafayette Square." Which constitutes quite too strong a temptation to summarize the attitude of the Commission relative to the seven streets which were planned to command vistas of the White House.

Two of the vistas—the central section of Pennsylvania Avenue and lower New York—are of third-rate quality because the avenues, at an angle, shoot past their supposed objective. Both are now stopped by buildings, and against this the Commission strongly protests.

Four vistas—Vermont, Connecticut, and the northern sections of Pennsylvania and New York Avenues—are of second-rate quality because they strike the White House at an angle. These four vistas are now stopped by trees which could easily be removed, but regarding these lost vistas the Commission says nothing.

One vista—Sixteenth Street—is of first-rate quality, on axis and practically clear. This vista the Commission proposes to block with a new building.

In justice to the Commission, however, it must be said that this proposal was not embodied in the published plans, which may well be construed as representing the more carefully studied judgment. If their feeling changed it may have been out of respect for L'Enfant's axial avenue; perhaps also because Lafayette Square is of such obvious beauty and value as an open square. Real "squares" are rare in Washington. There are plenty of so called "circles" and other open areas of various shapes at street intersections, but Lafayette is in quite another class. It is a court of honor before the White House, fortunate in its ample size and symmetrical plan, its freedom from bisecting pavements, its dignified houses reminiscent of the old time capital, and the relative continuity of its bounding wall, for an area loses half the value of being open if wide avenues lead out from every side. It is the bounding wall which esthetically creates the space, and well designed three-dimensional spaces are the finest fruits of the arts of architecture, city planning, and gardening.

But the bounding walls of the old square have begun a radical transformation. The Dolly Madison house, the Corcoran house where Webster lived, the homes Richardson designed for John Hay and Henry Adams, and St. John's Church (built in 1816 by Latrobe) must soon make way, in accordance with the recommendations of the Commission of 1901, for huge departmental office buildings. The old Arlington Hotel and the home of Charles Sumner have already been destroyed. The departmental building which has taken their place overtops the "President's church" and the trees on the square. The new Lafayette Square will be crowded with automobiles and trucks, the lawns will be dotted at noon with clerks and typists, street car tracks may even be laid in Sixteenth Street, and the usual tatterdemalion lunchrooms and little shops will cling to the skirts of the office buildings and spread back into the residence streets to the north, producing another of those anemic business districts of which Washington already has so many.

Is it not surprising that while New York is laboriously working out a zoning law largely with the purpose of protecting established residence districts, while Boston is at great expense preserving the scale of Copley Square, while historical societies in many states are protecting what has survived from our great period in architecture, while all England is deeply stirred by the threatened destruction of some of the old London churches, Washington is making a business district out of Lafayette Square? And for no better reason, one is bound to suspect, than that there's an idea in the wind that the president ought to be "surrounded by his official family"—in spite of the fact that, in the lump, the president probably detests the sight of his official family and the family itself would jolly well rather be near the station or up on a hill in the suburbs where Uncle Sam could afford to erect office buildings without hot and ugly interior courts.

Purely as a matter of design, it is surely to be regretted that the residence scale and atmosphere of Lafayette Square cannot be maintained, to connect the White House with the residence district of the city. It seems an ideal location for those unofficial White Houses, the national headquarters of clubs and societies—all of red brick, to preserve for the White House its dominance of scale and color.

The present treatment of the central planted area of the square is of course quite impossible. Its design is as poor as the design of a dollar bill. French-curve walks superimposed upon a florist's arboretum, plus the accu-

mulated vagaries of a dozen gardeners, and "Mr. Clark Mills's nursery monument to the equestrian seat of Andrew Jackson"—thus Henry Adams dubbed it—as the center and gem of it all. And this in a country where box thrives and elms grow gloriously and there was once a fine traditional garden-art whose simple materials were straight gravel walks and hedges and lawns!

These fragmentary—and quite consciously suggestive rather than conclusive—notes on the plan of Washington have been intended primarily to encourage an attitude of concreteness and reality toward L'Enfant's plan and toward the city. The plan and city form a mine of inspirational and exemplary material, but from it there is little of value to be dug by those who come with no more sturdy tools than a conviction that when L'Enfant laid down his draughting-pen his plan was perfect and complete, and a belief that the principal value of that plan is a mystical parallelism with the federal constitution, which it is unpatriotic to question. And those eyes are useless which have not the strength to search out and judge the real form which lies underneath that patina of historical association with which time covers everything, right or wrong, ugly or beautiful. What is needed now is the approach which cannot be diverted by an anecdote or a pretty bunch of trees, the unromantic attitude of the Renaissance, seemingly hard and cold but really warm with bodily life and personality, seeing clearly that beauty lies in arrangements of tangible things and not in general ideas, however grandiose.

Imperial grandiosity as an ideal—that is the great danger to Washington. Spacious monumentality may produce great beauty, but let there be a hair's breadth of deviation from good taste and nothing remains but pompous banality. Too great an emphasis on the national scale, the impersonally monumental, is more likely to produce dulness than grandeur. Lining the Mall, Capitol Square, and Lafayette Square with monumental buildings of granite and marble may be financial and administrative daring—it may also be artistic timidity. It is much easier to follow the generally accepted idea of the "right thing to do" than it is to create the unique expression of a rich personality. Until we overcome this small sector of our deadly national idealism and realize that art is something more than liberal expenditure and good intention, students of civic art will continue to study plans of the capital of the United States—and to make pilgrimages, seeking the living touch of beautiful cities, to Paris and Rome—to Bath, Richelieu, Nancy, Ludwigslust, and Pompeii.

FIG. 1203—WASHINGTON. THE ARCH OF VICTORY, 1919

Since the text of this chapter was written a new unit in the frame of Lafayette Square, the U. S. Chamber of Commerce, has been begun, and the Webster house has been torn down to make way for it.

LIST OF BOOKS

The illustrations in this book which have been published elsewhere are from the following list of books and periodicals. The list has been made as succinct as possible, since it is intended merely as first aid in consulting library catalogues and bibliographies. Nearly all of the books cited can be found at the Avery Library of Columbia University.

The illustrations not noted in the captions as being from the publications in this list are of various origins. Many have been prepared especially for this book. Among this number are Mr. Herding's drawings, most of which are pen renderings of the very interesting and carefully selected photographs published by A. E. Brinckmann in his "Stadtbaukunst." A large proportion of the modern American material was secured directly from the designers or from officials of cities and institutions. A number of the illustrations, mainly of modern European work, but also the reproductions of historical maps especially of Paris and Berlin, were collected by Mr. Hegemann during his service as the general secretary of the City Planning Exhibition held at Berlin in 1910 and were published in his "Staedtebau." Other illustrations, such for instance as the Tokio views on p. 225, are from photographs taken by Mr. Hegemann; yet others are from photographs and maps collected by Mr. Peets while in Europe in 1920 and '21.

Periodicals

AMERICAN ARCHITECT AND ARCHITECTURAL REVIEW. Semimonthly, New York.
ARCHITECTURAL FORUM. Monthly, Boston.
ARCHITECTURAL RECORD. Monthly, New York.
ARCHITECTURE. Monthly, New York.
ARCHITECTURE. Monthly, London.
DEUTSCHE BAUZEITUNG. Monthly, Berlin.
LANDSCAPE ARCHITECTURE. Quarterly, Brookline, Mass.
STADTBAUKUNST. Semimonthly, Berlin.
DER STAEDTEBAU. Monthly, Berlin.
TOWN PLANNING REVIEW. Quarterly, Liverpool.
DIE VOLKSWOHNUNG. Semimonthly, Berlin.
WASMUTHS MONATSHEFTE FÜR BAUKUNST. Monthly, Berlin.

Books

ADAM, ROBERT AND JAMES. Works of Architecture. London, 1822.
BLOMFIELD, REGINALD. Architectural Drawing and Draughtsmen. London, 1912.
BLONDEL, JACQUES-FRANÇOIS. Architecture Française. Paris, 1752.
BORRMANN, R. Handbuch der Architektur. Stuttgart, 1897.
BRINCKMANN, A. E. Stadtbaukunst des achtzehnten Jahrhunderts. Städtebauliche Vorträge, Vol. VII, No. 1. Berlin, 1914.
    Die Baukunst des siebzehnten und achtzehnten Jahrhunderts. Berlin, (1919?).
    Deutsche Stadtbaukunst in der Vergangenheit. Frankfort, 1921.
    Platz und Monument. Berlin, 1908.
    Stadtbaukunst. Berlin, 1920.
BROGI, GIACOMO. Disegni di Architettura, Galleria degli Uffizi. Florence, 1904.
BUEHLMANN, J. Die Architektur des klassischen Alterthums und der Renaissance.
BURCKHARDT, JACOB. Geschichte der Renaissance in Italien. Esslingen a. N. 5th edition, 1912.
CAIN, G. La Place Vendôme. Paris, (1890?).
CALLIAT, VICTOR. Hôtel de Ville de Paris. Paris, 1844.
CAMPBELL, COLEN. Vitruvius Britannicus or the British Architect. London, 1717.
CAYON, J. Histoire de Nancy.
CERCEAU, J. A. DU. Les plus excellents bâtiments de France. Paris, reprint, 1870.
CHOISY, A. Histoire de l'Achitecture. Paris, 1899.
COMMISSION MUNICIPALE DU VIEUX-PARIS. Paris. Annual Reports, 1909-1911.
COUSSIN, J. A. Du Genie de l'Architecture. Paris, 1822.
CRANE, EDWARD A., AND E. E. SODERHOLTZ. Examples of Colonial Architecture in South Carolina and Georgia. New York, 1895.
DASENT, A. J. History of St. James' Square. London, 1895.
DESHAIRS, LEON. Bordeaux. (Bordeaux, 1890?).
DOHME, ROBERT. Barock- und Rokoko- Architektur. Berlin, 1892.
DURAND, J. N. L. Recueil et Parallèle des Edifices de tout Genre, anciens et modernes. Paris, 1798.
ELDERKIN, G. W. Problems in Periclean Buildings. Princeton, 1912.
ELWELL, NEWTON W. The architecture, furniture, and interiors of Maryland and Virginia during the eighteenth century. Boston, 1897.
ENLART, C. Rouen. Paris, 1906.
D'ESPOUY, H. Fragments d'Architecture antique. Paris, 1905.
FAIRMOUNT PARK ART ASSOCIATION. Fairmount Parkway. Philadelphia, 1919.
FELIBIEN, J. F. Description de l'Eglise Royale des Invalides. Paris, 1706.
FISCHER, THEODOR. Sechs Vorträge über Stadtbaukunst. Munich, 1919.
FRAUBERGER, H. Die Akropolis von Baalbek. Frankfort, 1892.
GARNIER, CHARLES. Le Nouvel Opéra. Paris, 1878.
GEYMUELLER, H. VON. Sanct Peter in Rom. Vienna and Paris, 1875.
GROMORT, G. Grandes Compositions executées. Paris, 1910.
GUILHERMY, M. F. DE. Itinéraire Archéologique de Paris. Paris, 1885.
GURLITT, CORNELIUS. Geschichte des Barockstiles. Stuttgart, 1888.
    Handbuch des Städtebaues. Berlin, 1920.
HEGEMANN, WERNER. Der Staedtebau nach den Ergebnissen der allgemeinen Staedtebau-Ausstellung. Berlin, 1913.
    Report on a city plan for the municipalities of Oakland and Berkeley. Berkeley, 1915.

HEIGELIN, K. M. Lehrbuch der höheren Baukunst. 1828.
HESSLING, E., AND W. HESSLING. Le Vieux Paris. Paris, 1902.
KLOPFER, PAUL. Von Palladio bis Schinkel. Esslingen, 1911.
KUHN, WALDEMAR. Kleinsiedlungen aus Friderizianischer Zeit. Hanover, 1917.
    Kleinbürgerliche Siedlungen in Stadt und Land. Munich, 1921.
LANGE, WILLY. Land- und Gartensiedelungen. Leipsic, (1912?).
LE PAUTRE, PIERRE. Les Plans, Profiles, et Elevations des Ville et Château de Versailles. Paris, 1716.
LETAROUILLY, PAUL. Edifices de Rome Moderne. Paris, 1874.
    Le Vatican et la Basilique de Saint-Pierre de Rome. Paris, 1882.
LOFTIE, W. J. Inigo Jones and Wren. New York, 1893.
MAERTENS, H. Der optische Maassstab. Revised edition, Berlin, 1884.
MACARTNEY, MERVYN. English Houses and Gardens; Engravings by Kip, Badeslade, Harris, and others. London, 1908.
MACOMBER, BEN. The Jewel City. San Francisco and Tacoma, 1915.
MANGIN, A. Les Jardins. Tours, 1868.
MAWSON, THOMAS H. Civic Art. London, 1911.
MCKIM, MEAD, AND WHITE. The Monograph of the Work of McKim, Mead, and White. New York, 1917.
MAQUET, A. Paris sous Louis XIV. Paris, 1883.
MEBES, PAUL, AND WALTER COUT BEHRENDT. Um 1800. Munich, 1920.
MIGGE, LEBERECHT. Die Gartenkultur des 20. Jahrhunderts. Jena, 1913.
MUENTZ, E. La Renaissance en Italie et en France à l'époque de Charles XIII. Paris, 1885.
MULLGARDT, LOUIS CHRISTIAN. The Architecture and Landscape Gardening of the Exposition. San Francisco, 1915.
Muséum de la Nouvelle Architecture Française. Paris, 1795.
MUTHESIUS, HERMANN. Kleinhaus und Kleinsiedelung. Munich, (1919?)
NEW YORK COURT HOUSE COMMISSION. Competition drawings for the New York Court House. New York, 1913.
NEUFFORGE, SIEUR DE. Recueil Elémentaire. Bordeaux, (1800?).
OSTENDORF, FRIEDRICH. Sechs Bücher vom Bauen. Berlin, 1920.
PALLADIO, ANDREA. Treatise on Architecture. Translation by R. Ware, London, 1738.
PATTE, PIERRE. Monumens érigés en France à la gloire de Louis XV. Paris, 1765. (Also modern reprint.)
PINDER, WILHELM. Deutscher Barok; die Grossen Baumeister des achtzehnten Jahrhunderts. Düsseldorf and Leipsic.
PIRANESI, GIOVANNI BATTISTA. Antichità d'Albano. Rome, 1764.
    Antichita Romane. Rome, 1756.
PLATT, CHARLES A. Monograph of the Work of Charles A. Platt. New York, 1913.
RAMSEY, STANLEY C. Small Houses of the late Georgian Period 1750-1820. London, 1919.
ROBINSON, CHARLES MULFORD. City Planning. New York, 1916.
RUSKIN, JOHN. Studies in Both Arts. London, 1895.
SCHULTZE-NAUMBERG, PAUL. Kulturarbeiten; Band IV, Staedtebau. Munich, 1909.
SILVESTRE, ISRAEL. (Also spelled SYLVESTRE.) Divers Paisages faits sur la nature. Paris, 1650. (And other collections of engravings.)
SIMPSON, F. M. A History of Architectural Development. New York, 1911.
SITTE, CAMILLO. Der Städte-Bau. Vienna, 1889. (French translation. L'Art de Bâtir les Villes, by Camille Martin, Paris, 2nd. ed. 1912.)
STUEBBEN, J. Vom französischen Städtebau. Städtebauliche Vorträge. Vol. VIII, Nos. 2 & 3. Berlin, 1915.
SWARBRICK, J. Robert Adams and his Brothers. London, 1915.
TARBE, P. Reims.
TORNOW, PAUL. Denkschrift betreffend den Ausbau der Hauptfront des Domes zu Metz. Metz, 1891.
TRIGGS, INIGO. Town Planning, past, present, and possible. London, 1909.
UNWIN, RAYMOND. Town Planning in Practice. London, 1909.
VATOUT. Histoire Lithographique du Palais Royal. Paris.
VIOLLET-LE-DUC, E. E. Dictionnaire raisonné de l'Achitecture. Paris, 1884.
WARE, WILLIAM ROTCH, AND CHAS. S. KEEFE. Georgian Period. New York. (New edition announced for 1922.)
WEAVER, LAWRENCE. Houses and Gardens by E. L. Lutyens. London, 1913.
WOLF, PAUL. Städtebau. Leipsic, 1919.
WOOD, ROBERT. Palmyra and Balbec. London, 1827.
WREN, CHRISTOPHER. Parentalia. Reprinted, London, 1903.

INDEX

This is an index of illustrations only. It is arranged according to place-names. The names of designers are entered only in those cases in which no definite location can be assigned to the design—as, for instance, "ideal" town plans. Large estates and gardens not in towns or cities are entered according to the names by which they are commonly known; those in England are also grouped under the heading "English Estates." The numbers referred to are the page numbers.

During the compilation of the index a number of errors have been discovered. The group of engravings at the upper left hand corner of p. 161 ought to be captioned "Figs. 690-92—Street terminations. Market Building, arch, and pavilion." Of Fig. 927 the place-name should be Oldenburg instead of Dobbengelände. Of Fig. 1029 it might well have been made clearer that the sketch is a conjectural visualization of Wren's scheme for the setting of St. Paul's; in the third line of the caption the word "been" is omitted. The date in the caption to Fig. 249 should be 1586 and not 1686.